War Crimes, Genocide, and Justice

War Crimes, Genocide, and Justice

A Global History

David M. Crowe

First published in 2014 by
PALGRAVE MACMILLAN®
in the United States—a division of St. Martin's Press LLC,
175 Fifth Avenue, New York, NY 10010.

Where this book is distributed in the UK, Europe and the rest of the world,
this is by Palgrave Macmillan, a division of Macmillan Publishers Limited,
registered in England, company number 785998, of Houndmills,
Basingstoke, Hampshire RG21 6XS.

Palgrave Macmillan is the global academic imprint of the above companies
and has companies and representatives throughout the world.

Palgrave® and Macmillan® are registered trademarks in the United States,
the United Kingdom, Europe and other countries.

ISBN: 978–0–230–62224–1

Library of Congress Cataloging-in-Publication Data is available from the
Library of Congress.

A catalogue record of the book is available from the British Library.

Design by Newgen Knowledge Works (P) Ltd., Chennai, India.

First edition: January 2014

10 9 8 7 6 5 4 3 2 1

Contents

Acknowledgments

This work is the culmination of over two decades of research, writing, and work as an expert witness in various legal settings. My work on the Roma, for example, prompted requests from attorneys throughout the United States and Canada to work with them on a variety of asylum and other cases that dealt with the plight of minorities in Eastern Europe and Russia after 1989. I also dealt extensively with the legal status of the Roma in postcommunist Central and Eastern Europe in my *A History of the Gypsies of Eastern Europe and Russia*. Law was also a theme in my biography of Oskar Schindler, since I not only had to delve into the evolution of Nazi law vis-à-vis German and European Jews, but also the war crimes trials of several German and Austrian perpetrators, particularly Amon Göth. And toward the end of my research on Schindler's life, I was drawn indirectly into several of the law suits launched by Emilie Schindler in the struggle over the ownership rights of Oskar's private papers in Germany.

By the time I began work on my *The Holocaust: Roots, History, and Aftermath*, I had decided that I needed to look more closely at the whole question of the marriage of history and international criminal law. And since I had worked extensively in the Göth trial transcripts while researching the Schindler book, I was curious about the various war crimes trials conducted throughout Europe after the war. Consequently, I devoted much of the last chapter of the Holocaust book to this subject, which set the stage for this current study.

My interest in this topic was further stimulated by my participation in a two-week seminar for law school professors at the US Holocaust Memorial Museum in Washington, DC, on the question of the Holocaust and international law. I came away from that seminar with far more questions than answers, particularly when it came to the historical origins of international humanitarian law—a direct product of the atrocities and mass murders of World War II. Though there is ample literature on some of these roots, they often focus more on legal theory and precedent than the deeper historical roots of some of the core ideas that provide the basis for pre-IHL legal thinking. I finally decided that the only way I was going to be able to understand these deeper roots was to go back and look at them not only in their historical context, but also at the politics and other issues that often drove their developments. And since legal scholars often begin with modest discussions of precedents that often go back to antiquity, I decided I had to start at the beginning. But I was also concerned about charges of euro-centricity in international law, and wanted to be certain that any discussion I undertook looked at these historical roots globally and not regionally. Moreover, since international criminal law is a relatively modern field, I wanted to find out what rules or regulations, if any, guided armies or military institutions in the field in premodern times, particularly when it came to POWs and other noncombatants. I also wanted to look into the nature of the crimes committed in warfare going back to antiquity to determine the interrelationship of such rules and crimes. I knew that this would be an overwhelming undertaking, particularly since I wanted to start afresh and try, as much as possible, to look at primary source material through the ages to be certain that my interpretations were drawn from such sources, knowing, of course, of the bias often found in such works.

This has been an extremely rewarding undertaking, helped along by an outstanding editor, Chris Chappell, who has been extremely supportive of my work on this book. I would also like to thank the staffs at the law libraries of Duke University, George Washington University, Northwestern University, and Indiana University, where I spent long days poring over their vast collections of primary source material. I am particularly grateful to the Inter-Library Loan staff at the Walter Clinton Jackson Library, University of North Carolina, Greensboro, who often, on very short notice, came up time and again with obscure articles and books that I needed for my research. The Jackson Library is one of the best in the mid-Atlantic, and, time and again, whenever I needed a book or an article, they usually had it. This helped the pace of my research and writing immensely. It also did not hurt that my wife, Kathryn Moore Crowe, a scholar in her own right, is an associate dean at the Jackson Library. Her incredible loving support on many levels was the absolute key to the successful completion of this study.

This is a complex study that touches not only on many eras of history and law, but also on a wide variety of subjects and issues. For the most part, I followed a chronological and geographic approach in my first few chapters, but decided to fall back on the approach I use in my law school classes to discuss in separate chapters the Nuremberg and Tokyo IMT trials as well as the tens of thousands of military commission and other trials conducted throughout Europe and Asia from 1945 to 1956. Collectively, one could argue that they are the most important war crimes trials in history, particularly when one considers the vast death and destruction wrought during this global conflict. Moreover, with the exception of Nuremberg and a handful of other trials conducted by the occupation authorities in Germany after the war, little is known about the thousands of trials conducted by the victor nations in Asia and Europe in the decade or so after the end of World War II. While a few of them are discussed in the shadows of historical and legal scholarship, many of them established important legal and historical precedents that are still referenced in court cases today.

I adopted a modified case law approach for the last two chapters and tried, for example, to choose cases that showed interpretative contrasts when it came to questions of genocide and violations of IHL. I also tried to look at the diversity of legal proceedings domestically and internationally over the past few decades with examples from various major and minor trials. In the end, my hope is that, in the most modest way, this work will open up new doors of historical and legal scholarship.

Chapter 1

Crimes of War: Antiquity to the Middle Ages

I [Sung K'ang] *have heard that Ts'in and Ts'oo are fighting together, and I am going to see the king of Ts'oo and persuade* [them] *to cease hostilities...Mencius said: "What course will you take to try to persuade them?" Kang answered, "I will tell them how unprofitable their course is to them." "Master," said Mencius, "your aim is great, but your argument is not good."...* [While all will] *rejoice in the cessation of war* [it shall be driven by] *the pursuit of profit...* [But] *if you, starting from the ground of benevolence and righteousness, offer your counsels to the kings of Ts'in and Ts'oo...so as to stop the operations of their armies,...* [then all will] *find their pleasure in benevolence and righteousness.*[1]

—Mencius

War crimes and genocide are as old as history itself. So are customs, regulations, and laws that governed the behavior of armies in the field, particularly when it came to the treatment of individuals during times of war, be they combatants or civilians. Yet many scholars of international law do not think that these constraints or guidelines in antiquity fell within the confines of traditional interpretations of what constitutes an international legal order. According to Wilhelm G. Grewe, this could

only be assumed to exist if there is a plurality of relatively independent (although not necessarily equal-ranking) bodies politic which are linked to each other in political, economic and cultural relationships and which are not subject to a superimposed authority having comprehensive law-making jurisdiction and executive competence. In their mutual relations these bodies politic must observe norms which are deemed to be binding on the basis of a legal consciousness rooted in religious, cultural and other common values.[2]

Lassa Oppenheimer, whose 1905 work—*International Law: A Treatise*—is considered by some to be one of the most important works in international law, wrote that international law, "essentially a product of Christian civilization," is a body of rules on the relations between sovereign nations.[3]

Over the past few decades, a growing number of non-Western scholars have underscored the Eurocentricity of such definitions, and challenged the idea that the Western view of what is and is not international law was in itself a contradiction of the above definitions, since it was forced on many parts of Africa and Asia by nineteenth-century European colonial powers. Eric Yong-Joong Lee has gone so far as to conclude that "international law was regarded as just a skillful instrument for the advancing powers of the West to plunder Asian-African states."[4] But what Robert Cryer calls the world's first "international criminal law regime"[5] was, according to R. P. Anand, in many ways a form of victor's justice or "ruler's law" forced on Asia and Africa by the West in the nineteenth century.[6]

While it could be argued that such sentiments are a reflection of the deep, lingering scars of centuries of Western colonial conquest and abuse in the Americas, Asia, Africa, and the Middle East, they also represent what some legal scholars see as a dismissal of legal norms that date back five millennia. While few would argue that the various statements, for example, in ancient Near Eastern, Greek, Roman, Chinese, Muslim, Mongolian, or medieval European texts, regarding the behavior of armies in the field could be put in the same context as the modern laws of war, such expressions about the nature of war as well as the behavior of soldiers and armies during conflicts, regardless of their source, could be viewed as "cultural regulations of violence."[7] The nature of these sources, be they religious, literary, or historical, is and was a reflection of the societies that gave rise to such accounts and statements.

War in Antiquity

The Ancient Near East

The Holocaust, the Rwandan genocide, and Srebrenica have shown us that brutality in war has changed little over the ages despite the establishment of a sophisticated body of international law designed to prevent and adjudicate such atrocities. War in antiquity, particularly in the ancient Middle East, "operated in a world in which belief in the supernatural power of the gods was an omnipresent assumption."[8] Divination, which often included reading the entrails of animals, was considered an integral part of military planning. Oracles and various natural phenomena could also point to the displeasure of the gods and thus bring a campaign to a halt. In such cases, a monarch and/or his priests would make special offerings to "re-establish good relations with the gods."[9] Thus military campaigns took on a special military-religious spirit.

One of the early works on such campaigns is the *Epic of Gilgamesh*, a Sumerian-Akkadian epic poem whose earliest version dates to the twenty-second century BCE.[10] It centers around the story of the anthropomorphic king Gilgamesh, who, along with his friend Enkidu, undertakes a challenging odyssey that ultimately leads to a search for immortality. One part of the epic deals with a conflict with Humbaba, a Satan-like figure who guards the sacred fortress of the Cedar Forest. According to William J. Hamblin, the *Epic of Gilgamesh* "best reflects military practices of the late third or early second millennium," while the battle with Humbaba on Mount Lebanon "represents the military ideal, if not necessarily the reality," of warfare at the time.[11] After Gilgamesh and Enkidu slayed Humbaba, Enkidu "pulled out Humbaba's lungs and beheaded him. They then laid waste to his domain, the cedar forests of Mt. Hermon and Mt. Lebanon."[12]

Earlier descriptions of war in third-millennia accounts indicate that, at least theoretically, wars were not fought unless they were in self-defense or so commanded by "the gods." Once a military course of action was chosen, the result could be devastating. A ruler in Lagash, for example, warned the neighboring city-state of Umma:

> Be it known that your city will be completely destroyed! Surrender! Be it kno[wn] that Umma will be completely destroyed! Surrender![13]

Rimush, the son of Sargon of Akkad, who created the first united empire in Mesopotamia in the twenty-third century BCE, treated captives of war with great brutality. After defeating an army from Ur and Lagash, "he expelled 5,985 men [noncombatants] from their two cities and annihilated them." And after a rebellion in some of the city-states in his empire, he "filled the Euphrates River with their [the rebels'] bodies."[14]

Hamblin says that such treatment was common after wars in the ancient Middle East.

> Royal prisoners were often marched naked and in stocks back to the capital of the victorious king, where they were paraded in triumph, brought before the gods, and ritually debased by having the victorious king stand on their heads or bodies in the courtyards before the temples of the gods. The great hero Shulgi [twenty-first-century BCE neo-Sumerian ruler] boasts that he will "set my foot on his [the defeated king's] head...I will make him die amidst dripping blood; the enemy was ritually executed by being disemboweled in what probably amounted to a form of human sacrifice."[15]

In the realpolitik world of the ancient Near East, whether mythical or real, there was no room in war or politics "for considerations of moral obligations."[16]

Zimri-Lim, the eighteenth-century BCE king of Mari, used psychological warfare as a tactic. Most captives were enslaved, though some were tortured and mutilated "to terrorize enemies." Victorious troops would, on occasion, cut off the heads, legs, and arms of the enemy and send them to the king, who had the body parts put on display.[17] Others were brutally tortured. One officer

> pierced [a prisoner's] nose and placed a nose-rope [in it]. He opened [wounds] in both thighs, skinned his rib-cage, cut off his ears. He [the prisoner] passed through agonies. 30 times they took him [the prisoner] around the city...His [the prisoner's] father was present.[18]

One of antiquity's more storied leaders, Hammurabi, conquered Mari along the present-day Syria-Iraq border in 1761 BCE. Two years later, angry over continued resistance to Babylonian rule there, he ordered its city walls be torn down and "the land [turned] into rubble heaps and ruins."[19] His *Code of Hammurabi* underscored the militant nature of Hammurabi's threats against anyone who challenged his power. The gods, it said, called him "to destroy the wicked and the evil-doers," and gave him "mighty weapons" to "uproot" the enemy. And if anyone challenged his authority, Ishtar, the "goddess of fighting and war," would "create disorder and sedition for him, strike down his warriors, that the earth may drink their blood, and throw down the piles of corpses of his warriors on the field."[20]

Egypt

The predilection for violence was also a part of Egyptian warfare. Isolated and protected by deserts, warfare during early Egyptian history centered more around economically driven "military expeditions" into Nubia and the Sinai. Yet a sixth-dynasty account describes an Egyptian campaign against the Libyans under Pharaoh Pepy I (Phiops) as one of great brutality and destruction:

> This army returned in safety
> It had ravaged the sand-dwellers' land...
> It had flattened the sand-dwellers' land...
> It had sacked its strongholds...
> It had cut down its figs, its vines...
> It had thrown fire in all its [mansions]...
> It had slain its troops by many ten-thousands...
> [It had carried] off many [troops] as captives.[21]

One of the remarkable things about ancient Egypt was the durability of its political system. With the exception of the Hyksos era in northern Egypt in the seventeenth and sixteenth centuries BCE, Egypt enjoyed almost 1,600 years of political independence as an autonomous nation ruled by pharaohs. Warfare in ancient Egypt "was a heady mixture of violence, religious ritual, magic, and divine sanction and intervention." It was also a "ritual act by which the mythic combat of [the brothers] Horus [the sun god] and Set [god of chaos] was reenacted, and, through the king's ultimate victory, the cosmic balance of the universe maintained."[22] Though documentation is scarce, it is possible to get some sense of the customs of warfare when it came to the treatment of those captured in battle. Some of the earliest art from this period, for example, depicts the "ritual slaughter of prisoners of war."[23] Coffin Texts from the period immediately after the collapse of the Old Kingdom depict not only the extremely cruel treatment of POWs but even examples of "martial cannibalism." While these texts relate to mythical events, William J. Hamblin thinks that "there is no reason to think the Egyptian kings did not do these types of things to their real enemies."[24] One text, for example, tells how enemies of the pharaoh were treated after battle.

> I am stronger than they...their hearts fall to my fingers, their entrails are for the denizens of the sky [carrion birds], their blood is for the denizens of the earth [carrion animals]. Their heirs are [doomed] to poverty, their houses to conflagration...But I am happy, happy, for I am the Unique One, the Bull of the sky, I have crushed those who would do this against me and have annihilated their survivors.[25]

Hamblin states that such "texts represent a military world view in which retaliatory raids and personal revenge on enemies were a positive moral responsibility."[26] He adds that there were references to martial cannibalization in other Old and Middle Kingdom texts as well.[27]

The idea of martial cannibalism was not part of Egyptian warfare during Egypt's most imperialistic era, the New Kingdom. Egypt's wealth and greatness during this period rested on the spoils of war taken by its armies. Though Egyptian armies could be devastating and sometimes cruel in battle, they also placed great value on the importance of captives, particularly soldiers. Some POWs were integrated into the Egyptian military, which was strained by the responsibilities of occupying a vast empire. In the aftermath of one battle, Rameses II's troops "scattered all over the plain, spoiling the dead and collecting booty. The Egyptian does not usually decapitate his enemy: he cuts off the right hand or some limb, and carries it to the scribes, who inscribe it against his name."[28] But such brutality was more the exception than the rule, since pharaohs of this era were "risk-averse" and "not out to exterminate their enemies," since they were principally interested in preserving, to some extent, "the status quo in Asia."[29]

Israel and Judah

The Hebrews, a group of seminomads who slowly migrated from Mesopotamia into Canaan in the second millennium BCE, were deeply affected by Egypt's empire-building wars.[30] Warfare was an integral part of Jewish efforts to gain control of their promised homeland. The *Tanach*, or Jewish bible, abounds with references to atrocities committed during war. But, as Rabbi Joseph Telushkin has noted, such descriptions were merely a reflection of "how wars were fought in the ancient world."[31] The *Book of Deuteronomy* describes the killing of the entire population of the cities of Sihon and Og after their capture. The Israelites then despoiled both towns of all its valuable resources. According to the author of the *Book of Deuteronomy*, all of this was done with the support of the "Lord our God." The *Book of Joshua* carries this theme further, and discusses the atrocities committed by Joshua when he conquered Jericho. "They exterminated everything in the city, with the sword: man and woman, young and old, ox and sheep and ass." The only survivors were members of the family of a prostitute who had helped Israeli spies before the assault on the city.[32]

The heyday of ancient Israel as a unified state was from the tenth through the eighth centuries BCE. It was later divided into two kingdoms, Israel and Judah, with Jerusalem as the latter kingdom's capital. In 732 BCE, the Assyrians conquered Israel, and began to deport and resettle large numbers of Jews in the Assyrian hinterland.[33] After a series of rebellions in Judah,[34] Assyrian king Sennacherib, who had just conquered and destroyed Babylon, took the city of Lachish to the south of Jerusalem in 701, and had Jewish prisoners "impaled alive, flung naked upon the ground preliminary to being flayed, or had their heads struck off by swords."[35] According to *2 Kings*, he sent Hezikiah, Judah's ruler, a note warning him:

> You yourself have heard what the kings of Assyria have done to all the lands, how they have annihilated them and can you escape?[36]

But prior to the Assyrian attack on the city, Sennacherib's forces suddenly retreated.[37] According to Herodotus, the Assyrian army was "afflicted with the bubonic plague."[38]

Assyria

Battlefield atrocities, massive deportations, and resettlement were an integral part of Assyrian warfare. According to H. W. F. Saggs, such tactics were not used for "sadistic purposes, but psychological warfare."[39] Regardless of the motivation, the Assyrians were quite capable of committing horrible atrocities. In a ninth-century BCE Assyrian account, King Ashurnasirpal II wrote that after one battle,

> 3,000 of their combat troops I felled with weapons...Many of the captives taken from them I burned in a fire. Many I took alive; from some (of these) I cut off their hands to the wrist, from others I cut off their noses, ears, and fingers[?]; I put out the eyes of many of the soldiers. I burnt their young men and women to death.

In another campaign, he

> fixed up a pile (of corpses) in front of the city's gate. I flayed the nobles, as many as had rebelled, and spread their skins out on the piles...I flayed many with my hand and spread their skins out on the walls.[40]

After a city was taken, the victorious Assyrian king would set up his throne inside the captured city's walls, and hold court where the defeated monarch would be brought before him to be tortured. Some had their eyes put out or were put in a cage. Sargon II had the king of Damascus burned alive. There were also instances when Assyrian soldiers would massacre a captured city's population, and bring the severed heads of their victims to the king, particularly males. On other occasions, wives and daughters of a captured monarch would be forced into the royal harem, while those of nonroyal blood would be sold into slavery. Those males who somehow managed to escape these atrocities were often forced to work for the Assyrians as slave laborers on the empire's massive building projects. Others would be deported to other parts of the empire.[41] Simo Parpola has estimated that between 830 and 640 BCE, Assyrian rulers moved 4.5 million people from one part of their empire to another in an effort to destroy any sense of ethnic identity other than that of being an Assyrian.[42]

Persia and Greece

The Assyrians were briefly supplanted by the Neo-Babylonians (Chaldeans), whose empire existed for less than a century. They were overwhelmed by the Persians (550–330 BCE), whose empire provided a historical bridge between traditional antiquity and the emerging greatness of the Western-oriented Greco-Roman world.[43] Persia's greatest ruler, Cyrus II the Great, was known for his humane, tolerant policies, which stood in contrast to the "despotic cruelty" of most of his Near Eastern predecessors. According to Pierre Briant, some consider him "the inventor of 'human rights'"[44] because he chose to conquer and rule with "righteousness and justice."[45] But his humane policies had their limits. After Lydia rebelled against Persian rule, Cyrus ordered his troops to "ravage" her cities, execute Lydian rebel leaders, and enslave all captives.[46]

Cyrus' successors, Cambyses II and Darius I, adopted much harsher policies.[47] While Herodotus, whom Cicero dubbed the "father of [Western] history," admired Cyrus, he had little good to say about Cambyses or Darius. He wrote that after conquering Babylon, Darius had 3,000 of the city's "chief men" impaled or crucified, and he also ordered that 50,000 women be sent to Babylon to "propagate" the Babylonian race because the city's "chief men," worried about the city's food supply during the Persian siege, had "strangled their own women."[48]

But it was Darius' invasion of Greece in 492 BCE that has most intrigued scholars. By this time, Greeks had already developed the *koina nomina*, which Thucydides called the "common laws of the Greeks" in war. In addition to setting up guidelines for the general outbreak and customs of war, the *koina nomina* also dictated the treatment of the dead, POWs, and noncombatants. POWs were preferably to be ransomed off (as opposed to execution or mutilation) and noncombatants were "not [to be] primary targets of attack."[49]

Over the next few years, Greek and Persian forces met three times in battle with the latter suffering a final, devastating defeat on the plains of Marathon outside of Athens. A decade later, Persia's new monarch, Xerxes, led one of antiquity's largest invasion forces overland into Greece.[50] He was driven by just one thing—revenge—and told his generals that "the rest of the Persians will never stop until I have destroyed and burned Athens." He added that "those who are innocent in our sight and those who are guilty will alike bear the yoke of slavery."[51]

The Greeks were unable to decide on a common defense strategy, which led to desperate efforts by hundreds of Spartans and about 5,000–7,000 Greeks from other city-states to move north to Thermopylae to slow down the Persian advance. After three days of fierce combat, the Persians succeeded in taking the Thermopylae pass. Xerxes ordered his troops to cut off the head of the slain Spartan leader, Leonidas, and "put [it] up on a pole." The Persians also left the bodies of the fallen Greeks to rot in the sun, while burying their dead in mass graves. Other Greek POWs were "chained and branded."[52] As they moved southward, Persian forces ravaged central Greece, burning city after city and committing numerous atrocities. By the time Xerxes reached Athens, it was almost empty except for defenders on the Acropolis. Once taken, it was plundered and burned. The tables soon turned on the overextended Persians at the naval battle of Salamis. Xerxes fled to Persia, leaving a remnant of his army to the mercy of the Greeks.[53]

What followed was a growing conflict between Greece's two dominant city-states (Athens and Sparta)--the Peloponnesian War (431–421 and 415–404 BCE)--that led to the breakdown of the *koina nomina*. Alcidas, a Sparta admiral, cut the throats of most of his prisoners during his naval campaign during the first phase of the war, while in 427, the Corcyraeans, allies of the Athenians, butchered not only their Messenian captives, but also domestic opponents of their alliance with Athens. Several years later, the Corinthians did the same to Corcyraean sailors after a naval battle between the two city-states.[54]

The most heralded war crime of this conflict, which a few scholars have called an act of genocide,[55] took place in 415 BCE, when the Athenians, according to Thucydides, butchered "all the men of military age" on the island of Melos, a Spartan ally, and sold the Melian women and children into slavery.[56] The Melian tragedy did little to temper the deadlier passions unleashed during the Peloponnesian War. In 413, the Syracusans butchered the remnants of an Athenian force on the island of Sicily while they were "greedily drinking from the nearby dry riverbed." They also cut the throats of two captured Athenian generals and forced their Athenian captives to work as slave laborers in the harshest of conditions.

The Syracusans treated the men in the stone quarries very harshly at first. There were a great many men in a small, bare place, without a roof. In the beginning, the sun was still hot and they were oppressed by the stifling air. The cold nights that followed were just the opposite, it being autumn, and the shock to their systems made them sick. Because of the lack of space, they had to perform all their bodily functions in the same place, and the corpses of those who died from their wounds, exposure, and other causes were piled on top of each other. The stench was unbearable, and they were also afflicted by hunger and thirst, for they were given—some for up to eight months—only one cup of water and two cups of ground meal a day. They suffered every misery you could imagine among men in such a place. They all lived in those crowded conditions for seventy days, when all but the Athenians and any Sicilians and Italians who had fought with them were sold into slavery. It is difficult to say just how many prisoners there were in all, but there were at least seven thousand.[57]

Alexander the Great and Macedonia

Will Durant called the Peloponnesian War the "suicide of Greece,"[58] since it led to the destruction of one of the most fabled eras in antiquity, and paved the way for the most famous conqueror in the ancient Western world, Alexander the Great (Alexander III of Macedon). Alexander's father, Philip, created an empire in the Balkans and central Greece between 359 and 336 BCE, and brought an end to the Hellenic period of Greek history.[59] Alexander, like Philip, preferred the policies of conciliation over brute force and cruelty, though this had more to do with the practical needs of governing a vastly expanding empire than any strong ethical code of war or governance.[60] But if an enemy gave any hint of refusal to accept Macedonian domination, then he could be quite brutal. This was certainly the case after his conquest of Thebes in the fall of 335 BCE after the city-state rebelled against Macedonian domination and rejected Alexander's demands for renewed ties. Once in Thebes, Alexander allowed his non-Macedonian allies brutally to massacre "its helpless population," sparing, according to Arrian, "neither women nor children." James R. Ashley writes that Alexander's goal was "to terrorize the other Greek states into submission." The 30,000 Thebans who were not massacred were sold into slavery, while the city itself was destroyed.[61]

Alexander's next act of butchery took place in 334 after a seven-month siege of Tyre, one of the ancient Mediterranean's most important trading cities in what is now Lebanon. Once Tyre had fallen, Alexander allowed his troops to butcher, "without mercy...women, children or the elderly." He had 2,000 of Tyre's defenders crucified "along the coast, a grim warning of the futility of resisting the conqueror."[62] After taking Egypt, Alexander moved into Mesopotamia, where he sacked the Persian capital of Persepolis, and ravaged its population.[63]

He then moved into Afghanistan, western India, and Central Asia.[64] James R. Ashley has described Alexander's invasion of India as a campaign that "was brutal to the extreme and consisted, for the most part, of the storming of cities and citadels and the massacre and enslavement of their populations." His war in India was "a virtual war of extermination" where "terror and brutality became the order of the day." The reason was simple—the Indians resisted Macedonian dominance and fought to the death to maintain their independence. After defeating the Aspasians, his troops butchered all of their captives because Alexander had been wounded in the battle. After their victory in Sangala in the Upper Punjab, Macedonian troops murdered all of the sick and wounded and burned the city to the ground. Alexander's incessant campaigning drove his army to rebellion in 324 BCE, and a year later, he died in Babylon.[65]

India

After his death, Alexander's empire was divided among his generals, though northwestern India soon fell under the sway of Chandragupta Maurya.[66] Chandragupta is considered one of the greatest kings in Indian history, though some of his success can be attributed to his principal adviser, Kautilya, possibly the author of one of the ancient world's most important political treatises on the science of politics (*Arthaśāstra*). Its sections on military strategy should be seen in the same light as Sun Tzu's earlier *The Art of War*. Though many of the political ideas about rule and conquest are based upon eternal suspicion of all potential threats to state sovereignty and security, the *Arthaśāstra* was very humane when it came to the treatment of prisoners and noncombatants after battle. Though he used the term "extermination" frequently, Kautilya only meant it in the context of a rival monarch. A defeated enemy was to be treated well, he wrote, since postwar massacres only served to "frighten all those kingdoms that surround him and terrifies even his own ministers." A well-treated enemy will gain the victor "new and loyal subjects." Kautilya advised that after battle the victorious king should "'order the release of all prisoners and render help to the distressed, the helpless and the diseased.'"[67]

According to Roger Boesche, this idea very much reflected ancient Indian religious law (*Dharmasutra*) teaching that condemned

> the killing of those who have thrown down their weapons, who have disheveled hair, who fold their hands in supplication, or who are fleeing.[68]

Such humane treatment of the enemy or noncombatant is also mentioned in the *Law of Manu* (*Manusmrti*), another sacred Indian work that condemned the killing of anyone in battle

> who was on the ground if the other was in a chariot...nor the sleeping, nor a person without the attire, nor naked, nor unarmed...nor the one who is not fighting, nor a person but just watching, nor the one wounded.[69]

This also applied to the use of weapons in battle.

> Fighting in battle, [the king] should not kill his enemies with weapons that are concealed, barbed, or smeared with poison or whose points blaze with fire.[70]

In many ways, these ideas about humane treatment of the enemy and noncombatants affected imperial policy during the Maurya Empire, which reached its peak under Chandragupta's grandson Ashoka the Great, who, after militarily uniting India, converted to Buddhism and became an advocate of nonviolence and tolerance. He explains his change of heart in one of his Rock Edicts.

> When he had been concentrated eight years the Beloved of the Gods, the king Piyadassi [Ashoka] conquered Kalinga. A hundred and fifty thousand people were deported, a hundred thousand were killed and many times that number perished. Afterwards, now that Kalinga was annexed, the Beloved of the Gods very earnestly practised *Dhamma* [Buddhist enlightenment teachings], desired *Dhamma*, and taught *Dhamma*. On conquering Kalinga the beloved of the Gods felt remorse, for, when an independent country is conquered the slaughter, death, and deportation of the people is extremely grievous to the Beloved of the Gods, and weighs heavily on his mind. What is even more deplorable to the Beloved of the Gods is that those who dwell there, whether Brahmans [sages], *Bramanas* [wandering monks], or those of other sects, or householders who show obedience to their superiors, obedience to mother and father, obedience to their teachers and behave well and devotedly towards their friends, acquaintances, colleagues, relatives, slaves, and servants—all suffer violence, murder, and separation from their loved ones. Even if those who are fortunate to escape, and whose love is undiminished [by the brutalizing effect of war] suffer from the misfortunes of their friends, acquaintances, colleagues, and relatives. This participation of all men in suffering weighs down on the mind of the Beloved of the Gods. Except among the Greeks, there is no land where the religious orders of the brahmans and *Bramanas* are not to be found, and there is no land anywhere men do not support one sect or another. Today if a hundredth or a thousandth part of those people who were killed or died or were deported when Kalinga was annexed were to suffer similarly, it would weigh heavily on the mind of the Beloved of the Gods.[71]

Romila Thapar notes that after uniting India, there was little else for Ashoka to conquer. Yet regardless of the reasons behind his decision to renounce war as a tool of national policy, Ashoka's decision and his humane statements about the powerful impact of war on a civilian population are unique in antiquity.[72]

China

In many ways, it could be argued that the Mauryan empire of Chandragupta and Ashoka was a bridge between the ancient Near East and China, which itself was on the eve of unification under China's first emperor, Qin Shi Huangdi (r. 221–210 BCE).[73] His conquests and subsequent reign ended the Warring States era, and resulted in the "creation of the major political institutions that defined early imperial China."[74] Interestingly, Confucius, Mozi, Mencius, the Sophists, and Sun Tzu (Sun Wu) all wrote their classical works during the Warring States period.[75]

Sun Tzu is one of the world's most revered military strategists and theorists. His *The Art of War* has stood the test of time and is not only studied in prominent military academies like West Point but has also been used as a model for business executives. Sun Tzu was a general in the state of Wu who wrote that the "actions of the officers [are] responsible for bringing intelligibility and order to the collective behavior of the massed soldiery."[76] His principal themes were the importance of dynamism and "advantage" in battle, and the idea of "non-battling" in strategic thinking.[77] He thought that annexing a country or army was the best option, followed by destroying either. It was also important, he argued, to treat "captured soldiers well in order to nurture them [for our use]. This is referred to as 'conquering the enemy and growing stronger.'"[78]

Such theories, though admirable, did not necessarily translate into humane treatment of the enemy during or after battle. As Mark Edward Lewis has noted, the Qin state (and later empire) was "organized for war," while "slaying enemies or commanding victorious units" could result in promotion and other significant rewards.[79] *The Book of Lord Shang*, a fourth-century BCE book that influenced the pre-imperial Qin state, said that you could tell if a state was strong if the people, "on perceiving war, behave like hungry wolves on seeing meat...Generally, war is a thing that people hate; he who succeeds in making people delight in war, attains supremacy."[80] Post-battle rewards and promotions were based on the number of enemy heads captured and turned over to one's officers, who were now allowed to cut off heads themselves.[81]

Consequently, brutality was one of the hallmarks of war during the Qin dynasty. The *Shih-chi*, one of the standard histories of the era, noted that during the battle of Ch'ang-p'ing, Qin general Po Ch'i massacred 400,000 captives from the Chao state, allowing only "240 of the youngest [Chao] soldiers...to return to Chao."[82] Though these figures are exaggerated, such massacres were a standard part of warfare in China at the time.[83] After the collapse of the Qin (Chin, i.e., China) dynasty, Confucianist scholars accused Qin Shi Huangdi of committing horrible atrocities during his military campaigns.[84] Some contemporary Chinese historians, however, view him differently, calling Qin

> a farsighted ruler who destroyed the forces which has kept China divided, unified the nation, and established the first centralized state in Chinese history. In particular, he is praised for following the Legalist [taught belief in law that treated all men equally] policy of "emphasizing the present while slighting the past" and scorning the Confucians, who looked to the ancient past for their ideals and are portrayed as desiring to restore the old social and political order. His achievements in creating a unified, centralized government, it is now argued, justified his use of violence, in particular, "the burning of books and burying Confucian scholars alive, for which he had been castigated by centuries of Confucian historians."[85]

And, according to the *Basic Annals of Ch'in Shih-Huang*, once he completed his wars of unification, Qin ordered "all weapons [to be] collected and brought to the capital Hsienyang [Xianyang], where they were melted down to make bronze bells and 12 statues of giants, "and placed in the courts and palaces."[86] Eric Yong-Joong Lee adds that it was the Qin emperor who created that country's "first managed international legal order."[87]

Derke Bodde, however, argues that such arguments fail to take into account the dreadful human costs of the Qin wars. While he claims that "1,200,000 men, exclusive of Ch'in [Qin]'s own casualties, were killed or taken prisoner" during these campaigns, he notes that one of the principal lessons learned by Qin leaders during these wars was to be "absolutely ruthless in their warfare." It was a simple matter of "either conquer or be conquered." The result was a "fighting machine" that was "more relentless, more ruthless and more efficient than anything known in the other feudal states of China proper."[88]

The Qin dynasty collapsed after the death of its founder, and was followed by the Han dynasty, which existed for a little more than four centuries. China flourished during this period, but succumbed to various dynastic problems that saw post-Han China wracked by civil war before Jin rulers restored some sense of unity and stability.[89] It is no accident that modern China's principal ethnic group, the Han, takes its name from this dynasty.

Warfare during this was brutal and cruel. In 302 CE, a force led by the prince of Changsa attacked Luoyang, capturing the prince of Qi and butchering 2,000 of his supporters. Four years later, forces from Donghai captured the city of Chang'an and pillaged it, murdering 20,000 of its residents. The *History of the Jin Dynasty* describes the aftermath of the civil war.

> By the Yongjia period [307–312] trouble and disturbances were very widespread. From Yongzhou eastward many suffered from hunger and poverty. People were sold [as slaves]. Vagrants became countless. In the six provinces of You, Bing, Si, Ji, Qin, and Yong there was a bad plague of locusts...Virulent disease accompanied the famine. Also the people were murdered by bandits. The rivers were filled with floating corpses; bleached bones covered the fields...There was much cannibalism. Famine and pestilence came hand in hand.[90]

In 311, the Xiongnu, another tribe possibly related to the Huns, attacked the Jin state, reducing its army "to a mountain of corpses." This was followed by an attack on Luoyang, and the plunder of the Jin capital. Estimates are that "tens of thousands" of civilians died in the assault.[91] Once again, China drifted into chaos and disunity, not to be reunited until 589 under the Sui dynasty. Though short lived, this dynasty paved the way for what would become one of the most glorious eras in imperial Chinese history, the T'ang dynasty.

Rome

The period between the Qin and the T'ang dynasties is occasionally compared to the Roman Empire. And even though ties between these two great empires along the patchwork of trade routes, later dubbed the "silk road," were at best peripheral, they both were aware of each other's greatness. The Chinese referred to the Roman east as the Great Ch'in or Qin (*Ta Ch'in*), while the Romans, who were obsessed with Chinese silk, called the Chinese the silk people (*Seres*).[92]

Like the various Chinese dynasties, the Roman Empire was built on warfare and militarism. To the Roman Republic's citizen body, war was "the highest and most perfect fulfillment of the key values of the community."[93] Such ideals, though, did nothing to temper the brutal, savage nature of Roman warfare. This propensity for violence in combat was bred into the Roman soldier during training, which emphasized hardcore, severe discipline that at times bordered on cruelty.[94]

Rome's opponents were equally brutal. During the Second Punic War (218–201 BCE), for example, Hannibal, the Carthaginian general, ransomed Roman POWs and fed them only enough to keep them alive. On the other hand, he treated Roman allies better, and, on one occasion, "gathered them together, informing them that his war was against Rome, and for the liberty of Italy's people. With this he freed them all without ransom."[95] But after annihilating a Roman army at Lake Trasimene in 217, his troops refused to accept the surrender of some Roman soldiers, who "though lifting their hands and entreating to be spared in the most piteous terms...were finally dispatched either by the horsemen or in some cases by begging their comrades to do them this service."[96] The slaughter continued at Gerunim, where Hannibal ordered his men to kill what remained of the city's population after they refused his offer of peace terms.[97]

But it was at Cannae, 70 miles to the south, where the worst of Carthaginian atrocities took place in early August. In what Robert L. O'Connell calls a "pornography of violence," Hannibal's forces, after surrounding a Roman army of 65,000–70,000, decided to take no prisoners.

> If it is possible to conceive of hell on earth, this human abattoir at Cannae must have been the equal of any hell that history in all its perversity has managed to concoct. Thousands upon thousands packed together, unable to move, beset by the crimes of those in extremis, many of them dressed now in useless chain suits and cooking-pot helmets beneath the broiling sun, without prospect of water, only death offering any relief whatsoever. As time passed, more and more men would have fainted from the heat, slid to the ground, and been trampled beneath the feet of their comrades, their bodies and discarded shields tripping still others who would then have fallen similarly to their deaths. At the outer edges especially, but also in the interior, where javelins rained, the ground would have grown slick with Roman blood, which would have brought down still others. As at Lake Trasimene, the hopeless would have begged their fellows to finish them—presumably there was room for even a short sword thrust—or simply would have done the deed themselves. The stink of death and all the bodily functions that accompany it must have come to pervade the atmosphere and compound the wretchedness of those condemned to take their last breaths there. There was no place worse.[98]

Though Hannibal was ultimately driven out of Italy and defeated by Scipio Africanus, the Romans never forgot the havoc that Hannibal had wreaked throughout Italy. After taking the city of Nova Carthago in Spain, Scipio ordered his soldiers to kill everyone. His troops understood, of course, that while this meant full-scale plunder, one of the core reasons for serving in a Roman legion, it did not mean the outright butchery of everyone in the city. Noncitizen captives were enslaved, while Carthaginian citizens were promised liberty in return for "loyal service" to Rome.[99]

Such retribution did nothing to assuage Roman fears of Hannibal. The fact that he helped revive a defeated Carthage ultimately led to demands that the Carthaginians surrender him to the Romans. Hannibal fled Carthage to avoid arrest, and took poison in 182 or 181 as the Romans closed in on him. It was this paranoid fear of Carthage and Hannibal that led Cato the Elder to insist at the end of each of his speeches in the Senate, "Besides, I think that Carthage must be destroyed" (*Ceretum censeo delendam esse Carthanginem*).[100] Some Roman historians later joined in this chorus and demonized Hannibal, charging falsely that he had encouraged his troops, who were starving as they made their way from Spain to Italy earlier in the Second Punic War, to "eat [the] human flesh" of the local inhabitants.[101]

All of this ultimately led to the outbreak of the Third Punic War in 149 BCE, a conflict that the Carthaginians did everything diplomatically to stop, even offering *deditio*, which involved "the voluntary surrender by a State of all its rights and the placing of itself in the power (*postestas* or *dicio*) of another state."[102] After accepting Rome's terms, the Carthaginians learned that the Romans expected them to evacuate the city of Carthage, which the Romans planned to destroy totally. The Carthaginians now chose to resist. What followed was a three-year siege that resulted in the complete destruction and plunder of Carthage. Roman fury was partially driven by the decision of Hasdrubal, Carthage's military leader, to torture Roman prisoners on the city walls in full sight of the Roman army below. The 50,000 Carthaginians who managed to escape the final Roman onslaught were sold into slavery.[103] Such actions "molded a [Roman] ethos that raised the capacity for violence to the status of virtue."[104]

What is interesting about all of this is the later medieval fascination with the Roman concept of "just war," based on the idea of the principles governing going to war (*jus ad bellum*) and principles about the conduct of war (*jus in bello*).[105] According to Antonio Santosuosso, the basic Roman justifications for going to war centered around three scenarios—to halt a threat to national security, "to right a wrong, or at times civilize barbarians."[106] These concepts were drawn from Cicero's first-century BCE *The Republic*, which stated that

> wars are unjust when they are undertaken without proper cause. No just war can be waged except for the sake of punishing or repelling an enemy... no war is deemed to be just if it has not been declared and proclaimed, and if redress has not been previously sought.[107]

What is often missed in the discussion about Cicero's ideas about just war are his earlier comments about the negative side of Roman warmongering.

> Every empire is gained by war, which always involves harm for the gods of the conquered as well as for the conquered themselves... If there is such a thing as justice, it is the height of folly. If the Romans decided to be just and return other people's property, they would at once revert to poverty and live in huts. Your advantages are the disadvantages of others. Hence, building an empire involves expropriating other people's territory and enriching yourself at their expense. Aggressive generals are held to be the embodiment of valour and excellence. Teachers of philosophy give the cloak of tradition and authority to folly and crimes.[108]

Cicero lived in one of the most turbulent times in Roman history, an era of political decay that saw Roman republican traditions under assault by military leaders such as Pompey and Julius Caesar, whose power rested on the support of the army.

Civil war now became a fixture in the Roman political system and helped pave the way for the imperial system created by Rome's first emperor, Augustus (r. 27 BCE–14 CE). Roman armies now had several duties: defend and expand the borders of the empire and, increasingly, act as a force in the incessant political infighting that plagued the Western empire until its collapse in the fifth century CE. As a result, service in the army remained "the most important public service."[109]

The instability that often plagued the imperial period was exacerbated by constant rebellions on the borders of Rome's vast Mediterranean empire. Julius Caesar discussed one of these early revolts in *The Gallic Wars*. Triggered by what became a common theme in future rebellions—an effort to take advantage of perceived Roman political unrest and weakness—one Gallic leader, Vercingetorix, led a rebellion in Gaul in 52 BCE that presented Rome with its greatest threat since the Punic Wars. Savagery against civilians and soldiers alike became the hallmark of the rebellion. Vercingetorix used a scorched earth policy to prevent the Romans from living off the land and ensure full Gallic resistance to the Romans. According to Caesar, the Gallic chieftain explained the reason for this tactic—it would be "far worse to have their children and wives dragged off into slavery, and themselves be killed" if they were defeated.[110] In the end, Caesar prevailed. Vercingetorix surrendered and was taken back to Rome as a prisoner, where he was ultimately put on public display to celebrate Caesar's victory. By 50 BCE, all of Gaul was in Roman hands. As part of his program to pacify Gaul, Caesar resorted to "great ruthlessness" to bring the region under his control. After he conquered Uxellodunum, Caesar ordered the hands of all of its citizens to be cut off because they had earlier supported Vercingetorix.[111]

The Romans resorted to similar savagery during the Great Jewish Revolt in Palestine between 66 and 70 CE, triggered by the Roman capture of Jerusalem a few years earlier. Jewish disillusionment with Roman rule was exacerbated by Roman insensitivity to Jewish religious traditions and practices, the persecution of some Jewish groups such as the Zealots, and the growing influence of Hellenism.[112] It began when Jewish extremists massacred the Roman garrison in Jerusalem after the region's new proconsul tried to collect Temple taxes. Emperor Nero ordered his best general, Vespasian, to secure the Jewish countryside, which was completed by the latter's son, Titus, who also retook Jerusalem.[113] The Romans were extremely cruel throughout the rebellion and, after an uprising in Alexandria (Egypt), they massacred everyone in the Jewish quarter. According to Jewish historian Josephus, those not directly butchered by the Romans were forced into their homes, which were then set on fire.

> No mercy was shown to the infants; and no regard to the aged; but they [the Romans] went on in the slaughter of persons of every age, until all the place was overflowed with blood.[114]

The Jewish rebellion ended in 70 CE after a five-month siege of Jerusalem. Once inside the city, the Romans

> killed those whom they overtook without and set fire to the houses where the Jews had fled, and burned every soul in them and laid waste a great many of the rest; and when they were come to the houses to plunder them, they found in them entire

families of dead men, and the upper rooms full of dead corpses, that is, of such as died by the famine...they ran everyone through whom they met with, and obstructed the very lanes with their dead bodies, and made the whole city run down with blood, to such a degree indeed that the fire of many of the houses was quenched with these men's blood...they killed the aged and the infirm...but of the young men he chose out the tallest and most beautiful, and reserved them for the triumph.[115]

Afterward, Titus ordered the total destruction of the city and the Second Temple. According to Josephus, over 900 Jewish rebels fled to Masada with their families to avoid the "miseries" they expected at the hands of the Romans if captured. Later, when it was apparent that the Romans would take this mountain redoubt near the Dead Sea, the rebels committed mass suicide to avoid Roman "abuse" of their women and the enslavement of their children.[116] Antonio Santosuosso says that the message of the Romans was clear—"resistance to the legions meant inevitable destruction," adding that "Roman supremacy [was] based on a masterful combination of violence and psychological persuasion."[117] In the end, the western Roman Empire fell prey centuries later partially to its own culture of military violence. According to Will Durant, it "is easier to explain Rome's fall than to account for her long survival."[118]

War in the Post-Roman World and the Middle Ages

Islam and Byzantium

What arose from the ashes of the Roman Empire were the disparate states of Western Europe and the Byzantine Empire in the eastern Mediterranean. In the early seventh century, a new power arose in the Mediterranean world—Islam—that considered warfare an integral part of the spread of this new faith.[119] It also gave birth to the concept of *jihād* or "holy war," which has peaceful and militant connotations. The holiest of Muslim texts, the *Qur'ān*, which Muslims consider "the literal word of God [Allāh] revealed to the prophet Muhammed," mentions it primarily as an act of faith against unbelievers.[120]

> To those against whom war is made, permission is given (to fight), because they are wronged...(They are) those who have been expelled from their homes in defiance of right—(for no cause) except they say, "Our Lord is Allāh."[121]

Jihād rewards those who die in holy war for Allāh with "forgiveness and mercy" and togetherness with Allāh. Failure to fight *jihād* is strongly condemned, though those who are "infirm, or ill...blind" or "lame" are excused from combat. Fighting during *Ramadān*, the Muslim holy month of fasting and spiritual introspection, is frowned upon, though not as much as "access to the path of Allāh." The *Qur'ān* also contains guidelines for the treatment of POWs, who are to be bound upon capture and then either treated with "generosity" or ransomed. If an unbeliever asks for asylum, "grant it to him, so that he may hear the Word of Allāh." And if an enemy sues for peace, Muslims are to "incline toward peace, and trust in Allāh."[122]

What is not certain in all of this is whether *jihād* is a defensive action or applies to any form of military action against unbelievers. The *Qur'ān* states that believers should "fight in the cause of Allāh those who fight you, but do not transgress limits; for Allāh does not love aggressors." On the other hand, the *Qur'ān* states that Muslims should "fight and slay the Pagans wherever you find them, and seize them, beleaguering them, and lie in wait for them in every stratagem [of war]." Such fighting should continue until the unbelievers "pay the Jizya [head tax on non-Muslims] with willing submission and feel themselves subdued."[123]

It was from these concepts that Muslims developed their own codes of war. Abu Bakr, Mohammed's father-in-law and successor, laid down a firm set of laws of war for his troops that were about to move into territory under Byzantine control.

> Stop, O people, that I may give you ten rules for your guidance in the battlefield. Do not commit treachery or deviate from the right path. You must not mutilate dead bodies. Neither kill a child, nor a woman, nor an aged man. Bring no harm to the trees, nor burn them with fire, especially those which are fruitful. Slay not the enemies' flock, save for your food. You are likely to pass by people who have devoted their lives to monastic services; leave them alone.[124]

A century later, Islamic scholar Al-Shaybani wrote that soldiers in battle should "not cheat or commit treachery, nor should you mutilate anyone or kill children."[125] Yet according to Javaid Rehman, "certainly wars and other societal conflicts of early Islamic experience by their very nature were destructive and bloody."[126] Amir b. al-Tufayl, a contemporary of Prophet Mohammed, described in a poem an attack against one of his tribe's enemies.

> We came upon their host in the morning and they were like a flock of sheep on whom falls the ravening wolf...
>
> We fell on them with white steel ground to keenness: we cut them to pieces until they were destroyed;
>
> And we carried off their women on saddles behind us, with their cheeks bleeding, torn in anguish by their nails.[127]

Over the course of three centuries, Arab Muslim armies enjoyed dizzying success throughout parts of the Mediterranean world. However, by the late tenth century, Byzantine rulers began to push back against them, retaking territories along their eastern borders.[128] There was also a diminution of "the anxiety and fear of the unknown [enemy]" and the growth of "mutual respect for recognition of the warriors and their achievements."[129] In the midst of such changes, a new code of war developed between Muslims and Christians that took a more humane view toward POWs. The ransoming of prisoners, a practice that went back to Roman times, was replaced by a system of prisoner exchanges, though there were occasions when Byzantine commanders, weighed down by a large number of prisoners, would simply execute their captives. And both Muslims and Byzantines continued to practice forced conversions in certain instances.[130]

In the midst of these changes, a new Muslim power arose in the Middle East in the eleventh century—the Seljuk Turks. This led to a series of meetings between Roman Catholic and Western Orthodox leaders where the latter painted a dreadful, exaggerated picture of Muslim threats and persecution throughout the eastern

Mediterranean. Such stories, in league with various political and religious consid-erations, ultimately led Pope Urban II to issue the call for a holy war against the Muslims in the Middle East—the First Crusade.[131] Over the course of the next century or so, Western Europe responded with four major crusades designed to retake the Holy Lands from the Muslims. They pitted the best of Europe militarily against the Islamic world. With the exception of the First Crusade (1095–1099), which succeeded in retaking Jerusalem and a modest amount of territory around it, the Crusades were unsuccessful in achieving the complex goals envisioned by Urban II.[132]

In many ways, the atrocities committed by the Christian armies during the Crusades were merely an extension of the ferocious warfare that took place in Europe in the centuries leading up to the First Crusade.[133] This medieval European "culture of violence" targeted the "unarmed segment of the population, the church and the peasants."[134] Since churches, with their artifacts and priceless relics, were often the focus of knightly attacks, the Catholic Church sought ways to curb such militant violence. In 989, Rome issued a decree instituting the Peace of God (Pax Ecclesie), which forbade attacks against church property, the clergy, and Christian pilgrims. It later extended such prohibitions to peasants, their livestock, and businessmen.[135]

When these strictures failed to halt militant violence against noncombatants, Urban II instituted the Truce of God (Treuga Dei), which prohibited warfare from late Saturday evening until Monday, extending this limitation soon after to Thursdays and various Christian holidays. Such restrictions were extended through-out Christian Europe and in 1095, on the eve of the First Crusade, the Council of Clermont called for peace in Europe in preparation for a holy war against Muslims in the Middle East.[136]

> Now the Christian soldier was a warrior whose battles against the enemies of the faith were both ordered and glorified by the papacy.[137]

Not surprisingly, what these holy wars introduced to the Middle East was a level of brutality in warfare not seen since Roman times, particularly toward Muslims. Driven by what David Nicolle calls the "sheer [religious] fanaticism" of the crusad-ers, these Christian "holy warriors" committed untold atrocities against Muslim civilians. "Torture and mutilation became a feature of the early decades of crusader warfare in the Middle East."[138] After the battle of Antioch, the crusaders killed all of the men in the city and sold the women and children into slavery. They also killed all of the Muslims and Jews in Jerusalem because they "saw their God as a punisher" and their victims infidels. And even though recent scholarship has questioned the claims that the crusaders butchered over 70,000 Muslims and Jews when they took Jerusalem, the fact remains that the nature of the massacres, taking place as they did in one of the world's holiest cities, shocked both the Christian and Muslim worlds. Robert the Monk's account of what took place, though exaggerated, was read widely in Europe.[139]

> In no battle were there so many opportunities to kill. Many thousands of chosen soldiers slashed human bodies from head to abdomen...Those who did man-age to get away from such butchery and slaughter made their way to the Temple of

Solomon [Temple Mount and its Al-Aqsa Mosque and the *Dome of the Rock* (*Haram al-Sharif*)]...Our men...found a new rush of courage, broke into the temple and put its occupants to a wretched death. So much human blood was spilt there that the bodies of the slain were revolving on the floor on a current of blood; arms and hands which had been cut off floated on the blood and found their way to other bodies so that nobody could point out which body the arm had come from [or] which was attached to another headless body. Even the soldiers who were carrying out the massacre could hardly bear the vapours rising from the warm blood. Once they had finished this indescribable slaughter their spirits became a little gentler; they kept some of the young people, male and female, alive to serve them.[140]

Given these horrors, it is not surprising that several myths about Christian cannibalism arose after the First Crusade.[141]

How could such behavior take place in the early stages of the age of chivalry? For one thing, this code of honor between knights was just that, "little more of an insurance policy for the fighting upper classes."[142] In fact, in some ways, the age of chivalry—which reached its peak at the height of the Middle Ages—was a reaction both to the violence of early medieval warfare and the Roman Catholic Church's efforts to temper the indiscriminate violence of war. Different wars dictated different codes of conduct for knights. The war to the death (*guerre mortelle*), which meant either killing or enslaving the enemy, was waged "against Muslims and pagans."[143]

The atrocities committed by Christian knights during the Crusades stunned the Muslim world. They were driven not only by the idea that Muslims practiced a pagan faith but also by the stereotype that Muslims themselves were extremely violent. This image was drawn from Byzantine sources that expressed a deep hatred of Islam. European chroniclers fed off of these stereotypes. Hildebert of Lavardin's *Historia de Muhamete* is filled with crude tales about Prophet Muhammed and claims that upon his death, he was buried in an exquisite temple where his coffin was "suspended by magnets to trick his followers into believing he had miraculous powers."[144] Another medieval author, Alexandre du Pont, included many of the stereotypes about Muslims in his tale *Roman de Mahomet*, a fictitious account told from the perspective of a Muslim who converted to Christianity. Once again, the Muslim holy prophet was depicted as a scheming, tricky charlatan.[145]

The brutality of the First Crusade and the desecration of two of Islam's holiest sites on Temple Mount "have been etched deeply in the collective memory of Muslims." Saladin (Salah al-Din), who retook Jerusalem in 1187, was certainly more magnanimous than the crusaders.[146] He offered them peace terms before he besieged the city, which they originally rejected, but later accepted. They also told Saladin that if he did not offer them quarter, they would kill their 5,000 Muslim captives and destroy all of Islam's important shrines in the city. He responded by agreeing not to seek revenge for earlier atrocities committed by the crusaders in 1099, and allowed those residents who could afford to do so to pay a ransom for their freedom once the city capitulated. Those who could not afford the ransom were sold into slavery.[147]

Muslim armies, of course, could be just as brutal as their Christian counterparts. In 1153, after capturing the Christian fortress at Ascalon, the Turks beheaded a group of Knights Templars, sending their "heads . . . as trophies to Cairo."

Their bodies were left to decorate the wall of the captured fortress "as a ghastly gesture of defiance."[148] And on the eve of Saladin's capture of the crusader fortress at Bait al-Ahzan in 1179, the Christians asked for quarter. The Seljuk leader refused, and butchered at least half of the fortress' defenders. Saladin specifically ordered that all of the fortress' staunchest defenders, the crossbowmen, be executed. Such acts were deliberate and were not only driven by revenge but also as a warning to anyone who dared join in the fight against the Muslims.[149]

The Question of "Just War" in the Middle Ages

Given the militancy of the age, it is small wonder that church theologians and philolophers such as Gratian, considered by some to be the father of canon law, and St. Thomas Aquinas, weighed in on the whole question of warfare and, as a result, provided the early theoretical foundations of the Christian definition of "just war." Gratian addressed, directly and indirectly, the moral underpinnings of war and its justification throughout his twelfth-century *Concord of Discordant Canons* (*Concordia discordantium canonum*) or *Decretum*.[150] He drew many of his basic ideas from St. Augustine, who, in turn, relied on some of Cicero's concepts about just war. The Roman philosopher wrote that wars could be justified only if they were undertaken with "proper cause," which he said centered around "punishing or repelling an enemy."[151]

Though scholars differ quite a bit over the whole question of St. Augustine's ideas about just war, there is general agreement about his core principles.[152] He argued that just war had to be undertaken by "rulers and officials acting in the line of duty."

> War was justified when a people or a city neglected either to punish wrongs done by its members or to restore what it had unjustly seized.[153]

This was, according to Frederick H. Russell, an expansion on Cicero's more limited view of just war, which the Roman philosopher saw simply as a means to return to the *status quo ante bellum*. For Augustine, just war

> was thus total and unlimited in its licit use of violence, for it not only avenged the violation of existing legal rights but also avenged the moral order injured by the sins of the guilty party regardless of injuries done to the just party acting as a defender of that order.[154]

Gratian, drawing from Ivo of Chartres' writings on Augustine, described the "legitimate purposes of warfare."

> Peace was the desirable condition, while resort to war must only be in case of necessity. Military prowess, itself a gift of God, and warfare were instrumentalities of peace; for this reason warriors must be pacific even in warfare, for their goal is to return their enemy by conquest to a state of peace. Once victory was achieved, mercy should be shown to enemy captives. Thus wars are only licit when they are necessary to return to a peaceful situation. Good men go to war against violent attackers, and wage wars of pacification (*bella pacata*) to coerce the wicked and sustain the good.[155]

He added that any war that took place as an act of self-defense or to correct an "unjust situation" was just, though, in the latter case, it had to be undertaken by a "constituted authority," not a private individual.[156]

A century later, Aquinas argued that war was "always sinful" though some times justifiable.[157] Such wars had to be waged by one who held "supreme authority" in a state, and had to be fought to "avenge wrongs" and "have a rightful intention."[158] According to Gregory M. Reichberg, at the center of all of this is the idea of *prima facie* or "just cause," meaning that such justification must be based on the fact "that those who are attacked deserve attack on account of some fault."[159]

Eurasia and the Mongols

In the midst of these discussions, a new force threatened Europe—the Mongols—a group that became the scourge of Asia and parts of Europe throughout the thirteenth and fourteenth centuries. The Mongols were initially led by Temuchin (Temüjin), who united the nomadic tribes of Mongolia in the late twelfth and early thirteenth centuries. *The Secret History of the Mongols*, a collection of Mongol folk tales, tells us that after he defeated the Tartars (Turkic tribe from northeast Mongolia) as part of his unification campaign, Temuchin ordered his generals

> To avenge our fathers and forefathers,
> and requite the wrong, for them
> we shall measure *the Tatars*
> against the linchpin of a cart,
> And kill them to the last one,
> We shall utterly slay them.
> The rest we shall enslave:
> Some here, some there, dividing them among ourselves![160]

Clan leaders later rewarded Temuchin with the title Genghis Khan (Chinggis Khan; Great or Universal Leader).

Over the next few decades, his armies invaded the borderlands of China and parts of Central Asia, spreading terror wherever they went. After they conquered Zhongdu, the Jin (Jurchen) dynasty capital near Beijing, they plundered it and massacred thousands. Visitors from Central Asia later noticed a large white hill outside of Zhongdu, and were told that it was the "bones of the massacred inhabitants." They also saw an area "greasy from human fat" just outside the walls of the city, where the "air was so polluted that several members of the mission became ill and some died." Their guides told them that after the capture of Zhongdu, "60,000 virgins threw themselves to death from the fortifications in order to escape capture by the Mongols."[161]

Between 1215 and 1219, Genghis Khan sent missions to the sprawling kingdom of Khwarezm in Central Asia, which was ruled by Shah'Alá' al-Din Muhammad II, to establish diplomatic ties. Though these efforts were initially successful, in 1219 a regional governor had all members of a large Mongol trade mission executed.[162] Genghis retaliated by invading Khwarezm in 1219. One apocryphal story says that after his troops captured Otrar, Genghis ordered that "molten silver...be poured into" the eyes and ears of the commander of the Shah's troops.[163] Over the next four years, the Mongols conquered all of the kingdom,

> massacring, plundering and ravaging. With one stroke a world which billowed with fertility was laid desolate, and the regions thereof became a desert, and the greater part of the living dead, and their skin and bones crumbling dust; and the mighty were humbled and immersed in the calamities of perdition.[164]

This blend of terror and tolerance was a deliberate Mongol tactic. While the Mongols were adept at siege warfare, they preferred the quiet surrender of a city and let it be known that those who resisted would be treated brutally, while those who surrendered peacefully would be spared. This was certainly the case for Samarkand, where city leaders, opposed to efforts by a large Turkish-Tajik military force to defend the city against the Mongols, appealed directly to Genghis Khan to save their city. He agreed but massacred some of the Turkish and Tajik soldiers and sacked the city.[165]

Such tactics became widely known and helped feed rumors throughout Europe about Mongol barbarity. Matthew Paris, one of medieval Europe's most widely read historians, said in his *English History* that the Tartars (the Mongols) were "rude, lawless and inhuman beings," who were "educated in caves and dens, after expelling lions and serpents therefrom." To underscore Mongol savagery, Paris wrote that the Mongols "eat the flesh of horses, dogs, and other abominable meats, and, in times of necessity, even human flesh." Their goal, Paris claimed, was "to subjugate the whole world." Once they had ravaged it, he went on, the Mongols intended to depopulate and devastate the world to purify it.[166]

In early June 1223, the Mongols moved into southern Russia and defeated a Russian force at the battle of the Kalka River. Afterward, the Mongols convinced Russian prince Mstislav to surrender, promising him and his 10,000 men safe passage home in return for paying a ransom. Afterward, the Mongols slaughtered all of Mstislav's men and celebrated their victory with a banquet on a platform. Underneath were the three Russian princes who had commanded troops at Kalka. They were slowly crushed to death by the Mongol banqueters above them.[167]

In the central Volga region,

> they used fire and sword without mercy wherever they found men and property. They filled southern Russia with terror; they swept through the Crimea and ravaged it; they captured Bulgar on the Volga and ruined that opulent city. Sated with bloodshed and laden with booty they returned that same year to headquarters east of the Caspian.[168]

The Mongols then retreated to Mongolia after Genghis Khan's death in 1227. A decade later, his grandson, Batu, invaded the central Volga region of Russia, while other Mongol forces moved southward toward the Caucasus.[169]

He then moved northward, taking Riazan in late 1237. According to the *Tale of the Ravage of Riazan by Batu*:

> The churches of God they devastated, and in the holy altars they shed much blood. And no one in the town remained alive: all died equally and drank the single cup of

death. There was no one here to moan, or cry—neither father and mother over children, nor children over father and mother, neither brother over brother, nor relatives over relatives—but all lay together dead. And all this occurred to us for our sins.[170]

The medieval *Chronicle of Novgorod* was even more descriptive, noting that the "Tartars (Mongols)"

violated nuns, priests' wives, good women and girls in the presence of their mothers and sisters.[171]

Over the next four years, the Mongols completed the conquest of Russia, including its most important city, Kiev. Since Kievan leaders rejected the Mongols' terms of surrender, those who survived their onslaught were butchered, and the city destroyed. The Mongols then moved into Poland, Hungary, Bulgaria, Moldavia, and Wallachia, but eventually retreated to Russia in 1242.[172]

For the next century and a half, the Mongols' Golden Horde ruled Russia from its capital Old Sarai on the lower Volga. Yet it was China, not Russia, that was the principal focus of the Mongols during this period.[173] They conquered much of northern China in the years before and after Genghis Khan's death, though it would be almost 30 years after their conquest of Russia before they resumed their move into the rest of China.[174] After campaigns in the Middle East, East Asia, and southern China, the Mongols' new ruler—Khubilai Khan—overthrew the Song dynasty and became China's new emperor. He ordered his troops not to plunder the countryside and treated the Song royal family with dignity. He granted them generous allowances and homes, but sent the young four-year-old emperor Hsien to Tibet, where he ultimately became a Buddhist monk. By 1279, the new Mongol Yuan dynasty (1272–1368) controlled most of historic China.[175]

Conclusion

Crimes of war and acts of genocide date back to the beginning of history itself. The nature of warfare in early antiquity was excessively brutal and driven by the idea that warfare was something that was blessed by the gods. Over time, we begin to see more attention given to the enslavement of POWs and the treatment of refugees. In Egypt's New Kingdom, military brutality was tempered by the need to treat captured slaves well because of their importance to Egypt's growing manpower needs. Slowly, more humane, tolerant policies in war evolved, particularly in Persia and Greece. In the latter case, what Thucydides called the codes of war, the *koina nomina*, were used to guide the actions of combatants in battle. Similar hints of a more humane approach to warfare developed in India, particularly under Ashoka, a Buddhist who renounced war as a tool of national policy after he unified India. In China, Sun Tzu argued that it was best to treat the defeated enemy well to ensure stable rule afterward, while Qin Shi Huangdi introduced a ruthlessness in war that was to remain a constant in Chinese warfare for centuries.

Similar brutality was a feature of Roman warfare, which led Cicero, St. Augustine, and others to raise questions about the nature of a just war. Centuries later, Gratian and St. Thomas Aquinas discussed this question more deeply in response to failed church efforts to temper the harshness of warfare, particularly during and after the Crusades.

Chapter 2

War and Crimes in China and Postmedieval Europe

Over time, the overextended Mongol Empire collapsed, though its demise in Russia and Central Asia was far more gradual than in China. Like most Chinese dynasties, the Yuan or Mongol dynasty fell prey to a series of rebellions that began in the early 1350s. In 1368, Zhu Yuanzhang (Chu Yüan-chang), a poor Buddhist farmer who headed the Red Turbans, a secret Buddhist society, overthrew the last Yuan emperor, Toghon Temür. Zhu named his new dynasty Ming ("brilliant") and became the Hongwu (Hung-wu; "vastly martial") emperor. China blossomed under the Ming rulers, who fostered a cultural reawakening unmatched in the world at that time.[1]

Ming China was a hierarchical society led by Confucian-educated bureaucrats, royal eunuchs, and high-ranking military officers who held hereditary ranks. The military played an important role in the overthrow of the Mongol dynasty, and, over time, grew to a force of a million men. Yet the Mongols always remained a threat, which prompted Ming emperors to greatly expand the Great Wall and move the capital from Nanjing to Beijing to oversee better the defense of northern China.[2]

Warfare in China at this time was extremely brutal. The chronicle of Zhu Yuanzhang's reign, the *T'ai-tsu shih-lu*, offers numerous accounts, some exaggerated or fictional, about military practices, particularly the treatment of the enemy during combat. After a battle in 1360, Zhu lured the Mongol commander Ch'en Youliang (Ch'en yu-liang) into a trap that resulted in the latter's defeat during the siege of Hangzhou. In the midst of a rain storm, Zhu's "men ambushed Ch'ien's forces as pre-arranged, slaughtering and capturing more than twenty thousand of them."[3] In 1449, an Oirat Mongol force under Esen defeated a Ming army at T'u-mu, about 100 miles northwest of Beijing. About half of the 500,000 Ming troops died in battle, including all of their officers. Esen's troops also captured the emperor, Ying-tsung, and held him for ransom. The Mongols then unsuccessfully tried to take Beijing and, in retreat, ravaged the countryside.[4]

Success in battle in China at this time was gauged by the rank of the captured soldier or officer, or the number killed in battle,

verified by turning in either the captive or his head. The latter verification was far more convenient and more commonly used. The size of the reward depended on the war zone in which the act occurred. That is, the reward was graded according to the dangers accompanying the action and the fierceness of the enemy. Capture in battle of an enemy general or other commander brought special rewards. Otherwise enemy heads taken on the northern and northeastern frontiers brought the highest rewards, those taken on the western (Tibetan) frontier and in fighting against the southwestern aborigines ranked second, and heads taken from fellow Chinese while fighting bandits or rebels ranked last. In times of special crisis the system was altered to give higher rewards for heads of the most dangerous new enemies of the moment. That system had many critics, especially Confucian, pacifist-minded statesmen who recognized it as an encouragement to victimize the innocent—ruthless commanders were often accused of beheading unfortunate noncombatants in the war zone or even far behind the lines in order to magnify their records. Antimilitarist censors also often uncovered false claims from commanders who, unlike individual fighting men, benefitted from the total number of heads taken by their units when they announced "victories" and claimed rewards. But though often criticized, the system was not changed.[5]

Though Ming armies and the navy had been successful in toppling the Yuan dynasty, their military prowess ultimately suffered from the imperial decay that led to the collapse of the Ming dynasty in the seventeenth century. By the late sixteenth century, it became mired in its own inefficiency and corruption, which weakened Ming efforts to defend itself from a series of domestic and international threats. Though Ming armies thwarted two Japanese invasions of Korea between 1592 and 1597, they suffered humiliating losses on the battlefield. After the final battle in 1597, the Japanese claimed "they took 38,700 [Chinese] heads."[6]

Such atrocities were also a common problem during the peasant rebellions that took place during the final decades of the Ming dynasty. To some degree, this was caused by the lack of adequate military training of lower-level peasant commanders. One rebel leader, Teng I, was burned to death when he tried to discipline his troops. Because of the emphasis on captured heads as a means of gauging military success in battle, soldiers often murdered innocent civilians for their heads "as fake evidence of having garnered a victory." Looting and rape was also widespread among rebel armies.[7] Court officials were occasionally complicit in such atrocities. After Chinese troops put down a rebellion led by Yang Ying-lung in southwestern China in 1598, the court ordered his body be sent to Beijing "for desecration."[8] Forty-three years later, Ming officials sent a eunuch general to help lift the siege of Nan-gang. Though the eunuch and his troops arrived too late to help the city, they "seem to have set something of a record in looting, kidnapping women, and slaughtering peasants whom they claimed to be rebels. Their actions became so flagrant that an investigation was ordered, and the eunuch general was eventually executed."[9]

After the capture of Wuchang in 1643, rebel troops under Chang Hsien-chung butchered thousands of city residents and murdered more by forcing them into the Yangtse river. One source claimed "the fish devoured so many corpses as to become unfit for food." On the other hand, other sources state that Chang went to great lengths to aid the starving refugees. Chang adopted similar violent tactics after he conquered Chengdu in the fall of 1644, gaining a reputation as "a rebel leader who is an example *par excellence* of ruthlessness and savagery."[10] According to one legend, Chang promised his wife during a serious illness that he "would offer two 'heavenly candles' as a sacrifice if he recovered." His "sacrifice" was to have

> the small bound feet of many women cut off and placed in two piles, and since the feet of one of his own concubines were usually small, he had them severed and placed on top of each pile. Then, oil was poured on and both piles set afire in fulfillment of his promise to offer two "heavenly candles."[11]

According to Martin Martini, a Jesuit priest who worked as a missionary in Hangzhou from 1642 to 1651 and 1658 to 1661, Chang also struck out against those he suspected of opposing his reign of terror.

> [Chang] called all the students of the country to be examined for their degrees, promising to give those honours to whosoever should deserve them best, and the Chinese are so bewitched with the desire for these dignities that they did not conceive the perfidious stratagem of the tyrant. There appeared therefore in the public hall deputed for that ceremony about eighteen thousand persons all of which he commanded his soldiers to massacre most barbarously, saying that these were the people who by their caviling sophisms solicited the people to rebellion.[12]

There were also instances where Chang would order the death of an official for no other reason than he disliked the size of his mansion. There was also an occasion when he ordered the execution of 1,000 Buddhist monks whom he accused of hiding a Ming official in their monastery. Another account claims that Chang had 980,000 soldiers murdered because he doubted their loyalty. There were also reports that he brought "vicious dogs into court sessions and killed officials whom they [the dogs] sniffed at."[13] In the end, his reign of terror backfired, and Chang decided to flee to Chengdu. Before he left, he decided on a "scorched earth" policy to destroy the region. The *Ming shih*, the official history of the Ming state, claims that 600 million Chinese died in Sichuan province because of this policy, though scholars doubt that Chang ever initiated it. Yet one of his generals, Sun K'o-wang, appealed to Chang to stop the butchery:

> The king [i.e., Chang Hsien-chung] has been moving around and waging war for thirty years. Every place the king went through in the past was slaughtered, with the result that there is not even an inch of land left to depend on for our defense. That is not what the generals and the soldiers have aimed at in following the king's command. We struggled to take over this land at the risk of dying ten thousand times, and now we have got it. It is hoped that you will become a king and that the great business of overlordship can be accomplished. If the massacre of the people is attempted again in this area, what, then is the good for us to continue living? I would like to ask you to let me kill myself before the people with the sword with which you are holding in your hand.[14]

His plea fell on deaf ears. Jesuits in Chengdu, for example, talked about widespread looting and violence, particularly against women. James Parsons adds that the "slaughter of women by Chang's forces is mentioned so frequently in the sources that it seems to have been one of the stereotypical means employed by the rebels for displaying loyalty and valor, though it undoubtedly had more restrictive usage than the sources would indicate."[15]

Chang was finally defeated in early 1647 by a special Manchu "expeditionary force," one of the culminating acts in the Manchu reunification of China.[16] Three years earlier, the Manchu captured Beijing, and the new Manchu or Qing emperor, Shun-chih, in league with his uncle, Dorgan, unified China. Toward the end of their campaigns, the Manchus laid siege to the city of Yangzhou, and savaged it as a warning to anyone who dared challenge Manchu authority in the future.[17]

Our principal source for the atrocities that took place in Yangzhou is Wang Xiuchu's *An Account of Ten Days in Yangzhou* (*Yangzhou shiri ji*). Almost from the moment that Qing soldiers entered the city, they began killing people. Wang witnessed horrible atrocities as he tried to escape the rampaging soldiers.

> Several dozen people were herded like cattle or goats. Anyone who lagged were flogged or killed outright. The women were bound together at their necks with a heavy rope—strung one to another like pearls. Stumbling with each step, they were covered with mud. Babies lay everywhere on the ground. The organs of those trampled like turf under horses' hooves or people's feet were smeared in the dirt, and the crying of those still alive filled the whole outdoors. Every gutter or pond that we passed was stacked with corpses, pillowing each other's arms and legs. Their blood had flowed into the water, and the combination of green and red was producing a spectrum of colors. The canals, too, had filled to level with dead bodies.[18]

Wang watched as several Qing soldiers humiliated a group of seamstresses, forcing them first to undress and then fondling them as one was forced to measure the other women for new gowns. One soldier remarked,

> When we campaigned in Korea [in 1627 and 1636–1637] we captured women by the tens of thousands, and not one lost her chastity. How is it that wonderful China has become so shameless? Alas, this is why China is in chaos.[19]

The women who were fondled "felt so ashamed and awkward that they wanted to die."[20] Wang, who was frantically searching for his family, at one point hid in a mound of dead bodies. Over time, some residents seemed resigned to their fate, and when gathered for mass execution

> would all hang their heads and grovel, or stretch out their necks to receive the sword, and not a one would dare to flee.[21]

Wang described another scene where a soldier, dressed in red, grew angry when one of his captives, a young boy, begged his mother for something to eat. "The soldier grew angry and bashed in the child's skull with one blow."[22] Wang and his wife, who had a miscarriage during the rampage, became so desperate that they tried unsuccessfully to hang themselves. When soldiers reappeared in their home, they both fled. After the soldiers left, Wang searched for his wife, and found her with

> other women all lying on a woodpile, their bodies smeared with blood, gobs of excrement in their hair, their faces powdered with ashes. They looked like phantoms, and I could tell which one my wife was only by her voice.

They hid Wang under their bodies, and gave him a bamboo tube to use to breathe.[23]

Fires broke out in the city on the fifth day of the massacres, and many residents committed suicide by staying in their homes as the fires spread across the city. Wang said that

> when not trembling with fear, I quite lost my senses, and, on the whole, no longer knew whether I was still in the human world.[24]

The Qing soldiers seemed to take pleasure in violating women in Yangzhou. Wang watched as one group of soldiers gang raped a number of young women.

> Suddenly one of them hoisted one of the younger women and crudely copulated with her under a tree. Then the two other younger women were sullied while the two older ones wailed and begged to be spared. The three younger ones shamelessly thought nothing of it when about a dozen men took turns raping them before handing them over to the two soldiers who'd run up later. By that time one of the younger women couldn't even get up to walk.[25]

After ten days, the horrors ended. Wang Xiuchu's final words were

> All I intend is that people of later generations who are fortunate to live in a peaceful world and to enjoy uneventful times, but who neglect self-cultivation and reflection and are inveterately profligate, will read this and be chastened.[26]

While it would be unfair to see the early Qing dynasty totally through the prism of the Yangzhou massacre, such atrocities do underscore the extent to which Qing rulers were willing to go to send a signal about the price that would be paid by anyone who challenged Manchu rule in the future.

Born as it was in war and violence, it should not be surprising that "military affairs was one of the Qing state's most distinctive features."[27] The Qing dynasty's three greatest emperors, Kangxi (r. 1662–1722), Yongzheng (r. 1722–1736), and Qianlong (r. 1736–1796), all integrated martial themes with traditional Chinese culture to counter what they saw as the excesses of the late Ming dynasty. Qianlong became obsessive about "warfare and its trappings and uses," and saw "martial prowess" as "a mark of a superior civilization." He hoped that this emphasis on all things military would help create "a uniquely Qing form of nationalist ideology."[28]

Imperial China would, territorially speaking, reach its zenith during the Qing dynasty, in large part because of the expansion into Inner Asia—Mongolia, Tibet, and Chinese Turkestan. The dynamics of warfare changed during this period with the increasing use of artillery and, in the case of the Chinese Green Standard Army, and most of the Manchu Banner forces, matchlock rifles. On the other hand, the more elite Manchu Banner forces continued to rely "primarily on mounted cavalry." The end result of these wars of expansion, which finally secured China's far-flung borders, was the creation of a China far more secure than at any time in its recent history. "It was a very peaceful and prosperous land, a center of world trade exporting vast quantities of both agricultural and industrial (primarily handicraft) goods."[29]

But it was also a time of civil war, particularly during the early part of the reign of the Kangxi emperor. In some cases, particularly when the rebellions or challenges to his power involved disloyal generals or court officials, he adopted a "dual policy of marshaling force and offering amnesty at the same time."[30] But not all situations lent themselves to such a policy and, where necessary, the emperor could be as brutal as his predecessors. At the end of the War of the Three Feudatories (1673–1681), his advisers suggested that "large numbers of rebel leaders be executed and their families enslaved." Kangxi agreed, and though there was "no general bloodbath," he approved the execution of many rebel leaders. He also ordered that warlord Keng Ching-chung and a handful of other generals be sliced to death. Others were "hacked to death" in front of the emperor's troops. Some rebels were also executed, even though the emperor had promised them amnesty if they surrendered. Kangxi explained this contradictory policy in an imperial rescript to one of his generals.

> I think that whenever you are going to do something, you must think through both the background and the consequences. If it will be to the benefit of the state (*kuo-chia*), then you can take action. But lightly embarking on a dangerous course will inevitably lead to trouble. At the present time...the remaining rebel groups who are stretching out their necks in their desire to return to the right path cannot just be numbered by hundreds or thousands. If we now kill Keng Ching-chung, then not only will those who have already surrendered expect to receive the same punishment at a later date, but those who have not yet surrendered will note this example and grow cold at heart—with unknown consequences...If you are really able to do what I have ordered and get him to come to Peking, then everything will be settled peacefully.[31]

Kangxi was not pleased with the performance of his military during these conflicts, and in 1710 began to make changes in the state military examinations that future officials had to pass if they hoped to have a successful military career. These exams, which shared much with the civilian Confucianist exams, centered around the study and mastery of the *Seven Military Classics* (*Wu jing qi shu*), a body of military treatises drawn from Chinese antiquity. The emperor, who had read these works, was very critical of some of them and decreed the ones to be read by those studying for the military exams. He was particularly fond of Menzi (Mencius), Confucius' disciple, and wanted to integrate Menzi's teachings into the military curriculum to create "Confucian generals."[32]

Kangxi was drawn to Menzi because of the sage's criticism of the conduct of ancient Chinese warfare. Menzi criticized "people who say 'I am an expert at military formations; I am an expert at waging war,'" calling such statements "a grave crime." In a series of discussions with King Hui of Liang, Menzi criticized the monarch for his fondness for war. He suggested, instead, that Hui pay more attention to the general welfare of his people, reminding him that there was no difference between killing a man "with a knife and killing him with misrule."[33]

The Kangxi emperor's reforms were short-lived and later abolished by the Qianlong emperor, who was devoted to the "militarization" of Chinese culture.[34] Kangxi's son, Yongzheng, also faced the challenges of civil war, particularly, from the Zunghars (Junghars), a western Mongol group.[35] Devout Tibetan Buddhists, the Zunghars controlled much of western Mongolia and the Qinghai province. A treaty between China and Russia in 1689 forced the Zunghars into the territory claimed by China, and they became an irritant to a Chinese state determined to secure its far-flung borders.[36] In 1729, Yongzheng vowed "to exterminate the Zunghar state" but failed in his initial efforts to do so. Afterward, he wrote to Gen. Yue Zhongqi, who had commanded the emperor's troops during this campaign, and told him

> to kill as many of the enemy as possible...You may take measures on the frontier to rouse up the warrior spirit, and proclaim an advance to exterminate the enemy, stirring up the troops to kill before advancing.[37]

In 1738, the Zunghars agreed to a peace settlement with the Qing court, though this new relationship soon began to unravel.[38] This led to further conflicts and rebellions among other Mongol groups.[39] Consequently, in 1756, the Qianlong emperor ordered his generals to subdue the Zhunghars and "massacre...all Zhungarian captives."

> Show no mercy at all to these rebels. Only the old and weak should be saved. Our previous military campaigns were too lenient. If we act as before, our troops will withdraw, and further trouble will occur.

In a later edict, he added:

> If a rebel is captured and his followers wish to surrender, he must personally come to the garrison, prostrate himself before the commander, and request surrender. If he only sends someone to request submission, it is undoubtedly a trick. Tell Tsengünjav [a Mongol general in Qing employ] to massacre these crafty Zunghars. Do not believe what they say.[40]

He rewarded commanders who reported or oversaw such massacres. He praised one for "exterminating" the followers of a rebel leader, and punished others who failed to adopt such harsh policies. He told another general, Chebudengzhabu, to "take the young and strong and massacre them," and leave the women alive "as booty." Young men who surrendered were to be executed because "their ancestors had been chieftains."[41] Qianlong also ordered his commanders to starve the Zunghars, stating that it would be "easy to exterminate rebels because they had run out of provisions." The elderly, children, and women "would be spared and sent as bond servants to other Mongol tribes and Manchu bannermen." But they would no longer be identified as Zunghars.[42] This was part of a broader Qing policy to eradicate all hints of Zunghar history and culture.[43] Qing commanders were told that

> the captives must not be treated according to the usual rule for dealing with bandits: "These are not ordinary cattle rustlers. They must be captured and executed. Why should we have to distinguish leader and follower? These tribes have many bandits; if we do not completely exterminate them [*jiaomie jingjin*], it will be no good for the Mongols and merchants." The goal was not merely to put down a rebellion but to "cut off the roots" of the Zunghar resistance.[44]

Peter C. Perdue notes that such policies were a significant departure from earlier Qing efforts that emphasized "using barbarians to fight barbarians." The Qing, he adds, adopted this policy of "ethnic genocide" to achieve a "final solution" to China's northwest frontier problems, which lasted for a century. It worked. "The Zunghars disappeared as a state and as a people, and the Zungharian steppe was almost completely depopulated."[45] Perdue places blame for the

> obliteration of as many as a million Zunghars on a combination of starvation, battlefield death, Chinese massacres, epidemic disease, dispersed through flight, and enslavement to Chinese, Russian, Kazakh, and other warlords. Russian tacit acquiescence to the extermination of the Zunghar state was critical to Chinese success.[46]

Qing historian Wei Yuan

> estimated the total population of the Zunghars at 600,000 people, [and] stated, "Of several hundred thousand households, 40 percent died of smallpox, 20 percent fled to the Russians and Kazakhs, and 30 percent were killed by the Great Army. [The remaining] women and children were given as [servants] to others... For several thousand *li* [one-third of a mile] there was not a single Zungharian tent." Zungharia was left as a blank social space, to be refilled by a state-sponsored settlement movement of millions of Han Chinese peasants, Manchu bannermen, Turkestani oasis settlers, Hui, and others.[47]

Christopher I. Beckwith concludes that only 10 percent of the Zunghars survived Qianlong's extermination campaign.[48]

This significant departure from traditional Chinese policy reflects a certain imperial arrogance that would later prove to diminish many of the accomplishments of Qianlong's reign. His military campaigns ultimately led to serious budgetary problems, caused in part by corrupt military leaders. Such corruption became endemic throughout the Chinese state, and left the country unprepared for renewed efforts by Qing rulers to deal with a population that grew to over 301 million by 1790, and efforts by the West to gain a stronger foothold in China.[49]

Sadly, as Jonathan Spence has noted, the "signs of decay and even collapse" were embedded in the very greatness of Qianlong's long reign. The stage was now set for a dramatic clash of cultures that pitted a decaying, autocratic China with Western ideas about the rights and powers of states in a broad international context. It was also a clash of economic systems—one driven by the idea that China's greatness was such that it had little need of anything from the outside barbarian world—and the other by a rapacious Western desire for economic expansion and markets.

The Changing Nature and View
of War in Early Modern Europe

China's downward spiral in the late eighteenth and nineteenth centuries contrasted sharply with a significant change in military thinking in the West, accompanied by the development of new weapons that increasingly depersonalized the nature of warfare. To some extent, these changes and ideas about warfare should be seen through the prism of new, emerging ideas and laws about individual rights *vis-à-vis* those of the state. In other words, the development of civilized codes of war had to be preceded by the development first of domestic laws that offered some protection of individual rights in Europe's emerging national states. The linkage of war to the individual was a core part of the medieval concept of "just war," which was strongly based on a universal concept of natural law. The *Magna Carta* (1215) gives some hints of this new shift as does Emperor Charles V's *Constitutio Criminalis Carolina* (1530/1532) or the "Carolina of 1532."[50] The "Carolina" was centered on "'justice and the common good...' Justice had a transcendent moral dimension. The common good had a practical historical dimension."[51]

Such changes took place in the midst of the dramatic political, intellectual, and religious upheavals that swept Europe during the Reformation. Martin Luther's emphasis on what Richard Marius calls his paradoxical concept of the "priesthood of all believers" vis-à-vis that of the Roman Catholic Church gives a hint of the vibrant power of the idea of the individual in a spiritual context.[52] Luther embraced the notion

> that law—including both the moral law of the Bible and the civil law—is primarily an instrument of God's will for the earthly kingdom alone, and that, contrary to Roman Catholic doctrine, works of the law are not a path to salvation in the heavenly kingdom.

Luther thought that law should serve three divine purposes—"to define and condemn sins"; to use penalties to prevent people from committing such sins; and to teach people the "right conduct."[53] This, plus ideas about the individualization of authority, would, over time, also affect the nature of warfare.

Sadly, the Reformation was more than just a revolution of ideas—it was also an era of war—with widespread violence, torture, and other crimes. After the Peasants War of 1524, there was "torture and death for thousands [of rebels] who had survived mass slaughter on the battlefield."[54] Later that century, France's Catholics rose up against the country's Protestant Huguenots, and, after the St. Bartholomew's massacre in Paris on August 24, 1572, began a nationwide campaign of "savage killings and mutilations" that resulted in 5,000 deaths.[55]

But the worst of these religious conflicts was the Thirty Years War (1618–1648). According to C. V. Wedgwood, the "individual peasant suffered atrociously" in this conflict.[56] It began as a rather obscure Catholic-Protestant brush-up in Prague (the "defenestration of Prague") that soon exploded into what would become a series of religious and political wars that ultimately pitted the vast Habsburg empire against its greatest continental rival, Bourbon France. Yet what was it about the Thirty Years War that made it such a transformative force in the development of the laws of war and precedents for the later evolution of international humanitarian war? Part of the answer lies in the dramatic changes that had taken place in the nature of warfare during the previous century. This "military revolution" meant that the methods and tactics of fighting were now much more destructive and produced greater suffering for combatants and civilians trapped in the midst of a battle or campaign. It

> involved new techniques of fortification, a capacity to raise larger armies, and, above all, the effective use of firearms. Artillery became a fixture on the battlefield, firing solid balls, explosive shells, or canister: metal containers filled with bullets and scrap metal. Muskets appeared and, despite atrocious accuracy and cumbersome loading procedures, gained effectiveness through such techniques as the infantry volley (in which a long line of infantry fired together and then moved back to reload, its place taken by another line, allowing for a continuous barrage). The ringlock bayonet allowed soldiers to use their muskets both as firearms and as short, deadly pikes. As a result, by the eighteenth century, battles frequently involved the death of 40 percent of the participants, and, occasionally, much more.[57]

One of the most innovative developments was the creation of large standing armies made up of local recruits. Such armies were an early reflection of the emergence of nation-states during this period.[58] This was what led King Gustav II Adolf (Gustavus Adolphus; 1594–1632), Sweden's greatest monarch, to issue his *Articles of War* (*Krigsartiklar*), considered by some to be not only the basis of modern military law, particularly in the United States, but also of modern international humanitarian law (IHL). A great deal is made of articles 88–91 and 99–100 since they address questions of individual war crimes and violations of IHL or the laws of armed conflict. Gustav drew his code from past Swedish regulations as well as other European codes of war that were, according to Michael Roberts, "designed primarily for a national conscript army." Unfortunately, these humanitarian strictures did little to keep Gustav's army from committing crimes against civilians in the German states, though their excesses were far less severe than those of other armies at the time.[59]

One of the other things that changed the dynamics of the Thirty Years War was the "printing press, which had free rein, and events both major and minor [were] widely reported in contemporary newspapers, pamphlets, and broadsheets, often providing graphic descriptions in which sensationalism and propaganda [were] broadly distinguishable."[60] It was in this environment that Hugo Grotius wrote his monumental *The Rights of War and Peace* (*De Iure Belli ac Pacis libri*; 1625). Considered by some to be the father of international law, Grotius' ideas were a bridge between the medieval European laws of war and a new pre-Enlightenment insistence on a more civilized approach to industrially destructive wars. They also reflected the growing concern among scholars in the early modern era about the nature of war, its justification, and war crimes.

What gave rise to such concerns, historically speaking, was the emergence of the "nation state" and with it the "law of nations." Grotius gave voice to these changes, particularly the law of nations. According to Stephen C. Neff, there were two things that distinguished the new concept from the earlier law of nature or natural law (*jus naturale*)—the idea that there was "a set of universal norms applicable to all nations and peoples at all times."[61] The first was "that it focused on the rights and duties of states as such—i.e., that it was law applicable *only* to states." The second was that it concentrated on "the external actions of states," thereby forging "consideration of good faith and mutual attitude and the like." Natural law continued to guide thinking about warfare during this period, though, over time, the concept of the law of nations began to hold sway.[62]

Grotius' writings also "contained the first authoritative statement of the principle of humanitarian intervention—the principle that exclusiveness of domestic jurisdiction stops when the outrage upon humanity begins." Though these concepts can be found in the works of earlier legal scholars such as Francisco Suárez and Alberico Gentili, Grotius' statement about the "right of humanitarian intervention" made his contributions unique.

> We must also know that Kings, and those who are invested with a Power equal to that of Kings, have a Right to exact Punishments, not only for Injuries committed against themselves or their Subjects, but likewise, for those which do not peculiarly concern them, but which are, in any Persons whatsoever, grievous Violations of the Law of Nature or Nations... it is so much more honourable, to revenge other Peoples' Injuries rather than their own.[63]

According to Theodore Meron, this statement about "the right of humanitarian intervention... to punish the perpetrators of gross violations of human rights committed in another state," is "an important precursor to the recognition in modern international law of universal jurisdiction over such matters as genocide, war crimes and crimes against humanity."[64]

Also embedded in Grotius' writings about war was the idea that it was more rational than interpersonal. Enemy soldiers were "being killed not because of any personal wickedness or acts of wrongdoing on their part, but rather by virtue of their *status* as members of the opposing armed force." Such ideas can be partially traced back to the medieval concept of just war, which emphasized individual responsibility in fighting a just or unjust war. These perspectives are probably what prompted Gustav II to carry a copy of *De Iure Belli* with him in the field.[65]

All of this points to the significance of Grotius' work as an important intellectual bridge to the development of Enlightenment ideas about the nature and definition of war, particularly its justification. He laid out three just reasons for war—"*Defence*, the *Recovery* of what's our own, and *Punishment*."[66] According to Neff, Grotius' list of *justa causa* "acquired virtually canonical status, to be reverently endorsed by international lawyers for centuries to come."[67] Most important was Grotius' idea of punishment, which, grounded as it was in natural and not divine law, "provided the natural law foundation for his defence of a right to wage war on behalf of the oppressed."[68]

Grotius wrote at the end of what Peter Gay calls the "era of pagan Christianity," a period between 1300 and 1700 that embraced the "affinity of the Enlightenment to classical thought." This pre-Enlightenment era, he argues, "supplied the Enlightenment with its image of the past, both pagan and Christian, its vocabulary, its philosophical methods, and much of its program."[69]

This pre-Enlightenment era culminated with the work of Isaac Newton and John Locke, who influenced the scientific and legal revolutions that began in the second half of the seventeenth century.[70] Both men wrote during the Scientific Revolution and contributed to the three principal ideas of the Enlightenment—natural law governs the universe, intelligence and scientific inquiry can lead to solutions and fundamental questions—and, according to Locke—that one's environment opens the door to unlimited human improvement.[71]

Locke argued in his *Two Treatises of Civil Government* (1690) that, over time, governments, which theoretically existed as the collective will of the people, had occasionally abused their power. He proposed that when this abuse happened, people had the right to change it. Government, Locke said, never had any authority over people's lives, liberty, or property without their consent.[72] He added in his *Letter concerning Toleration*, written in exile several years before England's Glorious Revolution, that no one in a civil society should be deprived of their "civil enjoyments" because they belonged to a certain church or religion. In fact, "neither pagan, nor Mahometan [Mohammedan or Muslim], nor Jew, ought to be excluded from the civil rights of the commonwealth, because of his religion." Locke's ideas reflected the shift in thinking about the rights of individuals vis-à-vis that of governments in the late seventeenth century.[73]

Jean Jacques-Rousseau, an eighteenth-century French *philosophe*, added to this growing body of Enlightenment thinking about such rights by criticizing Grotius for writing that when "an individual can alienate his freedom, and enslave himself to a master, why could not a whole people alienate its freedom, and subject itself to a king?" Such ideas, Rousseau argued, "assume a people of madmen; madness does not make right." He believed that natural law made men free, and that to give up one's freedom was "incompatible with the nature of man, and to deprive one's will of freedom is to deprive one's actions of all morality."[74]

He also challenged Grotius' argument that in war "the victor has the right to kill the vanquished." Rousseau saw war

> not [as] a relationship between one man and another, but a relationship between the state and another, in which individuals are enemies only by accident, not as men, nor even as citizens, but as soldiers; not as members of the fatherland, but as its defenders. Finally, any state can only have other States, and not men, as enemies, inasmuch as it is impossible to fix a true relation between things of different nations.[75]

This differentiation between state and people was an important part of Rousseau's ideas about the primacy of the people's will vis-à-vis that of a temporal ruler. Given man's "naturally peaceable and timorous" nature, war was not something fought "between man and man." Instead, it was something fought between states where "no one has the right to dispose of his own or another's life."[76]

Newton, Locke, and Rousseau were writing during one of the most militant periods in European history. While the Thirty Years War did result in the emergence of France as Europe's most powerful state and reduced Habsburg lands principally to Central Europe, it did nothing to still the ongoing wars of nation and empire building in the second half of the seventeenth and most of the eighteenth centuries.[77] Yet David A. Bell argues that war during most of the latter century in Europe was limited by a number of factors that made it far less devastating than in the past. With the exception of Prussia, whose "precocious 'militarism'" transformed it into "an army which has a state," most of Europe was just beginning to develop new military systems distinctly separate from the rest of society. The officer caste in these new armies was usually drawn from the aristocracy, while military campaigns saw "soldiers and civilians mixed promiscuously together." Bell notes, for example, that when Sweden's monarch, Karl XII, invaded Russia in 1709 during the Great Northern War, almost a quarter of his force was made up of civilians. The officer was first and foremost a gentleman with little training in military science or battlefield tactics. French officers, in fact, often did not wear uniforms in campaigns, and considered it a breach of etiquette to wear a military uniform in court.[78]

Consequently, Bell disagrees with military historians such as John Keegan, who argue that a "warrior culture" dominated European armies during this period. On the other hand, war in the eighteenth century was a deadly serious undertaking and considered so normal that countries devoted the bulk of their revenues to it. Most importantly, Bell argues, "war is what the rulers did." It was the principal undertaking of a monarch and his nobility, and conducted with aristocratic values.[79] Jean-Paul Rabaut Saint-Etienne, an eighteenth-century Huguenot pastor, wrote that

> Wars are less bloody than among ignorant and savage peoples: armies slaughter each other politely; heroes salute before killing each other; soldiers of opposing armies pay each other visits before battles, as people lunch together before an outing. No longer is it nations which fight each other, but just armies and professionals; wars are like games of chance in which no one risks his all; what was once a wild rage (*fureur*) is now just silly (*une folie*).[80]

Such aristocratic values did nothing to temper the horrors of eighteenth-century war, which often saw casualty rates of 40 percent or more.[81] Consequently, many aristocrats were horrified by what they saw on the battlefield. The Marquis d' Argenson, who briefly served as Louis XV's foreign minister, noted that after the battle of Fontenoy in 1745, he vomited seeing "the corpses stripped naked, the enemies dying in agony, the awful scenes, the wounds steaming in the air." Triumph, he later wrote, "is the most beautiful thing in the world," though "its foundation is human blood and shreds of human flesh."[82]

Yet despite such horrors, writers such as Voltaire tried to capture the "aristocratic ideal of war" in their writings. What was important was not the experience or feelings of those involved, he argued, but how commanders and their troops "lived up to an impersonal aristocratic ideal of splendor, courage, and honor." The result was small, well-trained, and expensive armies whose size, fortunately, limited the devastation of war itself.[83] The wars of Frederick the Great, eighteenth-century Europe's "magnificent enigma," offer us a glimpse into the nature of such military campaigns.

During the Seven Years War (1756–1763), he had about 150,000 men under arms, and normally faced enemy forces that numbered about 250,000 troops.[84] This imbalance forced the Prussian monarch to fight wars of attrition to weaken his enemies before finally defeating them on the battlefield. At least a third of his troops were foreigners, while in any given battle, he had no more than 40,000 men under his command. His casualty rate per campaign was about 40 percent.[85]

Frederick and his opponents also brought their aristocratic ideas into battle. The Prussians, for example, captured 40,000 Austrian prisoners during the battle of Leuten in 1757, and carefully recorded the name, rank, and unit of each of the POWs, and indicated whether he had been wounded or was ill. Later, each would be exchanged for Prussian POWs.[86]

Frederick, one of eighteenth-century Europe's Enlightened Despots, was intrigued by the study of war. One of his most interesting works was *The General Principles of War* (*Les principes Généraux de la guerre*; 1748). He called war the "Roman discipline," which "now exists only with us; in following their example we must regard war as a mediation, peace as a rehearsal."[87] He opposed lengthy wars, particularly "in hostile lands," and preferred to fight one enemy at a time. While an offensive genius, he was prepared to adopt defensive measures if he suffered significant reverses. He believed strongly in treating his troops well and considered "discipline 'the foundation of the glory and conservation of the state.'" A good commander, he wrote, should "be their father, not their executioner," though he advocated severe punishment for deserters and troublemakers. Beyond this, he thought a good commander had to be a "man of reason . . . a worthy man and a good citizen."[88]

Frederick died in 1786, just three years before the outbreak of the French Revolution, which dramatically changed the nature of warfare. At the time, France had an army of only 150,000 men. This increased to 645,000 in the summer of 1793, and rose to 1,169,000 the following year, though only 730,000 were combat-ready. Between 1792 and 1815, about 3 million soldiers served in France's armies.[89] Perhaps nothing better underscores this change than a comparison of the size of the armies that invaded Russia in 1708 and 1812. During the earlier campaign, Karl XII of Sweden swept into Russia with a force of 22,000–35,000 men, while Napoleon Bonaparte began his Russian campaign with over 600,000 men. To some extent, this reflects the dramatic rise in population in Europe's major countries from 1700 to 1800, which rose from 125 million to 195 million.[90]

The changing nature of warfare also saw a new body of international law emerge that focused principally on the conduct of warfare. Several Enlightenment scholars such as Cornelius van Bynkershoek, a Dutch legal specialist and jurist, embraced the idea that customs and treaties were the basis of international law, while Christian Wolff, a German philosopher influenced by the work of Grotius and Gottfried Leibniz, married natural law with the law of nations in his *The Law of Nations Treated According to a Scientific Method* (*Jus Gentium Methodo Scientifica Pertractatum*; 1749). He argued that international law was based on natural and voluntary law and that the latter "required the positing of a community of nations or *civitas maxima*." He thought that such a "community" had collective interests in the "suppression of war," which was equal in importance to the needs of individual states. He argued that war should not be undertaken against a country "willing to submit its case to arbitrations." He added that neutrals had the right to assist another country waging a just war but not an unjust one. And if there was any doubt about the nature of such a conflict, a neutral could refuse to help either nation.[91]

According to Paul Guggenheim, Wolff was the first "to have transformed the principles of natural law, making them applicable to international law."[92] Wolff said that it was just to go to war when "a wrong has been done or is likely to be done," but unjust to fight a war "without precedent or threatened wrong."[93] He also thought it was important to settle international disputes amicably, with war being a last option if "one nation is not willing to accept a conference for an amicable adjustment or compromise, or to accept a submission to an arbiter."[94] He argued forcefully that countries not legally bound to two warring nations had the right to be neutral. He also wrote that

> We ought to love and cherish an enemy as ourselves. For every man is bound to love and cherish every other man as himself. Therefore, since he is your enemy who is at war with you, and since war can be waged without hatred towards him, consequently this does not stand in the way of love; we ought to live and cherish an enemy as ourselves.[95]

He underscored the importance of military law, and thought "that it is not allowable to kill the subjects of a belligerent, as long as they refrain from all violence and do not show an intention to use force."[96] The same was true for those who "surrendered unconditionally."[97] And while he seemed to support the idea of using terror as "a motive for ending war," he did not think this should include the killing of POWs.[98] Furthermore, stubborn resistance by an enemy was not a basis for killing him. All of this, of course, would be determined by the justness of a particular conflict.[99]

Such justifications would also help to determine the treatment of an enemy's property. "In an unjust war all destruction of the property of an enemy is illegal."[100] If the war was just, the opposite was true, for "without it we should not be able to pursue our right by force." This was not necessarily the case of captured "cities, towns, [and] villages," though such action was legal "if some special offence has before occurred which deserves such a punishment."[101] The destruction of tombs, monuments, and sacred sites was completely illegal.[102]

Wolff regarded pillaging as a debt that a "belligerent collects by right of war."[103] He differentiated between pillaging and plundering, which he defined as the "taking of booty...movable property of an enemy, both to collect a debt...and also to diminish his power of action." All captured booty, he added, "belongs to the sovereign powers which are at war."[104] He also described perhaps the most heinous of war crimes—rape.

> Since an enemy has no power over one who does not oppose him by force, since, moreover, women and maidens do not resist an enemy by force, especially when they have come into the power of the enemy, soldiers ought not to be allowed by their officers to commit rape on women and maidens, nor, since it is illegal by itself, does the right of war excuse it, much less justify it.
>
> The same thing is true whether the captive women are taken into camp to be prostituted to the soldiers, or whether they are raped after cities and territories are captured, or the soldiers rush into places not surrounded by a wall or entrenchment. It

undoubtedly is a foul crime, to be abhorred by all who have not thrown aside all sense of honour, and it is absolutely alien to the warlike force by virtue of which we secure our right. Compare what we have said above. Nor is there reason why you should object that rape is not allowed except when there is need of terrorizing. For here the same reason exists for not allowing it, by which we have proved above that, for the purpose of terrorizing, the persons of captives or of those who have surrendered or who wish to surrender themselves are not to be harshly treated.[105]

Perhaps the most controversial part of Wolff's study is his discussion of the use of poison in warfare. He argued that "it is allowable to destroy the enemy by poison," and regarded this as no different from killing him with a sword. "There is no reason why you should object that an enemy is killed secretly by poison, so that he cannot protect himself for that so easily as from open violence." He also thought it was allowable to use poisoned arrows or bullets, though illegal to "poison springs." On the other hand, he considered it legal to pollute the water sources of the enemy so that they could not be drunk.[106] Assassination was also legal since, he argued, it was simply a part of the "treachery and deceit" of warfare.[107] Emer Vattel, who relied heavily on Wolff's treaties for his own, more influential, work, *The Law of Nations* (*Les droit des gens*), disagreed strongly with him on both of these issues. He considered "assassination and poisoning…contrary to the law of war and equally condemned by the law of nature, and the consent of all civilized nations."[108]

Wolff ended his discourse on war by discussing peace, which he defined simply as a state "in which we are at war with no one."[109] While rulers were obligated "to strive in every way to preserve the peace" not only for his nation but also others, he also had an obligation to stop "disturbers of the public peace ['one who harasses other nations in reckless and unjust war']…until sufficient provision has been made for security in the future."[110] He saw rebellion as an "unjust" attempt to "deprive a ruler of his sovereignty…or…accept certain limitations on it." Civil war differed from a rebellion, Wolff concluded, since it involved subjects taking "up arms for a just cause against the ruler of a state," making it, unlike a rebellion, a just undertaking.[111]

Emer Vattel, Wolff's "admiring follower,"[112] borrowed heavily from Wolff in his *The Law of Nations*,[113] particularly Wolff's "definitions and general principles."[114] And even though both works "are strikingly similar,"[115] there were also differences. Wolff's study was grounded in traditional views of naturalism, whereas Vattel's work provided a more contemporary, practical view of the place of war in eighteenth-century Europe.[116]

But what is it that made Vattel's ideas so influential? Wolff wrote his work in Latin, limiting its readership, while Vattel's work was published in French and quickly translated into English. It soon found its way to the American colonies and influenced the early political development of the United States. According to Abraham C. Weinfeld, Vattel's *The Law of Nations* became "the bible of international law" because it gave the early founders of the United States a "book of a recognized authority." They were particularly drawn to Vattel's descriptions of

a category of international arrangement, called "accord, convention, pact," which were fulfilled by a single act and not by a continuous performance of acts; when the act in question was performed, such agreements were executed once and for all, if valid they brought about a permanent and irrevocable state of things.[117]

Yet even though some American lawyers at the time were fond of quoting Vattel when it was useful to them as "legal advocates...there is no evidence that they adopted Vattelianism *tout court* into their American theory of the law of nations."[118]

Vattel's ideas were also popularized through the various editions of James Kent's 1826 *Commentaries on American Law*, which Brian Richardson says US federal courts used as "a useful first port of call for establishing the exclusive authority of Vattel." He was recently cited, for example, in a US Supreme Court decision, *Sosa v. Alvarez-Machain et al.* (No. 03–339; June 29, 2004).[119] But Kent was quite critical of Vattel,[120] and noted that even though Vattel

> professed to have followed the voluminous work of Wolff on the Law of Nature and Nations, and to be enlightened and guided by his learning, with much improvement upon the doctrine of his great master...his topics are loosely, and often tediously and diffusively discussed, and *he is not sufficiently supported by the authority of precedents*, which constitute the foundation of the positive law of nations.[121]

According to Stephen C. Neff, Vattel's work introduced two major new concepts to the laws of war—the "even-handed treatment" of combatants on both sides of a conflict, and the "idea of a fixed set of rules for the conducting of hostilities."[122] In reality, similar ideas could be found in Wolff's *Law of Nations*. Vattel, like Wolff, thought that war should be fought only for "the most cogent reasons."[123] On the other hand, Vattel went beyond Wolff by laying some of the groundwork for the future concept of "total war" when he stated that one state had the right to deprive his enemy of "everything which may augment his strength and enable him to make war," and "destroying what we cannot conveniently take away."[124]

Wolff and Vattel wrote during what David Bell calls the "restrained" era of warfare in the eighteenth century. For the most part, he argues, wars were nothing more than a "theater of the aristocracy."[125] All this changed during the wars of the French Revolution, which saw a shift away from Frederick the Great's policies of attrition to Napoleon's "strategy of annihilation."[126] Carl von Clausewitz noted in his classic *On War* that Napoleon waged "absolute" war, which Clausewitz described as "war...without respite until the enemy succumbed, and the counter blows were struck with almost equal energy."[127] All that mattered, he went on, was "*final victory*."[128]

These dramatic changes in the nature of warfare, for the most part, can be attributed to both the ideological fanaticism that drove French remilitarization in the second phase of the revolutions that swept France between 1789 and 1799, and the incredible number of troops the Jacobins were able to raise during the *levée en masse* in 1793.[129] Earlier French army regulations dictated the waging of "lawful, civilized" wars, while the new French republic's National Assembly stated that its war against Austria and Prussia was fought to defend "the principles of justice and humanity." It ordered its generals "to conduct hostilities with restraint toward civilians and promises of humane treatment for prisoners."[130]

All this changed once the Jacobins came to power in 1793. What followed was what Simon Schama called a "Holocaust for liberty," a "reign of terror" that enveloped all of France and led to the execution of Louis XVI and his queen, Marie

Antoinette.[131] This, coupled with a rebellion in the Vendée (Poitou, Anjou, Brittany) in 1793, led to shocking reprisals by republican forces.[132] Gen. François-Joseph Westermann informed Paris after his troops retook the Vendée later that year that

> There is no more Vendée, citizens, it has perished under our free sword along with its women and children. I have just buried it in the marches and mud of Savenay. Following the orders that you gave me I have crushed children under the feet of horses, massacred women who at least…will engender no more brigands. I have no prisoners with which to reproach myself.[133]

Donald Greer called the "Vendeen war the most poignant tragedy of the Revolution…No war in French history, not even the Albigensian crusade [in the Middle Ages] was fought with more sheer cruelty on both sides."[134] According to Schama, once the area was pacified, the government initiated a "policy of extermination" that centered around the idea of massacring "virtually every living person who stood in their [republican] path." The violence was so indiscriminate that it even entrapped loyal supporters of the Jacobins. Schama adds:

> Every atrocity that one could imagine was meted out to the defenseless population. Women were routinely raped, children killed, both mutilated. To save powder General Cordellier ordered his men to do their work with the saber rather than the gun. At Gonnord on January 23 [1794], General Crouzat's column forced two hundred old people, along with mothers and children, to kneel in front of a large pit they had dug; they were then shot so as to tumble into their own grave. Some who attempted to flee were struck down by the hammer of a local Patriot mason. Thirty children and two women were buried alive when earth was shoveled onto the pit.[135]

He does, though, disagree with Reynald Sécher, who called these massacres genocide. This does not, Schama, added, diminish the nature and horror of the atrocities that took place there. He thinks the "exterminations practiced there were, in fact, the logical outcome of an ideology that progressively dehumanized its adversaries and that had become incapable of seeing any middle ground between total triumph and utter eclipse."[136] Estimates are that 220,000–250,000 "men, women, and children—over a quarter of the population of the insurgent region"—lost their lives in the Vendée in 1793–1794.[137]

The Vendéan campaign was, according to David Bell,

> the face of total war, which followed its own dynamic of radicalization. It was the place where the modern version of the phenomenon was first revealed to its full, gruesome extent…What made it total was rather its erasure of any line between combatants and noncombatants and the wanton slaughter of both—and at the behest of politics more than military necessity.[138]

And though he agrees with Schama that what took place in the Vendée was not genocide, he thinks that what happened there

> stirs memories of recent genocidal horrors—enough to make one think that it must have scoured every last trace of romance out of European warfare.[139]

The worst of the Vendéan campaign ended in the spring of 1794, followed by the toppling of the Jacobins several months later. A new constitution in 1795 gave power to a five-man Directory, which faced continued domestic and international threats. Napoleon Bonaparte, initially a staunch supporter of the Directory, who enjoyed its patronage, became France's most respected military figure after a series of successful military campaigns in Italy. This fueled his own political ambitions, and, in the aftermath of a failed expedition in Egypt, he was part of a coup that overthrew the Directory. He soon became First Consul, and in 1804, French emperor.[140] His brother, Lucien, wrote in 1792 that

> there are no men more hated in history than those who bend with the wind. I will say to you in full confidence that I have always detected in Napoleon an ambition that is not altogether selfish, but which overcomes his love for the common good; I truly think that in a free state, he would be a dangerous man...He seems inclined to be a tyrant, and I think he would be one if he were king.[141]

Though history has tended to buy into much of the romantic image of Napoleon Bonaparte, this should be balanced with his role as a dictatorial warmonger whose armies ravaged Europe.

Though scholars differ on the total number of deaths as a result of the Napoleonic Wars—1.5–5 million—most would agree with David Bell that they transformed "the scope and intensity of warfare."[142] The reason is quite simple—Napoleon used tactics designed to destroy the enemy totally, and used larger armies to defeat his opponents.[143] At Austerlitz in December 1805, Napoleon commanded an army of 207,000–210,000. Desperate for a victory, he ordered his troops to "take no prisoners at all—to leave no man standing, whether he surrendered or not." The French lost only 1,350 men during the battle, but killed 15,000 Prussian and Austrian soldiers.[144]

Initially, Napoleon had adopted the more humane wartime customs of the *Ancien Régime*, particularly when it came to the treatment of officers. But, as Gunther Rothenberg has noted, "the treatment of captives and wounded was less than satisfactory by all sides during the Napoleonic Wars. 'Military necessity' had more of an impact about the treatment of prisoners and the wounded" than any deep commitment to the customary rules of war.[145] This breakdown in traditional military values was poignantly highlighted during Napoleon's invasion of Russia in 1812, when a French coalition army of over 600,000 faced a Russian force of 409,000.[146] By the time his army took Moscow in mid-September, Napoleon only had 100,00 men under his direct command. After the city was destroyed by fire, Napoleon began a retreat westward, followed by Cossacks,[147] "who were ready to pounce" on stragglers, whom they robbed and killed.[148] By the end of the Russian campaign,

> one could see Cossacks with a couple of dozen of watches strung around their necks, wearing several rich uniforms and coats, bedecked with gold epaulettes, a variety of resplendent plumed hats, with an array of booty of every kind strung from their cushion-like saddles.[149]

The Cossacks treated officers no differently than enlisted men, while French POWs "were forced-marched, and if a man stopped to tie up his leggings or answer the call of nature," he would be beaten and, if he did not rejoin the column fast enough, killed.[150]

Those who avoided capture were more skeletal than human. According to one French officer, "the most ragged beggars inspire pity, but we could have inspired only horror."[151] And as conditions worsened, Napoleon's troops resorted to cannibalism.[152] In the end, all that remained of a French army of 600,000 was 43,000–120,000 troops.[153] "Total war," David Bell argues, "ends with an army transformed into a starving, skeletal, lice-ridden, barely human mass, covered mostly in rags, its eyes blank and hopeless."[154]

Napoleon was finally beaten outside of Leipzig in the fall of 1813, and exiled to Elba the following year. However, he soon got tired of the comfortable life of an exiled noble, escaped from Elba in February 1815, and returned to France to try to restore his monarchy.[155] The Allies, gathered in Vienna to deal with a Europe torn asunder by almost a quarter century of war, were stunned but resolute in dealing with Napoleon. Prince Clément Metternich of Austria declared:

> Napoleon appears anxious to run great risks; that is his business. Our business is to give the world that repose which he has troubled all these years. Go at once and find the Emperor of Russia and the King of Prussia; tell them that I am prepared to order my armies once again to take the road to France. I have no doubt that the two Sovereigns will join me in my march.[156]

The Allies agreed and passed a resolution that declared that by fleeing Elba, the former French dictator had destroyed the only legal title for his existence. And once he returned to France,

> he has cut himself off from the protection of the law…Accordingly, the Powers declare that Napoleon Bonaparte is excluded from civil and social relations, and, as an Enemy and Disturber of the tranquility of the World, that he has incurred public vengeance.[157]

Napoleon was quickly defeated near Waterloo several months later, and exiled to the remote British island of St. Helena in the southern Atlantic where he remained a British prisoner until his death in 1821.[158]

As they moved into France, the Allies had different ideas about how to deal with the French. The Prussians, who had suffered horribly during the Napoleonic Wars, wanted a "punitive peace," and Napoleon's head. According to French historian Henry Houssaye:

> From the Rhine to the Oder, the whole country [Prussia] resounded with the press's barking. "We were wrong to be merciful with the French. We should have exterminated them all. Yes, we must exterminate this bunch of 500,000 robbers. We must do more than that: we must outlaw the French people.…No treaties with the French. The proscription pronounced by the Congress [of Vienna] against their chief [Napoleon] must be extended to the whole nation. We must exterminate them, kill them like mad dogs."[159]

After their victory at Waterloo, Fld. Mshl. Gebhard von Blücher told the Duke of Wellington that he intended to execute Napoleon if he captured him.[160] Blücher's chief of staff, Count August Neithardt von Gniesenau, added:

> Bonaparte has been declared under outlawry by the Allied Powers. The Duke of Wellington may possibly (from parliamentary considerations) hesitate to fulfill the

declaration of the Powers. Your Excellency will therefore direct the negotiations to the effect that Bonaparte may be delivered over to us, with a view of his execution.

    This is what eternal justice demands, and what the declaration of March the 13th decides; and thus the blood of our soldiers killed and mutilated on the 18th and 19th will be avenged.[161]

Wellington would have none of this and argued as commander of the Allied occupation forces in Paris that such an act would hand down our names to history stained by a crime, and posterity would say of us, that we did not deserve to be the conquerors of Napoleon.[162] This same spirit was embedded in the Peace of Paris that ended Napoleon's Hundred Days. France lost a small amount of territory, paid an indemnity of 700 million francs, and had to support an Allied army occupation of 150,000 men for five years until the debt was paid off. Napoleon, who sought British protection after the fighting ended, was ultimately sent to St. Helena and eternal exile.

    It is difficult fully to describe the impact of the French revolutions and the Napoleonic era on Europe. The memory of devastation and trauma was such that as late as 1919, the British government ordered a study on the British decision in 1815 to exile the former French dictator to St. Helena instead of executing him or having him tried by the government of Louis XVIII. At the time, the government of David Lloyd George was trying to decide how to deal with Kaiser Wilhelm II, and sought guidance from the past. Ultimately, the Allies put article 227 into the Treaty of Versailles (1919), which accused the Kaiser of "a supreme offence against international morality and the sanctity of treaties" and created an Allied tribunal to try him for such crimes.[163]

Conclusion

The atrocities and war crimes committed during the French and Napoleonic Wars paled in comparison with those committed in China during the Ming and Qing dynasties. Yet there were also some interesting though distant parallels between Chinese efforts to wipe out the troublesome Zunghars in the second half of the eighteenth century and Jacobin efforts to deal with rebels in the Vendée several decades later. But one can at least catch a glimpse of a more humane approach to war in the dictates and ideas of Gustavus Adolphus, Hugo Grotius, Christian Wolff, and Emer Vattel based on Enlightenment ideas about the rights of the individual vis-à-vis the state. In the end, it would take more than a body of ideas to temper the horrors of war, particularly on the eve of pre–Industrial Revolution Europe. Nation-states under autocratic rulers such as Peter the Great, Frederick the Great, and Napoleon Bonaparte had little concern for the fate of the individual during times of war and, if David Bell is correct, it was Napoleon, the military dictator, who introduced the concept of "total war" to Europe. But if we consider Napoleon a mere child of the French Revolution, then, perhaps, we can see the seed for such concepts in the Jacobin campaign in the Vendée, where politics trumped ideals.

Chapter 3

Colonialism: The Americas, Asia, and Africa

The revolutions in France and the Napoleonic Wars cast a long shadow over Europe and paved the way for a century of great social, political, and economic upheavals. It was during this long century of dramatic transformation that a general body of international law evolved that addressed humanitarian issues during war. This was driven by a number of factors such as the Enlightenment with its emphasis on human and civil rights, the emergence of new, powerful nations in Europe, the rise of militant ethnic nationalism, the growing arms races triggered by new, impersonal industrial weapons of war and death, and growing conflicts between Europe's major powers in Europe, Asia, and Africa.

It should, however, be remembered that such conflicts, and their accompanying atrocities, began centuries earlier in the Americas when the Spanish, the Portuguese, the British, and the French began their push into the New World. What followed were policies that ravaged native populations, though some of the tribes they encountered in the Americas had some of their own violent traditions, which in turn affected European attitudes and policies toward some of the peoples they encountered in the New World. The savagery that such attitudes bred lingered well into the nineteenth century, and affected relations between Americans and the peoples they encountered as they pushed westward to the Pacific.

This was certainly the case with Rachel Plummer Parker, who was held for almost two years by the Comanches after being taken prisoner in 1836. She and four members of her family were enslaved after a raid and dragged behind Comanche horses from Texas to Colorado. Rachel became the property of one Comanche family, who forced her to do menial labor. She had been pregnant when captured, and after she gave birth to a son, one of the family members complained that the new child prevented Rachel from doing all of her chores. Soon, six warriors showed up and took the infant from her.

They "strangled the baby, then handed him back to her. When he showed signs of life, they took him again, this time tying a rope around his neck and dragging him through prickly pear cactus, and eventually dragged him behind a horse around a hundred-yard circuit." In her memoirs about her captivity, she wrote: "My little innocent one was not only dead, but literally torn to pieces."[1]

But Indians could be equally cruel toward one another. One Texas tribe, the Tonkawa (mortal enemies of the Comanches), reportedly practiced ritual cannibalism. According to one account,

> They [the Tonkawas after Plumb Creek; battle between Comanches and Texans-Tonkawas, 1840] cut him [a dead Comanche warrior] into slices and boiled him on sticks. Curiously enough the eating of flesh acted upon them as a liquor does upon other men. After a few mouthfuls they began to act as if they were very drunk, and I don't think there was much pretense or sham about it. They danced, raved, howled and sang, and invited me [witness, Robert Hall] to eat a slice of Comanche. They said it would make me brave. I was very hungry, but not sufficiently so to become a cannibal. The Tonkawas were wild over victory, and they did not cease their celebration until sunrise.[2]

Puckshunnubbee, a Choctaw Indian, said in a letter to the Fort Smith (Arkansas) *Herald* in 1851 that

> The Tonkawas are cannibals eating the body of those they kill, and those of their own tribe who are sickly and die. A short time ago, two or three weeks since, a young gentleman of my acquaintance passed their camps on Red River, about sixty or seventy miles above Fort Washita, and they were eating their own people; and when they were asked about it, said that he was sick, and would have died, and that they killed him to relieve him of his suffering, and themselves of hunger.[3]

Regardless of whether or not the Tonkawas actually practiced cannibalism, whites used such stories to justify their own attacks and savagery against various Indian tribes.[4] On the eve of the Sand Creek massacre in late 1864, Col. John Chivington, the commander of a number of Colorado regiments formed to fight hostile Indians, told critics of his plans to attack peaceful Cheyenne and Arapaho Indians at Sand Creek

> that it would be murder in every sense of the word…"Damn any man who sympathizes with Indians!" he cried. "I have come to kill Indians, and believe it is right and honorable to use any means under God's heaven to kill Indians."[5]

The Colorado units committed untold atrocities during the attack against defenseless women, children, and the elderly. Most were slaughtered indiscriminately, even if they begged for mercy. Robert Bent, one of the soldiers at Sand Creek, later wrote that he "saw one squaw cut open with an unborn child," while another soldier cut off the genitals of While Antelope, one of the chiefs who had earlier tried to negotiate a peaceful settlement in Denver. The soldier said that he intended to make a tobacco pouch out of the genitals. The Coloradans scalped most of their victims, and in some instances cut out the genitals of females, which they wore on their saddles or on their hats.[6]

Russell Thornton calls the Sand Creek massacre, along with the so-called battle at Wounded Knee 26 years later, a "genocide."[7] The latter genocide of hundreds of Sioux Indians in late December 1890 began after the US government decided to send troops into the Dakotas to deal with the looming "crisis"—rumors of an

Indian "ghost dance."[8] Prior to the massacre, the US Cavalry began to round up various groups of rebellious Sioux and force them to Wounded Knee Creek to await transport to the new Cheyenne River Reservation in north central South Dakota. When a number of Sioux warriors refused to surrender their arms, the cavalry opened fire with four Hotchkiss machine guns that killed over 300 Indians, most of them unarmed women and children.[9] The principal "crime" of the Indians—they were simply in the way of the rapacious flood of white settlers and developers who wanted their lands.[10]

Alexis de Tocqueville, the author of the classic *Democracy in America*, wrote his mother about the forced transfers of Choctaw Indians in 1831. What drove American policy, de Tocqueville argued, was the American sense that "God had bestowed upon them, as an unrestricted gift, the New World and its inhabitants." The Spaniards, he added, also shared this belief.[11] What de Tocqueville saw were not the bold Indian warriors of Little Big Horn or Comanche raids, but forlorn, dislodged Choctaws who

> carry their old parents in their arms; mothers hoist their children onto their shoulders; the whole nation begins to march, taking their most cherished possessions with them. It abandons forever the soil on which its forefathers lived for a millennium perhaps and settles in a wilderness where the Whites will be harassing it ten years from now. Can you see what becomes of a high civilization?[12]

He was particularly shocked by the plight of the elderly.

> Among the latter was a woman 110 years old. I have never seen such a horrifying figure. She was naked, except for a threadbare blanket revealing, here and there, the scrawniest body imaginable. She was escorted by two or three generations of grand-children. Having to leave one's land at that age and seek one's fortune in a foreign country—what an abomination! Amidst the old people was a young woman who had broken her arm a week earlier; for lack of care, the arm had frozen beneath the fracture. She was obliged nonetheless to join the march...This whole spectacle had an air of ruin and destruction; it spoke of final farewells and of no turning back. One felt heart sick watching it. The Indians were calm, but somber and taciturn.[13]

De Tocqueville's prescient observations are underscored by the high death toll among the Choctaw; 6,000 of the 40,000 Choctaw forced on this tragic migration west died en route.[14]

De Tocqueville also compared American treatment of the Indians with earlier Spanish *conquistadores*. He considered the Spanish

> real brutes, unleashing their dogs on Indians as they would on ferocious beasts; they kill, burn, massacre, pillage the New World like an army storming a city, pitilessly and indiscriminately. But one cannot destroy everything; fury spends itself. Indian populations that survive end up mingling with their conquerors, adopting their customs, their religion.[15]

Yet he found Americans even worse, a surprising conclusion given that he also found them "a rational people without prejudices." He felt, in general, that Americans were "more humane, more moderate, more respectful of law and legality, never blood-thirsty." But when it came to the treatment of the Indians, he found them "pro-foundly more destructive...than the Spanish."[16]

Spain and the *Leyendra Negra*

What de Tocqueville was describing, of course, particularly when it came to the Spanish, was the Black Legend (*Leyendra Negra*), the controversial indictment of Spanish policies in the New World linked not only to Spanish mistreatment of Indians but also to the introduction of slavery into the Americas.

When Christopher Columbus discovered land in the Caribbean in the early morning hours of October 12, 1492, after a horrible five-week voyage from Spain, he opened the floodgates of European conquest and colonial expansion that was to continue unabated for centuries. What drove the early Spanish and Portuguese *conquistadores* were tales of an unspoiled world of great riches and wealth. Many of them had read Marco Polo's memoirs about the vast riches of China during the Yuan dynasty.[17] According to John A. Crow, what was about to take place was

the greatest revolution ever effected in the history of mankind. It shifted completely the order of gravity of the known world, turned the eyes of civilization from the Crusades, the East towards the conquest of the West, marked the end of the Middle Ages and the beginning of the modern era, and above all altered and broadened the entire nature of man's thinking.[18]

What this revolution did not do was alter the religiously driven, racist European atti-tudes toward the people, civilizations, and cultures they found in the New World. The violent, crusading mentality of the Middle Ages was now transferred to the New World by the *conquistadores* who saw the native peoples as barriers to instant wealth, fame, and power.

In 1521, Hernan Cortés conquered the Aztec or Mexica empire, a complex civi-lization unified by a religious ideology that centered around human sacrifice. The sun was the center of Aztec life, and the center of an eternal struggle with other cosmic forces. The only way to keep these forces at bay was to sacrifice human beings whose *chalchihuatl* or "life energy" was essential to keep the sun, which was associated with the warrior god Huitzilopochtli (Huichilobos), shining bright. Over time, the Aztec's lust for this life force drove them to incessant warfare for prisoners, who became the principal sacrificial victims. According to Miquel Léon-Portilla, "imperial conquests were key to 'the moral combat against evil...The survival of the universe depended on them.'"[19]

Such sacrifices stunned the *conquistadores*, who first encountered signs of it in Cholula, where altars "were stained with [the] human blood of six thousand victims."[20] Bernal Díaz del Castillo, the principal chronicler of the Cortés expedi-tion, added that the Spaniards were so convinced that the Cholulans were about to kill them and "eat our flesh" that he ordered his Tlaxcalan Indian allies, long enemies of the Aztecs, to join in an attack against the Cholulans, erstwhile allies of the Aztecs. What followed was a dreadful two-day massacre that only ended after Cortés, "on account of the compassion we had felt [toward the Cholulans]," ordered a halt to the assault.[21]

Cortés then moved on Tenochtitlan, the Aztec capital (today Mexico City), which was ruled by Moctezuma (Motehcuzoma Xocoyotzin; Montezuma). What the Spaniards discovered was a city that was built on a series of lakes high in the mountains of central Mexico (7,300 feet). They saw

> enchantments they tell of in legends, Amadis [*Amadis de Gaula*; a late medieval Spanish tale of knightly chivalry], on account of the great towers and cues [temples] and buildings rising from the water, and all built of masonry. And some of our soldiers asked whether the things that we saw were not a dream.[22]

Though the Spaniards were entranced by the beauty of the Aztec capital and the courtesy of Moctezuma, Bernal Diaz was shocked by the horrors of cannibalism and human sacrifice. He claimed that in one house or temple where they kept idols of their most "fierce gods" were many beasts of prey: tigers, and two kinds of lions, and animals,

> something like wolves and foxes, and other small carnivorous animals, and all these carnivores they feed with flesh, and the greater number of them breed in the house. They give them as food deer and fowls, dogs and other things that they used to hunt, and I have heard said that they feed them on the bodies of the Indians who have been sacrificed. It is in this way: you have already heard me say that when they sacrifice a wretched Indian they saw open the chest with stone knives and hasten to tear out the palpitating heart and blood, and offer it to their Idols, in whose name the sacrifice is made. Then they cut off the thighs, arms, and head and eat the former at feasts and banquets, and the head they hang up on some beams, and the body of the man sacrificed is not eaten but given to these fierce animals. They also have in that cursed house many vipers and poisonous snakes which carry on their tails things that sound like bells. These are the worst vipers of all, and they keep them in jars and great pottery vessels with many feathers, and there they lay their eggs and rear their young, and they give them to eat the bodies of the Indians who have been sacrificed, and the flesh of dogs which they are in the habit of breeding.[23]

According to Ross Hassig, cannibalism was a common practice among the Aztecs after battle. They sacrificed some of their POWs by cutting their chests open and tearing out their hearts.[24] Others were skinned by priests who dried their flesh and placed skulls "on the skull rack (*tzompantli*)."[25] Some bodies were laid by the skull rack, and each warrior identified the one he had captured. Then, after skinning, the body "was taken to the captor's home, where it was eaten; the bones were hung in the house as a sign of prestige."[26]

When Cortés, Bernal Diaz, and other Spaniards visited the temple of Tlalelolco, where Moctezuma was sacrificing captives to Huitzilopochtli, the god of war, they noticed the walls of the temple were

> so splashed and encrusted with blood that they were black; the floor was the same and the whole place stank vilely...The walls were so clotted with blood and the soil so bathed with it that in the slaughter houses of Spain there is not such another stench.[27]

When Cortés told Moctezuma that such sacrifices were a form of devil worship, the Aztec leader responded that such practices were essential to appease Aztec gods, who were "very good, for they give us health and rains and good seed times and seasons and as many victories as we desire, and we are obliged to worship them and make sacrifices."[28]

But it was not the human sacrifices that led Cortés to imprison Moctezuma, but his belief that it was the only way to gain the upper hand over the large Aztec population. Though Cortés allowed Moctezuma to maintain his royal lifestyle and court in captivity, all of this changed after an Aztec uprising in response to the Spanish massacre of 600 Aztec chieftains who were taking part in a religious ceremony. Efforts by Moctezuma to quell the uprising failed and Aztec forces ultimately drove the Spanish eastward to Tlaxcala, where the Aztecs were defeated. Cortés regrouped and invaded Tenochtitlan in the summer of 1521. What followed was a 75-day siege of the capital that led to its complete destruction.[29] During one battle in the suburbs, the Aztecs carried the heads of five recently killed Spaniards before them into battle, crying out—"Thus we will kill you as we have killed Malinche [Cortes' interpreter and mistress] and Sandoval [Gonzalo de; one of Cortes' commanders] and all whom they had brought with them, and these are their heads and by them you may know them well."[30]

In the midst of the Tenochtitlan campaign, the Aztecs sacrificed several captured Spaniards in sight of some of Cortés' officers. The Aztecs forced the captives with

> plumes on the heads of many of them and with things like fans in their hands to dance before Huichilobos, and after they had danced [, they] immediately placed them on their backs on some rather narrow stones which had been prepared as places for sacrifice, and with stone knives they sawed open their chests and drew out their palpitating hearts and offered them to the idols that were there, and they kicked the bodies down the steps, and Indian butchers who were waiting below cut off the arms and feet and flayed the skin off the faces, and prepared it afterwards like glove leather with the beards on, and kept those for the festivals when they celebrated drunken orgies, and the flesh they ate in *chilmole* [spicy black soup]. In the same way they sacrificed all the others and ate the legs and arms and offered the hearts and blood to their idols, as I have said, and the bodies, that is their entrails and feet, they threw to the tigers and lions which they kept in the house of the carnivores.[31]

When the fighting ended, all that remained of this once beautiful city was "rubble." According to one *conquistadore*, "there was no house left to be burned and destroyed."

> Countless men and women came towards us and, in their eagerness to escape, many were pushed into the water where they drowned...we came across piles of dead and were forced to walk over them.[32]

This tragedy was compounded by the actions of Cortés' Indian allies, who began to slaughter thousands of Aztecs, sacrificing some of them to their gods. According to Bernal Diaz, "the cruelty of our allies was so great that on no account would they spare a life in spite of our reproofs and example."[33] Cortés later said: "There was not one man among us [Castilians] whose heart did not bleed at the sound of these killings."[34] Spanish losses were no more than a hundred, while some estimate that as many as 100,000 Aztecs and other Indians died during and after the long siege.[35]

Once they had taken Tenochtitlan, the Spanish turned to their primary objective—the search for gold and wealth. They accosted Aztecs in the streets, demanding their gold. They also seized pretty women, particularly

> those whose bodies were yellow, the yellow ones...Some women, fearful of rape and servitude, worked frantically to make themselves appear old and unattractive...[They] muddied their faces, and clothed themselves in old clothing, put rags on themselves as a shift. It was all only rags that they put on themselves.[36]

Desperate, Cortés tortured several Aztec leaders in an effort to find the "secret" Aztec treasure. He had them tied "to a pole" and, after dipping their feet in oil, set them on fire. In the end, they found little new gold nor the "treasure of Mexico." To the Aztecs, gold was no more valuable than jade or feathers, and was valued simply for its beauty.[37] Consequently, all the Spanish achieved in their lust for great wealth was the destruction of "the great Indian nations and civilizations that had flourished in Mesoamerica for almost two millennia."[38]

Cortés, of course, was not alone in paving this path of destruction throughout the Americas. Three years after he conquered the Aztec empire, Francisco Pizzaro moved south from Panama to find his own treasures in Peru. In late 1532, he followed Cortés' example and kidnapped the Inca leader Atahualpa, and massacred hundreds of his followers.[39]

In the hours following Atahualpa's arrest, the Spanish rounded up so many Inca captives that some of Pizzaro's troops suggested "putting them all to death, or, at least, cutting off their hands, to disable them from acts of violence and to strike terror into their countrymen." Though Pizzaro rejected this idea, he did allow his men to keep a large number of Incas as menial servants.[40]

The *conquistadores* then pillaged the countryside, destroying not only much of the area's llama population but stealing vast quantities of wool, gold, and silver. Atahualpa, shocked by this, told Pizzaro that if he freed him, he would fill the room where he was being held with gold. He also promised to fill a smaller room with silver.[41] Pizzaro agreed, but kept a close eye on the Inca leader. However, Pizzaro, concerned about rumors among his troops of an Inca rebellion, decided to court-martial Atahualpa in the summer of 1533 on a number of bogus charges despite the fact that there was no evidence of an uprising. The outcome of the "trial" was a forgone conclusion, and the tribunal ordered that Atahualpa be burned alive that night in the town square. While a handful of Pizzaro's men objected to the verdict, most agreed with Father Vincente de Valverde, Pizzaro's priest, that Atahualpa "deserved death."[42]

Stunned by the court's decision, Atahualpa pleaded with Pizzaro for his life, asking "what have I done, or my children, that I should meet such a fate? And from your hands." He promised the Spanish leader that he could double the amount of gold and silver if he spared his life. Pizzaro told the Inca leader that he had no control over the decisions of a court-martial. That evening, as the execution pyre was about to be lit, Father Valverde told Atahualpa that if he accepted Christianity and was baptized, he could be strangled to death instead of being burned alive. He agreed, and was baptized as Juan de Atahualpa. He then asked Pizzaro to protect his children. While Atahualpa was being strangled to death, Pizzaro's men "muttered their *credo* for the salvation of his soul!" Francisco Xerez, Pizzaro's secretary, later wrote that

> thus he paid the penalty of his errors and cruelties, for he was the greatest butcher, as all agree, that the world ever saw; making nothing of razing a whole town to the grounds for the most trifling offence, and massacring a thousand persons for the fault of one!

The Inca view was different. One Inca woman later stated that "on that fateful day, darkness fell at noon."[43]

These atrocities, in league with the rapid decimation of the Indian populations in Spanish America through enslavement and disease, shocked some Spaniards, who were concerned about the "rapacity of many of the *conquistadores*."[44] One of those who was sickened by the murderous policies of his fellow Spaniards was Bartolomé de las Casas, a young Spanish priest who became known as the "Defender of the Indians."[45] In 1515, he was granted an audience with King Ferdinand, and told him about the horrors that he had seen in the New World. In 1542, he wrote *A Short Account of the Destruction of the Indies* to inform Spain's new king, Philip II, of the atrocities being committed by his countrymen in the New World.

> It was upon those gentle lambs...that from the very first day they clapped eyes on them the Spanish fell like ravenous wolves upon the fold, or like tigers and savage lions who have not eaten meat for days. The pattern established at the outset has remained unchanged to this day, and the Spaniards still do nothing save tear the natives to shreds, murder them and inflict upon them untold misery, suffering and distress, tormenting, harrying and persecuting them mercilessly.[46]

Though scholars disagree about the nature of the deaths described by de las Casas, they do agree that the native peoples in the Americas suffered staggering losses that some call genocide. Estimates are that 8.4–112.5 million people lived in the Americas on the eve of the beginning of the European conquests.[47] And most accept the fact that within a century, 80–90 percent of the native populations in the Americas had disappeared. In what later became the United States, for example, there were over 5 million Indians in 1492. By the end of the nineteenth century, there were only 250,000 Native Americans in the United States.[48] And even though Robin Blackburn attributes most of these losses to disease, Ward Churchill considers such losses "a vast genocide." David E. Stannard goes even further, and considers this the "worst human holocaust the world has ever witnessed."[49]

While statistics seem to point to genocide, the fact remains that most Indian deaths were the result of interaction with Europeans who unknowingly introduced highly contagious diseases to Indian populations with no immunity to such diseases. While there is no question that the native peoples of the Americas suffered from horrible mistreatment at the hands of the European and American colonizers, most specialists do not think that native deaths were the result of genocide. Thornton blames these deaths on multiple factors all stemming from "European contact and colonization; introduced disease, including alcoholism; warfare and genocide; geographic removal and relocation; and destruction of ways of life."[50] He adds that while war and genocide were not the principal causes for the decline of the Indian population, these factors were extremely important in the destruction of certain tribes.[51]

The Qing Dynasty and the West

Sadly, the sense of racial and cultural superiority that drove Europeans and Americans to brutalize Native Americans and African slaves gained new life during European conquests in Asia and Africa in the nineteenth century. Though a handful of Western missionaries and adventurers had made their way into China centuries before Columbus discovered America in the late fifteenth century, they had little influence on what D. E. Mungello calls "a genuine cultural encounter."[52] At the time, China's relations with the outside world were governed by an age-old tribute system that "functioned to intermesh rather than to integrate the Central, East, and Southeast Asian societies that were derivative of, or peripheral to, China's and the region's predominant Confucian society and traditions."[53]

This system was driven by a Chinese ethnocentric view of the outside world as one of barbarians. China was the center of the world (Middle Kingdom, *Zhongguo*), while its emperor, the "Son of Heaven" (*Tainzi*), governed with the Mandate of Heaven. All nations beyond the pale of China's vast frontiers were treated as tribute states, with relations between the imperial court and the barbarian nations governed by a complex set of rituals that underscored the emperor's "benevolent paternalism."[54] As Mark Mancall has noted, China's hierarchical tribute system was based on moralistic Confucian ideas that saw the world only in civilized and barbarian terms.[55] Within this hierarchical world, there were three zones—a "Sinitic" one that included Asian states such as Korea, Vietnam, and Japan that had "borrowed extensively from Chinese culture"; an "Inner Asian" zone of non-Han peoples such as the Mongols, the Tibetans, the Uighurs, and others; and, finally, a zone of "outer barbarians" (*waiyi*) that included other parts of Asia and the West.[56] During the Qing dynasty, 500 or so tribute missions from 60 countries were permitted to travel to Beijing to pay homage to the imperial court.[57]

Initially, early European coastal incursions in southern Asia did little to challenge this system. The first took place in 1498, when Portuguese explorer Vasco da Gama landed in Calcutta in southern India. Four years earlier, Pope Alexander VI helped negotiate the Treaty of Tordesillas, which gave Portugal theoretical control over most of Asia, Africa, and Brazil, while Spain gained jurisdiction over most of the Americas.[58] The Portuguese established a foothold in southern China near Canton (Guangzhou) in 1514. Four decades later, the Chinese allowed Portugal to build a permanent trading post in Macao, which was returned to China in 1999.[59]

These initial Western incursions had little impact on the Chinese tribute system, and the only significant contact that the imperial court had directly with Westerners during this period was with Christian missionaries, particularly the Jesuits.[60] Francis Xavier, considered the "patron saint of all Catholic missions overseas," dreamed of establishing missions in China after his successes in India and Japan. But he died on an island just outside of Canton, never reaching the mainland of what he considered the Jesuit missionary field's "richer prize."[61]

The Jesuits quickly learned that to make headway in China they would have to master its language and customs, something that came to distinguish their efforts there. They also decided that the best way to appeal to the Chinese was to dress as Buddhist monks, and shave their heads and beards. This, they thought, would fortify the Chinese perception that the Jesuits were "a special sort of Buddhist."[62] No one better embodied this Jesuit approach to mission work in China than Matteo Ricci, a brilliant linguist who embraced Chinese culture and engaged Chinese scholars with in-depth discussions of Chinese classics in Mandarin. As Andrew Ross has noted, Ricci "lived as a scholar among Chinese scholars."[63] In 1601, he was permitted to live permanently in Beijing, transforming himself from a "tribute bearer to resident scholar with an imperial income."[64] Over the next nine years, he worked "to present Christianity as a faith that could be adopted by a Confucian scholar-administrator while he remained an official of the empire and a follower of the philosophy of Confucius."[65] When Ricci died in 1610, the Wanli emperor gave him a state funeral, and the plaque on his tomb reads:[66]

To one who loved righteousness
and wrote illustrious books,
to Li Madou [Ricci], Far-Westerner.
Erected by Huang Jishi
Governor of Beijing.[67]

The Jesuits continued their missionary work after Ricci's death, trying to "work from the top down in converting social classes." Their influence began to wane after the collapse of the Ming dynasty. They now had to compete with other Catholic religious orders such as the Franciscans, whose approach and unwillingness to seek accommodation with Chinese traditions and culture created conflicts in China. Government officials in Beijing became increasingly concerned about Franciscan efforts to create "religious brotherhoods and sisterhoods," something that Chinese officials equated with China's subversive secret societies.[68]

In the end, it was the controversy over the role of the practice of traditional Confucian rites, especially ancestor "worship," and the traditions of Christian belief and practice that ultimately led to the decline of Catholic missionary activity in China, particularly during the first century of the Qing dynasty. By the early eighteenth century, successive popes gradually drew a line in the sand when it came to such practices, insisting that Christians could not take part in such Confucian ceremonies, and rejected any Catholic accommodation with such traditions.[69]

In 1724, the Yongzheng emperor declared Christianity a "heterodox" sect, and 18 years later, Pope Benedict XIV forbade all Christians from taking part in "the Rites and Ceremonies of China."[70] Andrew Ross blames failed Jesuit efforts in Asia on the unwillingness of eighteenth-century Catholicism "to integrate Christianity and the indigenous culture so that there developed a pattern of Christian life which was Chinese or Japanese and not a replication of European Christianity." He adds that "to the arrogant imperialist expansionism of nineteenth century Europe it was nonsense."[71]

Overall, the impact of Christian missionaries in China was minimal, though they did introduce China to various aspects of Western science and technology. According to Immanuel C. Y. Hsü, the "feebleness of the Jesuit efforts, in league with the ethnocentric complacency of Confucian intellectuals, and the imperviousness of Chinese culture to outside stimuli, inhibited any process of modernization in China at this point."[72] This was certainly borne out in the imperial court's dealings with the Macartney mission in 1793, a misguided British attempt to establish formal diplomatic and economic ties with China.[73] The British, sensitive to imperial Qing court traditions when it came to dealing with foreigners, told the Chinese that Macartney's sole purpose was to bring birthday greetings from King George III to the Qianlong emperor, who was celebrating his eighty-third birthday.[74] In response, the imperial court ordered that Macartney be treated with exceptional courtesy, even allowing him to kneel on one knee before the emperor instead of the traditional *kou tou* (kow tow).[75]

The Qianlong emperor issued two imperial edicts for George III that rejected Macartney's efforts. The first explained that "we have never valued ingenious articles, nor do we have the slightest need of your Country's manufactures," while the second dealt specifically with what the Chinese viewed as the real purpose of Macartney's embassy—expanded trade rights in China.[76] The British emissary, Qianlong noted, failed "to recognize the Throne's principle to 'treat strangers from afar with indulgence,' and to exercise a pacifying control over barbarian tribes, the world over." Britain, he added, was not the only country with trade rights in Canton, and that if other countries made similar requests for expanded trade rights, how could he (Qianlong) "treat them with easy indulgence." The emperor said that he understood the reason for this ignorant request—England was a lonely, remote island "cut off from the world by intervening wastes of sea." The emperor concluded by warning that if the English king sent ships to Chekiang and Tientsin, they would be "subject to instant expulsion...Do not say that you were not warned in due time! Tremblingly obey and show no negligence! A special mandate!"[77]

This, for the most part, put the matter to rest for almost four decades. However, by the 1830s, the failure of the British government to find a diplomatic solution to its "China problem" dovetailed with another issue—the growing trade imbalance with China. Tea had long been the principal British export from China. By the end of the eighteenth century, the East India Company (EIC) was buying almost £27 million worth of tea from China, while the Chinese only bought £9.2 million worth of British goods. To counter this growing trade imbalance, the EIC began to smuggle opium into China.[78] Though all of the countries that traded with China were involved in this illegal trade, the EIC was "the father of all smuggling and smugglers." Chinese officialdom did what it could to stop the trade, though the British proved far more adept at promoting its sale there. No less a figure than the Duke of Wellington noted in 1838 that "Parliament had not only refused to frown upon the opium trade but cherished it, extended it, and promoted it."[79]

Several Chinese emperors tried to outlaw the sale and use of opium in the eighteenth century but their strictures did little to stop it. When the British Parliament formally ended the EIC's opium trade monopoly in the 1830s, it opened it to "all British subjects." The Qing court finally decided to outlaw the opium trade and sent Commissioner Lin Zexu to Canton to do whatever was necessary to stop it.[80] Lin wrote Queen Victoria two letters asking her to help him stamp out what he called the trade of "a poisonous drug." He also ordered the British and other foreign traders to turn over thousands of chests of opium, which he then destroyed. This led to a growing conflict with British merchants in Canton and Macao that ultimately led Lord Palmerston, the British foreign secretary, essentially to declare war on China without consulting Parliament.[81] Gilbert Kynymound (Lord of Minto), the First Lord of the Admiralty, wrote Lord Auckland, the governor general of British India, that the new China campaign was "nothing more nor less than the conquest of China."[82] Even critics of the war, such as William Gladstone, could not resist describing the war, which he called a "disgrace" caused by England's "'infamous and atrocious' opium trade," as one between "the pagans, the semi-civilized barbarians" against "we, the enlightened and civilized Christians," who were "pursuing objects at variance both with justice and with religion."[83]

The First "Opium War" was a one-sided affair that saw the Chinese quickly sue for peace.[84] The British-dictated Treaty of Nanjing (1842) forced China to pay a £21 million indemnity, establish a "fixed tariff," outlaw the major Chinese business firms (hong) system, open five new ports to the British, accept the British seizure of Hong Kong, and agree to "equality in correspondence."[85] The French and the Americans soon made similar demands on the Chinese, heralding a new era in Western relations with China.[86]

As China suffered through this first wave of Western humiliation, it also faced a new threat—the Taiping Rebellion—that was driven not only by a reaction to a Qing state ill-prepared to deal with a number of problems, particularly a dramatic increase in China's population, which rose from 150 million in 1700 to almost 430 million by 1850, but also new, distorted Western views of social equality that challenged traditional Chinese economic, political, and social policies.[87] One of the bloodiest civil wars in history—with 25 million dead—it was led by an unbalanced religious mystic, Hong Huoxiu (later Hong Xiuquan; Heavenly King), who saw himself as the brother of Jesus. Hong, who was from Guangxi, just to the west of Canton, was deeply affected by his repeated failure to pass the state Confucian exams and his distorted views of Christian teachings.[88] He preached "an iconoclastic monotheism potent enough to set up the Taiping theocracy but too blasphemous to win foreign missionary support, too intent on the one true god to permit cooperation with secret societies like the Triad (pro-Ming, anti-Qing Heaven and Earth Society), and too bizarre and irrational to win over Chinese literati, who were nominally essential to setting up a new administration."[89]

Over time, Hong's movement was transformed into an effective, anti-Qing fighting force centered in Nanjing, later the capital of what Hong called *The Heavenly Kingdom of Great Peace (Taiping Tianguo)*.[90] Initially, the Western powers were intrigued by Hong's movement because of its Christian and pro-Western overtones. However, over time they began to oppose it because it hurt trade and Western missionary work. In the end, the Allies decided to support the Qing government when it became apparent that they had more to gain by siding with Beijing than supporting Hong's movement.[91]

The British took advantage of the civil war to strengthen their position in China, and in 1856 transformed a minor naval incident (the *Arrow*) in Canton into a major international crisis to force the Chinese to consider revising the Treaty of

Nanjing and allow British entry into the walled city of Canton.[92] In late October, the British navy attacked a series of forts near Canton. When Chinese officials refused to give in to British demands to surrender, Admiral Sir Michael Seymour, who commanded the British fleet, wrote Yeh Mingchen, Canton's imperial commissioner: "The lives and property of the entire City population are at my mercy, and could be destroyed by me at any moment" unless Yeh agreed to meet with him.[93] When this failed to convince Yeh to surrender, the British began a full-scale assault on Canton.[94] Yeh urged everyone in the city "to assist the soldiers and militia in exterminating those troublous English villains, killing them wherever you meet them."[95]

British public reaction to this undeclared, one-sided war against China was heated. The *Times* noted that "a state of war with China costs us £10,000,000 a year in home revenue and commercial profits,"[96] while William Gladstone told Parliament that British commanders had driven "the whole might of England against the lives of defenceless people" when they attacked Canton. The crisis toppled the government of Lord Palmerston, who was soon returned to power by a British public drawn to his ideas about "the importance of upholding British honor and interests overseas."[97]

After taking Canton at the end of 1856, British forces under Lord Elgin and Baron Gros moved north, taking Tientsin (today Tianjin), which was just 80 miles southeast of Beijing, in the spring of 1858. The frightened Qing court agreed to talks, which resulted in another British-dictated accord—the Treaty of Tientsin. It included heavy indemnities, the opening of a large number of ports to the British with expanded trade privileges, new travel rights into the interior, and freedom of movement for Christian missionaries. The United States, France, and Russia soon took advantage of China's weaknesses and forced the Qing court to sign similar treaties.[98]

But the British were not satisfied with their new gains, and insisted on a new trade agreement that would be finalized in Beijing, something the Chinese resisted. To force the issue, Lord Elgin moved on Beijing and overthrew the government of Emperor Xianfeng, who had already fled the capital. Elgin, who soon learned of the arrest and torture of British representatives sent earlier to negotiate a settlement with the imperial court, ordered the looting and destruction of the emperor's Summer Palace.[99] These new humiliations rocked the Qing court, and the following year a coup brought Dowager Empress Cixi (Tz'u-hsi) to power, who adopted a two-prong policy of appeasing the West while trying to defeat the Taiping rebels. This "Restoration" (*zhongxing*) was ultimately successful, particularly in the latter case, and led to the bloody Qing capture of Nanjing in the summer of 1864. The goal of the Qing general, Zeng Guofan (T'seng Kuo-fan), was "the extermination of the whole movement through the death of its core leaders and followers." In his report to the emperor, Zeng mentioned:

> On the 17th and the 18th, Tseng Liang-tso...and others searched through the city for any rebels they could find, and in three days killed over 100,000 men. The Ch'in-huai creek was filled with bodies. Half of the false *wangs*, chief generals, heavenly generals, and other heads were killed in battle, and the other half either drowned themselves in the dikes and ditches or else burned themselves. The whole of them

numbered about 3,000 men. The fire in the city raged for three days and nights...not one of the 100,000 rebels in Nanking surrendered themselves when the city was taken but in many cases gathered together and burned themselves and passed away without repentance. Such a formidable band of rebels has been rarely known from ancient times to the present.[100]

Ultimately, though the "restored" court was able to stabilize the situation in China, and gradually embraced some Western ideas, particularly in the military field, it eventually led to the collapse of the Qing dynasty because of the ineffective leadership of an "ignorant and obscurantist Empress Dowager." As John King Fairbank and Merle Goldman have noted, the Qing court could not "overcome the inertia of the traditional Chinese policy," which, by the 1870s, was once again "conscientiously reviving the past instead of facing China's new future."[101]

As a result, over the next four decades, China's humiliation deepened as various European countries carved out autonomous enclaves along China's vast coastline. Many Chinese blamed the Dowager's ineffective government for many of the country's problems, which ultimately led first to the Hundred Days reform movement (1898), and the subsequent Boxer Rebellion (1899–1901).[102] The Boxers, a Western appellation used to describe members of the Society of Righteous and Harmonious Fists (Yihetuan), believed that blending martial arts with certain spiritual practices would protect them from harm in battle.[103]

The chain of events that led to the Boxer Rebellion began with the murder of two German Catholic missionaries in late 1897 in Shandong. What followed was the "'Great Powers' scramble for concessions, or the gua-fen, as the Chinese called it, the 'carving up of the melon.'" This, in turn, fed the anger that led to the violent uprising.[104] The response of some Chinese to these new Western incursions was swift and brutal. Missionaries and Christians, long a symbol of Western culture and humiliation, were now increasingly subjected to a growing crescendo of violence, which one Chinese observer termed "a carnival of crime."[105]

In late June 1900, hundreds of missionaries and thousands of Chinese Christians were massacred in Tai Yuan in Shanxi Province northwest of Shandong. Yung Cheng, a Chinese Christian, described what happened to one group of missionaries.

The first to be led forth was Pastor Farthing. His wife clung to him. But he gently put her aside, and going to the front of the soldiers, himself knelt down without saying a word, and his head was struck off by one blow of the executioner's knife.

He was quickly followed by Pastors Hoddle and Beynon, Drs. Lovitt and Wilson, all of whom were beheaded with one blow by the executioner. Then the Governor, Yü Hsien, grew impatient and told his bodyguards, all of whom carried big beheading knives with long handles, to help kill the others. Pastors Stokes, Simpson, and Whitehouse were next killed, the last one by one blow, the other two by several blows.

When the men were finished the ladies were taken. Mrs. Farthing had held the hands of her children who clung to her, but the soldiers parted them, and with one blow beheaded their mother. The executioner beheaded all of the children, and did it skillfully, needing only one blow; but the soldiers were clumsy, and some of the ladies suffered several cuts before their death. Mrs. Lovitt was wearing her spectacles and held the hand of her little boy even when she was killed. She spoke to the people saying, as near as I can remember, "We all came to China to bring you the good news of salvation of Jesus Christ; we have done you no harm, only good; why do you treat us so?" A soldier took off her spectacles before beheading her, which needed two blows.

When the Protestants were killed, the Roman Catholics were led forward. The Bishop, an old man, with a long white beard, asked the Governor Yü Hsien why he was doing this wicked deed. I did not hear the Governor give him any answer, but he drew his sword and cut the Bishop across the face [with] one heavy stroke; blood poured down his white beard, and he was beheaded. The priests and nuns quickly followed him in death.[106]

As this orgy of violence spread, other Boxers moved on Beijing, which spurred radicals in the imperial court to urge the Dowager to use them to force the foreign diplomatic corps to leave the capital. She followed their advice, and by June 20–21, the Qing court was essentially at war with the country's foreign community in Beijing. Fortunately, officials in southern China refused to abide by the court's new antiforeign decrees, which helped limit Boxer excesses to northern China, Inner Mongolia, and Manchuria. After the Boxers entered Beijing and attacked its foreign compound, the Allies sent over 18,000 troops to try to lift the siege. Once they took the capital in mid-August, they looted the Forbidden City and the city of Beijing of their most valuable treasures. The imperial court fled to Xi'an, where it remained until early 1902.[107]

Once the Allies restored order to the capital, they forced the Qing court to sign the Boxer Protocol (1901), which required China to pay them an excessively high indemnity. It also stipulated that the Qing government had to erect monuments to slain foreigners throughout the country, and suspend imperial exams in those parts of China where antiforeign violence had taken place. It also dictated an array of punishments, including executions, for officials responsible for the violence.[108]

In many ways, the Boxer Protocol represented the final phase of the Western world's humiliation of imperial China. While a great deal has been made of this uprising, only 231 foreigners died, many of them horribly, during the upheaval. Victor Purcell said that "Europe's treatment of China in the whole period from 1895 had been devoid of all consideration and all understanding."[109] William L. Langer was equally critical of Western policies.

Hardly anywhere in the diplomatic correspondence does one find any appreciation of the feelings of the Oriental or any sympathy for the crude efforts made at reform. The dominant note is always that force is the father of peace and that the only method of treating successfully in China is the method of the mailed fist. The Boxers were considered to be so many ruffians who deserved no better treatment than is ordinarily meted out to common criminals. When the trouble began, legation guards were rushed to Beijing, where evidently they took the initiative in shooting at Chinese troops. The American Minister thought that these "exhibitions of skill and courage" would serve as "good object lessons." In their negotiations with the Yamen [Zongli Yamen; Qing Foreign Office] the foreign ministers rarely bothered with the facts. Indeed, a careful student of the problem [George Steiger] has put on record his opinion that each of the decisive steps taken by the diplomats in Peking, or by their naval commanders at Taku, was taken on the strength of rumours which have never been substantiated: each has been justified only by appealing to subsequent events as "evidence of the wisdom and necessity of the act."[110]

India

But it was not just China that suffered at the hands of the Western powers. India, today an emerging global power, has, like China, a rich, diverse history dating back to antiquity.[111] During the fourth and fifth centuries CE, much of northern and central India enjoyed a "golden age" of cultural, scientific, and religious achievement under the Gupta dynasty.[112] Once it ended, internal strife spread throughout the continent, followed by Turkish-Afghan incursions in the eighth century that introduced Persianate cultural, religious, and political traditions to the northwest part of the country with an "Arabic patina" and a "Turkish frame." What followed were Muslim efforts to convert the region to Islam. One conqueror, Mahmud Ghazni, forced 10,000 Indian troops in the city of Kanauj to convert to Islam after he took it in 1018. This victory was quickly followed by the conquest of Krishna, where Mahmud ordered that "all the temples should be burnt with naptha and fire and leveled to the ground," thus destroying some of "the noblest monuments of ancient India."[113]

In 1024, Mahmud attacked the city of Somnath, which he intended to destroy "in hope that the Hindus would become Muhammadans." Though its Hindu residents put up a "desperate resistance," they were unable to stop his troops from taking the city. Over 50,000 people died defending the city, which now fell prey to the savagery of Mahmud's troops.[114] Historically, Indians remember him as "a bandit operating on a large scale...his raids had no lasting results in the interior beyond the destruction of life, property, and priceless monuments."[115]

He was succeeded by a series of Slave or Malmuk dynasties that had to face a new wave of Muslim attacks in the late twelfth century that led to the creation of the Delhi Sultanate.[116] One of the invaders, ʿAlāʾ-ud-din Husain, the chief of the Afghan kingdom of Ghur, attacked Ghazni.

> The unhappy city was given to the flames for seven days and nights, during which "plunder, devastation, and slaughter were continuous. Every man that was found was slain, and all the women and children were made prisoners. All the palaces and edifices of the Maḥmūdi kings which had no equals in the world" were destroyed, save only the tombs of Sultan Maḥmūd and his two relatives.[117]

Another Afghan invader, Muhammed Ghūrni, captured the state of Bihar, and killed all of what he thought were idolatrous "shaven-headed [Buddhist] Brahmans."[118] His troops destroyed many of Bihar's Buddhist temples, monasteries, and libraries. The destruction was so widespread that it effectively destroyed Buddhism in that part of India. Monks who managed to escape the Afghan terror campaign fled to Tibet, Nepal, and other parts of southern Asia. By the beginning of the thirteenth century, "the traces of Buddhism in upper India were faint and obscure."[119]

For the next three centuries (1206–1526), the Afghani "Slave" or "Malmuk" dynasty ruled much of northern India, the Land of Submission (*Dar-ul-Islam*). Qutb-ud-din Iltemish, the first Sultan, was "a devoutly religious monarch who preferred the tactics of persuasion and tolerance to those of naked power."[120] Yet he could be brutal toward his enemies. "His gifts were bestowed by hundreds of thousands, and his slaughters likewise were by hundreds of thousands."[121]

Over the course of its long history, the Delhi sultanate faced numerous threats from various invaders, particularly the Mongols. While Sultan Shams-ud-din is supposed to have diplomatically halted Mongol incursions in northern India in the early thirteenth century, future sultans were less successful, particularly when it came to attacks by Tamerlane [Timur-i-lenk; Temur or Temür the Lame], a Turkified Mongol who saw himself as a successor to Ghenghis Khan. During the latter part of the fourteenth and early fifteenth centuries, Tamerlane created a vast Central Asian empire.[122] In 1398, he invaded northern India and captured Delhi.[123] Once in control of the city, his troops began to ravage it "like hungry wolves falling on a flock of sheep or eagles swooping on weaker birds."[124] Persian historian Mahomed Ferishta described the Hindu response.

> The Hindus, according to custom, seeing their females disgraced, and their wealth seized by the soldiery, shut the gates, set fire to their houses, murdered their wives and children, and rushed out on their enemies. This led to a general massacre so terrible that some streets were blocked by the heaps of the dead; and the gates being forced, the whole Mongol army stormed inside, and a scene of horror ensured easier to be imagined than described. The desperate courage of the Dehlians [sic] was at length cooled in their own blood, and throwing down their weapons, they at last submitted like sheep to the slaughter...In the city the Hindus were at least ten to one superior in number to the enemy; and had they possessed souls, it would have been impossible for the Mongols, who were scattered about in every street, house, and corner, laden with plunder, to have resisted.[125]

After two weeks of plunder, murder, and rape, Tamerlane decided it was time to leave. His army, loaded with booty and "tens of thousands of slaves," slowly made its way back to his capital, Samarkand.[126] Delhi

> was so spent in the wake of his orgiastic attack that for months the city lay in the death throes of famine and pestilence, "not a bird moving."[127]

Tamerlane left the whole subcontinent "fragmented politically" and "divided spiritually into many religio-philosophical camps," conditions that paved the way for India's last great pre–British Empire—the Mughal (Mongol) dynasty.[128] It was founded by Zahir-ud-din Muhammed Babur (Babar), a Chaghatia Turk who traced his lineage to Genghis Khan and Tamerlane. His grandson, Akbar, initiated a series of reforms that established the basis of Mughal rule over the subcontinent over the next few centuries.[129] He abolished the enslavement of POWs, putting "an end to an inhuman practice, but also saved Hinduism from mass conversion of its adherents to an alien faith."[130]

Akbar's grandson, Shah Jahan, who built the famed Taj Mahal in memory of his wife Mumtaz Mahal, did away with many of his grandfather's reforms, preferring to rely heavily on *Sharia* (*Shari'ah*, God's law) to guide official state policy. He transformed Delhi into "a religious center of great sanctity for pious Muslims," which today is regarded as "India's noblest monument to Islamic culture."[131] After putting down a rebellion in Bundelkhand (today part of Madhya Pradesh in north central India) in 1628–1629, Jahan had the heads of Bundelkhand's ruler, Jujhar, and his son, Bikramajit, cut off and sent to him. Jujhar's other sons were given a choice—convert to Islam or die. Two chose conversion, while the third refused. He was then "put to a brutal death." Jahan also ordered Hindu shrines and temples in Bundelkhand desecrated and destroyed, and the temple at Orchla turned into a mosque.[132] Scholars differ on the impact of Jahan's orthodox Islamic views on the Mughal Empire. Ashirbadi Lal Srivastava, who sees Jahan as more progressive and less conservative than traditionally depicted, thinks that his policies planted the "seeds of reaction which became eventually the main cause of the downfall of his dynasty and the destruction of his empire. His religious bigotry and intolerance anticipated the reactionary reign of Aurangzeb."[133]

Aurangzeb, one of Jahan's sons, waged a bloody civil war against his father and several of his brothers. After defeating and capturing his father, he had him "paraded in public humiliation throughout the streets" of Delhi. Aurangzeb then had the head of one of his brothers, Dara, whom he had put to death on "grounds of apostasy from Islam and idolatry," delivered "in a box" to his father.[134]

Aurangzeb, a devout Sunni Muslim, ruled with an iron religious fist. He insisted that his empire become "a Muslim state government by the precepts of the *Sharia* for the benefit of the Indian Muslim community." His efforts to force non-Muslims to convert to Islam spurred considerable resistance to his rule. His son, Muhammed Akbar, joined Rajput Hindu rebels against his father, and ultimately established a stronghold in the Deccan state of Maratha.[135]

Aurangzeb invaded the Deccan plateau (covering much of central and southern India), where his troops plundered and burned at will. After taking Hyderabad, Aurangzeb ordered the destruction of all Hindu temples and replaced them with mosques to "put down all forbidden deviations from proper Islamic practice."[136] In 1688, he captured Shambhaji, the Maratha rebel leader, and, after torturing him for two weeks, had him "hacked to death and the pieces thrown to the dogs."[137] The rebellion, which continued until the early eighteenth century, resulted in as many as 100,000 deaths annually. It also left in its wake untold human misery and destruction. The fighting

> stripped the peninsula of India of any and all of its surplus grain and wealth throughout the quarter century of its intrusion. Not only famine, but bubonic plague arose to take countless more lives during this era of tragic conflict and waste. The macabre dimension of the drama seems somehow too great for seventeenth century warfare, sounding more modern in its unyielding butchery, its senseless massacre of human and animal life.[138]

In many ways, the Deccan wars were only the tip of the iceberg when it came to the problems that Aurangzeb faced during his long reign. Though successful in his early military campaigns in Bengal and parts of Afghanistan, he later had to deal with various rebellions that drained his treasury. In the end, his policies set the stage for the "destruction of the centralized imperial system" in India, which paved the way for Europe's colonial powers, particularly the British, to use Mughal instability to strengthen their hold on various parts of India's east and west coasts.[139]

Portugal was the first of the European nations to establish a foothold in India in the late fifteenth century. A century later, the Dutch arrived, displacing the Portuguese as the dominant trading power in the region.[140] The British East India Company (EIC) soon followed, and established its first settlement in Surat in western India in 1608, and Madras in 1641.[141] King George II leased Bombay island, a former Portuguese outpost, to the EIC, in 1668, and two decades later the EIC built Fort William in Calcutta. Initially, the British were interested principally in Indian textiles, though, over time, Chinese tea, and later, Indian opium, came to dominate EIC trade.[142]

Late Mughal India, with its considerable wealth, was very attractive to Europe's major colonial powers, and by the eighteenth century they flooded the subcontinent. The various Indian states that began to emerge in the midst of the Mughal Empire's decline sought alliances with Europe's colonial powers, though what transformed the British presence in India was the conquest of Bengal (today West Bengal, India, and Bangladesh) in northeast India in 1757.[143] What followed was the EIC's "unbridled and systematic economic exploitation" of Bengal,[144] which led to unsuccessful efforts by Mir Kasim, Bengal's ruler, to try to drive the British out. This led to further EIC incursions, which convinced other Indian rulers of the wisdom of seeking British "protection" in the future.[145]

Now in control of much of the lower Ganges, the British expanded their fiefdom northward and southward in a series of wars between 1766 and 1818. This process was pushed along by greater British efforts to regulate what now was a troublesome EIC, an "empire within an empire" that was "out of control and capable of wreaking havoc both in India and Britain."[146] Robert Clive, the governor general of Bengal, tried to defend the EIC when he told the House of Commons in 1772 that its policies were partly driven by the fact that

> Indostan was always an absolute despotic government. The inhabitants, especially in Bengal, in inferior status are servile, mean, submissive and humble. In superior status they are luxurious, effeminate, tyrannical, treacherous, venal, cruel.[147]

In other words, the nature of EIC rule was driven by the need to deal with an Indian system of government that it concluded was alien to British traditions.

The gradual British conquest of India followed no organized game plan and was driven both by EIC economic interests and the idea that to "stop is dangerous; to recede ruin."[148] From the British perspective, defeating India's armies handily enhanced their reputation among local rulers, while defeat or retreat had the opposite effect. This meant terrorizing not only the enemy but also local populations during battle. The future Duke of Wellington, known for his humanity during the Napoleonic Wars, ordered his troops to burn entire villages and loot them completely during a campaign in Malabar in 1800.[149]

Consequently, EIC expansion continued unabated through the first half of the nineteenth century as the British either annexed or conquered a number of Indian kingdoms. Most of these moves were successful, while others were problematic. One of the constants that began to emerge in the minds of British policymakers was what Capt. Arthur Conolly called the "Great Game," the Anglo-Russian conflict over control of Central Asia and the Himalayas.[150] Convinced that Russia was gradually moving toward northwest India and Afghanistan, the British mounted an invasion of the latter state in 1839. Expecting an easy go of it, the large British invasion force soon fell prey to Afghan tribesmen who

> ambushed isolated detachments and stole whatever they could get their hands on. Baluchi horsemen were particularly adept at hijacking strings of baggage camels. A blood-soaked rag was thrust in the face of a bull camel which, incensed, would rush off in pursuit of its tormentor, dragging along its companions. Stragglers were murdered and their bodies hideously disfigured by the Afghans. An officer of the 3rd Bengal NI (Native Infantry) came across the corpses of a pair of camp followers near Kandahar; one of the woman's breasts had been cut off and placed in her husband's mouth while his penis had been removed and laid in her mouth.[151]

By early 1842, the British, now in control of Kabul, the capital, decided it was best to retreat in the face of an increasingly volatile Afghan uprising. Afghan rebels killed most of the British soldiers as they tried to make their way back to India. The British responded with a retaliatory campaign in Afghanistan that

> destroyed villages, drove off or slaughtered stock, burned crops and storehouses, and hustled tribesmen and their families to the hills to perish. The severest chastisement fell on the inhabitants of those areas in which the refugees from Kabul had been massacred. The fortress and town of Ghazni were razed to the ground and during the brief reoccupation of Kabul, its bazaar was demolished.[152]

Once this "Army of Retribution" had done its dirty work, it retreated back to India.[153]

Such setbacks were more the exception than the rule for the British, and by mid-century, the EIC controlled much of India, either directly or through alliances with various principalities ruled by Hindu *maharajas* and Muslim *nawabs*. The bulwark of the EIC's success was its army, which was built around a strong cadre of British officers and large numbers of Sepoys, who were the backbone of the British forces in India. In 1830, for example, the EIC had an army of almost 225,000 men, which was led by over 30,000 regular army troops. The rest of the troops were Indian Sepoy foot soldiers and native cavalrymen. "By this time, the British high command had become mesmerized by its own military mythology, a combination of racial arrogance and past experience." This was based principally on the idea that an army led by "white soldiers would always sweep all before them, regardless of the odds."[154]

This "racial arrogance" was what drove British efforts to transform India in the nineteenth century, thus abandoning earlier ideas about respect for and working with Indian rulers and institutions. In what was nothing more than an exercise in imperial arrogance, the self-assured British, particularly in the decades leading up to the Sepoy Rebellion of 1857–1858, tried to transform and Christianize India along British lines.[155] These efforts had a deep impact on the Sepoys and their British officers, who began increasingly to distance themselves from their Hindu and Muslim infantrymen. This, in turn, fed growing Sepoy discontent about how they were being treated by their British officers. Between 1837 and 1846, there were a number of mutinies in the Bengal army, which made up a third of EIC forces in India, over such mistreatment and disrespect.[156] One British officer, Gen. Sir George Pollack, said as much to a House of Commons committee in 1853.

> The modern officer appeared indifferent to the welfare and customs of the Sepoys and, in consequence, enjoyed far less affection than his predecessors.[157]

Such discontent exploded into violence during the Sepoy or Great Indian Mutiny of 1857–1858. The rebellion, in turn, underscored the serious problems of British colonial rule in India, and forced Queen Victoria's government to step in and replace the EIC as the principal governing power in the subcontinent. According to Douglas M. Peers, what took place in India during the rebellion

> took on the attributes of a race war, one in which intensified racial and religious animosities caused participants on all sides to commit atrocities against each other.[158]

But, driven as it was by growing discontent with British rule, particularly in northern India, it was more than a military rebellion. This is why what began as a military uprising soon became a rebellion that involved Indians from all ranks of Indian society.[159]

This is also the reason for its widespread violence and destruction. Estimates are that 15 percent of the 40,000 Europeans living in India and as many as 800,000 Indians died during the rebellion. Property losses ranged from £60 to 100 million.[160] What shocked most observers were the terrible atrocities committed by both sides. The rebellion, which began with small brushups in the Bengal army in early 1857, soon spread throughout the region. It became more violent after Col. Edward Smyth of the 3rd Bengal Light Cavalry ordered 85 Bengali army Sepoys to load their Enfield rifles with cartridges that the Sepoys thought were covered with cow-and-pig grease. While tradition states that the Sepoys refused to use the cartridges because they thought it would violate their religion, the reality is that they had no problem using the rifles once the rebellion began, meaning that the cartridge dispute was simply a catalyst for an uprising driven by far "deeper causes."[161]

Smyth arrested the Sepoys who refused to load their rifles, and ordered their court-martial. This was preceded by a "ritual humiliation" before their peers on May 9. That evening, Sepoy cavalrymen broke into the stockade and rescued their comrades. Civilians from the nearby city of Meerut joined them in the attack on the local British garrison. The mob butchered every European they could find. When what remained of the garrison fled north to Delhi, the mobs were close behind. Once they took control of Delhi, they repeated what they had done in Meerut, murdering Europeans at will. The mobs desecrated anything that symbolized a Christian presence in the city, and murdered Indian converts. The mobs also captured 50 Europeans, mainly women and children, and "slaughtered [them] in the presence of the Bahadur Shah [king of Delhi] and his family."[162]

Several hundred miles to the south, another mob besieged the small British garrison in Cawnpore and the 1,000 civilians who had sought refuge there. Gen. Sir Hugh Wheeler approached the local ruler, the Nana Sahib, for peace terms. The latter agreed that in return for a British surrender, Wheeler, his men, and the refugees would be allowed safe passage out of Cawnpore. In reality, Nana had no intention of allowing them to escape, and attacked them as they fled down the river. Most were shot or drowned. The Sepoys also captured about 125 women and children, and imprisoned them in the home of the mistress of a British officer, the Bibighar, or "lady's house." Weeks later, the Indian rebels murdered all of the Bibighar captives and dumped their bodies into a nearby well. After the British retook Cawnpore, they searched for the missing women and children. One officer reported that "gore trailed and [was] smeared and spattered through the pillared rooms [of the Bibighar house] 'as if a hundred bullocks had been killed there.'" Another described the nearby well as "a mass of gory confusion."[163]

Afterward, one British officer pledged: "I have spared many a man in fight...but I will never spare another. I shall carry this with me in my holsters, and whenever I am inclined for mercy, the sight of it, and the recollection of this house, will be sufficient to incite me to revenge."[164] Many officers made similar pledges. The British retaliated with the cruel torture, humiliation, and execution of suspected Hindu and Muslim rebels. To Indian "onlookers," these "measures constituted a grotesque, nightmarish affirmation of the very fears that had incited them to rebellion in the first place: that the Feringhees [derisive term for foreigners or Europeans] intended to destroy their caste and their religions."[165]

Exaggerated tales of such atrocities included stories "of women raped, children tortured and...roasted alive and fed to their parents."[166]

> Stories about the violation of women had a powerful impact on the British public, who saw the uprising as "more than a violation of trust, it was a brutal assault on national ideals of womanhood and it placed the perpetrators beyond the pale of mercy." The violation of women, more than anything else, justified the retribution which was being handed out and reported in the press.[167]

All of this stirred British soldiers to "fight with a demonic energy and contempt" for an enemy that they saw as capable of "unlimited evil."[168] Such passions often expressed themselves in horrible reprisals. After the British captured Delhi in September, they committed "random massacres of sepoys and civilians."[169] Two of Bahadur's sons were captured and executed on the spot, while the city was thoroughly and brutally looted.[170]

The final campaign in the Sepoy Mutiny centered around the siege of Lucknow in early 1858. After two weeks of "brutal fighting," young British troops, who had seen the carnage at Cawnpore, unleashed their fury on their captives.

> One injured rebel was dragged out of a bombarded house and deliberately wounded by a united squad of Sikhs and Englishmen; they first tried to draw and quarter him, but when that did not work they stabbed him in the face with bayonets and then pinned him down in a small fire until he burned to death. In room after room, rebels died by the hundreds, shot down "in files" until "no living enemy was left to kill."
>
> The looting of Lucknow was second only to the sack of Delhi. Wading through rooms two feet deep in smashed mirrors and chandeliers, officers packed their kits and ammunition pouches with jewels and gold mohurs [coins] snatched from the burning houses of Oudh's aristocracy.[171]

Afterward, the British began a search for Sepoy fugitives, which one officer likened to "manhunting," since they used hunting methods to find rebels. Elsewhere, captured Hindu rebels were covered in "cows' flesh before being hanged or blown from the mouths of guns." There were other instances where Muslim rebels "were hanged in pigs' skins or forced to chew on pig fat before execution. Thousands of prisoners were hanged from trees in the *doab*, often on the flimsiest of evidence."[172]

Most of the blame for the rebellion was placed on the shoulders of the EIC. In 1858, the British Parliament passed the Government of India Act, which placed India under direct government rule, thus ending the Mughal empire. Unfortunately, it left in place most of the EIC bureaucrats, who now ran the new British *Raj* (Hindi, reign). A secretary of state for India, who was answerable to Parliament, oversaw Indian affairs from afar, while a Crown-appointed viceroy governed the *Raj* on a day-to-day basis from Delhi. In 1877, Queen Victoria was named Empress of India.[173]

What emerged, politically speaking, was a British-run state that included not only modern India but Pakistan, Bangladesh, and, at one time, parts of Burma and Singapore. Within the subcontinent itself, there were 500 provinces ruled directly by the Crown that enjoyed dominion status, and 175 princely states under the suzerainty of Her Majesty's Government. These kingdoms, which were scattered throughout India, had the right to select their own rulers. But other than that, they were firmly under British control. This system was set up to reward those Indian rulers who had remained loyal to the British during the mutiny, and there were many. From the British perspective, India's princes were "props of imperialism from whose class a self-governing and pro-British India might ultimately arise."[174]

None of these changes, though, could repair the damage of what the British called the "Indian Mutiny."[175] The racial prejudices that had begun to surface in the years before the uprising were now "confirmed and strengthened." Trust, at least on the part of the British, was gone, as were "more liberal assumptions concerning Indian progress and possible political developments."[176] What Lawrence James calls the "sinister side to the British memory of the Mutiny" would, he argues, "have repercussions in India and in other parts of the empire."[177] This would certainly be the case in Africa.

Africa

There are probably few areas in the world that have suffered more from colonialism than Africa. This has not only affected our views of this continent but also robbed us of the ability to see "Africa as a dynamic and exceptionally fecund entity, where the evolution of humanity is merely one of many developmental trajectories that are uniquely evident there."[178] Europe's colonial powers saw sub-Saharan Africa principally as a source of human labor and natural resources. The result was the creation of one of the most controversial and devastating institutions in the history of mankind—African slavery—an institution so destructive and dehumanizing that some have chosen to call it the *Maafa* or African Holocaust.[179] Between 1400 and 1900, 18 million Africans were captured, sold, and enslaved as part of Saharan, Red Sea, Indian Ocean, and New World slave trading ventures.[180]

The most infamous of these slave trading networks saw as many as 12 million Africans transported from Africa to the Americas between 1451 and 1870.[181] Sixty percent of the slaves shipped to the New World came from West Africa. Though the shipment of Africa slaves began soon after Europeans entered the New World, this trade did not increase substantially until the seventeenth century, when over 1.8 million slaves were shipped to the Americas.[182] These "slave exports" reached their peak in the eighteenth and nineteenth centuries, when almost 9.5 million African slaves were shipped abroad. During the latter period, the English were the principal "exporters" in this trade (2.5 million), followed by the Portuguese (1.8 million), the French (1.2 million), and the Dutch (350,900).[183]

While there is no question about the involvement of Africans in this trade, the real culprits in the American slave trade were the Europeans, and later the Americans.[184] The Portuguese, who established a strong foothold in Africa in the late fifteenth century, dominated the African slave trade until the first half of the seventeenth century, and terrorized towns and villages on the East African coast to force them to accept Portuguese rule. They argued that these attacks were justified as part of the "Christian war against Islam." John Reader says Portuguese onslaughts amounted more accurately to "crimes against humanity."[185] In the mid-seventeenth century, the Dutch, the British, and the French began successfully to challenge the Portuguese dominance of the slave trade, which reached its peak in the eighteenth century, when over 6 million African slaves were shipped to the Americas. Its demise over the next century was driven, as Eric Williams has noted, by economic, political, humanitarian, international, and social factors.[186]

To some extent, it could be argued that the seed for abolition can be found in the ideas of the Enlightenment. And even though the American *Declaration of Independence* of July 4, 1776, and the French *Declaration of the Rights and Duties of Man and Citizen* (1795) voiced similar Enlightenment ideals about equality and liberty, history would soon prove that there was a great difference between such ideals and their practical implementation when it came to the question of slavery and the slave trade.[187] But they helped to lay the moral groundwork for its abolition, which gradually took place in Europe and the United States in the nineteenth century. But even as abolitionists pushed to end this dreadful institution, the slave trade flourished.[188] Between 1801 and 1843, over 2.6 million African slaves were shipped to the Americas, though these figures declined dramatically by mid-century because of abolition efforts and the changing economic realities of Europe's new industrial age.[189]

The end of the African slave trade, however, did nothing to temper the European view that the African continent was still ripe for exploitation. Africa was now seen as a source of raw materials to feed Europe's growing industrial needs and new markets for goods produced in its factories. This led to Europe's late-nineteenth-century "scramble for Africa." It began when European explorers such as David Livingstone, a missionary who opened up the interior of Africa, and others made the Western world more aware of the exotic wonders of this intriguing, diverse continent. After his first expedition to Africa in 1841–1856, Livingston challenged an enthralled audience at Cambridge University

> to direct your attention to Africa; I know in a few years I shall be cut off in that country, which is now open: Do not let it be shut again! I go back to Africa to try to make an open path for commerce and Christianity; do you carry out the work which I have begun. *I leave it with you.*[190]

One of those intrigued by Livingstone's adventures was Belgium's king, Leopold, who became enthralled with Henry Morton Stanley's 1871 expedition to find Livingstone, who had disappeared into the interior of Africa six years earlier. Leopold followed Stanley's search in the press and was determined to convince the Welsh explorer and writer to help him set up his own kingdom in Africa.[191] In 1878, Leopold hired Stanley to explore the Congo (Kongo), arguing that it was to be mainly a philanthropic expedition. In reality, he hoped the Welsh explorer would establish a Belgian colony in the Congo for him.[192] Before Stanley left, Leopold told him "to lay the groundwork in the Congo for a 'confederation of free negro republics,' black tribes whose president would live in Europe and rule under the guidance of the Belgian king."[193] Stanley despised the Africans he encountered, and saw them as nothing more than future recruits "to the ranks of soldier-laborers."[194]

Leopold's ambitions conflicted with German imperial ambitions in Africa, and in 1884, Europe's major colonial powers met in Berlin to discuss this conflict. In the end, they decided to recognize his *Association international du Congo* (AIC)'s control over a Congo Free State (CFS) in return for free trading rights in the region. For all practical purposes, the Congo was now the personal possession of the Belgian king.[195]

Leopold was driven by one goal—to use whatever means necessary to rob the Congo of its natural resources, be it rubber, ivory, or other treasures. He created a village quota system for rubber and a *Force Republique* that used torture and other methods to ensure that these quotas were met. The result was a manmade criminal disaster that ultimately resulted in the deaths of between 3 and 5 million Congolese from 1880 to 1920. Adam Hochschild argues in his *King Leopold's Ghost* that while "the killing in the Congo was of genocidal proportions, it was not, strictly speaking, a genocide," since "the Congo state was not deliberately trying to eliminate one particular ethnic group from the face of the Earth." Instead, he argues, what took place in the Congo was "mass murder on a vast scale."[196]

The atrocities in the Congo gained widespread international attention. Joseph Conrad, who visited the Congo in 1890 and later captured the essence of the brutality there in his *Heart of Darkness*, blamed all of Europe for creating Kurtz, the novel's protagonist who proclaimed that they must "Exterminate all the Brutes!"[197] Conrad was part of a larger British effort to bring international attention to the tragedy in the Congo. In 1903, Roger Casement, the British consul to the Congo Free State, spent the second half of that year traveling throughout Leopold's kingdom to investigate charges about Belgian treatment of the Congolese population. This led to the creation of the Congo Reform Association, which, in league with considerable international pressure, prompted the Belgian government to take control of the CFS in 1908.[198]

Similar atrocities took place in German Southwest Africa (*Deutsch-Südwestafrika;* DSWA), today Namibia. In 1884, Germany officially acquired what became the DSWA and began immediately to exploit its human and natural resources.[199] Most of the good land in the DSWA was taken over by the German Colonial Society for Southwest Africa (*Deutsche Kolonialgesellschaft für Südwest-Afrika*), which was funded by a group of German bankers and industrialists. From the outset, imperial efforts in the DSWA were a losing proposition, since, according to some experts, the area was "unfit even for a penal colony."[200]

The DSWA was inhabited by three tribes: the Ovambo and the Herero, who made up 80 percent of the population, and the Nama (the Germans called them the *Hottentots*). From the outset, there were conflicts between German colonists and these tribes because the former coveted tribal grazing lands, native cattle, and labor. Over time, the tension exploded into a civil war. In early 1904, the Herero, led by Samuel Maherero, attacked German settlements throughout the DSWA, killing "every German man who could bear arms." On the other hand, they "spared the lives of German missionaries and German women and children, as well as all Europeans of other nationalities." Some of those who were killed during the early days of the rebellion were "tortured in macabre rituals."[201]

German reservists quickly put the rebellion down, though Kaiser Wilhelm II decided to send Gen. Lothar von Trotha to the DSWA to "crush the revolt...by fair means or foul."[202] He arrived in the DSWA in June and within a few months had driven the Herero to the edge of the Kalahari, which became a deadly Herero "prison." What followed would be "a great catastrophe" that some scholars call the first act of genocide in modern history. Von Trotha ordered his troops to poison the wells, erect guard posts along the Hereroland-Kalahari border, and shoot any Herero who tried to enter German territory. The Hereros who managed to survive were forced into slave labor camps where they were forced to work for German businesses. Thomas Parkenham described incarceration in such camps as "a death sentence."[203]

On October 2, 1904, von Trotha issued what has been called his extermination order (*Vernichtungsbefehl*):

> I, the Great General of the German soldiers, address this letter to the Herero people. The Herero are no longer considered German subjects. They have murdered, stolen, cut off ears and other parts from wounded soldiers, and now refuse to fight on, out of cowardice. I have this to say to them...the Herero people will have to leave the country. Otherwise I shall force them to do so by means of guns. Within the German boundaries, every Herero, whether found armed or unarmed, with or without cattle, will be shot. I shall not accept any more women or children. I shall drive them back to their people—otherwise I shall order shots to be fired at them.[204]

What followed was a Nama rebellion that escalated into a fruitless guerilla war that was almost over by the time von Trotha left for Germany later that year, claiming full victory in the DSWA. Estimates are that over 75 percent of the DSWA's Herero and about half of the Nama died during the conflict.[205] Isabel V. Hull concludes that Nazi Germany's "culture of violence" was

> simply the reification of practices and policies...that had become general from the old Imperial military culture. In the Third Reich they were easily harnessed for the ideological ends of even greater mass destruction and death.[206]

Unlike Belgium and Germany, Great Britain was not a newcomer to the African colonial scene. The British saw the southern tip of Africa as an important way station to India and the East. In the mid-seventeenth century, the Dutch EIC (*Vereenigde Oost-Indische Compagnie*) established a small settlement in the Cape of Good Hope region, which drew Dutch, German, and French settlers to the colony. Over time, these "Boer" (Dutch, farmer) colonists began to spread out in the Cape, which ultimately brought them in conflict with a number of tribes living in southern Africa. One of the tribes, the San, or bushmen, were "on the whole ruthlessly exterminated in the eighteenth and early nineteenth centuries after many decades of warfare."[207]

The British, who forced the Dutch out of the Cape in the early nineteenth century, also had conflicts with various tribes, particularly the Xhosa, who were determined "to drive the British back to the sea."[208] Yet the Xhosa were not willing to go to any extremes to do this, since Xhosa military tradition dictated that only men be killed, and that the lives of women and children be spared during a conflict. "Amakeia," a popular, nationalistic South African poem written in the nineteenth century, tells of a Xhosa servant who promised to save her white mistress's child at all costs. When she refused to give the child to a band of Xhosa warriors, they, according to the poem, killed both of them. In reality, no "such incident occurred."[209]

In early 1835, the British, aided by the Boers and Khoikhoi auxiliaries, began a war of attrition against the Xhosa. By European standards, the losses were moderate—100 colonists and Khoikhoi and 2,000–4,000 Xhosa. Yet the countryside was devastated, and the Xhosa "lost most of their cattle," much of it stolen during the early stages of the war.[210] After the fighting ended, the British government considered expanding further into Xhosa lands, which several British officials argued would lead to the "extermination" of the Xhosa. On the other hand, Britain's king, William IV, argued that the Xhosa were "irreclaimable savages," whose "ferocious and plundering character" was "the cause of the war." In the end, Lord Gleneg, the head of the British Colonial Office in London, argued in a detailed report to Lt. Gen. Sir Benjamin D'Urban, the governor of the Cape Colony, that

> the conduct of the colonists and government authorities during past years had given the Xhosa "ample justification" for the war. They had been harassed "by a long series of aggressions…which they had been the victims…they had a perfect right to hazard the experiment, however, hopeless, of extorting by force that redress which they could not expect otherwise to obtain."[211]

He ordered D'Urban to cease efforts to acquire further Xhosa land, "a conquest," he added, that was unjust.[212]

This led thousands of pioneers (*Voortrekers*) to move out of the Cape Colony into lands to the north and east. Viewed in Afrikaner history as an "act of civilian rebellion," it was, according to one *Voortreker*, Anna Steenkamp, a reaction against Britain's "perceived drift towards racial equality." She felt that

> the shameful and unjust proceedings with reference to the freedom of our slaves—and yet it is not their freedom that drove us to such lengths, as their being placed on an equal footing with Christians, contrary to the laws of God, and the natural distinction of race and religion, so that it was intolerable for any decent Christian to bow down beneath such a yoke; wherefore we rather withdrew in order to preserve our doctrines in purity.[213]

When the British tried to forestall the creation of an Afrikaner state in Natal, the new homeland of the *Voortrekers* northeast of the Cape Colony, the Boers split into various groups and moved further north, founding what later became the Transvaal or the South African Republic (SAR) and the Orange Free State (OFS).[214]

The result was a diverse collection of English and Afrikaner settlements that were sometimes a "melodramatic mixture of solid uncertainty and high risk."[215] Denis Judd and Keith Surridge likened some of these settlements to plantations in the American South, "serving...as fortresses of white supremacy."[216] The British, who wanted to create a united South Africa, were hindered not only by "the nature of white supremacy and need: namely, serious, perhaps long-term, trouble with the black tribes people," but also by the discovery of diamonds and gold in the region.[217]

The British intensified their unification efforts after the discovery of diamonds on the Cape Town–OFS border in 1869. After several failed efforts to convince Cape Towners and Afrikaners to join their confederation, London annexed the Transvaal in 1877.[218] Initially, Boer resistance was momentarily tempered by the Transvaal's economic problems. This was not the case with the Zulu nation, which occupied a key route to the diamond mines in the Transvaal. Though the British Colonial Office wanted to find a diplomatic solution to the Zulu question, Sir Bartle Frere, the British high commissioner for South Africa, wanted to go to war to annex the Zulu state, claiming that the Zulus threatened the newly annexed Transvaal.[219] He argued that what was taking place was a "war of race" driven by "insolent" Zulus "burning to clear out white men." Theophilus Shepstone, who oversaw the British annexation of the Transvaal, added:

> At this moment the Zulu power is a perpetual menace to the peace of South Africa; and the influence which it has already exercised and is now exercising, is hostile and aggressive; and what other result can be looked for from a savage people, whose men are all trained from their youth to look upon working for wages and the ordinary labour necessary to advance the progress of a peaceful country to be degrading; and to consider the taking of human life as the most fitting occupation of a man![220]

The only problem, Frere admitted, was how to make the Zulu appear to be the aggressor. The solution was simple. He adopted, despite local opposition, a policy of "coercion" that he hoped would draw the Zulu into war. The Zulu refused to react and seemed willing to go to any extreme to avoid a conflict. So Frere and Shepstone decided to create an incident based on the brief Zulu interrogation of two British surveyors in September 1878, who had wandered into Zulu territory. Two months later, the Zulu were presented with an ultimatum that would have resulted in the arrest of the brother and sons of a Zulu chief, Sihayo, a hefty fine, and a number of dramatic changes in the Zulu military and judicial system. If the Zulu had accepted the British proposal, they would have lost their autonomy and placed themselves directly under British rule.[221]

Yet the Zulu monarch, Cetshwayo, agreed to the arrests and fines, but asked for extra time to discuss the other demands with his advisers. Frere, who was determined to go to war, ordered troops into Zulu territory in early January 1879. The British, who "began looting cattle" once they entered Zulu territory, reported that the Zulu seemed to have no stomach for a fight.[222] On January 12, British troops destroyed Sihayo's homestead and stole all of his cattle. After hearing rumors of large Zulu contingents nearby, they set up camp at Isandlwana and sent out patrols that were unable to substantiate the rumors. This all changed late on January 21, when it became apparent that the Zulu were preparing to attack the British at the new encampment. The next day, 25,000 Zulus attacked and overwhelmed the British "in less than an hour." Almost 900 British troops lay dead, along with 500 black Natal Native Contingent (NNC) troops and 3,000 Zulus.[223]

After the battle was over, the "Zulu, as was their custom, took no prisoners and spared no lives, despite pleas for mercy." Though the Zulu later claimed that none of the British captives were tortured or mutilated before they were killed, there was evidence that they decapitated and scalped some of the soldiers. The British were particularly horrified by "the cruel fate of the little drummer boys, who were hung and butchered."[224] But what troubled the British most were the Zulu rituals of disembowelment and multiple spear wounds.[225]

After another battle at nearby Rorke's Drift, victorious British troops, aided by an NNC contingent, captured about 200 wounded or exhausted Zulus. They bayoneted, beat, or speared the captured Zulus to death because they were so short on ammunition.[226] Several weeks later, the British *Annual Register* called it

> a shock for which this nation was totally unprepared. It was as complete and almost as horrifying a surprise as the Indian Mutiny [of 1857], and nothing had occurred since then to stir public feeling about imperial affairs so profoundly. It was not indeed felt that there was any danger of a province being lost to the Crown, but there were the same fears for the safety of English colonists, an unarmed population exposed to the fury of overwhelming numbers of savage enemies.[227]

Though it took months for the British to respond, they finally did at the battle of Ulundi on July 4, 1879. As they marched into position, they found the "ritually disemboweled" bodies of a reconnaissance patrol sent out the day before. Though the British were greatly outnumbered by the Zulus (5,000 versus 15,000–20,000), they prevailed because of their artillery and superior fire power. When the Zulus began to flee the battlefield, the British pursued them savagely, killing even the wounded and burning nearby villages.[228] According to one British officer, "we all felt at last that the power of the Zulus had been destroyed."[229]

He was right. The Zulu lands were divided into 13 "independent chiefdoms," and the Zulu military system was done away with. These changes, in league with other dictated reforms, devastated the Zulu kingdom, which was "quickly plunged into chaos, the country lacking leadership, control and supplies."[230] Frere, who was widely blamed for what many considered "an unjust and unnecessary war," briefly kept his job, but was eventually recalled when it became apparent that he could not unite the various colonial states into a South African confederation.[231]

But this did not end British problems in South Africa. Boer leaders, frustrated by what they saw as the inequities of British rule in the Transvaal, initiated a series of conflicts over the next two decades—the First and Second Boer Wars.[232] Though the first ended with a Boer victory, the second, stimulated by British interest in recently discovered gold in the Transvaal, convinced London that the only way to resolve this ongoing conflict and create a united South Africa was "to push the crisis to the brink of war."[233] The Second Boer War, which began in the fall of 1899, pitted Transvaal and OFS irregulars against England's considerable military might. Though the British did not fare particularly well at the outset, the tide slowly shifted in London's favor, and by the summer of 1900, the British were in full control of the Transvaal.[234]

But what followed, a protracted guerilla war, haunted the British, who decided to fight fire with fire. Lord Kitchener of Khartoum fame was ordered to break the back of the Boer resistance. He adopted

a double sweeping operation: to flush out the guerillas in a series of systematic "drives," organized like a sporting shoot, with success defined in a weekly "bag" of killed, captured and wounded; and to sweep the country bare of everything that could give sustenance to the guerillas: not only horses, but cattle, sheep, women, and children.[235]

In the end, the decision to destroy Boer homes proved more harmful than helpful to British interests, since it antagonized Boer moderates and made "postwar reconstruction more difficult and ... much more expensive." It also created some immediate problems—what was to be done with the women and children whose homes had been destroyed by British troops.[236]

For Kitchener, the solution was simple—put them in *laagers* (Boer Afrikans, camp; Dutch, *leger*) or concentration camps that would prevent contact between Boer civilians and the guerillas, and also "protect the families of the Boers who were at risk because their menfolk had surrendered."[237] The British also opened separate camps for black South Africans. Kitchener, who later blamed this "policy of 'extermination'" on Sir Alfred Milner, the British high commissioner for South Africa, was widely criticized for such policies.[238]

Both Kitchener and Milner were attacked by two pro-Boer members in the British Parliament, C. P. Scott and John Ellis, who said these camps were similar to the *reconcentrado* camps used by the Spanish a few years earlier in Cuba.[239] Public outrage in the United Kingdom led Emily Hobhouse, a welfare activist, to visit some of the *laagers* in South Africa. When she returned, she wrote a scathing report on the plight of the women and children there, which she shared with the War Office and Parliament.

She described conditions in one of the camps as

wholesale cruelty. It can never be wiped out of the memories of people. It is hardest on the children. They droop in the terrible heat...with insufficient, unsuitable food...To keep these Camps going is murder to the children...I can't describe what it is like to see these children lying about in a state of collapse. It's just exactly like faded flowers thrown away. And one has to stand and look on such misery, and be able to do almost nothing.[240]

She also reported on

the wholesale burning of farms...the deportations...the burnt out population brought in by hundreds in convoys...deprived of clothes...the semi-starvation in the camps...the fever-stricken children lying...upon the earth...the appalling mortality.[241]

David Lloyd George, a future prime minister, asked why Great Britain was making

> war against women and children... "By every rule of civilized war we were bound to
> treat women and children as non-combatants... When children are being treated this
> way and dying, we are simply raising the deepest passions of the human heart against
> British rule in Africa... It will always be remembered that this is the way British rule
> started there, and this is the method by which it was brought about."[242]

A special government-appointed women's commission headed by Millicent
Fawcett looked further into these abuses and made extensive recommendations
about how to improve conditions in the *laagers*. It blamed most of the problems on
inadequate food, hygienic conditions, and lack of medical personnel. And though
conditions began to improve dramatically, these changes were too late to save the
lives of 20,000 Boers and 12,000 blacks imprisoned in the British concentration
camps.[243]

By the time the Fawcett Commission published its report in early 1902, the war
was almost over. Though the Boers lost, it left a bruised British Empire scarred not
only by the revelation of considerable military weaknesses but also charges of serious
war crimes. There were, for example, accounts of the rape of Boer women and the
murder of Boer POWs. This latter charge received considerable attention during the
1902 court-martial and execution of several Australian officers for such crimes.[244]
All of this also had a dramatic impact on British–Boer relations, and ensured that
the new South African confederation that emerged after the war lacked the loyal,
supportive underpinnings so important to such British efforts.

In the end, European colonial policy in Africa and Asia was driven by a new,
potent force of white racism that centered around ideas that Rudyard Kipling called
"The White Man's Burden"—the civilization of Kipling's "half devil/half child."
Josiah Strong said that the Anglo-Saxon move into Asia and Africa was the prelude
to the "final competition of races for which the Anglo-Saxon is being schooled."
According to Peter Gay, Strong, "the prolific American divine," had blended the
Social Darwinism of Herbert Spencer, who coined the term "survival of the fittest,"
with new nineteenth-century concepts of racism. Carl Peters, one of the founding
members of the Company for German Colonization, and the founder of German
East Africa, wrote in 1886 that colonial policy "is and remains the ruthless and determined enrichment of one's own people at the expense of other, weaker peoples."[245]

Such attitudes, particularly when faced with what appeared to be the "insolence"
of resistance by inferior peoples vis-à-vis the policies of superior white Europeans,
often led to various degrees of violence. Leander Jameson, for example, who, as
Rhodes' administrator in Mashonaland (today part of Zimbabwe), oversaw the
British invasion of Matabele territory during the brief Matabele War (1893–1894),
argued beforehand that he intended to treat the natives "like dogs and order the
whole *impi* [Zulu, armed body of men] out of the country."[246] And this is what his
forces did, destroying villages and "killing them [natives] wholesale." His rationale
was that "they had been 'impertinent and threatening.'"[247]

According to Isabella Hull, imperialism itself "*was* war" that bred an "economy
of violence" that rested not only on various racist and imperialistic ideas but also,
most importantly, on the idea of not appearing weak before people the Europeans

considered inferior.[248] To some extent, it could be argued, similar cultural, religious, and racist ideas also drove the European and American assaults against the native peoples in the Americas, Asia, and Africa.

Conclusion

The Western world truly came of age industrially and militarily in the nineteenth century. This was an era of dramatic overseas expansion into Africa and Asia, driven partly by the idea of a superior white civilization. Building on long centuries of European, and later, American dominance of slaves and native peoples, a new body of racism emerged that saw the peoples of Africa and Asia as mere objects in the way of a new era of international territorial expansion. This led to new conflicts in the Americas, Asia, and Africa that pitted Westerners against the native peoples of the lands they sought to conquer. Many of today's problems in Africa can be traced to this new era of European colonialism. And one does not have to dig too deeply into the collective Chinese, Indian, or Asian psyche to find negative historical memories of these long eras of brutish colonial rule. This was also an era that saw the development of new industrialized machines of war that were designed to protect ever-expanding American and European colonization efforts. This, coupled with the nationalism and other factors that drove such expansion, would provide the basis for a search for a body of law that would better define not only the nature of warfare but also the plight of the individual in such wars.

Chapter 4

Birth of the Modern Laws of War— Lieber to Versailles

In the midst of the debate in Great Britain about the concentration camps in South Africa, Sir Arthur Conan Doyle, the author of the Sherlock Holmes tales, defended British actions there in several books.[1] He argued in *The Great Boer War* (1902) that success in South Africa was key to the survival of the British Empire and the affirmation of the "virtues of our race." The war, he went on, has also "won for us a national resuscitation of spirit" that sealed "the blood brotherhood of the empire."[2] He continued this argument in *The War in South Africa*, blaming the worst of British policies on the guerilla tactics of the Boers, whom he likened to the French *franc-tireurs* (irregular military formations or guerillas) during the Franco-Prussian War. In fact, he added, from the outset of the war, "the Boers was [*sic*] entirely irregular as regards the recognised rules of warfare."[3] He added that though article 23 of Hague Convention II of 1899 made the destruction of enemy property illegal, it permitted such destruction if it was "imperatively demanded by the necessities of war."[4]

He considered the concentration camps as nothing more than temporary refugee centers that would protect Boer women and children from "all harm" while they waited for "the return of peace." He was extremely critical of Emily Hobhouse's report, and part of a larger effort "to poison the mind of the world against Great Britain." He devoted the latter part of *The War* to charges of war crimes against British troops. He argued that the British use of "expanding" and "hollow-headed" bullets was not a violation of the Hague Conventions, though Hague II did outlaw the use of "arms, projectiles, or material of a nature to cause superfluous injury."[5]

He returned to the *franc-tireur* question when he defended the British treatment of POWs. A belligerent, he stated, must be commanded by a superior, wear a "distinctive emblem recognizable at a distance," and "carry arms openly." The Boer guerilla, he argued, was no better than an assassin. And if there were occasions when British soldiers executed an "assassin" without superior orders, should one really consider such an action "outside the strict rules of warfare"? In the end, he concluded, given the "savage" nature of Boer guerilla tactics, the British acted with great discipline and humanity, refusing "to punish a whole nation for the cruelty and treachery of a few."[6]

Conan Doyle's continued references to the Boers' guerilla tactics and international law is remarkable, and underscores the contemporary impact, at least in public conversation, of efforts to develop a body of international laws that governed the behavior of armies in the field during wartime. While the works of Grotius, Wolff, and Vattel would lay the groundwork for such efforts, it must be remembered that these were the works of jurists and philosophers, not soldiers. Interestingly, it was an American conflict—the Civil War—not a European one that led to the creation of the first codified body of laws of war.

The *Lieber Code*

A little over a decade after the second Boer War ended, Senator Elihu Root, the recent recipient of the Nobel Peace Prize for his work in ending the Russo-Japanese War, delivered a speech before the American Society of International Law praising Francis Lieber, whom he called the "patron saint" of international law.[7] He was referring, of course, not only to Lieber's coauthorship of the Union Army's *Instructions for the Government of the Armies of the United States in the Field* (General Orders No. 100, 1863; the *Lieber Code*), but also to Lieber's later work in promoting an international gathering of legal scholars that would meet to create "a permanent institution or an academy of international laws."[8] Lieber, a native Berliner who served in the Prussian army and was wounded at the battle of Waterloo, later settled in the United States where he taught at South Carolina College (now the University of South Carolina), and later, at Columbia University.[9]

By the time the Civil War broke out, Lieber was a well-known scholar and political theorist. A strong supporter of the Union, he became particularly interested in "the treatment of the foe on the battlefield" because two of his sons served in the Union army (Hamilton and Guido), and a third (Oscar) in the Confederate military. He was particularly concerned over the question of the rights of rebels, whom some thought enjoyed no rights because of their treasonable actions.[10]

After researching this question, Lieber concluded that the nature of the rebellion did not change the fact that "for humanitarian reasons, even in time of rebellion, the customary rules of warfare and treatment of prisoners of war should continue."[11] But he was plagued by questions about prisoner exchanges, paroles, the treatment of "fugitive slaves," and other issues, particularly in light of the fact that for the average Union officer, the "laws of war...were no more than rhetorical expressions to justify one's own conduct and damn the enemy."[12] He insisted that the Union army adopt "co-ordinated rules" of war to ensure its operation as "a smooth-functioning, efficient military machine." He had been gathering materials for a course he hoped to teach at West Point, "The Laws and Usages of War," and integrated them, along with his chapter on war from his *Manual of Political Ethics* (1838–1839), into a series of lectures he delivered at Columbia in the winter of 1861–1862.[13]

He argued that wars should not be fought unless they were for a just cause. But once engaged, he went on, a belligerent should "use the most destructive means possible to injure an enemy, even if it means killing noncombatants and destroying property."[14] On the other hand, he thought that what was "allowed in injuring the enemy" was "that which serves the public." What was disallowed in war was

> that which serves private ends...I have not the right to injure my enemy privately, that is, without reference to the general object of the war...We do not injure in war in order to injure, but to obtain the general object of war. All cruelty, that is, unnecessary infliction of suffering, therefore, remains as cruelty among private individuals. All suffering inflicted upon persons who do not impede my way, for instance, surgeons, or inoffensive persons, if it can possibly be avoided, is criminal; all turning the war to private ends...all use of arms, of the power which I enjoy as a soldier, for private purposes, as, for instance, the satisfaction of lust; the unnecessary destruction of private property is criminal.[15]

The personal experiences of his sons deeply affected Lieber, particularly after he learned of the death of Oscar, who was killed at the battle of Williamsburg in the spring of 1862. Later that year, Gen. Henry Halleck, the Union army's new general-in-chief, and a renowned international lawyer in his own right, asked Lieber to write something about the treatment of guerillas.[16] The result was "Guerilla Parties Considered with Reference to the Law and Usages of War" (1862), which distinguished between the partisan, who was "entitled to the privileges of the laws of war," and guerillas, who carried on "petty war (guerilla) chiefly by raids, extortion, destruction, and massacre, and who cannot encumber themselves with many prisoners, and will therefore generally give no quarter." In such situations, he concluded, the laws of war, as they pertained to the capture of guerillas, were not applicable.[17]

Halleck later appointed a committee that included Lieber and several general officers to develop "a set of rules and definitions providing for the most urgent cases, occurring under the Law and Usages of War, and on which our Articles of War [1806] are silent."[18] The result was the *Lieber Code* (General Orders 100),[19] which Root called an erudite document written with clear definitions, and "injunctions and prohibitions that were 'distinct and unambiguous.'" It was also, he added,

> a practical presentation of what the laws and usages of war were, and not a technical discussion of what the writer thought they ought to be, which in all its parts may be discerned an instinctive selection of the best and most humane practices and an assertion of the control of morals to the limit permitted by the dreadful business in which the rules were to be applied.[20]

Theodor Meron, who considers the *Lieber Code* a document founded on "broad humanitarian principles" that explained "its tremendous impact both on later multilateral treaties codifying the law of war and on the development of customary law," saw it in a different light. The fact that it represented a certain balancing act between "humanitarian concerns with military necessity" did not mean that it necessarily "further[s] the dictates of humanity."[21]

The *Code*'s 157 articles discuss a wide range of subjects such as combatants, noncombatants, enemy property, partisans, guerillas, spies, POWs and their exchange, parole, peace, assassination, insurrection, civil war, rebellion, and armistices. It defines "military necessity" as the means a belligerent uses to secure "the ends of the war," including "incidentally *unavoidable*...destruction of life and limb of *armed enemies*." On the other hand, such necessity "does not admit cruelty." Retaliation was considered legal as long as it was not driven by "mere revenge." Yet article 30 admitted that "the law of war imposes many limitations and restrictions on principles of justice, faith and honor." Article 43 specifically declared free any slave who came under US military custody, while article 44 forbade "all wanton violence...against persons in the invaded country" and the "destruction of property not commanded by the authorized officer." These plus other acts of a violent or criminal nature, including rape, were punishable by death, a punishment that allowed a commander "lawfully" to kill a subordinate "on the spot."[22]

It defined POWs in article 49, while article 56 forbade the ill treatment of such prisoners. On the other hand, while article 60 spoke out firmly against giving no quarter, it did state that "a commander is permitted to direct his troops to give no quarter, in great straits, when his own salvation makes it *impossible* to cumber himself with prisoners." The *Lieber Code* laid out such circumstances in articles 61, 62, and 66, while articles 72–80 dealt with POWs. While they were to be treated humanely, armed groups not tied to an "organized hostile army" were to be dealt with as "highway robbers or pirates." The same was true of scouts dressed in the enemy's uniform, "armed prowlers," and "war-rebels."[23]

The Pathway to the Hague Conventions

Though the *Lieber Code* was distributed widely throughout the Union army, it is difficult to gauge its impact on its officers. President Lincoln, for example, felt that the *Lieber Code* "had to be applied flexibly" because "dealing with guerillas required unorthodox tactics."[24] On the other hand, Lieber was convinced that his code would be adopted by the British, French, and the Germans since, as he told Gen. Halleck, "it is a contribution by the United States to the stock of common civilization."[25] And, to some extent, he was correct. Johann Caspar Bluntschli, one of the giants in international law in the second half of the nineteenth century, and cofounder of the Institute of International Law (*Institut de droit international*), used the *Lieber Code* as the basis for his *The Modern Law of War* (*Das moderne Kriegsrecht*; 1866). He later wrote in the introduction to his own codification of international law, *Modern International Law (Das moderne Völkerrecht*; 1868), that the *Lieber Code* was what "prompted him to attempt 'to set forth the essentials of modern international law in the form of a codification' and that their correspondence encouraged him to see the 'risky undertaking' through to completion."[26]

Several years later, Bluntschli praised Lieber and a number of other legal specialists for proposing the idea that they come together to create "a permanent institution or an academy of international law."[27] Lieber, who corresponded regularly with Bluntschli, was, like many other international jurists, upset by both sides' violation of the 1864 Geneva "Convention for the Amelioration of the Condition of the Wounded in Armies in the Field" during the Franco-Prussian War. [28]

Such violations were, however, only the tip of the iceberg, so to speak, when it came to charges of war crimes during this conflict. In the midst of the German *juggernaut* that swept through France in the summer and fall of 1870, the French responded with "a new class of soldier called the *franc-tireur*, a French deserter or civilian who took up arms to obstruct the German advance or plunder the crops and homes needed to sustain the German army."[29] The French decision to create squads of *franc-tireurs* was an act of desperation when it became apparent that there was little the French army could do to stop the German advance on Paris. Leon Gambetta, the minister of the interior for Gen. Louis Truchu's new Government of National Defense, argued that the role of the *franc-tireur* was to

> harass the enemy's detachments without pause or relaxation [and] prevent him from deploying, restrict the area of his requisition, make him thin out before Paris, disturb him day and night, always and everywhere.[30]

Within a few months, the French had created 3,000 *franc-tireur* units with 57,000 active guerillas.[31]

When the war began, the Germans followed "generally accepted war conventions" when it came to the treatment of regular French soldiers."[32] However, Fld. Mshl. Helmuth von Moltke, chief of the Prussian and, later, German general staff, considered the *franc-tireurs* to be common criminals and ordered his troops to deal with them accordingly. According to Manfred Messerschmidt, German military thinking at the time was driven by a new sense of strength that devalued "international law, which was no longer seen as a binding authority but simply a tool of foreign policy that could be ignored at will." Prussian general Julius von Hartmann wrote: "The military war aim lies in the immediate aims of the act of violence in war itself," something that Messerschmidt thinks led to the development of the idea of war as an act of "extermination." This, he argues, was the type of war that Moltke fought in France in 1870–1871.[33]

Both sides felt that their actions were justified and legal. One German wrote that *franc-tireurs* should be shot on the spot and argued that his unit "was completely justified in seizing equally cruel countermeasures." Another was convinced that French guerilla units had poisoned the wells in one village and dumped rotten meat in them. "The French civilians are nasty people; they have fired on the wounded." After his squad lost a number of men during a *franc-tireur* attack on Christmas day, he reported that his unit set a nearby village on fire because they thought it was where the French guerillas were hidden. The French were equally critical of the German reprisals.

> Breaking into homes with axes, pillage, plunder, murder, and especially arson. All these atrocities continued during the whole night and the following day under the orders of a disciplined organization, which places the responsibility for this as high as the Prussian government.
>
> Long after the fighting, during the night and the following day, peaceful inhabitants, elderly people, the sick have been killed by the blows of guns and revolvers in their homes and at their doors. Some have been burned in their beds which had been set on fire; wounded people were thrown alive into the flames where they were burned to such an extent that it became impossible to recognize [them].[34]

For the Germans, there emerged a *franc-tireur* myth that affected military thinking for decades and centered around the idea of a guerilla driven by "reckless rage" who harassed "the enemy at his most vulnerable." On the eve of World War I, the German general staff considered the *franc-tireur*

> the antithesis of the German soldier, for they frequently had a criminal attitude, insulted and even attacked their officers, and carried out robbery, theft and murder. Their value in regular combat was low, for they ran away after the first shots were fired.[35]

This view of the *franc-tireur* clearly violated the spirit of operative international law at the time and would govern German actions in Belgium and France in the early months of World War I. This led the French and the Belgians to charge the Kaiser's forces with major war crimes.

Such violations of the laws of war were what prompted international jurists like Lieber, Bluntschli, and others to promote the idea of creating an international body of legal specialists who would look for ways "to promote the progress of international law." The result was the Institute of International Law, whose work would, they hoped "correspond to the legal conscience of the civilized world," and help lead to the "gradual and progressive codification of international law . . . in harmony with the needs of modern societies." Its founders hoped that it would also contribute "within the limits of its competence, either to the maintenance of peace, or to the observance of the laws of war." The Institute and its legal scholars could do this by offering "reasoned legal opinions in doubtful or controversial cases," and through "publications, public teaching, and all other means, in ensuring that those principles of justice and humanity which should govern the mutual relations of people."[36]

In 1874, Tsar Alexander II of Russia and William I of Prussia called for an international conference to discuss a draft proposal "concerning the laws and customs of war." Almost from the moment that it opened on July 27, 1874, the Brussels conference became embroiled in controversy, particularly over the authorship and purpose of the Russian draft proposal, which centered around the general idea of creating "binding rules of war" to mitigate war's "grave consequences."[37] Other nations saw it differently. The Duc la Rochefoucauld, the French ambassador to England, said the draft was

> calculated to guarantee conquering armies the advantages of their reorganization and their invading marching masses, and, on the other hand, to diminish the means of defence of populations surprised by such an invasion. It is, in truth, a code of conquest rather than one of defence.[38]

The British agreed, which underscored what many delegates thought was a German-driven gathering. In the end, though some delegates considered the conference a "shipwreck," most approved (but did not ratify) the conference's final *Brussels Declaration*.[39]

Consequently, despite the failure of the Brussels conference, the *Declaration* was the first collective European effort to agree on a common set of laws of war. And though it was not nearly as comprehensive as the *Lieber Code*, the *Declaration* was a starting point for European discussions about a modern, codified body of the laws of war. Its first eight articles dealt with the question of "military authority over hostile territory," which was the basis of suspicions that it was a "code of conquest." These articles generally corresponded to the first 47 articles in the *Lieber Code*, which

Bluntschli drew heavily on for his own work. Articles 9–11, which differentiated between "belligerent combatants and non-combatants," corresponded to the *Lieber Code*'s articles 74–85, while articles 12–14 were similar to the *Lieber Code*'s articles 68–71. There are also similarities between the *Declaration*'s sections on spies, the sick, and wounded, and the status of private property in a war zone. This is certainly the case of its 12 articles (23–34) on POWs, which correspond to the *Lieber Code*'s 19 articles on the same topic.[40]

Undeterred by the lack of enthusiasm for the *Brussels Declaration,* Bluntschli and others at the Institute set up a commission to study it and explore new ways to promote an internationally accepted code of war. The commission concluded that the Institute needed to find ways to improve the 1874 *Declaration*'s "rules of occupation and on reprisals and at the coordination of national military codes and of the rules on penal sanctions in case of the violation of the law of war." The commission's members saw such a code, particularly following the Russo-Turkish War (1877–1878), as a way, if adopted, to "greatly diminish the evils of war."[41] In 1879, the Institute set up another commission to draft such a code. *The Laws of War on Land (Manuel des Droits de la guerre)* or *Oxford Manual* (1880), written principally by Gustave Moynier, one of the Institute's founding members and president of the International Committee of the Red Cross (ICRC), it was meant as a guide to countries interested in considering "national legislation" on the "observation of the laws of war."[42]

The *Manual*, which was widely distributed abroad, noted in the preface that, in light of the failure of the international community to ratify the *Brussels Declaration*, it was time to revisit the question of a codified body of international laws of war. Though its authors did not mean it to be a proposal for an international accord, since there was little likelihood that it would be approved, they hoped it would be a guide for countries interested in adopting laws that embraced "the accepted ideas of our age" on the laws of war.[43] They also hoped that the passage of such laws would let people know of

> laws known among all people, so that when war is declared, the men called upon to take up arms to defend the causes of the belligerent States, may be thoroughly impregnated with the special rights and duties attached to the execution of such a command.[44]

Its authors noted that the *Manual*'s 86 articles were nothing more than a refined statement of accepted nineteenth-century laws of war. They were broken down into three general parts—two dealing with the general principles of war and their application during hostilities, the question of occupied territory, POWs, and internees in neutral territory, and a third with "penal sanctions."[45]

Not surprisingly, only one country, Argentina, initially adopted the *Manual*. Its staunchest critic was the German military. Gen. Julius von Hartmann, a member of the German general staff, wrote that the Kaiser's army preferred an "uncodified law in absolute terms," and considered the idea of "civilised warfare" to be unintelligible.

> For war destroys this very equilibrium...If military authority recognises duties it is because it imposes them upon itself in full sovereignty. It will never consider itself

subject to outside compulsion. *Absolute military action in time of war is an indispensable condition of military success.*[46]

Hartmann added that such regulations flew in the face of the "nature and the objects of every war," and, as such, were

> "obscene": When peace gives place to war, then passion and violence enter upon the great stage of history…the expression "civilized warfare," used by Bluntschli, seems hardly intelligible; for war destroys this equilibrium.[47]

Fld. Mshl. von Moltke, who received a copy from Bluntschli, wrote the Swiss jurist that

> perpetual peace is a dream, and it is not even a beautiful dream: war forms part of the universal order constituted by God. In war are displayed the most noble virtues, courage and abnegation, fidelity to duty, and the spirit of sacrifice which will hazard life itself; without war humanity would sink into materialism.[48]

Bluntschli responded by noting that, since antiquity, all laws had been suspended during warfare, which increased "the unavoidable sufferings and evils of war without necessity." A uniform code of international laws of war would address such wartime misery.[49]

Yet fear of such "misery" was not what drove Europe to consider more seriously such codes at the end of the nineteenth century. In his classic study on the causes of World War I, Sidney B. Fay discusses five issues—secret alliances, militarism, nationalism, economic imperialism, and the press.[50] Each of these complex, interrelated problems helped pave the way for what was to become, at least until World War II, the most devastating war in history. Two issues—militarism and imperialism—were particularly important because they bred increased friction between Europe's major powers as they struggled to open the vast resources of Asia and Africa. Such tension was exacerbated by an incredible late-nineteenth-century arms race. According to Arthur Eyffinger, in 1898, the Russians were spending 42 percent of their national revenue on arms, the Germans 51 percent, the British 37.5 percent, the French 27 percent, and the Austro-Hungarians 16.2 percent. These figures rose considerably in the years before World War I.[51]

The First Hague International Peace Conference (1899)

These costs were what ultimately led Tsar Nicholas II to propose, on August 24, 1898, an international conference whose purpose was to secure a "true and stable peace, and above all to put an end to the progressing development of armaments." The idea for such a gathering came from Sergei Witte, the tsar's finance minister, and Mikhail Muraviev, his foreign minister. Witte, in turn, was influenced by the work of his former boss, the wealthy Polish business magnate Jean de Bloch, whose *The Future of War* (1899) predicted that future wars would be disastrous and cause great social upheaval.[52]

The tsar's announcement was met with considerable international skepticism. The Kaiser, Wilhelm II, considered the proposal "utopian" and "hypocritical," while the Prince of Wales said it was "the greatest nonsense and rubbish I ever heard of."[53] Others doubted the tsar's moral sincerity, because, like Andrew White—the US ambassador to Germany—they knew of his "indifference to everything" and "lack of force even in the simplest efforts for the improvement of his people."[54] Yet while his motives might have been suspect, the tsar's timing was perfect, coming as it did in the midst of concern about Europe's out-of-control arms race.[55]

Nicholas II's proposal was embraced by various international peace movements, which, stirred by the idea of some sort of international gathering to discuss disarmament, pressured their governments to respond positively to the tsar's invitation.[56] The British prime minister, Lord Salisbury, embraced this spirit when he wrote Muraviev that

> the extreme costliness of modern warfare and the horrible carnage which ensued... had long served as a serious deterrent to war, but along with it the burdens imposed thereby upon the nations had produced feelings of unrest and discontent.

His government, Salisbury went on, would do everything possible at the conference to explore

> the most effective methods of securing the *continuance* of general peace and of putting *some* limit on the constant increase of armaments.[57]

What was missing in the Russian proposal, though, were specifics about the nature of such a gathering. Consequently, in early October, the Russian Foreign Ministry asked Fyodor Martens to prepare a draft program for the conference, which was circulated through diplomatic channels in early 1899. It suggested that the conference consider eight major questions.

1. Freezing of present military effectiveness and budgets for a fixed period, and examination as to the future reduction of both.
2. Immediate prohibition of any new firearms and explosives more powerful than the ones actually in use.
3. Restriction in wartime of existing explosives and prohibition of projectiles dropped from balloons or other aircraft;
4. Prohibition of submarine torpedo-boats and ram-equipped vessels.
5. Extension of stipulations of the 1864 Geneva Convention to the area of naval warfare.
6. Neutral status of ships employed in rescue operations during or after an engagement.
7. Revision of the still unratified *Declaration* of the 1874 Brussels Conference on the laws and customs of war.
8. Acceptance of the principles of mediation and facultative arbitration as a means of preventing or settling international disputes, and the establishment of a mode and uniform practice in these respects.[58]

It also asked for suggestions about where to hold the conference. Muraviev finally settled on The Hague after an invitation from the Dutch queen, Wilhelmina, to hold the conference at her summer residence, the House of the Woods (*Huis ten Bosch*).[59]

The International Peace Conference (May18–July29, 1899), which was attended by 100 delegates representing 26 countries, opened on Nicholas II's birthday. Baron G. G. Staal, the Russian ambassador to Britain, presided. The work of the conference was divided among three commissions that would study the questions of disarmament, accepting and or updating the 1864 Geneva Convention and the 1874 *Brussels Declaration*, and the settlement of international disputes through arbitration.[60]

The work of the disarmament commission was the most problematic since there was little sympathy among the great powers for any serious effort to begin a program of arms reduction. The tsar, for example, refused to consider a reduction in the forthcoming Russian army draft even before the conference began.[61] Regardless, the Russian delegation, which played a major role at the conference, focused its energies on proposals that would freeze the size of armies and military budgets for five years, and navies for three years.[62]

The Germans staunchly opposed these ideas, arguing that the build-up in armaments had not put an undue burden on the Reich's economy, and that the arms race would "not lead humanity to the brink of general war." One of the German delegates, Col. Gross von Schwarzhoff, added that there would also be technical problems trying to enforce such an accord, while anything that upset the current "military equilibrium...would really endanger peace."[63] The British were equally hostile to the idea of disarmament, particularly when it came to the navy. Sir Julian Pauncefote, the head of the British delegation, arrived in The Hague with strict cabinet instructions not to let anything take place that would affect Great Britain's "supremacy at sea."[64] In the end, all that the delegates on the disarmament commission were able to agree on was a rather meaningless statement that said

> the restriction of military charges, which are at present a heavy burden on the world, is extremely desirable for the increase of the material and moral welfare of mankind.[65]

The second commission, chaired by Fyodor-Martens, a Russian diplomat and jurist, discussed the Geneva Convention of 1864 and the 1874 *Brussels Declaration*. Two subcommissions dealt separately with these documents. The first discussed extending the terms of the 1864 convention to naval warfare, and the second dealt with a revision of the 1874 declaration on the laws of war. The first subcommission forwarded a 10-article proposal to the conference, and the second approved a 56-article proposal that was closely based on the 1874 *Brussels Declaration*.[66] Its articles on military authority in hostile territory, definitions of belligerents and nonbelligerents, the means of injuring an enemy, sieges and bombardments, spies, POWs, the sick and wounded, military power vis-à-vis private persons, taxes and requisitions, parlementaires, armistices, and interned belligerents and wounded cared for by neutrals were, with a few exceptions, almost identical to the articles in the 1874 declaration. The biggest changes centered around seven new articles on the treatment and rights of POWs.[67]

The subcommission also struggled with controversial articles 9–11, particularly the role of the *franc-tireurs* in the Franco-Prussian War.[68] When it became apparent to Martens that this could be a stumbling block for the overall passage of this key element in the Hague Convention, he proposed a statement be included in the subcommission's draft that would deal with these differing opinions and interpretations.

> The Conference is unanimous in thinking it is extremely desirable that the usages of war should be defined and regulated. In this spirit it had adopted a great number of provisions which have for their object the determination of the rights and of the duties of belligerents and populations and for their end a softening of the evils of war so far as military necessities permit. It has not, however, been possible to agree forthwith on provisions embracing all the cases which occur in practice.
>
> On the other hand, it could not be intended by the Conference that the cases not provided for should, for want of a written provision, be left to the arbitrary judgement of the military commanders.
>
> Until a perfectly complete code of the laws of war is issued, the Conference things [*sic*] it right to declare that in cases not included in the present arrangement, populations and belligerents remain under the protection and empire of the principles of international law, as they result from the usages established between civilized nations, from the laws of humanity, and the requirements of the public conscience.[69]

The latter part of this statement, the *Martens Clause*, was included in the final convention draft of July 29, 1899, while articles 9–11 of the *Brussels Declaration* now became articles 1–3 of the same accord.[70] According to Theodor Meron, the purpose of the *Martens Clause* was "to substitute principles of humanity for the unlimited discretion of the military commander."[71] Regardless of its meaning, the *Martens Clause* has proved interpretatively challenging to international jurists and has lent itself legally to a variety of international judicial decisions to this day.

The work of the third commission, on arbitration, considered by some scholars to be the most important undertaking of the conference, was equally successful, though its delegates had to contend with competing national interests. In many ways, the question of arbitration was the stickiest issue because there were few precedents for solving international disputes. Beyond this was the fact that each of the major powers had their own concerns about submitting a dispute to a neutral arbitrator.[72] The third commission appointed a Committee of Examination (*Comité d'Examen*) to try to find a middle ground on these issues. After considerable controversy, particularly over the creation of a Permanent Court of Arbitration, the Germans and others agreed to support an expanded Russian draft proposal that included phrasing that gave governments the freedom "to choose their arbitrators voluntarily from a list."[73] The end result was a 57-article draft that dealt with maintaining general peace, mediation, international commissions of inquiry, and international arbitration.[74]

Toward the end of the conference, the delegates approved three conventions, including the *Pacific Settlement of International Disputes* (Hague I, July 29, 1899),

Respecting the Laws and Customs of War on Land (Hague II, July 29, 1899), and *Adaptation to Maritime Warfare the Principles of the Geneva Convention* (Hague III, July 29, 1899), as well as three separate declarations in Hague IV on *The Prohibition of Balls which Expand in the Human Body, Prohibition of the Throwing of Projectiles from Balloons,* and *Prohibition of the Employment of Asphyxiating Projectiles.* Each of these separate documents was considered part of the Final Act of the conference, and gave the nations at the conference until December 31, 1899, to sign any or all of the accords. They would then go into force on September 4, 1900. The conferees expressed their own hope that "the restriction of military charges, which are at present a heavy burden on the world, is extremely desirable for the increase of the material and moral welfare of mankind."[75]

Such idealism, unfortunately, was not enough to garner support from some of the most important countries represented at the conference. While Britain, China, Germany, Italy, and Japan signed the Final Act, they did not sign the separate conventions and declarations. The United States, which had played a major role at the conference, approved the Final Act and signed the convention for the *Pacific Settlement of International Disputes* and the declaration on the *Discharge of Projectiles from Balloons.* In the end, France and Russia were the only major countries to sign the Final Act, the three conventions, and all of the declarations.[76]

While much of what was contained in the Hague II document was already part of the traditional customs of war, the Hague I document contained several innovative concepts for the resolution of international disputes, such as an International Commission of Inquiry and a Permanent Court of Arbitration (PCA). Its effectiveness, though, was weakened by the fact that Hague I had "no obligatory clause, without the sanction of armed force."[77] Regardless, the PCA reviewed four international cases between 1899 and 1907, while Britain and Russia agreed to submit the Dogger Bank incident during the Russo-Japanese War to an International Commission of Inquiry.[78]

Hague I again came into play at the end of the Russo-Japanese War, when both sides agreed to submit to American arbitration to end the conflict. The war itself was the most severe of the various colonial conflicts in Asia and Africa in the second half of the nineteenth and early twentieth centuries, and pitted two countries trapped by their own imperial ambitions in Manchuria and Korea, which were up for grabs in the midst of the collapse of China's decaying Qing dynasty.[79] Though Japan was winning the war, it could not sustain its military presence in southern Manchuria, and secretly sought President Theodore Roosevelt's help in bringing hostilities to an end.[80]

According to Martens, Roosevelt's actions were "absolutely in accord with the new and nobler ideas solemnly sanctioned by the Hague Conference of 1899." As a neutral, he went on, US efforts were "perfectly correct, based as it was not only on moral grounds, but also on solid legal grounds."[81] While there is no doubt that Hague I provided an idealistic instrument for US diplomatic efforts, Roosevelt was more concerned about protecting American interests in the Pacific than peace. Regardless, he played an active role in the successful Portsmouth, New Hampshire, peace talks in the summer of 1905 that brought an end to the war and garnered him the Nobel Peace Prize the following year.[82]

The Second Hague International
Peace Conference (1907)

In the midst of the Russo-Japanese war, Roosevelt's secretary of state, John Hay, sent a circular note to US diplomats in countries that had attended the 1899 Hague conference suggesting a new gathering in the Dutch capital. A week after the conclusion of the Portsmouth treaty, the Russian government asked that the tsar be given the privilege of officially issuing a call for the second Hague conference. The United States agreed, and on April 12, 1906, the Russian government sent out a detailed proposal that dealt with improving the 1899 accord in the areas of arbitration and the settlement of international disputes, additions to the laws of war, particularly those relating to the opening of hostilities and the rights of neutrals, and a new convention for various facets of maritime warfare.[83]

In the midst of the discussions for a second Hague conference, the Swiss Confederation, in league with the International Committee for the Red Cross, held a special conference in Geneva (June 11, 1906–July 6, 1906) to revise the 1864 Geneva *Convention for the Amelioration of the Condition of the Wounded and Sick in Armies in the Field*. The new convention expanded and better defined some clauses of the 1864 accord, and included new clauses on the transmission of information about those injured or killed in battle, and the burial of the dead. It also recognized the importance of allowing voluntary aid societies to help the wounded, and further clarified guidelines for aiding and repatriating the wounded, who were now considered POWs.[84]

The second Hague International Peace Conference (June 15–October 18, 1907) brought together 256 delegates representing 44 nations. Its work was divided into four commissions and a large number of subcommittees. One was given responsibility for dealing with arbitration, while the others worked on war on land, war at sea, and maritime law. Initially, it appeared that there was general consensus on the need for "compulsory" arbitration, even from the Germans. In reality, the Germans totally opposed such an idea, which effectively ended any serious discussion of this issue.[85] In the end, all the arbitration committee was able to agree on was a statement "admitting the principle of compulsory arbitration."[86]

There were also discussions about creating a Permanent Court of Justice (PCJ) and an International Prize Court (IPC) to deal with maritime issues. The arbitration delegates ultimately decided to put off discussion of a PCJ until a later conference, but did create a Prize Court with permanent members drawn from the world's major naval powers. Even though its work was initially hampered by the fact that there was, at the time, no universal code of maritime law, this was soon rectified at a London conference a year later that addressed the creation of such a law.[87] To some, the creation of a Prize Court was the conference's most important decision, since this was the world's first "truly international *court*."[88]

The second and third commissions dealt with questions of war on land and sea. The former looked into improving the laws of land warfare, particularly as they related to the declarations of the 1899 Hague conference, and issues surrounding the outbreak of war and the role of neutrals during war. Both subcommissions also revised the 1899 convention with a focus on the opening of "hostilities...without previous warning."[89] The commission on war at sea wrote conventions on the bombardment of undefended cities and the use of submarine mines. It also improved laws that dealt with belligerent ships in neutral territory and tried to provide guidelines for the belligerent status of merchant ships converted into military vessels. It also established better rules for the right of capture on the high seas, and further defined the status of neutral countries during a war.[90]

What none of the commissions dealt with adequately was the arms race and disarmament, in large part because the Russians and the Germans opposed placing these issues on the conference agenda. In the former case, Nicholas II's government would not support any agreement that limited its ability to rebuild its military after the Russo-Japanese War.[91] The United States and Great Britain, however, insisted that they reserved the right to raise these questions during the conference.[92] The British were particularly adamant about these issues, and reminded the delegates about the tsar's warning about the dangers of the arms race years earlier. One of the British delegates, Sir Edward Fry, said that his government was interested in finding ways internationally to reduce arms spending.[93] He followed this up by proposing that the conference accept the 1899 Hague statement on disarmament, which many delegates supported. Consequently, it was included in the conference's Final Act.[94]

> The Second Peace Conference confirms the resolution adopted by the Conference of 1899 in regard to the limitation of military expenditure; and inasmuch as military expenditure has considerably increased in almost every country since that time, the conference declares that it is eminently desirable that the governments should resume the serious examination of this question.[95]

The 1907 Hague conference's final collective document included a number of resolutions (2), recommendations (4), conventions (13), and a declaration dealing with a wide range of topics on various aspects of war on land and on sea. The best known are Hague I, *Convention for the Pacific Settlement of International Disputes*, whose 97 articles greatly expanded on the voluntary means of resolving international disputes through International Commissions of Inquiry and the Permanent Court of Arbitration; and Hague IV, the *Convention Respecting the Laws and Customs of War on Land*, and its *Annex*. Hague IV further defined belligerents, POWs and their treatment, various hostile actions, spies, and matters dealing with the conclusion of fighting. Eight of the conventions dealt with various aspects of naval warfare.[96]

International reaction to the Second Hague Conference was mixed. Some saw it as "disillusionary," and weighed down by just "small margins of progress" over the 1899 conference.[97] An American delegate, William Hull, naïvely wrote in 1908, though, that even if a country did not sign any of the conventions, only a nation that was "very bold and hardened" would "resist the international public opinion of the civilized world" and "resort to measures condemned by the Peace Conferences." He agreed with Alfred Lord Tennyson, who called it the nucleus of a "federation of the world," and hoped that a third conference, which the American delegation hoped would take place in June 1914, would build on the legal and moral edifices of the first two international gatherings.[98] Unfortunately, instead of a major peace conference in the early summer of 1914, Europe found itself on the edge of a terrible cataclysm that many had hoped the two Hague conferences would prevent.

The "War to End All Wars"

Alan Kramer argues in his *Dynamics of Destruction: Culture and Mass Killing in the First World War* that this tragic conflagration "produced the most extensive cultural devastation and mass killing in Europe since the Thirty Years War."[99] Yet what most thought would be a short war quickly became the most devastating war in history prior to World War II. Aleksandr Solzhenitsyn cited one Russian newspaper story in his *August 1914* that argued that "a protracted war in Europe is impossible," since in "previous wars . . . the decisive events took place within two months."[100] Instead, it lasted over four years and forever changed the course of world history. Four empires disappeared at the end of the war—Russian, German, Austro-Hungarian, and Ottoman—leaving in their wake untold political, ethnic, and religious conflicts that haunt parts of Europe to this day.

But it was the human losses—9–10 million soldiers, 6.8 million civilians, and as many as 20 million wounded—that traumatized Europe for a generation.[101] The British, who lost 723,000 men, later talked of a "lost generation" to explain the country's postwar doldrums. This "demographic deficit," as Ian F. W. Beckett calls it, yielded "a civilian death toll of 3.7 million and a birth deficit" of between 15.3 million and 24 million for the British, the French, the Germans, and the Austro-Hungarians.[102] The French mourned the loss of 1.3–1.7 million men, including 400,000 missing-in-action, and sought comfort during the 1920s with a national search for the identity of one former amnesiac soldier, Anthelme Mangin, who was in an asylum in Rodez. French journalist Paul Bringuier called the search "the most touching, the cruelest story of the war that I can tell, a story of the purest and most brutal symbolism."[103]

Russian military losses (1.7–1.8 million) underscored an ineffective military system that proved incapable of withstanding the German-Austrian onslaught. Growing frustration with the tide of war led to the collapse of the tsarist state and a Bolshevik victory in late 1917 that ultimately plunged the country into a devastating civil war that left another 8 million dead.[104] German (1.7–2 million), Austro-Hungarian (1 million), and Ottoman (325,000–337,250) military losses were also high though, as the defeated, their tragedy is often left out of the discussion of postwar trauma.[105] German psychoanalyst Ernst Simmel wrote of a postwar "neurosis" that was caused not only by the devastating experiences in a "bloody war" but also "the difficulty in which the individual finds himself in his fight against a world transformed by war."[106] In Austria, the chaos caused by the breakup of the empire into a number of new states created considerable social and economic upheaval while, over time, a wave of nostalgia swept this now small country that looked back fondly at the imperial virtues of Emperor Franz Josef.[107] In Turkey, growing opposition to Allied efforts to enforce the terms of the Treaty of Sèvres, which stripped the Ottomans of their vast empire, led to a war of independence that saw a new Turkish state emerge under Mustafa Kemal Pasha (Atatürk), and a new peace settlement, the Treaty of Lausanne (1923), which ended the Allied occupation of parts of the country.[108]

Yet, unlike World War II, where the culprits were easily identifiable, it is less the case with World War I even though the Allies claimed at the end of the war that the blame rested firmly on the shoulders of the Germans. Long unresolved international friction over colonies, the arms race, tension in the Balkans, nationalism, secret treaties, and a tendency to see military adventures as a key to diplomatic solutions could all be cited as causes. When it all ended in the fall of 1918, a bitter coalition of Allied victors sought not only justice but also compensation for their collective losses. They also hoped that the various treaties they forced the defeated Central Powers to sign would pave the way for a new era of peace, partially based on the old idea of disarmament and a new concept—justice for those convicted of the alleged crimes committed during the war.

Germany and the War Crimes Question

Though the Allies sought to bring alleged German and Turkish war criminals to justice in the immediate years after victory, they were particularly concerned about trying alleged German war criminals. Estimates are that the Kaiser's troops, stirred by memories of the *franc-tireurs* during the Franco-Prussian War, deliberately killed 6,427 civilians, most of them in Belgium, during World War I.[109] This, coupled with the forced deportation of tens of thousands of French and Belgian civilians to forced or slave labor situations in Germany, as well as outrage over stories about the indiscriminate German use of submarines during the war, laid the groundwork for the discussion of German legal accountability for war crimes during and after the war. Such discussions officially "waxed and waned" according to Allied successes and failures throughout the war. However, once the Allies became convinced that victory was within reach, they began a more serious discussion on how to deal with German criminality.[110]

This was all part of a larger effort to force Germany to accept full responsibility for causing the outbreak of the war and its associated horrors. What would follow would be a peace treaty that included reparations, German territorial losses, severe military restrictions, and the prosecution of those Germans responsible for the crime of destructive war. According to Gerd Hankel, the trials of alleged German war criminals should be seen as "einer zivilisatorische Errungenschaft," a civilizing achievement that would help prevent war crimes in the future.[111]

Initially, the question of German criminality focused on the Kaiser, who had hesitatingly abdicated on November 9, 1918, and fled to the Netherlands, where he lived until his death in 1941.[112] Soon after the armistice was signed on November 11, the British prime minister, David Lloyd George, brought the matter of war crimes trials up before his Imperial War Cabinet. Few supported the idea of trying the Kaiser for war crimes, but a majority agreed to ask the British attorney general, Sir Frederick E. Smith (1919, Baron Birkenhead), to appoint a committee of lawyers to look into the legality of such an undertaking. Eight days later, Smith told the War Cabinet that his committee approved the idea of indicting the Kaiser before an international tribunal made up of judges from the victor nations. To do otherwise, he noted, would undermine the "vindication of the principles of international law." It might also weaken efforts to bring lesser war criminals to justice, particularly if they chose "to plead the superior orders of a sovereign against who no steps had been taken."[113] The international court, Smith went on, should use British legal standards in league "with those of its liberal allies."[114]

The alternative, Smith argued, was to punish the German leader for "high crimes and misdemeanors," without a trial, thus avoiding "the risks of infinite delays and a long drawn-out impeachment." But this, he went on, while no doubt enjoying "the sanction and support of the overwhelming mass of civilization," would possibly rob the Kaiser of "the sanction of legal forms and the protection—in favor of the prisoner—of a tribunal whose impartiality can be established in the face of any challenge."[115] Smith's committee concluded that

> the Kaiser as head of the German armed forces could be charged with ordering or sanctioning violations of the laws of war as contained in the Hague conventions of 1899, and they suggested fifteen categories of applicable offenses, including unrestricted submarine warfare, execution of hostages, and ill treatment of prisoners of war.[116]

It also recommended, by a very narrow vote, the indictment of

> the Kaiser for having provoked or brought about an aggressive and unjust war.[117]

Smith's arguments won over the cabinet, and by early December, the French and the Italians readily agreed with its decision. They quickly discovered, though, that the American president, Woodrow Wilson, had grave concerns about such a trial.[118] Such differences quickly surfaced during the meetings of the Commission on the Responsibility of the Authors of War and on Enforcement of Penalties to the Preliminary Peace Conference. Created at the end of January 1919, and made up of representatives from Britain, France, Italy, Japan, and the United States, it was charged with investigating and preparing a report on:

1. The responsibility of the authors of the war.
2. The facts as to breaches of the laws and customs of war committed by the forces of the German Empire and their Allies, on land, on sea, and in the air during the present war.
3. The degree of responsibility for these offenses attaching to particular members of the enemy forces, including members of the General Staffs, and other individuals, however highly placed.
4. The constitution and procedure of a tribunal appropriate for the trial of these offenses.
5. Any other matters cognate or ancillary to the above which may arise in the course of the enquiry, and which the Commission finds it useful and relevant to take in consideration.[119]

Its March 29 report placed principal responsibility for the war on Germany and Austria, followed by Turkey and Bulgaria.[120] It concluded that the war was "premeditated" and that Germany and Austria rejected all conciliatory efforts to prevent its outbreak.[121] It was particularly critical of the German-Austrian violation of Belgium and Luxembourg's neutrality, and charged all of the Central Powers of using "barbarous or illegitimate methods [during the war] in violation of the established laws and customs of war and the elementary laws of humanity."[122] It added that various individuals in the defeated countries were "liable to criminal prosecution" for "offenses against the laws and customs of war and humanity," and that "the vindication of the principles of the laws of war and customs of war and the laws of humanity" would be "incomplete" if the Kaiser, among others, was "not brought to trial."[123] Yet the commission did not feel that "the acts which brought about the war" should be the basis of an indictment against Central Power leaders. On the other hand, it did conclude that a "high tribunal" should be created to try "all enemy persons alleged to have been guilty of offences against the laws and customs of war and the laws of humanity," and that an Allied Prosecuting Commission should be in charge of "directing and conducting prosecutions" before the tribunal.[124]

The United States and Japan wrote dissenting memoranda that were appended to the official report. While the United States agreed that the Central Powers were responsible for the outbreak of the war, and that Germany had violated Belgian and Luxembourg neutrality, it did not consider this a violation of international law. The American memorandum supported the idea of creating a future body of law that would define aggression as a war crime, and argued that national military tribunals had the right to try individuals who violated the laws and customs of war. On the other hand, it disagreed with any effort to try anyone who violated the ill-defined "laws of humanity." The US statement also opposed the creation of an international tribunal to try war criminals and argued that it should be left to national military tribunals to try such cases in individual countries. If such crimes involved more than one country, then a "tribunal...made up of the competent tribunals of the countries affected or a commission thereof possessing their authority" should try alleged war criminals.[125] Both memoranda opposed trying a head of state, and more specifically the Kaiser, based on the "doctrine of negative criminality (liability for failure to act)."[126]

The commission's report, with the dissenting opinions, was then used during talks of the Council of Four—Georges Clemenceau of France, David Lloyd George of Great Britain, Vittorio Orlando of Italy, and Woodrow Wilson of the United States. During the council's sessions at Wilson's Parisian villa from March 24 to June 28, 1919, the American president stuck to his guns when it came to the question of trying the Kaiser and referred time and again to American objections in the minority report.[127] And though Wilson agreed that the invasion of Belgium was a violation of international law, trying the Kaiser as the "author of the war" for such a "crime" was problematic since it was a crime "for which no sanction has been provided, because there is no legal precedent."[128] In the end, Wilson's arguments did little to sway the others, whose time was spent discussing far more pressing matters such as reparations and territorial changes and adjustments.

The Germans were shocked and dismayed when they received a copy of the proposed peace settlement on May 7, 1919, particularly its sections on war guilt. Ulrich Graf von Brockdorff-Rantzau, the foreign minister of the new Weimar Republic, sent the Allies the German response three weeks later. It suggested, for example, that when it came to the issue of war guilt, that there be

a neutral enquiry into the responsibility for the war and culpable acts in its conduct. An impartial commission should have the right to investigate on its own responsibility the archives of all the belligerent countries and all persons who took an important part in the war.

Nothing short of confidence that the question of guilt will be examined dispassionately can put the peoples lately at war with each other in the proper frame of mind for the formation of the League of Nations.[129]

The Council of Four responded to the German protest two weeks later with surprising harshness that underscored their deep bitterness toward Germany. They called

the war which began on August 1, 1914…the greatest crime against humanity and the freedom of peoples that any nation, calling itself civilized, has ever consciously committed.[130]

The council blamed the "rulers of Germany" and their "Prussian tradition" for their country's role in the war. These leaders, who were not satisfied with their own country's "growing prosperity and influence," sought "to dictate and tyrannize…a subservient Europe." The council also blamed Germany "for the savage and inhuman manner in which it [the war] was conducted." They pointed, for example, to Germany's use of poison gas (which the Allies later used), the "bombing and long distance shelling of towns for no military object," the killing of innocent women and children, the "piratical" use of submarines, slave labor, and the barbaric mistreatment of POWs. "The conduct of Germany," the Allied response went on, "is almost unexampled in human history."[131]

Consequently, the "Allied and Associated Powers believe that they will be false to those who have given their all to save the freedom of the world if they consent to treat this war on any other basis than as a crime against humanity and right." In the end, "justice, therefore, is the only possible basis for the settlement of accounts of this terrible war." They saw the draft peace treaty as "a peace of justice." Everything in the draft, be it reparations, territorial concessions and changes, war crimes trials, and the League of Nations, had to be seen through this prism. The council's response concluded by warning Germany that the May 7 draft was the Allies' "last word." If the German government refused to accept it, the Allies would "take such steps as they think necessary to enforce their terms."[132]

Unswayed, the Germans responded the following day, and expressed willingness to admit some responsibility for the Second Reich's role in causing the outbreak of the war, though it also pointed to the Russian decision to mobilize as the final action leading to the outbreak of the conflict. The German note also admitted to the ongoing perfidy of Prussia and the Second Reich, which historically had championed "force and violence, deception, intrigue and cruelty in the conduct of international affairs." But Weimar's leaders reminded the Allies of the recent people's revolution in Germany that overthrew a government that was "the enemy of freedom, justice, and equality at home."[133]

Germany lodged another protest on June 22 that accused the Allies of having little interest in making significant changes in the draft proposal, which violated the "principle of justice" that was supposed to be the cornerstone of the talks. The new Weimar government, the note went on, could not accept article 227, which accused the Kaiser of "a supreme offence against international morality and the sanctity of treaties," and created a special tribunal to try him for such crimes. It added that it could also not accept articles 228–230, which required Germany to recognize the right of the Allies to try and sentence other German war criminals "before military tribunals," turn over those accused of such crimes to these tribunals, and supply the Allied courts with all necessary documentation to determine the nature of these crimes and the individuals who committed them. The German note was particularly critical of article 231 (the *Schmachparagraphen*; paragraph of shame), which forced Germany to accept sole responsibility for itself and its allies for "causing all of the loss and damage to which the Allies and Associated Governments and their nationals have been subjected as a consequence of the war."[134] Weimar Germany, it added, was also unwilling to accept the "burdens" that would "be placed on her" if she accepted such terms.[135]

The Allies, who had already anticipated German hesitancy to sign the Versailles settlement, had decided on what Clemenceau described as "a vigorous and unremitting blow that will force the signing."[136] This would, if necessary, include marching on Berlin, overthrowing the government, and putting a new one in place that would sign the treaty. Plans were also laid for seeking the extradition of the Kaiser from the Netherlands, though it was finally decided that this could not be done until the treaty was signed, something a hesitant Weimar delegation did on June 28, 1919.[137] James Brown Scott, a prominent American jurist and a US delegate to the Second Hague Conference, called the Treaty of Versailles "the worst ever drawn, a great human tragedy. The statesmen have but given their people what they want and cry for…and have made a peace that renders another war inevitable."[138]

Such criticism was certainly applicable when it came to Allied efforts to bring suspected German war criminals to justice. An Allied Commission on the Organization of Mixed Tribunals (COMT) was responsible for overseeing the enforcement of the terms of articles 228–230, and by the end of 1919 had prepared a list of 1,590 alleged German war criminals that it wanted extradited for trial consideration, including the Kaiser. Simultaneously, the Allies sought the extradition of Wilhelm II from the Netherlands. This effort failed in large part because by the time a formal request for extradition was delivered to the Dutch government in early 1920, official and public interest in such proceedings had waned. It was also apparent that the Netherlands had no intention of surrendering the Kaiser for trial. In its official response to the extradition request on January 23, 1920, the Dutch government noted that it was not bound by the Versailles settlement, though if the new League of Nations did create "an international jurisdiction to judge crimes committed in war," it "would 'associate itself with this new regime.'" But for now, the Dutch note went on, it was the "government's duty to abide by Dutch law and the national tradition as a "'land of refuge for the vanquished in international conflicts.'"[139]

Dutch Queen Wilhelmina did issue a decree for the internment of Wilhelm in the province of Utrecht on the Rhine River just across from Germany in the spring of 1920 "as an alien dangerous to the public tranquility."[140] The Kaiser's "internment" consisted of life on a comfortable estate he had bought the year before in the village of Doorn. He was now able to "live like a prosperous lord in the country with forty-six people domiciled on the estate, including twenty-six servants."[141] Though the Allies would watch his movements for another year or so, he soon faded from public memory and lived in obscurity, ever bitter that postwar Germany's various governments did not welcome him home.[142]

Germany's new Weimar government was prepared for the request of extradition of suspected war criminals, and set up the General Committee for the Defense of Germans before Enemy Courts (*Haupstelle für Verteidung Deutscher vor Feindlicher Gerichten*) to aid those indicted by the Allies. It also created a parliamentary commission, the Committee of Inquiry into the Causes of Germany's Defeat during the World War (*Untersuchungsausschuß für Schuldfragen des Weltkrieges*), to blunt an Allied request to turn over suspected war criminals via a special court, the *Staatsgreichtshof*, which was charged with hearing any cases that came out of the Committee of Inquiry's investigations.[143] Over the next eight years, the Committee of Inquiry looked into German and Allied crimes and, in the end, published "a report whitewashing the German military." The Committee began its work in the fall of 1919, and interviewed such military stalwarts as Paul von Hindenburg, Erich Ludendorff, and others, who used the proceedings to promote the "stab in the back" (*Dolchstoßlegende*) myth—that Germany's defeat lay not with the military, but with lack of adequate support on the home front.[144]

These efforts strengthened German determination not to turn over any suspected war criminals to the Allies. This resistance dovetailed with growing Allied concern about the impact of any extradition request on the stability of the new Weimar government. Within months after the signing of the armistice, revolutionary violence had swept Germany. A brief *Spartikist* communist rebellion broke out in Berlin in January 1919, while a few months later a short-lived Bavarian Soviet Republic (*Bayerische Räterepublik*) had taken power in Munich.[145] A rightist *putsch* in the spring of 1920, which was partially driven by the extradition controversy, convinced the Allies that pushing for large-scale extraditions and trials could imperil the fragile Weimar Republic.[146]

Consequently, the list of 1,590 suspected German war criminals was gradually reduced to 45. Gone were the names of some of Germany's most important wartime leaders—former chancellor Bethmann Hollweg, Fld. Mshls. Hindenburg and von Bülow, Crown Prince Wilhelm, Prince Rupprecht of Bavaria, and Gen. Erich Ludendorff. In the end, only 10 of the alleged war criminals on this list were tried by the Imperial Court of Justice (*Reichsgericht*).[147]

The *Reichsgericht* trials took place in Leipzig from May 23 to July 16, 1921, in a courtroom that included Allied observers and antitrial Germans. The first trial involved four Germans, three accused by the British of abusing POWs, and one for the sinking of a British hospital ship, the *Dover Castle* (resulting in the deaths of six crew members). The three accused of the mistreatment of POWs received sentences of six to ten months, while Capt. Lt. Karl Neumann, who commanded U-67, the submarine that sank the *Dover Castle* in 1917, was acquitted. The court's ruling noted that when the war began, Germany respected the inviolability of hospital ships as established in "the 10th Hague Convention." However, it made exceptions to such regulations when it became apparent that the Allies were using such ships "for military purposes," thus "violating this convention." Neumann, the court ruled, was acting under superior orders that had placed limits on the movements of Allied hospital ships, and that, given the choice of following orders or violating criminal law, the superior order ruled supreme. Consequently, it found him not guilty of the charges.[148]

Yet in what seemed to be a gesture to the British, the Germans initiated their own proceedings at Leipzig that centered on the sinking of a Canadian hospital ship, the

Llandovery Castle. This case was particularly important because it involved not only the sinking of a hospital ship but also the deaths of many of the passengers onboard. Since the commander of the German submarine in question, Capt. Lt. Helmut Patzig, had disappeared after the war, two of his subordinates, Senior Lts. Ludwig Dithmar and John Boldt, were tried for the deaths of all but 24 of the 258 passengers on the *Llandovery Castle.* One high-ranking Canadian officer called the sinking "a crime surpassing in savagery the already formidable array of murders of non-combatants by the Germans," while the *New York Times* reminded its readers that the attack was a violation of the Hague Conventions.[149] Dithmar and Boldt received four-year sentences at hard labor but escaped en route to prison.[150]

The Leipzig court also heard four Belgian and French cases that involved six German defendants charged with crimes against civilians and POWs. The most sensational Belgian trial centered around accusations that a German military police-man and law student, Max Ramdohr, had arrested several underage boys and beaten them into confessing that they had sabotaged German trains. The court rejected the testimony of the boys because of their age, and acquitted Ramdohr. The Belgian delegation, outraged, called "the proceedings a travesty of justice," and left Leipzig, thus voiding their other cases before the German court.[151]

The French fared no better. Their principal case involved charges that Lt. Gen. Karl Stenger had ordered the shooting of all of his French POWs in August 1914. The French viewed Stenger as a symbol of "German military ruthlessness" during the war, though the Germans saw him as a war hero. At first, it seemed as though it would be easy to convict Stenger, since his subordinate and codefen-dant, Capt. Benno Crusius, testified that he had shot French prisoners on orders from Stenger. Other soldiers gave similar supportive testimonies, though these were not enough to convince the court to convict Stenger, who was acquitted. On the other hand, Crusius was found guilty of "killing through negligence," and sentenced to two years' imprisonment including time served. The French, like the Belgians, were outraged, and left Germany in disgust. Over the next three years, the French courts prosecuted 2,000 alleged German war criminals *in absentia* and convicted over 1,200 of them of war crimes. The Belgians followed suit with similar trials.[152]

The *Reichsgericht* continued its work and investigated over 1,700 cases between 1921 and 1927. In the end, the principal goal of the German court was "to exoner-ate" those Germans accused of war crimes, not to convict legitimate war crimi-nals.[153] According to Gerd Hankel, the cases were weakened by the political environment surrounding the trials, the newness of the concept of war crimes, and the weak enforcement mechanisms of international law. The trials, he argues, also legitimized German interpretations of military concepts such as war of necessity (*Kriegsnotwendigkeit*), customs of war (*Kriegsbrauch*), and acting under orders (*das Handelm auf Befehl*), which allowed the German court to conclude that most defen-dants were not liable for their actions because they were part of a legal military objective.[154]

This, in turn, he argues, helped spur extremist violence in Germany after World War I, and left the impression, at least legally and morally, that war crimes would not be effectively dealt with in German courts of justice. Hankel thinks this helped strengthen the legal and moral basis for Germany's barbarous conduct during World

War II. John Horne and Alan Kramer also see the Leipzig trials as a failure, while Jürgen Matthäus, who agrees with their conclusion, notes that those convicted were viewed as war heroes in Germany, which "contributed as much to the prevailing German unwillingness to confront crimes committed during the Nazi era as did the continuity of German elites, including officers and jurists." [155]

Nothing underscores these perspectives more than the roles that some of those initially on the Allies' "most wanted" list played in German society and the military after World War I. Fld. Mshl. Paul von Hindenburg was elected the president of Germany in 1925, and reelected to that position in a two-part election in 1932 that pitted him against Adolf Hitler, whom he later appointed chancellor.[156] Another alleged German war criminal was Qtr. Mr. Gen. Erich Ludendorff, Hindenburg's second-in-command. After the war, he became the darling and symbolic leader of Germany's right-wing extremists, and was an active participant in Hitler's failed Beer Hall *putsch* of November 8–9, 1923, in Munich. When he died in 1937, Hitler gave him a lavish state funeral.[157] Also on the Entente's list were Cmdr. Erich Raeder and his mentor Adm. Franz von Hipper, commander of the High Seas Fleet, Germany's principal naval force. Raeder, who became commander of Weimar Germany's *Reichsmarine* in 1928, wrote after World War II that he was not concerned about being on the Entente's list because provisions had been "made to provide safe sanctuary for the 'war criminals' at home and abroad."[158] Hitler made him head of Nazi Germany's *Kriegsmarine* in 1937 and promoted him to First Lord of the Admiralty in 1939. After World War II, the Nuremberg International Military Tribunal (IMT) convicted him of war crimes, crimes against peace, and crimes against humanity and sentenced him to life imprisonment.[159]

The Armenian Genocide and Postwar Justice

The failure of the Allies and the Germans to bring suspected war criminals to justice after World War I underscored a lack of political will to deal with this question internationally. The same was true when it came to international efforts to deal with the Armenian genocide—a massive wartime crime that resulted in the deaths of 800,000 to over 1 million Armenians.[160] This horror is the subject of continuing debate between those who support the idea that what took place in Anatolia and what is now Syria and Iraq during World War I was genocide, and those, principally the Turks and their apologists, who argue that Ottoman actions against the Armenians were a legitimate response to a rebellious, disloyal Armenian fifth column that tried to destabilize the country during the war. The official Turkish position, which is stated throughout *The Armenian "Genocide"?: Facts and Figures* (2007), traces the roots of this crime back to the early nineteenth century when, it argues, Russia sought to destroy the Ottoman Empire and expand its influence in the region.[161]

Yet who are the Armenians and how did they come to suffer one of the worst genocides in modern history? The Armenians are an ancient people living in the Caucasus region who embraced Christianity in the early fourth century CE. Over the course of the last two millennia, they have enjoyed periods of independence interspersed with eras of domination by powerful, regional empires. Through all of this they were able to preserve their distinct "ethnic presence as Armenians."[162] Though the Ottomans valued the Armenians as gifted businessmen and bankers with considerable international connections, the Armenians came to view the Muslim Turks, particularly in the repressive nineteenth century, with "bitter hatred if not racial contempt" and as an "Asiatic people, an inferior and uncultured people."[163]

By the 1820s, Ottoman Armenians began to flock to neighboring Russian Armenia in the hope of enjoying new freedoms in a Christian kingdom. They soon learned, though, that Russian rulers could be just as harsh as the Turks when it came to the various expressions of their national identity. This was particularly the case after the assassination of Russia's "tsar liberator" Alexander II in 1881. His successors, Alexander III and Nicholas II, imposed harsh russification policies on the Armenians, "the most loyal of the tsar's non-Russian subjects,"[164] and other ethnic minorities.[165]

Tensions between Armenians and Turks intensified after the Treaty of Berlin (1878), which gave the major powers, concerned over the lack of political and religious freedom throughout the Ottoman Empire, "collective responsibility for Ottoman reforms" that were now meant to address such issues.[166] The sultan voiced his own commitment to such reforms in the treaty, particularly the idea of maintaining "the principle of religious liberty." He also issued assurances that religion would play no role in excluding "any person" from the "enjoyment of civil or political rights."[167]

In reality, just the opposite happened. Stung by this humiliating treaty, Sultan Abdul Hamid II began to embrace a new Islamic "Ottomanism" that, while advocating that all individuals in the empire were first and foremost Ottomans, also promoted the idea that the once great Ottoman Empire was under siege by "Christian aggression." This new "Islamism" called "for a return to the fundamental values and traditions of the civilization of which the empire was the most modern expression." The sultan blended this with his own brand of Pan-Islamism that promoted an Islamic culture vis-à-vis the growing threat of Western ideas and customs in parts of his kingdom. Its anti-European and anti-Christian tenets created growing hostility toward non-Muslims throughout the empire.[168]

Consequently, the Armenians now found themselves increasingly isolated and threatened in an Islamic state that paid little attention to their cries for help against growing anti-Armenian violence in eastern Anatolia. This led to the creation of self-protection efforts among Armenian communities there. Ottoman specialists would later claim that such efforts led to the widespread assassinations of officials and massacres in "entire [Turkish] villages" by Armenian revolutionaries. Such claims are, for the most part, false, because most Armenians sought to bring about change "within the Ottoman legal structure." But such charges have become useful to Turkish apologists, who claim such actions laid the groundwork for similar tactics against the Armenians during World War I.[169]

By the end of the nineteenth century, tension between Christians and Muslims throughout the Ottoman Empire had intensified, and led to harsh, indiscriminate reprisals from the sultan's government. In 1894, the first prewar massacre of Armenians took place in the village of Sasun after Armenians refused to pay

harsh taxes to local Kurdish chieftains. Ottoman forces, Kurds, and military police
(*zapitye*)

> attacked and burned villages and wounded and killed, without regard to age or sex,
> all who fell into their hands.
>
> In a village called Semal, the Armenians, led by a priest who had received assur-
> ances from the colonel of the Turkish forces that they would be unharmed, gave
> themselves up. But as soon as they surrendered, the colonel gave the order to seize the
> priest, and they proceeded to gouge out his eyes and bayonet him to death. Then they
> separated the men from the women and that night raped the women. The next night
> they bayoneted the men to death, within [the] hearing of the terrified women. As
> [British] Consul [R. W.] Graves put it, things degenerated "from bad to worse, culmi-
> nating in a massacre of some three thousand Armenians in the district of Talori."[170]

According to one British diplomat:

> [The] Armenians were absolutely hunted like wild beasts, being killed wherever they
> were met, and if the slaughter was not greater, it was, I believe, solely owing to the
> vastness of the mountain ranges of that district which enabled the people to scatter,
> and so facilitated their escape. In fact, and speaking with a full sense of responsibility,
> I am compelled to say that ... [the object was] extermination, pure and simple.[171]

A British investigation concluded that this

> was the first instance of organized mass murder of Armenians in modern Ottoman his-
> tory that was carried out in peace time and had no connection with any foreign war.[172]

Western diplomatic intervention only intensified the situation, and a wave
of anti-Armenian violence swept the region. A year later, mobs swept through
Constantinople after Armenian protestors voiced support for European diplomatic
efforts to force the sultan to initiate new reforms to protect Armenians. Afterward,
Islamic mobs roamed the city, butchering hundreds of Armenians. When news
spread that the sultan had accepted the European-imposed reforms, Anatolia
exploded in a wave of anti-Armenian violence. In Van, the Turks and their collaborators staged an incident to justify a new wave of massacres there from June 3 to 11,
1896. Though the Armenians fought valiantly against four Turkish army battal-
ions, the fighting did not stop until the Ottoman government asked for British and
French help to bring an end to the violence. Negotiations led to an agreement that
stipulated that the Armenian defenders of Van, "the crème of the Armenian youth"
in the city, would be escorted by Ottoman troops to the Iranian border. Instead,
"they were massacred en masse by the troops and Kurdish tribesmen."[173] When
the horrors finally ended later that year, tens of thousands of Armenians were dead
and their property looted or destroyed.[174] The *New York Times* called what had just
taken place "another Armenian Holocaust."[175]

Sadly, Western interest in the plight of the Armenians soon faded, and, according to Stanford Shaw, the "Armenian Question was exhausted and lay dormant until
World War I." Turkish scholar Taner Akçam partially agrees, noting that it was
"removed from the international agenda until the 1908 [Young Turk] revolution."

Moreover, he goes on, Western intervention "produced no lasting reforms [in the Ottoman Empire], and played a significant part in both the killings of 1894–1896 and the Armenian genocide of 1915."[176]

Trapped as they were between two crumbling empires, most Ottoman Armenians realized that the only way for a more secure, stable life was through changes in the leadership of the empire itself. Initially, the Young Turk "revolution" of 1908 seemed to offer some hope for such change.[177] The Young Turks (*Les Jeunes Turcs; Jön Türkler*) were a "loosely formed coalition" of liberals from "many protest groups" that sought "fundamental political and social reforms."[178] Stimulated by the success of revolutionaries in Russia who forced the tsar to embrace constitutional reforms during the 1905 Revolution, the Committee of Union and Progress (CUP; *Ittihat ve Terakki Cemiyeti*) and other groups successfully initiated a constitutional revolution that forced the sultan to embrace constitutional reforms that promised expanded freedoms and improved interethnic relations in the empire.[179]

Armenian hopes soon faded after a brief conservative party counterrevolution in 1909 called for a "return of Islamic religious law, or Shari'a." Spurred by rumors that the Young Turks had been driven from power, Muslim reactionaries in Adana, where local Armenians were suspected of being Young Turks loyalists, went on a rampage from April 14 to 27, 1909, butchering 15,000–25,000 Armenians and plundering or destroying their property. Initially, the Turks blamed the Armenians for this violent uprising, though a parliamentary investigation later found the Armenians to be guiltless. Regardless, Turkish courts did try, convict, and sentenced to death 7 Armenians and 124 Muslims for their roles in the "uprising."[180] The counterrevolution was soon put down by the army, which remained, in league with the CUP, the dominant force in the empire.[181]

The return to stability did little to ease tensions between Christians and Muslims, which worsened in Anatolia, particularly during the First Balkan War in 1912–1913. The Turkish loss of Rumelia, the home of many of the CUP's leaders, was particularly humiliating, and laid the groundwork for what Taner Akçam considers the key to understanding the Armenian genocide a few years later—a resurgent Turkish nationalism driven by a sense of revenge and a determination to cleanse "Anatolia of 'non-Turkish' elements."[182] Ziya Gökalp, the CUP's leading ideologue, wrote that earlier reformers had erred in promoting equality between Muslims and non-Muslims. To be Turkish was to be Muslim and anything else weakened national unity and identity. Thus it was no accident that a year before the outbreak of World War I, the Ottoman government opened a Special Office for the Settlement of Tribes and Immigrants. Gökalp initiated a study for the Special Office that investigated the "Armenian Questions" and the deportation of this group.[183] Now all it would take to put words into practice would be war.

There were probably few major nations in Europe as ill-prepared for war as Ottoman Turkey. Initially, the CUP sought an alliance with the Entente and, after being rebuffed, signed an accord with Berlin, fully expecting a short war with Russia. Once Constantinople finally declared war on the Entente in mid-November 1914, its military forces were quickly placed under direct German command. Driven by calls for a holy war (*Cihat*), Ottoman forces were ordered to take the Suez Canal and invade the Caucasus. If successful, Ottoman leaders hoped the war would lead to the restoration of its old empire. But first they had to win, and early Russian successes in eastern Anatolia raised serious doubts about the realization of this dream. Tsarist forces invaded eastern Anatolia in early November 1914, taking the important town of Sarikamiş. Ottoman efforts to retake it ended in disaster in mid-January 1915, leaving the door open for a western Russian advance.[184]

According to Taner Akçam, it was the humiliating loss at Sarikamiş that prompted Enver Paşa, the minister of defense and commander of Ottoman forces at Sarikamiş, to conclude that a scapegoat was needed for the loss—the Armenians. He, in league with Talat Paşa, the minister of the interior, and Bahaeddin Şakir, the head of the Special Organization (SO; *Teskilât-I Mahsusa*), which oversaw the deportations of the Armenians from Anatolia for the ruling CUP, were the architects of the Armenian genocide.[185] Ottoman leaders used the poisoned atmosphere after the Sarikamiş defeat and the Entente's assault on the Dardanelles (Gallipoli; April 25, 1915–January 9, 1916) as the justification and "cover" for the deportations and mass deaths of the Armenians.[186] The Ottoman goal was to rid itself of a minority that its leaders considered would be a problem in creating a united postwar Turkey.[187] What followed were deportations in name only. SO killing squads, military and police units, Turkish civilians, Kurdish bandits, and Arab raiders attacked the Armenians, first in Anatolia, and then during their long, brutal forced marches from Anatolia into the deserts of Syria to the south. Those who somehow managed to survive this deadly trek then had to contend with equally harsh conditions in makeshift concentration and death camps in the Syrian desert.[188]

The litany of horrors faced by the Armenians during the "deportations" is heart wrenching and painful to describe. The first to die were innocent civilians who were murdered outright by SO units and their collaborators. The roundups and deportations began in eastern Anatolia, followed by similar actions in the western part of Turkey. The inhumanity of their mistreatment is well documented by many observers. The roundups, particularly in eastern Anatolia, were preceded by orders for Armenians to turn in their weapons. Males were arrested and tortured to find the location of alleged hidden arms caches. The Turks began with the "bastinado...beating the soles of the feet with a thin rod," followed by pulling out the eyebrows and other body hair, and then the finger- and toenails. There were also instances where recalcitrant Armenians were crucified, with their torturers crying out, "Now let your Christ come and help you out!"[189]

> The police fell upon them [Armenian families] just as the eruption of Vesuvius fell upon Pompeii; women were taken from the wash tubs, children were snatched out of bed, the bread was left half baked in the oven, the family meal was abandoned partly eaten, the children were taken from the schoolroom, leaving their books open at the daily task, and the men were forced to abandon their ploughs in the fields and their cattle on the mountain side. Even women who had just given birth to children would be forced to leave their beds and join the panic-stricken throng, their sleeping babies in their arms.[190]

Those who had a little more time were allowed to dispose of their property quickly, selling it to Turks at prices that "amounted simply to robbery." In most instances, though, their property was stolen by locals or confiscated by the government.[191]

For some, the forced marches ended quickly in death. Grigoris Balakian, an Armenian priest, described the murders of prominent Armenians from Ankara in western Anatolia in August 1915. After a seven-hour march into the countryside, SO units

> attacked from all sides, cutting and hacking off legs and arms and necks with axes and hatchets, ripping them off partly or entirely, and crushing heads with rocks. Then the bodies were thrown half alive, dead, or in the throes of death into prepared ditches and covered in lime. Those who were partly sticking out of the dirt and the lime made the heavenly arches resound with their cries of agony; more dirt was poured on them and they were buried alive.[192]

After murdering the men in Sungurlu in north central Anatolia, the women, girls, and young boys were taken to the countryside where an "armed mob of Turks," aided by

> police and police volunteers, set upon these poor, defenseless women – mothers, brides, virgins—and children. Just as spring trees are put down with bill-hooked hedge knives, the bloodthirsty mob attacked this group of more than four hundred with axes, hatchets, shovels, and pitchforks, hacking off their appendages: noses, ears, legs, arms, fingers, shoulders... They dashed the little children against the rocks before the eyes of their mothers while shouting, "Allah, Allah."
>
> The screams of the mothers and virgins and little children echoed across the valley and the surrounding rocky hills and caves. The children screamed, *"Mayrig, Mayrig* [Mother, Mother], help us, please!" But the mob, indifferent, continued to rip apart the bodies so that even the stones cried out. Finally, after four to five hours of carnage and plunder, night's black blanket covered this scene of blood, which would stir the envy of wild animals.
>
> With the fall of night, the Turkish mob, police, and police soldiers returned to town with their bundles of loot. Whatever they had left, hyenas, wolves, jackals, and other scavengers came to finish off. The precipices of the valley were strewn with corpses, naked or half-naked. It was a scene beyond all human imagination. Now and then, in the darkness of the night, the moans and groans of the badly wounded and the raspy drone of those giving up the ghost could be heard.[193]

Reports from diplomats and others who observed the roundups and deportations documented the horrors that took place throughout Anatolia. One German diplomat noted in mid-May that "with its barbaric methods, the government is obviously damaging the interests of the nation," while another described what was taking place as "extermination."[194] Talat Paşa confirmed this explanation in a meeting with Germany's Consul Gen. Johann Mordtmann, in mid-June 1915.

> This can no longer be justified by military considerations rather it is a matter of destroying the Armenians.[195]

Several months later the Turkish leader tried to justify the massacres by reminding Mordtmann that the Germans "had murdered 40,000 Belgians in Belgium."[196] Another German diplomat informed Germany's chancellor, Theobald von Bethmann Hollweg, a few weeks later that the Turks meant "to destroy the Armenians totally."[197]

Rape and forced human bondage was common. An Armenian Catholic report to the German embassy in Constantinople stated that Bedouins dragged off one group of women and girls, while another from the German consulate in Aleppo discussed the forced sale of children to Arabs and "all kinds of disgraceful acts of violence...on wives and girls."[198] Local police were actively involved in this "flourishing trade." For a "few Medjidiees [Turkish coin], anyone could take a girl of his choice for a short while or forever."[199] Hans Morgenthau, the US ambassador to the Ottoman Empire, discussed this in his memoirs.

> There are cases on record in which women accused of concealing weapons were stripped naked and whipped with branches freshly cut from trees, and these beatings were even inflicted on women who were with child. Violations so commonly accompanied these searches that Armenian women and girls, on the approach of the gendarmes, would flee to the woods, the hills, or mountain caves.[200]

The violations of women continued throughout the deportation phase of the genocide. Morgenthau told of Kurdish attacks against the deportation "caravans" where "pretty ones [Armenian women]" would be kidnapped and taken "off to the hills." As these "caravans" passed through Muslim villages, "Turkish roughs would fall upon the women, leaving them sometimes dead from their experiences [repeated rapes] or sometimes ravingly insane." The pretty ones who had been kidnapped were often "sold as slaves—frequently for a medjidie, or about eighty cents—and who, after serving the brutal purposes of their purchasers, were forced to lead lives of prostitution."[201]

The survival rate from these death marches was quite low. Morgenthau reported, for example, on a caravan of 18,000 Armenians that left eastern Anatolia for Aleppo in what is now Syria. After a 17-day forced march, only 150 Armenian women and children were still alive. "A few of the rest, the most attractive, were still living as captives of the Kurds and Turks; all the rest were dead."[202] Another report talks about the deportation of 1,000 families to the desert.

> There, without shelter, naked and famished, they are abandoned to their fate, and have to subsist on the morsel of bread which the Government sees good to throw to them.[203]

Those who did survive these "death marches" arrived with little or nothing other than the ragged clothes on their backs because the Turkish officials who oversaw their roundup and deportations had

> exerted themselves to carry off, for their own use, everything they could lay their hands on.[204]

The deportations, which began in the spring of 1915, lasted through 1916. The Turks, who seemed to have no clear plan for how to deal with the deportees, pushed them deeper and deeper into the Syrian desert along a line that ran down the Euphrates from Aleppo to Damascus. Time and again throughout 1916, German diplomatic observers noted that the Ottoman goal seemed to be the extermination of the Armenians. Their deadly tools were starvation, disease, and incessant raids by Turks, Arabs, and Circassians. One observed that "it may be a principle of government to let them die of hunger," while another, noting what seemed to be a systematic Ottoman policy of extermination in the desert, called this "cruel policy...a disgrace to Turkey" and one that would cause it great harm once the war was over.[205]

During this second phase of the genocide, large and small caravans of Armenians, most on foot but some in railroad cattle cars, trucks, or barges on the Euphrates, were pushed deeper and deeper into the desert. Temporary "concentration camps" were set up at isolated desert outposts near the rail line that ran to Damascus. By the time that most deportees reached these "camps," they could barely function and were starving to death. Walter Roessler, the German consul in Aleppo, traveled the deportation route from Baghdad to Aleppo in early 1916. He called what he saw a "Trail of Horror" filled with "the horrific parade of [dead] bodies."[206]

In reality, these detention "camps" were merely way stations of death, since the Ottoman government seemed to have no concrete plan on how to deal with the tens of thousands of Armenians trapped along this "Trail of Horror." Roessler, who visited some of the camps between Maskanah (today Meskéné, Syria) and Dayr al-Zawr (Deir ez-Zor) in the fall of 1916, described them as "a corner of hell" with "a thousand horrors."[207] Beatrice Rohner, a Swiss humanitarian worker, described what she saw in Maskanah earlier that spring.

> Sick and dying. Anyone who cannot manage to get a piece of bread by begging eats grass raw and without salt. Many hundreds of the sick are left without any tent covering, in the open, under the glowing sun. I saw desperate ones throw themselves in grave-trenches and beg the grave diggers to bury them. The government does not give the hungry any bread, and no tent to those who remain outside. As I was in Meskené, there was a caravan of sick women and children from Bab [Al-Bab to the northeast of Aleppo]. They are in an indescribable condition. They were thrown down from the wagons like dogs. They cried for water, they were given each a piece of dry bread, and were left there. No one gave them any water though they remained a whole day under the hot sun...Among the orphans there was a small boy of four years old. It was early in the morning and I asked him if he had eaten anything. He looked much amazed, and said "I have always gazed at the stars, and my dear God has satisfied me." On my questioning him where his father and mother were, he said simply that they were dead in the desert.[208]

A few weeks later, a Turkish pharmacist reported the deaths of 55,000 Armenians at Maskanah.[209]

The Ottomans operated another large detention camp at Dayr al-Zawr, which was originally supposed to be the terminus of the deportations. Araxia Dschebedjian wrote Beatrice Rohner that the camp had "become a desert for the deportees." Guards beat

> defenceless and exhausted children...with whips and clubs which she called the rule of the day...The persecution and oppression of the homeless has increased over the past few days to such an extent that only one thought fills my heart: who can bring relief to this wretched situation, and who can portray a picture of our condition to those who tolerate such violence and permit it.[210]

Hunger was rampant, and she asked Rohner to do what she could to inform

> our missionaries that their college children, young men and young girls, are dying of
> starvation here. People were so hungry that they were slaughtering and eating stray
> dogs. Recently they even slaughtered a dying man and ate him; that is what I was told
> by an eye witness. One woman cut off her hair to sell it for bread. I saw how a woman
> ate the dried blood of a dead animal on the street. Up to now they all ate grass, but
> that has dried up for the meantime. Last week we were in a house where the inhabit-
> ants had not eaten for 3 days. The woman held a small child in her arms to give it
> some bread crumbs to eat. But the child was so weak, it couldn't swallow any more, so
> it choked and died in her arm.[211]

Dschebedjian also wrote about reports that the deportees were being "sent to
the banks of the river Chebor [Khabur]," a tributary that flows into the Euphrates
south of Maskanah. Little did she know that by the spring of 1916, this remote desert area had become one of the new Ottoman killing fields of the Armenian genocide. In mid-April 1916, 19,000 Armenians were sent to the Chebor from Dayr
al-Zawr where most were murdered over a five-week period.[212] Several months
later, the Turks massacred another 20,000–30,000 deportees from several camps
along the banks of the Chebor. According to one survivor,

> Circassians on horseback came by and surrounded the caravans: they took everything
> away from them that they [Armenian deportees] were carrying with them and tore
> off the clothes off their backs...and distributed the clothes among the Arabs who
> appeared in crowds. The entire load, men, women, children, were driven naked for
> three hours until they reached a plateau on the north side of the Karadagh surrounded
> by hills, where they stopped. There, the Circassians threw themselves a second time
> at their victims, striking into the crowd with axes, sabres, knives until blood flowed
> like a river and the entire plateau was covered in mutilated corpses...When nothing
> moved any longer after the entire regiment had ridden across the corpses several times,
> the Circassians made off. [213]

A year later, several German engineers visited the killing site, and reported seeing a
"large number of bleached human skulls and skeletons" there. Some of them "had
bullet holes," while in other places "we found stakes, also with human bones and
skulls." Local Arabs estimated that "12000 Armenians...were massacred, shot or
drowned here alone." [214]

Similar massacres took place at the Ra's al 'Ayn (Ras-ul-Ain) concentration camp
along what is now the Turkish-Syrian border. According to Robert Roessler, the Turks
ordered the mass killing of the 14,000 Armenians at Ra's al 'Ayn. Each day, he reported,
"300 to 500 of them have been led out of the camp daily or almost daily and massacred about 10 kms away...The bodies were thrown in the river." When the killings
ended, there were only 2,000 Armenians left in the camp. They were then forced on a
trek across the desert where their "caravan" was attacked and "smashed to pieces." [215]

Part of the motivation for these particular massacres might have been the unstable Iraqi front to the south, where the British were trying to defend their oil wells
and refineries in southern Iran as well as new ones in nearby Al Mawşil (Mosul) and
Karkük (Kirkuk). The whole region was an active war zone, with threats from the
British and the Russians, particularly in central and southern Iraq, and there is no

doubt that the Ottoman government chose to use the war in this part of the empire as an excuse for their further mass murder of Armenians.[216]

The international reaction to the deportation and massacres of the Armenians was slow to develop, in large part because the British and others had initial doubts about the accuracy of the reports coming principally from Russian sources. But Russia's foreign minister Sergei Sazonov did everything possible to convince his Entente allies to voice in the strongest diplomatic language possible concern about the outrages taking place against Armenians throughout the region. His initial draft, which spoke of Turkish "crimes...against Christianity and civilization," was changed after British objections to "crimes against humanity and civilization."[217] The note, which was published on May 24, 1915, was presented to the Ottoman government on June 3 by Ambassador Morgenthau.[218] It warned Constantinople that the Entente would

> hold personally responsible [for] these crimes all members of the Ottoman Government and those of their agents who are implicated in such massacres.[219]

The Entente warning spurred a flood of reports from throughout Anatolia and Mesopotamia that documented the spreading genocide. Within weeks, Morgenthau received numerous reports from American diplomats that provided gruesome details of the massacres. He responded by organizing American relief efforts in the United States, and warned the State Department that the "destruction of the Armenian race in Turkey is rapidly progressing."[220] By 1916, Viscount Bryce, Britain's secretary of state of foreign affairs, was able, with the help of Arnold Toynbee, to publish a collection of 149 documents that underscored the breadth and horrors of the mass murders that had taken place in Anatolia and Mesopotamia.[221]

These were amply seconded by German reports from throughout the region, though the Kaiser's government seemed more concerned about its reputation as Turkey's ally, particularly in light of earlier accusations of German war crimes during the early days of the war. And while a handful of German diplomats and aid workers did what they could to report the crimes and/or provide what aid they could to help the Armenian deportees, Berlin's official position was similar to that voiced by its ambassador to the Ottoman government, Hans Freiherr von Wangenheim. A few days after the Entente published their statement about the genocide, Wangenheim informed the German foreign office that he opposed publishing any of the reports from his diplomats in the field about the spreading massacres because he thought it would "be disadvantageous to the Turkish government and the Muslim population; we would only supply the enemy press with welcome material in their campaign against the Turkish government."[222]

His successor Paul Wolff-Metternich was much more aggressive in informing Bethmann Hollweg about the massacres. In early December 1915, he had meetings with Enver Paşa and other top Ottoman leaders and warned them in "exceedingly sharp language" that their actions created "unrest and indignation" in Germany and "in allied foreign countries." If the atrocities were not stopped, he warned, "these circles would end up withdrawing all of their sympathies from the Turkish government." Ottoman leaders argued that the massacres were "necessities of war" and that the "revolutionaries needed to be punished." Metternich concluded that his

government's "protests were useless." He suggested Berlin put a note in the semiof-
ficial *Norddeutschen Allegemeinen Zeitung* condemning Turkish atrocities against
the Armenians, and demand they be stopped "immediately."[223] Bethmann Hollweg
totally rejected this idea, explaining:

> Our only aim is to keep Turkey on our side until the end of the war, no matter
> whether as a result Armenians perish or not.[224]

This settled the matter for the Germans, who stuck to the rationale they had
adopted since the genocide began—that the actions taken by the Turks against the
Armenians were for "military reasons" and, as such, were "justified."[225]

In the end, politics and the realities of the war trumped most international
efforts to do anything significantly to aid the Armenians. The American response
to the genocide, for example, became increasingly linked to the whole question of
American entrance into the war. Yet when the United States finally entered the war
in 1917, it refused to declare war on the Ottoman Empire, even though Germany
convinced its Ottoman ally to sever diplomatic ties with Washington. The reason
was simple—American fear that such a declaration would weaken US influence in
Turkey once the war was over.[226]

As the war neared its end, it seemed as though the Entente was going to follow
through on its 1915 statement and hold the Ottoman government accountable for
the Armenian deaths. But this pledge would be tempered by a series of agreements
signed during the war that would break up the Ottoman Empire and divide parts
of it into European spheres of influence. The Entente also promised Arab independence and the creation of a Jewish homeland.[227] In their January 10, 1917, response
to Woodrow Wilson's request for a statement of peace terms, the Entente stated that
one of its goals was the "enfranchisement of populations subject to the bloody tyranny of the Turks" and the "expulsion from Europe of the Ottoman Empire decid-
edly alien (...) to western civilization."[228] Arnold Toynbee paraphrased and further
clarified this statement on the title page of his book *The Murderous Tyranny of the
Turks*—"the expulsion from Europe of the Ottoman Empire *which has proved itself
so radically alien* to western civilization."[229] Woodrow Wilson declared a year later
in his Fourteen Points (January 8, 1918) that the Turkish portions of the Ottoman
Empire would "be assured a secure sovereignty," while "the other nationalities which
are now under Turkish rule should be assured an undoubted security of life and
absolute unmolested opportunity of autonomous development."[230]

The Armenian question remained on the front burner in postwar negotiations
between the Allies and the Turks. The March 29, 1919, report of the Commission
on the Responsibility of the Authors of the War, while placing principal responsibility for the war on Germany and Austria, also blamed Turkey for its outbreak. It
made reference to British, Armenian, and other documents as "abundant evidence of
outrages of every description…against the laws and customs of war and of the laws
of humanity." The report listed 32 specific war crimes committed by the Central
Powers. The first 15, which included "murders and massacres, systematic terrorism,"
"torture of civilians," "deliberate starvation of civilians," rape, "abduction of girls
and women for the purpose of enforced prostitution," "confiscation of property,"
and "illegitimate requisitions," were all in reference to the crimes committed during

the Armenian genocide. It concluded that those responsible for such crimes would be held "liable to criminal prosecution."[231]

Initially, there seemed to be widespread public support in Turkey to bring the perpetrators of the Armenian genocide to justice. Such support quickly fell prey to a groundswell of Turkish nationalism that arose in the midst of the growing Entente presence in Turkey and the slow carving up of what remained of the Ottoman Empire. Alleged perpetrators such as Enver Paşa and Talat Paşa, who, along with other prominent wartime leaders, had fled Turkey onboard a German submarine in late 1918, now became national heroes. In an effort to appease the Entente, Turkish officials began to arrest 50–100 prominent Turkish politicians and military figures in early 1919, arguing that Turkish courts were more than capable of investigating and trying them for the mistreatment of Allied POWs and the massacre of the Armenians. Over the next few months, further arrests followed, and by April 1919, there were 107 suspected Turkish war criminals in Turkish jails. Some, unfortunately, were there as political prisoners, not suspected war criminals.[232]

After this last wave of arrests, the Ottoman government created a special court-martial that conducted four major trials and a series of lesser trials that dealt with crimes committed during the Armenian genocide. In April, the military court convicted Kemal Bey and Maj. Mehmet Tevfik Ben of issuing deportation orders to their subordinates that resulted in the forced migration of Armenian women and children, and the premeditated murder of Armenian males in the Yozgat district. The court ruled that such crimes were

> against humanity and civilization which were not compatible in any manner to human considerations. Moslem supreme justice consider these events as murder, pillage, robbery and crimes of enormous magnitude.[233]

Kemal Bey was sentenced to death, while Maj. Tevfik Ben received a 15-year prison term. A shocked Turkish nation, already stunned by the harsh terms of an Entente-proposed peace accord, transformed Kemal's funeral into a wake for a person they now saw as an "innocent victim of the nation."[234]

The subsequent trial of the Ottoman Empire's principal wartime leaders, some *in absentia*, only made matters worse. According to the indictment:

> The principal subject matter of this investigation has been the event of the disaster befalling the deported Armenians.... The disaster visiting the Armenians was not a local or isolated event. It was the result of a premeditated decision taken by a central body composed of the above-mentioned persons; and the immolations and excesses which took place were based on oral and written orders issued by that central body.[235]

By the time that this trial opened in late April 1919, public support for these legal undertakings had completely vanished, though the trials continued. In July, the tribunal convicted Talat and Enver Paşa and several other Young Turk leaders of crimes against the Armenians and sentenced them to death (Talat and Enver *in absentia*). The other Turkish trials involved minor criminals or those accused of "disturbing national security."[236]

At the same time, the Turks began to release suspected war criminals, something that infuriated the British. In late May, the British seized 67 imprisoned Turks, including some very prominent CUP leaders, and jailed them on the islands of Mudros and Malta. Over the next 18 months, an additional 50 or so suspected Turkish war criminals were placed in British custody.[237] During the summer of 1919, other suspected Turkish war criminals either escaped from jail or were freed by the Ottoman government. Frustrated, the Entente decided to include the question of war crimes trials in the treaty being negotiated with the Ottoman government.[238]

Several clauses in the proposed Treaty of Sèvres alluded to the Armenian massacres, though they made no specific reference to Armenian victims. Article 144 required Turkey to recognize "the injustice of the law of 1917 in relation to Abandoned Properties," and to restore the homes and businesses of those forced to flee them "by fear of massacre or any other form of pressure" since January 1, 1914. Articles 226–229, which dealt with war crimes, required Turkey to recognize the right of the Allies to bring to trial before military tribunals individuals who violated the "laws and customs of war." Turkey was also required to turn over individuals accused of such crimes and to supply the military tribunals with all documents relating to such crimes. Article 230 specifically stated that Turkey was also required to turn over individuals "responsible for the massacres committed on Turkish territory since August 1, 1914."[239]

In the midst of these negotiations, Turkey drifted into a civil war that ultimately led to the collapse of the Ottoman Empire. The new government of Mustafa Kemal Atatürk refused to recognize the Sèvres accord. This, coupled with British disillusionment with Anglo-Turkish efforts to bring alleged war criminals to justice, led to the collapse of such efforts. By the spring of 1921, the British began to free suspected Turkish political prisoners on Malta and Mudros, and exchanged the rest for British POWs. In the end, "retributive justice gave way to the expediency of political accommodation."[240]

Such disillusionment was encased in the Treaty of Lausanne (July 24, 1923), which replaced the Treaty of Sèvres. It made no mention of Armenia or war crimes, though Turkey was required to grant full political and other rights to all Turkish citizens, regardless of their religion or ethnicity. Diplomatic efforts to force Turkey to agree to look for Armenian women or children forced into *harems* during the genocide failed, though article 6 of the treaty's Protocol on Amnesty did state that Turkey agreed

> not to contest the measures carried out under the auspices of the Allied Powers during the period between the 20th October, 1918, and the 20th November, 1922, with the object of re-establishing families scattered during the war or replacing legitimate proprietors in possession of their goods.[241]

On the other hand, the Entente rejected Armenian requests to send delegates to the peace conference and efforts to facilitate "the return of the surviving Armenians and establishing a 'national home for the Armenians' within Turkey." The question of prosecuting Turkish war criminals was now a dead letter. When asked why the Entente powers had abandoned the Armenians, one British diplomat explained that the reasons were simple:

The Armenian claims are not a vital question for the Allies, who are more concerned with the Straits issue. Allies will not sever their relations with Turkey for the sake of the Armenian question.[242]

Telford Taylor, the chief American prosecutor at the Nuremberg trials, later said that the best that could be said of failed Allied efforts to prosecute war criminals after World War I was that "the mountain labored and brought forth a mouse."[243]

Conclusion

If the First World War, and more particularly the Armenian genocide, proved anything, it was that international laws in and of themselves could do little to protect innocent civilians during wartime. International humanitarian law, statutorily speaking, was still in its infancy when war broke out in 1914. Efforts by the ICRC and the diplomatic achievements at the two Hague conferences were limited by the special military needs and interests of the major signatory powers, which tended to neutralize, in some instances, the effectiveness of the larger body of the laws of armed conflict in place at the outset of World War I. Such conflicting national interests also affected legal efforts after the war to bring German and Ottoman war criminals to justice, sending a strong signal internationally about the limits of enforcement of international accords created to prevent such crimes.

Chapter 5

Peace, Law, and the Crimes
of World War II

Soon after World War I broke out, British author and pacifist H. G. Wells wrote *The War that Will End War*. Wells, who sought to justify his country's entrance into this conflagration, called it

> a war for peace. It aims straight at disarmament...This, the greatest of wars, is not just another war—it is the last war.[1]

Though the phrase—the "war to end all wars"—was incorrectly attributed to American president Woodrow Wilson, who only used it once, it was used frequently in the decade after the "Great War" ended as the world searched for ways to address those issues that had led to its outbreak and the horrors that took place on the battlefield.[2]

Wilson was certainly at the forefront of these efforts. A scholar by training and temperament, he approached growing American involvement in World War I with caution, foreboding, and, ultimately, pragmatism. During the early months of the war, Wilson told Edward M. House, his trusted confidant, that there was "'great work to do for humanity in the readjustment of the wreckage that would come from the European war.'" Yet Wilson also thought that the United States had to be neutral both "in fact as well as in name."[3] But American neutrality was soon compromised by its growing trade with the Entente. By the time that the United States finally entered the war in the spring of 1917, its trade with the Entente (France, Italy, Russia, United Kingdom) totaled $2 billion, while that with the Central Powers (Austria-Hungary and Germany) was only $27 million.[4]

By late 1914, Wilson began to lay out the core ideas that he hoped would be the basis of any postwar peace settlement.

> A peace without victory...no nation shall ever be permitted to acquire an inch of land by conquest...the reality of equal rights between states small and great...the manufacture of munitions must no longer remain in private hands, [and] an association of

nations all bound together for the protection and integrity of each, so that any one nation breaking from the bond will bring upon herself war; that is to say, punishment, automatically.[5]

Yet even though Wilson had some fairly clear ideas about a postwar settlement, he was opposed to direct American involvement in the war and campaigned for reelection in 1916 on the slogan, "He kept us out of war."[6] But he could not keep war at bay for long, particularly after Germany's leaders decided to initiate unlimited German submarine warfare on the high seas on January 9, 1917. This, Gen. Erich Ludendorff told Chancellor Bethmann Hollweg, "was 'the very means of carrying the war to a rapid conclusion.'"[7]

Thirteen days later, a newly reelected Woodrow Wilson addressed the US Senate, unaware of the German campaign that was to begin on February 1. He noted that he had sent a note to all belligerents in mid-December 1915 offering American mediation of the war. In his Senate speech, he reiterated the point that any settlement had to be built around the concepts of "peace without victory" and "equality of nations."[8] He also laid out some of the core ideas that were later included in his Fourteen Points, which he discussed in another speech to Congress a year later.[9] He discussed the importance of addressing the problems of arms buildup as the "most immediately and intensely practical question connected with the future fortunes of nations and of mankind."[10] He added that "national armaments" had to be reduced "to the lowest point consistent with domestic safety." It was also essential, Wilson went on, to create "a general association of nations" to afford "mutual guarantees of political independence and territorial integrity to great and small nations alike" in postwar Europe. The Fourteen Points became the basis of the armistice signed between the Entente and the Central Powers on November 11, 1918, ending the war.[11]

Wilson's ideas were controversial. Maurice Hankey, the secretary to the British War Cabinet and later to the British delegation at the Paris Peace Conference, called them the "moral background" of any such settlement, while his boss, David Lloyd George, scoffed at Wilson's idealism, calling the US president "a missionary to the rescue [of] the heathen Europeans, with his 'little sermonettes' full of rather obvious remarks."[12] Stéphen Pichon, the French foreign minister, disagreed, telling Wilson, "We are so thankful that you have come over to give us the right kind of peace."[13]

Just before he left for what would be two trips to Europe in 1919, Wilson delivered his State of the Union address to Congress. He brushed aside objections to his role in the forthcoming peace talks, convinced that his presence in Paris was his "paramount duty." He said it was essential for him to be there to ensure a fair, just peace anchored by a League of Nations. He hoped the peace settlement would create "a new order, for new foundations of justice and fair dealing... it is international justice that we seek."[14]

Yet even though he was the driving force in getting the Covenant of the League of Nations included in articles 1–30 of the Treaty of Versailles, the League's history predated Wilson.[15] In fact, in many ways, it could be argued that the Covenant of the League of Nations was the child of the two Hague conferences, since its introduction and 30 articles gave body to many of the ideas included in the various documents created at both gatherings. Yet the Covenant was also a child of World

War I, since it directly addressed questions of peace and its maintenance in terms that directly reflected the failures of the Hague signatory states to ensure just that. The Covenant's introduction pledged the High Contracting Parties not "to resort to war," to maintain "open, just and honourable relations between nations," to firmly establish "international law as the actual rule of conduct among Governments," and observe by the "maintenance of justice a scrupulous respect for all treaty obligations in the dealings of organised peoples with one another."[16]

Article 3 added that the League's Assembly was partly to deal with issues "affecting the peace of the world," while article 8 stated that the "maintenance of peace requires the reduction of national armaments to the lowest point consistent with national safety." The League's Council, which was to be made up "of the Principal Allied and Associated Powers" as well as representatives from other member states, was charged "to formulate plans for such reduction" with member states. They, the Covenant went on, agreed "that the manufacture by private enterprise of munitions and implements of war is open to grave objections." Article 8 concluded by stating:

> The Members of the League undertake to interchanges of full and frank information as to the scale of their armaments, their military, naval and air programmes and the conditions of such of their industries as are adaptable to warlike purposes.[17]

Article 9 stipulated that the League would create a "permanent Commission to advise the Council on the execution of the provisions of articles 1 [membership] and 8 [arms reduction] and on military, naval and air questions generally."[18] Article 10 pledged League members to "undertake to respect and preserve as against external aggression the territorial integrity and existing political independence" of one another, while article 11 stated that member states were pledged to "take any action...to safeguard the peace of nations" against "any war or threat of war." Article 12 created a mechanism that allowed member states to submit such international disputes to "arbitration or judicial settlement."[19]

Articles 13 and 14 created the Permanent Court of International Justice, which would deal with any "dispute of international character" brought to it by member states. In cases where such disputes were not submitted for "arbitration or judicial settlement," channels were created that allowed the Council to investigate the matter, prepare a report on the issues surrounding the dispute, and recommend a solution. If Council members could not agree unanimously on such a report, then League members could "take such action as they shall consider necessary for the maintenance of right and justice." The matter could also be referred to the General Assembly, whose decisions had the same power as a Council report.[20]

Article 16 stated that any League members that resorted to war in violation of articles 12, 13, or 15 would be deemed at war "against all other Members of the League." This could lead to the severance of all economic and diplomatic relations with the rogue state, including the prospect of being forced out of the League. Article 17 dealt with similar situations between non-League and League member states, while article 18 stated that all international accords involving League members had to be registered with the secretariat to be considered valid.[21] Much of what was in articles 10–16 came from the pen of Woodrow Wilson.[22]

For better or for worse, the League's Covenant, particularly its clauses on disarmament and the maintenance of peace, made the League the arbiter of international peace over the next two decades. According to British foreign secretary Sir Edward Grey, the arms race had been the principal cause of World War I, making postwar "disarmament…essential to create security." The disarmament clauses in the Treaty of Versailles and in the treaties with the other defeated Central Powers were seen as merely the starting point for disarmament among the major powers globally.[23]

The introduction to Part V of the Treaty of Versailles, which dealt with German disarmament, set the tone for this.

> In order to render possible the initiation of a general limitation of the armaments of all nations, Germany undertakes strictly to observe the military, naval and air clauses which follow [articles 159–213].[24]

Yet, as the international community was soon to discover, achieving global disarmament was no easy matter because of the security and political needs not only of the Versailles powers but also of Europe's postwar pariahs—Germany and Soviet Russia.

In many ways, Peter Jackson argues, postwar disarmament "was a 'poisoned chalice' that created tensions between Britain, France, and the United States."[25] A rather cynical report by the French military in the spring of 1923 during the Ruhr crisis, which saw the French and the Belgians occupy this part of Germany "to insure the timely delivery of reparation goods," underscored Paris' suspicions about the effectiveness of disarmament, particularly in light of the fact that "mutual assistance and arms reduction 'have no value in themselves' but were instead dependent on the 'mentality of peoples and the nature of armaments.'" The French report added that neither "Germany nor Bolshevik Russia had demonstrated any respect for international law. France must therefore either maintain overwhelming strategic preponderance over Germany or secure a guarantee of military assistance from Britain."[26]

By the time this report was released, the short-term disarmament of Germany was almost complete and, from the British perspective, it was time for Germany to rejoin the "concert of nations and assist in checking Soviet Russia and postwar France." Such sentiments were very much a reflection of Britain's view that the role of disarmament was "continental containment and engagement."[27] The French, who were always suspicious of general military disarmament as a way of containing Germany, sought a much deeper "moral disarmament" that centered around not only giving "up the physical underpinnings of power, her war matériel, but of her potential to change her interests and, with Allied pressure and surveillance, let go of her virulent nationalism."[28]

The United States, which had rejected the Treaty of Versailles in late 1919 because of concerns over article 10 of the League's Covenant, was drawn back into the disarmament discussion a few years later by decades-old worries about Britain and Japan's competitive naval strength, particularly in the Pacific. The result was the American-sponsored Washington Naval Conference of 1921–1922, which concluded three major treaties that protected the *status quo* in the Pacific, voiced respect for the territorial integrity of China and the Open Door policy (equal trade and investment in China), and adopted a naval treaty between the United States, Britain,

Japan, France, and Italy, which included a 5–5–3.1.7–1.7 arms reduction ratio for capital ships. It also dictated size limits for aircraft carriers (27,000 tons), battleships (35,000 tons), cruisers (10,000 tons), and other naval armaments, including a ten-year ban on new ship construction.[29] The accord, which was to remain in effect until 1936, also stated that the status quo would be maintained when it came to existing "fortifications and naval bases."[30]

Though there were objections to these restrictions as well as others on submarines and the use of poison gas, this was still the most successful of the various disarmament efforts during the interwar period. Attempts to achieve further reductions in Geneva in 1927 failed, though the major powers were successful in agreeing to new limits on various naval vessels.[31] The London naval treaty three years later was more successful and created new definitions for aircraft carriers, cruisers, and destroyers, and set new tonnage limitation categories for these ships as well as submarines. Unfortunately, its enforcement fell prey to the darkening economic, political, and military clouds that swept the world during the Depression. This was particularly true in Japan, where the military criticized its government for giving in to a compromise on cruiser limits that they thought weakened the navy's ability to defend itself against threats "to Japan's position in Manchuria from Chinese nationalism and a Soviet military buildup in China." This controversy ultimately led to an increased role for the military in the discussion of Japan's defense policies.[32]

But efforts to reduce the size of the major powers' navies were only one dimension of international efforts to create a greater sense of global security and peace. This was particularly true after the Ruhr crisis of 1923–1924. The League's failure to create a system of "regional collective security agreements" led to the Geneva Protocol (1924), which provided for the peaceful settlement of international disputes. This, coupled with the Locarno treaties (1925), which restored Germany to the European "family of nations" and guaranteed the territorial status quo of Western Europe, helped create a new "spirit of Locarno" that seemed to point to a more systematic, peaceful, League-oriented way to handle international disputes.[33] This spirit was certainly embedded in the Kellogg-Briand Pact (1928), an American-French declaration that denounced war as a means of resolving international differences, and the League's *General Act for the Pacific Settlement of International Disputes* (1928), which provided for such resolution through a Conciliation Commission, the Permanent Court of International Justice, or an Arbitral Tribunal. Though flawed, these accords seemed to underscore the new sense of collective "responsibility" necessary "for helping in the maintenance of peace" through what seemed to be a mature, effective League of Nations.[34]

This idealistic, naïve approach to addressing various dimensions of international conflict can certainly be seen in the League's 1925 (Geneva) *Protocol for the Prohibition of the Use in War of Asphyxiating, Poisonous or other Gases, and of Bacteriological Methods of Warfare*. It outlawed the use in war of asphyxiating, poisonous, or other gases, and of all analogous liquids materials or devices[35] but did not do anything to address "their study, production or storage." The treaty also failed to set up any mechanism for "verification or enforcement." In addition, Britain, France, and the Soviet Union attached two reservations to the accord that allowed them freely to "use such weapons in retaliation" and only agreed to accept the treaty's restrictions in relation to other countries that signed the 1925 protocol.[36] In the end, national interests trumped international ones when it came to warfare and national security, an ill omen for what was to come in the 1930s.

By this time, the threat of war, particularly in Asia, loomed large, while the growing strength of Nazism in Germany underscored the urgency of a new, more serious discussion of disarmament, particularly in light of the economic trauma sweeping the world. Consequently, in 1932, the League opened a Conference for the Reduction and Limitation of Armaments (World or Geneva Disarmament Conference) on February 2, 1932. There was general hope when it opened that after years of discussion and preparation, a longed-for global treaty could finally be realized that would provide the underpinnings of world peace. In the end, though, the same national self-interests that had long haunted earlier efforts and dreams surfaced, and effectively ruined any chance of serious global disarmament.[37] After the Locarno conference, the League created a Preparatory Commission for the Disarmament Conference that prepared a draft treaty for the 1932 conference to consider. It was quickly "brushed aside," replaced by individual proposals from France, Italy, and the United States.[38] By the time that the first phase of the conference ended later that summer, all that most of the delegates could agree on was a resolution that voiced support for a "substantial reduction" in arms that would "reduce the means of attack." For the most part, the resolution was an admission that this phase of the conference has been a "dismal failure."[39]

Germany voted against the resolution and announced that it would not return until it had been given equality in "arms rights." Later that year, an Anglo-American–French declaration pledged equality of rights for all participants, and reaffirmed their commitment to the Kellogg–Briand Pact. This prepared the way for Germany's return to the conference in early 1933.[40] Adolph Hitler, Germany's new chancellor, pledged in a radio address general support for "the preservation and maintenance of peace," but also insisted on the restoration of Germany's equality of rights in international affairs. He added:

> As great as is our love for our army as the bearer of our arms and the symbol of our great past, we would be happy if the world, by limiting its own armaments, would never again make it necessary for us to increase ours.[41]

In the midst of these discussions, Germany's foreign ministry prepared a game plan for Hitler's cabinet that centered around the restoration of Germany's pre-1914 borders, the reacquisition of its lost colonies, the takeover of Austria, and the revival of Germany's dominant position in Central and Eastern Europe.[42]

In March 1933, the British presented a new proposal at the conference that would, among other things, replace "the Versailles disarmament obligations" and give Germany arms equality in five years. The outraged French insisted on changes to this proposal that would allow Germany to rearm in two phases over eight years.[43] In the end, this all played into Hitler's plans, as he used the talks "to secure whatever advantages they [Germany] could gain without committing themselves to agreements they would have to break consciously and quickly."[44] Rearmament was an absolute for Germany's new leader, and an essential part of his early strategic and economic planning.[45] But he was hesitant to pull the plug on the Geneva talks for fear of alarming the other major powers about his plans. He was simply waiting for the most opportune moment to withdraw and hoped it would come when France showed a "lack of intention to disarm."[46]

As the talks proceeded, Rudolf Nadolny, the German delegate at the conference, said privately that Germany was making plans to create an army of 600,000 men. If Britain or France tried to place limits on this, he added, Hitler's government was prepared to leave the talks and even walk out of the League of Nations.[47] Other proposals did nothing more than stall the inevitable,[48] even after President Franklin Roosevelt's efforts to breathe new life into the talks with letters to the US Congress, the delegates in Geneva, and later, the World Economic Conference in Lausanne. He proposed four steps to disarmament.

First, that through a series of steps the weapons of offensive warfare be eliminated.

Second, that the first definite step be taken now.

Third, that while these steps are being taken no nation shall increase existing armaments over and above the limitations of treaty obligations.

Fourth, that subject to existing treaty rights no nation during the disarmament period shall send any armed force of whatsoever nature across its own borders.[49]

Hitler responded in a Reichstag speech, arguing that the "degradation of a great people to a second-rate, second-class nation" after World War I "could not lead to the pacification of the world...Treaties which are concluded for the pacification of the lives of peoples in relation to one another have any real meaning only when they are based upon a genuine and honest equality of rights for all." The outbreak of a new war, he went on, would be "madness" and would "lead to the collapse of today's social and political order...It is the earnest desire of the National Government of the German Reich to prevent such an unpeaceful development by means of its honest and active cooperation."[50]

Germany, he claimed, had disarmed and has "fulfilled the obligations imposed upon it in the Peace Treaty to an extent far beyond the limits of what can be deemed fair or even reasonable." Consequently, Hitler argued, Germany had the "justified moral right to insist that other powers [should] also fulfill their [disarmament] obligations pursuant to the Treaty of Versailles," and pointed to the large arsenals of various European countries. Germany, he promised, was more than "willing to disband its entire military establishment and destroy those few weapons still remaining at its disposal, were the bordering nations to do the same without exception." But if they were unwilling "to comply with the disarmament provisions imposed on them by the Peace Treaty of Versailles, then Germany must, at the very least, insist upon its demand for equal treatment."[51]

Hitler assured his audience that he was not proposing "rearmament" but "the disarmament of other States." He was willing to consider the current British proposal and welcomed Roosevelt's message, which he saw as "incorporating the United States in European relations in the role as guarantor of peace." But, he warned, "Germany would never be coerced into signing anything which would constitute a perpetuation of Germany's degradation." Any such effort, he noted, could lead to Germany's withdrawal from the disarmament talks and the League.[52]

His speech was part of propaganda minister Joseph Goebbels' effort to deemphasize "sabre rattling" and reassure the West of Hitler's peaceful intentions.[53]

Several months later, Goebbels told the press that the world misunderstood the German position on disarmament, and that the Reich was not embracing a "policy of expansion by force." In fact, he said, "German foreign policy had nothing to do with war and *revanche*," words that should "be expunged from the international vocabulary."[54]

Hitler's speech and Roosevelt's letters did little to move the disarmament talks along, and they were postponed in June. During the summer, the British and the French agreed to a two-part, eight-year plan monitored by the Permanent Disarmament Commission.[55] Though German leaders did not reject this proposal outright, they raised so many objections that it was obvious it would almost be impossible to reach a compromise with the other major powers in Geneva. Hitler, who did not want the talks to end over this issue, finally decided in October after conversations with his cabinet, most of Germany's top diplomats, and President Hindenburg, that there was little room for further compromise.[56] On October 14, Goebbels officially announced that Germany would leave the talks and the League. The reason, he explained, was because the disarmament conference was determined to impose unequal "dictates" on Germany that reflected the "unjust and degrading discrimination of the German Volk." And though Hitler, he argued, was committed to peace,

> the final pacification of the world which all require can only be achieved when the concepts of victor and vanquished are replaced by the acceptable application of equal rights for all.[57]

Germany's withdrawal from the League followed Japan's exit seven months earlier and raised serious questions about the future of global peace and stability. Now free from constraints on their military development, Japan and Germany initiated conflicts in Asia and Europe that caused unparalleled human suffering, and some of the most horrendous war crimes in modern history.

Japan and Crimes of War, 1931–1945

These crimes would finally be addressed at the end of World War II, when the victorious Allies created two separate International Military Tribunals (IMT) to try major Japanese and German war criminals. They used crimes committed during war itself to justify such trials, which brought into play violations of the various Hague and Geneva conventions as well as the Kellogg–Briand Pact.[58] The IMT Nuremberg charter (August 8, 1945) indicted 24 German war criminals for four crimes:

> Crimes against peace, war crimes, crimes against humanity and a *common plan* or *conspiracy* to commit any of the foregoing crimes.[59]

Five months later, Gen. Douglas MacArthur, the supreme commander for the Allied Powers in Japan, decreed that the Allies would create a separate IMT to try "Far Eastern war criminals." Its April 26, 1946 charter, for what was officially known as the International Military Tribunal for the Far East (IMTFE) or Tokyo IMT trial, cited the same crimes as the Nuremberg charter, though, instead of defining war crimes in some detail, it simply mentioned "Conventional War Crimes," and married the IMT Nuremberg definition of crimes against humanity with the broader charge of conspiracy. The Tokyo tribunal indicted 28 Japanese defendants on 55 counts of crimes committed from January 1, 1928 to September 2, 1945. It also cited three dates, September 8, 1931, July 7, 1937, and December 7, 1941, as starting points for Japanese acts that violated various international laws tied to the waging of aggressive war.[60]

According to Neil Bositer and Robert Cryer:

[The] Tokyo IMT can be viewed as a legal response, broadly, to the military expansionist phase of Japanese foreign relations in the nineteenth and twentieth centuries or, more narrowly, to Japan's "fifteen year war" in East Asia and the Pacific...The roots of this military expansion of Japan's sphere of influence can be traced to the Meiji Restoration in 1868.[61]

Such expansion should also be seen in light of European and American incursions in the nineteenth century, first in China and later in Japan, which helped spur the evolution of Japan's "expansionist" foreign policy. But, unlike China, which was aggressively forced to open its doors to the West's major powers, Japan's leaders chose to welcome the West as a starting point for its own development as a competitive power in the slow carving up of China. This attempt to learn to "know the enemy" bred considerable opposition in Japan, and ultimately led to an uprising in the late 1860s that saw the collapse of the Tokugawa Shogunate, which had dominated Japan for almost three centuries. What followed, the Meiji Restoration, introduced an era of modernization and Westernization designed to transform Japan into a competitive Great Power in Asia. Over the next few decades, Meiji leaders dramatically transformed the face of Japan though not without considerable unrest, particularly from the Samurai, Japan's medieval warrior caste that had long enjoyed unique status and privilege throughout the country.[62] Though ultimately neutralized in a bloody civil war, their code *Bushidō*, with its emphasis on "loyalty, respect for superiors, valor, faithfulness, righteousness, and simplicity," remained an integral part of Japanese military values well into the twentieth century.[63]

Bushidō emphasized honor and loyalty above all else, and guided conduct in battle, though its more humane constraints, as emphasized in its *Regulations of 1412*, "proscribed the wanton taking of life and called for humane, courteous and kind behavior."[64] In the 1930s, the Japanese military moved away from these values and began to emphasize "brutal discipline" in its training and a deep hatred of Japan's enemies. *Bushidō* now emphasized loyalty to the emperor above all else. "Compassion for wounded enemies was discouraged, even forbidden...Victories would no longer be sought within honorable rules of war but by any means, no matter how bestial or deceitful."[65]

Meiji Japan became a constitutional monarchy in 1899 and began an experiment with democracy that many Western observers thought would ultimately fail. Two of the key elements in this failure were the army and the navy, which, using France, Germany, and Great Britain as models, rapidly modernized.[66] According to two top army commanders, Katsura Tarō and Kawakami Sōroku, the role of the army was not only self-defense, but also to preserve a country's independence. It also existed

> to display the nation's power, resorting to arms when necessary to execute national policy, as in the case of first-class European powers. Japan's aim is maintaining armed forces not that of the second-class nations but that of the first-class powers.[67]

From 1875 until the early years of World War I, Japanese leaders pursued an increasingly aggressive expansionist policy that saw Japan acquire the Kuril Islands, Taiwan, southern Sakhalin (Karafuto), Korea, the Liaotung Peninsula, and, when World War I broke out, Germany's modest colonial empire in the Pacific.[68]

Japan, which entered World War I as a British ally, overplayed their hand during the early stages of the conflict when they presented China with a list of 21 demands that, if accepted, would have robbed China of considerable autonomy and given Japan Shandong province as well as expanded interests in the Liaotung Peninsula and Manchuria. Fortunately, the United States, backed by Britain, sent Tokyo a firm note stating that it could "'not recognize'" such gains, a position it took again in 1931 and 1941. Japan withdrew its demands but remained hopeful that its role as an Entente ally during the war would strengthen its role in China once the war ended.[69]

Japan saw China as its special sphere-of-influence, something it hoped the United States would recognize at Versailles. However, the United States and Britain wanted to restore a balance-of-power in Asia and prop up "'young China'" as a counter-weight to Japan. They allowed Japan to retain control of Shandong province, which was considered by some to be the birthplace of Chinese civilization, though Tokyo agreed to return it to China in 1922 in return for concessions in the province. At the same time, Japan, which had expanded its military presence in northern China and southeastern Siberia during the war, agreed to withdraw its troops from Siberia, ending what some observers saw as an ambitious overextension of Japanese power in East Asia.[70]

These moves signaled a new phase in postwar Japanese diplomatic history. After the war, Foreign Minister Kijūrō Shidehara adopted a new foreign policy that centered around "international collaboration, economic diplomacy, and nonintervention in China's domestic affairs." Anchored by a new sense of international prestige gained after the Washington conference, Japan's leaders thought their country could compete economically in trade with China and with other international powers "without excessive political or military protection."[71]

The underpinnings of Shidehara's policies began to fade after Chiang Kai-shek decided to begin a series of military campaigns to unite China in 1926. The Japanese, already worried about earlier Soviet moves in Mongolia, were deeply concerned over the impact of Chiang's moves on their interests in northern China and Manchuria, and his alliance with the Soviets. Though Chiang's ties with the Russians collapsed in the midst of his assault on Shanghai in the spring of 1927, this did little to still Japanese concerns about their interests in the region, particularly in the aftermath of the earlier Nationalist assault against foreigners in Nanjing. Shidehara's failure to take an aggressive stance against the violation of Japanese interests and citizens during the "Nanjing incident" led to his dismissal. His successor, Giichi Tanaka, who served as both prime minister and foreign minister, adopted a new policy that centered around sending troops into China whenever Japanese interests there were threatened andaffirming Japan's special interests and position in Manchuria and Mongolia.[72]

When Chiang resumed his "unification" campaign in 1928, Tanaka sent two army divisions into Shandong province, triggering a minor clash with Chinese troops in Tsinan. As Chiang moved northward, the Japanese asked Tso-lin Chang, Japan's staunch Manchurian ally in northern China, to move his capital from Beijing to Mukden. Fearful of a Nationalist takeover of Manchuria, Japanese officers in the Kwantung Army, which was responsible for protecting Japanese interests in Manchuria, decided to stage an incident there to draw attention to the growing Chinese threat. On June 4, 1928, they assassinated Chang and blamed the murder on the Chinese. In the end, the incident failed because Tanaka refused to send more forces into Manchuria, which ultimately led to his dismissal.[73] According to the indictment at the Tokyo IMT trial, the plot by the Japanese army to murder Tso-lin Chang was the

> first step in a scheme of domination which later extended to other parts of China to the territory of the Union of Soviet Socialist Republics, and ultimately to a wider field, aiming to make Japan a dominant power in the world.[74]

War itself began three years later when officers from the Kwantung Army blew up a section of the southern Manchurian railway on September 18, 1931, without the knowledge or support of the Japanese high command and the government of Reijirō Wakatsuki. What followed, the "Mukden incident," saw the Kwantung Army gradually take over the rest of Manchuria, aided by reinforcements from Korea. By the end of the year, Wakatsuki's government fell, replaced by one more amenable to accepting the Japanese conquest of Manchuria.[75] The new government of Tsuyoshi Inukai announced in the spring of 1932 the creation of a Japanese puppet state, Manchukuo, which would be ruled by China's last Manchu emperor, Pu-yi. During the interim, the Kwantung Army hatched another plot in Shanghai that led to a clash between Chinese and Japanese forces, followed by the Japanese occupation of Shanghai.[76] F. P. Walters considers the Japanese invasion of Manchuria

> a turning point in the history of the League and the world. For the first time not only the action of the Council and Assembly, but the fundamental moral and political conceptions on which the Covenant was based were exposed to a powerful and determined attack—an attack that was none the less deadly for the protestations of good will and peaceful intentions by which it was accompanied.[77]

Three days after the Mukden incident, Dr. Alfred Sao-ke Sze, the Chinese delegate to the League, asked the League Council to invoke article 11 of the League Covenant.[78] Initially, the League hesitated because it was difficult to determine if the Kwantung Army had merely mounted "a violent demonstration with the object of bringing the Chinese in Manchuria to a more submissive frame of mind, or whether it had wider and more permanent ambitions."[79] This soon changed after Dr. Sze told the Council on September 22 that the situation in Manchuria was far more serious than initially thought. He asked the Council "to act with speed" and promised that China would abide by "whatever decision it might see fit to make."[80] Kenkichi Yoshizawa, Japan's Council representative, downplayed the threat and blamed the Chinese for the actions of the Kwantung Army. Several days later, his government informed the Council that

> there was no military occupation...Japan had no warlike intentions and no territorial designs [and] had withdrawn most of the troops back to the railway zone and intended to withdraw the rest as soon as the lives and property of Japanese subjects in Manchuria were no longer in danger, which it hoped would be very soon. His government was anxious to enter into direct negotiations with China; and the best thing the Council could do would be to refrain from all intervention.[81]

Dr. Sze said that his government was willing to do everything possible to protect Japanese lives and property in Manchuria and would be glad to begin talks with Tokyo once its troops had withdrawn from the region.[82] The Kwantung Army had no intention of withdrawing despite a Council resolution on October 24 that called for this course of action. A Japanese withdrawal, the resolution continued, would lead to talks between Nanjing and Tokyo.[83]

When the Council reconvened in Paris three weeks later, the situation in Manchuria was much worse because the Japanese had moved deeper into Manchuria. The Japanese reacted to growing criticism of their moves by suggesting the Council create a Commission of Inquiry to investigate the whole crisis. Dr. Sze welcomed such a move, but insisted that nothing could be resolved until Japanese troops pulled out of Manchuria. On December 10, 1931, the Council, frustrated by Japanese promises that they were trying to halt Kwantung Army movements in Manchuria, created a Commission of Inquiry to the Far East (the Lytton Commission) "to study and report on all the circumstances of an international character which threatened peace and good relations between China and Japan."[84]

This all became more complicated in early 1932 after reports of the murder of five Japanese Buddhist monks in Shanghai, possibly at the instigation of the Japanese military. The Japanese press became filled with lurid stories about the attack, followed by demands for vengeance. In the meantime, Japanese mobs marched through Shanghai, killing several Chinese and destroying shops. The Japanese demanded an apology and compensation for the monks' deaths, which Chinese officials readily agreed to. But the Japanese were determined to take the city, and in late January, 500 Japanese soldiers were sent ashore, followed by a naval and aerial bombardment of Shanghai.[85] According to Jonathan Fenby, this

> was the world's first air raid on an unprotected civilian target the size of Shanghai, setting the precedent for Guernica and the Second World War.[86]

The Japanese assault on Shanghai took place in full view of the large international community there. Western observers were horrified by the Japanese air and naval attacks on the heavily populated Chapei quarter of the city. Japanese bombs and artillery shells caused appalling civilian casualties and destroyed an area that included the highly regarded National Oriental Library. Japanese bombers also damaged the League of Nations Chinese National Flood Relief camp where over 10,000 refugees lived.[87] Though Chinese troops fought valiantly to save the city, they were no match for the Japanese forces, and by the end of February were forced to abandon Shanghai. Japanese troops then

> flung themselves into systematic destruction in the zones they were occupying. Whatever had not been razed by bombardment and fire was either mined or dismantled and loaded into Japanese ships.[88]

The League responded by creating a separate Investigation Commission (IC) to deal with Shanghai, while the General Assembly passed a resolution on March 3, which stated that League members would not recognize "any situation, treaty or agreement which may be brought about by means contrary to the Covenant of the League or to the Pact of Paris."[89]

The IC ultimately arranged an armistice in Shanghai in May but had to await the report of the Lytton Commission before it could begin to work on a solution to the Sino-Japanese crisis. The Lytton Report, which dealt with Manchuria and Shanghai, was completed in the fall of 1932. For the most part, it sided with China when it came to Japan's efforts to blame Nanjing for the crises in Manchuria and Shanghai. The report also rejected Japan's claim that the new "state" of Manchukuo was not "called into existence by a genuine and spontaneous [Chinese] independence movement." The General Assembly then adopted a resolution that "left no doubt as to Japan's violation of the [League] Covenant."[90] It also voiced support for China's claim of "sovereignty" in Manchuria and stated that Manchukuo "was neither legally constituted nor representative of the will of the inhabitants."[91] The report concluded by recommending that both sides enter into talks, with the League's help, to carry out the League's recommendations that Manchukuo be returned to China.[92] When the Assembly voted on February 24, 1933, to approve this resolution, Yosuke Matsuoka, Japan's delegate to the League, announced his country's withdrawal from the League.[93] According to Ikuhiko Hata:

> This meant that Japan had seceded from the Versailles system and had chosen "splendid isolation" instead. Italy and Germany, seeing the League's impotence, took a leaf from Japan's book and embarked on their own paths of expansionism.[94]

Japan's moves in Manchuria and Shanghai reflected two trends at the time—a resurgence of ultra-nationalism among the military and the adoption of a policy that was "a kind of Asian Monroe Doctrine" that essentially ended the disarmament structure of the Washington conference.[95]

> The Japanese government was by December 1933 committed to a policy which proposed to neutralize the influence of the Soviet Union, the Nationalist government of China, and the Anglo-American nations by a diplomacy rooted in the arrogance of Japan's military forces.[96]

Over the next few years, various Japanese military units moved more deeply into northern China and Inner Mongolia "to check the emergence of a strong and unified China." Economically, the Japanese adopted a policy of "ruthless...plunder" as it expanded its presence in China, which alienated the local populations, who saw the Japanese army as an "'army of locusts.'"[97]

In 1936, Japan joined the German-Italian Anti-Comintern Pact, and now became part of an alliance headed by two of Europe's militant, international pariahs.[98] In addition, its political system was now in the hands of bureaucrats who favored a defense policy that promoted the heavy development of "military industry and weaponry."[99] This, coupled with an unsuccessful revolution in 1936 by young officers critical of the political status quo, set the stage, in league with political changes in China, for the next phase of Japanese military aggression there.[100]

The War of Resistance

Unlike Europe, where the outbreak of war followed a predictable path, the course of war in Asia began with less foresight and planning. Many Japanese leaders saw the Soviet Union as their nation's greatest threat and discussed the importance of planning for a possible war with the Russians. However, after the unsuccessful military coup in 1936, they decided to pursue a more moderate diplomatic and military path to avoid "untimely conflicts with either the Anglo-American powers or the Chinese nationalist movement."[101]

This all changed on July 7, 1937, when a minor incident involving a reportedly missing Japanese soldier exploded into full warfare after a skirmish between Japanese and Chinese soldiers at the Marco Polo Bridge outside of Beijing. Though Japanese leaders, troubled by the new Nationalist-communist united front in China, did not want war, they saw the escalation of the crisis as an opportunity to enhance their military presence in the region. Chiang Kai-shek, who now saw the Japanese, not the communists, as the greatest threat to his regime, felt the Marco Polo Bridge incident gave him the opportunity "to drive 'the Japanese over the [Great] Wall.'"[102] In the meantime, the Japanese had moved 160,000 troops into the Beijing region. Chiang responded by moving troops into Shanghai to draw Japanese forces southward and out of northern China. Shanghai, China's most important business and trading center, now became the focal point of Chinese attempts to defeat the Japanese and drive them out of China. Unfortunately, the Chinese loss of this important coastal city after a three-month battle set the stage for one of the most gruesome campaigns in the history of World War II—the rape of Nanjing.[103]

The Tokyo International Military Tribunal (IMT) trial estimated that the Japanese butchered over 200,000 Chinese civilians and POWs in the first six weeks of the occupation of Nanjing (Nanking), the Nationalist capital, in late 1937 and early 1939. Iris Chang claims that 260,000–350,000 civilians were murdered by the Japanese, while Peter Li notes that another 300,000 Chinese were murdered en route to Nanjing.[104] Dr. Robert O. Wilson, a Harvard-trained American physician at the University Hospital in Nanjing, gave ample examples of the atrocities committed by Japanese soldiers during his testimony before the Tokyo trial. He noted that rumors of such atrocities were such that his staff begged for permission to flee in the wake of the Japanese occupation.[105]

Almost from the moment the Japanese entered Nanjing on December 13, Dr. Wilson observed first hand untold atrocities against Chinese civilians. Rape and savage executions were commonplace, and on one occasion he intervened to stop two Japanese soldiers from raping two women. He also treated a man who had a "bullet through his jaw" and severe burns over two-thirds of his body. Several Japanese soldiers, the man told Dr. Wilson, had poured gasoline all over his body and set him on fire. He died two days later.[106] On another occasion, Dr. Wilson treated another burn victim who told him that

> he was the only survivor of a large group who had been bound together, had gasoline sprayed over them, and were set afire.[107]

Chuan-Ying Hsu, an official with the Chinese Ministry of Railways, reported similar war crimes, particularly against women. Hsu, who headed the Housing Committee of the International Committee for the Nanking Safety Zone, which had been set up to protect Chinese civilians from the Japanese, testified that

> the action of the Japanese soldiers toward women are even worse, and we can never dream of in [sic] this civilized world. The Japanese soldiers—they are so fond of raping—so fond of women, and that one cannot believe.[108]

In one home he visited, Hsu stated that

> after raping, they [Japanese soldiers] put foreign stuff into the vagina and the grandmother showed me the stuff. The young girl was raped on the table; and while I was there the blood spilled on the table not dry yet. And we also see the corpses [of the rest of the family] because they were took [sic] away, not far away, only a few yards from that house, all the corpses there.[109]

He told the court of another incident where two Japanese soldiers boarded a boat and discovered several young women and girls onboard with their entire family. Both soldiers raped two young women in front of their families, then asked one of the grandfathers, "'Isn't that good.'" The soldier then ordered the old man to rape one of the young girls. The family, fearful of further outrages, jumped overboard and drowned.[110] The Tokyo IMT trial estimated that the Japanese raped 20,000 Chinese women during their initial occupation of Nanjing, while Iris Chang and other Chinese scholars claim that as many as 80,000 women were raped, making it, Chang argues, one "of the greatest mass rapes in world history."[111]

The Japanese also targeted men of military age and POWs. Though most of the 50,000 Nationalist troops fled the city just before the Japanese occupation, or escaped in civilian clothing to the International Safety Zone, the 30,000 or so captured outside the city were killed within a few days after Nanjing fell to the Japanese. Most were machine-gunned to death in groups and their bodies dumped into the Yangtze River. The murder and mistreatment of POWs became one of the hallmarks of Japanese occupation policies throughout Asia during World War II. R. J. Rummel estimates that of the over 19 million Chinese who died during the "China War," almost 4 million were "killed in cold blood by the Japanese." Of this number, 267,000–1,000,000 were POWs.[112]

The Japanese assumed that after the quick takeover of Shanghai, Nanjing, and other parts of central coastal China, the Nationalists would sue for peace. But Chiang Kai-shek, bitter over the failure of the League and the Nine Power talks in Brussels in November 1937 to give anything more than lip service to solutions for peace, adopted a policy of attrition toward Japan that traded "space for time—the Japanese would be ceded territory but the Chinese would win time to strengthen their resistance."[113] Consequently, China became a quagmire for the Japanese, who faced new threats to its power in Manchuria from the Soviet Union. This led to three "military confrontations" with the Soviets from 1937 to 1939.[114]

While there is ample evidence to document a variety of Japanese war crimes in China during this period, the Chinese prosecutorial team at the Tokyo trial chose to focus on crimes against women, with the "rape of Nanjing" its symbolically "representative case."[115] Women throughout Japanese-occupied Asia were forced to become prostitutes for the Japanese military. According to Saburō Ienaga, such defilement flowed from Japanese societal disregard for basic human rights.[116] In parts of China, women were lured to Japanese camps by promises of work, and were then sent to "comfort stations" as "comfort women" to serve the sexual needs of Japanese soldiers. According to the testimony of a British journalist, John Goette, who worked in Shanxi province in 1939–1940, Japanese officers often demanded that Chinese officials supply them with women for the Japanese military.[117]

At the end of 1999, the International Citizens' Forum on War Crimes and Redress (ICFWCR) held a conference in Tokyo to discuss "Japanese Atrocities in World War II and Redress." Driven by what the ICFWCR called Japan's refusal "to overcome the past 'Era of War'" and, unlike postwar Germany, pay reparations to victims of Japanese war crimes, the conference sought to strengthen the handful of cases before Japanese courts and draw attention to the depth and breadth of Japanese war crimes in Asia. The conference held a number of workshops that featured testimony from sexual victims of the Japanese.[118]

At the end of 2000, the Violence against Women in War Network Japan, "and other Asian women's and human rights organisations," held a new conference in Tokyo, the Women's International War Crimes Tribunal on Japan's Military Sexual Slavery, to help "identify those who were responsible for military sexual slavery." It also sought "to make a judgement on Japanese military sexual slavery before and during the Second World War from the perspective of international law and gender justice." It conducted a mock trial that featured eight prosecutorial teams from throughout Asia, and testimony not only from former "comfort women" but also from two Japanese soldiers who took part in mass rapes.[119] More than 20 women from 9 Asian countries testified before these mock tribunals.

> I was only twelve years old when I was taken to a comfort station. A Japanese soldier wanted to rape me but my vagina was too small; he cut my private part; it was so painful I fainted (a North Korean Survivor).
>
> I was taken to Manchuria…; when I resisted, the soldier put a hot iron on my body; the scar is still there. I don't want to die as the ghost of a virgin (a south Korean survivor).
>
> I was an anti-Japanese guerilla girl and, at the age of fourteen, I was forcibly taken to the enemy garrison and raped many times. Once I tried to escape, I was beaten by a baton, tied to a tree and hung; I was also thrown into a frozen river (a Chinese survivor).

I'm an aborigine woman of Taiwan. I was raped by many soldiers in a dark cave. I had to get an abortion. I went back to my village and got married without knowing I was pregnant again. My husband beat me violently and divorced me three times (a survivor from Taiwan).

I was thirteen when Japanese soldiers came into my house and took me. My father tried to protect me but was beheaded in front of me. I was raped by three or four men every night (a Filipino survivor).

I cried and cried. The soldier intimidated me "Do you want to live or die?" I obeyed in order to live. My life was like a prisoner in jail. Later I learned my father had been killed (an Indonesian survivor).

The first night, I was raped by ten men and bled so much I couldn't walk. I was treated like an animal. I came to Japan not to see the country but to tell the truth (an East Timorese survivor).

Even after I got married, I could never enjoy sex, because the memory of rape by Japanese soldiers had always haunted me. However, I feel I have to speak up, because I heard the same horrible thing was happening in Bosnia (a Dutch survivor).[120]

According to Yayori Matsui,

All these testimonies illustrated the vast geographical scale, from the Siberian-Chinese border in the north to the Pacific island in the south...[of] the brutality of sexual slavery and all kinds of sexual violence, including forced and deceptive recruitment, trafficking, deportation, confinement, enslavement, beating, intimidation, gang rape, mutilation, forced pregnancy and abortion, forced labor, unsafe environment, abandonment, and murder on an unprecedented scale.[121]

Many of the victims who testified in Tokyo in 2000 told of crimes that took place after the Japanese invaded southeast Asia (Indochina) in 1940–1941. Driven by the successes of the Germans in Europe in 1939–1940, the Japanese military thought that expanding their empire southward would not only help cut off European support for the Nationalists but also provide Japan with natural resources to maintain their military presence in China.[122] The German invasion of the Soviet Union in the summer of 1941 surprised the Japanese and presented its military with new challenges. Now that the Russians were bogged down in what many believed would be a war of attrition with Germany, there remained only one stumbling block to Japan's creation of its Greater East Asia Co-Prosperity Sphere—the United States. The failure of diplomatic efforts to resolve the growing differences with the United States, particularly after Washington's embargo against the sale of essential raw materials to Japan in 1940, ultimately led to Japan's decision to attack US naval installations at Pearl Harbor on December 7, 1941, followed by the invasion of the East Indies and the Philippines.[123]

The litany of Japanese war crimes continued in the new parts of Tokyo's expanding Asian empire. The principal foci of the Tokyo IMT trial were crimes committed against Allied POWs. According to trial transcripts, 27 percent of the 132,134 British and American troops taken prisoner by the Japanese died in captivity compared to only 4 percent of those imprisoned by the Germans and the Italians in Europe.[124] The court noted in its judgment the

Ruthless killing of prisoners by shooting, decapitation, drowning, and other methods; death marches in which prisoners including the sick were forced to march long distances under conditions which not even well-conditioned troops could stand, many of those dropping out being shot or bayonetted [*sic*] by the guards; forced labor in tropical heat without protection from the sun; complete lack of housing and medical supplies in many cases resulting in thousands of deaths from disease; beatings and torture of all kinds to extract information or confessions or for minor offenses; killing without trial of recaptured prisoners after escape or for attempt to escape; killing without trial of captive aviators; and even cannibalism.[125]

The Tokyo tribunal also pointed out that the Japanese military had opposed the ratification of the 1929 Geneva Convention on the treatment of POWs because they saw humane treatment as an invitation to intensified Allied bombings of Japanese cities. After the April 18, 1942 Doolittle raid (16 US B-25 carrier-based bombers attacked Japanese cities), Gen. Hideki Tōjō, now the prime minister, ordered the death penalty for all captured US pilots. He also ordered Gen. Hata, the commander-in-chief of the Expeditionary Force in China, to mount a massive campaign in Zhejiang and Jiangxi provinces to find any Doolittle pilots who had landed in China, and to do all that was necessary to discourage the Chinese from helping the downed US fliers. The Japanese sent 100,000 crack troops under Gen. Shiro Ishii into the region where they

> rampaged across the countryside...burning, killing, and raping equaling the savagery of the Rape of Nanking.

Before they left, the Japanese dropped

> cholera, typhoid, and paratyphoid bacteria...into wells and reservoirs; plague infested fleas and anthrax bacteria were spread throughout the rice fields. Contaminated sweet cakes and snacks were left for children to pick up and eat.

Estimates are that almost 250,000 Chinese died as a result of Japanese savagery in Zhejiang and Jiangxi provinces.[126]

Equally shocking was the infamous Bataan Death March that took place after the Japanese captured the Philippine island of Luzon in the spring of 1942. Over a third of the 76,000 Filipino and American POWs on this brutal forced march died en route to the Japanese facility at Camp O'Donnell. Many were bayoneted to death when they fell by the side of the road.[127] Others died from dehydration even though there "was water all along the route, plenty of it."[128]

> The men on the death march were drying up. As their bodies tried to conserve fluids, they stopped sweating and urinating. Their saliva turned adhesive and their tongues stuck to their palates and teeth. Their throats started to swell, and their sinus cavities, dry and raw from the dust and heat, pounded with a headache that blurred their vision. Some men got ear aches and lost their hearing. A guard could shout "Hey" (*Kora!*) all he liked, but a man down from dehydration, dazed and deaf with heat fever, would never hear the warning or sense the watchman's fatal approach.[129]

What drove the Japanese to commit such crimes were racial and historical stereotypes that viewed all captives as inferior barbarians. Consequently, they saw torture as the way to assert their sense of superiority and control over a hated enemy.[130]

> Sometimes a group of Japanese soldiers would drop what they were doing, form a long gauntlet on the road, and force a column of prisoners to run single file down the middle, shoving them back and forth and pummeling them so hard with ax handles and bamboo cudgels the prisoners could hear bones breaking.[131]

Those who survived the forced march and made it to Camp O'Donnell faced new horrors. Malaria and dysentery were rampant with a death rate of between 25 and 50 prisoners per day.[132] Dr. Paul Ashton, a US Navy surgeon, was sent by the Japanese in the summer of 1942 to treat the prisoners there. What he saw was ghastly.

> Everyone had diarrhea or dysentery; most had malaria too; a handful suffered from dengue fever and couldn't eat. Half the detail seemed to have some kind of respiratory problem, and several of these were developing pneumonia. Others were either yellow with jaundice or [were] covered with jungle ulcers, which were suppurating and attracting flies. A number of the infirm were infested with worms, nematodes, deposited as larvae by flies and mosquitos.[133]

What little food the Japanese supplied their prisoners

> was the dregs of each shipment. The grains [of rice] were often spoiled or moldy, each sack laced with worms, weevils, small rocks, dirt, rat droppings. Everything, of course, went in the pot. There were men who couldn't stomach the worms. They'd sit hunched over their ration, meticulously culling them out, white worms as long as a finger joint, with two tiny black spots near the head.[134]

The prosecution also presented evidence before the Tokyo tribunal on slave labor. Though slave labor was widespread throughout Japanese-occupied Asia, the prosecution paid particular attention to the atrocities that took place while building the Burma–Siam railway. Immortalized in David Lean's film *The Bridge on the River Kwai*, which was based on the novel by Pierre Boulle, the 258-mile railway between Ban Pong, Thailand, and Thanbyuzayal, Burma, was built to strengthen Japan's ability to supply its troops in Burma. Lean's highly fictionalized and criticized film, unfortunately, failed to capture the true depth of the horrors suffered by the 250,000 Asians and 60,000 Allied prisoners forced to build the railroad in harsh jungle conditions. Between 70,000 and 90,000 of the Asian slave laborers and over 12,000 Allied POWs died building it.[135] Their deaths were attributed to

> the constant driving, beating, torturing and murdering at the hands of their Japanese and Korean guards and the insanitary conditions in which the prisoners were required to live and work and the failure of the Japanese Government to furnish the barest necessities of life and medical care.[136]

The judges noted in their majority judgment that "the practice of torturing prisoners of war and civilian internees prevailed at practically all places occupied by Japanese troops, both in the occupied territories and in Japan."[137]

One of the first cases tried by a US military commission after the war charged Gen. Tomoyuki Yamashita with failure to control the murderous actions of troops under his command in the Philippines. The prosecution's two Bill of Particulars stated that

> from 9th October, 1944 to 1st May, 1945, troops under his command undertook and put into execution a deliberate plan and purpose to massacre and exterminate a large part of the civilian population of Batangas Province [Philippines], and to devastate and destroy public, private and religious property therein, as a result of which more that 25,000 men, women, and children, all unarmed non-combatant civilians, were brutally mistreated and killed, without cause or trial, and entire settlements were devastated and destroyed wantonly and without military necessity.[138]

Other charges included:

> The unjustified failure or refusal to provide prisoners of war...with adequate shelter, food, water, clothing, sanitation, medical care, and other essentials it being sometimes stated specifically that such omission caused malnutrition and death; abandoning, without care or attention helplessly sick, wounded or starved prisoners of war...; and deliberately profaning the bodies of dead prisoners of war and internees...deliberately and unnecessarily exposing prisoners of war...to gunfire and other hazards.[139]

Elsewhere, the Japanese also tortured and murdered civilians and POWs in their extensive biological warfare programs. The main biological and chemical warfare center was at Pingfang, south of Harbin in Manchuria. Established by an army physician, Shirō Ishii, the Pingfang (Ping Fan) facility, known first as the Kamo Unit or Togo Unit, and later, Unit 731,[140] was built "to develop weapons of biological and chemical warfare, including plague, anthrax, cholera and a dozen other pathogens." Working closely with the Japanese military, Ishii's unit "field" tested "plague bombs by dropping them on Chinese cities to see whether they could start plague outbreaks. They could."[141]

Though the Nationalists reported as early as 1937 that the Japanese were using biological and chemical weapons against them, they were initially "dismissed as propaganda" and seen as an excuse for China's "humiliating defeats by advancing Japanese armies." The first major documented "incident," though, took place not against the Chinese but against Soviet forces in the summer of 1939, when the Japanese army fired 2,000 shells "laden with bacteria" at the Red Army. The Japanese also used "suicide squads" to dump chemical and biological material in rivers and streams to infect Soviet troops. In 1989, three members of one of these squads told a Japanese reporter that

> with our own hands, we threw large quantities of intestinal typhoid bacteria into the river. The pathogens were cultured in a vegetable gelatin. We opened the lids, and poured the jelly-like contents of the cans into the river. We carried the cans back with us so we wouldn't leave any evidence.[142]

But it was the Chinese, not the Soviets, who suffered most from these "experiments." In the fall of 1940, a sole Japanese plane dropped wheat that contained "plague-infected fleas" on the city of Ningbo in southern China.

> People began to sweep it up to use to feed their chickens, not knowing that the wheat contained plague-infected fleas.

Within days, bubonic plague began to spread and those infected were taken to a special hospital in the sealed-off city center. The situation became so dire that in early December, Chinese officials decided that the only way to halt the spread of the plague was to burn this part of Ningbo to the ground. Similar raids took place over other Chinese cities using "wheat, grains of rice, cotton padding, strips of paper, and other unlikely objects." There were also cases where the Japanese released thousands of infected rats into a city.[143] According to Tien-wei Wu, the Japanese killed 20,000 Chinese in Heilungchiang and Kirin provinces by releasing infected rats into the area toward the end of the war. Two other Chinese scholars, Peter Li and James Yin, estimate that anywhere from 748,000 to 2 million Chinese were killed by Japanese biological weapons.[144]

Sheldon H. Harris says that the Japanese killed another 10,000–12,000 men, women, and children at its 12 biological warfare facilities throughout Asia.[145] Unit 731, for example, also did experiments to determine the "consequences of frostbite." Lt. Col. Nishi Toshihide, one of the 12 defendants tried by the Soviets in Khabarovsk in 1949 for their involvement in Japan's biological and human experimentation program, testified that he watched one experiment, which was being filmed, where people were brought from the prison and placed outside with bare arms. The temperature was 20 below zero and a fan was used to make it colder.

> This was done until their frozen arms, when struck with a short stick, emitted a sound resembling that which a board gives out when it is struck.[146]

Other medical experiments, some done at Kyushu Imperial University's medical school, involved

> replacing blood with sea water; excising lungs, stomachs, livers, and other organs from POWs; interrupting blood flow from arteries to the heart to determine [when] the time of death would occur from such a procedure; and drilling holes in craniums, then inserting scalpels into the brain to determine what, if anything, medically useful could be discovered from the procedure.[147]

Some of these experiments were done surgically on living or recently murdered captives. One Japanese lab technician who worked at several Unit 731 facilities remembered watching Japanese soldiers behead two suspected Chinese guerillas.

> "Blood from the cartoid artery shot up two meters into the air, as if it were gushing from a hose." The two men were immediately dissected. "The chest cavity was opened and the heart was removed and placed on a scale for weighing. The heart was still beating, and it made the scale weights clank together."[148]

The Japanese also used "comfort women" to study the effect of syphilis on the body and on occasion "engaged in 'live dissection to investigate how different internal organs are affected at different stages of the disease.'"[149]

Unit 731 also did such experiments on Allied POWs. Japanese physicians on the island of Truk, for example, took two captured American airmen and tied extremely tight tourniquets around their arms and legs. The tourniquets were taken off after seven or eight hours, and the men died of shock. Their bodies were immediately dissected, and their skulls were kept as souvenirs by the medical commander on the island, Capt. Iwanami Hiroshi.[150] Similar experiments were conducted on eight American POWs at Kyushu University.

> In one operation, which took place in a crude dissecting facility in the university's Anatomy Department, a lung was removed from each of the two prisoners. On a second occasion, doctors removed the stomach, heart, and liver from two other POWs. The third experiment led to the death of an airman whose brain was damaged in the course of surgery to examine the function of the trigeminal nerve [facial sensation and cranial sensory nerve]. Three American fliers were used in the fourth and final test. The doctors operated on stomachs, gall bladders, livers, and hearts. All eight men used in the experiments died on the operating table.[151]

What is particularly troubling about all of this is that most of the principal Japanese officials involved in these medical experiments were never brought to trial. The US government, and more particularly the US Army's Chemical Warfare Service and the Intelligence Division at Ft. Detrick, Maryland, were desperate to get their hands on Ishii's experiments on human subjects. The use of this scientific "forbidden fruit" was illegal and unethical because the experiments were conducted on subjects without their consent. On the other hand, the State Department's State-War-Navy Coordinating Committee (SWNCC), which was "responsible" for coordination of occupation policy in Japan, thought it was essential that "Japanese BW [Biological Warfare] experts provide American scientists with all the data they had previously amassed."[152] SWNCC was also determined to do what it could to prevent the Soviets from acquiring this information.[153] Yet how was the United States to deal with the possibility that Ishii and his colleagues had committed war crimes and could be prosecuted for such crimes? This was the subject of a SWNCC report in the summer of 1947, which stated that

> experiments on human beings similar to those conducted by the Ishii BW group have been condemned as war crimes by the International Military Tribunal for the trial of major Nazi war criminals in its decision handed down at Nuremberg on 30 September 1946.[154]
>
> This Government is at present prosecuting leading German scientists and medical doctors at Nuremberg for offenses which included experiments on human beings which resulted in the suffering and death of those experimented on.

Regardless, the report concluded that the "'interests of national security'" overrode any consideration of a war crimes trial, because BW intelligence would probably be disclosed in such a forum. Consequently, this course of action would "'not be advisable.'"[155] This, the fear of disclosure, was one of the reasons that United States decided not to prosecute the Ishii team.[156]

Nazi Germany

Experiments on human subjects were also an integral part of Nazi Germany's program to create an Aryan-pure Europe. This, and ridding itself of those it deemed a threat to this goal, resulted in untold atrocities, particularly against the Jews, whom Nazi leaders deemed the greatest threat to Nazi racial purity. And even though Nazi racial ideology played a role in the commiting of these crimes, the nature of Nazi German racial hatred was much more focused and defined than in Japan, in large part because it was a central political and ideological theme of Nazism's prophet, Adolph Hitler.

At a distance, Hitler would seem to be an unlikely founder of a movement that would dominate Germany for 12 years. He was a high school dropout and financial deadbeat who fled Austria for Germany in 1913 to avoid being drafted into the Austrian army. But when World War I broke out, he readily volunteered to fight in the German army. His service in the Kaiser's army proved to be a transformative experience for Hitler, and after the war he took over and transformed a small right-wing political movement in Germany, the German Workers' Party (*Deutsche Arbeiterpartei*; DAP) into the National Socialist German Workers' Party (Nazi; *Nationalsozialistische Deutsche Arbeiterpartei*; NSDAP).[157]

According to Ian Kershaw, Hitler was a gifted public speaker and propagandist who was able "to advertise unoriginal ideas in a original way."[158] One of the central themes in Hitler's speeches and writings was the threat of the Jews, who he called "a racial tuberculosis of the nations."[159] Over time, he blended his deep anti-Semitism, a late-nineteenth-century term that identified the Jews as a race, with his hatred of communism. He stated in *Mein Kampf,* which he wrote while serving time in prison for trying to seize control of the city hall in Munich during the Beer Hall *putsch* in late 1933, that the goal of Marxism, which he considered a Jewish doctrine, was "systematically to hand over the world to the Jews."[160] Consequently, one of the principal goals of the Nazi movement was to destroy Jewish Bolshevism. It could only be achieved, he argued, through a "war of extermination," which would result in the "annihilation and extermination of the Marxist *Weltanschauung* (world view)." From Hitler's perspective, this "world view" was synonymous with "the Jew."[161]

Hitler and the Nazis' political fortunes waxed and waned throughout the 1920s, and were linked to the economic well-being of Weimar Germany. For the most part, his political movement remained on the fringe of German politics until the Depression overwhelmed Germany in the early 1930s. Hitler, who had transformed his movement after the failed 1923 coup into a viable political party designed to achieve power through the ballot box, was well positioned to take advantage of the unstable socioeconomic situation in Germany. Official unemployment rose from 8.5 percent in 1929 to 29.9 percent three years later.[162] These dire economic figures and their social implications, in league with a political system that seemed unable to deal with the growing crisis, played directly into Hitler's plans. Nazi political fortunes peaked in the spring and summer of 1932, when Hitler ran second in two political campaigns for the presidency of the Weimar Republic against Paul von Hindenburg, and Reichstag elections that saw the Nazis win 37.3 percent of the popular vote.[163]

But Hindenburg's refusal to appoint Hitler (whom he considered no better than a "former corporal") chancellor, coupled with growing public concern about the violence associated with Hitler's movement, saw Nazi political fortunes wane considerably in the November 1932 Reichstag elections.[164] In the end, Hitler's appointment as chancellor three months later had less to do with his political skills and vision than with the political whirlwind surrounding Hindenburg, who was convinced by some of his cronies that appointing Hitler as chancellor with a few cabinet seats would give Hindenburg a conservative majority in the Reichstag that hopefully could stabilize the political and economic situation in Germany. Hindenburg and his advisers, who hoped to control Hitler politically, sorely miscalculated his political vision and drive. Within months after he became chancellor in early 1933, Hitler and his allies were well on their way to creating a dictatorship that would completely Nazify Germany.[165]

Though the first targets of the Nazis were their political enemies, it did not take long before Hitler agreed to mount a national boycott of Jewish businesses. Though this quickly failed, the Nazis were able to put into place a series of laws in the spring of 1933 that stripped Jews of their government jobs or severely limited their ability to work in the medical or legal professions. Other laws limited Jewish enrollment in public schools and severely restricted their ability to work as writers, film makers, and artists. By the end of 1933, one Jewish newspaper, the *Jüdische Rundschau*, noted that it had been a devastating year for Germany's Jews, "many of [whom] have lost their economic base of existence."[166]

Over the next few years, Nazi policies toward the Jews waxed and waned in severity. The situation seemed to stabilize in the fall of 1935 when Hitler insisted on a series of laws that better defined the status of Jews in Germany. Written in haste during the annual Party Days (*Parteitage*) in Nuremberg, the two principal Nuremberg Laws—the Reich Citizenship Law (*Reichsburgergesetz*) and the Law to Protect German Blood (*Blutschutzgesetz*)—stated that only someone of German or related blood could enjoy full citizenship rights and marry other Aryans. Non-Aryans such as Jews could only enjoy rights as subjects of the state (*Staatsangehöriger*). Over the next eight years, the government would issue a number of supplementary decrees that would more clearly define Jewishness. According to Nazi officials, there were 400,000–500,000 full or three-quarter Jews in Germany, and 300,000 *Mischling*, quarter or half Jews. A third Nuremberg Law, the Marital Health Law (*Ehegesundheitsgesetz*), required couples who wanted to marry to obtain a Certificate of Fitness to Marry (*Ehetauglichkeitszeugnis*), which would determine whether either applicant might "racially damage" the marriage because of a history of feeblemindedness, epilepsy, venereal disease, or other "racially" contagious diseases.[167]

This concern over the "racially unfit" was also what drove the Nazis to sterilize hundreds of thousands of handicapped Germans in the early years of Nazi power. Such practices had roots in late nineteenth- and early twentieth-century scientific thinking and practice in the Western world. Hitler wrote in *Mein Kampf* that

it is a half-measure to let incurably sick people steadily contaminate the remaining healthy ones...The demand that defective people be prevented from propagating equally defective offspring is a demand of the clearest reason and if systematically executed represents the most humane act of mankind. It will spare millions of unfortunates undeserved sufferings, and consequently will lead to a rising improvement of health as a whole.[168]

In the spring of 1933, the Nazis adopted Germany's first sterilization law, the Law for the Prevention of Genetically Diseased Offspring (*Gesetz zur Verhütung erbkranken Nachwusches*), which allowed the state forcibly to sterilize individuals suffering from a long list of mental, emotional, physical, and inherited diseases that ranged from "feeblemindedness" to blindness and alcoholism. Other laws expanded coverage to the Roma. Special "health" courts, the *Erbsesundheitsgericht*, made up of two physicians and a lawyer, were created to review proposed sterilization cases submitted to the "court" by physicians and other health professionals. Estimates are that Hitler's government sterilized 375,000–400,000 Germans, most of them in the immediate years before the outbreak of World War II.[169]

The Roma, or Gypsies, were also caught up in the evolution of Nazi policy toward the Jews and the handicapped. Though there were only 20,000–26,000 Roma in Germany when Hitler came to power, they were universally despised for what most Germans believed were their lazy, criminal ways. By 1933, there was already a mature body of restrictive anti-Roma laws throughout Germany that placed severe restrictions on their movements under the watchful eye of the police. These laws were such that the Nazis felt all they needed to do was enforce them more rigorously as part of their efforts to deal with what they called the Gypsy plague (*Zigeunerplage*).[170] The Germans also created a special office to deal with the Roma, the Reich Center for Combating the Gypsy Nuisance (*Reichszentrale zur Bekämpfung des Zigeunerwesens*), and set up a special research institute under Dr. Robert Ritter to gather information on the Roma and others who lived an itinerant lifestyle. Ritter's institute was also charged with determining who was a Roma. It ultimately developed a detailed Roma classification scheme that ranged from full-blooded Gypsy (*Vollzigeuner*) to Part-Gypsy (*Zigeunermischling*) to Non-Gypsy (*Nicht-Zigeuner*).[171]

Ritter, who advocated the sterilization of the *Zigeunermischlinge*, argued that only one group of Roma, the Sinti, was not a threat to Aryan racial purity. On the other hand, he concluded, the other group, the Roma, newcomers to Germany from Eastern Europe, were a threat to the racial vitality of the Nazi state. Consequently, Heinrich Himmler, the head of the SS (*Schutzstaffel*) who saw himself as the protector of Germany's racial purity, issued the Combating the Gypsy Plague (*Bekämpfung der Zigeunerplage*) decree on December 8, 1938, which ordered police to register all Roma and Sinti over six as well as those who lived an itinerant lifestyle. This information would be used by the Reich Criminal Police (*Reichskriminalpolizei*; Kripo) to determine each Roma and Sinti's racial category. Himmler's decree and subsequent codicils required Roma and Sinti to carry special identification papers and placed new travel restrictions on them. Foreign Roma were either to be expelled from the Reich or forbidden to enter the country. The purpose of this policy was to isolate the Roma from the rest of the German population, something that had already begun a few years earlier with the opening of Gypsy concentration camps (*Zigeunerlarger*) on the eve of the 1936 Summer Olympics in Berlin.[172]

Himmler's decree came in the aftermath of Nazi Germany's most violent assault against the Jews, the *Kristallnacht* pogrom of November 9–10, 1938. To some extent,

Kristallnacht was an expression of the Nazi elite's frustration with their inability to force large numbers of Jews to leave Germany, and the continued role of some Jews in the German economy. Beginning in late 1937, the Nazis initiated a new wave of anti-Jewish policies designed to further isolate Jews and force more to leave the country.[173]

Though there were considerable differences of opinion within the Nazi leadership about how to achieve these goals, the highly charged anti-Semitic environment in Germany throughout 1938 helped lay the groundwork for *Kristallnacht*, which began days after the assassination of a German diplomat, Ernst vom Rath, in Paris, by Herschel Gryszpan, a young Jew who was distraught over the forced expulsion of his parents to Poland. What followed was a carefully orchestrated national pogrom that damaged or destroyed 1,500 synagogues and thousands of Jewish homes and businesses. Scores of Jews were injured or murdered by German thugs, while total property damage was over $15 million. The German leadership blamed the country's Jewish community for the pogrom and imposed a 1 billion *Reichsmark* ($400 million) fine on it for the damage. To underscore its disillusionment with the country's Jewish community, the Gestapo rounded up 30,000 Jewish males days after *Kristallnacht* and sent them to concentration camps. Germany was condemned internationally for its actions, and Joseph Goebbels, who blamed the world's Jews for this criticism, stated that if it continued, the result could "be digging the graves of the Jews in Germany."[174] Hitler underscored this point in a speech before the Reichstag on January 30, 1939.

> Europe cannot find peace until the Jewish question has been resolved...if the Jewish financiers in and outside of Europe should succeed in plunging the nations once more into a world war, then the result will not be the Bolshevization of the earth, and thus the victory of Jewry, but the *annihilation of the Jewish race in Europe.*[175]

Germany and World War II

A Social Darwinist at heart, Hitler saw war as an essential element in his plan to provide Germany with the lands it needed to create his Aryan-pure, thousand-year Reich. Beginning with his announcement in early 1935 that Germany would rearm in violation of the Treaty of Versailles, Hitler gradually prepared his nation for war by adopting increasingly aggressive moves that brought him the Rhineland, Austria, the Sudetenland, and the rest of Czechoslovakia between 1935 and 1939. His invasion of Poland on September 1, 1939, not only plunged Europe into a new world war, but also provided the cover for a new racial war against Jews, the Roma, and Christian Poles.[176]

The new phase of the Nazi "war" against the handicapped and the disabled began in 1938 when the Knauers, a family in Leipzig, wrote their *Führer*, asking permission to "euthanize" their seriously handicapped child. Hitler sent his personal physician, Dr. Karl Brandt, to examine the child. After Brandt approved the parents' request, Hitler asked him, along with Philipp Bouhler, the head of the Führer chancellery (*Führerkanzeli*), to develop a program that would oversee the "euthanization" of German children with serious physical or mental handicaps. Several weeks before Germany's invasion of Poland, the new organization that oversaw this program, the Reich Committee for the Scientific Registration of Severe Hereditary Ailments (*Reichsaansschuss zur Wissenschaftlichen Erfassung von erb- und anlagebedingten schweren Leiden*), sent a directive to German physicians and midwives to report on any children under the age of three (this was later expanded to include older children) who suffered from a long list of physical and mental handicaps. Special forms denoting each child's disabilities were to be filled out , and then sent to the committee. By the time the war ended, 5,000 children were murdered under the guidelines set up by the Reich Committee.[177]

Hitler also oversaw the creation of a similar program for adults. While the Germans had no problem finding physicians interested in working for the adult "euthanasia" program, some were afraid they could be prosecuted for murder under pre-Nazi German criminal codes. Consequently, in October 1939, Hitler signed a brief statement backdated to September 1 that authorized such a program.

Reichsleiter Bouhler and Dr. Brandt, M.D., are charged with the responsibility of enlarging the authority of certain physicians to be designated by name in such a manner, so that persons who, according to human judgement, are incurable can, upon a most careful diagnosis of their condition of sickness, be accorded a mercy death.

[signed] A. Hitler

During the first two years of the war, the Germans opened six "euthanasia" killing centers throughout Germany for what was called the T-4 program. By the time they were shut down officially in the summer of 1941, T-4 specialists had murdered 70,000–80,000 Germans in these centers. Many of the physicians and technicians involved in this program were later transferred to the new "Final Solution" mass death camps created by the Germans in occupied Poland in 1941–1942.[178]

Hitler's statement authorizing the adult euthanasia program was dated to coincide with Germany's invasion of Poland. Hitler considered Christian Poles to be that "dreadful [racial] material" and Polish Jews "the most horrible thing imaginable." When the war broke out, there were 3.3–3.5 million Jews in Poland out of a population of 35 million.[179] Just days before Hitler invaded Poland, he told his military commanders that they were to kill "without pity or mercy all men, women, and children of Polish descent or language...Only in this way can we obtain the living space [*lebensraum*] we need."[180] What followed was a multifaceted campaign that centered around wiping out Poland's political, intellectual, and religious elite and, ultimately, the mass murder of its Jews. Though there is some debate about the number of Poles who died under German occupation, estimates are that 1.8–1.9 million Polish Christians and 3.2 million Polish Jews died as a direct result of Nazi racial policies.[181]

Soon after the Germans conquered Poland with the help of the Soviet Union, an ally of the Reich from late August 1939 until June 1941, they collectively erased Poland from the map of Europe. The Russians got a little over half of Poland, while western Poland was integrated directly into Germany proper. What remained was reconstituted at the General Government for the Occupied Areas of Poland (*General-gouvernement für die desetzen polnischen Gebiete*) with its capital in Kraków. The General Government quickly became not only Nazi Germany's "racial laboratory" but also its "dumping ground" for what the Germans considered to be Europe's racial inferiors. In 1941, it also became Germany's principal killing field for the Final Solution of the Jewish question.[182]

The Germans saw the Christian Poles as a key source of forced labor. On the other hand, they wanted to isolate Poland's Jews from the rest of the Polish population and strip them not only of their citizen rights but also their jobs, economic resources, and homes. Once Germany and the Soviet Union completed the conquest of Poland in early October, only about two million Jews remained in German-occupied Poland. Almost from the outset of the German occupation, Nazi officials struggled with the question of what to do with this large, increasingly impoverished Jewish population. In the summer of 1940, the Germans developed several plans to deport them to Madagascar, though there are some questions of the seriousness of such plans. In the end, the Germans finally decided to establish ghettos in the General Government's large and small cities. They created Jewish Councils (*Judenräte*) to govern the ghettos and act as liaisons with German officials. The ghettos were expected to be, for the most part, self-sustaining, and provide the Germans with a source of cheap slave labor. The largest ghettos were in Warsaw (445,000), Łódź (204,800), Kraków (64,348), and Lublin (40,000). Over time, they became bastions of slow death from disease, hunger, and physical abuse.[183] But once the Germans began to develop a new program to deal with its growing Jewish population—the Final Solution—in the early months of the invasion of the Soviet Union in 1941, they decided to close the ghettos.

In many ways, war between the Soviet Union and Germany was inevitable because Hitler saw Russia, with its large Slavic and Jewish populations, as the seedbed of "Jewish Bolshevism."[184] But the conquest of the Soviet Union was also an essential part of his larger plan to gain *lebensraum* for his burgeoning Aryan empire. It also had abundant natural resources, something Hitler needed desperately to maintain control over his large empire in Europe. Girded by his incredible military successes over Poland and Western Europe in 1939 and 1940, Hitler was convinced he would be able to conquer Russia in four or five months.[185]

In the spring of 1941, he told his top generals that what was about to take place was

> a life and death struggle between two races and two ideologies...National Socialism and the criminal code of Jewish Bolshevism, which constitutes the greatest threat to the future of civilization...The ultimate objective of this war was not only the destruction of the Red Army in the field but the final elimination of the Russian-Bolshevik menace.[186]

The German armed forces (*Wehrmacht*) issued a number of directives in the spring and early summer of 1941 that reminded its officers and men that this was an ideological war against "Bolshevik agitators, guerillas, saboteurs, and Jews, and the total elimination of all active or passive resistance." The infamous Commissar Order of June 6, 1941, added that the *Wehrmacht* should expect the Russians not to "act in accordance with the principles of humanity or international law," particularly the country's "political commissars," who used "barbaric, Asiatic fighting methods on the battlefield." Consequently, German troops "would be mistaken to show mercy or respect for international law towards such elements." When captured, political commissars were to be shot on the spot.[187] Germany's military leadership thought this decree freed German soldiers from legal responsibility for their actions against important communist operatives. It also helped set the tone for the savage fighting that took place in Russia from 1941 to 1945.[188]

The *Wehrmacht* would also play an important supportive role in Heinrich Himmler and Reinhard Heydrich's mass killing programs in the Soviet Union, aimed first at Jews but later the Roma and the handicapped. The first phase of this campaign involved the murder of Jews by *Einsatzgruppen*, specially trained killing squads that swept into the Soviet Union just behind the *Wehrmacht*. Estimates are that by the end of 1941, these units, aided by the *Wehrmacht*, murdered 500,000–800,000 Jews.[189]

These *Aktions* are well documented in the *Einsatzgruppen Reports*. On July 7, *Einsatzkommando* 8, operating in Belorussia, informed Berlin that

> According to instructions by RSHA [*Reichssicherheitshauptamt*; Reich Security Main Office; Himmler's super police organization headed by Heydrich], liquidations of government and party officials, in all named cities of Byelorussia, were carried out. Concerning the Jews, according to orders, the same policy was adopted.[190]

The methods of mass murder, as well as the makeup of the killing squads, varied from community to community. In Tarnopol (Ternopol, Ukraine), Ukrainian nationalists, in league with *Einsatzkommando* 4b, murdered hundreds of Jews in reprisals for the supposed murder of three German soldiers. According to Maj. Gen. Otto Korfes:

> We saw trenches 5 m [16 feet] deep and 20 m [66 feet] wide. They were filled with men, women, and children, mostly Jews. Every trench contained 60–80 persons. We could hear their moans and shrieks as grenades exploded among them. On both sides of the trenches stood some 12 men dressed in civilian clothes. They were hurling grenades down in the trenches...Later, officers of the Gestapo told us that those men were Banderists [Ukrainian collaborators].[191]

In Jedwabne in northeast Poland, the village's Christian population murdered its Jews just weeks after the invasion began while the Germans looked on. After looting their homes and businesses,

> they took healthier men and chased them to the cemetery and ordered them to dig a pit, and after it was dug out, Jews were killed every which way, one with an iron bar, another with a knife, still another with a club.

Frustrated by the inefficiency of this method of death, villagers drove 1,500 Jedwabne Jews into a barn and set it on fire. Afterward, according to the testimony of one of the villagers, Wasersztajn, he, along with others, dug through the charred remains,

> trying to search the corpses, looking for valuables sewn into clothing. I touched a Brolin shoe-polish box. It clinked. I cut it through with a shovel, and some coins glittered—I think tzarist five-ruble coins. People jumped over to collect them, and this drew the attention of onlooking [German] gendarmes.[192]

Efficiency, along with secrecy and a growing sense of invincibility, would soon propel the Germans to the next phase of their massive killing campaign—the Final Solution of the Jewish Question (*Endlösung der Judenfrage*). By mid-July, Hitler, euphoric over what seemed to be another incredible military victory, held a meeting with some of his top leaders to discuss the administration of post-victory captured Soviet territory. He wanted to turn the country into a "Garden of Eden" and advocated all means necessary "to exterminate anyone who [is] hostile to us."[193] Several days earlier, Himmler met with Rudolf Höss, the commandant of the Auschwitz concentration camp in the General Government, and told him that Hitler had recently ordered the implementation of a Final Solution. He said that Adolf Eichmann, the Gestapo's Jewish specialist, would soon contact him about plans to develop facilities to initiate this new killing program. Himmler ended his conversation with Höss by reminding him that

> the Jews are the eternal enemies of the German people and must be exterminated. All the Jews within our reach must be annihilated during this war. If we do not succeed in destroying the biological foundation of Jewry now, then one day the Jews will destroy the German people.[194]

On July 31, Göring issued a decree that gave Heydrich the authority to begin planning for the Final Solution.[195]

> To supplement the task that was assigned to you on 24 January 1939 [creation of Reich Central Office for Jewish Emigration], which dealt with the solution of the Jewish problem by emigration and evacuation in the most suitable way, I hereby charge you with making all necessary preparations with regard to organizational, technical and material matters for bringing about a complete solution of the Jewish question [*Gesamtlösung der Judenfrage*] within the German sphere of influence in Europe.
>   Where other governmental agencies are involved, these are to cooperate with you.
>   I request you further to send me, in the near future, an overall plan covering the organizational, technical and material measures necessary for the accomplishment of the final solution of the Jewish question [*Endlösung der Judenfrage*] which we desire.[196]

Over the next few months, the Germans experimented with various techniques of mass death at Auschwitz (Zyklon B, a rat poison) and Chełmno (*Kulmhof*, asphyxiation by gas van). At the same time, the SS transferred T-4 specialists to occupied Poland to help with preparations for developing the killing operations at the six death camps there.[197] By the time that Heydrich met with Nazi Party and government officials in Wannsee (a suburb of Berlin) on January 20, 1942, planning for the Final Solution was almost complete.[198]

The Germans opened six death camps in Poland. Three—Auschwitz, Chełmno, and Majdanek—were meant to be permanent, at least until they had murdered all of the Jews of Europe. The other three—Belzec, Sobibór, and Treblinka—were part of *Aktion Reinhard*, a temporary program designed to murder the Jews in the General Government. Estimates are that the Germans murdered 3.5 million Jews in these camps as well as tens of thousands of Roma.[199]

Auschwitz, originally a concentration camp for Poles, has come to symbolize the horrible dimensions of the Final Solution since, over time, it was expanded to add a death camp, Auschwitz II-Birkenau, and a slave labor camp, Auschwitz III-Buna/Monowitz. Estimates are that the Germans murdered over a million Jews in Auschwitz as well as thousands of Poles, Roma, and Soviet POWs.[200] Most were killed in Birkenau's four crematoria-gas chambers. Höss described one of these gassings in his postwar memoirs.

> The door would now be quickly screwed up and the gas discharged by the waiting disinfectors through vents in the ceilings of the gas chambers, down a shaft that led to the floor. This insured the rapid distribution of the gas. It would be observed through the peephole in the door that those who were standing nearest to the induction vents were killed at once. It can be said that about one third died straightaway. The remainder staggered about and began to scream and struggle for air. The screaming, however, soon changed to the death rattle and in a few minutes all lay still…The door was opened half an hour after the induction of the gas and the ventilation switched on…the special detachment [of Jewish prisoners] now set about removing the gold teeth and cutting the hair from the women. After this, the bodies were taken up by elevator and laid in front of the ovens, which had meanwhile been stoked up. Depending on the size of the bodies, up to three corpses could be put into one oven at the same time. The time required for cremation…took three minutes.[201]

Auschwitz I and II were also the sites of horrible medical experiments. Two physicians, Dr. Carl Clauberg and Dr. Josef Mengele, conducted extensive, cruel medical experiments on hundreds of Jewish and Roma prisoners at both camps. Clauberg, a gynecologist, was interested in finding inexpensive, quick ways to sterilize patients. He would inject

> a caustic substance into a woman's cervix in order to obstruct the fallopian tubes. His subjects were married women between the ages of 20 and 40, preferably those who had proven their fertility by bearing children. After injecting them with an opaque liquid, he then x-rayed them to exclude prior blockage or impairment.[202]

Mengele's experiments were more wide-ranging and included research on twins, dwarfs, and Roma children with noma, a facial disease that ate away the skin. Mengele, a decorated *Waffen-SS* physician, became chief physician at Birkenau's Gypsy Family Camp, where he opened a kindergarten for the children. They lovingly called him "Uncle Pepi" because he gave them candy on the playground, unaware that some of them might be soon operated on without anesthesia.[203] Mengele's Jewish assistant, Dr. Miklos Nyiszli, described the "angel of death's" experiments on twins and dwarfs. They were

> exposed to every medical examination that could be performed on human beings: blood tests, lumbar punctures, exchanges of blood between twin brothers, as well

as other examinations, all fatiguing and depressing. Dina [Gottliebova-Babbitt], the painter from Prague, made the comparative studies of the structure of the twins' skulls, ears, noses, mouths, hands and feet. Each drawing was classified in a file set up for that express purpose, complete with all individual characteristics; into this file would also go the final results of this research. The procedure was the same for the dwarfs...Twin brothers died together, and it was possible to perform autopsies on both...They had to die together and in good health.[204]

Elsewhere, the air force (*Luftwaffe*) conducted medical experiments on prisoners at Dachau, the first of the Nazis' major concentration camps near Munich. These included cruel compression chamber experiments to test the limits of high-altitude flights for air crews, and tests to determine the effect of drinking salt water on sailors and downed pilots. In the fall of 1944, one of Dachau's SS physicians, Dr. Wilhelm Beiglboeck, fed 40 Roma prisoners a saltwater diet for several weeks. Over time, some of his patients "became raving mad; they foamed at the mouth." When a few refused to drink the salt water because it made them sick, Beiglboeck forced a tube down their throats and force-fed it to them, despite their pleas to stop.[205]

But such crimes were not limited to Germany. Nazi-allied countries such as Croatia, Hungary, Italy, Romania, Serbia, Slovakia, Romania, the Soviet Union, and France's Vichy regime all played an active role in implementing Hitler's deadly racial policies during the war. Ante Pavelić, the head of the Independent State of Croatia (*Nezavism Drzava Hrvatska*; NDH), waged a horrendous racial war against the Jews, Roma, and Serbs throughout NDH-held territory. His Jasenovac concentration camp was one of the most brutal in Europe. Though estimates vary, over a third of the 125,000 Serbs murdered by the Croats during the war died in Jasenovac.[206] Slovakia, which survived the breakup of Czechoslovakia in 1939 as a Nazi puppet state, was run by a triumvirate that included President Jozef Tiso, a Roman Catholic priest. In the fall of 1941, the Slovak government acceded to Germany's request to deport its Jewish population and send them to camps throughout the Third Reich. About 100,000 Slovak Jews died during the Holocaust, though most of its Roma population survived.[207]

Romania, like Slovakia and Croatia, was run by a harsh dictator, Ion Antonescu, who supported Germany's racial policies toward Jews and Roma. In addition to implementing Nazi-style racial policies in Romania, Antonescu committed most of his country's military to the invasion of the Soviet Union in 1941. His troops would play a major role in the mass murder of Jews and Roma in their areas of operation. Antonescu also set up a separate reserve for Jews and Roma in Transnistria, where 250,000 Jews died. Estimates are that 280,000–380,000 Romanian and Ukrainian Jews died in areas under Romanian occupation during the Holocaust. Raul Hilberg later noted that "no country, besides Germany, was involved in massacres of Jews on such a scale."[208] Another 135,000 Romanian Jews died in territory under Hungarian control.[209] Estimates are that over 10 percent of Romania's prewar Roma population died during the Holocaust.[210]

Hungary's role in the Holocaust was particularly tragic even though, as a German ally, its government had initially refused to deport its 750,000 Jews (and 100,000 Jewish converts to Christianity) and 100,000 Roma to Nazi death camps. On the other hand, Hungary's leaders did adopt a series of

Nuremberg-style laws that placed severe economic, political, and social restrictions on Jews that caused widespread suffering. This all changed in the spring of 1944 when the *Wehrmacht* invaded Hungary. Adolf Eichmann soon followed, and orchestrated the deportation of Jews, now concentrated mostly in ghettos in Budapest, to Auschwitz and death. There were heroic efforts by a number of Jewish operatives, diplomats, and others such as Hannah Szenes, Joel Brand, Per Anger, and Raoul Wallenberg to save Hungary's Jews. Unfortunately, they were unable to stop the mass murder of two-thirds of Hungary's Jews in the spring and summer of 1944.[211]

Italy and Vichy France, two of Hitler's West European allies, were also involved in the murder of Jews and others in their areas of occupation during the war. But Italy's crimes were not just limited to its mistreatment of Italian Jews. Italy committed numerous crimes during its invasion of Ethiopia and occupation of Libya in North Africa as well as parts of Greece and Yugoslavia before and during World War II.[212] In a personal address before the League of Nations in the summer of 1936, Ethiopian emperor Haile Selassie accused Italian forces of using

> tear gas and then mustard gas...to vast areas of Ethiopian territory, drenching not only soldiers but also women, children, cattle, rivers, lakes and pastures with this "deadly rain," systematically killing all living creatures.[213]

The following year, his government asked the League to appoint a commission to look into other war crimes such as the killing of POWs and "the massacre of over 6,000 persons in Addis Ababa...in February 1937."[214] For the most part, the emperor's pleas fell on deaf ears, particularly in light of the ineffective sanctions and arms embargo initiated by the League against Italy in the fall of 1935. According to Cristiano Andrea Ristuccia, the "failure of the sanctions can be numbered among the factors that accelerated the deterioration of international relationships which eventually led to the Second World War."[215]

This colonial mentality, to some extent, explains some of the war crimes committed by Italian forces in Greece and Yugoslavia in World War II. Mussolini invaded Greece in late October 1940, hoping to add it to his Mediterranean empire. The Greeks proved to be tough adversaries, and quickly pushed the Italians back into Albania. The British promised to move troops to Greece to shore up defenses, which prompted Hitler successfully to invade Greece in April 1941. Italy, which was given control of most of central and southern Greece, adopted a policy of revenge that governed their occupation policies throughout the rest of the war. In addition to rapacious plunder, the Italians set up a number of concentration camps where prisoners lived in "subhuman conditions." Torture "was common practice, often with unheard acts of sadism" against those suspected of being or aiding partisans.[216]

> Some of these died under torture, others suffered permanent mutilation. In some cases, the prisoners were tied up by their feet, hung head down, and beaten into unconsciousness. Or, having been suspended by a rope tied around their wrists, they were subjected to excruciating stretching of the limbs, after having heavy weights attached to their ankles. Sometimes, after having had their bodies slashed with nails, razors and knives, ice water was poured into the wounds.[217]

To combat the growing threat of guerillas in north central Greece in 1942–1943, the Italian military adopted indiscriminate policies against the civilian population that involved:

> Bombing and burning of villages, destructions of habitats, plundering food reserves and farm implements, and the deportation of hostages were the tragic consequences of the collective punishments inflicted on the rural populations after it was decided to subtract terrain from the partisan movement by uprooting and destroying the village communities.

By early 1943, Italian military directives

> obliterated any distinction between the civilian population and combatant groups, identifying communities and partisan bands under the single indistinct category of "enemies" to be eliminated with every means and at all costs.

Using the concept of "collective responsibility,"

> the repression of partisan guerilla activity coincided with the war against civilians, both for the broadening of subjects who were identified as objectives of military violence and the amplification of the techniques of repression. In addition to the mass execution of able-bodied men, the deportation of women and children and the summary execution of helpless civilians, now whole villages were firebombed, blown to pieces by artillery fire, or starved.[218]

The Italians adopted similarly harsh tactics against guerillas in their zones of occupation along the Dalmatian coast and Slovenia. Gen. Mario Roatta, commander of the Second Italian Army, found himself trapped in an intense three-part civil war involving Croat, Serb, and communist forces. He considered the latter "'the scum of the earth'" and issued guidelines ("3C") to guide his forces in dealing with Josef Broz "Tito's" partisans. Roatta, sensitive to German criticism that Italian troops were not up to the task of destroying the guerillas, adopted policies that viewed all "civilians as potential 'rebels.' In this climate, civilian and insurgent, male and female, parent and child were indistinguishable as potential killers of Italian troops."[219] Roatta let his officers know that in established war zones

> excessive reactions, undertaken in good faith, will never be prosecuted.[220]

Roatta's policies were particularly harsh in Slovenia, where he told his commanders that

> at whatever the cost Italian domination and prestige must be restored, even if all Slovenes have to be shot and Slovenia destroyed.[221]

By early 1943, Roatta ordered his troops "in operation zones" to shoot all males aged 18 and over. Everyone else was to be arrested and sent to concentration camps. H. James Burgwyn estimates that "the Italians managed to imprison and detain close to 90,000 Slav peoples during their occupation of parts of Yugoslavia during the war.[222]

Such policies contradict the mythical view of what Lidia Santarelli calls the *"italiani brava gente*...Italians as eternal nice guys."[223] This was certainly the case when it came to Mussolini's treatment of Jews in Italy. Though his Fascist National Party (*Partito Nazionale Fascista;* PNF) initially had Jewish members, the Italian dictator fell increasingly under Hitler's spell and in 1938 adopted Nuremberg-style racial laws that devastated Italy's Jewish community. Things got worse after Mussolini was deposed in 1943 in the midst of a successful Allied invasion and conquest of southern Italy. The northern part of the country, now firmly under German control, found most of Italy's 42,500 Jews trapped in the Nazi zone, where they were severely persecuted before the Allied liberation of Rome in the summer of 1944. During this interim, the Germans managed to deport 7,500–10,000 Italian Jews to Auschwitz and death.[224]

France's Jews, particularly those trapped in the collaborationist Vichy zone, suffered an equally harsh fate. Initially, most of the country's 330,000–340,000 Jews lived in northern France, which was quickly occupied by the *Wehrmacht* in the late spring and early summer of 1940. Many fled south, and by the fall of 1940, there were about 150,000–195,000 Jews living in Vichy France. Both French zones adopted Nuremberg-style laws, while one of Eichmann's loyal subordinates, *SS-Hauptsturmführer* Theodor Danneker, and Vichy France's Xavier Vallat developed policies that stripped French Jews of most of their civil, professional, and economic rights. Marshal Phillipe Pétain, Vichy's ruler, fired Vallat because Pétain thought he was too soft on the Jewish question, replacing him with Darquier de Pellepoix. Himmler made similar changes among his staff in France in preparation for a deportation campaign that ultimately led to the forced transfers of 75,000 Jews to Auschwitz, where all but 5,000 perished.[225]

Like France, the Soviet Union was both an ally and an enemy of Nazi Germany during the war. Josef Stalin, frightened by the prospect of war with Germany, did everything he could from August 1939 to June 1941 to play the part of loyal Germany ally. Yet he was also determined to strengthen the Russian presence in his new sphere-of-influence along his western borders, and do what he could to stifle any element that might be problematic to Soviet rule in the region. In April and May 1940, the Soviet secret police, the NKVD, began what they called the "wet work" (*mokraya rabota*), executing about 22,000 Polish POWs and civilian prisoners at Katyn Forest west of Smolensk.[226]

The Soviets committed similar atrocities after they invaded the Baltic states—Estonia, Latvia, and Lithuania—now part of Stalin's sphere of influence—in June 1940. Each country was rapidly sovietized in preparation for their forced integration into the USSR in August as the country's thirteenth, fourteenth, and fifteenth Soviet Socialist Republics.[227] Andrei Vyshinsky, Stalin's prosecutor-general during the infamous Purge "show trials" of the 1930s and later head of his "Secret Commission for Directing the Nuremberg Trials," oversaw the communization of Latvia.[228] Though estimates vary widely, between 1940–1941 and 1944, when the Soviets regained control of the Baltic states from Germany, Stalin's government

> deported or executed 12,000–60,000 Estonians, 15,000–34,000 Latvians, and 34,000–75,000 Lithuanians. Estonia lost 100,000 people, Latvia 150,000, and Lithuania 450,000 as a result of "deportations, executions, and guerilla warfare" after the second Soviet takeover of the Baltic states in 1944.[229]

Nicolas Werth has estimated that by the beginning of 1941, there were over 1.9 million prisoners in Stalin's vast gulag and prison system, a quarter of them from the newly conquered areas along Russia's vast western border. Many would die in these camps or suffer from untold hardships.[230] Such crimes would be conveniently set aside once Germany invaded the Soviet Union in the summer of 1941. The perpetrator now became a victim in Western eyes.

Conclusion

No one envisioned at the end of World War I that a far more devastating war would begin in Asia just a decade or so after the "war to end all wars" ended. Traumatized politicians thought that by addressing what many of them saw as World War I's principal cause—arms—they would protect the world from future conflagrations. Such ideals, of course, proved to be illusory and did not take into account the dynamics of the politics and the militaristic ambitions of leaders in Japan and Nazi Germany. Little was done in the interwar period to address some of the deeper issues that led to the outbreak of World War II though, in fairness to the world's visionary leaders who created the League of Nations, there was little short of preventive war that could have stopped the growing aggression of Japan and Germany in the 1930s. This was doubly so given the economic tsunami that swept the world in the 1930s and a public traumatized by fear of another international conflagration. The world was not prepared for growing Japanese and German aggression built around a concept of total war that targeted civilians in a way not seen in modern history. The level of brutality in the various campaigns initiated by the Japanese from 1931 onward horrified a world unwilling or unable to stop it. When the League finally objected to the Japanese conquest of Manchuria, Tokyo simply withdrew its membership, something Hitler did later. Short of war, the major powers, wracked by their own internal political and economic problems, were left with few options other than protesting Japan and Germany's growing violations of the modest body of international law that dealt with such crimes. These crimes would become the central focus of Allied war crimes prosecution efforts at the end of World War II.

Chapter 6

The Nuremberg IMT Trial

To some extent, it is almost impossible to find words to describe the horror that was World War II. While statistics certainly give us a hint of the murderous depth of this tragedy, they fail to put a face on its global human losses. Michael Ondaatje, the author of the *English Patient*, "compared the war in Europe to a chasm, a deep rift that demarcated two worlds." Diana Lary says that this was particularly true in China, where the "old world was gone for good, the new one in uncertain gestation."[1] The war in China, she goes on, led to a tremendous amount of "social dislocation" already under way before the outbreak of war in 1937. The devastation of war robbed the Chinese of any deep sense of victory, particularly since a civil war between the Nationalists and the communists seemed imminent.[2]

The trauma of what the Chinese call the War of Resistance steeled them to survive equally great horrors in the coming decades, while memory, whether it be public or private, has, particularly in the former instance, been carefully orchestrated by the country's communist leaders. Privately, the long years of silence about the horrors of World War II in China has finally ended, and over the past decade, scholars have begun to interview survivors to insure that the history of the War of Resistance is preserved.[3]

In the Soviet Union, war memory became an integral part of the government's efforts to remind the Soviet people of the role of the communist party in defeating the hated German "fascists." Any visitor to the Soviet Union in the 1970s and 1980s was always taken to one of the many war memorial and mass grave sites scattered throughout the western parts of the country where, in many instances, somber funeral music reminded one of the sacred nature of this place of death. Victory Day (May 9) on Red Square in Moscow was and is still used by the government to remind its citizens of Soviet sacrifice and victory during what the Russians call the Great Fatherland or Great Patriotic War. And while the dynamics of memory were and are quite different in China and Russia, their losses are not. Estimates are that between 20 and 30 million Chinese and 26 and 28 million Soviets citizens died during World War II, most of them civilians.[4] Other Allied and Axis deaths were equally devastating.

France (592,000–600,000)
Poland (5–5.4 million, including 3 million Jews)
United Kingdom (350,000–400,000)
United States (405,400)
Germany (6–6.5 million)
Hungary (430,000–436,000)
Italy (286,900–500,000)
Japan (2.1–2.4 million)
Romania (721,000)[5]

Pathway to Nuremberg

This was particularly true in the Soviet Union, where the Germans waged a dreadful racial war in what they considered the homeland of Jewish Bolshevism. It was no accident, then, that almost from the outset of the German invasion in the summer of 1941, the Soviets played a key role in developing policies first to bring collaborators to justice, and later German war criminals. Josef Stalin's government adopted the 1925 Geneva Protocol on the use of gas and similar weapons during wartime,[6] but not the 1929 Convention, arguing that the terms of the Hague Conventions were sufficient to protect POW rights. During and after World War II, Soviet jurists argued that the Hague Conventions were merely the codification of the customary laws of war, and that the Soviet Union "recognized all laws and customs of war, since they were directed towards the humanization of war, and that it insisted on its observance."[7]

However, early Soviet law did not specifically refer to "war crimes," even though the idea of "crimes against humanity" was first voiced by the Russians during the Armenian genocide. Instead, Soviet law referred to military crimes (*voinske prestupleniia*)—high crimes that included espionage and "violence against the civilian population." Soviet military tribunals were responsible for dealing with such crimes, and, once a new military statute was adopted in 1927, they were directed to deal harshly with "Soviet military personnel and civilians who committed crimes against wounded and sick POWs, and against the population in the theater of military operations."[8]

This was certainly the case after the Germans invaded the Soviet Union in 1941. Stalin's government declared martial law throughout the country and military tribunals were given the authority "to prosecute all crimes against the state as well as against public order." Such justice was swift since defendants were to be tried within 24 hours after they were indicted. These military courts also had the authority to try non-Russians throughout the USSR. Articles 318–320 of the Russian Soviet Federative Socialist Republic's (RSFSR, which comprised a large part of the country) Criminal Process Code stated "that sentences were to 'be based on the evidence presented in a trial and, more important, on the judges' inner conviction.'" The principal goal of the Soviet military court system was to prevent Soviet collaboration with the Germans.[9]

The early months of the German invasion seemed to point to a quick German victory as Soviet losses mounted. On October 25, President Roosevelt criticized the wanton German execution of "innocent hostages in reprisal for isolated attacks on Germans" throughout Europe, while Churchill warned that "retribution for these crimes must henceforth take its place among the major purposes of the war."[10] On November 6, Stalin pointed to "flagrant [German] violations of the rules of war," and warned that if the Reich continued waging "a war of extermination, they will get it." His foreign minister, Vyacheslav Molotov, followed suit a few weeks later and warned that "accountability for these crimes rested entirely with the German State."[11]

In early 1942, the Allies created the Inter-Allied Commission on the Punishment of War Crimes (IACPWC) and issued the Declaration of St. James, which, referring to Hague IV (1907), stated that they opposed retribution "by acts of vengeance on the part of the general public." But

> in order to satisfy the sense of justice of the civilized world...The Nine Powers [Big Three plus six governments-in-exile] place among their principal war aims the punishment, through the channel of organized justice, of those guilty of or responsible for these crimes, whether they have ordered them, perpetuated them or participated in them, [and] resolve to see to it in a spirit of international solidarity, that (a) those guilty or responsible, whatever their nationality, are sought out, handed over to justice and judged, [and] (b) that the sentences produced are carried out.[12]

Later that year, the Allies created the United Nations War Crimes Commission (UNWCC) to begin to gather evidence of Axis war crimes. Stalin, however, refused to work with this investigative body, instead creating his own, the Extraordinary State Commission for Ascertaining and Investigating Atrocities Perpetrated by the German Fascist Invaders and Their Accomplices (*Chrezvychainaia gosudarstvennaia komissiia*, ChGK), which provided the Soviets with the evidence they would use at Nuremberg and in other postwar trials.[13]

Stalin, Churchill, and Roosevelt all warned the Germans in the fall of 1941 that those found guilty of such crimes would be brought before international courts or tribunals.[14] On the other hand, little was done seriously to gather evidence of such crimes outside of the Soviet Union other than the creation of several committees in the United Kingdom that identified three categories of war crimes, discussed the role of superior orders in the commitment of such crimes, the capture and extradition of alleged war criminals, and the type of tribunal to try them.[15]

The Allies also did little to strengthen the investigative potential of the London-based UNWCC, which was politically weak, understaffed, and underfunded. Its only strength was its delegates from individual member states, who were able to provide accurate information about the war crimes being committed in Europe and Asia.[16] Such weaknesses were exacerbated by British qualms over the whole question of war crimes trials, particularly in light of the failure of the Leipzig and Turkish trials after World War I. This led to London's rejection of a Soviet proposal in November 1942 of a trial for "'major war criminals.'" A year later, Churchill sent Stalin and Roosevelt a proposal that became the basis for the Moscow Declaration of November 1, 1943. It left the impression that the European theater's major war criminals would be brought to justice and warned:

> Let those who have hitherto not imbued their hands with innocent blood beware lest they join the ranks of the guilty, for most assuredly the three Allied Powers will pursue

them to the uttermost ends of the earth and deliver them to the accusers in order that justice may be done.

The above declaration is without prejudice to the case of the major war criminals whose offences have no particular geographical location and who will be punished by a joint decision of the Governments of the Allies.[17]

The final paragraph made it clear that such decisions would be made jointly by the Big Three (the United States, the United Kingdom, and the Soviet Union).[18]

Churchill, Roosevelt, and Stalin met in Tehran three and a half weeks later, and while there was no official discussion of war crimes, Stalin did raise the question during a small dinner party. According to Churchill's account, Stalin stated that the whole "German General Staff... must be liquidated." The strength of Hitler's armed forces, he went on, "depended on these fifty thousand officers and technicians." If they were executed at the end of the war, "German military strength would be extirpated." Stunned by Stalin's comments, Churchill told the Soviet dictator that

the British Parliament and public will never tolerate mass executions. Even if in war passion they allowed them to begin, they would turn violently against those responsible after the first butchery had taken place. The Soviets must be under no delusion on this point.

Stalin replied that "fifty thousand must be shot." Churchill countered that:

I would rather be taken out into the garden here and now and be shot myself than sully my own and my country's honour by such infamy.

Roosevelt tried to lighten the mood by saying that they would only shoot 49,000 Germans. His son, Col. Elliott Roosevelt, echoed his father and said that he strongly approved of Stalin's suggestion. Angry, Churchill left the room, followed quickly by Stalin and Molotov, who laughingly assured him that "they were playing, and that nothing of a serious character had entered their heads."[19]

The British leader's qualms were shared by some in the Roosevelt administration. In preparation for a meeting in Quebec in September 1944 to discuss the occupation and reconstruction of a post-Nazi Germany, Supreme Headquarters Allied Expeditionary Force (SHAEF) prepared a handbook for the occupation of Germany. Hans Morgenthau, the secretary of the Treasury, was shocked when he read it because he feared it would quickly restore Germany to its "prewar estate."[20] Roosevelt agreed, arguing that:

The German people as a whole must have it driven home to them that the whole nation has been engaged in a careless conspiracy against the decencies of modern civilization.[21]

In the end, the SHAEF handbook was rewritten and excluded any reference to the economic rebuilding of Germany unless it affected the military occupation.[22]

Morgenthau then developed his own plan for Roosevelt and Churchill to discuss at Quebec. His *Suggested Post-Surrender Program for Germany* would have, if fully implemented, turned "post-war Germany into a primarily pastoral community" too weak to threaten Europe and the world.[23] It sent shockwaves throughout the Roosevelt administration and led to the resignation of Secretary of State

Cordell Hull. Churchill was also stunned when he learned of it in Quebec. He told Morgenthau that:

> I'm all for disarming Germany…but we ought not to prevent her living decently. There are bonds between the working classes of all countries, and the English people will not stand for the policy you are advocating. I agree with Burke [Edmund, 1775]. You cannot indict a whole nation. What is to be done should be done quickly. Kill the criminal, but don't carry on the business for years.[24]

Churchill preferred another approach, which became known in British circles as the "Napoleonic precedent." Discussed at the Quebec conference, it proposed that Germany's major war criminals "be disposed of by suicide or the action of the German people." If this did not pan out, it then suggested that those on a "previously prepared" British list " be executed on proof of identity and on the basis of a political decision."[25]

Morgenthau had already proposed the creation of a list of German war criminals in Appendix B of his plan. It would include easily recognizable "arch-criminals" who would "be apprehended" as soon as possible once the war ended. Once their identity was verified, they would be "put to death forthwith by firing squads made up of soldiers of the United Nations." Simultaneously, the Allies would set up military commissions to arrest and quickly try prisoners responsible for deaths in "violation of the rule of war, hostages killed in reprisal for the deaths of other persons, [and] the victim of death because of his nationality, race, color, creed or political conviction." Those convicted of such crimes were to be executed, though, in rare cases, mitigating circumstances could lead to lesser sentences.[26] Morgenthau's plan also specified that all members of the SS, the Gestapo, and "high officials" from the Reich's various police, security, and paramilitary organizations, the bureaucracy, the party as well as "leading public figures" with close ties to the Nazis should "be detained until the extent of the guilt of each individual is determined."[27]

It also suggested the registration of all males over age 14 to help determine whether they belonged to various Nazi organizations. Furthermore, membership in the SS, the Gestapo, and "similar groups" would "constitute the basis for inclusion into compulsory labor battalion[s] to serve outside Germany for reconstruction purposes." Morgenthau also discussed the dissolution of all Nazi organizations in Germany, the dismissal and disenfranchisement of members of such organizations, including *Junkers* and Wehrmacht officers. He also wanted to prohibit "any person resident in Germany from leaving or attempting to leave Germany" unless permitted by Allied occupation authorities. Any violation of this regulation would be considered "an offense triable by [the] Allied military commission and could result in the death penalty."[28] Though Roosevelt was able to get Churchill ultimately to accept the Morgenthau Plan, its effectiveness was reduced considerably when news about its details became public.

The war crimes issue came up again five weeks later during the meeting between Churchill and Stalin in Moscow. The British prime minister wrote Roosevelt afterward that,

> Major War Criminals. U. J. [Uncle Joe] took an unexpectedly ultrarespectable line. There must be no executions without trial otherwise they would say we are afraid of

them. I pointed out the difficulties in international law but he replied if there were no trials there must be no death sentences, but only life-long confinements. In face of this view from his quarter I do not wish to press the memo I gave you which you said you would have examined by the State Department. Kindly treat it as withdrawn.[29]

Roosevelt replied that he found the prime minister's note most "interesting" and said that the war crimes issue would be discussed further at the Yalta conference in February.[30]

To a large extent, Stalin's perspective was driven by the certainty of victory over the Germans and the success of Soviet military tribunals in bringing to justice German war criminals and Soviet collaborators. Stalin had initially broached the idea of some sort of international tribunal to try Germany's major war criminals in late 1942. However, it was not until the following year, when reports of the Katyn massacre became public, that Moscow began to press the ChGK to become more active in responding firmly to allegations that it was the Soviets, not the Germans, who were responsible for the Katyn massacres. [31]

The ChGK, which was created partially to give Soviet war crimes investigations a veneer of "international legitimacy," was also a tool of Kremlin propaganda.[32] The "éminence grise" behind all of this was Andrei Vyshinsky, Stalin's chief prosecutor during the show trials in the 1930s, and later the head of Moscow's Secret Commission for Directing the Nuremberg Trials.[33]

Once the ChGK was up and running, the Soviets launched a series of war crimes trials for collaborators in Krasnodar, Krasodon, and Maripol in the summer and fall of 1943. The legal basis for the trials was a Supreme Soviet decree of April 19, 1943, that called for the death penalty or long prison terms "for Axis personnel and their accomplices found guilty of crimes against civilians and POWs."[34] It did not define war crimes, instead referring to "'atrocities' or 'evil deeds (zverstva or zlodeianiia).'" The accused would be court-martialed while those sentenced to death were to be hanged quickly, and their bodies

> left on the gallows for several days so that everyone will be aware that [harsh] punishment will befall anyone who inflicts torture and carnage on the civilian population and betrays his Motherland.[35]

The most famous military "show" trials took place in Krasnodar from July 14 to 16, 1943. The court accused 11 Soviet citizens of collaboration with the Germans, though its subtexts were the German officers and "the leaders of the gangster Fascist Government of Germany and the German Command" who were responsible for

> torture and sadism, for the mass executions and massacres by the inhuman means of asphyxiation with toxic gases in specially equipped machines for the burning and other methods of exterminating of innocent Soviet citizens, including the old men, women, and children.[36]

The "innocent Soviet citizens," of course, were Jewish victims of Hitler's Final Solution.

Such crimes, Soviet prosecutors argued, were "an integral part of a total and unpremeditated plan basic to the whole fascist way of life." The Krasnodar court found all of the defendants guilty and sentenced them to death or long prison terms.[37] These trials set the stage for Stalin's growing insistence that the Allies use judicial means to bring German war criminals to justice, though his view of such trials was more propagandistic than legal. According to Francine Hirsch, what he sought at Nuremberg was "an exercise in education and enlightenment—a show trial extraordinaire."[38]

Consequently, in the weeks leading up to the Yalta Conference in February 1945, the Soviet press adopted an extremely aggressive tone when it came to German war criminals. Ilya Ehrenburg, one of Soviet Russia's most prominent writers and a member of the Jewish Anti-Fascist League, repeated the hate-filled attacks on all Germans that had first appeared in his 1942 poem—"Kill." He argued that the Soviets should use forced German labor to "restore devastated" territory, and "hang the criminals, spare the children."[39] At a reception hosted by Averell Harriman, the US ambassador to the Soviet Union on January 12, 1945, Ehrenburg asked one of the Western diplomats what he would do if he found a German standing beside a Christmas tree. A British general overheard Ehrenburg's question and responded—"Shoot him." The Soviet writer replied "'That is too good for him. You should hang him from the Christmas tree.'" But he went on to explain that he did not think such a harsh punishment should apply to any German under 16.[40]

Though the question of war criminals was not one of the major topics of discussion at Yalta, Churchill raised the issue and stated that he regretted his role in drafting the Moscow Declaration. He called this "an egg I have laid myself." He now insisted that the Allies "agree on a list of Nazi war criminals who would be shot upon capture and identification."[41] Stalin wanted to know if Rudolf Hess, Hitler's former vice chancellor now in prison in the United Kingdom, would be on the list. The Soviet leader, fearful that the British might use Hess "for separate peace talks with the Nazis," also asked if POWs could be tried for war crimes. Churchill responded that Germans who had violated the laws of war should "always be liable to be tried." He then asked Stalin if he was advocating a "judicial rather than a political act?" Stalin replied that this was what he was thinking.[42] Roosevelt added that "the procedure should not be too judicial," and thought that no journalists should be allowed in the courtroom.

The official communiqué and protocol released at the end of the Yalta conference underscored the Big Three's different views on war criminals, and stated that "all war criminals [would be brought] to justice and swift punishment." The protocol noted that "the question of the major war criminals should be the subject of enquiry by the three Foreign Secretaries for report in due course after the close of the conference."[43] Stalin followed this up with a new propaganda campaign about the trials of major war criminals. One propaganda poster depicted Hitler and other top Nazis behind bars with the caption:

> An inevitable date. War criminals. A realization of the unshakable decisions of the Allied conference in the Crimea. The din of battle is growing ever louder in Germany—the organizers of fascist crimes are approaching their end.[44]

For the next few months, the question of war crimes trials remained unsettled. Just before his death on April 20, President Roosevelt sent Judge Samuel Rosenman to London to discuss this question with the British and the French. Both seemed to still favor summary executions of major German war criminals, though on April 12, the British War Cabinet concluded that "for the principal Nazi leaders a full trial under judicial procedure was not out of the question."[45] All of this quickly changed after the deaths of President Roosevelt and the suicides of Hitler and Goebbels a week and a half later. The president's successor, Harry Truman, a lawyer, made it clear that he opposed summary executions and wanted a war crimes tribunal to try Nazi leaders. On May 3, the British War Cabinet voted, with some hesitancy, to support the American and Soviet positions on this question.[46]

By the time the war in Europe ended on May 8, there was considerable confusion in Washington about which government organization should be in charge of the war crimes trials. Roosevelt had already backed away from supporting the Morgenthau Plan, a decision he called "a boner."[47] This gave the upper hand to his secretary of war, Henry Stimson, who sent Hull and the president several memoranda in October and November 1944 advocating the creation of military tribunals under the office of the Judge Advocate General (JAG). These ideas were transformed into legally viable plans by Col. Murray C. Bernays, a member of the Army General Staff, whose memo of September 15, 1944, tried to find a legal basis for prosecuting prewar crimes and the tens of thousands of members of Nazi organizations responsible for war crimes. Bernays noted, for example, that the UNWCC considered prewar crimes outside its jurisdiction and acknowledged that the mistreatment of Jews and other groups before September 1, 1939, did not constitute war crimes. He also argued that summary executions could lead to the martyrdom of Nazi leaders like Hitler and contradict "the very principles for which the United Nations had taken up arms." He added that "'stream-lined trials were also problematic."[48]

The basic goals of the trials, Bernays went on, should be to reach judgments that "alleged high interests of state are not acceptable as justification for natural crimes of violence, terrorism, and the destruction of peaceful populations." Such trials would also underscore the dangers of "racism and totalitarianism," and force Germans to face their own national guilt as well as "their responsibility for the crimes committed by their government."[49] If the trials failed to achieve these objectives, he added, then "Germany will simply have lost another war," meaning that the "Fascist potential will thus remain undiminished in Germany and elsewhere, and its scope unimpaired."[50]

He recommended that an international court charge the Nazi government, the Nazi Party, and various state organizations such as the SS, the SA, and the Gestapo "with conspiracy to commit murder, terrorism, and the destruction of peaceful populations in violation of the laws of war."[51]

Evidence in such trials should be sufficient to prove both the "guilty intent (Nazi doctrine and policy) as well as criminal conduct (atrocious acts in violation of the laws of war)."[52] Individuals "representative of the defendant organizations" would be put on trial, while proof of guilt "would require no proof that the individuals affected participated in any overt act other than membership in the conspiracy."[53] This meant, he argued, that any member of the above organizations could be arrested, tried, and convicted by various United Nations national courts. An individual could also be held accountable for criminal acts other than conspiracy. This charge, he concluded, would include all crimes committed from the inception of the act of conspiracy itself.[54]

The charge of criminal conspiracy, an Anglo-American legal concept that involved two or more people engaged in "unlawful conduct," was not an accepted concept in European law, though Aron Trainin, a Soviet professor of criminal law, argued in his 1944 study, *The Criminal Responsibility of the Hitlerites*, for the use of the charge of "conspiracy" in war crimes indictments. He noted that Vyshinsky, who wrote the introduction to Trainin's work, had used this charge in his 1938 Moscow show trial.[55] Trainin's work was widely circulated among Allied jurists and cited by Bernays in a January 4, 1945, memo. Bernays noted Trainin's categorization of two types of international crimes, "interference with peaceful relations between nations" and "offences connected with war."[56] Yet even though Trainin represented the new, Western drift of Soviet law, he was first and foremost a creature of Vyshinsky, who answered to Molotov. Stalin admired Vyshinsky's role as procurator general during the Moscow show trials of 1937–1938, particularly his "eloquence [and] the accusatory tirades with which he literally paralyzed his victims in the dock."

Bernays' ideas met with some opposition from the State and Justice departments, particularly the idea of conspiracy and the use of a "treaty court." There were also problems with the UNWCC's proposal that aggressive war be prosecuted as a war crime. The JAG's office further complicated this discussion by arguing that there was no legal basis for prosecuting German war criminals for aggressive war because it was "not a crime under international law."[57] Similar concerns were voiced by the Justice department, which argued that Bernays' proposal was an attempt "to apply ex post facto law," particularly when it came to the charge of conspiracy.[58]

American attitudes changed after news that the Waffen SS had massacred 84 American soldiers at Malmedy on December 17, 1944, during the battle of the Bulge. The White House now voiced support for the "aggressive war" charge, which led Bernays to draft a new memo in mid-January 1945 that called for the prosecution of German leaders and their organizations for "joint participation in the formulation and execution of a broad criminal plan of aggressive warfare" as well as "a conspiracy to achieve domination of other nations and peoples by the foregoing unlawful means."[59]

After further tweaking, Bernays sent a final draft to President Roosevelt on January 22, 1945, with the signatures of the US adjutant general and the secretaries of State and War. Titled *Trial and Punishment of European War Criminals*, it suggested two possible approaches to dealing with German and Italian war criminals (Italian criminals were not in the initial draft)—"political disposition without any trial or hearings," or a "judicial method." If the president chose the latter approach, Bernays proposed the creation of an international court by a UN treaty or an "International Military Commission or Court" appointed "by the Supreme Military Authority in the field" to try the accused. He also suggested that "prime leaders" be "charged as principals for violations of the law of war." He then listed 15 specific types of war crimes liable for prosecution. His draft concluded by stating the "prime leaders" should be tried by an "international military court," while other Axis war criminals be tried by "national or military courts." They were to be "charged with war crimes, including conspiracies to commit war crimes, as defined and established by international law."[60]

On February 1, US secretary of state Joseph Grew responded to press criticism about internal administration conflicts over US war crimes policy, by stating that the government intended

> to punish Germany's leaders and their associates for their responsibility "for the whole broad criminal enterprise devised and executed with ruthless disregard of the very foundation of law and morality, including offenses wherever committed against the rules of war and against minority elements, Jewish and other groups and individuals."[61]

The British government, startled by Grew's statement, spent the next few months discussing the war crimes question, while an American effort in April to create a common American–British position on this issue fell prey to the shock of President Roosevelt's death.[62] This, coupled with the execution of Benito Mussolini on April 28, and the suicides of Hitler and Joseph Goebbels on April 30–May 1, 1945, prompted President Harry Truman to appoint Associate US Supreme Court Justice Robert H. Jackson as the US chief counsel to prepare and prosecute "the leaders of the European Axis powers" on charges of "atrocities and war crimes before an international military tribunal."[63]

What followed over the next few months—the creation of perhaps the most important war crimes tribunal in history—was nothing short of miraculous, particularly in light of the fact that there were no serious legal precedents for such an undertaking. Jackson addressed the strengths and weaknesses of this court—the International Military Tribunal (IMT), Nuremberg—soon after its proceedings ended in the fall of 1946 in a report to President Truman. Though the trial was meant to do

> constructive work for the peace of the world and for the better protection of persecuted peoples…many mistakes have been made and many inadequacies must be confessed. I am consoled by the fact that in proceedings of this novelty, errors and missteps may also be instructive to the future.[64]

The Nuremberg IMT Trial, 1945–1946

The fact, as Jackson noted, that "errors and missteps" took place had as much to do with the hasty creation of the original IMT tribunal and the trial itself as with the conflicting nature of the legal systems and wartime histories and experiences of the countries sitting in judgment of the various Nazi war criminals in the dock. Beyond that was the fact that what took place in Nuremberg from October 18, 1945 to October 1, 1946, was essentially a civilian criminal trial conducted under the auspices of a four-power military occupation force in Germany. It used some aspects of military procedural law that relied on the convening authority for appeals. There was also a marriage of military and civilian law in article 10 of the charter, which allowed cases under the criminal organization count to be tried later in "national, military, or occupation courts."[65]

But the overriding principle of this marriage of civilian and military law was the conduct of a fair trial.[66] Several weeks before his appointment, Justice Jackson delivered a speech before the American Society of International Law that laid out his views on this question.

> I have no purpose to enter into any controversy as to what shall be done with war criminals, either high or humble. If it is considered good policy for the future peace of the world, if it is believed that the example will outweigh the tendency to create among their own countrymen a myth of martyrdom, then let them be executed. But in that case let the decision to execute them be made as a military or political decision. We must not use the forms of judicial proceedings to carry out or rationalize previously unsettled political or military policy. Farcical judicial trials conducted by us will destroy confidence in the judicial process as quickly as those conducted by any other people. Of course, if good faith trials are sought, that is another matter...all experience teaches that there are certain things you cannot do under the guise of judicial trial. Courts try cases, but cases also try courts.
>
> You must put no man on trial before anything that is called a court, if you are not prepared to establish his personal guilt...But, further, you must put no man on trial if you are not willing to hear everything relevant that he has to say in his defense and to make it possible for him to obtain evidence from others...Any United Nations court that would try, say, Hitler or Goebbels, would face the same choice... *The ultimate principle is that you must put no man on trial under the forms of judicial proceedings if you are not willing to see him freed if not proven guilty. If you are determined to execute a man in any case, there is no occasion for a trial.*[67]

At the same time, the United States circulated several proposals about the creation and conduct of such trials at the United Nation's Conference on International Organizations in San Francisco. Though the conference made no formal decisions on the trials, the British, French, Soviet, and US governments (the Big Four) decided to deal judicially, not politically, with Germany's major war criminals, to return alleged war criminals to the countries where they had committed their crimes, to create an IMT to try such criminals, and to create a committee of the Big Four to lay the groundwork for the trials.[68]

Once Jackson officially assumed his new role, he laid out many of the basic guidelines he thought the court should follow in several reports to President Truman throughout the summer. While he supported the idea of a proper defense for the defendants, they should not be allowed to use the "obstructive and dilatory tactics" employed in American criminal trials. He also thought defendants should not be able to hide behind the defense of superior orders, particularly if one were a voluntary member of a "criminal or conspiratorial organization, such as the Gestapo or the S.S." The overall case, he added, should center around a "Nazi master plan," and not "individual barbarities and perversions." It also "must be factually authentic and constitute a well-documented history of what we are convinced was a grand, concerted pattern to incite and commit the aggressions and barbarities which have shocked the world." The key charge of the proceedings, he added, was that Nazi crimes must be considered within the context of the "crime of making unjustifiable war" or "launching an aggressive war."[69] This meant that only crimes committed after September 1, 1939, by the Nazis could be considered by the court.

Once the war ended in Europe on May 8, Jackson began to put together a legal team that tapped into the research and documentation-gathering skills of investigative teams in the United States and Europe. He soon discovered, though, that they had gathered little evidence linking alleged Nazi war criminals "with the crimes to be charged."[70] Consequently, he told President Truman on June 6 that he would have to go to London to begin work with members of the British prosecutorial team.[71] Jackson's staff, which included Bernays, worked closely with the UNWCC and newly appointed British attorney general Sir David Maxwell-Fyfe, who became the principal British representative to the four-power IMT discussions.[72]

Jackson had his first meeting in London with representatives from Britain, France, and the Soviet Union in late June to decide on the rules that would guide the proceedings. The top Soviet delegates, Gen. Ion N. Nikitchenko and Feodor Trainin, took an active part in the discussions, though they were less concerned about legal niceties than a "judicial spectacle...that would lay bare all of the evilness of the Nazi system by detailing in public the criminal career of its leading personages."[73] Though Jackson initially thought that it would be easy to reach an accord, he and the other delegates quickly discovered that this would not be the case. Only two of the delegates, Jackson and Maxwell-Fyfe, had official appointments as chief prosecutors, which hindered the discussions. There were also differences between the Anglo-American and continental legal traditions, particularly when it came to the presentation of evidence, conspiracy, and other issues. Uncertainty over the impact of British parliamentary elections on the British delegation also proved problematic.[74]

Though these interpretative differences never really threatened the talks, they did require considerable explanation and, particularly when it came to the Soviets, careful translation. The Russians, for example, struggled with terms like "prosecutor" and their role in issuing an indictment.[75] Jackson assured them that he was not advocating the adoption of an American system, but simply one that would allow trying those cases "in a reasonable length of time and without undue difficulties."[76] The Soviets also had problems with the idea of trying organizations, something Jackson explained was key to the heart of the US proposal—the idea of conspiracy. Nikitchenko said his delegation was most concerned about trying organizations before trying its individual members. He preferred the reverse.[77]

There were also differences about the location of the Allied Control Council, the supreme Allied occupation authority in Germany, and the IMT trial. The Soviets suggested Berlin, which was in their zone of occupation, while Jackson began to push for Nuremberg, which was in the American zone. He pointed out that Nuremberg had a Palace of Justice, which was still standing, and a prison just yards from the courtroom.[78] In the end, the fact that the Americans and the British had 18 of the 24 defendants in custody in their zones helped sway Nikitchenko to agree that the trial would be held in Nuremberg, though Berlin would remain the administrative center of the tribunal, where the court's first session would be held.[79]

By this time, Jackson had become increasingly frustrated with the Soviets and their continued concern over a number of issues, particularly article 6 of the American draft of the proposed IMT charter, which stated that "initiating aggressive war was a crime under international law."[80] The Soviets and the French submitted counter proposals that specifically referred to such crimes that took place "in the service of any of the European Axis Powers."[81] Jackson, of course, was quite sensitive to both countries' collaboration with the Germans during the war, Katyn, and the Soviet invasions of Poland and the Baltic states in 1939–1940. But he told the committee on July 25 that the principal goal of the trial was to show the world "that launching a war of aggression is a crime and that no political or economic situation can justify it." He added that

> It may become necessary to abandon the effort to try these people on that basis, but there are some things worse for me than failing to reach an agreement, and one of them is reaching an agreement which would stultify the position which the United States has taken throughout [regarding war as an international crime].[82]

The next day, he flew to Potsdam to discuss these questions with American officials preparing for talks between Truman, Churchill (after July 30, Clement Atlee), and Stalin. Secretary of State James F. Byrnes told Jackson to stand firm on the aggressive war question, but to do what he could to reach a compromise with the Russians as long as it did not "derogate from fundamental axioms of justice."[83] In the end, the conference's chairman, Maxwell-Fyfe, whose gifted leadership insured its success, was able to craft a number of compromises that proved "crude but…workable."[84]

Article 6 of the Potsdam Protocol of August 1, 1945, announced the results of the London discussions.

> The Three Governments have taken note of the discussions which have been proceeding in recent weeks in London between British, United States, Soviet and French representatives with a view to reaching agreement on the methods of trial of those major war criminals whose crimes under the Moscow Declaration of October, 1943 have no particular geographical localization. The Three Governments reaffirm their intention to bring these criminals to swift and sure justice. They hope that the negotiations in London will result in speedy agreement being reached for this purpose, and they regard it as a matter of great importance that the trial of these major criminals should begin at the earliest possible date. The first list of defendants will be published before 1st September.[85]

The London delegates met the following day, and over the next six days, the conference's drafting committee pieced together the Agreement and charter for the IMT, which was officially approved and signed on August 8, 1945.[86]

It stated that the object of the new accord was to set up a tribunal to try "major criminals of the European Axis," though its sole focus would be German war criminals. Each of the signatory states was to share investigative documentation, while the August 8 agreement would in no way prevent the "return of war criminals to the countries where they committed their crimes." The accompanying charter was meant to set out the "constitution, jurisdiction and functions of the International Military Tribunal."[87]

The IMT charter stated that the court would be made up of four members and four alternates appointed by the individual signatory powers. The four permanent judges would select one of their own as president to preside over the tribunal. The court's decisions would be decided by majority votes by the permanent judges. The court had the authority to try individuals or members of organizations for one of three crimes (crimes against peace, war crimes, and crimes against humanity) as well as a "common plan or conspiracy" to commit these crimes.[88] Article 6, sections a–c, defined each of these crimes.

> *Common Plan or Conspiracy:* Leaders, organizers, instigators and accomplices participating in the formulation or execution of a common plan or conspiracy to commit any of the foregoing crimes are responsible for all acts performed by any persons in execution of such plan.
>
> *Crimes against Peace:* namely, planning, preparation, initiation, or waging of war of aggression, or a war in violation of international treaties, agreements or assurances, or participation in a common plan or conspiracy for the accomplishment of any of the foregoing.
>
> *War Crimes:* namely, violations of the laws or customs of war. Such violations shall include, but not be limited to, murder, ill-treatment or deportation to slave labor or for any other purpose of civilian population of or in occupied territory, murder of or ill-treatment of prisoners of war or persons on the seas, killing of hostages, plunder of public or private property, wanton destruction of cities, towns or villages, or devastation not justified by military necessity;
>
> *Crimes against Humanity:* namely, murder, extermination, enslavement, deportation, and other inhumane acts committed against any civilian population, before or during the war; or persecution on political, racial or religious grounds in execution of or in connection with any crime within the jurisdiction of the Tribunal, whether or not in violation of domestic law of the country where perpetrated.[89]

The charter added that superior orders and being a head of state or "responsible officials in Government Departments" did not prevent one from being charged with any of the above crimes. The court also reserved the right to declare any organization criminal, meaning its members could be tried by "national, military or occupation courts." It also set up a Committee for the Investigation and Prosecution of Major War Criminals (CPC), which would be made up of chief prosecutors appointed by the four signatory powers. They would decide whom to indict and draw up the draft rules of procedure, which would then be sent to the tribunal for final approval. The chief prosecutors would oversee the collection of evidence and the examination of "all necessary witnesses," and employ special representatives to aid with this investigative process. The charter also guaranteed all of the defendants a fair trial including complete copies of all documents referred to in the indictment in his native language. Each defendant could have an attorney of his own choosing or defend himself. He could also present evidence in court that strengthened his case, and had the right to cross-examine prosecution witness.[90]

The tribunal enjoyed all of the normal functions and rights of traditional Western criminal courts. It was not bound by "technical rules of evidence," and reserved the right to review any evidence before it was presented in court to determine its relevance. The final portions of the charter discussed details about the course of the trial's proceedings, followed by articles on judgment and sentencing. The Control Council for Germany (CCG) reserved the right to review the sentences and, though it could reduce individual sentences, could not increase their severity. The CCG could also decide to bring new charges against a defendant if new evidence surfaced against him during the trial.[91]

Once the charter was signed, the chief prosecutors created subcommittees to identify prospective defendants and prepare cases against them. The British would be responsible for the cases involving aggressive war, while the French would handle the question of war crimes in Western Europe. The Soviets would cover German crimes in Eastern Europe and the Soviet Union, while the United States would deal with the question of a common plan and conspiracy. While the list of defendants was being prepared, Nikitchenko expressed concern that there were too few defendants of "notoriety" on it. Hitler's name, for example, had been removed after his death, though with the proviso that if found alive, he would be brought to justice. Regardless, on August 29, the chief prosecutors released the names of 24 defendants.[92]

Nuremberg IMT Trial Defendants

Martin Bormann (1900–1945). Headed Reich Chancellery. Tried *in absentia*. Counts 1, 3, 4. *Death.*

Karl Dönitz (1891–1980). Supreme Navy Commander. President of Germany, 1945. Counts 1–3. *10 years.*

Hans Frank (1900–1946). Governor General, General Government. Counts 1, 3, 4. *Death.*

Wilhelm Frick (1877–1946). Headed Interior Ministry. Reich Protector Bohemia and Moravia. Counts 1–4. *Death.*

Hans Fritsche (1900–1953). Headed radio division, Propaganda Ministry. Counts 1, 3, 4. *Acquitted.*

Walther Funk (1890–1960). Reich Economics Minister. Counts 1–4. *Life.*

Hermann Göring (1893–1946). Reich Marshal. Headed Luftwaffe, Four Year Plan. Counts 1–4. *Death.* Committed suicide before execution.

Rudolf Hess (1894–1987). Deputy Party leader. Head of Party Chancellery. Counts 1–4. *Life.*

Alfred Jodl (1890–1946). Chief of the Wehrmacht Command Staff. Counts 1–4. *Death.*

Ernst Kaltenbrunner (1903–1946). Headed RSHA, Security Police, SD. Counts 1, 3, 4. *Death.*

Wilhelm Keitel (1882–1946). Head of Wehrmacht High Command (OKW). Counts 1–4. *Death.*

Gustav Krupp (1870–1950). Military Economy Führer. Counts 1–4. *Not tried because of ill health.*

Robert Ley (1890–1945). Head of German Labor Front. Counts 1, 3, 4. *Committed suicide.*

Konstantin von Neurath (1873–1956). Foreign Minister till 1938. Counts 1–4. *15 years.*

Franz von Papen (1879–1969). Vice Chancellor. Ambassador to Austria, Turkey. Counts 1, 2. *Acquitted.*

Erich Raeder (1876–1960). Supreme Navy Commander to 1943. Counts 1–3. *Life.*

Joachim von Ribbentrop (1893–1946). Foreign Minister. Counts 1–4. *Death.*

Alfred Rosenberg (1893–1946). Head Party Foreign Office. Reichminister Ostland. Counts 1, 3, 4. *Death.*

Fritz Sauckel (1894–1946). Gen. Plenopotentiary for Labor Deployment. Counts 1–4. *Death.*

Hjalmar Schacht (1877–1970). Headed Reichsbank. Economics Minister. Plenipotentiary for War Economy. Counts 1, 2. *Acquitted.*

Baldur von Schirach (1907–1974). Youth Führer. *Gauleiter* and Reich Governor, Vienna. Counts 1, 4. *20 years.*

Arthur Seyss-Inquart (1892–1946). Reich Governor, Austria. Reich Commissioner, the Netherlands. Counts 1–4. *Death.*

Albert Speer (1905–1981). Reich Minister, Armaments and Munitions. Counts 1–4. *20 years.*

Julius Streicher (1885–1946). *Gauleiter* of Franconia. Editor, *Der Stürmer.* Counts 1, 4. *Death.*[93]

The indictments were read in Berlin on October 18, followed by the formal opening of the trial in Nuremberg on November 20. During the interim, Jackson threw himself into the trial's preparation and suggested that the CPC move from London to Nuremberg, where most of the evidence was being collected and studied. When the other prosecutorial teams balked, he moved ahead with these plans to move his prosecutorial team to Nuremberg, where the 24 defendants were now imprisoned.[94]

Discussions about the indictments were tense, particularly when it came to American insistence that the German General Staff (GGS) and High Command of the German Armed Forces (HCGAF) be included in the indictment. Jackson argued that they were "'as guilty as any organization of aggressive warfare, and it seems peculiar to convict others of aggressive warfare if they are innocent.'"[95] British and American prosecutors stated that together, both groups were made up of about 130 high-ranking officers who "held certain positions in the military hierarchy" from February 1938, when Hitler took full control of the Wehrmacht as supreme commander.[96] One of the interesting twists in the negotiations was the suggestion that the term "genocide" be included in the indictment.[97] This idea was prompted by Raphael Lemkin, a legal adviser to Jackson. Lemkin had coined and defined genocide in his *Axis Rule in Occupied Europe* (1944), and thought it better described the nature of some of the crimes committed by the Nazis. Though it was not adopted as one of the core charges, it was included in count 3 (War Aims), section a, to describe, in part, the "systematic genocide" of civilian populations.[98]

The "polygeneric" indictment that the chief prosecutors approved on October 4 was a complex, lengthy document with three appendices. The 24 defendants as well as the Reich Cabinet, the leadership corps of the Nazi Party, the SS, the SD, the Gestapo, the SA, and the GGS and the HCGAF were charged with one or more of four crimes explained in detail in the indictment. Appendix A outlined the various charges against each of the 24 defendants, while Appendix B discussed the crimes of the Nazi Party, the Nazi government, and the various military organizations. Appendix C dealt with the violation of various international accords by each of the defendants.[99]

After the indictments were read, the chief prosecutors agreed that all eight judges would be involved in every phase of the trial, though only the permanent judges would vote on the fate of the defendants and indicted organizations.

- Lord Justice Lawrence (UK), president
- Francis Biddle (US)
- Professor Henri Donnedieu de Vabres (France)
- Major General Nikitchenko (USSR)[100]

By the time the trial began on November 20 in Nuremberg, there were only 20 defendants in the dock, and each of them pleaded not guilty. Robert Ley had committed suicide a month earlier, and Gustav Krupp had been excused because of bad health. Bormann was tried *in absentia*, despite efforts by his attorney to have proceedings postponed until he was captured.[101]

The trial was held in courtroom 600 on the second floor of the annex in Nuremberg's Palace of Justice (*Justizpalast*). US Army engineers worked furiously to reconstruct what was an active German courtroom to fit the special needs of the tribunal. Yet even with its expansion, it remained a very small, uncomfortable space. Ten military policemen stood behind and beside the defendants, while film and sound crews were scattered throughout the courtroom. A small, separate booth was set up for the translators, while the press sat in a separate gallery at the rear of the courtroom. The army engineers also built a small gallery for visitors.[102]

Jackson opened the prosecutorial phase of the trial on November 21, and thanked the court for the privilege of "opening the first trial in history for crimes against the peace of the world," a responsibility he considered grave.[103] The crimes of the defendants, he added, were "so malignant and so devastating, that civilization cannot tolerate their being ignored because it cannot survive their being repeated."

> This inquest represents the practical effort of four of the most mighty of nations, with the support of seventeen more, to utilize International Law to meet the greatest menace of our times—aggressive war.

It was a trial that "the world has demanded" and, while admitting the tribunal's inequalities, he thought there was no other choice but to allow the victors to judge the vanquished. The alternative was to leave the defeated to judge themselves. "After the First World War, we learned the futility of the latter course."[104]

He then went into considerable detail about the evolution of Nazi ideology and the role that it played in the planning of aggressive war and its resulting crimes.[105]

> [The] ultimate step in avoiding periodic wars... is to make statesmen responsible to law... This trial is part of the great effort to make the peace more secure.

The defendants, he went on, represented "the darkest and most sinister forces in society—dictatorship and oppression, malevolence and passion, militarism and lawlessness... Their acts have bathed the world in blood and set civilization back a century... The real complaining part at your bar is civilization."[106] Civilization, he concluded,

> asks whether law is so laggard as to be utterly helpless to deal with crimes by criminals of this order of importance. It does not expect that you can make war impossible. It does expect that your judicial action will put the forces of International Law, its precepts, its prohibitions and, most of all, its sanctions, on the side of peace, so that men and women of good will in all countries may have "leave to live by no man's leave, underneath the law."[107]

Albert Speer later called Jackson's opening remarks "devastating."[108]

The trial began in earnest on November 26 when the United States began its case on aggressive war. This was followed by the British, who tackled crimes against peace, and later joined with the United States to do joint presentations against each defendant. In mid-January, the French began their case on war crimes and crimes against peace, followed three weeks later by the Soviets, who presented evidence about crimes against humanity in Eastern Europe and the Soviet Union. The prosecution finished its presentations on March 4, and four days later the defense began its cases, which lasted until July 25. The prosecution gave its closing arguments a few days later, followed by its monthlong case against the organizations. The defense followed suit on August 9, resting its cases on August 28.

Almost from the outset, there were problems caused by the prosecutions' failure to provide the defense with exact copies of all documents, including translations and briefs. Sir Lawrence constantly insisted the prosecution meet these essential legal standards, and ultimately ruled that these documents be translated into the tribunal's four official languages before being read into the court record.[109] From the outset, the German defense attorneys, chosen because they had no damaging ties to the Nazis, were at a disadvantage. They were understaffed and had little time to prepare an adequate defense, particularly in light of the large body of evidence constantly flowing into Nuremberg. On the other hand, Anglo-American ignorance of the continental legal system, the German language, and Nazi Germany's complex administrative and military system played into the hands of the defense. This, coupled with widespread American blunders during the early weeks of the trial caused one defense attorney to wonder: "If they keep it up it may be possible to get the Gestapo declared not guilty."[110] To their credit, the judges bent over backward to insure that the defense attorneys had adequate time to present their cases, which added to the length of the trial.

One of the challenges for the defense was not being aware of how much, if any, the testimony of prosecution witness might hurt their individual clients. Maj. Gen. Erwin Lahousen, who headed Abwehr's Section II (sabotage, subversion, and special duties) under Admiral Wilhelm Canaris from 1939 to 1943, was privy to Germany's war plans, key elements in the charges of conspiracy and waging aggressive war. Lahousen, who kept copious notes, gave particularly insightful testimony about a meeting between Keitel, Ribbentrop, and Canaris on September 12, 1939, during which they discussed the "extermination" of Poland's religious, political, and intellectual leaders. He also testified that Keitel ordered Canaris to initiate an uprising in Galicia that would result in the mass murder of Poles and Jews, an order Canaris never carried out.[111]

Lahousen also testified about a meeting he attended just after the Reich invaded the Soviet Union with Gen. Hermann Reinecke, who oversaw OKW's POW branch, and Heinrich Müller, the head of the Gestapo. Reinecke explained that this was not an ordinary war and that the Soviet soldier must be viewed as an "ideological enemy" of Germany. He reminded Müller of the Commissar Order, and ordered that all Soviet commissars as well as Soviet POWs who identified closely with Bolshevism should be shot. Lahousen went on to testify about the horrible conditions of Soviet POWs.[112] His testimony shocked the defendants and their lawyers, who were not told of his appearance until the last minute. Lahousen later wrote Jackson that this was one of the pitfalls of testifying for the prosecution. Such reactions, he warned, might prevent other witnesses from doing the same. The only way the defense could counter such testimony was to find ways to "bludgeon" it and lessen its impact on the judges.[113]

The American prosecutors followed this up with evidence to support the charge of conspiracy to commit crimes against humanity. They had already shown a graphic, Allied-made film on the Dachau, Buchenwald, and Bergen-Belsen concentration camps, which set the stage for some of the more gruesome testimony presented during the trial. Raeder thought the film was shown to lay the groundwork for a political verdict, while Speer said the images haunted him for the rest of his life.[114] The United States finished this phase of their case with an SS film that showed the mistreatment of Jews and a shrunken head of a Polish police officer. They also showed the court pieces of tattooed skin from Buchenwald.[115]

The principal thrust of this portion of the trial was to support the idea of intent or purpose in the commitment of a crime, which was key to proving conspiracy. From Jackson's perspective, the conspiracy charge was an integral part of all four charges. Unfortunately, the American team drew much of their evidence from a disorganized body of documents that occasionally had little bearing on some of their presentations. This ultimately led the bench to ask Jackson's prosecutors about the relevance of some of their evidence to the case at hand.[116]

The British did a much better job in their initial phase of the trial, and presented a much more coherent, succinct presentation on crimes against peace. It centered around German violations of various pre–World War II treaties between 1939 and 1941. Sir Hartley Shawcross, the chief British prosecutor, handled this phase of the British case, but chose not to bring up the Nazi-Soviet pact of 1939, particularly after Jackson had angered the Russians by alluding to it in his opening remarks. Instead, Shawcross focused on the role of individual German leaders and their role in making war.[117]

Once the British finished their case in December, the Americans resumed theirs on conspiracy, and then introduced the case against German organizations. The British followed suit in mid-January with presentations against some of the defendants. The British and the Americans worked closely together throughout the trial, sharing evidence and courtroom time on their interrelated cases. They also split the cases against the defendants without consulting the French or the Soviets because the latter had opposed the idea of collecting evidence for each defendant on counts 1 and 2. Jackson and Fyfe concluded that French and Soviet opposition would weaken the overall cases against many of the defendants, and hurt the real thrust of this phase of the trial. Consequently, they decided that the United States would handle the cases for Göring, Kaltenburnner, Rosenberg, Frick, Funk, Schacht, Schirach, Speer, and Fritsche, the British Hess, Ribbentrop, Streicher, Neurath, Papen, Jodl, Raeder, and Doenitz, the French Sauckel and Seyss-Inquart, and the Soviets Keitel and Frank. [118]

The presentations themselves were, for the most part, unimpressive, "carried out at random either when there was the odd hour to spare during the organizations case or when the prosecutor has his material ready."[119] The British presentations on conspiracy to commit aggressive war, for example, were interspersed with efforts to link Raeder and Doenitz to these crimes. Their efforts were handicapped by the fact that the "laws of naval warfare were notoriously vague, and dangerously open to conflicting interpretation" once fighting began.[120] The case against Doenitz focused on the U-boat war, while the case against Raeder was stronger despite defense efforts to use the *tu quoque* argument in which

> the accused attempts to justify their actions by pointing to the fact that the state, being inflicted with harm or the state making the accusation of wrongdoing is behaving in the same (possibly illegal) way as the accused state and its responsible leaders.[121]

From the defense's perspective, Germany and the United States practiced unlimited submarine warfare and engaged in the same protective measures for their ships.[122]

The cases against Doenitz and Raeder lasted only a few days, followed by the French presentation on war crimes in Western Europe later that month. The chief French prosecutor, Francis de Menthon, ably documented the horrors of the German conquest and occupation of Western Europe, which left "a legacy of poverty and hunger."[123] Other French prosecutors presented details about the horrors of the concentration camps, the use of forced labor, depopulation, and destruction of property, and the seizure of foodstuffs that created a "regime of slow starvation, leading to death."[124]

By this time, the judges were growing impatient by what many felt was an endless and, at times, disorganized body of presentations. Judge Birkett noted in his diary in late January that the French evidence was "a complete waste of valuable time. The case has been proved over and over again."[125] But, according to Telford Taylor, the French and the Soviets understood "more clearly than their British and American colleagues" the importance of creating "a trial record that would do full justice to their evidence of Nazi Crimes throughout the full reach of Festung Europa [Fortress Europe]."[126]

The Soviets, who had suffered the most during the war, certainly agreed with this approach, and their presentations would be the most stunning of the trial. The Soviet chief prosecutor, Gen. Roman A. Rudenko, opened the Russian case on February 8 to a packed courtroom. He provided ample evidence of German plans to initiate an extermination campaign throughout the Soviet Union, and cited statements by Goebbels, Göring, and Rosenberg to underscore what he called the "rapacious crimes of the war launched by Germany against the U.S.S.R."[127] But what shocked the court was his description of some of the camps liberated by the Soviets. The "Hitlerites" constructed

> special concentration camps where they kept tens of thousands of children, women who were unfit for work, and old men. The approaches to these camps were mined. No buildings or shelters of any kind existed within the areas of the camps, not even

any barracks, and the internees had to camp on the bare ground. The internees were
punished with death for the slightest attempt to infringe upon the established ruthless camp regulations. Many thousands of typhus patients were found in these camps.
The population forcibly brought there from the surrounding villages was systematically infected with this disease. [128]

He also discussed the German use of gas vans in their killing operations and introduced a report from Dr. August Becker, an RSHA gas van inspector, to his superiors
about how to operate a gas van's killing machinery.

> The procedure of poisoning by gas is not always carried out in a correct manner. So as
> to end the business as quickly as possible, the drivers always open the throttle wide. As
> a consequence of this measure the condemned die of asphyxiation rather than falling
> asleep as had been originally intended. As a result of my orders death follows more
> rapidly, if the lever is set correctly, and in addition, the condemned people drop off
> peacefully to sleep. Distorted faces and defecations, two symptoms which formerly
> had been noticed, were no longer observed.[129]

He added that while the court was now familiar with the names of Auschwitz
and Majdanek, which the Red Army had liberated, he also mentioned German
mass killings in Smolensk, Kiev, Novgorod, Kaunas, Riga, and other cities where
"hundreds of thousands of Soviet nationals, both civilian and military" were tortured to death by the Hitlerites."[130] He then went into details about the gassings in
Auschwitz, and the murder of Soviet POWs as part of the overall plot to exterminate
the Soviet people.[131] He also alluded to the German war against the Soviet intel-
ligentsia, and reminded the court that it was his country that "bore the main brunt"
against the Nazi war machine. He ended his presentation by saying that,

> In sacred memory of millions of innocent victims of the fascist terror, for the sake of
> the consolidation of peace throughout the world, for the sake of the future security
> of nations, we are presenting the defendants with a just and complete account which
> must be settled. This is an account on behalf of all mankind, an account backed by
> the will and the conscience of all freedom loving nations.
> May justice be done![132]

The high point of the Soviet case was the testimony of Fld. Mshl. Friedrich von
Paulus, who surrendered his Sixth Army at Stalingrad on February 2, 1943. Paulus,
who had been in Soviet custody ever since, had turned against Hitler after Stalingrad,
and made broadcasts on Soviet radio critical of the Nazi leadership. The defendants
were shocked by his appearance in court as a prosecution witness. Göring, in fact,
asked his attorney "if he knows that he is a traitor."[133] Rudenko questioned Paulus
on February 11–12, followed by cross-examinations by several defense attorneys.
The main thrust of Paulus' testimony dealt with preparations for the invasion of
the Soviet Union, and Hitler's goals once he had conquered Russia. At one point,
Rudenko asked Paulus who he considered "guilty of the criminal initiation of the war
against Soviet Russia?" When Paulus asked for clarification, Rudenko stated:

> Who of the defendants was an active participant in the initiation of a war of aggres-
> sion against the Soviet Union?

Paulus answered:

> Of the defendants, as far as I observed them, the top military advisers to Hitler. They are the Chief of the Supreme Command of the Armed Forces, Keitel; Chief of the Operations Branch, Jodl; and Göring, in his capacity as Reich Marshal, as Commander-in-Chief of the Air Forces and as Plenipotentiary for Armament Economy.[134]

Several defense attorneys countered this by asking Paulus if he was aware of the fact "that you belong to the circle of the defendants," and if he understood that the attack on the Soviet Union was a violation of international law. Paulus said that it was only a violation of the 1939 German–Soviet Pact. After a few questions from the judges, Paulus was returned to Soviet custody until he was released from prison in 1953; he settled in East Germany.[135]

On February 19, Chief Councillor of Justice L. N. Smirnov presented evidence about the mass killings at Auschwitz, Majdanek, Riga, Kaunus, Belorussia, Yugoslavia, and elsewhere. Though he only mentioned Jews once or twice, it was apparent to the court that most of the victims were Jews. He ended his presentation with a film *The Atrocities by the German Fascist Invaders of the U.S.S.R.*[136] Dr. Gustav Gilbert, one of the two psychiatrists at the nearby prison, later wrote that the film was

> even more terrible than the one presented by the Americans as it showed acres of corpses of Russian POW's murdered or left to starve in the fields where they had been captured; the torture instruments, mutilated bodies, guillotines and baskets of heads…the crematoria and gas chambers; the piles of clothes, the bales of women's hair at Auschwitz and Majdanek.[137]

A week later, Smirnov introduced a new film that was made up of photographs that dealt with the persecution of Jews. He explained that this should be coupled with earlier US evidence about the operations of *Einsatzgruppe* A in Belorussia, Estonia, Latvia, and the Baltic states. Much of what he presented was drawn from the detailed reports of *Einsatzgruppen* commanders, who sent them to Berlin. He also discussed the murder of Jews in Czechoslovakia and estimated that the Germans killed about 3,000,000 Jews in Poland.[138]

He then discussed the medical experiments in Auschwitz, particularly the sterilization of the Roma (Gypsies) and the involuntary "euthanasia" of the handicapped and mentally ill. One inmate, Severina Shmaglevskaya, a slave laborer, testified that children born in Auschwitz were immediately killed, and remembered an order that children from recently arrived transports "were to be thrown into the crematory ovens or the crematory ditches without previous asphyxiation with gas." Smirnov asked her if this meant they were "thrown into the ovens alive or were they killed by other means before they were burned?" The children, she responded, "were thrown in alive. Their cries could be heard all over the camp."[139] Smirnov followed this with a description of what he called the "secret centers for the extermination of people." One witness, Samuel Rajzman, discussed the process of mass murder at Treblinka, where the Germans murdered 874,000 Jews and several thousand Roma. Smirnov also presented evidence about another death camp, in Chełmno, where the

Germans murdered 147,000 Jews and 5,000 Roma before the Red Army liberated it on January 17, 1945.[140]

Smirnov also discussed the German persecution of Christians throughout Eastern Europe and the Soviet Union, which included the "sacrilegious desecration of churches, destruction of shrines connected with the patriotic feelings of the Russian people, and the murder of priests."[141] Such crimes, he concluded,

> brought shame upon themselves by their mockery of the religious feelings and faith of the people, by persecuting and murdering the priesthood of all religious creeds.[142]

For the most part, this was nothing but show, given Stalin's ongoing persecution of Christians, Jews, and others during his long years in power. He briefly reversed these policies during the war to rally the nation, but resuscitated them in 1944.[143]

The defense began its cases in early March. From the outset, the prosecution tried to do what they could to "curtail [the defenses' cases] as much as possible." The judges, though initially sympathetic to incessant defense requests for documents, lists of witnesses, and more time to prepare its cases, ultimately decided that while witnesses could first be questioned by their own counsel, and then by the prosecution, they would not be given the same rights when it came to prosecution witnesses. According to Taylor, this was done to hasten the pace of the trial.[144]

Over the next four and a half months, the court heard the cases of each of the defendants. The most important was Hermann Göring, since his case, at least from the prosecution's perspective, "was almost a microcosm of their entire indictment."[145] Though he fell out of favor after the Luftwaffe failed to destroy the Royal Air Force during the battle of Britain in 1940, Göring had been a key Nazi Party member well before Hitler took power in 1933. He had been in his first cabinet and was head of the Four Year Plan, which was created to prepare Germany for war. In fact, there were few major developments in Nazi Germany, at least until 1941, that did not involve Göring. He was even technically responsible for the "Jewish question," and signed the decree in late July 1941 that gave Reinhard Heydrich permission to begin planning the Final Solution. In the end, there was no one in the dock who had been so integral to the complex operations of the Nazi state.

Göring did little during his early days on the stand to help his case, and readily admitted his importance in the Nazi movement prior to 1933. He also did little to negate the prosecution's charge that he was actively involved in Germany's waging of aggressive war and the Luftwaffe's commitment of war crimes.[146] He continually reasserted his close ties to Hitler and at one point stated that "at best only the Führer and I could have conspired. There is definitely no question of the others."[147] He even admitted that he wished he had studied the 1899 and 1907 Hague conventions more thoroughly, but added that air warfare was not included in either of them. "Modern and total war," he went on, is fought "along three lines."

> The war of weapons on land, at sea, and in the air; economic war, which has become an integral part of every modern war; and third, propaganda war.

Modern warfare, he added, drew "everyone, even the child...into the experience of war through the introduction of air warfare."[148]

All this changed on March 18, when Jackson began his cross-examination of Göring, which some observers considered the low point of the trial. Maxwell-Fyfe noted in his memoirs that the

> sixth sense of the cross-examiner which subconsciously anticipates the working of a witness' mind was necessarily rusty. Moreover he [Jackson] had not the familiarity with European history and the workings of European governments which proximity and parliamentary experience produce. The result was that, although in fact the documents put by Jackson drove home Goering's complicity in conspiracy to make aggressive war on any who resisted the Nazi plans, Goering scored heavily in the verbal encounters; Jackson's prestige was sensibly lowered both at Nuremberg and in America, and Jackson himself had to appeal unsuccessfully to the Tribunal for assistance.[149]

Norman Birkett added that "the cross-examination had not proceeded more than ten minutes before it was seen that he [Göring] was the complete master of Mr. Justice Jackson." Fyfe later wrote that Birkett was too critical of Jackson, and that if the judges had intervened and forced Göring to answer the questions and not branch "off into monologues," Jackson would have regained control of the cross-examination.[150]

Biddle blamed part of Jackson's failure on his temper and the fact that he was "overburdened and tired." And instead of confronting Göring "eyeball to eyeball," the American prosecutor periodically appeared confused and looked at his notes when Göring responded to a question. This left the impression that Jackson "was not thoroughly prepared."[151] Biddle added afterward that a frustrated Jackson came to see him and John J. Parker, an alternate American judge at the tribunal, and asked why the bench was always ruling against him. He told them that it was best if he resigned his position and returned home. Biddle, who later praised Jackson's work at the tribunal as "thoughtful, lawyer like, and wise," convinced him to stay.[152]

Jackson began his cross-examination of Göring by asking him if he was "aware that you are the only living man who can expound to us the true purposes of the Nazi Party and the inner workings of its leadership." "Yes," Göring replied, "I am perfectly aware of that."[153] They then discussed the Leadership Principle (*Führerprinzip*), which Göring expounded on in some detail. Jackson even got the former air marshal to admit that the concentration camp system was initially created "to eliminate opposition." However, as time went on, Jackson became frustrated with Göring, whom the court allowed to respond freely to prosecution questions. At one point Jackson even asked him if he could simply "answer 'yes' or 'no?'"[154] Time and again, Jackson asked Sir Lawrence to require the defendant to answer the questions directly, and accused Göring of an

> arrogant and contemptuous attitude toward the Tribunal which is giving him the trial which he never gave a living soul, nor dead ones either.[155]

This question arose again when Otto Stahmer, Göring's attorney, began to ask his client questions that Jackson complained would lead to speeches and long-winded answers. In fact, Jackson argued, much of what was in the defense documents was Nazi propaganda. The judges, after admitting that they had given the defendant great leeway, added that they would not "allow any other defendants to go over the same ground in their evidence except insofar as it is necessary for their own defense."[156]

Jackson's frustration was compounded by the fact that Göring often lied or distorted the truth, something not noted by some trial observers. Unfortunately, Göring was quite aware that there was no one else in the courtroom with more detailed knowledge about the inner workings of the Nazi state.[157]

Jackson regained the upper hand when he changed the subject and began to ask Göring about the Jewish question. He was able to link him to numerous anti-Jewish laws that, after some hesitation, Göring admitted that he had signed as president of the Reichstag. But he balked when asked if he had signed the July 31, 1941, Final Solution decree. After being shown a copy of it, Göring acknowledged his signature and then, arrogant as ever, insisted on correcting what he called the court's mistranslation of it.[158]

Jackson then asked Göring about his role in implementing more harsh anti-Jewish policies after *Kristallnacht*, particularly his ruling afterward that

German Jewry as a whole shall, as a punishment for the abominable crimes [Gryzspan's murder of Ernst vom Rath in Paris], *et cetera*, make a contribution of 1,000,000,000 [$401 million] marks. That will work. The pigs will not commit a second murder so quickly. Incidentally, I would like to say again that I would not like to be a Jew in Germany.[159]

Jackson followed this up with questions about the theft of Jewish and non-Jewish art throughout Europe, and Göring's private collection of such art. Jackson also questioned him about his use of Soviet and French POWs in the armaments industry.[160]

Maxwell-Fyfe followed Jackson with questions about the Luftwaffe's executions of POWs.[161] Unfortunately, he was unable successfully to tie Göring specifically to several SS documents about these alleged crimes.[162] Rudenko's questions to the former air marshal were much more broad and led to exchanges that were more like a fight "with heavy clubs rather than rapiers."[163] Why? Because the Soviet prosecutor's questions were "harsh, assertive, and harassing... like a heavy armoured column."[164]

Rudenko was particularly interested in the air marshal's role in planning Operation Barbarossa. When Göring proved evasive, he showed him a document that provided details of a meeting with Hitler where the Führer laid out the specific territorial goals of the invasion.[165] Then Rudenko asked Göring if Germany's "war aims were aggressive?" Yes, he replied, "The one and only decisive war aim was to eliminate the danger which Russia represented to Germany." After questions about Göring's role as head of the Four Year Plan, which was charged with the "economic exploitation of all the occupied territories, as well as the realization of those plans," Rudenko asked if he used this authority to order that every resource possible be squeezed out of the conquered territories? "Yes," Göring answered, "so that the German nation may live."[166] And was he responsible, Rudenko went on, for "the deportation to forced labor of millions of citizens from the occupied territories?" "Yes," Göring admitted, "to the extent that I was informed." Finally, Rudenko wanted to know, was this "slavery?" "No," Göring replied, "they were forced laborers, not slaves."[167]

Rudenko returned to plans for the invasion of the Soviet Union and asked Göring if he was aware of the OKW's May 13, 1941 directive, which gave "German officers [the right] to shoot any persons suspected of a hostile attitude towards the Germans without bringing that person to court." Göring said he was unaware of such orders, which annoyed Rudenko. "How could you," he wanted to know, as the "second man in Germany...have been unaware of these things."[168] When Göring tried to sidestep the question, Sir Lawrence told him that he had to answer clearly whether he knew about such orders. Göring explained that he only knew of orders that came directly from Hitler or were issued himself. "Did the orders," Rudenko asked, "show that prior to the invasion of the Soviet Union, the German government and military had a prepared plan for exterminating the Soviet population?" "No," the former air marshal answered. All it showed was that "the struggle with the Soviet Union would be an extremely bitter one, and that it would be conducted according to other rules and there were no conventions." But, Rudenko told him, "these rules of warfare are well known to us." Finally, the Soviet prosecutor wanted to know if Göring knew about Himmler's plan to "exterminate" 30 million Slavs and the mass murder campaign of the *Einsatzgruppen* of "Soviet citizens?" "Nothing," Göring responded.[169]

Maxwell-Fyfe resumed his cross-examination of Göring on March 21, and concentrated principally on POWs and the campaign against partisans and civilians, particularly in Auschwitz and other death camps. How was it, Fyfe asked, that "a minister with your power in the Reich could remain ignorant that this was going on?" Himmler kept such operations "very secret," Göring explained, and even Hitler was not aware of "the extent of what was going on." But, Fyfe added, the murder of 10 million people (6 million Jews, 4 million non-Jews) was broadcast in the foreign press. So how could he not know? Göring questioned the figure of 10 million and added that he never read or listened to the foreign press or broadcasts. But, as head of the Four Year Plan, Fyfe went on, how could he not know of the vast collection of stolen gold, clothing, and other goods taken from the Jews and packed in storehouses in Auschwitz and Majdanek? The defendant explained that he was only responsible for the broad outlines of the economy, which "did not include the manufacture of mattresses from women's hair or the utilization of old shoes and clothing."[170]

Maxwell-Fyfe then introduced several documents that indicated that he and Hitler, for example, were well aware of the mass murder of Hungary's Jews. One was the minutes of a meeting between Göring and Admiral Horthy, Hungary's leader, Ribbentrop, Hinrich Lohse, the Reich Commissioner for the Ostland (Baltic states and part of Belorussia), and others on August 6, 1942. Horthy asked what he was to do with his Jews. Ribbentrop replied that they should either be "exterminated or taken to concentration camps." Lohse noted that "tens of thousands of Jews had already been disposed of" in the Ostland, with only "a few Jews left alive." How, Maxwell-Fyfe, wanted to know, could Göring claim that he or the Führer did not know of these mass murders in light of these and other documents presented as evidence in court? "I only knew of a policy of emigration, not liquidation of the Jews," Göring answered.[171]

Once the prosecution completed its questioning of Göring, the whole complexion of the trial changed, since the cases of defendants who followed him were, for the most part, far less dramatic. On the other hand, there were still moments of high drama and shocking testimony. After Göring, the cases were heard as they were listed in the indictment with the exception of those against Seyss-Inquart and von Papen. The prosecution chose this order because it felt that the evidence against Göring, Hess, and the other German defendants was sufficient to find each of them guilty of crimes that would result in the death penalty.[172]

What followed—the defense presentations for Ribbentrop, Keitel, Kaltenbrunner, Rosenberg, Frank, Frick, and Streicher—were, for the most part, vain legal efforts to defend war criminals in the face of an overwhelming body of evidence presented by the prosecution months earlier. What is often forgotten about the trial is the extremely close physical environment, and the impact that derisive comments by the defendants had on their fellow co-conspirators. This, coupled with the uncertainty of what defense witnesses would say on the stand, added to the tension in the dock. While one witness might be on the stand to testify for one defendant, what they said often affected the cases of others.[173]

This was certainly the case during Fld. Mshl. Wilhelm Keitel's defense testimony. He admitted, for example, that despite his earlier claim that he had little real power, that, by carrying out certain criminal, illegal orders, he was violating "existing international law" as well as one of the "basic principles" of his "professional soldier's code."[174] Keitel's lawyer, Dr. Otto Nelte, tried to counter this admission by calling Hans Lammers, the former head of the Reich Chancellery, to the stand. Lammers testified that Keitel had little to do with "political matters." On the other hand, his answers about the relationship between Frank and Himmler damaged the former, since, after all was said and done, Frank, though occasionally objecting to Himmler's Jewish policies, tried to "fulfill them."[175] And though Frank bragged that he knew "a great deal about the final solution of the Jewish question," Lammers testified that Frank told him that whenever he brought the matter up with Hitler and Himmler, they always assured him that this only dealt with the evacuation of Jews, not their mass murder.[176]

The Final Solution came up again during the defense's case for Ernst Kaltenbrunner, who headed the Reich Main Security Office (*Reichssicherheitshauptamt*; RSHA) and the security police (*Sicherheitsdienst*; SD) after the assassination of Reinhard Heydrich. Kaltenbrunner, like his predecessor, actively promoted the mass murder of Jews throughout Europe during the last three years of the war.[177] One of the prosecution's witnesses was Otto Ohlendorf, the head of *Einsatzgruppe D* in southern Russia, who was later tried and sentenced to death during the 1948 *Einsatzgruppen* trial in Nuremberg. After describing in detail the methods of death, particularly the use of gas vans, and the disposition of corpses, Dr. Ludwig Bubell, one of the attorneys for the SS and the SD, asked Ohlendorf who gave him his "orders for the liquidation of the Jews?" He got them from Bruno Streckenback, Himmler, and Heydrich, he answered.[178] And when Bubell asked if he had "any scruples in regard to the execution of these orders?" Ohlendorf replied "Yes, of course," because he found it "inconceivable that subordinate leaders should not carry out orders given by the leader of the state." He added that the legality of such orders was never questioned, and he and other subordinates had "sworn obedience to the people who had issued the orders." To refuse to obey such orders, Ohlendorf said, "could have been a court-martial with a corresponding sentence."[179] He concluded his testimony by stating that all of his equipment and men came from the RSHA.[180]

Rudolf Höss, the former commandant of Auschwitz and Treblinka, also testified during Kaltenbrunner's proceedings. He admitted that while he only met Kaltenbrunner once in 1944, he did receive execution orders from Kaltenbrunner, though most of them were signed by Himmler or Müller.[181] Höss added, when asked about the mass murders at Auschwitz and Treblinka during cross-examination, that "all mass executions by gassing took place under the direct order, supervision, and responsibility of RSHA. I received all orders for carrying out these mass executions from RSHA."[182]

Alfred Rosenberg, the Reich minister for the Occupied Eastern Territories (Baltic states, Belorussia, and Ukraine), was asked similar questions about his role in the Final Solution and the use of forced and slave labor. Rosenberg, who fancied himself as the Nazis' top "theoretician on race," denied that he had ever discussed the mass murder of Jews with anyone, despite the fact that he took part in early meetings on the subject in Berlin in July 1941 and later at the Wannsee Conference.[183] His attorney, Dr. Alfred Thoma, tried to depict his client as a proponent of peace who

> advocated respect for all races... advocated freedom of conscience and a sensible solution of the Jewish problem, even giving certain advantages to Jews. In particular, he called for equality and justice in this matter.[184]

On the other hand, Rosenberg did admit that Jews were murdered in the Occupied Eastern Territories and that he had used forced labor.[185] But he denied that he had ever talked to anyone about the "extermination of the Jews," even after he was shown a document that showed that he discussed such a concept with Hitler. [186]

The final cases of what Telford Taylor called "murderers' row"—Hans Frank, Wilhelm Frick, and Julius Streicher—were far less dramatic. Frank, once the Nazis' top lawyer, was the head of the General Government, Nazi Germany's "racial laboratory" and home to five of its six death camps. Frank openly admitted his guilt and said that he was determined "to reveal that responsibility... to the world as clearly as possible."[187] Was he, his lawyer asked, "guilty of having committed crimes in violation of international conventions or crimes against humanity?" That, Frank answered, was "a question that the Tribunal has got to decide."[188] But, he added, after being in court for five months, he had "full insight into all the horrible atrocities which have been committed." As a result, "I am possessed by a deep sense of guilt."[189] He added that he played a role "in the annihilation of the Jews," and though he never "installed an extermination camp for Jews, or promoted the existence of such camps," he was guilty of the crime.[190]

But it was not just damning testimony that affected the dynamics and outcome of the court proceedings. There was also the issue of the physical appearance, demeanor, and reactions of some of the defendants not only to some of the testimony but also to their whole attitude toward the proceedings. Though justice is theoretically blind, the overall demeanor and comport of each of the defendants seemed to play a role in the court's decisions, at least in the eyes of some of the trial's participants and observers. In a recent study of such factors in death penalty cases, Michael E. Antonio concluded that "how a defendant appears inside the courtroom significantly impacts the punishment decision reached by jurors in capital trials."[191]

This would certainly be the case when it came to the court's decisions about Julius Streicher and Albert Speer.

Streicher was the virulently anti-Semitic *Gauleiter* of Franconia, Reichstag member, and editor of the *Der Stürmer* (Stormer/Militant), a weekly newspaper which always displayed in bold letters at the bottom of the front page Heinrich von Treitschke's phrase "Die Juden sind unser Unglück! (The Jews Are Our Misfortune)."[192] Streicher had been put on the list of top war criminals by the British "to stand for the Party racists," despite the fact "that he had little to do with the formal implementation of genocide and had been forced from public office well before the Holocaust [Final Solution] was unleashed."[193] According to a report by the British Foreign Office, Streicher's presence in the dock "'would help to deal with the issue of anti-Jewish activities of the Nazis at an early stage and in a conclusive manner.'"[194]

Streicher was indicted for conspiracy in helping bring the Nazis to power and consolidating it once Hitler became chancellor. He was also charged under count 4 of crimes against humanity for his "incitement of the persecution of the Jews."[195] But the judges and prosecution knew that his case raised "the first and only serious questions of criminal guilt arising among the defendants on 'murderers' row."[196] According to Taylor, the problem with the case against Streicher was that it was brought "against a private newspaper owner and journalist to punish him for publishing statements in which he believed." Consequently, once the case ended, "neither direct nor cross-examination had resolved the difficulties of deciding Streicher's fate."[197] The reason was simple. According to Richard Overy, Streicher played almost no role in carrying out the genocide and could furnish no account of it.[198] Moreover, by 1940, he had fallen from power and lived in internal exile as a small farmer who had little to do with racial politics in the Reich.[199] Consequently, the prosecutors were so concerned about convicting him that they decided to focus principally on the incitement charge.[200]

In the end, Streicher's behavior, appearance, and testimony both in and out of court had as much to do with his conviction and death sentence as the evidence against him. He was intensely disliked by his fellow defendants because of his strange behavior and anti-Semitic outbursts.[201] His attorney, Dr. Hans Marx, even tried to withdraw from the case, a request Sir Lawrence turned down.[202] His testimony only underscored the fact that most in the courtroom found Streicher a disgusting individual. Justice Biddle later wrote that he was "mean and sullen with whom none of the other defendants would talk."[203] He added that Rebecca West saw Streicher "as pitiable, because it was plainly the community and not he who was guilty of his sins. He was a dirty old man of the sort that gives trouble in parks, and a sane Germany would have sent him to an asylum before long."[204] Another observer noted that "any juror would have convicted Streicher on sight."[205]

Though there was disagreement among the judges over the degree of his guilt, the strongest arguments against him centered around the idea that he was "an accessory before the fact and…a murderer" who was responsible for the deaths of 6 million Jews "even if the exact nature of his responsibility could not be pinned down." And there lay the crux of his conviction—could Streicher's words "be linked directly with others' deeds." One of the members of the American prosecution team later asked whether Streicher was convicted "strictly on the law," since he had never killed anyone, or "on the physical and moral revulsion he evoked?"[206] In the end, the judges seemed to embrace the ideas of an American judicial aide who argued that

> Streicher could not escape responsibility for the death of six million Jews even if the exact nature of his responsibility could not be pinned down. At the very least he had been "an aider and abetter". and could be compared (perhaps only by the Americans) to the cheerleader who "by his continual goading of the crowd to frenzied excitement...is a key personality in his team's success."[207]

The opposite could be said of Albert Speer, even though he oversaw a vast forced and slave labor network that resulted in the deaths of tens of thousands of Jews and others forced to work in inhuman conditions throughout the Reich. Unlike Streicher, Speer's demeanor throughout the trial was one of studied intelligence and sophistication. Justice Biddle considered him to be

> the most humane and decent of the defendants. His straightforwardness and honesty, his calm and remarkable bearing, his awareness of the moral issues involved, impressed the members of the Tribunal.[208]

Yet as Gitta Sereny and Don van der Vat have noted, Speer lied in court when he said that he knew nothing about the Final Solution until after the war. Sereny terms this Speer's *"Lebensfüge*, the Great Lie of his life."[209]

Speer played a key role in planning his defense, which centered around the careful selection and preparation of his witnesses as well as assuming "general responsibility" for the crimes of the Nazi state. This, coupled with Speer's plan to condemn the policies of the German government during the war was not only "cunning" but also a way "'to make the most favorable impression on the majority of the prosecutors and the judges.'"[210] The judges were also affected by the prosecution's weak case on the first two counts (Speer was charged on all four counts).[211]

In many ways, Speer's case was tied to that against Fritz Sauckel, who, as the Plenipotentiary General for the Allocation of Labor, supplied Speer with his vast pool of forced and slave labor. And even though Sauckel, like Speer, was charged on all four counts, the bulk of the case against the former centered around his role in putting together the vast labor forces needed to fuel the German wartime economy.[212] In the end, the evidence against Sauckel was so overwhelming that he was certain of a "very heavy sentence."[213]

Speer, on the other hand, depicted himself first and foremost as an architect thrust into the role of armaments minister. With carefully scripted questions, his attorney, Dr. Hans Fläschner, guided Speer's testimony along this path, which dealt in generalities when it came to sensitive or damning answers about the use of POWs and foreign laborers in that part of his client's vast industrial empire.[214] Speer, who admitted that he had 14 million workers under him, boasted that POWs, especially Russians, and concentration camp inmates who worked for him, were treated well in his factories.[215] He added that he disagreed with the violent methods used to round up foreign workers, arguing:

> I had no influence on the method by which workers were recruited. If the workers were being brought to Germany against their will that means, as I see it, that they

were obliged by law to work for Germany. Whether such laws were justified or not, that was a matter I did not check at the time. Beside, this was no concern of mine.[216]

Yet he admitted he was aware of the brutal conditions in some of the work and concentration camps in his factories.[217]

The turning point in the trial for Speer was his testimony about his efforts to thwart Hitler's scorched earth policy at the end of the war and plans to kill the *Führer* in early 1945. His attorney, Hans Flächsner, also brought up the fact that the July 20, 1944, assassins intended for Speer to become their provisional government's new armaments minister if they succeeded in killing Hitler. While Speer admitted that he played no role in this plot,[218] Flächsner wanted to know why he was "the only minister from the National Socialist regime...on the opposition list?" It was, he explained, because Speer was working closely with military leaders who were at the center of the plot.[219]

Fläschner then asked him to describe his own plot to kill Hitler in early 1945. Speer said he made this decision after he learned of Hitler's "scorched earth" policies that would entail "the ruthless destruction of all animate and inanimate property on the approach of the enemy."[220] His plan, which he admitted never got past the initial planning stage, was to put poison gas in the chancellery's air conditioning system.[221] Several decades later, Speer admitted in interviews with Gitta Sereny, that the plot was more fictitious than real.[222]

Jackson brought up none of this during his questioning of Speer, instead underscoring the criminal nature of Speer's operations.[223] Later in the trial, Jackson and his deputy, Thomas J. Dodd, sent the judges a memorandum that demanded that "Speer should receive the maximum penalty for his crimes."[224] In the end, though, the judges, who were seriously divided over whether to find him guilty on all counts, compromised, and found him guilty on counts 3 and 4, and sentenced him to 20 years in prison.[225]

Both Sauckel and Speer had their own special ties to Hitler and the Nazis. Sauckel told US interrogators before the trial that he had "been a convinced National Socialist since 1921 and agreed 100 percent with the program of Adolf Hitler," whom "I never doubted but obeyed his orders blindly."[226] Speer seemed to have had a father-son relationship with the *Führer*, something his defense team played down during the trial. Other defendants in the dock—Colonel Gen. Alfred Jodl and Arthur Seyss-Inquart—also had close ties to Hitler, and that worked against them during the trial. The prosecution considered Jodl, the head of the Wehrmacht's Command Office (*Führungsamt*), "the actual planner of the war and responsible in large measure for the strategy and conduct of operations."[227] Consequently, the prosecution was particularly interested in Jodl's role in issuing the June 6, 1941 Commissar Order, which decreed that the military was not "to show mercy or respect for international law towards [Soviet] political commissars." It added that commissars were to be executed immediately upon capture.[228]

The prosecutors were also interested in the October 18, 1942, Commando Order (CO; *Kommandobefehl*), which had been issued in response to Allied commando raids in German-occupied territory in Western Europe.[229] Signed by Jodl, it called such raids violations of the "International Convention of Geneva," since the commandos were under orders "to kill out-of-hand unarmed captives" who might "hinder them in successfully carrying out their aims." Consequently, Hitler ordered that

> all enemies on so-called commando missions in Europe or Africa, challenged by German troops, even if they are to all appearances soldiers in uniform or demolition troops, whether armed or unarmed, in battle or in flight, are to be slaughtered to the last man...Even if these individuals, when found, should apparently be prepared to give themselves up, no pardon is to be granted to them on principle.[230]

The *Führer* explained in a supplementary order, which Jodl also signed, that "sabotage troops...who have orders ruthlessly to remove any German soldiers or even natives who get in their way," assumed that if caught they would "theoretically fall under the provisions of the Geneva Convention."[231] Hitler added that this was "a misuse in the worst form of the Geneva agreements, especially since part of these elements are even criminals liberated from prisons, who can rehabilitate themselves through these activities."[232]

Jodl said the idea for the CO came up after the Wehrmacht learned that the British had "shackled" German POWs after the British landed on Dieppe in August 1942.[233] He admitted that he had serious "doubts about its legality,"[234] though his principal role in the matter was "distributing this order, or having it distributed, in accordance with express instructions."[235]

Throughout his testimony, Jodl made a point of his deep respect for international law, and noted that well before the war broke out, his staff was quite concerned "with the conception of international law."[236]

> Jodl explained that he recognized and valued international law with which I was well acquainted, as a prerequisite for the decent and humane conduct of war. Copies of the Hague Rules of Land Warfare and the Geneva Convention were always lying on my desk. I believe that my attitudes toward the Commissar Order, toward lynching, and toward the intention to repudiate the Geneva Convention—bluntly rejected by all Commanders-in-Chief and all branches of the Wehrmacht, and by the Foreign Office—I have proved that I tried, as far as it was possible for me, to observe international law.[237]

If this was the case, one British prosecutor asked, Why did he support the illegal invasion of Western Europe in the spring of 1940 and Hitler's terroristic orders prior to his invasion of the Soviet Union in the summer of 1941?[238] This had nothing to do with international law, Jodl argued, since this policy in the East was aimed at partisans, and "the principle of such warfare is an eye for an eye and a tooth for a tooth, and this is not even a German principle."[239]

Arthur Seyss-Inquart, Hans Frank's former deputy in the General Government and later the Reich Commissar in the Netherlands, was, like Jodl, a staunch Nazi who did everything he could to promote Nazi racial and other policies during his long years in office.[240] Though they indicted him on all four counts, the prosecution was never able to prove conclusively that Seyss-Inquart was guilty of conspiracy. On the other hand, the prosecutors found it easy to prove the other charges against him because, for the most part, he openly admitted his crimes.[241] He told the court that Jews were a physical and "spiritual" threat to Germany and Germans, which partly explained his harsh anti-Jewish policies in the Netherlands.[242] Estimates are that 98,000–120,000 Dutch Jews died during the Holocaust out of a prewar population of 140,000. This was the highest death toll in Western Europe.[243]

What followed were the defense presentations for Franz von Papen, Hans Fritsche, and Martin Bormann. The case against von Papen, a former chancellor who helped arrange Hitler's appointment as chancellor in early 1933, was weak because his later positions were a vice chancellorship and a posting as German ambassador to pre-1938 Austria and Turkey. The judges thought that his greatest "sin" was one "against political morality," something that was not considered a crime under the IMT charter. This, coupled with the fact there was not sufficient evidence to prove that he was involved in the "planning of aggressive war," led to his acquittal.[244]

The court also acquitted Hans Fritsche, the head of the propaganda ministry's news service, and later its radio division. The judges concluded that there was insufficient evidence to prove that his activities fell "within the definitions of the common plan to wage aggressive war as set forth in this judgement." They added that despite his anti-Semitism, there was insufficient evidence to prove that his broadcasts promoted the "persecution or extermination of Jews," or that "he took part in . . . originating or formulating propaganda campaigns."[245]

Martin Bormann, Hitler's secretary, and head of the Nazi Party organization, wielded vast influence over affairs of state and policy.[246] His lawyer, Friedrich Bergold, told the court that it was impossible to defend him because he was "not at our disposal."[247] He then presented evidence to prove that Bormann had died on May 1, 1945, a fact later substantiated in the early 1970s, when his skeleton was found in Berlin.[248]

After three weeks of defense summaries, the prosecutors presented closing arguments in late July. Tensions were high among the defendants when Jackson began his comments on July 26, in large part because they had just learned that a US military court in Dachau had found 73 members of the Waffen SS guilty of the massacre of over 300 American soldiers and 100 Belgian civilians during the battle of the Bulge. The military court sentenced 43 of the Dachau defendants to death. Jackson did little to ease the minds of those in the dock, and, toward the end of his two-hour presentation, addressed the common defense of most of those on trial— ignorance of what had been going on around them during the war.

> These men saw no evil, spoke none, and none was uttered in their presence. This claim might sound very plausible if made by one defendant. But when we put all their stories together, the impression that emerges of the Third Reich, which was to last a thousand years, is ludicrous . . .
>
> The defendants have been unanimous, when pressed, in shifting the blame on other men, sometimes on one and sometimes on another. But the names they have repeatedly picked are Hitler, Himmler, Heydrich, Goebbels, and Bormann. All of these are dead or missing. No matter how hard we have pressed the defendants on the stand, they have never pointed the finger at a living man as guilty. It is a temptation to ponder the wondrous workings of a fate which has left only the guilty dead and only the innocent alive. It is almost too remarkable.[249]

Sir Hartley Shawcross followed Jackson, and called the defendants "common murderers,"[250] whose crimes were "so frightful that the imagination staggers and reels back at their very contemplation."[251] Each of them were part of a "common plan" that resulted in the horrible crimes committed throughout Europe.[252] While random atrocities were commonplace in warfare, what took place in Europe went beyond the normal definitions of murder.[253] They were calculated acts of genocide, a term he used four times in his statement.[254] He spent a considerable amount of time discussing the Holocaust, the Final Solution, and the numerous ethnic victims of Germany's mass murder program,[255] and the roles played by each of the defendants in these crimes.[256] He concluded by calling all of them "mad scoundrels" for whom history and civilization demanded justice.[257] The defendants, who were angered by Jackson's remarks, were stunned by Shawcross' comments.[258]

Gen. Rudenko was the last to speak, and, like his fellow prosecutors, he dealt with the alleged crimes of each of the defendants. He criticized the defense for using witnesses who were under indictment for their own criminal actions, and underscored the principal crimes of the Nazi state—"enslavement and genocide."[259] Each of those in the dock, he argued, played a role in Hitler's efforts "to exterminate millions of human beings, to enslave mankind in order to achieve their criminal aim of world domination."[260] He concluded that,

> I consider all of the charges against the defendants as fully proven. And in the name of the sincere love of mankind which inspires the peoples who made the supreme sacrifice to save for the world freedom and culture, in memory of the millions of innocent human beings slaughtered by a gang of murder[ers] who are now before the court of civilized mankind, in the name of the happiness and the peaceful labor of future generations, I appeal to the Tribunal to sentence all the defendants without exception to the supreme penalty—death. Such a verdict will be greeted with satisfaction by all progressive mankind.[261]

What followed was the least dramatic part of the trial: the month-long case against the six indicted German military, state, and Nazi Party organizations. Early in the trial, Jackson explained the reason for trying these organizations—to segregate "the organized elements from the masses of Germans for separate treatment."[262] To "punish a few top leaders," he went on, "but to leave this web of organized bodies in the midst of a post-war society would be to foster the nucleus of a new Nazidom."[263] He added that "organizations with criminal ends are everywhere regarded as in the nature of criminal conspiracies, and their criminality is judged by application of conspiracy principles."[264] He also reminded the court of the last lines of article 6 of the IMT charter.

> Leaders, organizers and accomplices' participation in the formulation or execution of a common plan or conspiracy to commit any of the foregoing crimes [crimes against peace, war crimes, crimes against humanity] are responsible for all acts performed by any persons in execution of such plan.[265]

The "very essence of the crime of conspiracy," he argued,

> or membership in a criminal association is liability for acts one did not personally commit, but which his acts facilitated or abetted. The crime is to combine with others and to participate in the unlawful common effort, however, innocent the personal acts of the participants, considered by themselves.[266]

Ultimately, Jackson explained, the six indicted organizations were chosen because "collectively they were the ultimate repositories of all power in the Nazi regime; they were not only the most powerful, but the most vicious organizations in the regime; and they were organizations in which membership was voluntary."[267]

Jackson then described the complex system set up by the tribunal to identify potential defendants in the organization phase of the trial, and efforts to interview the tens of thousands of POWs who had responded to queries about their roles in the indicted organizations.[268] Soon after the war ended, notices were posted throughout Germany giving members of Nazi organizations the opportunity to present evidence defending their membership in such groups.[269] Special Allied commissions and defense counsel for the indicted organizations interviewed possible witnesses. Over 600 were brought to Nuremberg for further consultation, with a much smaller group selected as prosecution and defense witnesses.[270] The Allied commissions also received over 300,000 affidavits, most of them dealing with the case against Nazi political leaders (155,000) and the SS (136,213). Only 90 were selected for full translation, though the Allied commissions reserved the right to screen and review all of the witnesses and affidavits chosen by the defense, which raised serious questions about the fairness of this phase of the trial.[271]

The charges against each of the indicted groups and organizations were laid out in Appendix B of the indictment.

Reich Cabinet (*Die Reichsregierung*).

Members of "ordinary cabinet...*Ministerrat fuer die Reichsverteidigung* (Council of Ministers for the Defence of the Reich)...[and] Members of *der Geheimer Kabinettsrat* (Secret Cabinet Council)...Members of these groups possessed and exercised legislative, executive, administrative and political powers...of a very high order" and, in this capacity...were responsible "for the policies adopted and put into effect by the government." Indicted on all four counts.

Leadership Corps of the Nazi Party (*Das Korps der Politischen Leiter der Nationsozialistischen Deutschen Arbeiterparti*).

"Persons who were at any time...*Politischer Leiter* (Political leaders) of any grade or rank...The Nazi Party was...the central core of the common plan or conspiracy set for tin Count One..." As such, they also "joined in the common plan or conspiracy...set forth in Counts One, Two, Three and Four."

SS and SD (*Die Schutzstaffeln der Nationalsocialistschen Deutscher Arbeiter Partie* including *Die Sicherheitsdienst*).

The SS, "a repressive police force," in league with the SD, "served as the instrument for insuring the domination of Nazi ideology and protecting and extending the Nazi regime over Germany and occupied territories. Indicted on all four counts.

Gestapo (*Die Geheime Staatspolizei*).

"It acted to suppress and eliminate tendencies, groups and individuals deemed hostile or potentially hostile to the Nazi Party, its leaders, principles and objectives, and to repress resistance and potential resistance to German control in occupied territories." Indicted on all four counts.

SA (*Die Sturmabteilung der Nationalsozilaistischen Deutschen Arbeiter partei*).

This "vast private [Nazi] army" created "disorder" and terrorized and eliminated "political opponents." Once Hitler's "wars of aggression began," the SA "provided auxiliary police and security forces in occupied territories, guarded prisoner-of-war camps and concentration camps and supervised and controlled persons forced to labour in Germany and occupied territories." Indicted on all four counts.

German General Staff and High Command of the German Armed Forces [GSHC].

Individuals who made up this group were the commanders-in-chiefs of the navy, the army, and the air force, the chiefs of the general staffs of the army and the air force, the chief of the High Command of the Armed Forces, the Chief of the Operations Staff of the High Command of the Armed Forces and his deputy, and the commanders-in-chief in the field (*Oberbefehlshaber*) of the Wehrmacht, navy, army, and air force. These individuals as a group "had a major responsibility for the planning, preparation, initiation and waging of illegal wars." Indicted on all four counts.[272]

The prosecution's case against the Leadership Corps of the Nazi Party focused principally on trying more fully to link it to the broader conspiratorial goals of the Nazi leaders. In the end, all the prosecution was able to show was that it was different from "the quasi-military agencies in the Himmler complex."[273] This was followed by the case against the various "Himmler complex" groups—the SS, the SD, and the Gestapo. What complicated these cases was confusion over the interrelationship of the SS with various organizations such as the SD and the Gestapo that were part of Himmler's super police organization, the RSHA. The defense used this to its advantage, contending that the Gestapo, for example, was not "the most important instrument of power of the Hitler regime."[274] Rudolf Merkel, the attorney for the Gestapo, called it an ordinary police organization that, for the most part, carried out "quite normal police work."[275]

There was no such confusion when it came to the role of the SS. According to the prosecution it was

> the very essence of Nazism. For the SS was the elite group of the Party, composed of the most thorough-going adherents of the Nazi cause, pledged blind devotion to Nazi principles, and prepared to carry them out without any question and—at any cost—a group in which every ordinary value has been so subverted that its members can ask, "What is there unlawful about the things we have done?"[276]

According to US assistant counsel Maj. Warren Farr, it was a key element in the Nazi conspiracy to dominate Europe.[277] And once achieved, the SS played a key role in the "extermination" of the Jews.[278] He then detailed efforts by various SS organizations, including the Waffen SS, to achieve this goal.[279] He concluded that the SS "was a single enterprise—a unified organization" that was at the heart of the Nazi system of power and rule. Its death head units were involved in the running of concentration camps created initially to "terrorize their opponents," while its various paramilitary organizations were "professional combat organizations." The SS was a key element in the mass murder of the Jews, and at the center of

> the murder and ill-treatment of civilian populations in occupied territory, the murder and ill-treatment of prisoners of war, and the germanization of occupied territories.[280]

The defense tried to depict the SS as a complex organization "of independent units" with Himmler as the only unifying force. Moreover, only a small percentage of SS members, it claimed, were involved in war crimes and crimes against humanity.[281] The defense also argued that Himmler's empire was made up of many different organizations, meaning the prosecution and the indictment was placing crimes at the feet of the SS that it did not commit.[282] It also claimed that the "decisive error" in the indictment against the SS was that most of Himmler's "spheres of activity...are considered as activities of the SS."[283] In the end, the defense argued, SS power rested solely in the hands of one man—Heinrich Himmler—particularly when it came to its alleged crimes.[284] In reality, the defense concluded, the SS was primarily "a unit of farmers, mechanics, students, workers, and representatives of all the professions."[285]

Moreover, most members of the SS knew nothing about the atrocities committed in the concentration or death camps nor, for that matter, the actions of the *Einstazgruppen*,[286] since most SS members were "employed at the front" during the war.[287] The same held true for the biological experiments in various concentration and death camps.[288] Given all of this, the defense argued there should be some "limitation of responsibility," with a "line...drawn between moral and legal responsibility."[289]

Comparatively speaking, the case against the SS was much easier to prove than the one against the General Staff and the High Command, which took place several weeks earlier. Telford Taylor, who handled the bulk of the prosecution's case against this small group of German military leaders, had doubts about the legality of such an approach, particularly when it came to the applicability of article 9 of the charter and the definition of "group" as it applied to the GSHC.[290] The British opposed trying the Wehrmacht's command structure, but gave in to US insistence that it was essential to put these groups on trial to better explain war planning. Once the trial began, Taylor had a change of heart, but decided to follow through with the case so that it "did not appear to be an exoneration of German military leadership."[291]

The principal focus of the prosecution's case was the GSHC's involvement in the planning and waging of aggressive war and crimes against peace as well as its collaboration and support of Hitler's "essential Nazi objectives."[292] Both groups, Taylor argued, also "became wedded to a policy of terror," and actively planned and engaged in, separately and in league with the SS and the SD, the "commission of War Crimes."[293] Though we now know that the Wehrmacht played a "direct and massive" role in the "implementation of the Final Solution,"[294] this was far less evident at the end of the war. Yet one prosecution witness, former SS Lt. Gen. Erich von dem Bach-Zelewski, who was the Higher SS and police leader for central Russia in 1941–1942, and then chief of anti-partisan combat units, testified that the Wehrmacht played a significant role in the SS campaign against partisans. These indiscriminate actions, he added, resulted "in the unnecessary killing of large numbers of the civilian population,"[295] though there were no instructions or Wehrmacht orders about how to deal with partisans, particularly after their attacks on military units.[296] He also testified that the "Wehrmacht Command" was well aware of "the methods for fighting the partisan movement and for destroying the Jewish population."[297]

The defense relied heavily on the affidavits and testimony of Col. Gen. Walther von Brauchitsch, the commander-in-chief of the army from 1938 to 1941, Field

Marshal Erich von Manstein, a brilliant field commander during the invasion of Western Europe and the Soviet Union, and Fld. Mshl. Gerd von Runstedt, who headed various army groups on the western and eastern fronts during the war, for its portion of the case. Each of them countered some testimony in earlier affidavits that weakened the prosecution's claim that neither group was "one unified organization."[298]

Hans Laternser, the attorney for both groups, argued in his closing argument that the case was an example of victor's justice since the Allies were trying defeated generals, something usually done by national courts, not international ones.[299] Indicting the GSHC, he went on, was like the Roman Catholic church indicting the Jesuits, when in reality it meant to indict the College of Cardinals. In the end, Laternser concluded, it was wrong to consider a disparate group of high-ranking officers an organization.[300]

All that remained after the prosecution finished its case against the GSHC was the case against the Reich Cabinet. The principal difficulty in finding this organization guilty was that it had, for all practical purposes, ceased to exist in 1938.[301] The defense's principal argument, which seemed to sway the judges, was that,

> An organization can be declared criminal only if all the individual members conceived a common plan for an unlawful war, or if they joined in a war which gave rise to the crimes will by the planners, as stated in the Charter.[302]

This would require the court to explore the individual guilt of each member of the accused organization to avoid the indiscriminate verdict of guilt for individual members.[303] Egon Kubuschok, the Reich Cabinet's attorney, also argued that there had to be proof of

> a cohesive connection between the persons who are indicted as members of the Reich Cabinet. Only such a connection would justify any acts charged to the Reich Cabinet being considered as having been committed by the Cabinet as a whole.[304]

In the end, the tribunal agreed, noting that after 1937, the Reich Cabinet never "really acted as a group or organization," and that its membership was "so small that members could be conveniently tried in proper cases without resort to a declaration that the Cabinet of which they were members was criminal."[305]

The trial concluded with the prosecution's final arguments on August 28–30.[306] These remarks were anti-climatic, brief, and to-the-point. Maxwell-Fyfe focused on party leaders, the SA, and the SS, and essentially called most of the defense witnesses liars.

> On the face of it, the evidence which has been given by almost all the witnesses called before your Commissioners is untrue.[307]

He added:

> The evidence on all of them is the same. They are asked if they knew of the persecution and annihilation of the Jews, of the dreaded work of the Gestapo, of the atrocities

within the concentration camps, of the ill-treatment of slave labor, of the intention and preparation to wage aggressive war, of the murder of brave soldiers, sailors, and airmen. And they reply with "the everlasting No." You may be reminded of the words of a great Irishman: "falsehood has a perennial spring." (Edmund Burke, 1774)[308]

While admitting that the bulk of the SA's crimes took place between 1933 and 1934, Maxwell-Fyfe noted that the SS was involved in

almost every one of the crimes, great and small, of which you have now heard daily over the course of almost 10 months. It may all be summarized, even if understated, in the words of their leader, Himmler. I quote:

"I know there are some people in Germany who become sick when they see these black coats. We understand the reason and do not expect that we shall be loved by too many."[309]

Thomas J. Dodd added during his summary that finding the SS and the other organizations guilty would let "mankind... know that no crime will go unpunished because it was committed in the name of a political party or of a state... no criminals will avoid punishment because there are too many."[310]

Gen. Rudenko closed for the prosecution on August 30, and argued that the tribunal should find all six indicted organizations criminal because each of them were integral parts of Hitler's "bandit Government."[311] He asked the court to see its verdict as a condemnation of "the whole criminal system of German Fascism." Their decisions would be seen as "the Judgement of the Nations—severe but just." His hope, he ended, would be that this "judgement fall harshly on 'these Fascist hangmen.'"[312]

The following day, each of the defendants was allowed to make a statement. Göring told the court:

The only motive that guided me was my ardent love for my people, its happiness, its freedom, and its life. And for this I call on the Almighty and my German people to witness.[313]

Frank said that the German nation's "turning away from God" paved the way not only for its crimes but also its destruction.

I beg of our people not to continue in this direction, be it even a single step; because Hitler's road was the way without God, the way of turning from Christ and, in the last analysis, the way of political foolishness, the way of disaster, and the way of death.[314]

An unrepentant Streicher denied any role in the mass murder of Jews, arguing that he opposed the use of violence to settle the "Jewish problem."

Your Honors! Neither in my capacity as Gauleiter nor as political author have I committed a crime, and I therefore look forward to your judgment with a good conscience.[315]

Albert Speer totally avoided the question of innocence or guilt, instead talking about dictatorship and the "danger of being terrorized by technocracy."[316] He applauded German cultural achievements of the past, and said they would create new "cultural values" in the future.

> It is not the battles of war alone which shape the history of humanity, but also, in a higher sense, the cultural achievement which one day will become the common property of all humanity. A nation which believes in its future will never perish. May God protect Germany and the culture of the West.[317]

The last defendant to speak, Hans Fritsche, denied that any of his actions were criminal, and that the only connection between himself and Nazi Germany's true criminals was that "they merely misused me in a different way than they misused those who became their physical victims." With that, the president, Sir Geoffrey Lawrence adjourned the court until September 23, when the tribunal would announce its judgment. The judges later decided to delay the judgment until September 30.[318]

The justices had begun working on the judgment months earlier. President Lawrence asked Justice Birkett to write the historical sections, while Justice Biddle handled questions of law and the innocence or guilt of each of the defendants.[319] Though all eight judges were involved in the judgment's discussions, only the four permanent judges could vote on the fate of the indicted individuals and organizations. They were guided by article 4.c. of the IMT charter which stated that

> the Tribunal shall take decisions by a majority vote and in case the votes are evenly divided, the vote of the President shall be decisive: provided always that convictions and sentences shall only be imposed by affirmative votes of at least three members of the Tribunal.[320]

At a meeting on September 9, the judges, against Nikitchenko's wishes, agreed that a tie vote would result in an acquittal on a particular charge.[321] However, to their credit, the judges were well aware that they were what Biddle called "a jury as well as a court," and worked hard to reach consensus on each of their decisions.[322]

One of the principal stumbling blocks to such decisions were questions raised by de Vabres about the theory of conspiracy, something unknown in international law. He considered it an *ex post facto* idea that should be thrown out.[323] A compromise was finally reached that stated that "conspiracy must be 'clearly outlined in its criminal purpose' and not 'too far removed from the time of decision and action.'"[324] In addition, the judges decided to use November 5, 1937, the date when Hitler met with his top military commanders to discuss future aggressive plans, as the benchmark date for the charge of conspiracy to wage aggressive war.[325]

The judges also found ways to finesse embarrassing episodes like the Munich accord, the Soviet Union's two-year alliance with Germany, its invasion of Poland and the Baltic states, Katyn, and French collaboration.[326] This was extremely important, given the problems with the question of crimes against peace and the definition of aggression. Since they were never able to reach an agreement on the meaning of aggression, the judges decided to go into great detail about every dimension of the planning and execution of acts of aggression from November 5, 1937, to the end of the war.[327]

The judges also found it difficult to decide which of the indicted organizations were criminal. Biddle suggested dropping the criminal charges against all of them, since to pursue such charges was "to convict men without trial."[328] Instead, he suggested a formula that "restored the necessity of providing individual guilt," which the other judges accepted.[329] The judges expressed such reservations in the early part of the judgment on organizations:

> In effect, therefore, a member of an organization which the Tribunal has declared to be criminal may be subsequently convicted of the crime of membership and be punished for that crime by death. This is not to assume that international or military courts which will try these individuals will not exercise appropriate standards of justice. This is a far-reaching and novel procedure. Its application, unless properly safeguarded, many produce great injustice.[330]

They had far less difficulty dealing with the question of war crimes and crimes against humanity, given the large body of evidence on both charges. Once the judges had reached a uniform decision about the general "legal framework" for the first two counts, they were more comfortable dealing with the cases against each of the indicted individuals.[331] There was little disagreement about defendants like Göring, Ribbentrop, Keitel, Streicher, Jodl, and Rosenberg, who were all condemned to death.[332] On the other hand, von Neurath, who was also indicted on all four counts, received only a 15-year sentence because his policies in the Protectorate of Bohemia and Moravia were, comparatively speaking, far less deadly than those in other parts of Nazi-occupied Europe.[333]

The five other defendants ultimately sentenced to death—Kaltenbrunner, Frank, Frick, Sauckel, and Bormann (*in absentia*)—were not convicted on all counts, though their involvement in war crimes and crimes against humanity were sufficient, in the judges' minds, to sentence them to hanging.[334] There were, though, considerable differences about Speer, whom the British and French thought should be spared death because of his appearance in court and his alleged anti-Nazi activities during the latter part of the war. Biddle and Nikitchenko thought he deserved death, though the former finally agreed to a far lesser sentence.[335] Hess did not fare as well, and, like Walther Funk and Erich Raeder, was sentenced to life imprisonment. Admiral Doenitz ultimately got ten years because the judges could not agree on the specifics for convicting him, since, as the judgment noted,

> In actual circumstances of this case, the Tribunal is not prepared to hold Doenitz guilty for his conduct of submarine warfare against British armed merchant ships

It added that,

> the sentence of Doenitz is not assessed on the grounds of his breaches of the international law of submarine warfare.[336]

Three of the defendants—Schacht, von Papen, and Fritsche—were acquitted, though, like many of the other decisions, there was considerable disagreement between the judges about their fate. The British thought, for example, that Schacht should be acquitted, while Nikitchenko wanted no acquittals. In mitigation, it was pointed out that Schacht was 70 years old, had not been involved in the planning of aggressive war, and had been imprisoned after the July 20, 1944 assassination plot. The British also argued that Schacht was "a respectable man, a banker, not like those other ruffians."[337] This helped pave the way for a tie vote, which meant acquittal. The judges had no trouble acquitting Fritsche, whom de Vabres considered "the least guilty of all the defendants" in a three to one vote.[338] The vote on von Papen was split and he was, like Schacht, given an "acquittal by impasse."[339]

Each of the permanent judges read part of the 190-page judgment on September 30 and October 1. It began with an overview of the charter, the indictment, and a discussion about the evidence gathered during the trial. It also discussed in some detail the history of Nazi rule in Germany and the legal basis for the various charges. This was followed by the decisions on the indicted organizations, and, on October 1, the individual defendants. The judgment also included Nikitchenko's dissenting opinions on the acquittals of Schacht, von Papen, and Fritsche, as well as the decisions on Hess, the Reich Cabinet, and the GSHC.[340]

Each of the defendants found guilty had four days to file an appeal with the Allied Control Council. Speer and Kaltenbrunner refused to do so, while the lawyers for Göring, Frank, and Streicher filed appeals against the wishes of their clients. All of the petitions for clemency were turned down on October 11, and five days later those sentenced to death were hanged in the prison gymnasium. Göring escaped hanging by committing suicide just before he was to be led from his cell to face the hangman. Those who escaped death remained in the courthouse prison until July 18, 1947, when they were transferred to Spandau prison in Berlin. Over time, the prison was slowly emptied as the various Nuremberg defendants were freed after serving their sentences, some on early release. By the early 1980s, Hess remained the only prisoner there. Western and German efforts to convince the Soviets to release him on humanitarian grounds fell on deaf ears, and he remained the sole prisoner in Spandau until his death on August 17, 1987. Afterward, the prison was torn down to prevent it from becoming a neo-Nazi shrine.[341]

Conclusion

Though flawed, the Nuremberg IMT trial remains the most significant international criminal trial in history. While it certainly was a case of victor's justice, this does not invalidate its proceedings and efforts by the Americans, the British, the French, and the Soviets to try to conduct a trial that was reasonably fair. This determination, to at least try successfully to conduct a trial with a mixture of Anglo-American, Continental, and Soviet legal traditions, was no small undertaking or achievement, particularly in light of the onset of the Cold War. The IMT's groundbreaking proceedings established important legal precedents that are still cited by various international tribunals today. Equally important, the vast body of evidence and other documents gathered during the trial provided the basis not only for our own understanding of much of the war in Europe, but also for the basic crimes of the Holocaust and the Nazi Final Solution. This alone makes what took place in Nuremberg not only a precedent-setting legal undertaking, but also a major, transformative trial in history.

Chapter 7

The Tokyo IMT Trial

In the midst of the opening of the Nuremberg trial, plans were being made in Japan for what would become a much more immense legal undertaking in Tokyo—the International Military Tribunal for the Far East (IMTFE), or the Tokyo trial.[1] Far less is known about this trial than its German counterpart, and few scholars have studied its transcripts, which remained closeted in a handful of archives until the early 1970s, when R. John Pritchard began a 14-year editing project that resulted in the publication of a 124-volume set of the Tokyo trial records.

Though Germany faced certain defeat by early 1945, the Allies felt that the war against Japan would last for another year or two. This all changed with the US decision to drop atomic bombs on Hiroshima and Nagasaki on August 6 and 9, 1945. The Allies had always considered the European theater their most important front, and relied on the United States to deal principally with the war against Japan. Consequently, Allied warnings about responsibility for war crimes almost exclusively focused on the Germans. Initially, the Big Three said little about Japanese war crimes throughout Asia. On the other hand, Chiang Kai-shek's Nationalist government did everything possible to bring to the world's attention those crimes being committed by the Japanese throughout much of eastern and central China. Wunz King, the Chinese delegate to the Inter-Allied Commission on the Punishment of War Crimes (IACPWC), stated after the issuance of the Declaration of St. James in 1942 that his government embraced the ideals of this statement, and "intended to apply the same principles to the Japanese authorities in China when the time came."[2] The Allies later condemned Japanese aggression as a "violation of all the standards of international law which proscribed and condemned the use of force."[3] And on November 1, 1943, they warned that

those who have hitherto not imbued their hands with innocent blood beware lest they join the ranks of the guilty, for most assuredly, the Three Allied Powers will pursue them to the uttermost end of the earth and deliver them to their accusers in order that justice may be done.[4]

A month later, Churchill, Roosevelt, and Chiang Kai-shek issued the Cairo declaration, which warned the Japanese of future "military missions" designed "to bring unrelenting pressure against their brutal enemies by sea, air, and land." The "three Great Allies," it went on, were "fighting this war to restrain and *punish* the aggression of Japan."[5]

Up until this point, little had been done internationally to investigate Japanese war crimes in China. The only exception was Chiang Kai-shek's government, which had begun to collect evidence of such crimes as early as 1941, and later set up the *Kangzhan Sunshi Diaocha Weiyuanhui* (War Damage Investigation Committee) to collect such evidence.[6] In the spring of 1944, his government, in league with the UNWCC's new Far Eastern and Pacific Commission (FEPC), set up a special subcommission in Chongqing (Chungking), the temporary Chinese capital, to gather further evidence, which was then sent to the UNWCC in London.[7]

The Australians were also interested in crimes committed against their nationals, particularly POWs, and would play a leading key role throughout the war in investigating and providing the Allies with detailed evidence of Japanese war crimes. Sir William Webb, a prominent Australian jurist who would later become presiding judge at the Tokyo IMT trial, served on three Australian war crimes investigative commissions from 1943 to 1945. In early 1945, he presented the UNWCC with the results of two of these investigations. The UNWCC, however, was hesitant to publicize the results of these commissions for fear that the Japanese would retaliate against Allied POWs.[8]

Such fears did not prevent the Allies from warning the Japanese about their responsibility for such crimes. Soon after the United States and Great Britain learned of the Bataan death march in early 1944, both separately informed Tokyo that they would "not forget these acts" or "relent in its determination to mete out just punishment" for those responsible.[9] In May 1945, Charles DeGaulle, the head of France's new postwar government, issued a similar warning, followed by one from the United States through the Swiss embassy in Tokyo. But it was the Potsdam Declaration of July 26, 1945, that laid the basis for the decision to mete out "stern justice . . . to all [Japanese] war criminals, including those who have visited cruelties upon our prisoners." It warned Japan that the Allies were about "to strike the final blows" against Tokyo if it did not accept unconditional surrender.[10]

President Truman's decision to support this declaration was particularly driven by the knowledge that if Japan did not accept these terms, the Allied determination "to prosecute the war against Japan until she ceases to resist" was backed by more than just veiled threats.[11] But the Japanese, who somehow hoped that the Soviets would act as an intermediary in talks that would lead to less harsh surrender terms, responded to the Potsdam Declaration with a "mandate to *mokusatu* (kill it with silence)." This led to the decision to drop the first atomic bomb on Hiroshima on August 6, followed by Nagasaki three days later. At this point, against the advice of some in his government, Emperor Hirohito agreed to the Potsdam demands, which he announced to his stunned nation on August 15.[12]

On September 2, Japan signed the US-dictated Instrument of Surrender (IS) onboard the *U.S.S. Missouri* in Tokyo Bay. Gen. Douglas MacArthur, the recently appointed Supreme Commander for the Allied Powers (SCAP) in Asia, orchestrated the signing.[13] Afterward, he declared that he would do everything possible "to see that the Japanese people are liberated from this condition of slavery" as a prelude to what he hoped would lift Japan "from its present deplorable state into a position of dignity."

The pathway to such a transformation would be democracy, which he declared was "on the march globally."[14] One dimension of such a transformation would be to hold those responsible for Japan's "deplorable state" accountable for their crimes.

The IS ordered all Japanese forces to "surrender unconditionally" and obey "all proclamations, and orders and directives" issued by MacArthur as SCAP. It also required the emperor and Japan's new leaders "to carry out the provisions of the Potsdam Declaration."[15] The IS was prepared by the US State, War, and Navy Departments' Coordinating Committee (SWNCC), which was responsible for overseeing US policy toward Japan and other areas in the Pacific under US occupation. Six days after Hirohito accepted unconditional surrender terms, the United States invited Australia, Canada, China, France, the Netherlands, New Zealand, and the United Kingdom to join the Far Eastern Advisory Committee (FEAC) to help advise the United States about occupation policies in Japan. The Soviets refused to join because of the FEAC's advisory nature.[16]

In early September, SWNCC sent its *Initial Post-Surrender Policy for Japan* directive to MacArthur, which stated,

> Persons charged by the Supreme Commander or appropriate United Nations Agencies with being war criminals, including those charged with having visited cruelties upon United Nations prisoners or other nations, shall be arrested, tried and, if convicted, punished. Those wanted by another of the united nations for offenses against its nations shall, if not wanted for trial or as witnesses or otherwise by the Supreme Commander, be turned over to the custody of such other nation.[17]

It followed this up a month later with its *Directive on the Identification, Apprehension and Trial of Persons Suspected of War Crimes* (later retitled *Policy of the United States in Regard to the Apprehension and Punishment of War Criminals in the Far East*). It stated:

> Any such plan [for an international military tribunal for the Far East] should provide for the use of rules of procedure and the application of principles in accord with those adopted for use by the International Military Tribunal for Europe established by the Agreement executed 8th August 1945, except where change is necessitated by differing circumstances in the Far East.[18]

MacArthur was given the authority to "arrange the trial of major Japanese war criminals" but was to keep their arrest secret until they were in custody. The directive defined war crimes as crimes against peace, conspiracy as well as "orthodox war crimes," and crimes against humanity. The time frame for the commitment of such crimes was to begin with the Mukden Incident of September 18, 1931. MacArthur was also given sole authority

> to appoint special international military tribunals...[for trial]...of Far Eastern war criminals where the alleged offenders are appropriately to be tried in an international court; and to prescribe or approve rules of procedure for such tribunals.

However, he was not to create panels for crimes against peace and conspiracy to commit such crimes until he received final approval from the US Joint Chiefs of

Staff.[19] The United States was in the early stages of developing its war crimes and conspiracy cases against the Germans in Nuremberg, and it was hesitant to allow MacArthur to proceed with cases involving these particular charges until they learned more about Jackson's success with such charges in Germany. Finally, the directive ordered MacArthur to "take no action against the Emperor as a war criminal pending receipt of a special directive concerning his treatment."[20]

The US allies in the Pacific were not informed of this document until late October. In early November, the United States issued several new directives that allowed SCAP to arrest war criminals and plan trials for them. The second stated that while the US' allies had been approached about participation in an international trial against alleged Japanese war criminals, Washington planned to move ahead unilaterally if they chose not to take part in such a trial or sought to delay it.[21] On December 26, the foreign ministers of the United States, the United Kingdom, the USSR, and China agreed that MacArthur should oversee the occupation of Japan and the creation of a Far Eastern Commission (FEC) to succeed the FEAC, which now added representatives from the Soviet Union and the Philippines. The United States, the United Kingdom, the USSR, and China had veto power over all FEC decisions, while the FEC had the right to review SCAP's policies in Japan. On the other hand, MacArthur still had the right to issue his own "directives" or make decisions on all aspects of the occupation of Japan.[22]

Soon after he arrived in Japan, MacArthur proposed the trial of the Japanese cabinet of Prime Minister Hideki Tōjō for "causing the murder of nationals of a country with which their nation was still at peace in the attack on Pearl Harbor."[23] The White House rejected this idea, which prompted MacArthur to propose the trial of Gen. Tomoyuki Yamashita, a Japanese war hero who had commanded the Fourteenth Army Group in the Philippines during the last year of the war. After he invaded the Philippines in 1944, Yamashita's troops committed horrible atrocities against civilians and American POWs. MacArthur ordered him tried before a military commission of five army generals in Manila, none of whom had any legal training, for "violations of the laws of war."[24] Yamashita was formally charged with unlawful disregard and failure

> to discharge his duty as commander to control the operations of the members of his command, permitting them to commit brutal atrocities and other high crimes against people of the US and of its allies and dependents; particularly the Philippines; and he, General Tomoyuki Yamashita thereby violated the laws of war.[25]

This trial was unique because there "was no precedent in U.S. military law for this charge [now command responsibility or *respondent superior*] against" Yamashita, since he was not charged with giving orders to commit such crimes or even knew of them. His alleged criminality centered simply around the fact that he was in command when the crimes took place.[26]

For the most part, the results of the trial (October 29–December 7, 1945), which was hastily staged and concluded in a circus-like atmosphere in Manila (scene of some of the Fourteenth Army's worst atrocities), were a foregone conclusion. Robert Shaplen, a *Newsweek* reporter, wrote that almost every reporter covering the trial was convinced that the military "commission went into the courtroom the first day with the decision already in its collective pocket."[27] The fact that the generals chose to announce their guilty verdict on December 7, 1945, certainly one of the most horribly symbolic dates in American history, underscores the highly politicized nature of the Yamashita trial. Yamashita's attorneys quickly appealed the commission's death penalty decision to the US Supreme Court, which ruled against Yamashita on February 4, 1946. However, Associate Justices Wiley Rutledge and Frank Murphy wrote dissenting opinions that pointed out that the structure and haste of the trial robbed Yamashita of the most elemental rights of due process guaranteed by the Fifth Amendment of the US Constitution.[28]

A week later, they wrote similar dissenting opinions for the case of Gen. Masaharu Homma, the commander of the Fourteenth Army during the battle for Corregidor in 1942, who was also charged with command responsibility. The fall of Corregidor and the subsequent Bataan Death March deeply affected MacArthur, who later wrote that the "bitter memories and heartaches [of these losses and tragedies] will never leave me."[29] He had Homma, who had retired from the Japanese military in 1943, arrested in September 1945, and brought to Manila for trial, which opened on January 3, 1946. Homma admitted during the trial that he was "morally responsible" for the crimes committed by his troops but neither "knew about nor condoned them."[30] A new five-general military commission found him guilty on 48 counts of war crimes on February 11, 1946, and condemned him to death. The same day, the US Supreme Court denied his appeal, though Rutledge and Murphy again wrote dissenting opinions condemning this decision using arguments similar to those voiced in their Yamashita trial opinions.[31] MacArthur, as he had done in the Yamashita case, supported the commission's decision, and argued that "no trial could have been fairer than this one." Homma, he argued, "lacked the basic firmness of character and moral fortitude essential" to leading men in the field.[32] The night before his execution on April 3, Homma, who had always maintained an air of calm throughout the trial, said: "I am being executed for the Bataan incident. What I want to know is: Who is responsible for the burning of 150,000 innocent civilians at Hiroshima—MacArthur or Truman?"[33]

It is difficult to determine exactly what impact these decisions had on the development of the IMT Tokyo proceedings. By the time the trial opened on May 3, 1946, Yamashita and Homma were dead, though the uproar over their trials was just beginning. In the summer of 1946, several similar cases (Mariano Uyeki, Teodoro Cantos) were being considered by the US Supreme Court. Associate Justice Hugo Black told Col. Frederick B. Weiner, who was handling these cases, that he and other justices now had doubts about the "legal underpinning[s]" of the Yamashita and Homma cases. In fact, Black went on, if the cases now came before the court, he and at least three or four of the other justices would "vote against the rationale of the earlier decisions." Given growing doubts about the fairness of both trials, Secretary of War Robert Patterson ordered a disgruntled MacArthur to turn the Uyeki and Cantos cases over to the new Philippine government.[34]

This disillusionment with MacArthur's handling of these early trials seemingly affected many of the judges appointed to the Tokyo court, who chafed at MacArthur's attempts to inject himself into the operation of the tribunal. For the most part, MacArthur acted singularly in issuing the January 19, 1946, proclamation announcing the creation of the Tokyo IMT. He appointed the nine judges nominated by the Allies the following month (and then informed the FEC), and added judges from India and the Philippines in early April. The Nuremberg-modeled charter of April 26, 1946, as well as the accompanying "Rules of Procedure" were, for the most part, American documents with modest FEC revisions that invested great "nominal" authority in MacArthur.[35]

But such power was limited by the fact that this was an Allied tribunal made up of judges nominated by their respective governments, meaning that MacArthur could not select whom he wanted. The same was true of the selection of the tribunal's chief of counsel and president. He also had limited powers to review sentences since he had to consult with "the Allied Council for Japan and the Representatives in Japan of other Powers, members of the Far Eastern Commission" before making a final decision on the tribunal's findings. For months he tried to find a way to gain more authority over the court, including the suggestion that he be allowed to make an "inaugural speech" when the trial opened. Sir William Webb, the tribunal's president, along with other members of the court, rejected this idea. MacArthur then let it be known that he would give the "Court instructions upon the interpretation of the Charter from time to time as occasion might arise," since "he was the originator of the Charter and was entitled to interpret it." The IMT judges were appalled by this idea, and Webb wrote MacArthur in early March that he would resign if he in any way attempted to interfere with the operation of the court.[36]

This prompted a meeting between MacArthur and the judges. He told them that all this was a misunderstanding and that he had no intention of meddling in court affairs since he thought it important that the court be independent of his authority. Though he did occasionally try to get the court later to move things along, he never again tried to interfere in its deliberations. According to Yuma Totani, the Tokyo IMT trial "turned out to be one of the rare events in occupied Japan that retained little of MacArthur's personal imprint."[37] MacArthur totally glossed over this conflict in his memoirs, and stated that after January 19, 1946, he was "relieved of all responsibility having to do with the actual trial procedures" of the IMT. His only duties once the trial began was "to pass on the final judgements of the tribunal and enforce the sentences."[38]

But MacArthur did have an important role in deciding whether or not to try Emperor Hirohito for war crimes. The day after the United States bombed Nagasaki, the Japanese government sent the United States a cable via its embassies in Bern and Stockholm accepting unconditional surrender

> with the understanding that the said declaration does not comprise any demand which prejudices the prerogatives of His Majesty as a Sovereign Ruler.[39]

President Truman met with his cabinet the same day (Japan is 13 hours ahead of the United States) to discuss the Japanese proviso. They agreed to it since they regarded the emperor as "an invaluable military asset" who could be useful in helping maintaining stability in Japan once the US occupation began. The British also agreed to accept it as long it was tied to unconditional surrender. Australia's leaders, though, already miffed at being left out of the major decisions at Potsdam, felt it essential that the emperor admit his guilt for waging aggressive war and its accompanying atrocities at the moment of surrender. Canberra regarded his continued presence on the throne as a "great military *threat*," and argued that he should not be exempt from war crimes prosecution. On the other hand, while the Australian government felt that the Allies should depose the emperor, they thought the fate of the imperial system should be left to the Japanese people.[40]

The Americans and the British brushed aside some of Australia's arguments and told the Japanese that from the moment of surrender

> the authority of the Emperor and the Japanese Government to rule the state shall be subject to the Supreme Commander of the Allied powers who will take such steps as he deems proper to effectuate the surrender terms.

The emperor would be required "to authorize and ensure" his government's "signature of the surrender terms" and order all Japanese military forces to cease operations and surrender their arms, while his government would immediately have to release all POWs and civilian internees and transport them safely to Allied control.[41]

This lenient treatment of the emperor, who was not even required to appear onboard the *Missouri* on September 2, did not sit well with the American public. The question of the fate of the emperor had bedeviled American officials since 1943, when the State Department began to discuss the issue. As the debate raged, all those involved in it agreed that "the Emperor was clearly an important figurehead in the Japanese consciousness."[42] MacArthur, who recalls in his memoirs the almost universal call for the dissolution of the imperial system when he arrived in Japan in late August, added that he had already decided when he was appointed SCAP that he would implement his reforms of Japan "through the Emperor and the machinery of the imperial government."[43] Moreover, he was convinced that if the emperor was tried and hanged as a war criminal, guerilla war would probably break out, which would require "at least one million reinforcements should such action be taken."[44]

MacArthur was also concerned about any gesture, such as summoning the emperor for a meeting, that might make Hirohito a martyr in the eyes of the Japanese people. So he decided to wait until the emperor asked for a meeting with him. When they finally met at the emperor's request on September 27, Hirohito, at least according to MacArthur, accepted full responsibility "for every political and military decision made and action taken by my people in the conduct of the war."[45] He then explained that he was a constitutional monarch and, as such, must do what his ministers advised him, "even if I don't like it."[46] But John W. Dower, using the highly secretive minutes of the meeting prepared by Katsuzō Okumura, the emperor's household interpreter, says that "at best," this was "a creatively ornamented version of what actually was said," meaning the emperor never accepted responsibility for the war. All he probably expressed were regrets for the war, not full responsibility, since he was quite aware of international sentiment regarding his role as a war criminal.[47]

There is ample evidence, of course, to suggest that Hirohito, as the supreme political figure in Japan, was fully responsible for the war. Prince Fumimaro Konoe, Tōjō's predecessor, told one of his aides after he resigned as prime minister in October 1941,

> When I told the emperor that it would be a mistake to go to war, he would agree with me, but then he would listen to others and afterwards say that I shouldn't worry so

much. He was slightly in favour of war and later on became more war-inclined...As prime minister I had no authority over the army and could appeal [only] to the emperor. But the emperor became so much influenced by the military that I couldn't do anything about it.[48]

MacArthur, of course, refused to consider such evidence, but chose instead to recast the image of the emperor as "the First Gentleman of Japan in his own right."[49] In this context, his efforts dovetailed nicely with those of the imperial court, which was doing everything possible to prevent a trial of the emperor. This included trying to get several of the Tokyo IMT's defendants to accept full responsibility for the war.[50]

However, this did not end the debate about how to deal with the emperor. Ten days before MacArthur's first meeting with Hirohito, Senator Richard Russell of Georgia introduced a resolution in Congress calling for trying the emperor as a war criminal.[51] But MacArthur, strengthened by SWNCC's directive to take no actions against the emperor until further notice, was determined to follow his own instincts on this matter, even after the SWNCC ordered him in late October to begin secretly collecting evidence to determine Hirohito's role in the war and his "culpability" as a war criminal. The October 29 directive added that

Hirohito is not immune from arrest, trial and punishment as a war criminal. It may be assumed that when it appears that the occupation can proceed satisfactorily without him, the question of his trial will be raised. It may also be assumed that if such a proposal will serve a purpose, it may be raised by one or more of our allies.[52]

MacArthur, however, had no intention of overseeing the trial of the emperor, and refused to mount a serious investigation of the emperor's "culpability," or, for that matter, interrogate him.[53]

The Australian government, however, was adamant that the emperor be put on trial, and asked the UNWCC to adopt a formal statement naming Hirohito as a war criminal. On January 9, 1946, Canberra presented the commission with a detailed study of Japanese war crimes with a list of 62 major war criminals, including the emperor, whom the report accused of crimes against peace and crimes against humanity. The United States and Great Britain opposed Australia's efforts, and ultimately the matter was turned over to the FEC's highly ineffective Allied Council for Japan and SCAP's badly led International Prosecution Section (IPS).[54] The FEC finally decided to adopt the SWNCC's October 29 directive, which effectively ended any further Allied discussions about the matter. Consequently, the IPS dropped the idea of voting on a proposal about whether to include the emperor in the list of proposed defendants in the IMT trial.[55] In the end, this played directly into the hands of the United States, MacArthur, and Japan, who would do everything possible to protect the emperor from being prosecuted as a war criminal.

As the debate over the fate of the emperor waned, MacArthur moved ahead with plans for the trial, and issued the Charter and its Rules of Procedure on April 25–26, 1946. Though modeled on the Nuremberg IMT Charter, there were considerable differences between the two documents, in part because the United States wanted to avoid some of the problems that its prosecutors had faced in Germany. Though similar in length, the IMTFE charter consisted of 17 articles instead of Nuremberg's

30 articles. And it was broken down into five sections as opposed to Nuremberg's seven. The Tokyo tribunal did not have a specific "constitution" like its German counterpart. Instead, its constitution was laid out in articles 1–4. The tribunal's jurisdiction was discussed in articles 5–7 (Nuremberg 6–13), while the question of a fair trial was touched on in articles 9–10 (Nuremberg 16). The question of the "powers of the tribunal and conduct of the trial" was discussed in articles 11–15 (Nuremberg 17–25), while "judgement and sentence" were laid out in articles 16–17 (Nuremberg 26–30). The nine "Rules of Procedure" were somewhat compromised by article 9, which allowed the court to amend or change any of these rules to ensure "a fair and expeditious trial."[56]

The charter gave SCAP the power to appoint judges, the trial's president, and the general secretary, whose Secretariat would

> receive all documents addressed to the Tribunal, maintain the records of the Tribunal, provide necessary clerical serves to the Tribunal and its members, and perform such other duties as may be designated by the Tribunal.[57]

Diplomatically, of course, MacArthur still had to rely on nominations from the 11 countries chosen to provide judges for the court since, without their support, the trial could not have proceeded smoothly. He appointed Sir William F. Webb, the chief justice of the Supreme Court of Queensland, Australia, to the tribunal's presidency. MacArthur knew Webb from his time in Australia during the war, and was impressed by his experience with war crimes investigations. Unfortunately, Webb proved to be a controversial figure on the court. While he had no qualms standing up to MacArthur and stopping him from interfering with the trial, he was, at least according to the Dutch judge B. V. A. Röling, considered the "most subtle of the judges on the tribunal,"[58] a "very arrogant and dictatorial man."[59] Erima Northcroft, the New Zealand judge, agreed, calling Webb "brusque to the point of rudeness." By 1947, several judges had become so disillusioned with Webb that they considered resigning from the court because of his "lack of experience and ability."[60]

MacArthur also appointed the tribunal's chief of counsel and his 10 associate counsels from candidates nominated by the 11 countries participating in the trial. President Truman intervened and insisted that MacArthur appoint Joseph B. Keenan as chief of counsel. It became pretty clear once the trial began that Keenan was not up to the job. Members of his own American team as well as other nations' associate counsels complained constantly about his prolonged absences, penchant for publicity, lack of focus and organizational skills, and a drinking problem. Some even suggested his dismissal.[61]

Edward Behr argues, however, that this was never a possibility, because Truman wanted Keenan, who was close to Roosevelt and J. Edgar Hoover, the head of the FBI, "no longer [to] haunt the White House corridors."[62] Yet it would be a mistake to dismiss his importance to the trial. First of all, Keenan and his staff drew up the IMT Tokyo charter and also played a key role not only in ensuring that the emperor was protected from prosecution, but also from any implications of criminality throughout the trial.[63] Just prior to his departure for Tokyo, Keenan, who had initially supported the idea of prosecuting Hirohito, received a note from Truman telling him to "lay off Hirohito, and that meant laying off the whole Imperial

Household as well." Robert Donihi, a member of Keenan's staff, said that Keenan told him personally "not [to] attempt to interrogate any of them."[64] He told his staff that if anyone did not agree with this decision, then they "should 'by all means go home immediately.'"[65]

Yet, at times, Keenan seemed to undercut efforts to protect the emperor during the trial. During his cross-examination of Kōichi Kido, the Keeper of the Privy Seal and Hirohito's personal adviser, Keenan pressed him on the emperor's role in the attack on Pearl Harbor, a key element in the US prosecution's case. His questioning became so intense that Webb, who felt the emperor should be tried as a war criminal, intervened, reminding the chief counsel that "we are not trying the Emperor."[66] Keenan regained his footing during the defense phase of the case for Tōjō. When questioned by Sir William Webb, the court's president, about Hirohito's role during the war, the former prime minister admitted that no one in Japan had the power to oppose the emperor. Did this, Webb continued, mean that Hirohito could have stopped Japan's drift to war? Keenan quickly rose to the emperor's defense and got Tōjō to retract his statement.[67]

For the most part, though, Keenan was successful in protecting the emperor during the trial, though at considerable damage to the credibility of the tribunal. In a separate opinion written by Webb at the end of the trial, he argued:

> The Authority of the Emperor was proved beyond question when he ended the war. The outstanding part played by him in starting as well as ending it was the subject of evidence led by the Prosecution. But the Prosecution also made it clear that the Emperor would not be indicted. This immunity of the Emperor, as contrasted with the part he played in launching the war in the Pacific, is I think a matter which this Tribunal should take into consideration in imposing sentences.
>
> The Emperor's authority was required for war. If he did not want war he should have withheld his authority...The suggestion that the Emperor was bound to act on advice is contrary to the evidence. If he acted on advice it was because he was fit to do so. That did not limit his responsibility.[68]

The French judge, Henri Bernard, was even more forceful in his dissenting opinion, arguing that the failure to try Hirohito "nullified" the trial and made the accused mere "accomplices."[69]

Yet despite considerable concern about this issue before the trial began, the United States went to great lengths to recast Hirohito's image throughout the trial, a move that contrasted sharply with that of Hitler during the Nuremberg trial. The German dictator was described as the evil genius of the Nazi state, while Hirohito was protected by a former enemy that had suffered a great deal trying to bring imperial Japan to its knees. The United States, in league with the royal household, worked hard to ensure that the emperor was not only absolved of any responsibility for the war and its crimes, but also "turned into an almost saintly figure who did not even bear moral responsibility for the war." Yet there were those close to Hirohito that thought he should accept some responsibility for the war and its crimes. Kido advised his former master just after the war ended, for example, that he should accept responsibility for Japan's humiliating defeat, and apologize to the Japanese people for their suffering during the "war waged in his name." He also hoped that Hirohito would abdicate in the aftermath of such an apology, which never came.[70] His failure to do so and refusal to take any responsibility for the war set the tone for his nation's refusal to accept similar responsibilities, a failure that haunts Japan to this day. The decision not to prosecute Hirohito also made it much more difficult for the prosecution to prove the five conspiracy charges "without the constitutional leader to either anchor it or provide evidence against its de facto leaders."[71]

When it became readily apparent that Hirohito would not be indicted, Keenan's Executive Committee (EC), which was made up of Keenan, his associate prosecutors, and their staffs, moved ahead with the selection of defendants. They were guided by article 5 of the charter, which stated that the tribunal had the right to

> try and punish Far Eastern war criminals who as individuals or as members of organizations are charged with offenses which include Crimes against Peace.[72]

What made this process difficult, particularly given the fact that 36 of the 55 counts in the indictment dealt with crimes against peace, was the lack of focus and infighting among many of the Japanese political and military leaders during the long years of the war. The president of the EC, British associate prosecutor Sir Arthur Comyns-Carr, laid out the general outline of the trial in several memos to the other prosecutors. The predominant theme in each of the trial's ten phases was Japanese aggression throughout Asia and crimes associated with such aggression.[73] The principal goal of the trial, he noted, was to determine Japanese criminality for the planning and waging of such acts of aggression. He thought that the prosecution should be less concerned about developing cases against alleged war criminals than selecting a group of 15 or so defendants who were "representative of the responsibility of the various criminal acts or Incidents." He added that while the Japanese public generally supported the prosecution of such criminals, this could quickly change if there was a prolonged trial. Equally important, Comyns-Carr argued, was the fact that a trial in Japan would not enjoy the interest or prestige of the Nuremberg proceedings, and once the German trial was over,

> world interest, as distinct from the purely Japanese interest, in the whole subject of International Trials, will fall to a vanishing point.[74]

He also thought that whether one was or was not a major war criminal was a question "of degree." Defendants would be selected from a larger list of alleged Japanese war criminals. The prosecution would investigate everyone on this list, and then select a smaller number for trial. It was important, he went on, to have representatives from each phase of Japan's various acts of aggression, while those whose alleged guilt spread beyond a single phase of the trial would be given prosecutorial preference over those whose crimes took place during a single phase of the prosecution's case. Those selected for trial would be Japan's "principal leaders" who bore the "primary responsibility for the acts committed," and for whom the prosecution's case was "so strong as to render negligible the chances of acquittal." In the end, at least theoretically, those selected for prosecution would be members of the highest organs of state and war, including the emperor's Imperial Conference and Privy Council.[75]

Though Keenan supported Comyns-Carr's plan, many on his team questioned using organizational or institutional ties to select what were now being termed "Class A" war criminals (those whose crimes were principally those against peace) as opposed to those selected because evidence pointed to their individual criminality.[76] Keenan responded by suggesting that there might have to be more trials for those not included in the first group of defendants. But he reminded his staff that he, Truman, and MacArthur thought the trial's principal goal was to

> establish as a matter of law, as a matter of tradition, and as a matter of fact that those individuals of a Nation who cause the Nation to break the peace of the world in violation of treaties are committing a crime which puts them in the category of Class-A criminals, whose infringement upon the rules of civilization have brought a world war.[77]

Using this criteria, that the principal crimes of the Class A war criminals were crimes against peace, the EC began to winnow down the list of 100 Class A Japanese wartime leaders incarcerated at Sugamo prison in Tokyo. In the end, it chose to indict 28 for trial. The United States, which now had responsibility for the remaining Class A suspects, released 15 of them over the next year. The rest remained under investigation, though a year after the IMT trial began, MacArthur asked the War Department what to do with them, reminding Washington that lengthy incarceration was a violation of "any accepted concept of justice."[78]

Keenan, whom MacArthur blamed for this problem, finally decided in August 1947 to hold a second Class A trial, much to the chagrin of the Allied prosecutors, who argued that they were overwhelmed with the current IMT proceedings. Several months later, the IPS stated that 19 of the detainees were eligible for trial, and argued that the rest should be released. In the midst of all of this, Keenan changed his mind, and decided that such a trial would be repetitive. He suggested that the legal section of the US occupation forces take responsibility for the remaining detainees and try them as Class B/C war criminals (those accused of crimes other than crimes against peace).There was also talk of a Pearl Harbor trial and several individual trials. In the end, though, these plans were dropped when Kenneth C. Royall, secretary of the army, told MacArthur that he wanted all US trials in the Pacific over by August 31, 1948. Ultimately, a number of Class A war criminals were set free, which put additional importance on the Tokyo proceedings.[79]

The indictment, which was written principally by Comyns-Carr, was broken down into three categories—crimes against peace (counts 1–36), murder (counts 37–52), and conventional war crimes and crimes against humanity (counts 53–55). Comyns-Carr later explained that the prosecution decided to include murder because

> it was felt to be simpler and better that those who initiate aggressive wars should be recognized as ordinary murderers as well as being in a special criminal category of their own.

He also argued that

> if this view of their conduct is accepted it removes any possible doubt as to the charge being *ex post facto* or based upon a legislative act of the victorious Powers [since]

murder is defined in the long-established law of all civilized countries as the intentional killing (including orders to kill) of a human being without lawful justification or excuse.[80]

Behind the scenes, MacArthur pushed hard for the murder charges, which he considered an important response to the Japanese attack on Pearl Harbor. Initially, the United States had been interested in trying Tōjō and his cabinet not only for "conspiracy to wage aggressive war," but also for killing US nationals at Pearl Harbor "without declaration of war." It finally decided to drop this approach because it might slow down the proceedings. The direct murder charges seemed to be a way to achieve the same end more quickly.[81]

In the end, the tribunal rejected many of the counts (18–26, 39–53) because they were "stated obscurely" or were redundant. This, in turn, was linked to problems associated with the widespread Japanese destruction of incriminating documents in the two-and-a-half-week interim between the acceptance of unconditional surrender and the signing of the peace accord on September 2, 1945. Estimates are that the Japanese destroyed 70 percent of the army's records during this brief period, which severely affected the prosecution's efforts to "prepare their war crimes cases." This, coupled with the fact that Keenan preferred his staff to interrogate war crimes suspects and witnesses instead of searching for incriminating documents, further weakened the prosecution's strategy throughout the trial.[82]

The prosecution's overarching plan during the trial was to argue that war crimes and crimes against humanity were so widespread throughout Japanese-occupied Asia that one could draw only one conclusion—"those in leadership circles must have authorized the commission of war crimes as a general policy of the Japanese war and military occupation."[83] Australia's associate prosecutor, Alan Mansfield, argued during the trial that

> this similarity of treatment throughout the territories occupied by the Japanese forces will lead to the conclusion that such mistreatment was the result not of the independent acts of the individual Japanese Commanders and soldiers, but of the general policy of the Japanese forces and of the Japanese Government.[84]

Keenan said as much in his statement opening the prosecution's case on June 4, 1946.

> Mr. President, I have no inflammatory purpose in reminding this Tribunal that there was much bloodshed of the flower of our youth at Nanking, at Pearl Harbor, at Hong Kong, in Malaya, at Guadalcanal, at Iwo Jima, at Okinawa, on the Island of Luzon in the Philippines, and in other parts of the world. There was the unloosening of cruel and inhuman forces in China and in other parts of Asia. It was all part of one grand pattern, and the vice of it consisted in the exhibition of utter contempt for the lives of blameless and helpless individuals all over the world.[85]

The 55-count indictment included 5 appendices that laid out the various aspects of each of the counts. The most extensive were appendices A, B, and C, which dealt with Japanese military and economic aggression throughout Asia from January 1, 1928, to the end of the war. These documents also dealt with the military's gradual takeover of the government and transformation of public opinion to prepare the nation for war, Japanese-German-Italian collaboration, the violation of numerous international treaties, and Japanese violations of various assurances of nonbelligerency to various countries.[86]

Appendix D dealt with conventional war crimes and crimes against humanity, emphasizing Japanese violations of earlier international accords relating to such crimes. Appendix E was a "Statement of Individual Responsibility for Crimes Set Out in the Indictment," and listed 14 specific dates in which one or more of the defendants was present at "conferences and cabinet meetings" from June 25 to December 1, 1941. Each one, it claimed, used "the power and prestige of the position which he held and his personal influence" in such a way that "he promoted and carried out the offences set out in each Count of this Indictment in which his name appears." It then went on to name each defendant and provided details about his specific role in the Japanese government and military from 1928 to 1945, with numbers used to identify the specific conferences and cabinet meetings he attended as a co-conspirator in the lead up to the "unlawful war" that broke out on "7th/8th December 1941."[87]

The defense immediately criticized the badly translated indictment for its failure to cite specific facts or particulars to document the different counts in the indictment. One of the American defense attorneys, Capt. Samuel Kleiman, argued that he wanted more specific details about when and how his client, Baron Kiichirō Hiranuma, was involved in the alleged conspiracy. Webb turned down his objection, arguing that such matters had to be dealt with in a broad manner.[88]

The trial, which formally began with the prosecutions' filing of the indictment on April 29, took place in the auditorium of Japan's prestigious Imperial Army Officers School in Tokyo's Ichigaya district. MacArthur ordered the Japanese government to completely renovate the future trial site, outfitting it with air conditioning and seats for 500 spectators.[89] Years later, Dutch judge B. V. A. Röling wrote that the Tokyo trial was

> like a huge-scale theatrical production. I didn't see that at the time, and I didn't see that there were more "Hollywoodesque" things around than there should have been. It was a big trial, that's true, and it was staged in a very ceremonial way, in a big courtroom, with very large audiences.[90]

In January 1947, the War Department told Maj. Gen. Myron C. Cramer, who replaced John P. Higgins as the US judge on the Tokyo tribunal in July, that it initially expected the trial to be over by Christmas 1946.[91] Instead, it lasted until November 12, 1948. And though it bore some resemblance to the Nuremberg trial, particularly when it came to the dominance of Anglo-American legal traditions, there were also differences.

> The Tokyo trial was a military court, and the procedural rules were based on American military commissions set up for the trial of aliens and reviewed in *Ex Parte Quirin* in 1942 [US Supreme Court decision that upheld the right of US military commissions to try German saboteurs]. These commissions applied a summary procedure that denied the accused the advantages of Anglo-American evidential and procedural rules; this simple non-technical approach was adopted in the London Charter and then carried over to Tokyo. Its rules of procedure governed.[92]

This meant, for example, that the Tokyo trial suspects were interrogated for hours without counsel. Tōjō, the central figure in the trial, was interrogated for 124 hours without a lawyer present. About 20 hours of this material was later used in the trial against him. And when the accused were finally allowed to select a lawyer, they were handicapped not only by considerable language barriers but also by the fact that Japanese lawyers were trained in European legal traditions and not Anglo-American adversarial traditions. Fortunately, the court soon realized the seriousness of this problem, and, with MacArthur's approval, asked for an American lawyer for each of the defendants. Unfortunately, the Japanese and American lawyers disagreed over how to defend their clients. The former wanted to prove the legality of Japan's actions from 1931 to 1945, while the American lawyers preferred an individual defense for each of their cases that would "ensure acquittal at trial or on review." The court looked askance at defense efforts it considered "technical and obstructive to the greatest degree." The end result was considerable "abuse...by the bench."[93]

The tribunal's judges were

- Sir William Flood Webb (Australia)
- Edward Stuart McDougall (Canada)
- Ju-Ao Mei (China)
- Henri Bernard (France)
- Delfin Jaranilla (Philippines)
- Bernard V. A. Röllins (The Netherlands)
- Erima Harvey Northcroft (New Zealand)
- Maj. Gen. Ivan M. Zaryanov (USSR)
- Lord Patrick (United Kingdom)
- Radhabinod Pal (India)
- J. P. Higgins/Maj. Gen. Myron C. Cramer (United States)

For the most part, they were trained as criminal lawyers, though few knew much about international law or, for that matter, had experience with military commissions. Six of the eleven were trained in Anglo-American law, which would have a considerable impact on the trial. There were no alternate judges, which meant that when a judge was absent, there was no alternate from his country present in court.[94]

All of this was further complicated by the same problem that haunted the defense at Nuremberg—adequate time to prepare a defense. This, coupled with lack of translators, basic secretarial and stenographic staff, and space meant that defense lawyers were constantly asking for delays and adjournments, which prolonged the trial and annoyed the judges. This ultimately raised serious questions about the "fair trial criteria under international law."[95]

The language problem was particularly significant and remained so throughout the trial.[96] Though English and Japanese were the official languages of the trial, all documents had to be translated into four other languages to accommodate the judges, witnesses, and others. But it was the translation of documents into English or Japanese that most plagued the proceedings, and ultimately resulted in the creation of a Language Arbitration Board (LAB) to deal with this issue. This was one of the reasons the trial took so long. Once the LAB became operational, each witness, lawyer, or judge had to stop his or her comments at the end of each sentence to await translation into English or Japanese. According to one of the prosecution staff, this meant that "when witnesses were being examined, the speed of the trial was reduced to one-fifth of its normal pace."[97]

The defense was also crippled by the fact that few of the defendants' Japanese attorneys spoke English or were familiar with Anglo-American legal principles. The result was, at least according to Röling, a certain "clumsiness" during the trial's early stages. This led the Japanese government to request help from the United States. MacArthur quickly responded and asked the Judge Advocate General (JAG) to provide him with 25 American lawyers "of suitable experience and qualifications to ensure the Japanese defendants proper representation and adequate defense."[98] Yet squabbles between the judges and MacArthur over this issue meant that once the trial began, there were only eight American military lawyers on the defense team. Ultimately, as the trial proceeded, more US military and civilian lawyers arrived to serve as co-counsels for the defendants.

> The Americans assigned to the Defence made a huge difference in the quality of legal representation which the Defendants received and earned the lawyers huge respect in Tokyo. Twelve of these lawyers were granted the unique honour of being the only foreigners ever admitted to practice at the Bar of Japan and several of them remained and did very well for themselves there throughout the remainder of their professional careers.[99]

Consequently,

> the Defence did better than anyone truly expected and the Defence interpretation at Tokyo was more trustworthy than that of the Prosecution on the more hotly contested issues that came before the Court.[100]

The greatest challenge for the prosecution was to prove that there was a core group of long-standing leaders involved in a "grand conspiracy...to expand Japan's empire through force." This approach "reflected a prosecutorial theory of total responsibility for all harm attaching to those who conspire to start illegal wars."[101] Consequently, though there was ample testimony about numerous atrocities, war crimes, and crimes against humanity, even rape, they were all filtered through the conspiratorial aggressive war theme, and did not play the role in the Tokyo trial that they did at Nuremberg. To prove this key point, the prosecution used a lot of "circumstantial evidence," while the defense countered with an equally insignificant body of "irrelevant material" that prolonged the trial. In the end, the judges and the lawyers were, to a very large degree, "victims of the material and temporal scope of the Charter."[102]

Tokyo IMT Trial Defendants

General Sadao Araki (1877–1966). Minister of War, 1931–1934; Supreme War Council, 1934–1936; Cabinet Advisory Council, 1937, 1940. Counts, 27, 29, 31–33, 35–36. *Life.*

General Kenji Doihara (1883–1948). Commander, Kwantung Army Intelligence Agency (1931—); Mayor of Mukden; Commander-in-Chief, Eastern Army (1943); Commander-in-Chief, Seventh Area Army, Singapore (1944–1945)—in charge of POWs and labor camps. Counts 1, 27, 29, 31–33, 35–36, 54–55. *Death.*

Colonel Kingorō Hashimoto (1890–1957). Army General Staff (1933); commanded artillery regiment during the rape of Nanjing; writer and influential publicist who advocated aggressive war. Counts 1, 27, 29, 31–32, 54–55. *Life.*

Field Marshal Shunroku Hata (1879–1962). Inspector General of Military Education (1937); Commander-in-Chief of the Expeditionary Force in Central China (1938, 1940–1944); member of Supreme War Council (1939). Counts 1, 27, 29, 31–32, 35–36, 54–55. *Life.*

Baron Kiichirō Hiranuma (1865–1952). Vice President (1930–1936) and President, Privy Council (1936–1939, 1945); Prime Minister (1939). Counts 1, 27, 29, 32–33, 35–36, 54–55. *Life.*

Baron Kōki Hirota (1878–1948). Foreign Minister (1933–1938); Prime Minister (1936–1937); Cabinet Advisory Council (1940). Counts 1, 27, 29, 31–33, 35, 54–55. *Death.*

Naoki Hoshino (1892–1978). Chief, General Bureau of Finance, Manchukuo; Chief of General Affairs, Finance Ministry, Manchukuo; Vice Minister Finance, Manchukuo (1936); Chief Secretary and Minister of State (1941–1944). Counts 1, 27, 29, 31–33, 35, 54–55. *Life.*

General Seishirō Itagaki (1885–1948). Chief of Staff, Kwantung Army; Minister of War (1938–1939); Chief of Staff of the Army in China (1939); Commander, Japanese Army in Korea (1941–1945); Supreme War Council (1943). Counts 1, 27, 29, 31–33, 35–36, 54–55. *Death.*

Okinori Kaya (1889–1977). Minister of Finance (1937–1938, 1941–1944). Counts 1, 27, 29, 31–32, 54–55. *Life.*

Marquis Kōichi Kido (1898–1977). Lord Keeper of the Privy Seal (1940–1945); confidential adviser to the emperor. Counts 1, 27, 31–33, 35–36, 54–55. *Life.*

General Heitarō Kimura (1888–1948). Vice Minister of War (1941–1944); Supreme War Council (1943); Commander-in-Chief Japanese Army, Burma (1944). Used POWs to build Burma–Siam railway. Ordered death penalty for Allied pilots. Counts 1, 27, 31–32, 54–55. *Death.*

General Kuniaki Koiso (1880–1950). Chief of Staff, Kwantung Army (1932–1934); Commander Japanese Army, Korea (1935–1936); Prime Minister (1944–1945). Counts 1, 27, 29, 31–32, 36, 54–55. *Life.*

General Iwane Matsui (1878–1948). Commander-in-Chief, Japanese Forces in Central China (1937–1938); Cabinet Advisory Council (1938–1940). Counts 1, 27, 31–32, 35–36, 54–55. *Death.*

General Jirō Minami (1874–1955). Commander, Japanese Army, Korea (1939); Minister of War (1931); Supreme War Councillor (1931–1944); Commander-in-Chief Kwantung Army (1934–1936); Governor General of Korea (1936–1942); Privy Council (1942–1945). Counts 1, 27, 29, 31–32, 54–55. *Life.*

General Akira Mutō (1883–1948). Senior Officer, Military Affairs Bureau (1935–1936); Headquarters staff in Central China and Kwantung Armies (1937; 1939–1942); Chief of Staff, 14th Area Army in Philippines under General Yamashita (1944). Counts 1, 27, 29, 31–33, 36, 54–55. *Death.*

Admiral Osami Nagano (1880–1947). Delegate, Geneva Naval Conference (1930); Supreme War Council (1933); Chief Japanese Delegate, London Naval Conference (1935); Navy Minister (1936–1937); Chief of Naval General Staff (1941–1944); Supreme Naval Adviser to Emperor (1944–1945). *Died during trial.*

Admiral Takasumi Oka (1890–1973). Navy General Staff (1930); Chief, General and Military Affairs Bureau of the Navy (1940–1944). Counts 1, 27, 29, 31–32, 54–55. *Life.*

Shūmei Ōkawa (1886–1957). Director General of East Asia Research Institute of South Manchurian Railway (1926–1945); organizer of Mukden incident (1931); written works advocated aggressive war and expulsion of white race from Asia; Army Corporal. *Case dropped against him on the grounds of mental illness.*

General Hiroshi Ōshima (1886–1975). Ambassador to Germany (1938–1939; 1941–1945); played key role in conclusion of Anti-Comintern and Tripartite Pacts with Germany. Counts 1, 27, 29, 31–32, 54–55. *Life.*

General Kenryō Satō (1895–1975). Chief of Military Affairs Bureau (1941–1944); close adviser to Tōjō. Counts 1, 27, 29, 31–32, 54–55. *Life.*

Mamoru Shigemitsu (1887–1957). Ambassador to China (1931); Ambassador to Soviet Union (1936–1938); Ambassador to Great Britain (1938–1941); Foreign Minister (1943–1945). Initially prosecution witness; Soviets insisted he be tried. Counts 1, 27, 31–33, 35, 54–55. *7 years.*

Admiral Shigetarô Shimada (1883–1976). Navy Minister (1941). Counts 1, 27, 29, 31–32, 54–55. *Life.*

Toshio Shiratori (1877–1949). Ambassador to Italy (1939); helped craft Tripartite Pact with Germany and Italy; wrote works that advocated war to establish "New Order" in Asia. Counts 1, 27, 29, 31–32. *Life.*

General Teiichi Suzuki (1888–1989). Chief of Political Affairs Division of China Affairs Board (1938–1941) and Director (1940–1945); President of the Cabinet Planning Board and Minister without Portfolio (1941–1943); cabinet adviser (1943–1944). Counts 1, 27, 29, 31–32, 35–36, 54–55. *Life.*

Shigenori Tōgō (1881–1950). Ambassador to Germany (1937); Ambassador to Soviet Union (1938); Foreign Minister (1941–1942; 1945). Signed Instrument of Surrender, 1945. Counts 1, 27, 29, 31–32, 36, 54–55. *20 years.*

General Hideki Tōjō (1884–1948). Chief of Staff, Kwantung Army (1937); Minister of War (1940–1944); Prime Minister (1941–1944). Counts 1, 27, 29, 31–32, 36, 54–55. *Death.*

General Yoshikirō Umezu (1882–1949). Commander, Japanese forces in China (1934); Vice War Minister (1936–1938); Commander, Kwantung Army and Ambassador to Manchukuo (1939–1944); Chief of Staff (1944–1945). Counts 1, 27, 29, 31–32, 36, 54–55. *Life.*

Matsuoka Yosuke (1880–1946). Graduate, University of Oregon Law School (1900); Principal Japanese delegate to League of Nations (1932–1933); President of South Manchurian Railroad Company (1935–1939); Foreign Minister (1940–1941). *Died June 26, 1946.*[103]

The prosecution began its case on June 4, 1946, with Keenan's opening statement and ended its portion of the trial on January 24, 1947. The defense's initial presentations lasted from February 27 until January 12, 1948. From the outset, the court seemed to favor the prosecution over the defense. For example, all prosecution evidence was considered admissible even if it was hearsay, while defense evidence was allowed only if it proved that the defendants "did not do or say the things alleged against them." The court also rejected half of the defense's evidence, arguing that it lacked probative value.[104] After the trial, Japanese scholars published an eight-volume set of rejected defense evidence, arguing that what actually took place in Tokyo "was a kangaroo court at which vengeful victors meted out punishment."[105]

Some observers certainly feel this was the case with the prosecution's use of the diaries of Kinmochi Saionji, the last surviving member of Japan's meritorious elders (*genrō*), as rebuttal evidence in January 1948. Saionji, who served as prime minister and held cabinet posts in six different governments, wielded considerable political influence at one time, though by the early 1930s he was regarded as "a sad, isolated, and increasingly irrelevant figure."[106] Regardless, the fact that he had a hand in the appointment of all prime ministers in the 1930s (Saionji died in 1940) convinced Keenan to use his diaries, which were written by his personal secretary, Kumao Harada, during his direct examination of Kido to counter his claims that he had tried to stop Japan's drift to war against China in the 1930s.[107] Kido, who was charged with all counts in the indictment, also played a key role in the meetings about the Pearl Harbor attack in the fall of 1941.[108]

A lot of what we know about these meetings and, for that matter, at least from the prosecution's perspective, the inner workings of the higher levels of the government from 1931 to 1945, came from the Saionji-Harada diary. Given this, the direct examination of Kido, who had willingly turned his own diaries over to Allied investigators after the war and proved most cooperative, should have gone far in strengthening certain aspects of the prosecution's case against the emperor's closest adviser and other defendants. Unfortunately, at the last minute, Comyns-Carr, who had spent a year preparing for the prosecution's direct examination of Kido, was pushed aside by Keenan, who had recently returned to Tokyo after seven months in the United States. Keenan did little to prepare for his examination of one of the prosecution's most important witnesses and it showed in court. Consequently, he was able to elicit little from Kido that enhanced the case against him and other defendants.[109]

On the other hand, Comyns-Carr was able to present supplemental evidence from the diary about the important meeting on November 29, 1941, which dealt with going to war against the United States. His purpose was simple—to emphasize comments from several of those in attendance who urged caution about attacking the United States. Former prime minister Renijiro Wakatsuki, for example, worried about Japan's ability to sustain a long war and, while sympathetic to Tōjō's arguments about the "preservation and self defense of the Empire," argued that

> it is dangerous indeed to execute state policy or to make use of the national strength to achieve such ideas to the "Establishment of the Greater East Asia Co-Prosperity Sphere" or of the "Stabilizing Power of East Asia" ideals. I pray that Your Majesty will give careful consideration to this point.[110]

Prince Fumimaro Konoe, who served as prime minister from 1937 to 1941, expressed similar doubts. He apologized for not being able "to do anything toward the adjustment of Japanese-American relations" and, while he considered "the further continuation of diplomatic negotiations would be hopeless," wondered about the wisdom of going to war even without such talks. Perhaps, down the road, he added, there would be an opportunity "to later find a way out of the deadlock by persevering to the utmost under difficulties." Hirota, one of the defendants, urged similar caution.

> Granting that it was inevitable, I believe we should always be on the watch to seize the opportunity for a solution by diplomatic negotiations even though blows have been exchanged.[111]

In the end, most of those in attendance urged caution though there were also strong voices supporting war. Afterward, Hirohito asked Kido what he should do. He told the emperor that if he had any doubts, he should talk to Admiral Osami Nagano, the navy's chief of staff, and Adm. Shigetarô Shimada, his navy minister, who had also expressed doubts about the wisdom of such a move. But on this occasion they voiced support for Tôjô's plans.[112] On December 1, a fully engaged Hirohito met with his cabinet and other key leaders to discuss the December 7/8 surprise attacks on Pearl Harbor and Kota Bharu in British Malay. The emperor sat silently for an hour as various officials discussed the reasons for the decision to go to war—the US November 26 demand that Japan withdraw its military and police forces from China and Indochina—and military plans for the attacks against the United States and Great Britain. At the end of each presentation, the emperor simply "nodded in agreement." Efforts to clarify American demands were brushed aside or distorted, and at the end of the meeting, Tôjô stated that

> Once His Majesty decides to commence hostilities, we will all strive to meet our obligations to him, bring the government and the military ever closer together, resolve that the nation united will go on to victory, make an all-out effort to achieve our war aims, and set his majesty's mind at ease.[113]

Though Comyns-Carr did not mention the December 1 meeting in his supplemental presentation, he did submit an excerpt from Kido's diary on December 8, "X" day to the Japanese government. As he awaited news of the attack on Pearl Harbor, Kido noted that it "was an unusually fine day." At 7:30 a.m. he met Tôjô and the heads of the army and the navy. He wrote that he was pleased to hear

> about the good news of the grand success of the surprise attack on Hawaii. I deeply felt the blessings of Divine Grace.

Several hours later, Kido met with the emperor, who had just issued his imperial rescript declaring war on the United States and Great Britain, "perfectly calm and absolutely unperturbed."[114]

William Logan, the principal defense attorney for Kido, used the diary to try to show that his client "had absolutely no participation in any premeditated plan for aggressive war either in general or in detail." Kido, he noted, had advised Konoe on September 7, 1938, that he should try to come to terms with Chiang Kai-shek over the "China Affair," and added that

> At no time did I ever vote for initiating any war nor did I vote for the continuance of any war.

Logan also noted that Kido had stated in his earlier affidavit that

> At no time did I ever have any conversation with any of the other accused or anyone else involving the planning, scheming, and conspiracy as alleged in the Indictment.[115]

At this point in the trial, the prosecution, as it often did, raised objections about the introduction of this portion of Kido's affidavit. Webb backed the defense in this case, which led Logan to criticize the prosecution for submitting documents into evidence that the defendant never had the opportunity to read or be "confronted with." If this tactic continued, he went on, "we will have to apply to reopen this case and put our accused on the stand and explain various items such as this which they should have offered in their case." Webb agreed with Logan, who complained that the prosecution continued to introduce such documents in court after they had completed their case, arguing that "it was lost among our documents" or "we weren't aware of it," when everyone knew that they had them in their possession "for many months." While Webb agreed with Logan's assertions, he also reminded him that "we must allow for the very unusual circumstances associated with the prosecution of such a case."[116] Logan brought the diary up again later in the trial in response to prosecution efforts to use excerpts from it to challenge Kido's credibility and his loyalty to the emperor.[117] His purpose was to point out inconsistencies in the Saionji-Harada diary in an effort to raise doubts about its accuracy and value as evidence.[118]

Once the defense finished its surrebuttal of the prosecution's rebuttal, Logan informed the court that he would now offer "evidence in mitigation," a move he hesitated to take since Anglo-American legal tradition dictated that such evidence be given after a verdict was reached in a trial. This issue had been raised by the defense and the prosecution in early February 1948. There was considerable disagreement between the judges over this issue, but it was finally decided that evidence could be offered in mitigation "immediately after all other evidence is received." The problem with this, Logan noted, was that offering such evidence could be an "intendant inference of guilt." Consequently, in countries where such a practice was allowed, there was "no implication of guilt." He wanted to know if this rule would apply in the Tokyo trial. Webb assured him that this would be the case and that there would "be no such implication" if he chose to offer such evidence. This assurance did little to assuage the fears of the other defendants, all of whom chose not to follow Kido's lead.[119]

After objections by Comyns-Carr, Logan underscored efforts by Kido to "restore peace" once war broke out and later bring it "to a close."[120] One deposition by Sotaro Ishiwata, the imperial household minister, stated that from the moment he took office in early July 1945, Kido emphasized the need for peace negotiations, even if it led to his death.[121] After the bombing of Nagasaki, Ishiwata testified, Kido told him that the emperor was ready to make a broadcast declaring the "termination of the war." Several days later, an Imperial guard unit laid siege to the Imperial Household Ministry building, and declared that it was looking for Kido and Ishiwata in an effort

> to rid the Throne of the Lord Keeper of the Privy Seal, who is a traitor, trying to terminate the war![122]

On the early morning of August 15, Kido told Ishiwata that

> We may be discovered and killed at any time. But history has already turned to a new direction. The war will be closed. I am completely ready to be killed now![123]

After further objections from Comyns-Carr, the court rejected this deposition. Logan replied that he would present no more mitigating evidence for Kido.[124]

In his summation several weeks later, Comyns-Carr used the diary as well as testimony from other Japanese officials to underscore the prosecution's claims that, from 1937 on, Kido was a key figure in the Japanese conspiracy to wage aggressive war, both as a cabinet member and Lord Privy Seal.[125] He even tried to tie Kido's role as minister of education in 1937 to 1938 to such charges, arguing that as a cabinet member he was responsible for its policies as well as those pursued educationally in trying to promote a "Japanese spirit" that "justified Japanese policy in China, and condemned the Chinese government for not yielding to Japan."[126]

Logan attempted to counter these charges in his defense summary in early April 1948. He termed the prosecution's case against Kido "aimless wandering in the wilderness of complicated and detailed factual matter." This, he argued, forced him to look at these charges in some detail because of "our inability to see the forest because of nearsighted examination of the trees."[127] He bemoaned the fact that, unlike Nuremberg, the Tokyo tribunal was weighed down by 55 charges instead of 4, which made it "almost humanly impossible to touch upon the Indictment allegations with the fullness they deserve."[128] In the end, given that his client was neither a "soldier in the field nor a formulator of policy" regarding war crimes and crimes against humanity, the real case against him centered around a simple charge—"whether the accused is responsible for the accomplishment of aggressive war."[129] The truth, Logan argued, lay in a careful reading of Kido's diary, not the random selections made by the prosecution that were often taken out of context or mistranslated.[130]

Logan also tried to argue that Kido had no "criminal mind," and that he did everything possible to try to stop the efforts of "radical positivists" to drag the nation into war. His involvement in internal Japanese affairs had one goal, "i.e. world peace."[131] Logan then addressed the prosecution's efforts to determine Kido's "mental attitude on a number of occasions." Of particular importance, he went on, was his mindset about "internal quarrels in Japan," its alliance with Germany and Italy, and "in securing agreement, no matter what it was," between the army and the navy in the fall of 1941.[132]

> The law in this case is that the burden of proof is on the prosecution to prove guilt beyond a reasonable doubt.[133]

Yet in attempting to prove that the former privy counselor was

> part of a conspiracy to wage declared or undeclared war or wars of aggression...or the waging thereof; or whether it was for a defensive war or peace or any halfway measure,

the prosecution only seemed satisfied to prove that in

> advocating *some* decision be reached, KIDO was perfectly satisfied if it was a decision to commit some act not charged in the Indictment—for example, peace.

The only conclusion to draw from this, Logan argued, was that the prosecution has admitted that it

> has failed to sustain the burden that he conspired to commit or committed the acts set forth in the Indictment. Furthermore, in so far as the conspiracy is concerned, any

contention that he did not resign even though his counsel was not taken is immaterial. Under the theory of conspiracy one must conspire ahead of time, not after the act is completed.[134]

In fact, if anything, Logan concluded, his decision to stay in office instead of resigning underscored the

> necessity of public officials assuming office to fight the forces of evil. The prosecution's attempt to create law to fit KIDO's case does not pass the test of reason. By saying with respect to his advice, "He did not so much mind what they agreed upon as long as they agreed," we submit the prosecution admits it has failed to sustain its burden. On the basis of the prosecution's own contention, the counts should be dismissed as to KIDO.[135]

In the end, some of the defense's arguments were able to sway the tribunal to spare Kido's life.

This was not going to be the case with Gen. Hedeki Tōjō, to many the most important defendant in the dock. With the exception of the emperor, Tōjō, whose bespectacled image appeared on numerous Allied propaganda posters as well as on the cover of *Time* magazine on November 3, 1941, was the person most closely associated not only with the attack on Pearl Harbor but also the principal figure that led Japan to war. A gifted career army officer, Tōjō had risen quickly through army ranks after graduation from Japan's top military academy in 1905. He saw service in the Russo-Japanese War and later in various Japanese adventures in Manchuria and China before his appointment as Chief of Staff of the Kwantung Army in 1937. After his successful campaigns during the early phases of the China War in 1937–1938, he became vice minister of war in the Cabinet of Seishirō Itagaki. A strong supporter of the war in China, Tōjō became army minister in two of the three cabinets of Fumimaro Konoe in 1940–1941 and, at the request of the emperor, was appointed prime minister on October 18, 1941, a position he held until the summer of 1944.[136]

He was indicted on all counts but two—25 (aggression against the Soviet Union in 1938) and 45 (rape of Nanjing). He was also charged in Appendix E of participation in 12 of the 14 meetings that took place between June 25 and December 1, 1941. From the prosecution's perspective, these were key to the preparation and outbreak of war on December 7/8, 1941.[137] In many ways, the case against Tōjō was made easier by the fact that during the early stages of his defense case, he admitted to full "administrative responsibility" as minister of war from the "beginning of the Pacific War up to 22 July 1944," and as Chief of the General Staff from February to July 1944. Such responsibilities involved the treatment of POWs and civilians under Japanese control during his tenure in these posts.[138] Tōjō made a similar admission in his prison diary, when he stated, "I should bear entire responsibility for the war in general."[139] Yet, despite such admissions, he proved to be an astute witness who time and again befuddled Keenan who, despite court rules, insisted at the last minute that he be allowed to step in and cross-examine Tōjō.[140]

Tōjō tried to commit suicide soon after the war ended, and apologized to Hirohito in a suicide note for his failure to see the war through successfully. He also apologized for the "countless number of bodies of his faithful subjects." He had, he went on, "dishonored our glorious history," though there was no way he could atone "for the injury sustained by the national dignity in being subjected to the disgrace of control by enemy nations. This will have a detrimental effect on the national soul." Regardless, he concluded, he believed firmly in the "rightness... of the Greater East Asia War."[141] This unbowed spirit permeated Tōjō's testimony, who proved to be a challenging and, at times, maddening witness. From the outset, Tōjō seemed unfazed by the trial and his time on the witness stand. He showed little patience for what he considered ridiculous or inappropriate questions. During questioning by one of his defense attorneys in late December 1947, he was asked if he had requested that the navy suggest a new minister for his cabinet "who would blindly follow any decisions by you?" The former general replied, "I never asked such a stupid thing—I never heard of such an absurd proposition," something his attorney reminded him was the "prosecution's assertion."[142]

But it was Keenan's bewildering questioning that most seemed to raise Tōjō's ire.[143] From the outset, Keenan showed total disrespect for Tōjō, and told him when he began to question him that he would not address him as general "because, of course, you know there is no longer any Japanese army."[144] This initial show of disrespect set the tone for the almost private *tête-à-tête* between the chief prosecutor and the former prime minister. Over the course of several days of questioning, Tōjō kept his American adversary continually off-balance by responding to questions with a question, and often refusing to answer queries directly.

At one point, Keenan asked the former prime minister if he knew that aggressive war was a crime.[145] After one of the defense attorneys objected to this question, Webb told Keenan that "we are getting no help from this type of cross-examination."[146] Keenan, however, insisted that the defendant's state of mind and awareness that he was "committing a crime at the time he did so" was important, since it might lead to "an admission of guilt on the witness stand." Webb responded that

> He was not invited to make any admission of guilt. Now, this is the position; His honest and reasonable, though mistaken, belief in the existence of a state of facts is a defense. His opinion or beliefs as to the law is not a defense and is irrelevant except on the question perhaps of mitigation if he is found guilty.
>
> The only man found guilty of aggressive war and of aggressive war along, at Nuernberg was not sentenced to death; so Nuernberg may have thought that belief as to the law, mistaken belief, may be a circumstance of mitigation, but they did not say so. I am only stating the fact.[147]

George F. Blewett, another defense attorney, reminded the tribunal that it was improper for the prosecution to use the cross-examination to ask Tōjō if he was guilty or innocent because he had already pleaded not guilty at the outset of the trial. Webb explained that Tōjō was not being specifically asked this question, only "an opinion on the law." Blewett argued that such a question was still improper under cross-examination, and Webb agreed, sustaining his objection and ordering the question to be "disallowed."[148]

Sadly, as Keenan continued his line of questioning, first about Japan's decision to draw closer to Germany after Hitler's successes in Europe in the spring and summer of 1940, and then about the impact of such victories on Japan's global view, he seemed to lose focus. At one point, when Keenan asked Tōjō to explain the fall of the cabinet of Admiral Mitsumasa Yonai in the summer of 1940, Webb intervened, telling Keenan, "I don't think any Member of the Tribunal wants this explanation."[149] The chief prosecutor then asked Tōjō about the decision by the new Konoe Cabinet to adopt policies based on the fact that, according to a cabinet policy statement, "The world is now on the threshold of a stupendous historic change."[150] And while questioning Tōjō about the meaning of this phrase, Keenan drifted confusingly into questions about Japan's role in World War I, which confused Tōjō, who thought he was still talking about World War II.[151] The point Keenan was trying to make was that Japan's alliances in 1917 prevented war from breaking out in the Pacific. His efforts, unfortunately, to draw a line between these ties and Japan's World War II alliances prompted Tōjō to tell Keenan, "I can't quite comprehend where the point in the question is."[152]

Keenan also briefly questioned Tōjō about the emperor's role in his appointment as prime minister, and differences in his testimony and those noted in Kido's diary. He also asked him about the importance of the Tripartite Pact with Germany and Italy (September 27, 1940) and its impact on Tokyo's relationship with the United States. Did Japan in 1940 see the United States as a threat? At the time, Tōjō responded, Japan was under considerable "economic pressure," which was exacerbated by the US abrogation of its commerce and navigation treaty a year earlier.[153] Militarily,

in May 1940...a large United States fleet was concentrated in Hawaii, its smokestacks exuding black smoke, its personnel active and on the alert. That fact alone should be clear enough.[154]

Did the presence of US naval vessels at Pearl Harbor, Keenan wanted to know, mean that Japan was in danger of being attacked by the United States? Tōjō replied that he was asked for an example of such a threat, and the above description was just "an illustration" of such a threat.[155]

He also described other US threats against Japan, including the "increase in armed forces" in the Philippines, Malaya, Burma, the Dutch East Indies, as well as aid to China that strengthened Nationalist resistance efforts against Japan. Why did Japan consider such moves threatening, Keenan asked, particularly in light of Tokyo's claims that its actions in China were defensive? Tōjō said such a question was "quite inconsistent," and that, in reality, there were two separate questions to consider. Japan saw the strengthening of US forces as threatening, while Tokyo's actions in China were to protect Japanese citizens and thus acts of "self-defense," points already introduced by the defense earlier in the trial.[156]

Though the thrust of Keenan's questioning of Tōjō centered on questions about his role in the buildup to war with the United States, he did bring up the question of war crimes. While war crimes never received the same attention as they did in Nuremberg, they were touched on during the trial, though it often proved difficult to link these crimes directly to some of the defendants. This was not going to be the case with Tōjō, who, the court later ruled, was guilty, as "head of the War Ministry...[and] Home Ministry...wilfully refused" to enforce the "performance of the Laws of War." In its decision, the tribunal made specific reference to the Bataan Death March and the abuses that took place during the construction of the Burma-Siam railway.[157] When Keenan questioned Tōjō about the latter crimes, he only admitted to authorizing the use of POW labor, but denied any criminal responsibility for the treatment of these workers because the railway was far behind the front lines and far away from any significant military operations. He added that there was no consistent policy of abuse of POWs and civilians throughout Japanese-occupied Asia. Moreover, Tōjō added, Japanese soldiers worked side-by-side with prisoners who "were treated properly and in accordance with international standards." He admitted, though, that there were isolated instances of abuse, but added that many of them were dealt with by the authorities.[158]

Keenan had tried initially to get the war crimes charges dropped because he knew that it would be difficult to tie individual atrocities to different defendants. When this effort failed, the prosecution decided to try to establish a common pattern of mistreatment during the individual national prosecutorial presentations early in the trial.[159] Chinese prosecutors, for example, focused on three collective crimes, the rape of Nanjing, war crimes elsewhere in China, and the Japanese introduction of addictive drugs into China that were meant

(1) to weaken the stami[n]a and undermine the will to resist on the part of the Chinese people;

(2) to provide substantial revenues to finance Japanese military and economic aggression.[160]

The principal goal of Chinese prosecutors was to use these and other crimes in China as documented instances of the "widespread" nature of "Japanese perpetrated atrocities." Webb, however, noted that the facts presented by the Chinese, at best, presented a "mere *prima facie* case…which contained a minimum amount of facts, just enough for a very limited purpose."[161]

The Chinese prosecution did, though, do a good job of documenting major war crimes against women including rape and sex slavery as well as the widespread Japanese use of slave labor.[162] One witness, G. J. Hsu from Shanghai, testified that in addition to watching Japanese soldiers mass murder over a thousand Chinese civilians along the Burma–Yunnan highway in the spring of 1942, he saw

four Japanese soldiers take two women into the hills and when the women came back they were both crying. They told me they had been raped.[163]

Another witness, Hsieh Chin-Hun, testified via affidavit that after the Japanese entered Changsha in the summer of 1944, they "freely indulged in murder, rape, incendiarism and many other atrocities throughout the district."[164] Mr. Liu, a witness from Hopei Province, testified in court that after the Japanese took over this area in the fall of 1937, they committed horrible war crimes, including rape.

I saw a Japanese soldier raping a woman who was then pregnant. He afterwards ripped her body with [a] bayonet and killed her. I also saw eight Japanese soldiers rape a 13-year old girl. She died.[165]

The Chinese prosecutors also introduced evidence from other war crimes tribunals in Asia that were trying alleged Japanese war criminals. David Sutton, an American lawyer who assisted Chinese prosecutors, introduced the statement of Col. Kiang Cheng Ying, which had been given earlier to a military court in China. It underscored widespread crimes (and atrocities) committed by Japanese military and nonmilitary units "against Chinese noncombatants" in Hubei province.[166] These included:

> Compulsory sexual intercourse of men and women who were strangers to each other. If they refused to do as ordered, they were immediately shot to death.
>
> Pretty women were accused to be members of the Communist Army. Burning matches were applied to the hair on delicate parts of their bodies just to poke fun out of their shyness, evasiveness and pain . . .[167]
>
> Another one of the tortures inflicted on women victims was to make them sit over a heated charcoal stove during the period of menstruation. The woman victim was stripped of her lower garment and made to sit over the stove with hands and feet bound.[168]

The Philippines' chief associate prosecutor, Pedro Lopez, documented similar atrocities in his country. He used evidence from the trial of Yamashita and Homma to document the Japanese abuse of Allied POWs and Filipino civilians, particularly during the Bataan Death March. His presentation was extremely detailed because he was able to use over 14,000 pages of US Army investigative material put together just after the end of the war. This enabled him to provide a clear picture of the widespread Japanese atrocities committed throughout the Philippines.[169]

Some of the most gruesome testimony dealt with Japanese acts of cannibalism that involved not only POWs and civilians but other Japanese soldiers as well. One Japanese document, *Memorandum Concerning the Training of All Officers and Men for the Prevention of Starvation* (November 18, 1944), gave instructions about eating human flesh. It stated that

> Although it is not prescribed in the criminal code, those who eat human flesh (except that of the enemy) knowing it to be so, shall be sentenced to death as the worst kind of criminal against mankind.[170]

A Japanese POW later told his Australian interrogators that in late 1944 the 18th Army Headquarters issued an order that stated that

> troops were permitted to eat the flesh of Allied dead but must not eat their own dead.

He added that at "the time rumors were prevalent that troops were eating their own dead."[171] The reason for the order was an attempt to dissuade desperate Japanese soldiers from eating their former comrades, and instead eating Allied POWs or civilians.[172] According to one US JAG report,

> In the early part of August 1945 six Japanese soldiers were seen going to the home of PITLUNGAY in Sitio Lilong [Philippines]. Two men fled and hid nearby as the Japanese approached but the Japanese bayonetted [*sic*] to death all occupants of the house, one

of whom was a three-year-old girl. The six Japanese ate the flesh from some of the bodies of their victims during the two-day period that they stayed in the house. The first evening, the flesh of the little girl was cut into small pieces, put on the end of sticks, and roasted over an open fire. The next morning, the flesh of another victim was roasted or boiled with native vegetables. The flesh of three of the victims was consumed in this manner. The body of one of the victims was later thrown into the river that ran in front of the house. The bodies of the two other victims were not touched. After the Japanese left, the two observers went into the house and saw a piece of human flesh inside of a bag left by one of the Japanese and also inside one of the kettles that had been used by the Japanese.[173]

The question of cannibalism also came up during a US military commission trial in the summer of 1946 on Guam. One of the defendants, Maj. Sueo Matoba, testified that he and his officers had eaten human flesh at a party in late February 1945. Earlier that month, Gen. Yoshio Tachibana told some of his subordinates that the coming invasion was the last battle before the "invasion of Japan." We must, he added, "fight even though we had no supplies and no food, and that we should fight and live on the flesh of our comrades and that of the enemy, whom he referred to as "*kiahiku* (beasts)."[174] On another occasion, he was ordered by Admiral Tomoichi Mori to bring him the liver from the "body of the next flyer to be executed by the 308th Battalion," which was later served in the "officers' mess."[175] During the meal, Admiral Mori mentioned that "during the Chinese-Japanese war human flesh and liver were eaten as a medicine by the Japanese troops. The medicine made from the liver was named Seirogan."[176]

According to Yuki Tanaka, such practices were widespread through Japanese-occupied Asia. They were not, he added, random acts caused by the chaos, disorganization, and starvation that occurred among the Japanese forces toward the end of the war. Instead,

cannibalism was often a systematic activity conducted by whole squads and under the command of officers. Throughout periods of starvation and cannibalism, discipline was maintained to an astonishing degree.[177]

He places the blame for such acts on Japanese Imperial Headquarters, which adopted a "'self-sustaining policy'" for its troops in the southwest Pacific when it could not supply them with adequate food or materiél. Of the 157,646 Japanese troops sent to eastern New Guinea during the war, only 10,072 survived the war. Most of the rest died of "starvation and tropical disease."[178]

British Commonwealth prosecutors also introduced evidence of cannibalism and medical experimentation, but focused principally on Japanese war crimes throughout Asia, particularly those involving Burmese, Chinese, Malays, Tamils, Thais, and others. Yuma Totani has estimated that "half of its [Commonwealth] war crimes cases had to do with crimes against civilians and prisoners of war with non-Caucasian backgrounds."[179] This was part of broader British efforts "to restore its moral authority by pursuing justice on behalf of its colonial subjects."[180] The British were particularly sensitive to the humiliating fall of Singapore to Gen. Yamashita in February 1942, and the 5,000 Chinese murdered by Japanese forces afterward.[181] These atrocities played a big part in the Commonwealth's case in Tokyo as well as a separate trial in Singapore, the center of the British war crimes trials in Asia after the war, in the spring of 1947. Of the 304 war crimes trials conducted by the British in Asia, 131 were held in Singapore involving 465 alleged Japanese war criminals.[182]

One of the principal Commonwealth cases was the Japanese murder of Australian nurses on Banka Island near Sumatra. The nurses, who had fled Singapore just before it fell to the Japanese in early 1942, were onboard the *Vyner Brooke*, which was sunk by the Japanese. The nurses survived and took refuge on Banka Island about 200 miles south of Singapore. When it became apparent that escape would be impossible because of the wounded and children, the survivors, most of them Australian nationals, surrendered to the Japanese.[183] The Japanese shot and bayoneted the soldiers to death, and then, according to the testimony of Vivien Bullwinkel, ordered the women

> to march into the sea. We had gone a few yards into the water when they commenced to machine-gun from behind. I saw the girls fall one after the other, when I was hit. The bullet that hit me struck me in the back at about waist level and passed straight through. It knocked me over, and the waves brought me in to the edge of the water. I continued to lie there for ten to fifteen minutes, and then I sat up and looked around, and the Japanese party had disappeared. I then took myself up into the jungle and became unconscious.[184]

The Commonwealth prosecution also presented detailed evidence on the Sandakan death marches in Borneo. The Japanese established a POW camp at Sandakan on the northeastern coast of Borneo to supply slave labor for the construction of an airfield there. Of the 2,500 Australian and British POWs sent there during the war, only six survived. Most of the guards at Sandakan were Taiwanese under the command of Japanese officers. Though the prosecution focused principally on a series of Sandakan death marches at the end of the war, war crimes in the camp were widespread. The Japanese military police (*Kempeitai*), who oversaw surveillance in the area, were convinced that an uprising was imminent in the camp and tortured some of the POWs there to gain information. They used extremely cruel methods including water torture and severe beatings with wet sand, which

> was smeared over the victim and was pressed into the skin when he was beaten with a wooden sandal. This abraded the skin and made the whole beaten area red, raw, and bleeding.[185]

They also force fed some of their victims large amounts of rice after days without food, and then made them drink large quantities of water that caused the rice to expand. The result was

> excruciating pain as the stomach stretched to its limit, and the pain would often continue for days as the rice was digested. The resulting stress on the digestive tract would also cause internal and rectal bleeding.[186]

The Japanese later tried the alleged ring leaders of the plot and sentenced them to death or long prison terms.[187]

In early 1945, the Japanese decided to move some of the POWs to other parts of the island for new construction projects. What followed were three death marches—one that began in late January 1945, the second in late May, and the third a month later. According to the testimony of Australian Warrant Officer William H. Stiepewich, who was on the first death march, only 6 of the 500 POWs on the January march survived by escaping their captors. When the second death march began, there were 824 POWs still in the camp, though only 536 could walk. Once the march began, those who fell by the wayside were shot or bayoneted by their guards. By the time the second march reached its destination, Ranau, there were only 183 survivors. Another 75 POWs from Sandakan died during a third death march in June. By July, most of the remaining prisoners in Sandakan were dead, and those that were still alive were either executed or died from disease or malnutrition.[188]

One of the principal Dutch prosecutors, a former POW, Sinninghe Damste, documented similar atrocities in his presentation on Japanese crimes in the Dutch East Indies (DEI). Like the other prosecutors, his goal was to show that the "Japanese armed forces committed the same kinds of war crimes repeatedly in various theaters of war."[189] The DEI colony in Indonesia became a prime target of the Japanese because of its large oil reserves. One Japanese historian has called it "the most important strategic jewel in the South Pacific."[190] The Dutch adopted a very firm war crimes trial agenda after the war not only because of the extremity of Japanese cruelty against "internees" but also against the native peoples throughout the DEI. The Dutch tried 308 alleged Japanese war criminals in military courts and condemned a third of them to death, the highest percentage among the Allied national courts in Asia.[191] They also refused to sign the 1951 San Francisco peace treaty ending the occupation of Japan, instead insisting on a special accord that allowed the Netherlands "to demand reparations [from Japan] on behalf of Dutch civilian victims."[192]

One of the principal themes of the Dutch case in Tokyo was sexual slavery. Damste documented three specific cases involving the creation of a large number of brothels in Borneo where local women were forced to "service" the sexual needs of Japanese sailors and civilians. In early 1944, for example, the Japanese made a group of Dutch girls and women in internment camps in Java have sex with Japanese military personnel for three weeks. They did the same thing in Timor, forcing local leaders to provide women for their brothels. If they refused, the Japanese explained, they would use their wives and daughters in the brothels.[193]

Unfortunately, Damste, like other prosecutors, chose to give only summaries of a larger body of testimony, which provided the court with only a glimpse of the depth and horror of Japanese sexual crimes.[194] The more detailed accounts were in the court records, such as the *Report on Enforced Prostitution in Western Borneo, N. E. I. during Japanese Naval Operations*. It described, in part, some of these crimes against women.

> In their search for women the Tokei Tai [navy special police] ordered the entire female staffs of the Minseiby [civil administration bureau] and the Japanese firms to report to the Tokei Tai Office [*tokkeitai*, navy special police], undressed some of them entirely and accused them of maintaining relations with Japanese. The ensuing medical examination revealed that several were virgins. It is not known with certainty how

many of these unfortunates were forced into brothels. Women did not dare escape from the brothels as members of their family were then immediately arrested and severely maltreated by the Tokei tai. In one case it is known that this caused the death of the mother of the girl concerned.[195]

This failure to present full documentation into the court record led to charges afterward that the Allies were only concerned about such crimes when they dealt with Caucasian victims. While this might be the case with some of the national war crimes trials in Asia, this was certainly not the case with the Tokyo trial, which amply documented Japanese sexual crimes against Asian women.[196]

However, documenting such crimes and actively prosecuting them are quite different issues. The Women's International War Crimes Tribunal on Japan's Military Sexual Slavery noted in its December 4, 2001, judgment that the responsibility for this failure

> rests with the World War II Allied states which did not prosecute Japanese officials for these crimes before the International Criminal [Military] Tribunal for the Far East (IMFTE), in the trial in Tokyo from April 1946 to November 1948, despite the fact that they possessed ample evidence of rape and sexual slavery in the "comfort system." That a court, especially an internationally constituted court, would deliberately ignore a systematic atrocity of this dimension is unconscionable and profoundly discriminatory.[197]

According to Yayori Matsui, part of the reason for this failure, beyond the fact that, at the time, "international law didn't consider wartime rape and other sexual violence as violations of the human rights of women themselves," was that all of the judges and lawyers at the IMFTE were men. This failure, she goes on, was merely a case of gender bias.[198]

Once the prosecution had finished its presentation in late January, the defense spent several days trying to convince the tribunal to dismiss the case against its clients. On January 27, David F. Smith asked for a mistrial against 11 of the defendants, which Webb refused to entertain. Smith then presented a motion of dismissal for each of the defendants and questioned the tribunal's jurisdiction. He added that the defense was prepared "to go to the federal courts in Washington, if necessary, to get this question resolved."[199] Smith then presented what he called the "Supreme Commander" motion, which Webb refused to be allowed to be read in the record since he thought it was meant to "publically challenge" MacArthur.[200] What followed were a number of motions to dismiss charges for individual defendants, which were rejected by the tribunal.[201]

The defense then began its presentation, which lasted from February 24, 1947, to January 12, 1948. Most of the scholars who have studied the Tokyo trial have paid little attention to the defense case, instead focusing on the prosecution's efforts and the lengthy tribunal judgment and dissenting opinions. According to Yuma Totani, who has written one of the better histories of the trial, the defense "did little to contest" the prosecution's charges of "mass atrocities across the Pacific theater." On the other hand, he notes that the defense did challenge the prosecution's contention that "their clients were individually responsible for the widespread atrocities," arguing that there was no evidence to suggest "that these crimes were committed with the knowledge, or on the orders, of the central government."[202] While his latter assertion is correct, a careful reading of the trial transcripts shows that the defense did mount a strong but unsuccessful case using a sophisticated body of international law that challenged the charge of widespread atrocities across Japanese-occupied Asia. And at the center of many of the defense's arguments were not only questions of Western and Japanese cultural and legal traditions, but also the heritage of European colonialism in Asia and its interpretative impact on Japan, both domestically and internationally.

The lengthy defense case was dominated by American lawyers, who put "forward a convincing case in the defense of their clients." Prominent Japanese lawyers also played an important part in certain phases of the trial, though few rarely "came to the microphones" because there "were few whom the court found tolerable."[203] Somei Uzawa, the chief Japanese defense attorney, for example, set the tone for much of the defense's case by arguing that the prosecution's charges were no better than a traditional "hat trick."[204] When the hat is lifted, he explained, the

> tribunal swarms with new-born little doctrines drawn from odds and ends of municipal law, to the extreme amazement of us all. Where the prosecution got them is immaterial. They were surely not in our silk hat. The prosecution put them there.[205]

Kenzo Takayanagi, a professor of law at the University of Tokyo who had studied at Harvard University, was a bit more diplomatic but also challenged many of the assertions of the prosecution, particularly the question of a pattern of widespread Japanese atrocities throughout Asia.

> Even if the alleged atrocities or other contraventions assume a similar singular pattern of acts, it cannot justify such an assumption. Such a pattern may have been a sheer reflection of national or racial traits. Crimes no less than masterpieces of art may express certain characteristics reflecting the *mores* of a race. Similarities in the geographic, economic, or strategic state of affairs may in part account for the "similar pattern" assumed. The existence of a command from above, and from whom it issued, has certainly to be proved beyond any reasonable doubt in a case of this grave character. The impression prevails after listening to the testimony of the witnesses alleging atrocities, that they follow not a uniform pattern but manifold patterns according to the nationality of the witnesses, not only negating "orders from above" but telling an entirely different story.[206]

But it was the aggressive war charges, not atrocities, that dominated Japanese defense efforts.

Dr. Uzawa noted in his summation that war was "one of the most serious and dangerous phenomena in human society." Yet, he added, despite international efforts "to exterminate war," nothing had proven effective to stop it, while "war of aggression" was still not an "international crime" under "world law."[207] Dr. Takayanagi raised the same questions, directly challenging Keenan's assertion that aggressive war was an international crime. In a careful discussion of the evolution of international law going back to the mid-nineteenth century, he noted that various countries, including Great Britain, had raised questions about the applicability of the Kellogg-Briand Pact and its effect on the ability of individual states to wage wars of "necessary self-defense." Japan was not Nazi Germany, he reminded the court, and while the Nuremberg tribunal had little difficulty proving the "aggressive" character of Hitler's war making, the case against Japan was quite different. The court would have to subject any charge of aggressive or defensive war against Japan to the "charge of *ipso dixit* [asserted but not proven], if not subserviency to popular prejudices or a wilful travesty of history."[208]

But it was Ichirō Kiyose, the future speaker of Japan's House of Representatives, who laid out the key elements in the Japanese case in his opening remarks. He challenged the prosecution's charge that "Japan...continuously committed alleged international crimes," noting that there were

> three vital considerations which should be outlined in this opening statement in order properly to comprehend the exact nature of the internal and external policies of Japan during the period covered by the Indictment. These are independence, abolition of racial discrimination and fundamental principles of diplomacy. These are not merely the policies of any particular cabinets, of which there were many, nor are the principles of specific political parties. Rather, they are national, long standing, and firm aspirations universally subscribed to and cherished by the entire Japanese nation since the opening of the country to foreign intercourse in 1853, and are important to the Japanese as are free speech, free education and freedom of religion in America.[209]

He went on to explain that one of the principal goals of Japanese leaders after the forced opening of Japan in 1853 by the United States was to "preserve the nation as a perfect independent and sovereign state."[210] Kiyose considered the charges of racial discrimination absurd, noting that Japan's goal throughout East Asia had always been to maintain that "standard attained by Europeans and Americans."[211] He reminded the court of Western efforts to carve up China into "spheres of influence," which prompted Japan to become "a stabilizing power in the East," a role supported and "recognized by the great powers."[212]

Kiyose also challenged the idea that Japan was involved in a conspiracy with Germany and Italy to conquer the world. The confusion, he argued, centered on the idea of *hakko ichiu*, which was included in the Japanese version of the Tripartite Pact Treaty and the Imperial Rescript that was issued after it was concluded. The latter document, he explained, stated that

> It is indeed a great teaching of our Imperial ancestors that the Great Cause shall be propagated all over the eight corners of the world and the whole humanity on earth shall be deemed one family. To this august teaching we endeavor to adhere day and night.[213]

Kiyose explained that

> "The Great Cause" here means "universal truth." To be "propagated" here means that the said idea be made plain and manifest by all the world. "To be in one family" means that whole mankind is to live together with the feeling of fraternity in one household. As said before, the culture is of a different origin from that of the West and, therefore, the expression is necessarily very different or even quaint to Europeans and Americans.[214]

The defense, he added, would show that regardless of Germany and Italy's intentions in the treaty, Japan "had no intention to conquer the world in cooperation with" its two Allies.[215]

Kiyose also challenged the prosecution's interpretation of the term "new order"—in the pact with the two countries, which the prosecution saw as "an idea to destroy democracy and freedom and the respect for personality."[216] The "intrinsic content of the idea of the new order," he explained, is the *Ko-do* or Imperial Way—"benevolence, righteousness and moral courage. It respects courtesy and honor," which is "the opposite to the idea of militarism and despotism."[217]

Kiyose was equally troubled by the idea of conspiracy, which he considered unique to Anglo-American law and difficult to understand, particularly since the prosecution relied heavily on the "decisions of inferior [US] federal courts" to define the term.[218] In Japan, he explained, "it is rather exceptional to punish the preparation of a crime and plot thereof before the commission of a criminal act."[219] He also differentiated between Anglo-American and Roman law, and noted that "to constitute a plot or conspiracy as an independent crime, the date and place of a plot or conspiracy must be specified to an intelligible extent." It was inconceivable that a country that did not have an Anglo-American legal system could be charged with conspiracy from "January 1928 to September 2, 1945."[220] Law based solely on Anglo-American traditions, he added, "cannot be deemed to constitute international law," and, given this lack of universality, cannot be applied by the IMFTE.[221] The defense, Kiyose went on, would also "refute the charge of conspiracy" against each of the accused not only because they varied in age, position, and rank, but also because they

> never had a chance to meet as a whole with any special object in view. They never had an occasion as a group to exchange their opinions on any such matters. As a matter of fact there were real differences and divisions of opinion among some of them.[222]

He then addressed the murder charges, arguing that the "loss of lives due to the act of war" was not murder.[223] International law, he argued, differentiated between "war as an act of sovereign states and acts of brigands or pirates." If war is "waged by the will of the state, it becomes an important question in international law whether individuals who are in official positions of the state are ipso facto criminally responsible."[224] If, as the Allies argued, World War II was fought to maintain international law, then such law as it existed from 1928 to 1945 "imparts no responsibility to individuals in official positions for the act of the state." His point, of course, was that the prosecution was trying to use *ex post facto* law to prosecute the defendants.[225]

Kiyose also questioned the validity of the prosecution's efforts to compare acts of "terrorism and atrocities" with those committed by Nazi Germany, and the idea that these were "not [individual] incidental errors" but "premeditated acts committed in pursuance of a national policy."[226] Japan's military, he went on, "strongly desired" that its troops strictly observe the laws of war. He did admit, though, that during the latter part of the war, when chaos reigned on the battlefield and at home, criminal acts might have occurred. But the "intentional violation of human decency as was alleged to have been committed against the Jews was never present in Japan."[227] Moreover, many of the

> atrocities and cruelties alleged to have been committed by Japanese forces against prisoners of war did not come to the knowledge of many of those accused until they were disclosed by this Tribunal. Others had no knowledge to restrain them even though they were aware of the fact... others did their best to restrain and punish the perpetrators of such crimes.[228]

Most importantly, no defendant "ever formulated a common plan, or ordered, or authorized or permitted atrocities or deliberately and recklessly disregarded his legal duty to take steps to prevent observance of the laws and customs of war in this respect."[229]

One of the key elements in the defense's case centered around the prosecution's interpretation of international law. During the early part of the trial, Dr. Takayanagi argued that the crimes laid out in the charter were not "declaratory" and were not the "law of nations." The defense considered such law "the formula of crimes unilaterally decided upon by the policy of the Allied Governments."[230] He noted that the Nuremberg court had rejected "some of the interpretations placed thereon by the prosecution,"[231] meaning that the Tokyo court had to decide on the relationship between the "law of the Charter and the Instrument of Surrender."[232] He reminded the court that the Instrument of Surrender meant that while Japan was obligated "to perform all of the demands" of the Allies, it also had the "right to insist" that the Allies not go beyond the bounds of their legal rights laid out in this document.[233]

A case in point, he went on, centered around the idea of "criminal conspiracy, the so-called crimes against peace and crimes against humanity (apart from cases which form part of the 'war crimes')... crimes unknown to the law of nations."[234] Initially, Keenan had used a broad definition of conspiracy based on several US cases such as *Marino v. U.S.*, a 1937 US Circuit Court of Appeals case. Citing *Marino*, Keenan defined conspiracy as

> a combination of two or more persons, by concerted action, to accomplish a criminal or unlawful purpose, or some purpose not in itself criminal or unlawful, by criminal or unlawful means... The purpose of the conspiracy may be continuous, that is, it may contemplate commission of several offences, or overt acts.[235]

When the defense challenged this definition, the prosecution provided a more succinct one during summation that described it as

> a machinery with a detailed plan of actions, with a distribution of roles and functions, with a system of subordination to a single directing center.[236]

The defense countered that to prove a conspiracy, it had to be shown that an alleged conspirator was part of a specific group of policymakers with specific knowledge of the conspiracy guided by the intention to undertake such a crime. It argued that the Nuremberg tribunal confirmed in its decision on the General Staff and High Command that simply holding an important position in authority when "a certain incident broke out does not establish that said accused is guilty of a crime against peace."[237] Conspiracy, the defense argued, was the "plotting or...conspiring, the breathing together to achieve an unlawful end."[238]

While the defense was correct in its reading of the Nuremberg decision, which found the German General Staff and High Command not guilty based on the fact that the tribunal did not consider it a criminal organization,[239] the Nuremberg tribunal did note in its judgment that

> it has heard much evidence as to the participation of these officers in planning and waging aggressive war, and in committing war crimes against humanity. This evidence is, as to many of them, clear and convincing. They have been responsible in large measure for their miseries and suffering that have fallen on millions of men, women, and children. They have been a disgrace to the honorable profession of arms...Although they were not a group falling within the words of the Charter, they were certainly a ruthless military caste.[240]

Takayanagi's goal in all of this was to challenge Keenan's assumption that conspiracy was an accepted concept in international law. He thought that this was based on nothing more than the chief prosecutor's assertion early in the trial that the "Charter creates no new law."[241] And by law, Takayanagi went on, he must mean the "law of nations," even though he only cites a US federal court case.[242] In reality, he argued, conspiracy was not found "in other legal systems,"[243] while the idea of "collective responsibility harked back to the tribal age of mankind," and could, if applied as the prosecution intended, mean that once a war was declared to be aggressive, anyone who had served his country, regardless of his motives, could be "held responsible for murder and for all shocking crimes by others, even if he is totally unaware when, where, and by whom these crimes were committed."[244] The Nuremberg tribunal, he added, ruled that under its charter, it had no jurisdiction to try a "person's participation in a common plan to commit war crimes or crimes against humanity." It ruled that "conspiracy must be clearly outlined in its criminal purpose. It must not be too far removed from the time of decision and action."[245]

Takayanagi was correct when he noted that the basic legal precedent for the prosecution's charge of conspiracy, *Marino v. U.S.*, was an obscure US federal court appellate case involving efforts by six defendants to have their conviction for liquor smuggling from Mexico into the United States overturned. The prosecution, which relied heavily on a lengthy US Department of Justice study on the law of conspiracy, chose the *Marino* case because, at least from the perspective of the lawyers who wrote the study, it fit the peculiar legal needs of the Tokyo prosecutors. But Takayanagi erred when he said that conspiracy was not found in other legal systems. Both the Department of Justice study and works by Peter Gillies and Sir Robert Samuel Wright have underscored the deep historical roots of criminal conspiracy in American and English common law. There is some question, though, about the applicability of *Marino* as a legal precedent, since it dealt with smuggling and relied heavily on a US criminal code definition of conspiracy as a crime by two or more persons who sought to harm or defraud the United States.[246] This, of course, all became moot once the Nuremberg court reached its decision in 1946, thus establishing new legal precedents for use by the prosecution and judges at the Tokyo trial.

Takayanagi also dealt with questions about the war crimes charges raised initially in Kiyose's opening remarks. The latter was particularly concerned about the validity of the prosecution's efforts to compare acts of "terrorism and atrocities" with those committed by Nazi Germany, and the idea that these were "not [individual] incidental errors" but "premeditated acts committed in pursuance of a national policy."[247] The defense argued that Japan's military leaders "strongly desired" its troops strictly to observe the laws of war. Kiyose did admit, though, that during the latter part of the war, when chaos reigned on the battlefield and at home, criminal acts might have occurred. But Japan did, he added, follow the rules of war when it came to the treatment of POWs.[248]

In fact, he went on, many of the defendants first learned of these alleged crimes during the trial. Some had no authority to deal with such crimes even if they were aware of them, while other defendants did what they could "to restrain and punish the perpetrators." He reiterated that there was ample evidence to prove that none of the defendants were involved in formulating "a common plan, or ordered, or authorized or permitted atrocities or deliberately and recklessly disregarded legal duty to take steps to prevent observance of the laws and customs of war in this respect."[249] In the end, he thought that the atrocities committed by some Japanese troops were "unduly magnified and in some degree fabricated," and that there was ample evidence to document this.[250]

Unfortunately, Takayanagi's later efforts, first to challenge the murder charges, and then the question of "conventional" war crimes, was weak. Regardless, he continued to disagree with the prosecution's definition of war crimes[251] and murder, likening the latter to a "hat trick" where, once the hat was picked up, out swarmed "little doctrines drawn from odds and ends of municipal law, to the extreme amazement of us all."[252] Takayanagi considered Allied efforts to try Japanese war criminals a form of "negative criminality," which the American delegation at the Paris Peace Conference in 1919 defined as "responsibility for failure to prevent 'conventional' war crimes, and that negligence in preventing death is only non-capital manslaughter in England."[253]

The defense also challenged the prosecution's contention that the applicable Hague and Geneva conventions were part of the larger body of customary international law. This was particularly the case with the 1929 Geneva convention, which Japan had signed but had not ratified. The prosecution countered that since Japan had assured the Allies that it would abide by the 1929 convention's terms, its provisions would be applied to Japan *mutatis mutandis*.[254] Takayanagi disagreed, and stated

> that it was immaterial what the reservation "mutatis mutandis" meant. Just as one tourist may tell another, "I am going to the *Kabuki* tomorrow—what about you?," and the other may reply, "Yes, that's my idea too." There is no pretence of any agreement or understanding whether in morals or law.[255]

One of the defense attorneys, Maj. Bruce Ben Blakeney, had argued early in the trial that "war is not a crime," and that the operative laws of war were not applicable until December 1941.[256] Takayanagi reiterated these points, and questioned whether the Hague Convention of 1907 was applicable to individuals and individual responsibility. The "main object" of the 1907 convention, he argued, "was to secure the responsibility of the state."[257] It did not deal with individual responsibility or "any new liability of high government officials."

> Therefore, it declared that a signatory state could not escape responsibility by shelter-ing itself behind the arbitrary judgement of its military commanders. That such a dec-laration, followed by a provision that a delinquent state should pay compensation, and no word concerning ministers, shall be distorted as implying personal liability on the part of government officials, will serve as a warning for future statesmen against the dangers of international agreements unless drafted with the patient care of a chancery barrister or a land title specialist. International agreements have hitherto been drafted in the broad spirit of agreements between friends who have a common background of ideas.[258]

He added that the prosecution's efforts to equate the word "governments" with "individuals momentarily running the government in various capacities" was, at best, "a transparent equivoque," and that it was the state and the state alone that was "liable for the breach of the provisions of the convention."[259]

William Logan took the defense's case in a different direction during his sum-mation on March 10, 1948. He gave full voice to a key argument that had rested just below the surface throughout the defense's presentation—that it was the Allies not Japan that brought war to the Pacific by provoking Japan "into a War of Self-Defense."[260] Led by the United States, the Allied powers took this course of action by adopting policies that affected Japan's economic stability. He argued against the idea that the war in the Pacific, at least on the part of Japan, was premeditated. Such an idea was foolish, given that Japan could never hope to dominate and con-quer "the great powers upon which it had depended with almost childlike faith for its economic sustenance."[261] In reality, the Pacific War was merely an attempt by "Japan to exercise its internationally recognized sovereign right of self-defense against encroachments by foreign powers which threatened its very existence—a decision which no authority questions as being their prerogative."[262]

The prosecution, he argued, would have the court believe that the blockade in 1940–1941 was simply aimed at diminishing the flow of military supplies to Japan. In reality, this

> was the act of all powerful and greatly superior economic states against a confessedly dependent island nation whose existence and economics were predicated upon world commercial relations.[263]

Moreover, Japan and Japan alone had the right to determine if such a blockade was "an act of war against it."[264] Japan's troubles, he reminded the tribunal, began when the

> Western Powers with their so-called civilization including a long history of wars and conquest by force, opened its doors and brought to its shores trade, commerce and con-tacts with the outside world. Colonization by force and imperialism was in full swing. It is not passing strange that after being compelled to emerge from its long retirement Japan found itself embroiled in world affairs, intrigues and wars. It became awakened

to new interests in life. Its population increased rapidly and its home resources were not sufficient to support its people.[265]

To deal with what became a demographic crisis, Japan had to industrialize and trade abroad. Being an island nation with little arable land and limited natural resources, Japan became dependent on foreign trade to deal with its "teeming population" vis-à-vis its own inadequate resources.[266] He might have added that Japan faced two other choices in the nineteenth and twentieth centuries—to become a "doormat" for the Western imperialists, who carved up China into foreign enclaves, or become a competitive economic power in East Asia that shared in the gradual destruction of imperial China.

Logan argued forcefully against the prosecution's charge that Japan's leaders entered "a conspiracy of economic preparations for war" in 1928, noting that planned economies were a common staple of modern, industrialized twentieth-century nations.[267] He then returned to the question of the US-led blockade of Japan from 1938 to 1941, reminding the court of the statement of Secretary of State Frank B. Kellogg, the coauthor of the Kellogg-Briand Pact that renounced aggressive war as national policy.[268] During the negotiations to determine if the United States would ratify the accord, he was asked by Senator Claude A. Swanson of Virginia,

> "Suppose a country is not attacked—suppose there is an economic blockade . . ." Secretary Kellogg replied: "There is no such thing as a blockade without you are [*sic*] in a war." A senator [David A. Reed, Missouri] then said, "It is an act of war," and Secretary Kellogg concurred saying, "An act of war, absolutely."[269]

In essence, Logan was using these comments and what he considered the court's own interpretation of international law, to justify Japan's attack on Pearl Harbor and other territories in southeast Asia in December 1941.[270] He also argued that US military support of China, which led to the "spilling of Japanese blood on Chinese soil," was further evidence of Japan's need to react "against the military ring being forged around her. The facts amply demonstrate she had just provocation to strike in self-defense."[271] Japan's effort diplomatically, he added, to deal with this military and economic encirclement failed because of the US determination not to compromise with Japan and end the economic stranglehold that drove Japan "into doing that which any other self-respecting nation would have done."[272]

> Having accomplished the avowed purpose of goading Japan into an attack it would indeed be a black mark in history to record this attack as other than one of self-defense.[273]

But it was the Japanese lawyers, not their American colleagues, who addressed most eloquently what to all of the defendants was one of the prosecution's most offensive ideas, voiced first by Keenan, that the trial was "a part of the determined battle of civilization to preserve the entire world from destruction."[274] From the prosecution's perspective, "there was a juridical concept of 'civilization' that demanded the prosecution of aggression."[275] The idea that the war in the Pacific and the Tokyo trial was a "battle for civilization" is something that still infuriates Japanese scholars. Yasuaki Ōnuma asks if the Allied powers [were] in a position to arrogate themselves the title of "civilization at large," while Masajirō Takigawa, a member of the defense team, later wondered if the tribunal had "judged the vanquished arbitrarily in the name of 'civilization' with the primitive idea of retaliation, but without any self-examination on their part."[276] Takayanagi said as much in his comments before the court on March 3–4, 1948. Kiyose added that

> Both Mr. Keenan and Mr. Comyns-Carr have said that this trial must be conducted in order to protect civilization. On this point, I, too am in complete agreement. But, by "civilization," do you not include the terms "respect for treaties" and "impartiality of trials[?]."[277]

In the end, of course, such arguments fell on deaf ears, since the tribunal, with one exception, did not address the question of the civilizing nature of the trial. The majority judgment did note, in reference to the idea that the tribunal was fulfilling the terms of Hague IV (1907), that judges "were animated by the desire, even in the extreme case, to serve the interests of humanity and the needs of civilization by diminishing the evils of war."[278] On the other hand, the Indian judge, Radhabinod Pal, who voted to acquit all of the defendants,[279] was adamant when it came to the idea that the trial was a "battle of civilization."

> The so-called trial held according to the definition of crime now given by the victors obliterates the centuries of civilization which stretch between us and the summary slaying of the defeated in war. A trial with law thus prescribed will only be a sham employment of legal process for the satisfaction of a thirst for revenge. It does not correspond to any idea of justice. Such a trial may justly create the feeling that the setting up of a tribunal like the present is much more a political than a legal affair, an essentially political objective having thus been cloaked by a juridical appearance. Formalized vengeance can bring only an ephemeral satisfaction, with every probability of ultimate regret; but vindication of law through genuine legal process along may contribute substantially to the re-establishment of order and decency in international relations.[280]

He argued that it was the Western powers that had set the stage for Japanese moves in Asia through their coinage and use of euphemistic terms like "protectorate" and "annexation." And had not this constitutional fiction served its Western inventors in good stead?"[281] Yet another Asian judge, Delfin Jaranilla, who argued that the tribunal had been too lenient in imposing penalties on the defendants, added that the nature of the Japanese crimes, particularly war crimes and crimes against humanity, had to "transcend national considerations if civilization is, as it should, survive."[282] In the end, the majority of the judges sided principally with Jaranilla in their November 4–12, 1948, judgment, noting that

> prior to the year 1930 ... [Japan] claimed a place among the civilized communities of the world and had voluntarily incurred the above obligations designed to further the cause of peace, to outlaw aggressive war, and to mitigate the horrors of war. It is

against that background of rights and obligations that the actions of the accused must be viewed and judged.[283]

Several years earlier, the judges discussed the process of reaching judgment. They agreed that all decisions would be made by majority vote and that there would be no "separate or dissenting opinions."[284] However, when Judge Pal joined the court, he let it be known that he would write a dissenting opinion, which essentially scuttled this agreement.[285] Over the next two and a half years, considerable differences of opinion arose among the judges over questions about the legality of the idea of crimes against peace, conspiracy as a crime in international law, natural versus positivist concepts of international law, and the law as expressed in the tribunal's charter. Some of the judges thought that they were there simply to uphold the law as stated in the charter, while others saw this as an opportunity "to write learned treatises on international law in defence of the charter, but each on different grounds. Still others...deny the law of the charter and our right to try those accused at all."[286] In the end, it was decided to let a committee headed by Justice Cramer write the majority decision, with separate opinions by Webb, Jaranilla, Bernard, Röling, and Pal.

The 1,443-page judgment was divided into 10 chapters, which focused principally on aggressive war. There was a single chapter on war crimes and others on applicable law, findings on the counts of the indictment, and a final chapter of verdicts, which included the separate concurring and dissenting opinions, and, in the case of Pal, a separate judgment.

The tribunal's majority judgment relied heavily on Nuremberg IMT precedents for its interpretation of international law.

> In view of the fact that in all material respects the Charters of this Tribunal and the Nuremberg Tribunal are identical, this Tribunal prefers to express its unqualified adherence to the relevant opinions of the Nuremberg Tribunal rather than by reasoning the matters anew in somewhat different language to open the door to controversy by way of conflicting interpretations of the two statements of opinion.[287]

It added, in reference to defense challenges about the question of aggressive war in international law prior to 1945, that "aggressive war was a crime at [sic] international law long prior to the date of the Declaration of Potsdam." This essentially shut the door on defense challenges against this interpretation of tribunal rights as expressed in article 5 of the charter.[288]

The majority also rejected much of the defense evidence, condemning the defense for delays caused by rigorous translation issues and "a tendency for counsel and witnesses to be prolix and irrelevant."[289] Webb stated after the trial that if the "Japanese lawyers had been more proficient in English, or the interpreters had been more competent, it might have affected the judgment of the trial." Kayoko Takeda disagrees with this conclusion, and notes that another Japanese scholar, Noboru Kojima, "believes that the problems with the interpretations disrupted the proceedings, limited the ability of the defendants and their counsel to express themselves and negatively affected the judges' understanding of the testimony."[290]

Neil Boister and Robert Cryer also point to the fact that many of the justices probably thought that United Nations Resolution 95 (I), *Affirmation of the Principles of International Law Recognized by the Charter of the Nürnberg Tribunal* (December 11, 1946) buffeted the majority's interpretation of aggressive war as an integral part of international law. However, they point out, since this and the Nuremberg judgment took place after the Tokyo court "had rejected the defence motions to jurisdiction in early 1946, Tokyo's reliance on Nuremberg was, in the final analysis, either adventitious, or betrays the initial rejection of the defence motions" challenging the question of whether "the Charter reflected existing law on crimes against peace." Such a rejection by the court, they argue, was "done thoughtlessly."[291]

All of this, of course, raises questions about the principal focus of the judgment and, for that matter, the trial itself—the question of Japanese violations of international treaties in waging a war of aggression, and the conspiratorial role of each of the defendants not only regarding aggressive war itself, but also the war crimes committed during the long conflict. In reaching its judgment, the majority of the judges concluded it was unnecessary to prove the "charge to wage aggressive war," since such "acts are already criminal in the highest degree."[292]

But linking this to the individual responsibility of the defendants was a different matter. The defense's position was that in international law, responsibility rested with the state, not individuals.[293] The court's majority, however, rejected this idea, noting that the charter, which it accepted as the guiding legal standard for tribunal decisions, would not permit a defendant to hide behind such a concept. It added that "the fact that a defendant acted pursuant to an order of his Government or of a superior shall not free him from responsibility but may be considered in mitigation of punishment."[294]

The focus then was on the ten charges of the indictment not rejected by the tribunal that dealt with the charges of conspiracy to wage aggressive war. Each of the defendants was ultimately convicted of one or more of these charges.[295]

Count 1—participation in a common plan or conspiracy to wage aggressive declared or undeclared wars of aggression in East Asia, the Pacific, and the Indian Ocean.

Counts 27, 28, 29, 31–33, 35, 36—all defendants waged illegal wars of aggression against China, the United States, the British Commonwealth, the Netherlands, France, the USSR, and Mongolia between 1931 and 1945.

Count 54—19 of the defendants (Dohihara, Hata, Hoshino, Itagaki, Kaya, Kido, Kimura, Koiso, Muto, Nagano, Oka, Oshima, Sato, Shigemitsu, Shimada, Suzuki, Togo, Tōjō, and Umezu) "ordered, authorised and permitted" those cited in count 53 (the same defendants as listed in counts 54–55) "to commit the breaches of the Laws and Customs of War" against "thousands of [Allied] prisoners of war and civilians" from December 7, 1941, to September 2, 1945.

Count 55—it added that the above defendants, "by virtue of their respective offices responsible for securing the observance of the said Conventions and assurances and the Laws and Customs of War towards Allied POWs and civilians...deliberately and recklessly disregarded their legal duty to take adequate steps to secure the observance and prevent breaches thereof, and thereby violated the laws of war."[296]

But the most surprising and fascinating part of the judgment were the separate opinions and in the case of Pal, judgment. Though not read in court, they deserve some discussion because they addressed some of the fundamental principles of law and evidence used during the trial to convict the defendants.[297] Webb, for example, while supporting the rights of the court as laid out in its charter, argued that the question of Hirohito's immunity should be taken into consideration when determining sentences. And though he did not agree with all of the sentences, he concluded that none appeared to "be manifestly excessive or manifestly inadequate."[298]

Justice Bernard considered the trial procedurally "defective," particularly when it came to the application of rules "essential to the defense of the Accused." This was also true, he noted, when it came to the issue of crimes against peace and conspiracy to commit aggressive war. At no point during the trial, he argued, was any

> direct proof furnished concerning the formation among individuals known, on a known date, at a specific point, of a plot the object of which was to assure Japan the domination unaccepted by its inhabitants of some part of the world. The only thing proven is the existence among certain influential classes of the Japanese nation of the desire to seat at all costs the domination of Japan upon other parts of East Asia.[299]

At best, with the official outbreak of the Pacific War, the defendants, Bernard thought, could be seen as "accomplices" of the "principal author" (Emperor Hirohito) of this crime, "who escaped all prosecution."[300] In the end, he concluded, the nature of the prosecution and the tribunal's "defects" were such that he could not come to any "definite opinion" about the charges of "crimes against peace...conventional war crimes and crimes against humanity." On the other hand, he did not doubt that certain defendants bore "a large part of the responsibility" for the "most abominable crimes...committed on the largest scale by the members of the Japanese police and navy."[301]

Röling, who also disagreed with some of the court's findings, later explained that the principal reason for writing his dissent was to induce MacArthur, under article 17 of the charter, to reduce the sentences of Hata, Hirota, Kido, Shigemitsu, and Togo, who he thought should have been acquitted.[302] He also wrote that none of the defendants should have been condemned to death "for having committed crimes against peace." Life imprisonment was sufficient punishment for this crime. The same was true for those convicted of involvement in a "conspiracy to wage a war of aggression, or of waging a war of aggression, but not found guilty of any conventional war crimes." On the other hand, Röling thought Oka, Sato, and Shimada should have been found guilty of committing war crimes and sentenced to death. He concurred with the death penalty sentences for Doihara, Itagaki, Kimura, Matsui, Muto, and Tōjō.[303]

But it was Pal, who voted to acquit all of the defendants, who attracted most of the attention with his lengthy, and, at times, brilliant dissenting judgment. Radhabinod Pal was one of only three Asian judges on the tribunal, and some have attributed his perspective to this fact. A specialist in "traditional Hindu law" who was serving as a judge on the Calcutta High Court when he was appointed to the IMTFE, Pal was well versed in international law. Like many legal scholars in India at the time, he was a "strict constructionist who went by the letter of the law."[304] He was a Bengali, and some have simplistically attributed his dissent as a product of Gandhi's "theory of passive resistance or of no resistance into judicial terminology."[305] Others see in his ideas a Pan Asiatic sympathy drawn from his experiences in colonial Bengal, a hotbed of ethnic and religious tension during India's long path to independence.[306] All of these factors affected his view of the trial and the plight of the defendants.

Pal questioned not only the authority of the tribunal but its charter. He also challenged the idea that aggressive war was illegal, arguing that the Kellogg-Briand Pact, a key legal document in the prosecution's arsenal, did not change the "position of war in international life."[307] Nor, for that matter, did documents such as the Cairo and Potsdam declarations, which were nothing more than "mere announcements of the Allied Powers."[308] Consequently, he thought that if the international legal basis of the trial was invalid, then the trial itself was

> only a sham employment of legal process for the satisfaction of a thirst for revenge. It does not correspond to any idea of justice. Such a trial may justly create the feeling that the setting up of a tribunal like the present is much more a political than a legal affair, an essentially political objective having thus been cloaked by juridical appearance.[309]

The result, he argued, was an international trial based on *ex post facto* law that allowed the victor to "define a crime at his will and then punish for that crime."[310]

> A victor state, as sovereign legislative power of its own state, might have the right to try prisoners of war within its custody for war crimes as defined and determined by the international law. But neither the international law nor the civilized world recognizes any right in it to legislate defining the law in this respect to be administered by any court set up by it for the purpose of such trial.[311]

Pal also challenged the prosecution's charge of aggressive war, arguing that "no category of war became criminal or illegal in international life" before the end of World War II. Prior to this time, individuals "comprising the government and functioning as agents of the government" incurred "no criminal responsibility in international law for the acts alleged." He added, though, that if one accepted aggressive war as a crime, one test of its criminality was its justification. Assisting a nation that has been invaded would be justified *just* as assisting a country "subjected to [an] aggressive act of domination" would be "equally justifiable."[312] His reference, of course, was to the Western world's century-old colonial domination of much of Asia, and Japan's claim that its military actions in Asia were partly driven by the desire to drive out the colonial "aggressors." Finally, he argued, the "international community has not yet reached a stage which would make it expedient to include judicial process for condemning and punishing either states or individuals."[313]

The Indian justice also pointed out the hypocrisy of the Allied victors, who either through policies of colonial domination, boycotts, and the use of weapons such as atomic bombs, could be accused of committing international crimes. He also paraphrased Justice Jackson at Nuremberg, who called the preparation by one nation to dominate another "the worst of crimes." If such a crime was illegal prior to World War II, Pal wrote, "there was hardly a big power which was free from that taint."[314] He added that the Allied boycott of Japan, which was "engaged in war…a direct participation in the conflict."[315]

Pal also challenged the court's decision on conspiracy, concluding that the prosecution was never able to prove there had been an ongoing, "comprehensive" conspiracy among those so charged between 1925 and 1945 "or during any other period." More importantly, the evidence failed to prove that any of the defendants had been part of any conspiracy.[316] To prove conspiracy, he went on, the prosecution had to prove that

1. the persons charged must be leaders, organizers, instigators, or accomplices in the formulation of the plan;
2. the object of the plan was that Japan should secure the military, naval, political, and economic domination of the countries named;
3. the persons who participated as leaders, etc., in the formulation of execution of the plan must also be shown to have conspired that, for the purpose of the above domination, Japan should wage declared or undeclared war;
4. that such war need not be against the country sought to be dominated but against any country which might oppose their purpose.[317]

Conspiracy, he argued, was not a part of international law, at least since 1928, while "no authoritative attempt has been made to extend international law to cover the condemned and forbidden conduct of individuals."[318] He saw conspiracy as "fundamentally a mental offense" in which "will and reason" are the starting point in "making any agreement." Both were key to analyzing

> the nature of the conspiratorial agreement...is an inchoate act for which the essential act is slight. It involves an intent to commit a further act...The essential element in the principle of the law of conspiracy is thus the desirability as also the possibility of prevention of the design contemplated by the conspirators.[319]

He then quoted Professor Francis Bowes Sayre of Harvard law school, who called criminal conspiracy "the evil genius of our law" that hopefully would become "nothing more than a shadow stalking through past cases."[320]

Justice Pal also discussed the murder charges and challenged Comyns-Carr's statement that every leader who ordered his "army to attack and kill an enemy, even in legitimate warfare, fulfills all of the conditions of murder if it was done without lawful justification." He then alluded to comments in *Oppenheim's International Law* (6th ed.), which stated that

> Whatever may be the cause of war that has broken out, and whether or not the cause be a so-called just cause, the same rules of international law are valid as to what must not be done, may be done, and must be done by the belligerents themselves in making war against each other...The rules of International Law apply to war from whatever cause it originates.[321]

There was no evidence, he went on, to prove that any of the defendants indicted on the murder counts had ordered, authorized, or given permission "to slaughter the inhabitants contrary to international law...beyond, of course, the order to attack these territories."[322]

Pal also disagreed with the idea that the similarity between atrocities that took place throughout Japanese-occupied East Asia reflected a "general policy of the Japanese forces and of the Japanese government."[323] In fact, he argued, many of these stories bore striking resemblance to some of the "baseless atrocity-stories designed to arouse animosities" during the American Civil War.[324] He also alluded to some of the propaganda films shown in court as evidence of the Allied use of such propaganda.[325] And what about the charges in counts 54 and 55, which held some of the defendants responsible for ordering, authorizing, and permitting Japanese naval and military forces to commit war crimes against POWs and civilians?[326] The prosecution often used hearsay evidence or propaganda to prove such charges, while the accuracy of testimony by "excited or prejudiced" witnesses about atrocities often went unchallenged.[327] Some stories, in fact, though horrible,

> were perpetrated. But those who might have committed these terrible brutalities are not before us now. Those of them who could be got [sic] hold of alive have been made to answer for their misdeeds mostly with their lives. We have been given by the Prosecution long lists of such criminals tried and convicted at different forums. The very length of such lists is sufficiently assuring that no mistaken clemency towards these alleged perpetrators of all such foul acts could find any place anywhere. We are, however, not considering the case of persons who had no apparent hand in the perpetration of these atrocious deeds.[328]

He concluded by challenging the prosecution's charge that the mistreatment of POWs was "part of the policy of the Japanese Government," and that in cases where the government was not involved, it was "indifferent" to the commitment of such crimes.[329] He focused on the claim that Japan was bound by the terms of the 1907 Hague and 1929 Geneva conventions, even though it had not ratified the latter. Interpretative differences over this question centered around Japanese "domestic law, peace law, army and navy penal codes and courts martial law, which were in some respects not compatible with the Geneva Convention," and the "difficulties Japan would face due to the vastness of the area of East Asia."[330]

Pal also criticized the propagandistic nature of some of the prosecution's evidence, and argued that there was no "similarity of patterns of crimes" across Japanese-occupied East Asia.[331] He did not deny that such abuses took place, and considered the Bataan Death March "an atrocious brutality."[332] But he also argued that it was "an isolated instance of cruelty" that could not be blamed on any of the defendants, particularly since the man responsible had been executed for his involvement in these crimes.[333] He made a similar argument for the treatment of POWs building the Burma–Thailand railway, and questioned the validity of some of the evidence, particularly as it related to charges against some of the defendants.[334]

The failure to prevent such crimes was not a criminal matter, since "failure does not imply fault."[335] In the end, given what he considered the inability of the prosecution to define aggressive war, the only real option legally was to fall back on article 43 of Hague IV (1907), which gave the international community the right to "remove any of the accused from any sphere of life where there would be any possibility of his doing any future mischief."[336] He pointed to the cases of Napoleon Bonaparte and Adolf Hitler, noting that none of the accused could be compared to either man, since each of the defendants came to power legally in a recognized sovereign constitutional state. He saw the case against individuals as a political undertaking, not a legal one. In the end, "a victor can dispense to the vanquished everything from mercy to vindictiveness; but the one thing the victor cannot give the vanquished is justice." The prosecution used the "language of emotionalized generalities" that was designed not to educate but rather to "entertain." In the end,

> When time shall have softened passion and prejudice, when Reason shall have stripped the mask from misrepresentation, then justice, holding evenly her scales, will require much of past censure and praise to change places.[337]

Conclusion

Though seldom studied or discussed, the Tokyo IMT stands as an example of the flaws of victor nations attempting to try leaders of a defeated nation based on an inadequate focus on generalized legal concepts and weak precedents. While the Nuremberg IMT trial was an imperfect model to copy, it at least had some core legal principles that worked vis-à-vis the special nature of the Nazi system of rule and ideology. This would not be the case in Tokyo, where it was hard to prove that a similar mind set drove Japanese policy during the long years of Japan's expanding interests in China and Asia. War crimes and other criminal acts took a backseat to the prosecution's efforts to filter what were originally 55 charges through the concept of illegal aggressive war. The tribunal's problems were further exacerbated by the US insistence on appointing a weak chief prosecutor and a judicial panel bent, at times, more on revenge than justice. Moreover, the failure of the tribunal to address some of the same lack of adequate defense rights that haunted the Nuremberg tribunal further underscored some of the serious flaws in this international legal undertaking. The fact that some of the most fascinating legal arguments from this trial are found in the dissenting opinions instead of those of the majority underscores many of the problems with the conduct of the trial and many of its judgments. In the end, despite some of the fascinating legal arguments from the prosecution and the defense, the Tokyo IMT trial stands as an example of how not to conduct an international criminal trial involving what would now be violations of International Humanitarian Law (IHL).

Chapter 8

Post–World War II National Trials in Europe and Asia

The Tokyo and Nuremberg IMT trials, though flawed, are some of the most important in history, and established important legal precedents and points of law that are still studied and cited today. It should be remembered, though, that they are only the tip of the "legal iceberg," so to speak, when it comes to the thousands of war crimes trials globally after World War II.

In early 1948, the UNWCC reported that the United States, Britain, France, Greece, the Netherlands, Norway, Poland, and Yugoslavia had conducted 969 trials involving 3,470 alleged war criminals. Czechoslovakia, it added, had conducted an unknown number of trials involving 18,496 alleged war criminals and Nazi collaborators. In Asia, it went on, the United States, Britain, Australia, and the Dutch had conducted over a thousand war crimes trials involving 2,794 defendants.[1] More recent studies, particularly by the Phillips Universität Marburg's *Forschungs-und Dokumentationszentrum für Kriegsverbrecherprozesse* (ICWC) point to a much more extensive body of trials throughout Europe and Asia.

We now know, for example, that the Dutch ultimately convicted 14,500 suspects of various war-related crimes in Europe, including collaboration, and sentenced 109 to death. Most of those convicted later had their sentences reduced, and, by 1960, few remained in prison.[2] Collaboration was also a key charge in the extensive war crimes trials in France, the Soviet Union, China, and other countries. The Soviet Union, for example, tried thousands of its own citizens for this crime, particularly during the latter months of the war, and condemned 5,000 to death. The same was true for a large percentage of the millions of Russians and others forcibly repatriated to the Soviet Union at the end of the war. The Nationalist government of Chiang Kai-shek was equally harsh on collaborators, and tried 25,000 Chinese for this crime. On the other hand, the Nationalists, and later the Communists, were far more lenient when dealing with alleged Japanese war criminals. This was not going to be the case in Europe, or, for that matter, elsewhere in Asia, where the victor nations used a series of military commissions and national courts to bring tens of thousands of German and Japanese war criminals to justice.

Denazification and War Crimes Trials in Occupied Germany

The American, British, and French decisions to conduct war crimes trials in each of their occupation zones in Germany was part of overall Allied efforts to denazify Germany and prepare it for a return to democracy. They argued that Control Council Law No. 10 gave them such rights, and used the Nuremberg charges to help define the basic charges in these trials.[3] Denazification efforts were guided by the Allied Control Council's directive, "The Arrest and Punishment of War Criminals, Nazis, Militarists, and the Internment, Control, and Surveillance of Potentially Dangerous Germans." It listed five categories of Nazis:

1. *Major Offenders*—anyone who committed crimes against victims or opponents against national socialism. *Sanctions*: death to 5 years imprisonment.
2. *Offenders*—Nazi political activists, militarists, or profiteers who actively advanced the national socialist tyranny. *Sanctions*: up to 10 years imprisonment.
3. *Lesser Offenders*—anyone, including former members of the Wehrmacht, who did not belong to the group of major offenders, but seems to be an offender, without, however, having manifested despicable or brutal conduct. *Sanctions*: up to 2 years probation.
4. *Followers*—anyone who was not more than a nominal participant in or a supporter of the national socialist tyranny. *Sanctions*: limits on travel and reparations payments.
5. *Exonerated Persons*—anyone who, in spite of his formal membership or candidacy or any other outward indication, not only showed a passive attitude but also actively resisted the national socialist tyranny to the extent of his powers and thereby suffered disadvantages. *No Sanctions*.[4]

Unfortunately, these guidelines, though helpful, could not ensure that all of the legitimate war criminals and lesser criminals would be trapped in the denazification net. This question was further complicated by the growing tensions between the occupying powers in the early stages of the Cold War. Regardless, Allied and German denazification courts dealt with 3,660,648 denazification cases from 1945 to 1949, and found 1,667 Germans to be *major offenders* and over 23,000 as *offenders*. Another 150,425 Germans were found to be *lesser offenders*, and over a million Germans were deemed Nazi *followers*. These courts also exonerated 1.2 million Germans and amnestied, failed to classify, or left uncharged another 1.26 million Germans. In other words, less than 5 percent of the 3.6 million Germans in the Western occupation zones who "were considered the hard core of the Nazis were charged accordingly."[5]

During the same period, the Americans, British, and French convicted more than 5,000 Germans of war crimes, sentencing over 800 to death, though executing only about 500. Dick de Mildt estimates that "the grand total of Germans and Austrians called to account for their involvement in Nazi crimes before the various courts of the formerly occupied European countries as well as those of the four main Allies, amounted to 60,000 persons." The "larger part" of those convicted were in Eastern Europe, particularly Poland and the USSR. In the Soviet occupation zone in Germany alone, for example, "Russian military tribunals sentenced nearly 18,000 persons in *secret* proceedings during the immediate post-war years."[6]

War Crimes Trials in the US Zone

The United States tried 185 alleged German war criminals in the "subsequent" Nuremberg trials from 1945 to 1948. It tried another 1,672 alleged German war criminals before military commissions in 489 separate legal proceedings during the same period.[7] Over half of the defendants in these proceedings were tried before US Military Commissions in the former Dachau concentration camp. According to the UNWCC, the United States based its right to conduct such trials on various statutes passed by the US Congress, particularly the 1920 Articles of War.[8] It tried its first German war criminals in a 1942 military commission trial in Washington, DC, and sentenced all eight to death for sabotage and other crimes. Several of the defendants appealed their conviction to the US Supreme Court, which ruled in *ex parte Richard Quirin*, 317 US 1 (1942) that the use of such tribunals was legal.[9] President Roosevelt added in a July 2, 1942, directive that anyone charged with committing "sabotage, espionage, hostile or warlike acts" against the United States, or violating the "laws of war, shall be subject to the law of war and to the jurisdiction of military tribunals." Joint Chiefs of Staff Directive 1023/10 of July 8, 1945, and a letter from the commander, United States Forces, European Theater (USFET), on July 16, 1945, titled "Trial of War Crimes and Related Cases," further strengthened US rights to conduct such trials. Five weeks later, Gen. Dwight David Eisenhower, the Supreme Commander of Allied Expeditionary Forces (SCAEF), issued his own directive authorizing the use of Military Commissions in the European Theater of Operations to

> try persons who are charged with violations of the laws of war and customs of war, of the law of nations or of the laws of occupied territory, or any part thereof.

A separate directive for military commissions in the Mediterranean Theater simply stated that their jurisdiction was limited to violations of the "laws or customs of war."[10]

The US military commission trials were to be conducted as General Courts-Martial, the highest level of military tribunals with the authority to impose the death penalty. According to the US Army's 1943 court-martial manual,

> Courts-martial are lawful tribunals, with authority to determine any case over which they have jurisdiction, and their proceedings, when confirmed as provided, are not open to review by civil tribunals, except for the purpose of ascertaining whether the military court had jurisdiction of the person and subject matter, and whether, though having such jurisdiction, it had exceeded its powers in the sentence pronounced.

The manual went on to explain that a General Court-Martial had the right

> to try any person subject to military law for any crime or offense made punishable by
> the Articles of War, and any other person who by the law of war is subject to trial by
> military tribunals.[11]

The military commissions, which were to use this manual to guide their proceedings, were not totally obligated to follow its rules, particularly when it came to the punishment of war crimes.[12]

Each US military commission trial would have a judge advocate who would serve as prosecuting attorney and a defense attorney "with such assistants as may be required."[13] Unfortunately, directives issued by the European command and SCAP did not require military commissions to adhere strictly to court-martial guidelines, other than to guarantee, as SCAP did in one directive—to adhere

> to a fair, expeditious hearing of the issues raised by the charges, excluding irrelevant
> issues or evidence and preventing any unnecessary delay or interference.[14]

Unfortunately, the commissions made hasty and at times deadly judgments that have raised serious questions about the fairness of such legal undertakings. This was particularly the case when it came to evidence. President Roosevelt's July 2, 1942, directive stipulated that evidence in such trials

> shall be admitted as would, in the opinion of the president of the commission, have
> probative value to a reasonable man.[15]

Postwar military directives in Europe and Asia embraced the spirit of this order but also allowed written statements, affidavits, depositions, letters, diaries, or copies of such documents as well as photographs, copies of papers "without proof," and "confessions...without proof of circumstances or that they were voluntarily made."[16]

They were also allowed to consider evidence from a previous trial of a "military or naval unit, or any group or organization" that centered around "an offence involving concerted criminal action."[17] It would be viewed "as *prima-facie* evidence that the accused is likewise guilty of that offence."[18] This would be particularly applicable where the defendant was a member of a group charged with "mass atrocity."[19] The military commissions could impose penalties ranging from death to fines, though they could not be carried out until they were approved "by the appointing authority" and, in the case of death sentences, the "Theatre Commander." Their decisions would be based on "a review and recommendation" of the Staff Judge Advocate who would study the facts of the trial and "its points of law" in consultation with "trained legal advice as to what, in right and justice, should be done."[20]

Yet a study of some of these early military commission trials that took place just weeks after the war ended in Europe and Asia shows that there were serious legal flaws in some of these proceedings. Very often defendants were convicted in hastily thrown together trials that bore little resemblance to the fair trial standards practiced at the time in civil courts. On June 1–2, a US military commission conducted the first postwar trial of German civilians accused of war crimes in Ahrweiler,

Germany. The defendants, Peter Kohn, Matthias Gierens, and Matthias Krein, were tried for beating to death an unknown US flyer near the village of Preist. Prior to the beatings, the pilot had been shot by another villager, Peter Back, who was tried a few weeks later for the same crime. Gierens and Krein were tried for the "violation of the laws and usages of war" as civilians, while Krein was accused of being an accessory to murder. The key to the prosecution's case was the testimony of a number of villagers who watched the crime unfold. The body of the unknown airman, which had been exhumed just a few weeks before the trial, provided some physical evidence of the beatings. All three defendants, who were represented by a JAG officer and a German attorney, Dr. Fritz Mehn, pleaded "not guilty." Two interpreters were present throughout the two-day trial.[21]

While a number of local villagers gave extremely brief testimony about what they saw, the defense could only come up with one witness, a local priest, Johann Delges.[22] Kohn admitted that he lost control during the incident, and was driven by the memory of Joseph Goebbels' statement about how to treat downed Allied pilots—"The one who kills them and the one who brings them off this world will not suffer any punishment."[23] Before the trial began, Dr. Mehn argued that Gierens, who delivered the death blow with a hammer, was mentally unstable, and asked the commission to have him examined by a psychiatrist. He was found to be sane not only at the time of the murder but also on the eve of the trial.[24]

Krein testified that he tried to stop Back from shooting at the pilot, but choose not to further challenge him because he was afraid Back would shoot him. In his review of the trial, Col. Julien C. Hyer wrote that Back was the "moving genius" behind this crime, while Kohn was "a mobster type as old as Caiaphas' judgement." Gierens, Hyer added, was "the morbid embodiment of all that the Nazi philosophy exemplifies."[25] The military commission found two of the defendants guilty of the murder, and Krein an accessory to murder. All three were ordered to "be hanged by the neck until dead." Hyer, well aware that this was the first conviction of German civilians since the war ended, confirmed the verdict for the Fifteenth US Army Office of the Army Judge Advocate on June 16, but stayed the executions while awaiting "further orders."[26] Back was found guilty of the same charges on June 16, and sentenced to death, which Hyer stayed pending "further orders."[27]

Three days earlier, another military commission convicted two German soldiers, Lt. Gunther Thiele and Grn. George Steinart, of the execution of an American POW, Capt. Peter M. Cummins, on April 17, 1945. According to the prosecution, which had signed statements from Thiele and Steinart, Cummins was captured after a firefight with Thiele's and Steinart's unit. Their commander, Capt. Johann Schwaben, who was acquitted two years later by a German Military Government Court in Dachau for involvement in the executions, ordered them to execute Cummins. Thiele questioned the order, while others suggested his subordinate, Steinert, carry out the execution, which he agreed to do. That evening, Cummins

was told to return to his car. "Steinert, who stood somewhat aside, followed with the machine pistol in order to carry out the order originally given by Captain Schwaben." After a few minutes shots were heard and Steinert returned and said, "the *Captain* is dead." Steinert had been told to shoot the Captain in such a way as to make it appear that he had fallen in combat. After Steinert had reported, several men stated that the Captain was not dead. The Lieutenant then sent Steinert to shoot the Captain through the heart. Another shot was heard and Steinert again reported. He was asked where he had shot and replied "in the right side." The Lieutenant then said "But that is not the heart," and Steinert fired again. The body was then carried to the vehicle, placed beside that of the "major" [Bennett; killed in the firefight] and covered with a shelter half from the bedroll.[28]

Thiele explained in court that Cummins was executed because his unit was "encircled" and was trying to avoid detection, something it could not do if it had to care for a wounded prisoner. He added that he was trained to follow orders and could not protest it until 48 hours after it had been carried out. If not, "Captain Schwaben would have shot him." Steinert made the same argument.[29]

To back up their claims, the defense introduced sections of the German Military Penal Code (*Deutsches Militärstrafgesetzbuch*), which stated that

> (1) If in the execution of an order relating to Service matters a penal law is violated, the commanding officer is solely responsible. Nevertheless, the subordinate obeying the order is subject to penalty as accomplice: 1. If he transgressed the order given, or 2. If he knew that the order of the commanding officer concerned an action the purpose of which was to commit a general or military crime of misdemeanor (2) if the guilt of the subordinate is minor, his punishment may be suspended.[30]

The commission rejected the idea of superior orders, and said German military law, when it came to this particular case, was "contrary to international law" and the accepted laws of war. It pointed to the Llandovery Castle case in Leipzig after World War I as justification for rejecting this point of defense. It also rejected the idea of "military necessity" and efforts by German jurists and others to justify what it called the "atrocities committed by Germans during the World War as well as the present war."[31] The commission found both men guilty of war crimes and ordered that they be hanged. In reviewing the case, Staff Judge Advocate Col. P. G. McElwee argued that such punishment served two purposes—appropriateness vis-à-vis the crimes and the deterrence "of further acts of a similar nature," something that was important "in the eyes of the civilized world, and particularly the Christian world, the most important." He added that

> in this case the source of evil was the commanding officer, Captain Schwaben, for it was he who conceived the original criminal plan to shoot the deceased and who issued the orders that set the fatal machine in motion. Captain Schwaben has not been tried for his crime. If the present accused are executed, the two most damning witnesses against him will be gone.[32]

Consequently, McElwee recommended the reduction of the sentences to life to ensure Thiele and Steinert would be able to testify against their former commanding officer.[33]

What is troubling about these early military commission and other trials is their haste. While these cases were chosen for their ease of conviction, they established a precedent in future US trials both in Europe and Asia where quick resolution was the legal watchword. While the pace of trials is less of an issue in instances where the defendants were charged and convicted of lesser charges and given brief sentences, it became extremely problematic when the charges were more serious.

The United States also conducted a series of major trials in Nuremberg and Dachau. The 12 "subsequent" Nuremberg trials involved some of Nazi Germany's most important organizations and individuals. These were specifically designated as military tribunal trials whose organization and powers were laid out in Ordnance No. 7 of October 18, 1946, which was issued by the US Military Government in Germany. It allowed for joint trials with the other occupying powers in Germany, and, unlike the military commissions, adopted more liberal guidelines to ensure better defendant rights when it came to questions of indictments and associated documents, translations, choice of counsel, ability to introduce evidence, and the selection of defense witnesses. But the tribunals were under orders to move their proceedings along expeditiously, and had the power to take whatever reasonable action was necessary to ensure this. They were not bound by "technical rules of evidence" and could admit any evidence that had "probative value." They also had the right to review any evidence beforehand to determine its "relevance." Once these tribunals reached a decision, it had to be forwarded to the military governor, who had the right "to mitigate, reduce, or otherwise alter the sentence imposed by the tribunal." A subsequent ordinance provided for joint sessions of the tribunals to discuss common legal rulings, precedents, or decisions.[34]

One of the most important military tribunal proceedings was the *Einsatzgruppen* trial (*U.S.A. v. Otto Ohlendorf et al.*; July 3, 1947—April 10, 1948), which involved 24 of the *Einsatzgruppen*'s most important leaders. All of the defendants, who pleaded not guilty, were charged with crimes against humanity, war crimes, and membership in a criminal organization. The principal defendant, Otto Ohlendorf, who commanded *Einsatzgruppe* D and had earlier testified at the IMT trial, argued that he considered almost all of the 90,000 Jews his unit murdered to be security threats to the Wehrmacht.[35] When asked about Jewish and Roma children, Ohlendorf explained that they were killed because they would "grow up, and surely, being the children of parents who had been killed, they would constitute a danger no smaller than that of their parents." He justified these crimes by noting: "I have seen very many children killed in this war through air attacks for the security of other nations."[36]

The court found 22 of the defendants guilty of all charges, and sentenced 14 of them to death by hanging, while the rest received prison sentences ranging from life to 10 years. Only four of the defendants—Paul Blobel, Dr. Werner Braune, Erich Naumann, and Ohlendorf—were ever executed. The others had their death or life sentences commuted and, after serving just a few years in prison, were released. The same was true of the two defendants who initially got life sentences. In fact, with the exception of those hanged, all of the *Einsatzgruppen* defendants found guilty never served their full terms.[37]

Equally important was the Doctors' Trial (*U.S. v. Karl Brandt et al.*; October 25, 1946—August 20, 1947), which charged all of the 23 defendants (20 of them were physicians), all of whom pleaded not guilty, with conspiracy to commit war crimes, crimes against humanity, and membership in a criminal organization. The principal defendant, Dr. Karl Brandt, had served as Hitler's personal physician and was one of the architects of his "euthanasia" program. Another defendant, Viktor Brack, headed this program.[38]

Brandt worked closely with Dr. Wolfram Seviers, the head of the SS's Ancestral Heritage office, and the Institute for Military Scientific Research (*Institute für Wehrwissenschaftliche Zweckforschung*). Seviers was also involved with some of the gruesome medical experiments in Dachau and helped fund the work of Dr. August Hirt, the chair of anthropology at the University of Strasbourg. Hirt collected human skulls and skeletons and sent Seviers a report in early 1942 about collecting the skulls of Jewish Bolshevik commissars in the Soviet Union. Hirt considered Jews "a repulsive, yet characteristic subhumanity," and suggested that the skulls be turned over to a physician or medical student, who would

> take a certain series of photographs and anthropological measurements...the origin, date of birth, and other personal data on the prisoner...He will separate the head from the torso and will forward it to its destination point in a preservative fluid within a well-sealed tin container especially made for this purpose. Based on the photos, the measurements and other data on the head, and finally the skull itself, the comparative anatomical research, research on racial membership, the pathological features of the skull from the form and size of the brain, and many other things, can now begin.[39]

Other defendants did medical experiments for the Luftwaffe at Dachau, which included the murder of 70–80 prisoners in high altitude compression chambers and the forced ingestion of saltwater.[40] The court sentenced Brack, Brandt, Gebhardt, Seviers, and three other defendants to death, acquitted five, and sentenced the rest to life imprisonment or terms of 15–20 years. All of the prison sentences were later reduced.[41]

In response, the World Medical Association issued its Declaration of Geneva (1948) for physicians to address the issue of medical experiments on human beings.

> I will not permit considerations of age, disease or disability, creed, ethnic origin, gender, national affiliation, race, sexual orientation, social standing or any other factor to intervene between my duty and my patient;
> I will not use my knowledge contrary to violate human and civil liberties, even under the threat.[42]

The United States also prosecuted 18 members of the Economic-Administrative Main Office (*Wirtschafts—Verwaltungshauptamt*; WVHA), which ran the concentration and death camps in the Pohl or WVHA Trial (*U.S. v. Oswald Pohl et al.*; April 8, 1947—November 3, 1947), charging all of the defendants except Hans Holberg with war crimes, crimes against humanity, and membership in a criminal organization. Three were acquitted while four, Pohl and his three deputy chiefs, August Frank, Georg Lörner, and Heinz Karl Fanslau, were sentenced to death. All except Pohl had their sentences commuted, while the rest got terms ranging from 10 years to life.[43]

Three trials, *U.S. v. Friedrich Flick et al.* (April 19—December 22, 1947), the *U.S. v. Alfried Krupp et al.* (December 8, 1947—July 31, 1948), and the I. G. Farben trial (*U.S. v. Carl Krauch*; August 27, 1947—July 31, 1948) involved cases against 42 bankers and industrialists who were charged with war crimes, crimes against humanity, crimes against peace, plunder, membership in a criminal organization, and, in the case of the Flick trial, being a member of Himmler's "Circle of Friends." The Krupp trial dealt with the role of the family's industrial complex in the Reich's military buildup before World War II and the use of slave laborers, while the I. G. Farben trial centered around its use of slave laborers and the manufacture of Zyklon B gas by one of its subsidiaries, Degesch. The Flick tribunal acquitted three of the defendants, while the rest received light sentences. All of the defendants in the Krupp trial were found guilty of the slave labor charge, though most received light sentences. Alfried Krupp, who was sentenced to 12 years imprisonment and forfeiture of his property, regained some of it after his early release in 1951. Thirteen of the I. G. Farben defendants were acquitted while the rest received light sentences including time served.[44]

The most extensive American military tribunal trials took place at Dachau. They were divided into four main categories:

1. main concentration camp cases;
2. subsequent concentration cases;
3. flier cases;
4. miscellaneous cases.[45]

The main concentration camp trials—six cases involving 200 defendants—focused on staff from the Dachau, Buchenwald, Flossenburg, Mauthausen, Norhausen, and Muehldorf *Konzentrationslager* in Germany and Austria. The subsequent concentration camp proceedings centered around 250 trials of about 800 staff members from subcamps that were attached to the above six camps. The 200 "flier" cases involved about 600 Germans, mostly civilians, who were charged with the deaths of 1,200 US military personnel, mainly downed pilots. The miscellaneous cases included the trials of 73 SS men involved in the Malmedy massacre of 84 Americans during the Battle of the Bulge in late 1944, the trial of staff members at the Hadamar asylum who were charged with the murder of almost 400 Polish and Russian nationals, and the trial of ten officers of the 150th Panzer Brigade who were charged with wearing US uniforms in an attack against US forces during the Ardenne Forest offensive in the fall of 1944.[46]

One of the earliest trials took place before a General Military Government Court (GMGC) from November 15 to December 13, 1945. It involved 40 guards and staff members from Dachau including its former commandant, Manfried Gottfied Weiss. They were each charged with

wilfully, deliberately and wrongfully aiding, abetting and participating in the subjection of civilian nationals of nations then at war with the German Reich, to cruelties and mistreatments including killings, beatings and tortures, starvation, abuses and indignities.

The defendants in the *Weiss et al.*-Dachau trial were also charged with abuses against "surrendered and unarmed prisoners of war in the custody of the then German Reich."[47] All of them pleaded not guilty, while those who took the stand argued that they were simply following orders that came directly from Richard Glücks' concentration camp inspectorate (Department D, WVHA) in Berlin.[48]

The prosecution focused on the widespread abuse, torture, murder, human experimentation, serious overcrowding, malnutrition, and inadequate medical care so severe that it led to a typhus epidemic that resulted in the death of 1,500 prisoners.[49] The defense based its case on two issues—superior orders and questions about jurisdiction, claiming that their clients enjoyed certain legal rights as POWs that protected them from prosecution. The judges considered the first argument "erroneous," and noted that the Yamashita decision gave the tribunal the right to try each of the defendants.[50] They found all but four of the defendants guilty of all charges and ordered them hanged. Upon review, the Deputy Theater Judge Advocate upheld most of the sentences, but reduced several of the death sentences to lengthy prison terms. The death sentences were carried out in Landsberg prison on May 27–28, 1947.[51]

Two other GMGC trials involved 69 staff and guards from the Mauthausen concentration camp. While Dachau was certainly one of the deadliest camps in Germany (15–17 percent of the 188,000–206,000 of those incarcerated died while in confinement),[52] death rates at Mauthausen and its subcamps were much higher. Between 50 and 60 percent of the 200,000 prisoners in Mauthausen died there during the war, including 38,120 Jews.[53] In the first trial, *United States v. Hans Altfuldisch et al.*, the court, drawing from the precedent set in the *Weiss et al.* case, ruled

> that the circumstances, conditions, and the very nature of the Concentration Camp Mauthausen, combined with any and all of its by-camps [there were 49], was of such a criminal nature as to cause every official, governmental, military and civil, and every employee thereof, whether he be a member of the Waffen SS, Allgemeine SS, a guard, or civilian, to be culpably and criminally responsible...any official, governmental, military, or civil...in any way on control of or stationed at or engaged in the operation of the Concentration Camp Mauthausen, or any or all of its by-camps in any manner whatsoever, is guilty of a crime against the recognized laws, customs, and practice of civilized nations and the letter and spirit of the laws and usages of war, and by reason thereof is to be punished.[54]

> The essence of the prosecution's case centered around a long list of crimes that included medical experimentation and what it described as "every known form of killing." This included gassing, hanging, clubbing, heart injections, driving inmates in the electric fence, kicking in genitals, being buried alive and by putting a red hot poker down the throat...A special form of killing took place in the "shooting gallery" where the victims were apparently having their pictures taken or heights measured...The main camp at Mauthausen was surrounded by an electric fence...When touched, a light would burn in the "shoe house." Sometimes the current would merely keep the victims hanging to the wire for several hours and finally they would start to burn. Later the current might be increased causing electrocution, or the victims would be shot...Guards would beat prisoners and drive them toward the fence so they would grab it in desperation.[55]

Others died at the "Vienna Ditch," a stone quarry where inmates

> were forced to carry heavy stones up the 185 steps...Many of these personnel were beaten, thrown down the cliff or driven through the guard chain to be shot...Intellectuals were ordered to the quarry so they would die of overwork.[56]

Mauthausen also had a gas chamber, which used Zyklon B, a gas van, and three crematoria.[57] Two of the defendants, SS Dr. Eduard Krebsbach and SS Capt. Erich Wasicky, played central roles in the gassing operations, and in the case of the former also conducted medical experiments on inmates. One witness even testified that Krebsbach had killed two tattooed prisoners and later displayed their tattooed skin in his office.[58] Though he did not take the stand, Krebsbach did admit

> to having participated in the shooting of hundreds of prisoners, as well as the selection for the gas chamber of hundreds of others.[59]

They were, along with 60 of the 69 defendants in the two trials, found guilty of all charges and executed, despite several appeals for clemency. On review, nine of those condemned to death had their sentences reduced to life imprisonment. On May 27, 1947, the US military conducted "the largest mass execution in the history of the American war crimes trial program" in Landsberg prison 40 miles west of Munich.[60]

War Crimes Trials in the British Zone

The *Royal Warrant* (RW) of June 18, 1945, gave the British jurisdiction over 500 trials in their occupation zone. However, it limited such rights to trials involving "violations of the laws and customs of war."[61] British Military Commissions (BMC) were to be made up of no less than two officers and a president. Procedurally, they were to follow, as much as possible, the Field Court-Martial of the British Army, with rules of evidence dictated by the traditions of English civil courts. This meant that the prosecution had to prove "beyond a reasonable doubt" the guilt or innocence of the accused.[62] This partially explains the much higher acquittal rates in BMC trials vis-à-vis American military commission trials—28.3 percent versus 15.3 percent. On the other hand, at least through early 1948, the British imposed slightly higher death penalities on German defendants than the American tribunals—25.5 percent versus 23.5 percent.[63]

The most significant BMC trial (*Trial of Josef Kramer et al.*) took place from September 17 to November 17, 1945, and centered on the prosecution of 45 former administrators, guards, and *Kapos* at Bergen-Belsen and Auschwitz. The tribunal charged all of the defendants with "having committed individual murders and other offences against the camp inmates," and "of having knowingly participated in a common plan to operate a system of ill-treatment and murder in these camps."[64] Though most of the defendants had worked at only one of the two camps, several had been stationed at both of them. Another distinctive facet of the trial was that almost half of the defendants were women, many of them Poles. Moreover, many of the defendants were accused of committing crimes against "Allied nationals."[65]

The principal defendant was *SS Hauptsturmführer* Josef Kramer (1906–1945), known in the British press as the "beast of Belsen." Kramer began his SS career as a guard at Dachau, and quickly moved up the ranks of the concentration camp bureaucracy, holding important positions at Sachsenhausen, Mauthausen,

Auschwitz, Dachau, and Natzweiler concentration camps.[66] One survivor testified that while at Auschwitz, Kramer took an active part in the *Selektions* for the gas chambers, sometimes "loading the victims into vehicles, and beating them if they cried because they knew what was awaiting them."[67]

The most famous female defendant was Irma Grese (1923–1945), a women's camp supervisor nicknamed the "Bitch of Belsen." Like Kramer, she rose rapidly through the ranks and became the Senior Supervisor (*SS Oberaufseherin*), the second most important female leader in Auschwitz. One survivor, Ilona Stein, testified that Grese, on her ever-present bicycle, took part in the selections at Auschwitz II-Birkenau and beat or shot anyone who tried to hide or escape during selection.[68]

One of the Polish defendants, Stanislawa Starotska, had originally been a member of the Polish underground *Armija Krajowa*. She was sent to Auschwitz where she was beaten and almost starved to death. According to the defense, she volunteered to be a Block Senior (*Blockälteste*) and later became a Senior Camp Administrator (*Lagerälteste*) because she was convinced that she would be able to help other prisoners. Her job was to maintain order as newly arrived prisoners were marched off to the nearby gas chambers.[69] She was transferred to Bergen-Belsen in February 1945, where she served in a similar role, and later transferred to the Prison Camp Police (*Lagerpolizei*). While the defense tried to depict her jobs in these camps as rather benign, the prosecution presented one witness who remembered Starotska as "a notorious collaborator with the S.S.; people seemed more frightened of her than of the S.S."[70] Another testified that Starotska

> used to make them kneel with their hands in the air holding a stone. She beat women until they lost their senses, thus causing their death. She placed a woman between live electric wires and killed another by forcing her head under water. She was perfect in causing slow death. She sent ill and old people to the crematorium.[71]

The defense responded to these charges by raising questions about the BMC's jurisdiction and also argued that the alleged offenses were not war crimes since they did "not fall within the limited categories of war crimes which could be committed by civilians." It also pointed out that many of the victims were not Allied nationals.[72] The prosecution countered this by arguing that all of the defendants were "members of the German armed forces" and that the concentrations camps were meant "to further the German war effort." It added that it was not necessary to identify specific victims to prove the charge of murder.[73] Moreover, "the Polish accused must be regarded in the same light as the ex-enemy accused since they had by their acts identified themselves with the S.S. authorities."[74]

In the end, the court found 30 of the defendants guilty—26 for crimes committed in Bergen-Belsen and 4 for crimes in Auschwitz. After review, the British sentenced Kramer, Grese, and eight other defendants to death, and one to life imprisonment. The rest, including Starotska, received punishments that ranged from 1 to 15 years in prison.[75]

The British also tried three German civilians in Hamburg March 1–8, 1946 for their involvement in the manufacture of Zyklon B. The principal defendant was Dr. Bruno Tesch, the owner of Tesch & Stabenow (Testa), one of the two German firms that made Zyklon B for the SS and other Nazi organizations. His codefendants were his managers, Karl Weinbacher and Dr. Joachim Drösihn. During the war, Tesch produced over 43,000 lbs. of Zyklon B for Auschwitz, Groß Rosen, Majdanek, and other SS camps.[76] Tesch claimed that he knew nothing about the killing of human beings at the camps with Zyklon B, which his stenographer testified was untrue.[77]

In reaching its decision, the tribunal considered three facts before passing judgment:

> First, that the Allied nationals had been gassed by means of Zyklon B; secondly, that this had been supplied by Tesch and Stabenow; and thirdly, that the accused knew that the gas was to be used for the purpose of killing human beings.[78]

It also asked whether Drösihn's "subordinate position in the firm" put him "in a position either to influence the transfer of gas to Auschwitz or to prevent it." If not, "no knowledge of the use to which the gas was being put could make him guilty." The court concluded that Tesch and Weinbacher must have known that the shipment of such large quantities of Zyklon B to Auschwitz was for something other than delousing or disinfecting buildings, and sentenced both to death. Its decision was in part based on the idea that "any civilian who is an accessory to a violation of the laws and customs of war is himself also liable as a war criminal."[79]

The British also tried a number of senior military leaders for war crimes, including Col. Gen. Nikolaus von Falkenhorst, who led the German invasion of Denmark and Norway in the spring of 1940, and later commanded Wehrmacht forces in the latter country. He was charged with using the "Commando Order" of December 18, 1942, to execute British POWs. The court rejected his argument of superior orders and the idea that the executed commandos were saboteurs. It found him guilty of eight of nine charges and sentenced him to death, which was later commuted to 20 years imprisonment. He was pardoned in 1953.[80]

The British also tried Luftwaffe Fld. Mshl. Albert Kesselring, who served as Supreme Commander for the South, which included Italy and North Africa. Kesselring was accused of being responsible for the murder of 335 Italians at the Adreatine Cave massacre in 1944 and the deaths of countless partisans. The court considered two issues in reaching its decision—was the military or the SD responsible for the deaths, and were the shootings in the Adreatine Cave "a legitimate reprisal or a war crime?" Though the court found him guilty of both charges, they were unable to answer the question of whether it was legal to kill "innocent persons as a reprisal." He was condemned to death but commuted his sentence to life imprisonment. He was released from prison for ill health in 1952.[81]

War Crimes Trials in France and the French Zone

France, unlike the United Kingdom and the United States, suffered directly from German occupation during the war, and conducted war crimes trials in France and in their small occupation zone in Germany. Trials in France focused principally on collaborators in the immediate years after the war ended. After liberation in 1944, some French collaborators were quickly tried and executed, often by resistance groups.

Estimates are that special "kangaroo courts" tried and executed 9,000 Frenchmen who were accused of collaboration.[82] Once the political environment stabilized, new laws helped spur an "anticollaborationist" purge throughout France that saw courts initiate investigations of over a half million Frenchmen. About 25 percent of those tried were found guilty of collaboration, though few were ever executed.[83]

What followed were a series of "show trials" in 1945 and 1946 that convicted some of Vichy France's most infamous leaders and collaborators such as Marshal Philippe Pétain, the head of the Vichy government, Pierre Laval, who served as prime minister in 1940 and 1942–1944, Charles Maurras, the leader of *Action Français*, a right-wing, anti-Semitic group that strongly supported the Vichy government,[84] Joseph Darnard, the pro-Nazi head of the *Milice*, the Vichy government's paramilitary police, and Rene Bousquet, who played a key role in the roundup and deportation of Jews in 1942 and 1943 as head of the Vichy police.[85]

Pétain, a major World War I hero, was convicted of collaboration and sentenced to death, which Charles de Gaulle commuted to life imprisonment. Laval was convicted of "plotting against the security of the state and [sharing] intelligence with the enemy," and found guilty. He was executed before a firing squad after a failed suicide attempt.[86] Maurras, like Pétain, was given a death sentence for collaboration, though it was later commuted to life imprisonment. Darnard, who fled to Germany in 1944, was found guilty of his crimes and executed in 1945. Four years later, Bousquet was acquitted of the charge of compromising national security, but found guilty of national indignity (shameful behavior toward the nation; *Indignité national*) and sentenced to five years in prison, a term the court immediately commuted because of his contributions to the resistance. His case resurfaced in the early 1990s and French prosecutors indicted him again for war crimes. However, several months before his trial was to begin, he was murdered in his apartment in Paris. His killer told the press he had "killed a serpent."[87]

French military courts drew their authority from an ordnance issued on August 28, 1944, by Charles de Gaulle's new interim government that gave "French military tribunals" the authority to try "enemy nationals" for crimes committed in France or its territories against "a French national, or a person under French protection, or a person serving or having served in the French armed forces, or a stateless person…or a refugee residing in French territory, or against the property" of such persons, "and against French corporate bodies."[88] The *Code de Justice Militaire* and the *Code Pénal* provided the general guidelines for the conduct of such trials. A *Juge d'Instruction* would investigate a case and decide whether it should be given to a military tribunal, which was made up of five judges. A Public Prosecutor (*Commissaire du Gouvernement*) would then present the accused with the indictment and initiate legal proceedings.[89]

There were few trials in the French zone in Germany. Most of them took place in Dijon, Lyon, Metz, and Strasbourg, and focused on a variety of charges including the illegal arrest and mistreatment of French civilians, illegal deportations, theft of private property, the murder of French guerillas, pillage, destructions of monuments, "abuse of confidence," and illegal requisitioning. The most prominent trial involved Robert Wagner, the brutal *Gauleiter* of Alsace, and six other members of his government, who mounted a forced "regermanization" campaign in the region that included the forced conscription of Alsatian Germans. They were charged with crimes ranging from forcing Frenchmen to "bear arms against France," recruiting Frenchmen to bear arms against their own nation, and restriction of individual liberty to premeditated murder.[90] Wagner was also accused of wielding "the same powers in respect to Alsace as Hitler did in respect of the Reich," a catch-all charge that made him responsible for all war crimes in Alsace from 1940 to 1944. This included "the power of final decision in the administration of justice" as well as "the privilege of mercy."[91]

The most serious charge was murder and complicity in murder, including judicial murder.[92] Wagner and his codefendants were found guilty of murder and other charges, and condemned to death. All except one of the defendants appealed their sentences, arguing that they never had access to prosecution documents, and that they were charged under retroactive criminal and international law. All appeals were turned down except for that of one of the defendants, who was handed over to the British for further investigation. He escaped while in custody.[93]

War Crimes Trials in Soviet East Berlin and the German Democratic Republic

The denazification program in the Soviet-controlled portion of Germany began almost immediately after the war ended. The Soviets mounted a major purge of suspected "fascists" and created 262 denazification commissions overseen by the zone's Communist Socialist Unity Party (*Sozialistisches Einheitspartei*; SED). By early 1948, the Soviets claimed that its denazification efforts were finished, and that it had dismissed 520,000 former Nazi Party members from their jobs.[94]

The Soviets also imprisoned 240,000 Germans under article III of Control Council Directive No. 38 that allowed the Allies to punish anyone who after May 8, 1945, "has endangered or is likely to endanger the peace of the German people or of the world, through advocating national socialism or militarism or inventing or disseminating malicious rumors."[95] The Soviets also set up special courts to try war criminals in eastern Germany that convicted over 12,500 Germans of war crimes. In 1950, the Soviets turned over 14,000 suspected Nazi war criminals to the East Germans, and sent about 20,000 to the Soviet Union, placing a third of them in POW camps there. A significant number of those sent to East German or Soviet camps or prisons died there.[96]

The new German Democratic Republic (*Deutsche Demokratische Republik*; DDR) tried and convicted almost 13,000 former Nazis of various war crimes between 1948 and 1964. In 1997, Judge Irmgard Jendretzky, one of the judges for the Waldheim trials, which took place in 1950 and tried over 4,000 alleged Nazi war criminals, was tried for her role in these trials. She stated that she deeply resented being prosecuted for what she felt was an "international obligation to prosecute Nazis." Instead of being punished, her attorney argued, Judge Jendretsky should receive "recognition and appreciation, not punishment."[97]

War Crimes Trials in the Soviet Union

The whole question of war crimes trials in the Soviet Union, a nation that lost 26–28 million lives during World War II, was complicated by the growing Stalinistic paranoia that swept the country at the end of the war. Consequently, anyone with the vaguest ties to the hated German "fascist" regime, including Soviet POWs, were viewed with suspicion. During the war, about 80 percent of the Soviet POWs in German camps died there. Many of those who survived served "in [the] German ranks" during the war, while another 1.8 million Soviet civilians worked for the Germans as forced laborers. When the war ended, the Allies and the Soviets forced or repatriated 5.5 million Soviet citizens back to the USSR. About 60–65 percent of the returnees were tried and convicted of various acts of collaboration; 20 percent were given death sentences or long prison terms, while 40–45 percent got shorter terms or were sent into exile or forced to work on special Soviet rebuilding projects. The rest found it difficult to find work because of the cloud of suspicion over their heads because of their former incarceration in German-held territory.[98]

In 1942, Stalin created the ChGK to gather materials on Nazi crimes, and a year later the Supreme Soviet, the country's "legislature," issued a decree that ordered public executions or lengthy prison terms for Axis soldiers and collaborators who committed

> crimes against [Soviet] civilians and POWs. Military courts would judge such cases, while the bodes of those publicly hanged would "be left on the gallows for several days so that everyone will be aware that [harsh] punishment will befall anyone who inflicts torture and carnage on the civilian population and betrays his Motherland.[99]

This was quickly followed by three "show trials" in Krasnodar, Krasnodon, and Maripol. The 11 defendants in the Krasnodar trial were accused of treason for collaborating with *Einsatzgruppe* D's *Sonderkommando* 10a in the northern Caucasus. They were accused of

> torture and sadism, for mass executions and massacres by inhuman means, asphyxiation with toxic gases in specifically equipped machines, for the burning of and other methods of extermination of innocent Soviet citizens, including old men, women and children. The responsibility [for these crimes] rests on the leaders of the gangster Fascist Government, Germany and the German command.[100]

All of the defendants pleaded guilty for crimes their lawyers blamed on their "Nazi superiors." The real criminals, the defense argued, were "Hitler and his criminal band of generals."[101] An unsympathetic tribunal sentenced 8 to death and the rest to 20 years of hard labor.

Stalin saw such trials as political theater, and in late 1943 began the first public trials for captured Germans accused of war crimes.[102] Guilt was a foregone conclusion since these trials were meant to highlight the crimes of the Nazi leadership. The prosecution said as much during closing arguments, rejecting claims by the defendants that they were just following orders.

> Hitler, Göring, Goebbels, Himmler and their ilk—these are the principal inspirers and organizers of the wholesale murder and atrocities committed by the Germans on Soviet soil, in Kharkov, in Krasnodar and in other cities.
>
>   Obergruppenführers and Gruppenführers of the SS—the Dietrichs and Simons, the chiefs of garrisons, commandants and gendarmes, leaders of the Gestapo of all ranks and positions among the German butchers—these are directly responsible for the deaths of hundreds of thousands of Soviet citizens.

All four defendants in the first of these trials were found guilty and sentenced to death.[103]

The United States and Britain asked Stalin to halt these "show" trials because they could be used by Goebbels for propaganda purposes. However, he continued to try suspected German war criminals in secret. In 1943–1944, Soviet military courts also tried and sentenced 5,200 collaborators to hard labor, while another 5,000 alleged Soviet collaborators were sentenced to death by Russian military, secret police, and other courts for similar crimes during the last months of the war. Once the war ended, the Soviets also tried prominent members of the Polish underground in the Trial of the Sixteen in Moscow. Lured to the Soviet capital under false pretenses, the Polish defendants were charged with terror, subversion, and other crimes while under orders from the "so-called Polish emigre 'Government' in London." After a three-day trial, the Military Collegium of the Supreme Court of the USSR found 13 of the 16 defendants guilt of various crimes, sentencing them to terms of between four months and ten years.[104]

The Soviets also unsuccessfully sought the extradition of prominent Wehrmacht and German industrial leaders such as Col. Gen. Heinz Guderian, the Chief of the Army General Staff (*Chef des Generalstabs des Heeres*), Fld. Mshl. Gerd von Runstedt, and Col. Gen. Georg-Hans Reinhardt (1887–1963), who commanded German army corps during the invasion of the Soviet Union, as well as Col. Gen. Franz Halder, Alfried Krupp, and others. On the other hand, the Soviets were able to convince the Americans to turn Lt. Gen. Andrei Vlasov, the head of the Russian Liberation Army (*Ruskaya Osvobditel'naya Armiya;* ROA), over to them. Vlasov, a highly regarded Soviet field commander, won the prestigious Order of Lenin in 1941 and was given the responsibility of defending Kiev, the Soviet Union's third most important city, in the summer of 1941.[105]

Vlasov was captured by the Germans in the summer of 1942 and convinced to work with them, first as a recruiter for Soviet POWs interested in joining the Wehrmacht.[106] The Germans also allowed him to promote his Russian Liberation Movement (*Russkoe Osvoboditel'noye Dvizhenie*; ROD) on radio, which infuriated the Soviets, who now saw him as the ultimate symbol of collaboration. He was tried in a three-day "show trial" (July 30–August 1, 1946), charged with voluntary surrender to the enemy, anti-Soviet agitation, the creation of the ROD and ROA, and training of anti-Soviet espionage agents to wreak havoc and terror throughout the Soviet Union. Vlasov claimed that he had never been involved in any anti-Soviet terrorist activities. He was found guilty of all charges and hanged on August 13, 1946.[107]

War Crimes Trials in Poland

With the exception of the Soviet Union, no other nation suffered more than Poland during World War II in Europe. Hitler saw Christian Poles as that "dreadful [racial] material" and Polish Jews as "the most horrible thing imaginable."[108] This is the reason that so many Poles—3.2 million Jews and 1.8–1.9 million Polish

Christians—died during the long German occupation.[109] After the war, the Polish government tried over 20,000 Germans and others for war crimes.[110] In 1943, the Polish government-in-exile created a War Crimes Office (WCO) to work with the UNWCC. During the war, the WCO provided the Allied war crimes commission with the names of 36,529 suspected war criminals. The Polish underground Home Army (*Armija Krajowa*; AK) created its own courts to deal with war criminals in Poland. They tried and convicted 5,000 Poles for war crimes, and condemned over 3,000–3,500 to death.[111]

In 1944, the Soviet puppet Committee of National Liberation (*Polski Komitet Wyzwolenia Narodowego* Polish; PKWN) declared that it would prosecute war criminals for the

1. murder of civilians and prisoners of war, their ill-treatment and persecution;
2. arrest and deportation of persons wanted or persecuted by the occupying authorities for whatever reason it may be, save their prosecution for common law crimes, including such acts committed against persons residing on Polish territory irrespective of their nationality or race; and
3. blackmail with intent to profit under threat of arrest or handing over to the occupying authority.

Those convicted of crimes 1 and 2 could be sentenced to death, while conviction of crimes under category 3 could result in a prison term of up to 15 years.[112] The PKWN created Special Criminal Courts (SCC) made up of a judge and two "lay-judges" that would "dispense justice in a 'just and swift' manner." Defendants would receive the indictments 48 hours before their trial, which often meant they appeared in court without defense counsel. The decisions of these courts was final with no right of appeal.[113]

These courts were abolished in the fall of 1946, and, with the exception of those now under the jurisdiction of the new Supreme National Tribunal (*Najwyzszy Trybunal Narodowy*; NTN), were turned over to "ordinary criminal courts."[114] Between 1946 and 1948, the NTN held 7 public trials of 17 major German war criminals. The charge of genocide, a crime coined and defined by Polish American lawyer Raphael Lemkin, figured prominently in four of these trials.

The first trial took place in Poznan (Posen) from June 21 to July 7, 1946, and involved *SS Obergruppenführer* Arthur Greiser (1897–1946), the *Stattshalter* of the Wartheland Gau, which included Danzig, Łódź, and the Chełmno death camp. He was charged with trying "through violence, waging of aggressive war and the commission of crimes" to establish in Europe, and in his particular case, Poland, "the national-socialist régime" and its incorporation into Reich territory. The NTN also charged Greiser with the mistreatment, persecution, and murder of civilians and POWs, the systematic demonization and destruction of Polish culture in an effort to germanize the country, and the theft of Polish property. The indictment also accused him of playing a role in the use of concentration and extermination camps to achieve his deadly ends not only against Christian Poles but also against the country's Jews through widespread "persecution and whole extermination."[115]

His two Polish defense lawyers argued that though he was a member of the Nazi Party and the SS, he was merely a functionary of the Nazi state who was specifically following orders, particularly those of Adolf Hitler and Heinrich Himmler. The court rejected this argument and mitigating evidence meant to show his "benevolent' attitude toward Polish people," noting simply that "this duality of character . . . is typical" of the Germans. Here we see, the judges argued, both the German "public soul" and the "private soul." The latter focused on the "ethical correctness of the 'decent person' in private life," and the former a mind set that placed "Germany above everything." This, the judges concluded, was "an attitude that often amounted to complete moral insanity."[116] In reaching their decision, they did not go into specific "questions of law," but instead relied on documentary evidence. They found Greiser guilty of all charges except one and condemned him to death by hanging.[117]

Five weeks later, the NTN tried Amon Göth, the infamous, sadistic commandant of the Płaszów concentration camp made famous in *Schindler's List*. He was accused of various crimes, including murder and the theft of his victims' property, in Kraków, Płaszów, and Szebnie.[118] The principal witness against Göth was Mietek Pemper, a Jewish inmate who was forced to work for Göth as his personal stenographer and interpreter in Płaszów.[119] Pemper discussed Göth's arrest by the SS in the fall of 1944 on various charges including theft, murder, and the mistreatment of prisoners.[120]

Another witness, Dr. Aleksander Bieberstein, testified about Göth's abuse of prisoners. One of the commandant's favorite cruelties was the crew train (*Mannschaftzug*), which required female prisoners, working in 12-hour shifts, to pull small train cars containing 9,000 kilograms (19,800 pounds) of stone for road work up a very steep incline. Teams of 35 women normally hauled 12–15 loads per shift. Göth was so proud of the *Mannschaftzug* that on Christmas Eve, 1943, he had a group of women haul one of them past his balcony for SS party goers. His guests were uniformly disgusted by this display, and he ultimately let the women return to their barracks.[121]

The prosecution argued that Göth was liable for a series of murders under the 1932 Polish Civil Criminal Code and Hague IV (1907). It also contended that these were not only crimes against humanity but also genocide. This crime, the prosecution added, was well within the "scope" of the PKWN August 31, 1944, decree, since it provided for the punishment "of murder and ill-treatment not only of individual persons, but moreover of large groups persecuted on specific grounds."[122]

The court agreed with the prosecution, and in its judgment on September 5, stated that Göth's

> criminal activities originated from general directives that guided the criminal Fascist-Hitlerite organization, which under the leadership of Adolf Hitler aimed at the conquest of the world and at the extermination of those nations, which stood in the way of the consolidation of its power.
>
> The policy of extermination was in the first place directed against the Jewish and Polish nations.
>
> This criminal organization did not reject any means of furthering their aim at destroying the Jewish nation. The whole extermination of Jews and also of Poles had all the characteristics of genocide in the biological meaning of this term, and embraced in addition the destruction of the cultural life of these nations.[123]

Göth's efforts to deny these charges, and his claims that, as a soldier, he was only obeying orders, fell on deaf ears, as did his claim that the punishments he meted out in Płazów were within "his disciplinary jurisdiction as commandant of the camp, and were in accordance with the German regulations in force." The court ruled that this did not exempt him from "criminal responsibility" for his actions, and rejected his argument that such actions were driven by "military necessity." His crimes, the judges ruled, took place

> without any military necessity and in flagrant violation of the rights of the inhabitants of the occupied territory as protected by the laws and customs of war.[124]

His trial, which was broadcast outside the courtroom on Senacka Street in Kraków, was intently followed throughout Poland. The court's verdict, guilt and death, which Göth unsuccessfully appealed, was met with a sense of relief.[125] He was hanged in Kraków on September 13, 1946, and cremated.

Six months later, the NTN tried Rudolf Höss, Auschwitz's principal commandant during the war. After his capture in 1946, he testified against Ernst Kaltenbrunner in the Nuremberg IMT trial and in the subsequent Nuremberg WVHA and I. G. Farben trials. He admitted that he was responsible for the mass murder of Jews and others, and the theft of his victims' property.[126]

But, he added, he had not actually killed anyone and was only carrying out orders.[127] The prosecution also reminded Höss that he was responsible for the medical experiments at Auschwitz and other horrible crimes.[128]

In many ways, Höss' trial was similar to Göth's, though in the former proceedings the court only dealt generally with genocidal crimes. It noted in its ruling that one of the goals of the Nazi Party was the "biological and cultural extermination of subjugated nations, especially of the Jewish and Slav nations." The medical experiments were considered part of this larger destructive plan, and "violated general principles of criminal law as derived from the criminal laws of all civilized nations." The court also saw such crimes as "preparatory to the carrying out of the crime of genocide." Needless to say, Höss was found guilty of all charges and sentenced to death.[129] He was hanged in Auschwitz I on April 16, 1947. In his final letter to his wife, he admitted,

> I was totally responsible for everything that happened there [Auschwitz], whether I knew it or not. Most of the terrible and horrible things that took place there I learned only during this investigation and during the trials itself. I cannot describe how I was deceived, how my directives were twisted, and all the things they had carried out supposedly under my orders. I certainly hope that the guilty will not escape justice.[130]

Allied Trials in Asia

The United States

Between 1945 and early 1948, the United States tried 202 cases involving 574 defendants in Asia, most of them before military commissions. These trials continued until 1949, with a large number of them—1,061—in Yokohama, Japan. Most of those convicted received relatively short prison terms, while a much smaller group of defendants were either acquitted or given life or death sentences.[131]

One of the most important trials took place in the Marshall Islands on December 7–13, 1945, and centered around charges that Rear Admiral Nisuke Masuda and four of his junior officers had shot or stabbed to death three downed American pilots on Jaluit Atoll. Admiral Masuda committed suicide before the trial began, but left a note confessing that he had ordered the execution of the pilots a month after their capture in early 1944. The Navy Judge Advocate who prosecuted the case said the crimes violated article 23 of the 1907 Hague Convention and the 1929 Geneva Convention.[132] The prosecution based its case on not only a number of US legal precedents but also regulations issued by SCAP. One of them, which had been adopted by the Judge Advocate General of the Navy, stated that

> The official position of the accused shall not absolve him from responsibility, nor be considered in mitigation of punishment. Further, action pursuant to the order of the accused's superior, or of his government, shall not constitute a defense but may be considered in mitigation of punishment if the commission determines that justice so requires.[133]

Japanese defense lawyers countered by arguing that the sitting military commission had no right to try the defendants using *ex post facto* laws that "did not exist" at the time the alleged crimes were committed. Furthermore, the rules issued by SCAP for such trials were "both substantial and procedural" violations of US law. Defense counsel also demanded that the trials be held in Japan before a "civil tribunal," not a US military commission. All of the defendants pleaded not guilty, and though admitting their part in the executions, argued that they were acting under superior orders.[134] One of the Japanese defense attorneys, himself a former officer, explained that an Imperial Rescript decreed that

> Subordinates should have the idea that the orders from their superiors are nothing but the orders personally from His Majesty the Emperor.[135]

Consequently, he went on, given the unique role of the emperor in Japanese society, "it was impossible to apply therein the liberal and individualistic ideas which rule usual societies unmodified to this totalistic and absolutistic military society."[136] He added that the accused asked not to be part of the execution squad, but when told that the order came from a Rear Admiral, they had little choice but to obey. If not, "everyone would have fallen upon them."[137]

The military commission, which was made up of seven US Navy officers, took little time reaching a decision, since a number of witnesses provided ample details about the executions and the disposal of the bodies, which were cremated. The judges rejected all of the defense's arguments, citing a number of laws and legal precedents to justify their decisions. The judges concluded that shooting POWs who were behaving properly was a "war crime under customary international law," and found three of the defendants guilty of all charges and sentenced them to death by hanging. The fourth, Ensign Tasaki, was sentenced to ten years imprisonment since he did not play a direct role in the executions. The findings of the commission were quickly approved by Rear Admiral William Keene Harrill.[138]

A month and a half later, an equally important trial took place in Yokohama. The prosecution charged Isao Fukuhara, the commandant of the Omuta POW camp on Kyuchu (Kyushu; one of the four Japanese "home" islands), of

> cruel and brutal atrocities against prisoners of war, and of failing to discharge accused's duty as camp commander to control and restrain members of the command, permitting them to commit cruel and brutal atrocities and other offenses against certain prisoners of war.[139]

The Army Judge Advocate who prosecuted the case cited 34 instances of such acts of cruelty including the deaths of three POWs and the brutal disfigurement of several others. Fukuhara was also charged with using slave labor in coal mines under extremely inhumane conditions.[140] What is unique about this case is that an American Navy officer, Lt. W. N. Little, worked for the Japanese as a "stool-pigeon." In return for extra food, Little reported any transgressions to Fukuhara and recommended "severe punishment for them."[141]

Fukuhara, who was charged with personally taking part in some of the beatings and torture, testified that he was not guilty of any of these crimes, though he did admit that he did discipline US corporal Walter R. Johnson because Johnson

> talked to Koreans and had a newspaper in his possession in violation of strict regulations [as well as his] "General attitude and the way he sat was bad."[142]

On the other hand, while denying that any of the alleged atrocities took place, Fukuhara did testify that he had "instructions from his superiors to adopt sterner measures against problematic prisoners.[143] He quoted Tōjō, who said in orders issued on June 25, 1942, that

> You should not for even a day allow any P.O.W. to lay idle and just feed him, but you must utilize every strength and technical ability of the P.O.W. for the increase of production of our country to carry out the Great East-Asia War. Moreover, at this time you should consider the circumstances surrounding the respective camps to which you are assigned and especially try to let the Japanese citizens around the proximity [of the camp] to understand the superiority of the Yamato [term popularized in late-nineteenth-century Japan to designate country's dominant ethnic group] race through your handling of P.O.W.s.[144]

Fukuhara cited other documents and orders that authorized him to use corporal punishment on his prisoners to emphasize the "strictness of…Japanese army discipline."[145] The tribunal found Fukuhara guilty on all counts after a 17-day trial. A review of the case by Assistant Staff Judge Advocate Lt. Col. Ralph W. Yarborough found the evidence, which included 79 sworn affidavits and other testimony against Fukuhara, overwhelming. Though Yarborough dropped one of the charges, he felt the evidence, despite petitions of clemency from Fukuhara's relatives and former colleagues, sufficient to uphold the death penalty. But, as he noted, final judgment would be withheld pending SCAP regulations.[146]

China

While there are legitimate questions about the fairness of these US military commission trials, they were, for the most part, at least conducted with a modicum of respect for accepted legal traditions. The same could not be said for war crimes trials in China, which were driven by the vicissitudes of the changing political landscape in China from 1945 to 1957. The principal defendants in the Nationalist trials from 1944 to 1947 were Chinese collaborators, not alleged Japanese war criminals. In fact, both the Nationalists and the Communists, who took power in 1949, were quite moderate in their treatment of Japanese war criminals in large part because they felt a spirit of forgiveness would lay the groundwork for closer relations with Japan.

China suffered horribly during its long war with Japan, and the Chinese demanded swift justice after the war for alleged Japanese war criminals and those who worked closely with them. While one would assume, given the atrocities committed by the Japanese in China, that the principal villains in these trials would be Japanese soldiers and civilians, just the opposite was true. Chiang Kai-shek's government chose to focus its legal energies on Chinese collaborators or *Hanjian*—"traitor[s] to the Han race."[147] From November 1944 to October 1947, the Nationalists investigated 45,679 cases involving alleged *Hanjian*, and initially decided to prosecute over 30,000 of them. In the end, they tried over 25,000 *Hanjian*, and found almost 15,000 of them guilty of various crimes. They executed 369, condemned 979 to life sentences, and sentenced 13,570 to lesser prison terms. Another 14 were given fines.[148] The principal reason for this emphasis on trying Chinese collaborators was politics. Chiang Kai-shek sought to use the trials to "re-establish national discipline and dignity, and finally to build a new nation."[149] Public opinion was clamoring for such trials and was becoming increasingly impatient with the time it was taking to bring the *Hanjian* to justice.[150]

These legal efforts contrasted sharply with Nationalist trials of Japanese war criminals. Driven by a policy of "treating those who are harmful with forgiveness and kindness," Chiang Kai-shek's government, for the most part, treated alleged Japanese war criminals far more leniently than the *Hanjian*.[151] Scholarship on the Chinese trials of Japanese war criminals, even when it is focused on the crimes themselves, is scant, and it is difficult to know exactly how many were actually investigated, tried, and convicted. The United Nations War Crimes Commission's 15-volume *Law Reports of Trials of War Criminals* mentions only one trial of a Japanese war criminal by a Nationalist court. Another study by M. Kajimoto states that the Chinese established 13 war crimes tribunals to try alleged Japanese war criminals. These courts tried 650 cases, and convicted 504 Japanese citizens of war crimes. Of that number, 149 were condemned to death. Yun Xia says that the Nationalists "processed about 2,200 cases" against alleged Japanese war criminals, including 145 involved in the Nanjing massacre. About 400 were convicted of war crimes.[152]

Several months after Japan invaded China in 1937, the Nationalists adopted the first of its anti-*Hanjian* laws, "Regulations on Handling *Hanjian* Cases," which "clearly labeled '*hanjian*' as the most serious crime against the nation."[153] Up until 1944, *Hanjian* were subject to military law and could, in certain situations, be punished by the military or the secret police without recourse to legal proceedings. Such punishments were announced publically by Chiang's government to discourage similar acts of collaboration.[154] In 1940, the Nationalists made further changes to the "Regulations" to undermine the new puppet Government of National Salvation under Jingwei Wang, which was based in Nanjing, calling itself the Republic of China.[155]

When the war ended, new efforts to try *Hanjian* were complicated by the fact that various organs of state now vied for some role in the *Hanjian* investigative and legal procedures as a way of strengthening "political influence."[156] Though a series of new postwar regulations were issued to deal with *Hanjian,* the most important one limited the military's role in cases involving officers who served Wang's government or directly worked with the Japanese armed forces. These regulations identified ten areas of civilian and military service in the Wang government that would help investigators to determine if an individual could "be considered as *hanjian* and prosecuted." Convicted *Hanjian* who worked for the resistance or "conducted activities beneficial to the people" could have "their penalty reduced accordingly."[157]

According to Yun Xia, there were four principal categories of *Hanjian* trials— major collaborators, economic collaborators, cultural collaborators, and "traitorous monks."[158] The most serious, of course, were the trials of *Hanjian* who had held important posts in Wang's Nanjing government. Many of these trials were, for the most part, "show trials" where "guilt was a forgone conclusion."[159] The reasons were simple—Wang was one of the most important figures in the early history of Nationalist China, and Chiang Kai-shek wanted to use the trials to underscore the depth of Wang's collaboration. Chiang also saw the trials as an opportunity to show the nation that his Nationalist government had been the "leader of the War of Resistance and [was] the only qualified government in China."[160]

Though there were trials of major *Hanjian* in Shanghai, Nanjing, Tianjin, Jinan, and Xiamen from April 1946 to September 1948, the most important ones took place before the Jiangsu Higher Court in Suzhou, an ancient Chinese city just to the west of Shanghai.[161] Dongyoun Hwang has divided the collaborators into three different groups—those who described themselves as national heroes or...patriots, on par with those who had resisted the Japanese..."; those who felt coerced to work for the Japanese; and those who collaborated for financial gain.[162] The major charges against the *Hanjian,* which varied from case to case, were

1. establishing various puppet organizations including the Nanjing Collaborationist government;
2. signing "traitorous treaties" with the enemy;
3. providing the enemy with war-materials;
4. issuing "puppet" government banknotes (*zhebiquan*);
5. poisoning (*duhua*) Chinese people in the occupied areas by selling them opium;
6. providing slave-making (*nuhua*) education to the people; and
7. establishing a puppet army (*weijun*).[163]

The Nationalist government argued that the nature of these crimes was such that they seriously "crippled its resistance efforts," and, since they had done serious harm to national interests, were acts of "national criminals."[164]

Three of the most highly publicized trials took place in April 1946. One involved Gongbo Chen (Kung-po Chen), one of the founders of the Chinese Communist Party (CCP) in 1921 who later joined the leftist faction of the *Guomindang* (Kuomintang; GMD) led by Jingwei Wang. Chen, who earned an MA in economics at Columbia University, was a vocal critic of Chiang Kai-shek's growing dictatorial and military powers. Regardless, he served as Chiang's minister of industry from 1932 to 1936, but resigned after an assassination attempt on Wang's life in 1935. Though initially hesitant to join Wang's collaborationist government in 1940, Chen explained during his trial that Wang convinced him that to do so was a patriotic act and, by implication, was "actually supporting Chiang Kai-shek and Chongqing [the wartime Nationalist capital] by advocating peace and collaboration with Japan." After Wang died in late 1944, Chen replaced him as head of the Nanjing collaborationist government. Immediately after the war ended, he contacted Chiang Kai-shek and warned him of the communist threat in the Nanjing area. He suggested that Chiang appoint him head of the collaborationist army to maintain Nationalist control in the region. Chiang never replied, and Chen fled to Japan. He was ultimately extradited to China for trial.[165]

The Nationalists not only considered Chen the "head traitor," but also a dangerous figure politically because of his past roles in the GMD and Chiang's government. To prove its case against Chen, the prosecution used over 50 volumes of documentation that it hoped would show

> How Chen organized the collaboration government and a puppet army, negotiated peace with the Japanese, forged secret contacts with the enemy, gave up Chinese sovereignty, resisted the central authority, disturbed the financial order and enslaved the people through educational means.[166]

The Chinese press, which covered all of the major *Hanjian* "show trials" extensively, depicted Chen as the Philippe Pétain of China.[167] Pétain, the former collaborationist Vichy French leader, was tried in France from July 23 to August 15, 1945. While Chen explained that Wang had decided to ally with the Japanese to preserve the "national vitality" of China,[168] Vichy apologists argued that Pétain collaborated to "reconstitute the national soul and rebuild the nation's past grandeur on the unshakable rock of French unity."[169] And like Chen, who thought his collaboration was a way ultimately for China to defeat Japan,[170] Petain said during his trial that "while General [Charles] de Gaulle, outside our frontiers, carried on the struggle, I prepared the way for liberation, by preserving an unhappy but living France."[171] But what Pétain never addressed were his crimes against the Jews, the shipment of French workers as forced laborers to Germany, and the terror of the French secret police—the *Milice*.[172]

To his credit, Chen did not turn on Wang and defended him as a "man of meritorious service" who was not present to defend himself.[173] Chen argued in court that he "was sure that the establishment of the Nanjing collaborationist government had served China for a certain period by preserving the vitality of the nation and its people."[174] At least, he added, it brought some semblance of Chinese rule to areas under Japanese occupation and, though not completely successful, tempered some of the harshness of Japanese rule in areas under Nanjing's control. Moreover, Chen went on, Wang's government stopped communist efforts to gain a foothold in these regions. In the end, though, he admitted that his arguments meant less in court than the opinions of Chiang Kai-shek, who would determine his guilt or innocence based on talks between the GMD and the communists. If they continued without conclusion, then Chiang would need him to maintain party unity. If they failed, he "would be eliminated followed by a civil war between the two parties."[175] Though a cease-fire between the GMD and the CCP had been declared just a few months before Chen's trial began, it became readily apparent to Chiang that Mao had no intention of abiding by it. In other words, Chen was of little use to the Nationalists as they faced growing communist aggression.[176] Chen was sentenced to death on April 12, and decided not to appeal his conviction. However, his wife intervened, and filed one with the Supreme Higher Court, asking for a new trial. The court refused her appeal on May 16, and Gongbo Chen was executed by firing squad on June 3 in Suzhou.[177]

Four days after Chen was condemned to death, Bijun Chen (Pi-chün Chen), the wife of Jingwei Wang, was tried for her collaborationist crimes. Considered the country's "number one female traitor,"[178] her trial was, according to Kaori Yamada, "the final stage of the internal political struggle between the two sides of the GMD of Chiang Kai-shek and Wang Jingwei."[179] Though Chen had served as the political director of Guangdong province during her husband's tenure in office, her real crime was being Wang's wife, something prosecutor Weiqing Wei emphasized in his charges against her. Beginning in 1938, he stated,

> she had helped him strengthen the enemy's invasion and weaken China's resistance. Once in power in Nanjing, Wei added, as his wife, "the accused could not but assist and support the sycophantic puppet from the side."

According to Charles Musgrove, what took place during the brief trial in Suzhou was an

> indictment of the martial unit...In addition to her own crimes, Chen had to stand trial for both of them.[180]

From Wei's pespective, Chen was an extremely ambitious, power-hungry woman who was manipulated by the Japanese in their effort to destroy the GMD underground in Guangdong province. What was interesting about his accusations against her is that he did not think she wielded any significant power in Guangdong, arguing that she was always under the control of "Japanese overseers." In the end, all that she had

> accomplished in her complicity was severely to compromise Chinese sovereignty by giving in to humiliating demands and allowing herself to be used.

Consciously or unconsciously, he was laying the groundwork for an appeal and later commutation of a death sentence.[181]

When Wei finished his presentation, chief judge Honglin Sun gave Chen an opportunity to speak. Like her husband, this former "revolutionary heroine" was a political activist who worked closely with Dr. Sun Yat-sen (father of modern China), and helped raise funds for his movement in Asia and the United States. Her "revolutionary marriage" to Wang in 1912 meant she was with him at every step of the way as he became more and more important in GMD politics. Wang was with Dr. Sun in Beijing when he died in 1925, and seemed to be in line to succeed him, though he was soon outmaneuvered by Chiang Kai-shek.[182] Afterward, Wang formed his own leftist government in Wuhan, but eventually returned to the GMD mainstream, holding numerous positions in Chiang's government. Chen, who was a political force in her own right, served as a member of the GMD's powerful Central Supervisory Committee during this period. Both continued their struggle with Chiang Kai-shek, and finally left China for France for medical treatment after Wang was wounded in an assassination attempt in 1935.[183]

Wang and Chen returned to China the following year, and became advocates of negotiations with the Japanese to avoid war, feeling that such a conflict "would bleed China dry."[184] After the outbreak of war in 1937, Wang created "an informal group of peace advocates in the KMT [GMD]," and Chiang Kai-shek authorized them to enter into secret talks with the Japanese about the prospect of peace. Chiang said he would step down from power if Japan withdrew all of its troops, while Tokyo countered secretly to Wang that he should form a new government to negotiate a peace accord.[185] Wang did what he could to have Chiang removed from power, and continued to talk to the Japanese about a peace settlement. He fled to Hanoi in late 1938, but hesitated to accept Japan's offer to set up a new "National government" in Nanjing until *Guomindang* agents attempted to murder him in Hanoi in the spring of 1939. Instead, the assassins killed his closest friend, Zhongming Zeng, which convinced Wang that the best way to challenge Chiang Kai-shek's authority was to work with the Japanese. This, he explained, was also the only alternative to halting the communization of China.[186]

Chen testified that her husband did not think his new government in Nanjing was "subversive," and instead saw it as a "faction within the Guomindang."[187] It was, she added, " an alternate and equally legitimate representative of an important segment of [the] Chinese people, and had cooperated with Chiang's government."[188] On the other hand, she argued that she was not involved in her husband's decision to work with the Japanese, though she did support his decisions. She also denied that she was involved in any "secret police activities or military planning."[189] While there is scholarly evidence to suggest that Wang's government was able to temper some of the more excessive and cruel Japanese occupation policies, the Chinese who lived in areas occupied by the Japanese suffered from hopelessness, fear, and socioeconomic policies that spread famine and disease.[190] And, in the end, at least according to R. Keith Schoppa, what mattered to the Chinese peasant, particularly the refugee, was not the state or nationalism, but mere survival for "themselves, their families, and their native places; the local, not the nation, became the focus."[191]

Regardless, there is also some evidence to support Chen's claim during the trial that her policies in Guangdong province did have some "beneficial effect," something that seemed to touch the spectators in court.[192] This was a key element in her defense, the idea that she and her husband had not abandoned the Chinese people.

Instead, she argued quite strongly, it was Chiang Kai-shek who had abandoned the masses.

> Everything Mr. Wang did was to take from the hands of the enemy and return rights back to the people who had been betrayed. He was merely tending to the land you high-level military officials abandoned when you were running for your lives.[193]

When the audience began to murmur among themselves about the idea of "abandonment," one of the judges, Meiyu Shi, demanded they stop. Undeterred, Chen continued her attack against Chiang's government.

> How can we say Wang Jingwei sold his country out? The area that Chongqing controlled, it was not up to Wang to sell. The three provinces of the Northeast were not his to sell either. Weren't they Chiang Kai-shek's to give to the Japanese? As for Guangdong, at the time that the Japanese invaded, the high-level officials of the provincial government fled on hearing the news. Who had the responsibility to protect the land with all of his strength? This was Chiang Kai-shek's responsibility. Was it Wang Jingwei's responsibility?[194]

In fact, she went on, not only did Chiang abandon China

> in the face of Japanese aggression, now in order to prop up his illegitimate power, he was selling the country out to the Americans. "Yes, I was opposed to cooperation with the English and Americans. This was fully in line with Sun Yat-sen's ideas of Asian solidarity. Up to today, how have England and American helped us at all?"

All the Western powers were interested in, she added, was "in maintaining their special privileges in a new guise." The United States, she claimed,

> would never have entered the war if the Japanese had not attacked Pearl Harbor. Who could have predicted that?[195]

Chen cleverly tapped into a strong reservoir of anti-GMD, anti-Western sentiment throughout China in her effort to underscore the contradictions of a political system that had "just returned from its safe haven inland and hypocritically accused virtually the entire population that stayed behind of being tacit collaborators."[196] Moreover, it was a regime considered by many to be driven by "five preoccupations: gold bars, automobiles, houses, women, and face." GMD corruption was so widespread that one liberal Chongqing newspaper, the *Dagong bao*, proclaimed five weeks after the defeat of Japan that

> We have lost the hearts of the people of Nanjing and Shanghai within a short span of twenty or more days.[197]

John Leighton Stuart, an old "China hand" who became US ambassador to China a few months after Chen's trial began, clearly saw that corruption, and Chiang Kai-shek's inability or unwillingness to do anything about it, "was a major cause of China's enormous troubles."[198]

The judges took her comments personally, particularly when the audience voiced its approval. They ordered her to shut up and asked the bailiffs to remove those who were causing a commotion. Chen told the judges that they knew nothing about "basic law" and were "making fools of themselves." And when she added that

> on the battlefield, Chiang Kai'shek uses generals who often lose, while in the rear he has all these brain-dead and diseased officials,

the audience applauded.[199] The prosecution responded with a long history of traitors in China over the past 2,000 years that was so boring that the judges decided it was time to end the proceedings.[200] As Chen left the court, she was overwhelmed by well-wishers who asked for her autograph.[201]

Six days later, Bijun Chen returned to court for sentencing. The GMD-dominated press said nothing about this phase of her trial, while Shanghai papers, some of them already stigmatized by charges of what Yun Xia calls "cultural collaboration," covered both phases of the trial in some depth.[202] Since her guilt had already been decided beforehand, the judges' ruling was somewhat moot. However, to give the trial an air of legitimacy, the judgment discussed testimony from others that underscored her guilt. They totally rejected her argument that her husband's government was in any way connected to the Nationalist government or that Chiang Kai-shek had "abandoned" the Chinese people when he retreated with his government to the safety in Chongqing during the war. According to the judgment, Chen, in league with her husband, had "served as the claws of the tiger" by helping the Japanese to control the region's vast resources.[203] Moreover, it stated that she played a key role in encouraging her husband, and that their collective roles damaged the ability of the Nationalist government to wage war more effectively against the Japanese. On the other hand, the judges stated that there was no evidence to support the prosecution's charge that she "still controlled a secret police force." Moreover, because she was Wang's wife, she was forced into a situation that made her "echo his opinions." Consequently, because of her "mindless discipleship of her traitorous husband," she was condemned, not to death, but to life in prison.[204]

The Communists inherited all of the GMD's prisoners when they took power in 1949, including Bijun Chen who was in Shanghai's Tilanqiao prison.[205] According to Charles D. Musgrove, Qingling Song, the wife of Sun Yat-sen, and Xiangning He, both members of the leftist wing of the GMD later honored by the CCP for their revolutionary credentials,[206] approached Mao and Zhou Enlai about pardoning Chen. Mao agreed, but only on condition that she "confess her crimes as a traitor." Chen refused and died in prison in 1959. Recent studies in the People's Republic of China have moved away from the GMD view that she was a woman under the influence of her husband and was not responsible for her actions. Instead, she is now depicted as a domineering, power-hungry shrew who dominated Jingwei Wang.[207]

Chiang Kai-shek's government adopted a very different approach to its treatment of alleged Japanese war criminals. While GMD courts sentenced almost 60 percent of the 25,000 *Hanjian* to various prison sentences, only 18 percent of the Japanese war criminals convicted by Nationalist courts received prisons terms. The reason was simple—Chiang Kai-shek insisted that the latter be treated with "forgiveness and kindness."[208] This was not to be the case with some of the US trials in Shanghai, which took place with the approval of Chiang's government, thus raising questions of jurisdiction.[209]

The first trial took place from February 27 to April 15, 1946, before a US military commission and involved charges against Lt. Gen. Shigeru Sawada, who commanded the 13th Chinese Expeditionary Army from 1940 to 1942. He, along with three codefendants—Lt. Ryuhei Okada, Lt. Yusei Wako, and Capt. Sotojiro Tatsuta—were charged with denying eight captured American pilots POW status after a successful bombing raid over Japan on April 18, 1945. Though initially held and tortured in Tokyo, the pilots were transferred to Shanghai's Kiangwan Military Prison, where they were court-martialed under Military Order No. 4 (the Enemy Airmen's Act) of August 13, 1942. Their trial, which only lasted a few hours, ended with death sentences for the eight airmen—a sentence later reduced to life imprisonment for five of the pilots.[210]

The defense raised questions about the jurisdiction of the commission, but also challenged the prosecution's claims that the American pilots were denied a fair trial. It also claimed that the defendants were simply acting under superior orders, which the commission rejected, pointing out not only the *ex post facto* application of the Japanese "Enemy Airmen's Law," which allowed the "passing of the death sentence on certain captured fliers," but also the failure of the defendants to resist orders they knew violated international law.[211] On the other hand, the US judges did take into consideration the nature of the Japanese military command system, and used this as a mitigating factor in reaching their decision. It ruled that the crimes of the defendants, who were involved in various phases of the detention, court-martial, or execution of three of the airmen, centered around their "obedience to the law and instructions of the government and their Military Superiors." Sawada was found guilty for his failure to intervene and alter the sentences of those condemned to death, and sentenced to five years of hard labor. Wako and Okada, who served as judges at the court-martial, were sentenced to nine and five years of imprisonment, while Tatsuta received a five-year sentence for his role as warden in the prison where the airmen were executed.[212]

Several months later, another US military commission tried Lt. Gen. Isayama Harukei and seven other defendants for denying POW rights to 14 American airmen and later executing them. What complicated all of this was that the 14 crewmen were tried by a Japanese military court, while the pilots of their downed aircraft were sent to Tokyo where they were interrogated but not tried.[213] All of the Japanese defendants were charged with playing various roles in this illicit trial. The prosecution charged that one of the defendants, Harukei, did "'permit, authorize and direct an illegal, unfair, unwarranted and false…Japanese Military Tribunal." He was also responsible, the Bill of Particulars went on, not only of ordering and directing the military court "to sentence to death these American" POWs but also to execute them.[214] His subordinate, Col. Seiichi Furukawa, was the chief prosecutor during the trial. After interrogating the airmen, he informed Tokyo that they had all confessed to their "crimes." He was told to try all of them and reach a "severe judgement." It was essentially left up to Furukawa to determine their fate.[215]

On the morning of 19th June, 1945, the American fliers were lined up in front of an open ditch, shot to death and then buried in that ditch.[216]

The American military court, which had access to the May 21 Japanese "trial" records, concluded that the US airmen were denied the most basic defense rights and that their conviction was a legal sham. It found all eight defendants guilty and condemned two of them, Furukawa and Lt. Col. Naritaka Suguira, the chief judge at the airmen's "trial," to death. Isayama and Capt. Yoshio Nakano, an associate judge who interrogated the airmen before their "trial," were given life sentences. The rest of the defendants were given sentences ranging from 20 to 40 years though, upon review, the death sentences were commuted to life, and those against Lt. Jitsuo Dayte and Lt. Ken Fujikawa overturned.[217]

A third American military commission trial took place in Shanghai from August 13 to September 3, 1946, and centered around charges that Gen. Hisakasu Tanaka, the governor general of Hong Kong and commander of the 23rd Japanese army in China, Maj. Gen. Haruo Fukuchi, his chief of staff, and four others were guilty of the illegal trial and execution of Maj. David Henry Houck, a US Army Air Force pilot. The Japanese charged Houck, the commander of the 118th Tactical Reconnaissance Squadron stationed in Sichuan Province, China, with sinking a Chinese civilian vessel in Hong Kong harbor in January 1945. For the next three months, Houck was periodically interrogated, and finally tried on April 5, 1945, for violation of Order No. 4.[218] He was never afforded the most basic legal rights during his two-hour military trial, something backed up by several Japanese witnesses during the *Tanaka et al.* trial. Houck explained that during the attack on Hong Kong harbor, he went into a dive (he was flying a P-51 Mustang) and bombed one destroyer. He added that the antiaircraft fire was very intense and while in the dive, the plane was hit and crashed into the sea. He denied intentionally bombing any civilian boat, or seeing such a ship sunk.[219]

The American court found five of the six defendants guilty and condemned Tanaka and Fukuchi to death for permitting the torture, trial, and death of Houck. Two other defendants were given 15-year prison terms, while another, Capt. Koichi Yamaguchi, the driving force behind the decision to condemn Maj. Houck to death, received a life sentence. Tanaka's conviction was overturned on appeal because he was "absent from command" during the entire period of Houck's trial and execution.[220] However, he was soon turned over to a Chinese military tribunal in Nanking where he was charged with war crimes while commander of the 23rd army. He was found guilty and shot in Guangzhou (Canton) on March 22, 1947.[221]

In the midst of the American military commission trials in Shanghai, Chiang Kai-shek's government began to investigate and arrest alleged Japanese war criminals. By the spring of 1946, Chinese investigators had uncovered over 30,000 cases of Japanese atrocities just in Shanghai. Given the widespread nature of these crimes, the Nationalists set up 13 military tribunals throughout China to try the Japanese accused of such crimes.[222] Two years earlier, Chiang's Ministry of Justice issued *Regulations on Prosecuting Special Criminal Cases*, which stated that only military courts could prosecute members of the Japanese military.[223] The government also issued rules that stated that the "principal source of substantive law for Chinese war crimes tribunals is international law." In cases where these regulations did not apply, the courts were to apply the new Chinese criminal code of 1935, which laid out harsh punishments for those who harmed the nation or its people.[224] These regulations were further defined by a new *Law Governing the Trial of War Criminals* of October 24, 1946.[225]

The first major trial of a high-ranking Japanese war criminal had one defendant—Lt. Gen. Takashi Sakai—who was charged with crimes against peace, war crimes, and crimes against humanity during his long years as a military commander in China dating back to 1931. According to the tribunal's transcripts, Sakai's criminal activities began in 1931 when he created a Chinese gang to "organize terrorist activities" including assassinations of journalists, politicians, and military figures in Shanghai, Tianjin (Tientsin), and Hebei (Hopeh) province, which adjoins Beijing and Tianjin.[226] Later, he was involved in the Kwantung Army's successful plans to expand its influence southward and force Chiang Kai-shek to withdraw "Chinese military, party, governmental, and secret service organizations and personnel from Hebei province, Beijing, and Tianjin."[227] He was also charged with having

> incited or permitted his subordinates to indulge in acts of atrocity. Between November, 1941, and March, 1943, in Kwantung and Hainan over one hundred civilians were massacred by shooting or bayoneting; twenty-two civilians were tortured; women were drowned after severe beating and one expectant mother was tortured; two women were raped and mutilated, and their bodies were fed to dogs; civilians were evicted from their homes and seven hundred houses were set on fire; rice, poultry and other foods were plundered. On 17th and 18th December, 1941, in Hongkong, thirty prisoners of war were massacred at Lyumen and twenty-four more prisoners were killed at West Point Fortress. On 19th December, 1941, the personnel of a British medical unit were massacred—twenty persons in all. Between 24th and 26th December, 1941, seven nurses were raped and three mutilated, and sixty to seventy wounded prisoners of war were killed. Valuable collections of books were pillaged from libraries.[228]

Sakai pleaded not guilty, and argued that he was acting under the "stipulations of the International (Final) Protocol of 1901 [Boxer Protocol and annexes]," which allowed "eleven foreign powers...to keep troops in certain areas in China in order to maintain free communication between Peking and the sea."[229] He added that this accord, which included Hebei and Tianjin, also stipulated that local governmental and military leaders were to do everything possible to protect foreigners from harm, on penalty of removal from office. He also argued that the alleged crimes took place during a "war of aggression," and that he was simply acting "upon the orders of his government."[230]

In reaching its decision on the charge of crimes against peace, the Chinese tribunal used but did not reference the definition of such crimes in the Allied Control Council Law No. 10 as well as the Nuremberg and Tokyo IMT trials. Sakai's guilt, the tribunal stated, was based solely on the fact that "he had taken part in the war of aggression against China."[231] It also concluded that he was guilty of war crimes and crimes against humanity as defined in Hague IV (1907) and the 1929 Geneva Convention. The Chinese tribunal rejected Sakai's claim of superior orders, and cited Yamashita and other postwar cases to back up its decision. It sentenced him to death at the end of his one-day trial on August 29, 1946, a decision upheld by Chiang Kai-shek. He was executed several weeks later by a firing squad "before a large, approving public audience."[232]

Four months after Sakai's execution, the Nationalist government began the first of four trials in Nanjing of four officers involved in the atrocities committed there in 1937–1938. The most important defendant was Lt. Gen. Hisao Tani, the commander of the Japanese 6th division that was accused of committing some of the worst atrocities in the city. Iris Chang, the author of *The Rape of Nanking* (1997), even claimed that Tani personally raped 20 women there.[233] But several Japanese historians question the accuracy of these charges. Masahiro Yamamoto, for example, states that most of the 6th division's operations were outside the city walls, and it "did not engage in extensive mopping-up operations within the city." [234] Another historian, Tokushi Kasahara, questions the evidence against Tani, arguing that if authorities had thoroughly investigated the Nanjing massacre, "higher-level commanders, army leaders, and even the emperor would have been implicated."[235]

According to Yamamoto, Tani was chosen to be the criminal scapegoat for the massacre to protect Iwane Matsui, the commander of the Shanghai Expeditionary Army that attacked Nanjing in early December 1937, who was on trial in Tokyo. Tani's superior, Lt. Gen. Kesago Nakajima, who commanded the Japanese 16th army during the battle for Nanjing, bore much of the direct responsibility for the crimes committed there. Various scholars have described Nakajima, who died soon after the war ended, as a "small Himmler of a man, a specialist in thought control, intimidation and torture,"[236] a "sadist" and a "beast."[237] His superior officer was Prince Yusuhiko Asaka, Hirohito's uncle and overall commander of Japanese forces that invaded Nanjing.[238] Yamamoto suggests that there were some former officers in China who campaigned to have Tani prosecuted to protect Prince Asaka, who ultimately was granted immunity from prosecution because of his family ties.[239]

Tani was arrested by the United States in Japan in early 1946 and questioned at Sugamo prison. The Chinese asked for his extradition, and he was sent to Nanjing for trial, which began on December 31, 1946. He was charged with "having killed 'several hundreds of thousands [of] victims' for the purpose of 'crushing our nation's [China's] will to resist.'" The prosecution also claimed that his troops "had committed massacres and rape in multiple locations outside of the Chunghua [Nanjing city] Gate," crimes that it considered a "blot on the history of modern civilization." The indictment also listed a number of specific examples of executions, stabbings, "group massacres," rape, property damage, and other specific crimes that resulted in hundreds of deaths.[240]

Tani pleaded not guilty and said he knew nothing about the atrocities committed in Nanjing. He blamed them on Nakajima's units. Scores of witnesses testified during the trial, some of them with missing limbs or scars. The prosecution also presented evidence from the recent excavation of a number of mass grave sites in Nanjing and displayed a mound of skulls in the courtroom.[241] At one point during the trial, a packed courtroom and several thousands spectators outside shouted "Kill them [Tani and his attorney] immediately" after hearing this gruesome testimony.[242] Needless to say, few were surprised when he was found guilty on February 6, 1947. His sentence was read to a packed courtroom a month later.

Hisao Tani, having been convicted of instigating, inspiring and encouraging during the war the men under his command to stage general massacres of prisoners of war and non-combatants and to perpetrate such crimes as rape, plunder and wanton destruction of property, is hereby sentenced to death.

Chiang Kai-shek quickly approved this decision and on April 26, 1947,

> spectators lined the streets and sidewalks as guards led Tani Hisao, his arms bound behind his back, to the execution grounds at Yuhuatai, or Rain Flower Terrace, an area just south of Nanking. There he met his death by gunfire.[243]

The Nanjing court also tried three other officers—Capt. Gunkichi Tanaka, 2nd Lt. Toshiaki Mukai, and 2nd Lt. Tsuyoshi Noda—and found them guilty of the mass murder of hundreds of Chinese POWs and civilians. They were sentenced to death and executed on January 28, 1948.[244]

Chiang Kai-shek's decision to approve Tani's execution was met with widespread support in a city whose wartime trauma had come to symbolize China's suffering during the War of Resistance. The same could not be said of his intervention in the conviction of Gen. Yasuji Okamura, the last commander of Japanese forces in China. According to *China Press*, many considered Okamura the top Japanese war criminal in China who pulled the "strings behind the puppet Wang Ching-wei regime in Nanking."[245] In fact, when the war ended, Okamura was also number one on the Communists' list of Japanese war criminals because of his "three alls" annihilation campaign—burn all, kill all, steal all (*sankō sakusen*)— which devastated their stronghold in Shaanxi province.[246] But Okamura's crimes began well before he took command of the North China Area Army in late 1941. In the spring of 1939, he was given permission to begin to use gas in his upcoming military campaigns "to restore the reputation of the troops and to give them 'the feeling of victory.'"[247]

In late 1944, Okamura was appointed commander-in-chief of the China Expeditionary Army. At the end of the war, Yingqin He, the commander of Nationalist forces in China, ordered the Japanese generals in northern and eastern China to hold their positions and defend them against the communists until Chiang's forces arrived to accept their surrender. Rumors abounded in Nationalist circles that Chiang had entered into secret agreements with the Japanese that would lead to a joint common front against the communists well before the war ended.[248]

Okamura quickly offered to surrender all Japanese forces to Chiang personally once Nationalist troops took over Japan's widespread positions throughout China. Negotiations for the formal surrender were handled by Okamura's deputy chief of staff, Maj. Gen. Takeo Imai, who met a number of his former Chinese students who were now top Nationalist generals when he arrived in Nanjing for surrender talks. They treated their former teacher (*sensei*) with deference and respect. Once surrender talks began, the Nationalists asked for Okamura's help in securing control over eight Chinese cities—Beijing, Guangzhou, Hong Kong, Nanjing, Shanghai, Tianjin, Qingdao, and Wuhan. Okamura said that he would help out in any way he could, but urged the Nationalists to move as quickly as possible to take over Japanese positions because of the growing threat of communist forces.[249] At the formal surrender ceremony on September 9, Gen. He, Okamura's former student in Japan, apologized for subjecting his former *sensei* "to the indignity of surrender." His interpreter, Maj. Yaowu Wang, was shocked by this statement and told an American adviser that it seemed as though "his countrymen had forgotten about the rape of Nanking."[250]

Okamura remained in China and, according to one Chinese observer, was "still enthroned in the Foreign Ministry building" in Nanjing in the spring of 1946.[251] For the next few years, Okamura served as an unofficial adviser to Chiang, which enabled him, like other Japanese officers who remained in China, to ship back to Japan the vast wealth he had accumulated during the war.[252] In the end, though, political expediency forced Chiang to agree to put Okamura on trial in Shanghai in August 1948. According to the president of the five-man military tribunal, Meiyu Sheh, this widely publicized, filmed trial was to "occupy an important page in the annals of the Chinese military commissions."[253] He added that it would be fair and not governed by revenge or leniency but by the "evidence deduced."[254] The prosecution charged Okamura with waging a war of aggression, violation of article 46 of the Hague Convention, and "tolerating the massacre of Chinese civilians and burning houses by Japanese troops and other crimes."[255] The chief prosecutor argued that senior commanders like Okamura had to accept responsibility for all actions of their subordinates.

> If Okamura should be let go free, what would the Chinese nation think of this tribunal? What would the relatives of victims of Japanese brutalities think of this military commission?[256]

He ended by insisting that Okamura be found guilty of all charges and condemned to death.[257]

Okamura's attorney countered that the prosecution had not produced any evidence directly linking him to any of the alleged crimes, and that it was Japanese troops' "immediate superiors," not senior commanders, who were responsible for the actions of their troops. Okamura sent written "supervisory orders" to his commanders that prohibited Japanese troops from "killing, committing arson, and attacking innocent people." He added that "We are here to try Okamura with law. Since there is no evidence against him, he should be released." The court then adjourned *sine die* toward the end of August because Okamura was ill, possibly of tuberculosis.[258]

In the interim, the political and military landscape in China changed dramatically, and most of the Nationalists' military leaders were convinced that the "situation [against the communists] was hopeless." Chiang Kai-shek and others were making plans to flee to southern China or Taiwan, while Vice President Zongren Li pushed for a cease-fire and talks with the communists. The White House and Gen. MacArthur concurred, and, realizing that the game was up for the Nationalists, decided that any further US aid to Chiang's forces in China would be totally wasted. [259]

Consequently, when Okamura's trial reconvened on January 26, 1949, the court ruled that he was not guilty because of "lack of evidence." It explained that since Okamura had taken command of Japanese forces in China just eight months before the defeat of Japan, he could not be held accountable for that country's war crimes based simply on the argument that they had been committed by his subordinates. It also noted that he had "acted commendably in ordering his men to surrender their arms and cease hostilities after V.J. Day."[260] The military tribunal's decision had little to do with law, since Chiang Kai-shek had already decided that Okamura and other Japanese officers should be hired as "advisers and military trainers."[261] His top generals strongly disagreed, but this did little to deter Chiang from using Okamura and other Japanese officers as his "drill masters" once he got to Taiwan.[262] According to *China Press* and the *New York Times*, Chiang arranged to have Okamura and 259 other Japanese POWs sent to Sugamo prison in Tokyo in early 1949 to "finish" their prison terms.[263] Once the Korean War began, the Japanese took over Sugamo and began gradually to parole the Japanese prisoners there.[264]

The public reaction to Okamura's acquittal was loud and vociferous. A Beijing radio station called it and the recent release of other Japanese war criminals "unjust."[265] On January 28, the CCP responded to Chiang's request for peace talks by demanding that the "reactionary Nanking government" rearrest Okamura and turn him and other Japanese war criminals over to the PLA (Peoples' Liberation Army). The Nationalists, it charged, had found him not guilty simply "to induce Japanese reactionaries to come to China and join you in massacring the Chinese people."[266] A week later, the CCP, aware that Okamura was in Japan, insisted that the recently repatriated Japanese war criminals be punished along with Chiang Kai-shek and other GMD "war criminals."[267] Japan never responded to these demands, and Okamura, who lived comfortably in Japan until his death in 1966, not only played an active role in the creation of Japan's new Self-Defense Forces, but also helped Chiang Kai-shek rebuild his military forces in Taiwan.[268]

The harsh tone of the CCP's attacks on Japanese war criminals was designed to play to the dark mood of a Chinese public dismayed by what seemed to be failed Nationalist efforts to deal more forcefully with Japanese war criminals. It was also a way for Mao's new government to link Nationalist criminality with Japanese war criminals. When the War of Resistance began in 1937, the CCP mimicked Nationalist policies toward *Hanjian* and Japanese war criminals. However, over time, CCP policies changed, and, in some cases, were even more severe because they allowed the "masses" more freedom of action in dealing with collaborators. Initially, Mao's policies toward suspected *Hanjian* in border areas stated that "once a *hanjian* is identified, anyone can immediately arrest him or her and hand in the *hanjian* to the local military or government."[269] These authorities, in turn, had the right to execute any *Hanjian* under their control without any concern for legal niceties.[270]

These policies evolved in the midst of the CCP's three-phased Yan'an Rectification Campaign that sought to unify the party and strengthen its discipline. One dimension of this program was "thought reform," a multistep process that broke down individualism through public humiliation and other means. For stubborn individualists, this could include prison isolation until he or she wrote a confession that analyzed "his evil conduct and his desire to change." The CCP hoped this would lead to a "new self" willing to conform to the "party line."[271] This new method of thought control was also used by the communists on suspected *Hanjian*, who were often held in "handicraft learning centers for self-renewal."[272] "Reeducation" efforts continued after the war, and a number of captured GMD generals, party officials, and Japanese war criminals confessed their crimes and testified about the successes of such transformative efforts. The CCP was particularly proud of the confession and successful "reeducation" of Pu Yi, the last Qing emperor and token ruler of Manchukuo.[273]

The CCP also used mass trials of *Hanjian* to stir up postwar propaganda against the collaborators. A trial in Chengde in 1946 employed many of the "thought reform" methods adopted earlier and was held before a crowd of over 15,000 Chinese workers, students, and others. During the accusatory phase of the "trial," those in attendance "exposed" *Hanjian* who not only worked with the Japanese but harmed other Chinese citizens. A group of thousands of railway workers, for example, told how a local rail station manager, Zhongxin Zhu, with the help of the Japanese military, "exploited and abused [Chinese] railway workers." He not only "embezzled" most of their salaries, they testified, but also fined them for "idleness." Consequently, local Communist officials fired Zhu and seized all of his property to compensate the workers for lost wages. Local Chengde merchants followed suit, and accused Kerang Ai, a politician and head of the local chamber of commerce, of similar crimes. This ultimately led to his loss of both positions. Similar mass trials took place elsewhere in communist-controlled China, where local party officials often seized the property of those found guilty, and redistributed it to the convicted individual's victims.[274]

Despite their harsh statements about the acquittal of Okamura and the return of several hundred other Japanese war criminals to Japan in early 1949, CCP policies toward alleged Japanese war criminals were similar to those of the Nationalists, who had a good track record when it came to the treatment of Japanese war criminals. Many Japanese POWs joined Mao's forces at the end of the war in northern China, and provided the CCP with needed military expertise. Those who were repatriated were first put through a CCP "reeducation" program designed to ensure their "commitment to communism."[275] Consequently, when the Soviets suddenly turned over almost a thousand alleged Japanese war criminals and *Hanjian* to the CCP in the early 1950s, the Communists had to develop more formal policies to deal with them as well as the scores of *Hanjian* still in prison. The most prominent *Hanjian* in this group was Pu Yi, China's last emperor. The rest were principally members of his royal entourage and Japanese officials who had served in Manchuria, which the Soviets had occupied at the end of the war.[276] Zhou Enlai, who was in charge of the transfer, was concerned about any public reaction to news that Pu Yi and other former top officials were now in China. Consequently, he not only ordered the windows of the train cars covered as they made their way to Fushun in China, but also insisted that the train take a "slow route" so he could prepare facilities for them. Ultimately, they were housed in two prisons in Fushun and Taiyuan just outside of Shenyang, the provincial capital of Liaoning province. Zhou vowed that none of them would die or escape while in custody, but also stated that "maybe in the future we can also consider the possibility of not killing any of them."[277]

In reality, Mao's government had no intention of harming any of the prisoners, particularly the Japanese POWs, because they might prove to be valuable diplomatic pawns in what Beijing hoped would be improved relations with Japan. They treated the Japanese POWs with "lavish leniency," and even tolerated their initial refusal to take part in the prisons' reeducation programs. Such policies greatly frustrated the guards at both prisons, and most of them applied for transfers just a few months after they opened. The prisoners' boldness was stimulated partly by news that Beijing did not intend to "hand down any death or life sentences" and that very few would even be put on trial.[278] These decisions also frustrated officials and the public in the region, who felt that the Japanese prisoners should be treated much more harshly. Both groups remembered Japanese atrocities during the war, which were kept alive by press reports of the 1949 Soviet trial in Khabarovsk that focused on Japanese medical and biological experiments on Chinese prisoners. These articles, which included a shortened version of the trial transcript, gave the Chinese public a rare glimpse into Japan's ghastly experiments on human subjects. Other Chinese publications attacked Emperor Hirohito, calling him "the most heinous, utterly despicable, and treacherous murder of humankind." According to journalist Fan Xiao,

> These thuggish Japanese war criminals must be punished without any mercy. Any talk of "leniency" would be the biggest crime of all.

Xiao also castigated Chiang Kai-shek for his "magnanimous and lenient treatment" of the Japanese POWs. Consequently, those who "died in the war were still 'rolling in their graves, unable to rest [peacefully].'"[279]

These tirades continued until the end of the Korean War, when Chinese policies toward the POWs began to change, largely because Zhou sought to use friction between the United States and Japan subtly to forge a new relationship with its former enemy. As ties between Beijing and Tokyo improved, visiting Japanese delegations kept bringing up the question of the repatriation of the Japanese POWs in Fushun and Taiyuan. By 1955, Mao and Zhou were convinced that a "lenient policy towards these Japanese war criminals will help us win over Japan and isolate American imperialism."[280]

The biggest challenge for China's leadership was to convince the public not only of the virtues of improved relations with Japan, but also the importance of adopting a more lenient, forgiving attitude toward the Japanese POWs. It began this process in 1954 when it repatriated 417 Japanese POWs to Japan. This was paired with an extensive number of cultural exchanges between both countries from 1954 to 1956 designed not only to improve Chinese public attitudes toward the Japanese, but also to strengthen ties between both countries. But the Japanese wanted more than the return of the remaining Japanese prisoners in Fushun and Taiyuan. In the summer of 1955, Tokyo wanted to know the fate of the 47,000 Japanese citizens currently in China.[281] Beijing responded that any Japanese who wanted to return to Japan could do so freely, while those suspected of war crimes would "be dealt with…in accordance with Chinese judicial procedures."[282]

A year earlier, the CCP had begun to lay the ground work for the trials of these alleged war criminals and ordered a detailed investigation of their crimes. Between 1954 and 1956, Chinese investigative teams gathered over 431,000 pages of evidence, which included the testimony of almost 27,000 witnesses. On March 14, 1956, Zhou announced that the government would try 51 (later 45) of the 1,063 alleged Japanese war criminals in Chinese custody. The rest would be sent back to Japan in "in three subsequent waves for maximum effect."[283] He admitted frustration with his government's inability to deal with this matter in a more timely manner, and closely linked its resolution to the official end of the war with Japan and restoration of diplomatic ties between both countries.[284]

One dimension of Beijing's plans to prepare the public for the trials and the acts of clemency to follow was to identify a new common enemy for both countries—the United States. This was made easier after the Americans detonated a nuclear bomb on the Bikini atoll in the spring of 1954.[285] The press also highlighted the visit by some of the Japanese war criminals to sites that were "evocative of Japan's past crimes," coupled with their heartfelt apologies. This, the Chinese press noted, marked the end of the long years of "political reeducation" that many of the POWs had undergone while incarcerated.[286] The final stage of this publicity campaign was coverage of a confessional gathering of some of the Japanese POWs. One of them, Ichiro Koyama, admitted killing a number of innocent Chinese civilians, and, along with others in the groups, asked for the death penalty for their crimes. Collectively, the group promised that if found guilty, they would cry out, "Long live the People's Republic of China.'"[287]

All of this led Zhou to conclude that the Chinese public was ready for the trials, which, like the earlier one, were carefully "choreographed" with severe restrictions on attendance. They took place in Shenyang and Taiyuan from June 9 to August 21, 1956. One of the most dramatic moments in the Shenyang trials was the appearance of Pu Yi, who testified against two former Japanese ministers in Manchukuo, Tadayuki Furumi and Rokuso Takebe. Furumi, the highest ranking Japanese official on trial, had been a deputy director of Manchukuo State Council's economic and general affairs departments, and played a major role in developing its economic and press policies.[288]

Some of those in the dock were on trial for far more serious crimes. Yoshikazu Sumioka and Lt. Gen. Keikyo Suzuki were charged with the murders of hundreds of Chinese civilians. After the war, Sumioka, and another defendant, Taiji Ono, led groups of bandits that regularly fought Communist forces, which helped the prosecution open the door to crimes committed not only during the War of Resistance but also during the postwar struggle against the GMD. In fact, of the 45 Japanese on trial, 8 were charged with crimes after the war, which not only allowed the CCP "to modulate conversations about the War of Resistance into areas advantageous" to the party, but also helped underscore the fate of those who opposed the party.[289] Suzuki's crimes were among the most horrific. He was charged with not only ordering his troops to rape and murder a large number of women in a rural Manchurian village, but also the murders of almost 1,300 villagers. Testimony revealed that when one of the women resisted, she was "taken to the river bank and hacked to death." When it was discovered that she was pregnant, a Japanese solider "slit open her stomach, took out the fetus, and cut it up." Suzuki was found guilty of all charges and sentenced to 20 years of imprisonment.[290]

Though witnesses often demanded the death penalty for some of the defendants, this did not fit into government plans to treat the worst criminals with leniency. In an effort to temper public outrage over the light sentences, the government carefully controlled news about the trials. People's Daily, for example, published only three short paragraphs on Suzuki's crimes, even though there were hundreds of pages of testimony and other evidence presented during his trial. The government also had legal experts explain in the press that "these Japanese war criminals do not bear chief responsibility for the prosecution of the Japanese imperialist invasion." Instead, they had been "forced by Japanese imperialists to participate in the war, and…their superior officers had ordered them to commit crimes."[291] Their crimes, the experts concluded, were of "lesser importance." In fact, according to Dingcheng Zhang, a state prosecutor, the worst of the Japanese war criminals had been tried and punished by the GMD and the Tokyo IMT. The only option for the CCP was to treat these "insignificant offenders" with leniency because "the Chinese people do not believe in revenge."[292]

In the end, the courts in Shenyang and Taiyuan sentenced the 45 Japanese war criminals on trial to terms ranging from 8 to 20 years. The other 1,018 Japanese POWS were granted exemption from trial and were sent back to Japan on August 21, 1956. Once back in Japan, many openly admitted their war crimes.[293] Ichiro Koyama told a *Japan Times* reporter in 2005 of these crimes, and praised the Chinese for his treatment while imprisoned there from 1950 to 1956. He was terrified during the trial and was willing to accept whatever fate was meted out to him. When the judge told him that he would be freed, "he cried and bowed to the judge."[294]

Conclusion

The question of World War II crimes and justice usually focuses on the Nuremberg IMT trial and, occasionally, on the 12 "subsequent" military trials in the US zone of occupation. Little is known about the tens of thousands of trials conducted throughout Europe and Asia. While many were short affairs with modest attempts at legality, some were of considerable length, though their outcomes were often tinged with politics. This was certainly the case with the *Hanjian* trials in China and those in the Soviet Union and East Germany. On the other hand, Poland conducted a remarkable series of reasonably fair trials in the few years that it remained truly independent at the end of World War II. Several of these trials, which are completely unknown in Western legal circles, tried and convicted several prominent German war criminals of genocide, a crime mentioned in Nuremberg and Tokyo but never really defined or addressed legally.

The real question about many of the hastily conducted military commission trials was—were they fair?—and, if not, did they really serve justice? While they certainly provided a legal basis for US military commission trials after 9/11, the similarities end there. Though these hastily called trials had all of the legal window dressing of the more mature trials in Nuremberg and Tokyo, they totally failed, for the most part, to offer those charged even the basics of accepted legal protection. In this sense, they were not much better than the "kangaroo courts" and show trials conducted in the Soviet Union and other authoritarian republics after the war.

Chapter 9

The Genocide and Geneva Conventions: Eichmann, Lemkin, Tibet, Guatemala, and the Korean War

The Chinese trials marked the end of the most dynamic phase of efforts globally to bring Axis war criminals to justice; such legal undertakings continue to this day, particularly in Europe. In 2011, a Munich court convicted John Demjanjuk, a native Ukrainian, of accessory to murder for being a "foreign helper" in the Sobibór death camp, where he abetted in "the murder of 27,900 Jews."[1] The Munich court sentenced him to five years in prison but immediately released him while he appealed his conviction. He died in a nursing home in Germany in the spring of 2012. Thus ended a long legal odyssey that had taken Demjanjuk from the United States to Israel, where he was convicted (later overturned on appeal) for being Ivan the Terrible, a brutal guard at Treblinka, back to the United States, and finally, Germany.[2] According to Thomas Walther, the "guiding spirit of this trial" was that the "crime of the millennium [the Holocaust] was not only perpetrated by Hitler and Göring and a handful of people," but also by "countless willing helpers who were also guilty of committing crimes."[3]

This was certainly the spirit behind the Israeli kidnapping and trial of Adolph Eichmann in the early 1960s. In some ways, it could be argued that the Eichmann trial was a bridge between the legal traditions, precedents, and concepts created in the various postwar trials in Europe and Asia, particularly at Nuremberg, and those embedded in the 1948 Genocide Convention and the four 1949 Geneva Conventions. Each of the Eichmann trial judges—Moshe Landau, Benjamin Halevi, and Yitzhak Raveh—were born in Germany, and, with the exception of Landau (who studied Law at the University of London), received their law degrees in Germany. Gideon Hausner, the chief Israeli prosecutor, was born in the Austro-Hungarian Empire and received his legal education at the Jerusalem Law School. Eichmann's principal defense attorney—Dr. Robert Servatius—served as defense counsel for Fritz Sauckel and the Leadership Corps of the Nazi Party at the Nuremberg IMT trial. Consequently, the Eichmann trial, which took place before the District Court of Jerusalem from April 11 to December 12, 1961, was very much a legal proceeding that brought together all of the major legal and legislative decisions that had taken place in the Western world since the end of World War II.

Eichmann was charged with 15 counts of crimes against the Jewish people, crimes against humanity, war crimes, and membership in a hostile organization. The prosecution relied not only on the 1950 Israeli Nazi and Nazi Collaborators (Punishment) Law (NNCL) but also on the judgment of the Nuremberg IMT tribunal, its charter, and Control Council Law No. 10 as the basis of the trial and its charges.[4] The judges cited not only these precedents in their decision, but also cases from Israeli criminal law as well as an extensive selection of international case law including decisions and precedents from the various trials conducted by the Allies in Europe and Asia after World War II. Most importantly, the judges argued that the charge of a "crime against the Jewish People" is "defined on the pattern of the genocide crime" mentioned in the United Nation's 1948 Genocide Convention.[5]

Eichmann, who was found guilty of all charges, and sentenced to death, appealed his decision to the Israeli Supreme Court. His appeal questioned the *ex officio* jurisdiction of the District Court as well as the legality of his abduction. The appeal even went so far as to cite the UN's 1948 Declaration of Human Rights and the subsequent Convention for the Protection of Human Rights and Fundamental Liberties to underscore what Servatius considered Israel's basic violation of such rights. The only country that had the right retrospectively to try Eichmann, Servatius argued, was West Germany.[6] The Supreme Court rejected these and other points of the appeal on May 29, 1962, citing Hans Kelsen and others about the legality of retroactivity in international law. It, like the District Court, also made reference to the Genocide Convention, the Nuremberg IMT tribunal, the Hague Conventions, *ex parte Quirin*, and even the Yamashita decision to justify the lower court's jurisdiction and decision.[7] In the end, the Supreme Court ruled that

> the appellant—by a variety of ruses, escape, hiding, false papers, etc.—succeeded in evading the gallows that awaited him, together with his comrades, at Nuremberg, also cannot afford him relief here, when at long last he stands his trial before an Israeli Court of Justice.[8]

Two days later, Israeli president Yitzhak Ben-Zvi turned down Eichmann's appeal for clemency. Several hours later, he was hanged, and his cremated remains secretly cast into the Mediterranean Sea in international waters.[9]

Raphael Lemkin and the Birth of the 1948 Genocide Convention

With the exception of the Geneva-based International Commission of Jurists 1960 study on the question of genocide in Tibet, the Eichmann trial was the first legal undertaking since the 1940s that addressed the question of genocide in a formal legal context. In reaching its judgment, the Jerusalem court noted that the concept of genocide was first laid out in Raphael Lemkin's 1944 classic, *Axis Rule in Occupied Europe*, and that he had proposed as early as 1933 that the "extermination of racial, religious and social groups be declared 'a crime against international law.'"[10] The Israeli court then looked briefly at the history of the Genocide Convention, noting that the UN General Assembly had adopted Resolution 95 (I) and Resolution 96 (I) in 1946 that affirmed the "principles of international law recognized by the Charter of the Nürnberg Tribunal and the judgement of the Tribunal," and that "genocide is a crime under international law."[11]

Oddly enough, during the trial itself, it was Servatius who first referred to the Genocide Convention, arguing that it, jurisdictionally speaking, was based not on the "universality principle, but on the territorial principle," meaning that only the state where the crimes took place has "jurisdiction over the offender."[12] Later, he challenged the idea that the crime of genocide was the same as a "crime against the Jewish people," and that the latter term "was framed too widely."[13] The judges rejected these arguments and made repeated references to the Genocide Convention in their judgment, particularly when it came to the question of the "universality of jurisdiction with respect of war crimes." They noted that while the authors of the Genocide Convention failed to address adequately the question of "universality of jurisdiction," they did content themselves with the "determination of territorial jurisdiction" as a "compulsory minimum."[14] The Israeli judges added that the Knesset was "inspired" by the Genocide Convention as its model for drafting section 1 of the NNCL, and that a person could be found guilty of such a crime if his intent, in harming "specific persons," was the result of "malicious intent against the whole group." But they also argued that

> the distinction does not lie only between the intention required in the crime of genocide and in the individual crimes of homicide perpetrated during the commission of that crime; but also the criminal act itself (*actus reus*) of genocide is different in its nature from the sum total of all the murders of individuals and the other crimes perpetrated during its execution. The people, in its entirety or in part, is the victim of extermination which befalls it through the extermination of its sons and daughters.[15]

Soon after Eichmann was brought to Israel in the spring of 1960, Israeli judge Emanuel Halevy mistakenly charged him with genocide, though this charge was soon changed to crimes under the NNCL since they took place before the convention went into effect.[16] The NNCL proved to be a much more precise law than the Genocide Convention, and included a detailed list of crimes drawn from the Israeli criminal code. It also defined "crimes against the Jewish People," war crimes, crimes against humanity, and crimes against persecuted persons. Since Israel had no death penalty at the time, the NNCL made provisions for one in cases in which an individual was convicted of a "crime against the Jewish People."[17]

The Genocide Convention is far less detailed than the NNCL and, as a result, has made genocide the most difficult of crimes to prove. This was not the case with Raphael Lemkin's initial definition of genocide in chapter 9 of his masterpiece *Axis Rule in Occupied Europe: Laws of Occupation, Analysis of Government, Proposals* (1944). Lemkin, a brilliant Polish Jewish lawyer who fled Poland just after the German invasion in the fall of 1939, had been troubled for some time by the lack of a legal term that defined crimes like the Armenian genocide. He settled in Sweden for several years after fleeing Poland, and began to collect copies of Nazi occupation documents, which he had shipped to the United States in 1941 after accepting an offer to teach at Duke University.[18] *Axis Rule* is simply his analysis of these documents, topically and country-by-country, throughout Europe. Chapter 9, which is wedged in between his discussion of "German Techniques of Occupation" and his section on such policies in Europe, contains not only the new word "genocide," which he described as "the destruction of a national or ethnic group," but also its two phases and "techniques."[19]

The two phases of genocide, he argued, were the "destruction of the national pattern of the oppressed group," and the "imposition of the national pattern of the oppressor." And though he argued that such practices were normally described as "denationalization," Lemkin thought this definition, which was often used simply to describe the deprivation of citizenship, was inadequate because it did not "connote the destruction of the biological structure" or the "imposition of the national pattern of the oppressor."[20] Genocide, he explained, was the "antithesis" of the Rousseau-Portalis Doctrine that was "implicit in the Hague Regulations." According to this doctrine, war was aimed against "sovereigns and armies, not against subjects and civilians."[21] According to Eyal Benvenisti, "war must wreak the least possible harm. As long as civilians keep themselves outside the war, it is not necessary to harm them."[22] According to Lemkin, the current war in Europe was not just against "states and their armies, but against peoples." Hitler's concept of genocide, he added, was based on "biological patterns," not cultural ones. Some groups such as the Jews were "to be destroyed completely."[23]

Lemkin then went on to define the eight "techniques" of genocide—political, social, cultural, economic, biological, physical, religious, and moral. He drew his examples from actual Nazi practice, with an emphasis on German policies in occupied Poland. He was extremely sensitive toward such policies against Jews and Christian Poles, particularly when it came to cultural, religious, and economic issues. The Nazis used biological and physical methods to depopulate and annihilate certain groups throughout Europe, particularly through forced malnutrition. They also practiced systematic religious persecution to destroy the idea of "religious leadership."[24] With the end of the war in sight, he proposed that amendments be made to the "Hague Regulations... expressly to prohibit genocide in any war which may occur in the future." Such amendments, he argued, had to

> consist of two essential parts: in the first should be included every action infringing upon the life, liberty, health, corporal integrity, economic existence, and the honor of the inhabitants when committed because they belong to a national, religious, or racial group; and in the second, every policy aiming at the destruction of the aggrandizement of one of such groups to the prejudice or detriment of another.[25]

He added that genocide was not just a problem "of war but also of peace," especially in Europe.

This was particularly true when it came to minorities, who were inadequately protected not only in their own countries but also abroad. Lemkin called for the creation of an "international multilateral treaty" that would provide constitutional and criminal code protections for minority groups in each country. The new criminal code provisions would protect "minority groups from oppression because of their nationhood, religion, or race," and include provisions "inflicting penalties for genocide practices." Lemkin, who proposed in 1933 that barbarity and vandalism be added to the offenses against the law of nations (*delicta juris gentium*), now suggested that genocide be included in such a list of crimes.[26]

Lemkin, who left Sweden in 1941 to teach at Duke University, accepted a job with the US government the following year, and published *Axis Rule* in late 1944, mostly to critical acclaim.[27] At the end of the war, he got a position in the JAG War Crimes Office, and spent time in London and Nuremberg working with Jackson's team. Lemkin says almost nothing in his memoirs about his time in London and Nuremberg, but does indicate that one of his jobs was to help prepare the indictment for the Nuremberg IMT trial.[28] Though he was not able to convince prosecutors to include the charge of genocide in the indictment because of British objections,[29] it was mentioned in count 3 (War Crimes), section a, as the

> extermination of racial and national groups, against the civilian populations of certain occupied territories in order to destroy particular races and classes of people and national, racial or religious groups, particularly Jews, Poles and Gypsies and others.[30]

When he returned to Washington in late fall 1945, Lemkin worked on the indictment for the Tokyo IMT trial, particularly the case of Gen. Karl Haushofer, a close associate of Rudolf Hess. Haushofer's *Geopolitik des Pazifischen Ozeans* (1925) strongly advocated closer military and political ties between Germany and Japan.[31] Lemkin argued that well before the outbreak of World War II, "Haushofer and his disciples saw...the battles at Pearl Harbor and Hong Kong."[32] The United States ultimately decided not to prosecute Haushofer because of illness and his advanced age. Lemkin returned to Europe in the spring of 1946 with the idea of remaining until the end of the Nuremberg trial.[33] Driven by recent news that he had lost most of his family, including his parents, in the Holocaust, he became relentless in his efforts to convince whomever would listen to him of the importance of convicting some of the Nuremberg defendants of genocide.[34] Needless to say, he was devastated by the news that none of them was convicted of genocidal acts, particularly against Jews.[35] But he could take solace from the fact that both the indictment and the judgment of the Nuremberg tribunal laid out details of the crimes that very much followed his eight "techniques" of genocide.

He now turned his attention to the United Nations, which was meeting at Lake Success in Long Island. By all accounts, he made himself a nuisance trying to convince the delegates and the press to support and promote his draft proposal for a genocide treaty.[36] Ultimately, his efforts paid off, and the UN's Sixth (Legal) Committee was charged with preparing a draft resolution on genocide, which the General Assembly approved on December 11, 1946. The secretary general then asked the UN's Economic and Social Council (ECOSOC) to study the prospects of preparing a draft for a genocide convention. It, in turn, asked the secretary general to oversee this initiative.[37] The Secretariat's Human Rights Division appointed a commission of three experts including Lemkin, Henri Donnedieu de Fabres, a former Nuremberg judge, and Vespasian V. Pella, a Romanian jurist, to help in the preparation of a draft convention. They were advised to make certain it did not "encroach on other notions," particularly when it came to crimes against humanity, which had been such an important feature of the recent Nuremberg judgment. The secretary general was also concerned about the impact of such a proposal on the draft of the Universal Declaration of Human Rights (UDHR), which was also being considered at the time.[38]

Much of the initial discussion among the committee of experts followed the general outline of Lemkin's book when it came to the questions of physical, biological, and cultural genocide.[39] The first few drafts also included proposals for an international court that would have jurisdiction on genocide and other "matters of international criminal law."[40] Pella and Lemkin also proposed that the signatory powers "take suitable steps likely to allay such racial, national, or religious antagonisms or conflicts that may lead to genocide," and create "special national offices…to centralize information on antagonisms between human groups and to transmit such information to the Secretary-General of the United Nations."[41] The draft was then sent to member states for comments, and then to the Sixth Committee. The matter was finally referred back to the ECOSOC, which created an ad hoc committee of representatives from China, France, Lebanon, Poland, the Soviet Union, the United States, and Venezuela, to prepare a draft genocide convention. The secretary general suggested that the committee consider several questions when it discussed the draft—which groups were to be protected, "what acts of genocide would be contemplated," and whether cultural genocide should be excluded from the draft.[42]

Though Lemkin, who by this time had joined the law faculty at Yale, was not officially a part of the ad hoc committee, he did, at least according to his memoirs, play a behind-the-scenes role in its preparation.[43] After considerable debate, the committee made a number of changes to the initial draft, including the elimination of the article on cultural genocide, which Lemkin considered a very important part of the convention.[44] It then sent its draft to the Sixth Committee, which approved it on December 2, 1948.[45] Seven days later, the three-part Genocide Convention (Resolution 260 [III]) was approved by the General Assembly. Attached to the convention was a separate statement that invited

the International Law Commission [ILC] to study the desirability and possibility of establishing an International judicial organ for the trial of persons charged with genocide or other crimes over which jurisdiction will be conferred upon that organ by international conventions.

It also requested the ILC "to pay attention to the possibility of establishing a Criminal Chamber of the International Court of Justice," the new successor to the League of Nations' Permanent Court of International Justice. Finally, the resolution asked that "parties to the convention extend its terms to their dependent territories 'as soon as possible.'"[46]

The heart of the 19-article *Convention on the Prevention and Punishment of the Crime of Genocide* were articles 2–4, which stated that

Article II

In the present Convention, Genocide means any of the following acts committed with intent to destroy, in whole or in part, a national, ethnical, racial or religious group, as such:

(a) Killing members of the group;

(b) Causing serious bodily or mental harm to members of the group;

(c) Deliberately inflicting on the group conditions of life calculated to bring about its physical destruction in whole or in part;

(d) Imposing measures intended to prevent births within a group;

(e) Forcibly transferring children of the group to another group.

Article III

The following acts shall be punishable:

(a) Genocide;

(b) Conspiracy to commit genocide;

(c) Direct and public incitement to commit genocide;

(d) Attempt to commit genocide;

(e) Complicity in genocide.

Article IV

Persons committing genocide or any of the other acts enumerated in article III shall be punished, whether they are constitutionally responsible rulers, public officials or private individuals.[47]

The convention's fatal flaw, of course, was that there was no international legal mechanism to investigate and try such crimes, something article 6 left to individual states or where "such international penal tribunals may have jurisdiction with respect to those Contracting Parties which shall have accepted its jurisdiction."[48] It would take another 40 years before the international community addressed this issue with the creation of the International Criminal Court. But this did not prevent the international community from investigating charges, and in the case of the Eichmann trial, including the crime of genocide in its legal proceedings in the early decades after the Genocide Convention went into force.

China, Tibet, and the Question of Genocide

This was certainly the case of the International Commission of Jurists' (ICJ) investigation of charges that the People's Republic of China (PRC) had committed genocide in Tibet between 1950 and 1959. Initially, China's new communist leaders dealt gingerly with Tibet, hoping a "soft touch," in league with social and economic reforms, would gradually convince Tibet's leaders of the virtue of accepting full assimilation into the PRC. What the communists failed to realize was the deep attachment of the Tibetans to a 1,300-year old religious-political system that centers around the Dalai Lamas.[49] Tibetans regard their special Lamaist, Gelugpa ("yellow hat") branch of Buddhism, "as a symbol of their country's identity and the superiority of their civilization." Each Dalai Lama is revered as the reincarnation of the "patron deity of Tibet," Chenrezig, "and the Buddha himself."[50] What complicated all of this at the time was the fact that Tibetans claimed a vast area—the Tibetan Plateau—that encompasses not only the Tibet Autonomous Region (TAR) but also portions of Gansu, Qinghai, Sichuan, and Yunnan provinces. Collectively, this region, which is home to about 5 million Tibetans, makes up about a third of China.[51]

But given the strategic importance of this region to China, and the fact that the Fourteenth Dalai Lama wielded vast temporal and religious sway over his deeply religious people, the communists quickly became impatient with the pace of assimilation, particularly when it became apparent that the Tibetans were resisting the communist takeover of their ancient homeland.[52] Tibetans were particularly afraid that the excessively chauvinistic Han Chinese intended to destroy Tibetan Buddhism.[53] Mao responded with People's Liberation Army (PLA) attacks against Tibetan monasteries and other centers of opposition, and by 1956, the situation had become so serious that the Dalai Lama asked for asylum in India. He was lured back by Zhou Enlai, who promised that Mao would delay the communization of Tibet until it was ready for such changes.[54] Though Mao initially kept his word, opposition to Chinese rule continued to grow throughout Tibet and exploded into violence after false rumors in March 1959 that the Chinese planned to kidnap the Dalai Lama. His Holiness, fearing for his life, fled into permanent exile in India in the midst of a harsh Chinese crackdown.[55]

The following year, the ICJ appointed a Legal Inquiry Committee on Tibet to investigate the genocide charges. Its 1960 report blamed the 1959 rebellion on years of pent-up Tibetan frustration with Chinese rule, and stated that the Chinese had committed horrible atrocities throughout the Tibetan Plateau during the rebellion.[56] What stands out in this report are the detailed statements of Tibetan refugees about the abuse of monks and lamas throughout the Tibetan Plateau since 1950. Communist operatives told monks from the monastery in Derge Dzongsar, for example, that "the monasteries and the lamas, and landlords and capitalists must be eliminated," which one monk interpreted to mean death. The monastery's leaders were then arrested and publicly humiliated.[57] At the Palzom monastery, a number of monks and one lama were taken to China, where they disappeared. Before he was taken away, Lama Kunga Pasang was forcibly humiliated in front of other Tibetans. The Chinese accused him of "accumulating wealth and exploiting the people." Tibetan women were forced to ride him like a horse, and he was made to eat grass and wear a bridle.[58] The abbot of the Tatsang monastery was tortured after he denied that there was any gold in the monastery. He was first forced to "carry human dung to the fields," and then tortured by being placed in cold water up to his waist. "His hands were locked together and bound by a sort of chain which tightened whenever he moved." When he continued to deny that there was gold in the monastery (it had been taken earlier by the Chinese), a gun was put to his head and he was told he would be shot if he did not reveal the location of the gold. Another monk from the Litang monastery said that the Chinese burned one Tibetan monk to death and crucified another.[59]

In addition to general pillaging of the monasteries, the ICJ report stated that the Chinese government also mounted a massive reeducation campaign in monasteries scattered throughout the Tibetan Plateau to force the monks to abandon their faith and the monasteries. A growing number of monks were also forced to work on public works projects. Part of China's reeducation program involved taking children from their families and sending them to schools in China. The Chinese explained that "the children would have to be separated from their parents, since their parents were religious and superstitious."[60] There are also accounts of rather crude Chinese efforts forcibly to sterilize Tibetan men and women.[61]

It is small wonder, after hearing these accounts, that the ICJ's Inquiry Committee concluded that

> acts of genocide had been committed in Tibet in an attempt to destroy the Tibetans as a religious group, and that such acts are acts of genocide independently of any convention obligation.

On the other hand, it

> did not find that there was sufficient proof of the destruction of Tibetans as a race, nation or ethnical group as such by methods that can be regarded as genocide in international law.[62]

The Committee explained that all of the evidence it reviewed "satisfied them that the Chinese in Tibet intended to destroy as such a religious group, namely Buddhists in Tibet."[63] The crimes committed by the Chinese against Tibetans, it went on, were driven principally by the latter's refusal to give up their faith. Such actions were not against the Tibetans as a "national, ethnical, or racial group. The dividing line is that a Tibetan who would not give up his religion was killed or ran the risk of being killed; he could never give up being a Tibetan." The report added that

> acts condemned as genocidal have been committed to destroy Buddhism in Tibet, and the intent is that there shall be no Buddhists left there.

The evidence underscored four principal facts:

1. that the Chinese will not permit adherence to and practice of Buddhism in Tibet;
2. that they have systematically set out to eradicate this religious belief in Tibet;
3. that in pursuit of this design they have killed religious figures because their religious belief and practice was an encouragement and example to others;
4. that they have forcibly transferred large numbers of Tibetan children to a Chinese materialist environment in order to prevent them from having a religious upbringing.

These practices, it concluded, were clear violations of article 2 of the Genocide Convention.[64]

Over the next 40 years, Tibet fell prey to the political and social vicissitudes of Chinese rule. With the exception of the Soviet Union, where tens of millions died partially as a result of what Norman Naimark called "Stalin's Genocides" during the 1930s and World War II, no country has suffered more in the twentieth century than China.[65] Scholars differ greatly over the actual number of deaths in the PRC during this period, with estimates ranging from 30 to 77 million. But all agree that the human losses were extraordinarily high and caused by a number of misguided economic, political, and social upheavals such as the Great Leap Forward and the Cultural Revolution. R. J. Rummell calls these deaths "democide," meaning genocide and mass murder.[66]

The Dalai Lama's government-in-exile claimed in 1996 that "over 1.2 million Tibetans have died as a direct result of the Chinese invasion and occupation of Tibet," a figure evidently taken from Rummell's 1991 study, *China's Bloody Century*.[67] Once again, scholars disagree on the actual number of losses during this period.[68] Robert Barnett, a prominent Tibetan scholar at Columbia University, admits that while such claims are unverifiable, there is "extensive evidence that the number of executions and prison and starvation deaths in some Tibetan areas was extremely high during this period."[69]

This underscores the fact that what has taken place in Tibet since 1950 has been a massive Chinese assault against an age-old, deeply entrenched Tibetan way of life that is dramatically changing throughout the vast Tibetan Plateau. The picture that emerges is one of an on again/off again oppression that has deeply affected Tibetan life, religion, and society. The situation became so severe that in 1987 the Dalai Lama told the US Congress' Human Rights Caucus that the illegal Chinese occupation of Tibet had inflicted a "holocaust" on his people.[70] This led to a series of Tibetan protests and a series of new Chinese policies, particularly after 1989, that saw Beijing reintroduce Cultural Revolution–style reeducation policies in monasteries designed "to promote the legal awareness of monks and nuns and dissuade them from being duped by separatist forces [the "Dalai clique"] and ensure the normal practice of Buddhism." Chinese authorities also decided to invest heavily in new economic ventures designed to improve the Tibetan way of life.[71] And while such investment has certainly improved the economic well-being of the Tibetans, it has also meant the growing Sinicization of Tibet. According to Elliot Sperling, while religion and culture are certainly important issues to Tibetans, the "underlying nationalist sentiment" among most Tibetans today is the "rejection of China's decades-long efforts to control the interpretations of Tibetan history." He calls this "a struggle . . . over historical time" and "historical memory."[72]

From the Chinese perspective, the Tibetans seem ungrateful for all of the largess invested in Beijing's efforts to transform what its leaders considered a backward, feudal kingdom that "groaned under a harsh rule" into a modern, integral part of China.[73] The Chinese blame most of this failure on the Dalai Lama, whom the PRC increasingly depicts as a "splittist" leader of a "Dalai cult" with one goal—Tibetan independence. According to Wei Jing, this was something

> both the Chinese government and people resolutely oppose. No attempt to separate Tibet from China's territory or damage the unity of the motherland and its nationalities can be tolerated.[74]

In 2009, China's *Fifty Years of Democratic Reform in Tibet* applauded the great changes that had taken place in Tibet despite efforts by the "Dalai clique" to hinder such growth. Tibet, it argued, enjoyed remarkable progress in economic, social, and political development. It also claimed that during this long era of "democratic reform," the "Law" protected "citizens' freedom of religious belief," as well as "patriotic and law-abiding monasteries."[75] *Fifty Years* also compared the struggle over Tibet to Abraham Lincoln's efforts to free the slaves during the American Civil War. The Dalai Lama, it inferred, was like Jefferson Davis, the president of the

Confederacy, who staged a "large-scale rebellion to retain the theocratic feudal serf-dom and to split the country."[76]

But various studies by the Dalai Lama's exile government painted a very differ-ent picture of religious rights throughout the Tibetan Plateau. One argued in 1996 that the Chinese had closed 6,251 monasteries, tortured and murdered over 110,000 monks and nuns, and "forcibly disrobed another 250,000 monks and nuns since 1950."[77] A year later, a new ICJ report claimed that the Cultural Revolution had virtually destroyed "all physical evidence of Tibet's previously pervasive Buddhist culture." Even Chinese scholars agree with much of this assessment.[78]

Yet religion is only one dimension of the various problems Tibetans face in an ever-changing Chinese economic and social landscape. There is still widespread poverty and illiteracy throughout the Tibetan Plateau.[79] This, coupled with what some see as growing Han Chinese domination of certain sectors of the region's busi-nesses and industries, and efforts to force a growing number of Tibetan nomads to settle in newly developed "urban developments," is seen by many Tibetans as simply another way to destroy the region's traditional way of life. John Isom considers the forced sedentarization program a form of "cultural genocide."[80] Such policies are driven partly by the Chinese view that Tibetans are backward with an "immature social system" that perpetuates "a vicious circle of poverty."[81]

Such policies are what helped trigger the riots in Tibet in the spring of 2008 months before the opening of the Beijing Olympics. The government responded with a harsh government crackdown throughout the Tibetan Plateau that led to the killing of hundreds of Tibetans by Chinese security forces. They arrested thousands more, particularly monks and nuns, and detained, tried, and imprisoned many of those involved in the protests. The government also forced thousands of monks and nuns to leave monasteries, and intensified a massive reed-ucation program that called the Dalai Lama a "de facto criminal."[82] These poli-cies triggered considerable international outcry and charges of "cultural genocide." Beijing responded by noting that

> on the contrary, the traditional culture of Tibet has been appropriately inherited, effectively protected, and vigorously promoted, while modern Tibetan culture, ori-ented toward modernization, the future and the rest of the world, has opened to the outside world and achieved rapid and all-round development propelled by Tibet's economic and social development. Tibetan culture is blooming with new vigor and energy in the new age and profoundly influencing the life of Tibetans and the devel-opment of Tibet's modernization through its diverse content and innovative forms.[83]

The Dalai Lama's government-in-exile countered this by arguing that, since 1950, PRC policies in Tibet set the stage for a "genocidal course meant to undermine Tibetan culture." This, it went on, was what led to the 2008 riots.[84]

Since then, Beijing's leaders have tried to walk a narrow path between tolerating some expression of Tibetan self-identity while also keeping a watchful eye on any further hints of Tibetan unrest. Government leaders, for example, seemed genuinely sensitive to the plight of the earthquake in Qinghai in 2010, though they also used the tragedy "to transform the disaster into a showcase of the party's benevolence and resolve."[85] At the same time, the party criticized the Dalai Lama, who had applauded Chinese relief efforts, for trying to "sabotage" them.[86] Simultaneously, the PRC began a major crackdown against Tibetan civic and intellectual leaders throughout the Tibetan Plateau. The principal ideological underpinnings of the government's new efforts to draw Tibet more deeply into the Chinese system have been driven by the ideals of the new "four adherences":

> Insist on adherence to the [Party's] leadership;
> Insist on adherence to the socialist system;
> Insist on adherence to the system of regional autonomy for minority nationalities; and
> Insist on adherence to a development path with Chinese characteristic and Tibetan traits.

A key element in this scheme was "to reshape and control Tibetan Buddhism" along what the CCP considered the proper socialist path.[87]

These policies, coupled with new restrictions on teaching Tibetan in schools in parts of the eastern Tibetan Plateau, are part of the reason for the recent wave of immolations, particularly in those provinces outside of the TAR with large Tibetan populations. Tsering Kyi, a gifted child of nomads who loved books, wrote before she took her life that she simply wanted "to do something for the Tibetan people."[88] Sonam Wangyal, a senior monk, stated that he was "giving away my body as an offering of light to chase away the darkness." Jampa Yeshil, a Tibetan refugee who set himself ablaze in New Delhi on March 26, 2012, wrote beforehand that

> The fact that Tibetan people are setting themselves on fire in this 21st century is to let the world know about their suffering, and to tell the world about the denial of basic human rights.[89]

Tamdin Thar, the oldest Tibetan to take his life, was, like Tsering Kyi, a nomadic herder from Qinghai province. According to Tsering Woeser, a Tibetan writer in Beijing,

> Many Tibetans think the pain of self-immolation is nothing compared to the pain of living without religious freedom.[90]

Beijing called those who took their own lives "outcasts and terrorists,"[91] and responded with a new wave of terror throughout the Tibetan Plateau that included sending thousands of party operatives into monasteries to keep a closer eye on monks and nuns. It offered those who accepted China's new gestures of friendship "health care benefits, pensions and television sets; the recalcitrant are sometimes expelled from their monasteries."[92] When these efforts failed to stop the immolations, the government adopted new tactics including statements by the official Buddhist Association of China that criticized them as a "serious sin,"[93] and harsh extra-legal policies designed to try and punish anyone directly or indirectly involved in the immolations. In late 2012, Beijing issued new prosecutorial guidelines that stated:

> people who burn themselves in public places will be charged with a public security offense and those who parade a corpse through the streets or gather to watch

the immolation without actively stopping the suicide will be subject to criminal prosecution.[94]

But is what has taken place throughout Tibet since 1950 cultural genocide? If we accept hypothetically that there can be acts of cultural genocide, then we must treat such acts in the same legal framework as those cited in the Genocide Convention. The key to such proof is the question of intent, a word cited twice (intent; intended) in article 2 of the convention. While "all true crimes require proof of intent," the standards for proving genocidal intent in international criminal law cases are particularly high.[95] Proof of intent is normally proven "as a logical deduction that flows from evidence of the material acts." In terms of cultural genocide, while not legally genocide,

> proof of attacks directed against cultural institutions or monuments, committed in association with killing, may prove important in establishing the existence of a genocidal rather than merely a homicidal intent.[96]

The failure to include cultural genocide in the Genocide Convention is one of the ongoing criticisms of this accord, even though, as Matthew Lippman has noted,

> the protection of a group's culture, as well as its physical integrity, is consistent with the prophylactic intent of the Genocide Convention. Both effectively extinguish a collectivity. Critics contend that a prohibition on ethnocide might impede assimilation. But, such policies are distinguishable from the deliberate destruction and desecration of icons, libraries, monuments and coerced religious conversions undertaken to with the intent to extinguish a group.[97]

Cultural genocide has been addressed in the United Nations' *Declaration on the Rights of Persons Belonging to National or Ethnic, Religious and Linguistic Minorities* (1992) and its *Declaration on the Rights of Indigenous Peoples* (2006–2007). What is tricky about applying such standards to nonmilitary attacks is that such assaults must be "widespread or systematic," and "in furtherance of a State or organizational policy to commit such attacks." However, as William Schabas has noted, there is controversy surrounding this latter issue about the role of non-State actors in the commitment of such crimes.[98]

And even though these declarations are not legally binding, they declare the importance of encouraging the development of full cultural, religious, ethnic, and other rights for national minorities. The *Indigenous Peoples' Declaration* addresses the issue of genocide and states that "all indigenous peoples and individuals have the right not to be subjected to forced assimilation or destruction of their culture." It also calls on countries to provide legal mechanisms to prevent or resolve such problems whose intent is to rob them "of their integrity as distinct peoples, or of their cultural values or ethnic identities."[99]

Given all of this, how are we to judge China's actions when they come to the charge of cultural genocide? In other words, has the Chinese government, in its treatment of the Tibetans, their religion, their culture, and their unique ties to the lands of the Tibetan Plateau over the past six decades committed genocide or crimes against humanity? What has taken place in Tibet and in other parts of China is, minimally, a major violation of basic human rights. The destruction of thousands of monasteries and other Tibetan religious and educational institutions has severely damaged the vitality and practice of Tibetan Buddhism, a key element in Tibetan ethnic identity. This, coupled with restrictions on the number of monks and nuns who can serve in these institutions and propagandistic efforts to force them to adopt extreme Chinese nationalistic ideals, has further eroded the dynamism of Tibetan Buddhism. This, in league with policies that are gradually replacing Tibetan as the principal language of instruction in schools throughout the Tibetan Plateau as well as programs of forced sedentarization and other socioeconomic policies have so dramatically changed the face of Tibetan life, religion, and society that one can only conclude that such policies could be seen as culturally genocidal. But, if history has taught us anything, it is that such policies will not necessarily lead to the total destruction of the multiple dimensions of Tibet's culture and religious traditions. They are simply too deeply embedded in the collective Tibetan soul not only in China, but globally.

Guatemala

Guatemala, like Tibet, has suffered from a long history of upheaval, particularly since it was conquered by the Spanish in the sixteenth century. And, like Tibet, Guatemala boasts a distinctive civilization—the Mayan—that some consider the New World's "greatest indigenous culture."[100] Though the Mayan civilization collapsed centuries before the arrival of European explorers, Mayans still make up the majority of the population in Guatemala.[101] According to Bartolomé de las Casas, the conquest of Guatemala was far more brutal and savage than any of the other conquests in Central America. After it was completed, the Spanish turned the region, once a veritable "paradise on earth," into "nothing but bare, ruined settlements."[102] The population was then enslaved and later forced to live on *reducciones*—settlements just for Indians. This facilitated not only their conversion to Christianity but also the "takeover of their lands by the settlers and the enforcement of the *encomienda* and *repartimiento* systems of forced labor." Once this latter system was set up, the Spanish government ruled that Indians had to be paid for their labor, which led to the creation of "forced indentureships" that lasted until the sixteenth century.[103] The *repartimiento* system allowed the Indians to return to their traditional villages, though widespread abuse continued, with the best land taken over by a small group of settlers with ties to the Spanish throne.[104] Over time, a rigid caste system evolved that separated Indios (Indians) from Spaniards.[105] Fortunately, the Maya, quite sensitive to their unique ethnic heritage, retreated into "closed, corporate communities" that enabled them and their culture "to survive the conquest and colonial periods."[106]

Spanish rule remained harsh and tyrannical throughout its long centuries of domination. This did not change after Guatemala gained its independence in 1821. In the late nineteenth century, the country's rulers began to seize control of Mayan land in the hills to grow coffee. Mayan efforts to resist these policies failed, which created "a climate of suspicion, hatred and resentment" between them, the Spaniards, and the Ladinos (Euro-Guatemalans).[107] Racial discrimination was widespread, rooted in the age-old idea that the Mayans were racially inferior.[108]

During the same period, the American United Fruit Company (UFC), was invited to open banana plantations in Guatemala. Over time, UFC gained control of the country's railway system and ports, and became a major player in the Guatemalan economy. It also created a forced labor system (*mandameinto*) to ensure it had a ready supply of cheap labor.[109] This, in turn, led to the creation of a "brutal model of capitalist development"[110] that not only treated native workers cruelly, but also paid them "slave wages."[111]

Efforts by several Guatemalan dictators to initiate liberal reforms before and after World War II did nothing to stop the UFC from taking over larger and larger tracts of land throughout the country, some of it from the Mayans. By 1945, the UFC was Guatemala's "wealthiest and largest employer,"[112] and owned more land in the country than the "combined holdings of half of Guatemala's landholding population."[113] In 1952, President Arbenz Guzmán initiated an agrarian reform program designed to allow more peasants to own land. His efforts were strongly opposed by Guatemala's wealthy landowning classes and the UFC, who were able to convince the United States that Guzmán's program was part of a larger communist effort to take over Guatemala.[114] A US-supported coup overthrew Guzmán in 1954, replacing him with Col. Carlos Armas, whose military dictatorship halted the agrarian and other postwar reform programs.[115] What followed was an "era of darkness" that led to a civil war in the early 1960s that would last for over 30 years. The country's military adopted a violent, racist campaign against the Mayans that was meant "to produce and maintain a climate of terror in the population."[116]

According to the UN-sanctioned *Report of the Commission for Historical Clarification* (RCHC; 1999) or *Memory of Silence*, the military was responsible for the murder or disappearance of over 200,000 Guatemalans, 83 percent of them Mayans, during what many Guatemalans refer to as *La Violencia*. The military was responsible for 93 percent of these deaths and the guerillas 3 percent. The military also used a "scorched earth" policy that resulted in the widespread destruction of Mayan villages, forcing 500,000–1.5 million persons from their homes.[117] In the Ixil region, a mountainous expanse in western Guatemala, for example, government forces destroyed 70–90 percent of the villages because guerillas used the region as a base of operations.[118] The military also created "model" villages in disputed areas that sought "to establish absolute control over populations considered to be the social base of the guerillas." One villager described the military's attitude toward the half million Mayans forced to live in these special villages:

> They really treated us with contempt. They would repeat their advice, the way you do a baby. They still despise us; we have no dignity. They definitely despise the indigenous people there—all of the poor. Now we are below them, because we have done wrong in their eyes, and they despise us. That's how they are with us now.[119]

Guatemalan soldiers, some trained by US Special Forces, also adopted counterinsurgency tactics that they called "hunting the deer (*cazando el venado*)" to force peasants to flee elsewhere from their villages. As they fled, they were met by armed troops who began to shoot them. According to Doña Eugenia,

> we were always asking each other, "Where should we go? Where can we go? Is there a place we can go? We were always looking for another safe place." Many elderly died

because we were climbing up and down steep mountains; the elderly cannot walk that much. They would stay behind resting. The army would find them and kill them. They killed lots of people: the elderly, children, babies, boys and girls, men and women, our youth. There was a señora with us. She had one child, a boy. We were running from the army, she was carrying her son, she was holding him in her arms. A bullet hit her in the back, it came out through her stomach and went through her baby. She died there with her son in her arms. They died together.[120]

In Cajixaj and Tuy Coral Cay the army executed villagers who surrendered because of hunger. The same happened to villagers from Tzalbal. According to the testimony from a villager who survived a massacre there,

In the beginning the Army began to burn some houses with everything in them, and the granaries where their corn was kept... Maybe it would be better if we went to the Army, because we can find food there and if they kill us, they kill us; what to do, but at least we won't die of hunger, the people would say... [they turned themselves in] when the Army was pissed off... "Oh! Good you all came in," was all the officer said; the Army took them, tortured and shot them, that's where they killed a group in Tzalbal because they gave up, they turned themselves in because they were hungry.[121]

Many of the victims were later tortured to death. Doña Elena, an Ixil refugee, later testified that after capturing and torturing her brother, they

put him in a hole for twenty-four hours. They threw ten buckets of water on top of him in that hole. They mixed soap, oil, and salt and forced my brother to drink it. After that, he was vomiting and vomiting in that hole. They threw him in that hole twice. They threw him in the river twice. They made him drink that mixture of soap, oil, and salt two times... My brother was very sad after all these tortures. He was so sad, so very sad. He was thirty-three years old. He became ill from susto [extreme fright] and the beatings. He died.[122]

The military was particularly harsh in villages it suspected of being sympathetic to the Guerilla Army of the Poor (*Ejercito Guerillero de los Pobres*; EGP), a Marxist-Leninist guerilla faction that played a major role in the civil war.[123] These campaigns against the EGP intensified in 1982–1983 under Presidents Fernando Romero Lucas García and José Efraín Ríos Montt. Garcia's plan

called for 100 percent random slaughter ("blindness and madness... brute force and nothing more") to a more systematic policy that called for a 30 percent "total kill" in the zones of conflict, combined with 70 percent "soft" pacification, including psychological operations and development projects.[124]

Ríos Montt, who overthrew Lucas Garcia in the spring of 1982, continued the same policies. A born-again Pentecostal Christian, Ríos Montt announced soon after taking power a new counterinsurgency plan, *Victoria 82*, or, as it was more commonly known, "rifles and beans (*Fusiles y Frijoles*)." It was more violent than Garcia's campaign, and emphasized an "intelligent killing" approach that resulted in mass murders throughout the Guatemalan highlands. According to Virginia

Garrard-Burnett, "nearly half of all the massacres and scorched earth operations" of the entire civil war took place during *Victoria 82*.[125]

One of the worst massacres took place in the village of San Francisco Nentón in the summer of 1982. The mass murders were so horrible that the Organization of American States' Inter-American Commission on Human Rights cited it in a 2001 report as one of 12 cases of genocide committed by the Ríos Montt government.[126] The genocidal actions began on June 22, 1982, when an army patrol entered the village and told the peasants not to help EGP. Twenty-five days later, the military returned in force, backed by three helicopter gun ships. Emphasis was now not just on "intelligent killing" but also on "a state of siege" mentality that included the suspension of most civil rights and much of the country's press freedom.[127]

Once the army surrounded Nentón, they told its residents to gather in the local square to receive food, reassuring them that nothing bad would happen to them. The women and children were placed in the local church. That afternoon, the women were taken from the church and put into houses where the soldiers raped them. According to one survivor,

> The men could hear their women's cries but could do nothing. But the cries stopped when the sounds of bullets and hand grenades commenced. *"Crack, crack. There was a lot of noise. All the little children were crying, crying."* When the women were dead, the soldiers burned their bodies inside the houses.[128]

The soldiers then returned to the church and brought the screaming children out in groups.

> They brought out the little kids—two, one, eight, five and six year olds they also brought out in groups. They took the groups and killed them with knife stabs. They picked the smaller ones up by their feet, "like you would a hen." They smashed their heads against pitchforks and against a cypress tree planted in front of the chapel. The soldiers ripped open the children's bellies with knives and tore out their intestines, tossing the small bodies into one of the houses located close to the church.
>
> When they brought out the last child, and he was a little one, maybe two or three years old, little—I saw this myself. They brought him out and stabbed him and cut out his innards. The little kid was screaming and because he wasn't dead, right there the soldier grabbed a thick stick and bashed his head. He cut out his guts and threw him away like shit. That's how the cabrones [bastards] did it. It's possible they killed the children like that so as not to waste their munitions, or perhaps as a game for the soldiers.

Once this savagery ended, the soldiers began to murder the men. First they killed the elders.

> Three old men. One, they stuck the unsharpened machete here [the throat], like you kill a sheep. "Aaaaay," they say. Just as we were watching they killed him...Inside the courthouse where we were—me, all of us. The old men's death cries amused some of the soldiers. "Like killing an animal; it made them laugh when they were killing. Poor people, the poor old men, they were crying and suffering."[129]

The remaining men were taken out in groups, blindfolded, forced to lie face down, and shot in the head. After a while, the soldiers got tired of this slow process, and "threw grenades and fired bazookas" into the courthouse to kill those still inside. Afterward, they cut out the heart of one of the bodies. They then dragged the bodies back inside the church and set it on fire. The final death toll was more than 300 villagers, with only one survivor. Nine thousand peasants in nearby villages fled the region because they feared they might be next.[130]

Months earlier, the EGP and Guatemala's bishops began to call what was taking place in the mountains genocide.[131] Once the civil war ended a decade later with the UN-brokered Oslo Accords between the Guatemalan government and a guerilla revolutionary coalition, a treaty-dictated Commission for Historical Clarification (*Comisión para el Esclarecimiento Histórico*; CHC) or Truth Commission, was created

> to clarify with objectivity, equity and impartiality, the human rights violations and acts of violence connected with the armed confrontation that caused suffering among the Guatemalan people.

Though its goal was not

> to judge—that is the function of the courts of law—but rather to clarify the history of the events of more than three decades of fratricidal war.[132]

Regardless, its conclusions substantiated the fact that some of the crimes committed during the long civil war were acts of genocide perpetrated principally by the various governments in power.

The commission's report, *Memory of Silence*, documented various "human rights violations and acts of violence," which included "extrajudicial executions and forced disappearances, torture, forced displacement, massacres, rape and sexual violence, genocide, and acts of violence."[133] It also focused on the "key actors" in the civil war (both government and guerilla), "their strategies," and the consequences of various aspects of the government terror campaigns. It ended with an extensive look at the impact of the civil war on various groups and institutions in Guatemala and the abuses committed by some of these groups during the conflict.

In many ways, the most important parts of the report were those on genocide and violations of international humanitarian law. The committee recommended that in cases where such crimes were "not extinguished" by the 1996 "Law of National Reconciliation," that

> crimes of genocide, torture and forced disappearance, as well as those crimes that are not subject to prescription or that do not allow the extinction of criminal liability, in accordance with domestic law or international treaties ratified by Guatemala

should be dealt with legally. This was particularly the case for those who bore

> various degrees of authority and responsibility for the human rights violations and acts of violence, paying particular attention to those who instigated and promoted these crimes.[134]

Memory of Silence also noted that Guatemala had ratified the Genocide Convention in early 1950 and that the CHC used the "legal framework of the convention and... jurisprudence, with particular reference to article 2 of the convention" to determine if acts of genocide had actually been committed. During its investigation, the CHC delved into the "general policies of the state," particularly those dealing with counterinsurgency, to determine the nature of the alleged crimes. It also looked at four different Mayan ethnic groups, and used four "selection criteria" to determine if they were victims of genocide:

- Intensity of violence (largest number of victims);
- Patterns of violence;
- Composition of victims (identifiable groups);
- Quantity of information.

The commission took great care to differentiate between causal and noncausal human rights violations as well as various independent variables such as

the command structure of the armed forces; the guerillas' political and military interest in the [four] regions analyzed; recognized norms of international humanitarian law; and the conditions of the noncombatant, civilian population.[135]

It decided that four Mayan tribes qualified under the convention as ethnic groups, and that the acts committed against them fulfilled the "in part" destruction section of article 2, which the committee understood to mean as "a reasonably significant number relative to the total of the group, such as all or a significant section of the groups, such as its leaders, that is, a substantial part of the group."[136] It then looked in detail at government policies in each of the regions where each Mayan tribe was located.[137] The report concluded that the nature of the violence committed by government forces against each of them was "massive and overwhelmingly impacted the Maya people." In some regions, government forces killed 98 percent (Ixil) to 100 percent (Rabinal) of the Maya population. The goal of the perpetrators was simply to kill the maximum possible numbers of the groups.[138]

In addition, government forces

systematically committed acts of extreme brutality, including torture and other cruel, inhuman, and degrading actions. The effect of these acts was to terrorize the population and destroy the basic elements of social cohesion between members, particularly when they were forced to witness or commit these acts themselves. Army units or *patrulleros civiles* [civil defense patrols] engaged in collective sexual violations against women, often committed in public and designed to harm the social reproduction of the group over time.[139]

In addition, government forces destroyed numerous villages, particularly in the Ixil region, where 70–90 percent of the "rural communities were destroyed."[140]

The commission concluded that these were "not isolated acts or excesses committed by troops out of control or improvised actions by mid-level army officers." Instead, these crimes "reflected high-level policies" that were "strategically planned, as is manifested by acts that express a coherent and logical plan."[141] These were acts of genocide committed by "agents of the Guatemalan State" and were the result of

> policies established by high-level commanders, rather than the material authors of these acts...the military authorities knew about the massacres committed by their agents. These acts were never investigated or sanctioned to ensure that they would not occur again. The failure to investigate these acts is the responsibility of the military authorities, competent judicial bodies, and political authorities.[142]

Memory of Silence was particularly critical of the state of Guatemala's failure "to investigate or sanction those responsible for these acts, despite the fact that many of them were well known publicly." It charged the state of Guatemala with violation of articles 4 and 6 of the Genocide Convention, which required "Contracting Parties" to try those responsible for such crimes before "a competent court of the state in whose territory these acts were committed or before a competent international criminal court."[143]

Yet the main purpose of the CHC report was not to lay the groundwork for extensive investigations and criminal proceedings, but to allow the truth to pave the way for national reconciliation. In fact, it was written deliberately "to avoid 'individualizing responsibility' and to delink it from the judicial process."[144] Consequently, while it certainly made a strong case for the nature of the crimes committed and those responsible, its principal thrust, similar to reports issued by commissions in Argentina, Chile, and El Salvador, was to

> formulate specific recommendations to encourage peace and national harmony in Guatemala. The Commission shall recommend, in particular, measures to preserve the memory of the victims, to foster a culture of mutual respect and observance of human rights and to strengthen the democratic process.[145]

It also proposed ways to compensate the victims for their losses and suggested the creation of a national body that would oversee implementation of these recommendations. Finally, the report suggested that the Guatemalan president issue a formal apology to the victims, their families, and their communities. However, though several presidents did apologize for these crimes, they meant little to the victims and their families because the country's leaders refused to accept responsibility for "past violations." To his credit, President Bill Clinton issued such an apology when he visited Guatemala in the spring of 1999, and stated that he regretted the role that the United States played in the civil war.[146]

In 2000, the Guatemalan Congress declared February 25, the day that the CHC released its report, to be the National Day for Victims' Dignity (*Día Nacional de la Dignidad de las Victimas*). While many have criticized the National Day's "low national profile" and the failure of successive governments significantly to invest in other memorial gestures, monuments, museums, those directly affected by the genocide have been far more critical of the government's failure adequately to address the reparations question. In 2003, the government did create a National Reparations Program (*Programa Nacional de Resarcimiento*; PNR), and, until 2006, spent its limited funds on "distributing land, building housing, and supporting a variety of development programs." In 2006, the government began to make single payments of $2,700 to rape victims and victims of other acts of "sexual violence." It also made single payments of $3,200 to the families of "victims of extrajudicial execution, death through massacres, or forced disappearance," and up to $5,900 for families who suffered multiple losses from the above crimes.[147]

The PNR also created a national registry of victims (*Registro Nacional de Victimas*) and sent thousands of case files to the public prosecutor (*Ministerio Púbico*) for further investigation and possible prosecution. Unfortunately, this program is hampered by government red tape and policies that hurt rural Guatemalans, particularly those who are illiterate or do not speak Spanish. To date, the PNR has failed not only to process the majority of claims it has received, but has also not sent thousands of claimants their reparations payments. On the other hand, it has paid out over $200 million to former members of civil defense patrols (*patrulleros*) who committed almost 20 percent of the crimes during the civil war. According to Daniel Rothenberg, this is far more than the government has paid the victims of the civil war. The Guatemalan government has also failed to heed another CHC recommendation to initiate an exhumation program for victims' bodies and create a special body to investigate the disappearance of 50,000 Guatemalans. Though there have been some exhumations, they have been done by various "civil society organizations," the driving force behind much of what has been done positively in Guatemala to deal with the complex aftermath of what some have called that country's "Silent Holocaust."[148]

But for many Guatemalans, the most serious failure of the government has been its unwillingness or inability to bring to justice those who committed these crimes. The reason is simple—the top perpetrators, both military and civilian—have continued to wield significant influence in Guatemala since the end of the civil war.[149] One has to look no further than the career of Guatemala's current president, Otto Pérez Molina, to understand the depths of this problem. Molina was a military intelligence officer in the Ixil region where the worst genocidal crimes took place in the early 1980s. He has been accused of torture and genocide while serving there, which he has denied. However, the nature of the charges are such that the Spanish National Court, which is conducting a case on the Guatemalan genocide, is investigating such charges. And though Molina has pledged to open new cases about the crimes committed during the civil war, some doubt his seriousness, particularly given his government's decision in the summer of 2012 to close the Peace Archives (*Archivos de la Paz*) and do away with its investigative team. Founded in 2008 to digitize 2 million documents relating to the civil war, the Peace Archives provided key documents in the investigation of human rights abuses in the civil war and in the current case against former president Montt.[150]

And even when the government permitted trials of some of the perpetrators, prosecutors faced "a tortuous series of legal obstacles and fraudulent 'experts' presented by the defense." This was certainly the case when three army officers and a priest were convicted in 2001 of the murder of Bishop Juan Gerardi, a prominent human rights activist. The two attorneys who prosecuted the case were later forced to leave the country for fear of their lives.[151] The following year, another officer, Col. Juan Valencia Osorio, was convicted of the murder of anthropologist Myrna Mack Chang, who had been doing field work with displaced Mayans. She was brutally murdered in 1990 by a government death squad because the government considered her an "internal enemy."[152]

Her sister, Helen Mack Chang, spent years seeking justice for her murder. The government did everything possible to prevent an investigation, first calling her death a political crime, and later "simply a robbery." The lead detective who completed the first report was shot to death outside police headquarters. Regardless, in 1993, a court did convict one of the assassins, Sgt. Noel de Jesús Beteta Alvárez, and sentenced him to 25 years in prison. But Chang was not able to convince the court to try some of the officers responsible for planning her sister's murder.[153] However, in 1994, the Guatemalan Supreme Court did order that the case against three officers allegedly involved in the planning of the murder—Gen. Edgar Augusto Godoy Gaitán, Col. Juan Valencia Osorio, and Col. Juan Guillermo Oliva Carrera—go forward. It later transferred their case to a military tribunal, but, after Chang's protests, returned it to a civilian court. In late 1997, Guatemala's Constitutional Court ordered that the case be prosecuted under the country's new Code of Criminal Procedure, which "vacated [all] earlier proceedings" against the three defendants. After further delays, the three defendants were tried, though only one, Valencia Osorio, was found guilty and sentenced to 30 years in prison. In the midst of several appeals, he escaped and is in hiding.[154]

Several years later, survivors of a massacre in Xamán successfully brought a case to trial that resulted in the conviction of 13 soldiers and 1 officer for their involvement in the murders. Other trials, backed by a Constitutional Court ruling that "forced disappearances was a 'permanent crime' due to the lack of a body" and did not fall under any statute of limitations, convicted five perpetrators in the forced disappearances of peasants in the village of El Jute between 1982 and 1984.[155]

All of this took place in a country that by the early twenty-first century had deteriorated into semi-chaos. The military remained a state within a state and crime was rampant. Racism and socioeconomic inequality was widespread, and the country became a major transit point for cocaine trade into the United States, which triggered a drug war between rival gangs. By 2007, the justice system had almost collapsed, and a desperate government asked the United Nations to help create an International Commission against Impunity in Guatemala (*Comisión Internacional contra la Impunidad en Guatemala*; ICIG) to help build a new justice system. Several laws and agreements over the past few years between various branches of the government have helped to do just that. These efforts were further strengthened in 2010 by the creation of the Transitional Justice Program (TJP) "to implement the mutually connected transitional justice mechanisms (criminal justice, truth-seeking, reparations, and institutional reform)." This set the stage for the appointment of a new attorney general, Claudia Paz y Paz, who was strongly committed not only to human rights issues but also bringing to justice those responsible for some of the worst crimes committed during *La Violencia*.[156]

While Paz y Paz has been untiring in her efforts to bring a multitude of criminals to justice, she has been particularly forceful in dealing with some of the major perpetrators of *La Violencia*. In July 2011, her office successfully prosecuted four members of the special forces (*Kaibiles*), whose training emphasized "a maximum level of aggression and courage." They served with larger military units but also acted independently in counterinsurgency operations. Members of the *Kaibiles* saw themselves as a "killing machine" dedicated to the protection of the homeland and the army from "foreign forces and doctrines."[157] The focus of this trial was the massacres at Dos Erres in December 1982. After they searched the village for communist literature and contraband, the *Kaibiles* murdered an estimated 350 villagers.

> They threw a three-month baby, alive, into an empty water well, then proceeded to smash the heads of infants against walls and trees. The skulls of older children were crushed with a sledgehammer.
> The villagers were then interrogated, then shot and dumped into the well. Women and girls were raped, then mutilated with machetes. The Kaibils shoveled dirt into the well; the survivors' cries still audible through the earthen seal.[158]

The court found each of the defendants guilty of all charges and sentenced them collectively to 6,060 years in prison, "or 30 years for each of the documented 201 men, women, and dozens of children slaughtered by the special unit plus 30 years for crimes against humanity."[159]

The following year a Guatemalan court charged Efraín Ríos Montt with genocide and crimes against humanity, and ordered him placed under house arrest. He had always denied responsibility for these crimes, stating in 2006 that

> During my government, the Army followed orders...But when they were not given orders, abuses were committed [*se cometió desmanes*], but I was never informed.[160]

His attorney added during Ríos Montt's first hearing in early 2012 that his client's only role in the civil war was "'to restore order and cooperation among the Mayan-Ixil.'" He had nothing to do with the "atrocities committed on the battlefield," and "did not determine the level of force the army used." The prosecution countered by noting that there was ample documentation to prove that he was well aware that "military documents...called for 'the extermination of subversive elements.'"[161] In a 1982 interview, for example, Ríos Montt told a journalist that

> Our strength is in our ability to respond to the chain of command, the army's capacity to react. Because if I can't control the army, what am I doing here?[162]

The legal woes of the former dictator continued when the judge handling the case, Carol Patricia Flores, ruled several months later that there was sufficient evidence to justify a second trial against Ríos Montt for his role in the genocidal crimes committed during the Dos Erres massacre. When his attorneys argued that he was not present at the crime scene, Judge Flores told them that "soldiers do not act without an order."[163] Ríos Montt responded by telling her, "It is under military law, your honor, that I declare I am innocent."[164]

The cases against Ríos Montt also had international dimensions. Thirteen years earlier Rigoberta Menchú Tum, a Mayan political activist and Nobel Prize Laureate (1992), and others had filed a complaint with the Spanish National Court (*Audencia Nacional;* SNC) against Ríos Montt and seven other former police and military officials "alleging genocide, torture, terrorism, summary execution and unlawful detention."[165] They were driven not only by frustration with the slow pace of justice in Guatemala, but also the murder of Bishop Juan Gerardi two days after he publicly announced the release of the CHC report in 1998. They were also heartened by the arrest of former Chilean dictator Augusto Pinochet in London later that year in response to an international arrest warrant issued by the SNC, which charged him with various war crimes and genocide.[166] After a number of appeals in several Spanish courts,[167] Spain's Constitutional Court ruled in 2005 that the case against Ríos Montt could not only go forward but was also open to "all complainants."[168]

> Spanish law establishes on a single limitation: the suspect cannot have been convicted, found innocent or pardoned abroad. It [Spanish law] contains no implicit or explicit hierarchy of potential jurisdictions and focuses only on the nature of the crime, not on any ties to the forum contemplating the concurrency of jurisdictions.[169]

The following year, the San Francisco–based Center for Justice and Accountability (CJA), which uses two US laws, the Alien Tort Statute and the Torture Victims Protection Act, "to hold perpetrators of international human rights abuses accountable,"[170] joined the case as lead counsel.[171] It was also working with a Spanish court on the case of Augusto Pinochet, who was indicted in Spain in late 1998 on charges of "genocide, terrorism, and torture" committed during his military dictatorship from 1973 to 1990.[172] And by 2007, it seemed as though Guatemalan courts were going to allow the extradition of Ríos Montt and his seven codefendants to Spain, though this decision was overturned at the last minute. Consequently, the Spanish judge handling the case, Santiago Pedraz, who had made an unsuccessful trip to Guatemala to interview witnesses, invited many of them to give testimony before his court in Madrid. During the interim, he issued international arrest warrants for Montt and the other seven defendants.[173]

Judge Pedraz held two court sessions for the witnesses from February 4 to 8 and May 26 to 30, 2008. One expert witness, Allan Nairn, described the methods the army used to torture people. Soldiers told him that

> they tortured people to make them talk: with a rope used as a garrote, by suffocation, near drowning, slicing with knives, burning with lit cigarettes, beating, electroshock, and mutilation. One soldier standing over recently killed bodies demonstrated how he would press a wooden club against the victim's throat until he was on the edge of death as a means of persuading him to talk.[174]

He added that

> Ríos Montt and his advisers openly suggested in interviews with Nairn [a journalist] that all Mayan people were potential subversives and therefore targets of the Army. Soldiers and massacre survivors alike told Nairn that the Army was ordered to kill Mayan children before they grew up to become subversives. The children were called "delincuentes subversivos" by the military. In addition to attacking Mayan communities, soldiers told him of killing their animals, burning their crops, and destroying their homes and possessions.[175]

Other witnesses told of the "use of rape by the Guatemalan soldiers and members of the civil patrol to abuse and humiliate the Mayan women" in their villages. One said that

> when the Army began showing up in her village, they camped out in front of her neighbor's house for three days, and raped her in front of her children. "I saw the soldiers enter the house of my neighbor, Maria Modesta, who lived with her children. They were shooting them."[176]

She fled the village, and when she returned,

> "'There were people outside their houses, crying. When we arrived in the center, I saw a huge pile of ashes and cinder, a pile of bodies, half of them still burning...The square was full of blood, I saw bullet shells scattered everywhere. We went back to my house again to get containers of water to try to put of [out] the fire. We tried but could not put it out. It continued to burn and the smell of the poor people burning was like burning chicken feathers"... She saw her neighbor and asked her what had happened? "She just looked at me and did not speak, because they had cut off her lips. This poor woman had been raped. She had no skirt, so I put a skirt on her and offered her water. She was like a child." They came upon corpses in the path, some half-eaten by dogs, and many other bodies lying face down next to the path.[177]

During the second round of testimony in May, Dr. Charles R. Hale, from the University of Texas, explained the historical dimensions of the "profound inequality between the Mayan community and Ladinos, or Euro-Guatemalans."[178]

> So when the military respond to the threat of insurgency, they are also responding according to this historical racism, with the idea that the indigenous traditionally act as a group and could at any time rise up against the Ladinos. The counterinsurgency was a marriage of the response against the guerilla and the deep perception of the threat of the indigenous. Understanding this helps explain the logic of the violence that was so much greater than what was necessary. It was a level of violence that had the clear intention to physically destroy or inflict crippling pain on members of specific indigenous communities, or groups of communities, without distinction. This partial destruction had a demonstrative effect on the rest of the Mayan population.[179]

Another expert witness, Dr. Marta Elena Casaús Arzú, a professor at the Autonomous University of Madrid, explained that such attitudes were part of a

> historical and [racist] structural element in Guatemala...The fear of rebellion and the overlapping desire to exterminate the "Indians" united in a historical-political moment that would lead to ethnocide. The elites believed that there was no other form to address the conflict than with systematic violence and genocide, and the racist attitudes of the army high command continued to the execution of the genocide acts.[180]

While there is no question that the Spanish helped spur efforts in Guatemala to take more aggressive action against the main perpetrators of the various crimes committed during the worst of *La Violencia*, it is not clear what impact these developments in Guatemala will have on the Spanish proceedings. From the moment that Pérez Molina took power in late 2011, many doubted that he would allow Paz y Paz to continue her investigations and prosecute his former colleagues, particularly given the fact that he does not think what took place in Guatemala in the early 1980s was genocide. This, coupled with the fact that he has former high-ranking officers in key government positions, and has stated that Paz y Paz can keep her job only if she fulfills it impartially, raises serious questions about the deeper commitment of his government finally to addressing the genocidal crimes of the government and military during *La Violencia*.[181]

However, in early 2013, a Guatemalan court ruled that there was sufficient evidence to move forward with a trial against Ríos Montt and his former intelligence chief, José Sánchez, who was charged with genocide and crimes against humanity.[182] Once the trial began with testimony from Mayan villagers, the defense focused its case on the prospect of an appeal based on the idea that Ríos Montt been "denied his constitutional right to a fair trial." Unfortunately, it has undermined its case by aggressively challenging the witnesses, and accusing them of being "guerillas" and "subversives." The army, the defendants' lawyers argued, were "merely trying to defend Guatemala against an insurgent threat."[183] The court concluded otherwise, and found Ríos Montt guilty of both charges, and sentenced him to 80 years in prison on May 10, 2013. Sánchez was found not guilty on all charges. However, a few weeks later, the Constitutional Court ruled that the proceedings be "rolled back to April 19 (2013)" over trial irregularities. In the end, given the confusion over this decision, it can only be resolved with a new trial of the former dictator.[184]

The Postwar Geneva Conventions and the Evolution of International Humanitarian Law

While the focus of some of the early investigations of the crimes committed in Guatemala during its long civil war dealt principally with genocide, many of the crimes committed there were also serious violations of international humanitarian law (IHL), something the Truth Commission referred to in its report. And the "heart" of IHL, a term first used by the International Committee of the Red Cross (ICRC) in 1953, are the 1949 Geneva Conventions and their additional 1977 protocols.[185] The International Committee of the Red Cross in Geneva, the "principal protector and enunciator of IHL,"[186] defines IHL as

> a set of rules which seek, for humanitarian reasons, *to limit the effects of armed conflict*. It protects persons who are not or are no longer participating in the hostilities and restricts the means and methods of warfare.[187]

And though the ICRC says that IHL and the Laws of Armed Conflict (LOAC) are the same, Gary D. Solis sees them more as "fraternal" twins.[188] And regardless of which term you use, he argues, their goals are the same:

> to confine fighting as closely possible to combatants and to spare noncombatants; to target those things having a military need for destruction and sparing property not necessary to achieve the military ends of the conflict.[189]

It is important at this point not to confuse IHL/LOAC with international human rights law (IHRL), which Steven R. Ratner and Jason S. Abrams define as

> the body of international law aimed at protecting the human dignity of the individual. Developed in the largest part since World War II, it principally seeks to guarantee the rights of persons *vis-à-vis* their own government, but also protects them against other actors in the international community that might violate their rights.[190]

Solis notes, however, that at least from the American perspective, "LOAC prevails on the battlefield to the exclusion of HRL." This distinction has faded, particularly after the issuance of the 1977 additional Geneva Convention protocols.[191] But, as Theodor Meron notes,

> It has become common in some quarters to conflate human rights and the law of war/international humanitarian law. Nevertheless, despite the growing convergence of various protective trends, significant differences remain. Unlike human rights law, the law of war allows, or at least tolerates, the killing and wounding of innocent human beings not directly participating in an armed conflict, such as civilian victims of lawful collateral damage. It also permits certain deprivations of personal freedom without convictions in a court of law. It allows an occupying power to resort to internment and limits the appeal of rights of detained persons. It permits far-reaching limitations of freedoms of expression and assembly.[192]

M. Cherif Bassiouni sees these overlapping imperfections as part of the "different political constituencies of these two legal regimes."[193] Each shared deep historical antecedents that date back to antiquity but were given more legalistic textures and body in the eighteenth and nineteenth centuries as more mature Western nations sought ways to address the growing inhumane, destructive nature of industrialized warfare. The first, which he calls the "Law of The Hague," is based on the 1899 and 1907 Hague conventions and make up what the introduction to the 1907 Hague IV Convention, "Respecting the Laws and Customs of War on Land," called "the interests of humanity and the ever progressive needs of civilization."[194] The "Law of the Hague" is now part of the body of customary law that has been integrated in the "Law of Geneva," the repository of "conventional international law" given birth in the 1949 Geneva Conventions.[195] One of the things that distinguishes these two legal regimes is the emphasis on international conflicts in the "Law of the Hague" traditions, and "a special regime applicable to conflicts of a non-international character" in common article 3 of the 1949 Geneva Conventions.[196] However, as David P. Forsythe and others have noted, common article 3, which, despite its emphasis on "humane treatment," is a "statement of 'affectionate generalities'" that lacks "precise" interpretative guidelines.[197]

What both "regimes" share is a commitment to try to diminish the inhumanity of war, particularly when it comes to noncombatants. Each of the major national and international accords or statements adopted since the second half of the nineteenth century have at least partially addressed this question. But what the international community was not prepared for, particularly in the 1930s, was a shift in military policies that deliberately targeted civilian populations. Between 1935 and 1938, the world watched in horror as aerial bombardments in the Italian invasion of

Ethiopia, the Spanish Civil War, and the brutal Japanese invasion of China resulted in the deaths of hundreds of thousands of innocent civilians.

The fate of civilians in war had been an ongoing concern of the ICRC and the League of Nations since the end of World War I. The plight of enemy civilians was brought up at the Fifteenth International Conference of the ICRC in Tokyo in 1934. The ICRC appointed a committee of experts to draft a convention on the subject that, though never approved because of World War II, was later partially integrated into the 1949 Fourth Geneva Convention, "Relative to the Protection of Civilian Persons in Time of War."[198] In 1938, the International Law Association appointed a draft committee to look into similar violations, particularly the question of whether armament workers should be considered combatants. The result was a draft convention that reaffirmed "fidelity to the obligations under the Pact of Paris of 27 August 1928." It was meant to "embody principles of humanity demanded by the conscience of civilization." Article 1 defined the civilian population as those not forming the "object of a state of war," meaning those neither "enlisted in any branch of the combatant services nor for the time being employed or occupied in any belligerent establishment." It also prohibited attacks and bombardment of undefended "towns, ports, villages or buildings" as long as they housed neither troops nor any sort of military facilities. If such attacks did take place, they had to be "directed at combatant forces or belligerent establishments or lines of communications used for military purposes." Air attacks aimed at "terrorizing the civilian population" were forbidden, as was the "use of chemical, incendiary or bacterial weapons." The draft proposal also called for the creation of "safety zones" to protect civilians, an illusion to such zones in Madrid, Nanjing, and Shanghai, that would "enjoy immunity from attack or bombardment by whatsoever means." Any state victimized by such crimes could report such violations to the president of the Permanent Court of International Justice, who would begin an investigation of such claims. Like the ICRC's 1934 draft convention, the ILA proposal fell prey to the outbreak of World War II.[199]

Tragically, the 1934 and 1938 proposals called for the very protections that might have prevented some of the most dreadful crimes committed during World War II. Consequently, all of the major international legal undertakings after the war addressed not only the horror of such crimes, but a recommitment to find ways to prevent them in the future. While most focus has been on the ICRC when it comes to such issues, the United Nations, which remained aloof from efforts to revise the laws of war because it feared to do so would "undermine confidence" in its ability "to maintain peace," has "exerted a considerable...influence on...efforts to bring about an international guarantee of human rights" from the moment it was created. The preamble of the United Nations Charter, for example, which was approved on June 26, 1945, in San Francisco, stated that

> We the peoples of the United Nations [are] determined to save succeeding genera-
> tions from the scourge of war, which twice in our lifetime has brought untold sor-
> row to mankind, and to reaffirm faith in fundamental human rights, in the dignity
> and worth of the human person, in the equal rights of men and women and of
> nations large and small, and to establish conditions under which justice and respect
> for the obligations arising from treaties and other sources of international law can
> be maintained.[200]

It reconfirmed this commitment in its Universal Declaration of Human Rights (UDHR), which was adopted by the General Assembly on December 10, 1948.[201] It underscored these ideals, and noted that

> disregard and contempt for human rights [which] have resulted in barbarous acts which have outraged the conscience of mankind.

Such rights, the UDHR added,

> should be protected by the rule of law.[202]

Consequently, it was left to the ICRC, long the "protector and enunciator" of IHL, to take the initiative to finds ways to "supplement" prewar "humanitarian conventions" with "a view to providing proper protection for the civilian population."[203] The ICRC began to make plans for such changes in 1944, though it did not send out a formal notice about this to various countries and national societies until February 15, 1945. Reaction to the letter from the ICRC president, Max Huber, was mixed, in large part because the war was still going on. Nine months later, Huber sent a new letter to the United States, the Soviet Union, the United Kingdom, France, and China proposing a meeting of experts to discuss such issues. The Soviet Union declined to participate, while delays in responses from the other five powers were such that the next meeting did not take place until April 14–26, 1947, in Geneva.[204]

The 1947 Geneva conference, which drew 70 delegates from 15 countries, decided at its opening session to entrust three commissions with the study of revising the 1929 *Convention for the Relief of the Wounded and Sick in the Armies of the Field*, the 1929 *Convention on the Treatment of Prisoners of War*, and the drafting of a new convention on the *Condition and Protection of Civilians in War-Time*. The commissions would spend the next nine days studying and revising their respective conventions, and then present them to the 70 delegates, who would collectively discuss and revise them. Once approved, they would be put in diplomatic shape by the ICRC in preparation for a Diplomatic Conference in 1948 that would make further revisions of these drafts before final consideration.[205]

What is remarkable about this convention is what it accomplished in just 12 days. The work of the commissions was helped by the ICRC's revisions of the 1929 convention on the wounded and sick in 1937. After the war, the ICRC revisited these revisions, and sought input from its various national organizations about further changes based on their wartime experiences. One of the most innovative proposals included in the 1937 draft was that it be applicable "to all cases of armed conflict between states, even if no declaration of war had been made." It was also suggested that the "humanitarian principles" included in the draft "be respected in all circumstances, even if the conventions were not legally applicable."[206] The plenary session of the 1947 conference recommended the adoption of these ideas without stating where it would be included in the draft conventions.

> The present Convention is applicable between the Contracting Parties, from the outbreak of any armed conflict, whether the latter is or is not recognized as a state of war by the parties concerned.

> In case of civil war, in any part of the home or colonial territory of a Contracting
> party, the principles of the convention shall be equally applied by the said party, sub-
> ject to the adverse Party also conforming thereto.
> The Convention is equally applicable to cases of occupation of territories in the
> absence of any state of war.[207]

Opposition from the British and others forced the conferees not to include these
provisions in any of the drafts.[208]

Thought was also given to expanding the convention of the sick and wounded to
civilians, but after considerable discussion it was concluded that it was best to write
a new convention on this subject, given the experiences of World War II. The third
commission suggested in its report that the ICRC study this matter, and submit a
report to interested governments with an eye toward possible consideration at the
forthcoming Diplomatic Conference.[209]

The next stage in the evolution of the 1949 Geneva Conventions took place at
the XVII International Conference of the ICRC in Stockholm from August 20 to
30, 1948. It drew delegates from 55 countries who represented not only their governments but also the national chapters of the Red Cross and related organizations.
The bulk of the conference was taken up with normal international Red Cross
business, though it did approve the revised conventions proposed by the 1947 conference with a few changes.[210] The delegates were particularly adamant about the
draft convention for the protection of civilians, and noted that it completed and
fine tuned

> what may be considered either as the customs of civilized nations or as ideas already
> embodied in former treaties, in particular the Hague Convention of 1907, or as the
> obvious demands of the world's conscience, draws especially the attention of govern-
> ments to the urgent necessity of ensuring the effective protection of civilians in time
> of war by a Convention, the lack of which was so cruelly felt during the last war,
> and urged that all States, immediately and without awaiting the conclusion off this
> Convention, apply its principles in the cases provided for.[211]

After further review by the ICRC's Legal Commission and the governments that
sent delegates to the Stockholm conference, the Swiss Federal Council convened a
Diplomatic Conference in Geneva, which met from April 21 to August 12, 1949, to
consider the final ICRC draft proposals. Their proposals centered around revisions
of the 1907 Hague Convention on maritime warfare, which was based on the principles of the 1906 Geneva Convention, the 1929 Geneva Convention, which dealt
with the treatment of POWs, and the creation of a new convention for the protection
of civilians during war. The conference drew delegates from 59 countries including
the Soviet Union and two of its constituent republics—the Byelorussian and the
Ukrainian Soviet Socialist Republics. Three of the new Soviet satellite states in
Eastern Europe—the Bulgarian, Hungarian, and Rumanian People's Republics—
also sent delegates to the conference, as did the Holy See (the Vatican) and the new
state of Israel. Chiang Kai-shek's Nationalists represented China even though the
communists were on the eve of the complete takeover of that country. There were
also delegates from Burma, India, Japan, Pakistan, and Thailand, while the rest
of Asia, still under colonial rule, had no voice at the gathering. The same was true

for Africa, which was still in the throes of colonial domination. There were also 14 delegations from throughout Latin America.[212]

Over the course of almost four months, the delegates studied and debated what would become the most important conventions in the history of international humanitarian law. To call their decisions monumental would be an understatement. Three committees oversaw the study of the four conventions under consideration.

(I) *Convention for the Amelioration of the Condition of the Wounded and Sick in Armed Forces in the Field.*

(II) *Convention for the Amelioration of the Condition of the Wounded, Sick and Shipwrecked Members of Armed Forces at Sea.*

(III) *Convention Relative to the Treatment of Prisoners of War.*

(IV) *Convention Relative to the Protection of Civilian Persons in Time of War.*[213]

One of the challenges these committees faced was defining the nature of the wars to which each of these conventions might apply. The tradition, of course, was to consider wars between individual states, though in the meetings after World War II with various Red Cross societies, serious consideration was given to making these conventions applicable to "civil wars and internal conflicts." In fact, according to the series of commentaries published by the ICRC after the four conventions were adopted, the idea of applying them to civil conflicts could be traced back to the XVI International Red Cross Conference in 1938.[214]

And even though such applications could be based only on the "essential principles" of the Geneva Conventions, the Preliminary Conference of the National Red Cross Societies recommended in 1946 that the following phrase be inserted in any future convention:

> In the case of armed conflict within the borders of a State, the Convention shall also be applied by each of the adverse Parties, unless one of them announces expressly its intention to the contrary.[215]

Unfortunately, the ICRC's Conference of Experts, which met in 1947, was not willing to embrace this idea fully, but did support the idea of the application of the "principles of the Convention...in civil wars by the Contracting party, subject to the adverse Party also conforming thereto."[216]

Consequently, the ICRC added a fourth paragraph to article 2 of the 4-draft conventions it submitted to the delegates to the XVII ICRC conference in 1948. It stated that

> In all cases of armed conflict which are not of an international character, especially cases of civil war, colonial conflicts, or wars of religion, which may occur in the territory of one or more of the High Contracting parties, the implementing of the principles of the present Convention shall be obligatory on each of the adversaries. The application of the Convention in these circumstances shall in no wise depend on the legal status of the Parties to the conflict and shall have no effect on that status.[217]

The conference approved this clause for the drafts of the first two conventions. This "made the application of the convention subject to the proviso that the adverse party should also comply with it" in the drafts of Conventions III and IV.[218]

Needless to say, these paragraphs caused considerable controversy at the 1949 Diplomatic Conference in Geneva. Committee II, which was dealing with POW convention (III), decided at its first meeting to discuss article 2 before article 1 because, according to Maurice Bourquin, the chairman, article 2 would "determine the scope of the convention."[219] The essence of the initial discussions centered around balancing the rights of the individual vis-à-vis the state in an internal civil conflict. How would one, for example, differentiate between a legitimate civil war and "forms of disorder, anarchy or brigandage" in terms of protections under Convention III? If not clarified, the protections of the conventions could give belligerent status to insurgents or even political opponents. There were also questions about a balance between humanitarian and legal principles when it came to this issue.[220] Leland Harrison, the head of the US delegation, stated that his country could not support the conventions "except in the case of war as understood in international law." Clear definitions had to be developed," he added, "to determine recognition of insurgents' belligerency," something he considered a potential "torturous" process.[221] One of the key questions raised by the United States was the definition of belligerency. On the other hand, the Soviets, backed by the delegates from their satellite states, fully supported article 2 and paragraph 4, noting that

> civil and colonial wars were often accompanied by violations of international law and were characterized by cruelty of all kinds. The suffering of the population in the instance of civil and colonial wars was as distressing as that which led Henry Dunant to realize the need for regulating the laws of warfare.[222]

Frustrated by a lack of consensus, the Diplomatic Conference's Joint Committee decided to appoint a smaller Special Committee to discuss the matter further. Over the course of two months, it considered a number of proposals that ranged from outright acceptance to full rejection. The ICRC delegate argued forcefully that the key point, particularly when it came to Convention IV, was that "all persons who were not nationals of the State where the conflict took place, or who did not take part in the hostilities, should be protected."[223] On the other hand, there was a general consensus that any broad application of article 2 that centered around the wording "'in all cases of armed conflict' was too comprehensive and would presuppose the inclusion of all cases of minor rebellion."[224] It was finally decided to appoint a smaller Working Committee to prepare two separate proposals for the civilian convention (IV) and Conventions I–III. Plinio Bolla, the chair of the Special Committee, stated that the time had come first to discuss the group's views on whether the conventions should be extended to non-international conflicts, the definition of non-international conflict, and the criteria for determining such conflicts. Once the committee had voted on these points, it then had to determine a number of other points that included reciprocity, the ICRC's "Discretionary Clause," application of humanitarian principles in situations where "conflicts [were] not expressly stipulated," the "juridical status of parties to the conflict," and the "situation of the insurgents at the close of a conflict."[225]

A week later, the Working Committee presented a draft to the Special Committee that was roundly criticized by some of the delegates. The French, borrowing from an earlier Italian suggestion, responded with a compromise draft that integrated parts of the above draft with new phrasing.

> In the case of armed conflict not of an international character occurring in the territory of one of the High Contracting Parties, each Party to the conflict shall *apply the provisions of the Preamble to the Convention for the Protection of Civilian Persons in Time of War.*[226]

The preamble, which would be included in each of the four conventions, stated that

> Respect for the personality and dignity of human beings constitutes a universal principle which is binding even in the absence of any contractual undertaking.
>
> Such a principle demands that, in time of war, all those not actively engaged in the hostilities and all those placed "hors de combat" [outside the fight] by reason of sickness, wounds, capture, or any other circumstance, shall be given due respect and have protection from the effects of war, and that those among them who are in suffering shall be succoured and tended without distinction of race, nationality, religious belief, political opinion or any other quality.
>
> The High Contracting Parties solemnly affirm their intention to adhere to this principle.[227]

Unfortunately, the key element in the French proposal was based on the draft Preamble, which was never approved by the Diplomatic Conference. This, coupled with the fact that some saw the proposal as too general when it came to specifics about principles, made parts of the French draft unworkable.[228]

Consequently, the Special Committee decided to create a second Working Committee to study the French proposal and come up with a draft that better clarified applicable "humanitarian principles and a minimum of mandatory rules."[229] This group developed a new proposal that ultimately became the basis of common article 3 in each of the four conventions.[230]

> In the case of armed conflict not of an international character occurring in the territory of one of the High Contracting Parties, each Party to the conflict shall be bound to apply, as a minimum, the following provisions:
>
> (1) Persons taking no active part in the hostilities, including members of armed forces who have laid down their arms and those placed 'hors de combat' by sickness, wounds, detention, or any other cause, shall in all circumstances be treated humanely, without adverse distinction founded on race, colour, religion or faith, sex, birth, or wealth, or any other similar criteria.
>
> To this end, the following acts are and shall remain prohibited at any time and in any place whatsoever with respect to the above-mentioned persons:
>
> (a) violence to life and person, in particular murder of all kinds, mutilation, cruel treatment and torture;
> (b) taking of hostages;
> (c) outrages upon personal dignity, in particular humiliating and degrading treatment;

(d) the passing of sentences and the carrying out of executions without previous judgement pronounced by a regularly constituted court, affording all the judicial guarantees which are recognized as indispensable by civilized peoples.

(2) The wounded and sick shall be collected and cared for.

An impartial humanitarian body, such as the International Committee of the Red Cross, may offer its services to the Parties to the conflict.

The Parties to the conflict should further endeavour to bring into force, by means of special agreements, all or part of the other provisions of the present Convention.

The application of the preceding provisions shall not affect the legal status of the Parties to the conflict.[231]

Overall, there are a number of "common articles" in the four 1949 Geneva Conventions (i.e., Convention I, 1–3, 47, 49, 50; II, 1–3, 46–53; III, 1–3, 129–132; IV, 1–3, 144–149) that emphasize some of the key elements in each of them. Article 2, for example, states that while the provisions of each convention "shall be implemented in peacetime," they

shall apply to all cases of declared war or of any other armed conflict which may arise between two or more of the High Contracting Parties, even if the state of war is not recognized by one of them.

The Convention shall also apply to all cases of partial or total occupation of the territory of a High Contracting Party even if the said occupation meets with no armed resistance.

Although one of the Powers in conflict may not be a party to the present Convention, the Powers who are parties thereto shall remain bound by it in their mutual relations. They shall furthermore be bound by the convention in relation to the said Power, if the latter accepts and applies the provisions.[232]

Some of the most significant and innovative parts of these common articles deal with the question of "grave breaches" and applicable "penal sanctions." The ICRC was at the forefront of insisting that any convention that dealt with a revision of the "laws and customs of war must necessarily include a separate Chapter on the repression of violations of its provisions." And while it argued that the "complete and loyal respect for the Conventions must be based on the imposition of effective penalties for those guilty of violating them," it was hesitant "to propose punitive penalties."[233] One of the draft articles the ICRC prepared for its XVII international conference proposed that certain violations of the conventions "were to be considered as war crimes, and laid down the manner in which those guilty were to be punished."[234] The conference asked the ICRC to continue to work on this issue, and it prepared four articles (39, 40, 40a, 40b) for consideration at the 1949 Diplomatic Conference.[235]

But even before the 1949 conference opened, it was apparent that there was widespread opposition to include the idea of war crimes in any of the conventions, in large part because it was feared that the

Soviet Union and its allies would stretch the meaning of "crimes" to cover whatever *they* believed to be crimes...this seemed very likely to include the planning of, and the participation in, whatever they classified as aggressive war, and the conduct of whatever they chose to call mass extermination.[236]

In the end, the delegates at the 1949 conference were very careful

> to avoid any reference to crimes or to make any particular reference to any interna-tional tribunal or to create a precedent which would conflict with existing interna-tional law.[237]

Consequently, though much of what was proposed in draft article 39, which dealt with a commitment of the signatories to the conventions to search for and prosecute those who committed "grave breaches," was included in the initial "grave breaches" article in the final conventions, there was no mention in these final documents of draft article 40's proposals that such violations be punished "by any interna-tional jurisdictions, the competence of which has been recognized by them."[238] According to the ICRC, the subject of draft article 40 was of "particular gravity," and was the

> first step towards the introduction of penal legislation of an international character, since it defines as crimes "sui generis" [of its own kind; unique] offences known in ordinary parlance as "war crimes."

This would, in turn, provide "a firm legal foundation for any future prosecutions."[239]

The Diplomatic Conference's rejection of the idea of an international tribunal to try "grave breaches" disappointed the ICRC. It had worked with legal consultants on the draft articles, who concluded that

> an International Tribunal would doubtless be the instrument best qualified to judge similar breaches. Pending the establishment and regular functioning of such a court, it seems preferable to rely upon the joint responsibility of all signatory States for the repression of crimes against the law of nations. The guilty persons would thus be sub-ject to various jurisdictions and have less chance of escaping punishment.
> Submission to international jurisdiction is also provided for, subject to the approval of the said jurisdiction by the Contracting Parties.[240]

But by 1949, the delegates, aware of the criticisms of the Nuremberg and Tokyo IMT courts, which were not mentioned in the conventions, were comfortable only with national trials with rights of international jurisdiction.[241] Such obligations were laid out in common articles 49, 50, 129,146 in each convention, and obligated each of the signatory states

> to search for persons alleged to have committed, or to have ordered to be commit-ted, such grave breaches, and shall bring such persons, regardless of their nationality, before its own courts. It may also, if it prefers, and in accordance with the provisions of its own legislation, hand such persons over for trial to another High Contracting Party concerned, provided such High Contracting Party has made out a *prima facie* case...
> In all circumstances, the accused persons shall benefit by safeguards of proper trial and defence, which shall not be less favourable than those provided by Article 105 [which dealt with defendant rights of POWs] and those following the Geneva Convention Relative to the Treatment of Prisoners of War of August 12, 1949.[242]

Another innovation rejected by the delegates was draft article 40 (a), which dealt with the question of "superior orders," a "principle recognized in various military penal codes, that orders received from a superior exculpate the subordinate who has carried them out."[243] While the ICRC admitted that this draft article did not go as far as the 1945 London Declaration on this question, it did provide a middle ground by stating that

> *The fact that the accused acted in obedience to take orders of a superior or in pursuance of a law or regulation shall not constitute a valid defence, if the prosecution can show that in view of the circumstances the accused had reasonable grounds to assume he was committing a breach of this Convention. In such a case the punishment may nevertheless be mitigated or remitted, if the circumstances justify.*
>
> *Full responsibility shall attach to the person giving the order, even if in giving it he was acting in his official capacity as a servant of the State.*[244]

From the ICRC's perspective, draft article 40 (a) underscored the "moral duty to oppose any patent atrocity, such as the massacre of defenceless women and children," though it added that the "onus of proof lies on the prosecution" to prove such a crime.[245] The ICRC also argued that it was "inseparably linked" to the other three draft articles by providing a "safeguard" against "all extraordinary jurisdiction." It also ensured that all of those tried before an "enemy tribunal" would be guaranteed a "fair trial."[246]

In the end, the most innovative ICRC proposal to survive the "drastic surgery" of the 1949 conference was the concept of "grave breaches," which is cited in each of the four 1949 Geneva Conventions.

Convention I, Article 50; Convention II, Article 51:

wilful killing, torture or inhuman treatment, including biological experiments, wilfully causing great suffering or serious injury to body or health, extensive destruction and appropriation of property, not justified by military necessity and carried out unlawfully and wantonly.[247]

Convention III, Article 130:

wilful killing, torture or inhuman treatment, including biological experiments, wilfully causing great suffering or serious injury to body or health, *compelling a prisoner of war to serve in the forces of the hostile Power, or wilfully depriving a prisoner of war of the rights of fair and regular trial prescribed in this Convention.*[248]

Convention IV, Article 147:

wilful killing, torture or inhumane treatment, including biological experiments, wilfully causing great suffering or serious injury to body or health, *unlawful deportation or transfer or unlawful confinement of a protected person, compelling a protected person to serve in the armed forces of a hostile Power, or wilfully depriving a protected person of the rights of fair and regular trial prescribed in the present Convention, taking of hostages and extensive destruction and appropriation of property, not justified by military necessity and carried out unlawfully and wantonly.*[249]

Collectively, these articles represent one of the more "remarkable and, by all humanitarian, liberal, and non-militarist criteria, progressive elements" in the 1949 Geneva Conventions.[250]

The Korean War and the Geneva Conventions

The first test of the spirit of the new conventions came ten months after they were approved by the Diplomatic Conference. In the early morning hours of June 24, 1950, almost seven divisions of crack North Korean troops invaded South Korea.[251] Five years earlier, the Allies agreed at Potsdam to divide Korea into American and Soviet zones at the 38th Parallel, with the idea that both zones would ultimately be united into a single country. In 1947, the United Nations was invited to oversee elections for this purpose, but could not gain access to Soviet-controlled North Korea. The following year, American and Soviet forces withdrew from their respective zones in Korea, leaving two separate countries, the autocratic Republic of Korea (ROK) in the south and the communist Democratic People's Republic of Korea (DPRK) in the north.[252]

The Korean War, which S. L. A. Marshall called the "century's nastiest little war," resulted in the deaths of 1.5 million Chinese and North Koreans, 415,000 South Koreans, and 33,000 Americans.[253] Soon after the invasion began, the UN Security Council, prodded by the United States, passed several resolutions, first calling the North Korean invasion a "breach of peace," and later asking its members to come to the aid of the ROK's efforts "to repel the armed attack." The United States, which headed the United Nations' Unified Command, entered the fray a few weeks after it began.[254] Within a month, DPRK troops had pushed deep into southeastern Korea. This all changed over the next month as UN forces flowed northward, taking Seoul, the ROK capital, and Pyongyang, the DPRK capital, on October 20. The Chinese, concerned not only about US successes in Korea but also the movement of the US 7th Fleet in the Taiwan Straits, began to express concerns about what it saw as potential US aggression against China. Such worries intensified after US forces moved beyond the 38th Parallel on October 1.[255]

At this point, Joseph Stalin and Mao Zedong, who had encouraged North Korea's leader, Kim Il-Sung, to invade the south, panicked. Stalin, unwilling to risk an open conflict between the USSR and the United States, encouraged Mao to defend North Korea from what they saw as "American aggression."[256] During the first three weeks of October, Zhou Enlai, who oversaw Chinese foreign policy for Mao, warned US troops about their drive northward, and declared that if it was not stopped, "they would encounter Chinese resistance."[257] On October 25, Chinese troops, which had secretly entered North Korea a week earlier, attacked ROK troops, and by the end of the year had regained control of North Korea. What followed was a bloody stalemate that by mid-1952 had come to resemble the

> worst of the First World War: trench warfare, days and nights of living under constant artillery barrages, men caught in the wrong place at the wrong time with almost all meaning subtracted from the fighting and the dying.[258]

When what David Halberstam calls this "difficult, draining, cruel war" finally ended with a truce on July 27, 1953, the division of Korea remained much the same as it had been before the war began three years earlier.[259]

While some hints of the cruelty of this war were apparent as it progressed, it would take decades before a full understanding of the depth of such horrors surfaced. Initially, most of the war crimes committed during the war were attributed to the North Koreans and the Chinese. However, after the ROK established its short-lived Truth and Reconciliation Commission (TRC) in 2005 to investigate wartime atrocities in the Korean peninsula since the early twentieth century, it became apparent that UN forces, principally ROK troops, committed some of the worst atrocities during the Korean War. Though estimates vary, there is evidence to suggest that ROK troops killed between 100,000 and 200,000 civilians in the early months of the war who they suspected of being leftists or communists. Lee Young Jo, the TRC's last president, estimated that North and South Korean forces each "killed about 150,000 civilians."[260]

The Truth Commission also charged the United States of using "indiscriminate force" in a series of napalm bombings that "violated international conventions of war." The commission also heard testimony that US ground forces had killed innocent civilians whom they suspected of being communist sympathizers. It demanded that the ROK government officially ask the United States for compensation for such violations of international law. While declassified US military documents have shown that American commanders issued "blanket orders to shoot civilians" during the early months of the war, the commission ultimately concluded that US "large scale killing of refugees . . . arose out of military necessity."[261]

The crimes committed by the North Koreans and the Chinese were equally heinous. While most attention has centered on the mistreatment of UN POWs, we now know that the North Koreans kidnapped 83,000 South Koreans, mostly males, in the early months of the war. Most of them were well-educated professionals they hoped to use either to help rebuild the country after the war or to "neutralize" any they suspected of anti-communist sentiments. This, coupled with South Korean estimates that the North Koreans killed 59,000–122,800 South Korean civilians during the war, underscores the latter's severe violations of Geneva Convention IV.[262]

But the depth of North Korean and Chinese war crimes runs much deeper. Both adopted Russian-style torture methods reminiscent of those used by the Germans against Soviet POWs and Jewish slave laborers during World War II. The North Koreans, for example, used extremely brutal, overtly harsh methods, including forced marches and the housing of prisoners "in disease-ridden shelters and water-filled cases."[263] A US Senate investigation in 1954 identified some of these methods.

Various acts of torture, i.e., perforating flesh of prisoners with heated bamboo spears, burning prisoners with lighted cigarettes and inserting a can opener into a prisoner's open wound.[264]

Once peace talks began, the Chinese took control of all POWs, and, sensitive to the importance of the POW question to UN negotiators, gradually moved away from "overt" torture. Instead, the Chinese used successful brainwashing techniques that by 1953 saw 70 percent of the 7,190 US POWs criticize "the American war effort."[265] For those US POWs who refused to cooperate, the Chinese resorted to

beating, forced running, forced standing with a rock over one's head, standing at attention for hours in freezing weather, forced kneeling in snow as guards poured water over the body. Forced standing lasted up to thirty hours. Sometimes guards forced prisoners to stand in water-soaked holes; the water would freeze gradually around the feet. Other times, guards marched prisoners onto the Yalu and poured water over their feet, leaving them standing for hours with their feet frozen.[266]

There were also systematic mass murders of American troops and Koreans captured by the North Koreans in the early months of the war,[267] which the Senate investigation concluded was "a calculated part of Communist psychological warfare" that violated the 1929 Geneva Convention as well as article 6 of the Nuremberg IMT charter.[268] A US congressional study noted that in mid-August 1950, the North Koreans took 45 American POWs to a ravine, stripped all of them of their clothing and personal possessions, tied their hands behind their backs, and executed each of them. Six weeks later, DPRK troops murdered 60 American prisoners in the Taejon prison. A week earlier, they also executed 5,000–7,000 South Korean civilians and soldiers at the prison.[269] That fall, 80 American POWs, survivors of what was called the "Seoul-Pyongyang death march," were taken northward by rail where they rode "unprotected in the raw climate for 4 or 5 days." Once they reached the Sunchon tunnel outside of Pyongyang, they were taken off the train and told they would be fed. Instead, they were taken in groups of 40 to nearby ravines where they "were ruthlessly shot by North Korean soldiers, using Russian burp guns."[270] The Senate investigation concluded that the North Koreans and the Chinese had committed numerous "war crimes and crimes against humanity" and violated "virtually every provision of the Geneva Convention governing the treatment of war prisoners."[271]

All of this, of course, underscored the impossibility of enforcing international humanitarian law at the time, even in light of the fact that none of the principal combatants during the Korean War had officially embraced them. On the other hand, the ICRC did everything possible to fulfill its role under Convention III as a "humanitarian organization" and undertook the "protection of prisoners of war" by providing "relief" for them.[272] While the ICRC worked successfully with North Korean and Chinese POWs in UN-run POW camps, the North Koreans and the Chinese would not allow them access to their POW camps because they wanted to hide their abuse of UN prisoners.[273] This did not, however, prevent Andrei Vyshinsky, now the Soviet foreign minister, from demanding in 1952 that UN forces abide by the 1949 Geneva Convention on POWs, particularly article 118, which stated that

Prisoners of war shall be released and repatriated without delay after the cessation of active hostilities.[274]

His comments could not sway UN negotiators to consider blindly turning POWs over to the North Koreans and the Chinese. The Allies were well aware of the fate of repatriated Soviet POWs at the end of World War II, and adopted the principle of "no forced repatriation," particularly after interrogations of 170,000 Chinese and North Koreans indicated that only 40 percent wanted to be repatriated.[275] Ultimately, only 8,000 of the 80,000 ROK troops captured by the North Koreans were repatriated. On the other hand, the ROK repatriated 76,000 North Koreans, while 1 million North Koreans refused to return home. Of the 7,140–7,190 Americans captured by the Chinese or the North Koreans, 2,700 died in captivity and the rest were repatriated except for 21 who initially chose to stay in North Korea. Most chose to return home later.[276]

The Geneva Protocols Additional

The refusal of the North Koreans and the Chinese to abide by the new Geneva Conventions underscores what Dietrich Schindler argues was their "almost lapse into oblivion" in the years after their creation.[277] Moreover, the Korean War underscored, at least from the perspective of the ICRC, the fact that while Convention IV theoretically protected civilians "against arbitrary enemy action," it did not, "except in the specific case of the wounded, hospitals, and medical personnel and material," protect them from the the "effects of hostilities." This, coupled with the fact that the Hague Conventions had not "undergone any significant revision since 1907," convinced the ICRC's Board of Governors to ask the organization to propose a text for the forthcoming XIX international conference in New Delhi in 1957 that would "protect civilian populations efficiently from the dangers of atomic, chemical, and bacteriological warfare." Beforehand, the ICRC drew up a set of Draft Rules (DR) that proposed the prohibition of incendiary, chemical, bacteriological, radioactive, or other agents, and more clearly defined the terms "attacks" and "civilian population." The DR also addressed the question of "precautions in attacks on military objects" as well as the question of "open towns" and "installations containing dangerous forces."[278] After the delegates discussed these proposals in some depth, they recommended that the DR be distributed to member governments. Unfortunately, there was little international response to the proposals because they touched on the highly sensitive subject of nuclear weapons.[279]

Eight years later, the ICRC's XX international conference in Vienna passed a resolution noting its

> profound anxiety with regard to the suffering endured by the populations of a number of countries where armed conflicts are being waged.
>
> It also expressed deep concern [with] the repeated use of force against the independence or the right to self determination of all peoples and urged governments to settle their international disputes by peaceful means in the spirit of international law.

Finally, it asked all governments to do what they could to "ban all nuclear weapons tests" and seek "complete [nuclear] disarmament."[280]

These efforts received a considerable boost in 1968 when the UN-sponsored First International Conference on Human Rights (ICHR) approved Resolution XXIII that expressed concern over the "widespread violence and brutality of our times." It also stated "that even during periods of armed conflict, humanitarian principles must prevail." The resolution asked the secretary general of the United Nations, after consultation with the ICRC, to remind all UN members of the "existing rules of international law" relating to "all armed conflicts," and to adopt

> new rules of international law relating to armed conflicts, to ensure that in all armed conflicts the inhabitants and belligerents are protected in accordance with

"the principles of the law of nations derived from the usages established among civilized peoples, from the laws of humanity and from the dictates of the public conscience."[281]

Resolution XXIII also addressed some of the concerns of a new "loose coalition of Third World countries that comprised the nonaligned movement." Some of them were involved in conflicts whose roots could be traced back to their colonial past. The resolution made direct reference to this, noting that there were "minority racist or colonial regimes that refused to comply with the decisions of the United Nations and the principles of the Universal Declaration of Human Rights."[282] This statement gave voice to the concerns of "a collection of militarily weak and economically impoverished states" in what was then known as the Third World, who felt that the major powers were not applying IHL to conflicts in the newly emerging states in their former colonies in Africa, Asia, and the Middle East. This represented a dramatic shift in global human rights policies that would be particularly important during the discussions about the drafting of the 1977 *Protocols Additional* a few years later.[283]

This concern over the plight of civilians in these burgeoning civil wars was what led the United Nations to adopt resolution 2444 at the end of 1968, which emphasized the importance of making a "distinction...between persons taking part in the hostilities and members of the civilian population to the effect that the latter be spared as much as possible."[284] According to Frits Kalshoven, the UN resolution was a "starting shot...for an accelerated movement which brought the three currents: Geneva, The Hague and New York, together in one main stream."[285]

Over the next three years, the ICRC began an intensive study of the Hague and Geneva Conventions with an eye toward confirming, supplementing, or improving various sections of each accord.[286] In 1971, the ICRC convened a Conference of Government Experts that did an intensive study of each one over the next five years. One of its proposals, *Rules Applicable in Guerilla Warfare*, suggested drafting a number of

> standard minimum rules which would be applicable in all conflicts not corresponding entirely to the conventional definition envisaged in Articles 2 and 3 of the Geneva Conventions and which—and herein lies the original aspect of the rules—would in no way influence the designation of the conflict or the legal status of the parties.[287]

These roles dealt with the

> definition of combatants and their treatment in the event of capture or surrender, a definition of civilian population and its protections in the event of military occupation or against the dangers arising from hostilities, principles and rules of behaviour between enemy combatants, and procedures for the implementation of the rules.[288]

Needless to say, this proposal met with stiff resistance, particularly the idea that it would be applicable to both international and non-international conflicts. The Conference of Experts concluded that this proposal was too radical, and that "the issues of guerilla warfare would be better dealt with in the context of other forms of armed conflict."[289]

After an experts' meeting in Geneva in 1972, the ICRC drew up two draft proto-cols for further discussion—one dealing with international conflicts, and the second with non-international conflicts.[290] The following year, the ICRC's International Conference in Tehran approved the general draft protocols, which were forwarded to the Conference of Experts for further review, and then to a Diplomatic Conference for final study and approval.[291]

Officially known as the Diplomatic Conference on the Reaffirmation and Development of International Humanitarian Law Applicable in Armed Conflicts, it met four times from 1974 to 1977. All parties to the 1949 Geneva Conventions and members of the United Nations were invited to the conference sessions. Though attendance varied, 700 delegates from 107 to 124 nations attended all or some of the sessions.[292] Though some of the delegates from new states or groups like the PLO (Palestinian Liberation Organization) and the ANC (African National Congress) had no voting rights, they "had significant influence over states sympathetic to their goals." According to Gary D. Solis, their "goals often involved scaling back and constricting the power and influence of the major powers."[293] This reflected the considerable tension at the conference between various political and humanitarian interests.[294] It also underscored the fact that the traditional Cold War alliances of the postwar period were now giving way to a new body of alliances among emerg-ing countries globally who, in some cases, had fought their own wars of liberation against the former colonial powers, but now faced threats from groups that saw themselves as "national liberation" movements.

The work of the conference was divided into three plenary committees, an ad hoc committee on conventional weapons, and various working groups.[295] From the out-set, there was tension between the major powers and the emerging or developing countries over the rights and protections in "wars of national liberation" in the new draft protocols. Among the most contentious was *Protocol I*'s article 1 (4), which stated that it was applicable to

> armed conflicts in which peoples are fighting against colonial domination and alien occupation and against racist régimes in the exercise of their right of self-determi-nation, as enshrined in the Charter of the United Nations and the Declaration on Principles of International Law concerning Friendly Relations and Co-operation among States in accordance with the Charter of the United Nations.[296]

Those who supported including "wars of liberation" in the new protocols felt that such recognition had already "been conferred" on such conflicts "by the world com-munity through various UN and other resolutions."[297] Some of the countries that opposed this section of article 4—France, Italy, Israel, Japan, the United Kingdom, and the United States—argued that it would give "rebels," whom they regarded as

> trouble-makers, brigands, and armed criminals groups—the full panoply of Geneva Convention protections.[298]

Suggestions by the United Kingdom, West Germany, and other Western-aligned nations that the Martens Clause would cover "wars of liberation" fell on deaf ears, and *Protocol I*, article 1 (4), was ultimately approved by the conference.[299]

Equally contentious was the idea of granting "'freedom fighters'" POW status if captured. The *Lieber Code*, Hague IV, and article 4.A (2) of the 1949 Geneva Convention III had each provided clear, similar definitions for those considered to be "combatants who may be considered lawful belligerents," and, as such, could be afforded the "combatant's privilege, or to be a POW upon capture."[300] Article 1, for example, in the annex to Hague IV on the "qualification of belligerents," was "repeated almost verbatim" in article 4.A (2) of Geneva Convention III (1949). It stated that to be considered eligible for POW status,

> members of the armed forces…militias or volunteer corps forming part of such armed forces including those of organized resistance movements, belong to a Party to the conflict and operating in or outside their own territory,

had to fulfill the "following conditions" to be granted POW status.

(a) that of being commanded by a person responsible for his subordinates;
(b) that of having a fixed distinctive emblem recognizable at a distance;
(c) that of carrying arms openly;
(d) that of conducting their operations in accordance with the law and customs of war.[301]

Protocol Additional I's article 44 changed this formula, and stipulated that, in certain situations, an "armed combatant" would no longer be required to "distinguish himself" with a "fixed distinctive emblem recognizable at a distance." While it still required combatants to "distinguish themselves from the civilian population" in preparation for or during combat, article 44 said that if the nature of "the hostilities" prevented a combatant from distinguishing himself, he still had protections as a combatant if "he carries his arms openly."[302] According to Philip Sutter, this "effectively erases the distinction between lawful and unlawful combatants and gives prisoners of war protection to all combatants regardless of their conduct in respect to the law of war."[303]

These concerns, however, did not deter 172 countries from ratifying *Protocol Additional I* by the spring of 2013. The United States, however, is not one of them. President Ronald Reagan, who asked the Senate to ratify *Protocol Additional II* in 1987, said in an introductory statement that his administration could not support ratification of *Protocol I* because it was, according to the Department of State, "fundamentally and irreconcilably flawed." The State Department was particularly concerned that it "would grant recognition and protection to terrorist groups, and would result in a 'politicization' of humanitarian law by such organizations."[304] The Pentagon's Joint Chiefs of Staff concurred, and stated that *Protocol Additional I* would grant irregulars a legal status that was stronger than that accorded regular forces.[305]

Hans-Peter Gasser, a senior legal adviser for the ICRC and editor-in-chief of its *International Review of the Red Cross*, challenged the US idea that *Protocol Additional I* "was fundamentally and irreconcilably flawed." From his perspective, it considerably broadened protections for the military and civilians, and extended "minimal fundamental guarantees to all persons affected by an armed conflict."[306] He also strongly disagreed with critics who thought that Third World delegates had dominated the Diplomatic Conference.[307]

Moreover, he was critical of anyone who suggested that *Protocol Additional I* gave "any radical group" certain protections, since it was not a statement about the "legal status of groups." And while it did afford protection to "secessionist" movements that somehow saw a "struggle against the central government...as a war of national liberation," article 96 stipulated that in a war of liberation between a high contracting party and a non-contracting party that fulfilled the criteria as an "armed conflict," both sides had to assume the *"same rights and obligations under the Geneva Conventions and Protocol I."*[308] This meant that each had to care for the wounded, POWs, and "refrain from attacking civilians." He added that article 1 (4) did "not recognize or grant legitimacy to any armed conflict or to any group or its claims. *Humanitarian law,*" he argued, *"never legitimizes any recourse to force."*[309]

Gasser also strongly disagreed with American criticisms of article 44, and noted the subtle but differing interpretations of 44 (3). There was nothing in its phrasing, he noted, that could lead one to conclude that it would "further terrorism." He felt that taking the "worst case" approach to an article that sought to distinguish between combatants and civilians was "not an appropriate way to understand an international agreement as delicate as a humanitarian law treaty," particularly given that the United States signed off on it in Geneva.[310] He was quite sensitive to the fact that the US position was in part dictated by its experiences during the Vietnam War, but noted that during that conflict

> members of Vietcong guerilla units who were captured while actually engaged in combat ("carrying arms openly") were *treated* by the U.S. Military Assistance Command as prisoners of war (but not granted formal POW status), whereas a Vietcong who had committed an act of terrorism did not receive that treatment. In a nutshell, that practice is identical with what is required by Protocol I, and the new rules thus go no further than American practice in Vietnam. Officers who served in Vietnam...have told the present writer that, according to their experience, the system adopted by Article 44(3) should work in practice.[311]

While US POW policies in Vietnam were based on the hopes of reciprocity on the part of its adversary,[312] Washington's ultimate rejection of *Protocol Additional I* did not mean that the United States does not abide by its dictates, given that, according to the State Department, almost two-thirds of its articles are part of international customary law. Moreover, since most of the conflicts involving the United States since 2001 included allies who had ratified *Protocol I,* the United States has found itself bound by many of its provisions by virtue of such relationships. During the Persian Gulf War, the Department of Defense concluded that since many of its "provisions are 'generally regarded as a codification of the customary practice of nations, and binding on all,'"[313] the United States

> can disregard Protocol I only when engaged in armed conflict on its own and without allies—and then it can disregard only those provisions which are contended to not be customary law.[314]

Many of these customary provisions deal with the expanded protections afforded civilians, the wounded, the sick, the shipwrecked, and those missing or dead. They also include important new articles on the question of "proportionality." Article 51 laid out specific guidelines for the protection of civilians from indiscriminate attacks, including those meant to terrorize civilians.[315] Article 57.2 (iii) added that "in the conduct of military operations," combatants must

> take all feasible precautions in the choice of means and methods of attack with a view to avoiding, and in any event to minimizing, incidental loss of civilian life, injury to civilians and damage to civilian objects.[316]

Article 85.3 (b) stated that

> launching an indiscriminate attack affecting the civilian population or civilian objects in the knowledge that such attack will cause excessive loss of life, injury to civilians or damage to civilian objects, as defined in Article 57, paragraph 2 (a) (iii),

was considered a "grave breach" as "defined in Article 11."[317] Each of these articles, including the expanded list of "grave breaches" in article 11, is considered part of customary law. The new "grave breaches" deal with the "physical or mental health and integrity of persons who are in the power of the Adverse party or who are interned, detained or otherwise deprived of liberty." Article 11 also prohibited subjecting persons in such situations to

(a) physical mutilations;
(b) medical or scientific experiments;
(c) removal of tissue or organs for transplantation [except in situations where it involved the state of health of the "person concerned," followed "accepted medical standards," and were "given voluntarily and without any coercion or inducement"].[318]

Protocol II, which was far less extensive than *Protocol I*, dealt solely with non-international conflicts. But this did not prevent it from being as controversial as its sister protocol, because many of the developing countries at the Diplomatic Conference feared that it would "grant international rights—and international legitimacy—to potential rebels and their supporters."[319] Consequently, most of them suggested rejecting *Protocol II* or "inserting a high jurisdictional threshold to ensure its infrequent application."[320] Most of the protections in *Protocol II* are already guaranteed in the 1949 Geneva Conventions' common article 3. And, since the latter is part of customary law (*Protocol II* is not), it has been used more frequently by ad hoc tribunals "to bring criminal charges" against alleged war criminals.[321] Jelena Pejic goes a step further and argues that regardless of the "formal classification or geographical reach" of a non-international armed conflict, common article 3 applies "to all parties to an armed conflict…as a matter of customary law."[322]

Regardless, *Protocol II* does provide new protections, for example, to children (article 4.3) and better clarifies legal protections for the "prosecution and punishment of criminal offenses related to the armed conflict" in article 6.[323] And article

14 prohibits the "starvation of civilians as a method of combat," something permitted in the *Lieber Code*.[324] These additional protections, however, do nothing to address some of the problems created by the scope of *Protocol II's* article 1, which states that it is applicable only in armed conflicts that

> take place in the territory of a High Contracting Party between its armed forces and dissident armed forces or other organized armed groups which, under responsible command, exercise such control over a part of its territory as to enable them to carry out sustained and concerted military operations and to implement this Protocol.[325]

While this article is meant clearly to prevent it from being applied to "internal disturbances and tensions," it has not been applied to "armed conflicts with a substantial element of civil war" in state party countries like Columbia, El Salvador, Guatemala, Liberia, Rwanda, Sierra Leone, Russia, and the former Yugoslavia.[326] Consequently, there are few instances since 1977 when *Protocol II* has been applied to legitimate situations by state parties. According to Theodor Meron, the fault often lies not with the conventions themselves, but with the

> refusal by States to apply the conventions in situations where they should be applied. Attempts to justify such refusals are often based on differences between the conflicts presently encountered and those for which the conventions are supposedly adopted.

Richard Baxter adds that "[t]he first line of defense against international humanitarian law is to deny that it applies at all."[327]

Conclusion

The failure of some nations to uniformly embrace these conventions, however, should not take away from the incredible achievements of the ICRC in the field of international humanitarian law after the end of World War II. While the earlier Geneva and Hague conventions were important in developing some of the core ideas and protections that gave birth to IHL, it was the 1949 conventions and their later protocols that really formed the nucleus of a body of international law that is still evolving. These achievements are equally remarkable given the diverse political and military landscape that developed globally after World War II. It was and is far more complex than that of the late nineteenth century and the first half of the twentieth. Part of the reason, of course, is that a much larger community of new countries were able to find common ground when it came to the search for ever newer protections for noncombatants in the context of national and international wars. This speaks volumes about the growing importance of the rule of law globally. However, as the situations in Tibet, Guatemala, and the Korean War show, the creation of a body of IHL did not ensure its actual enforcement. This would come much later as the international community, no longer crippled by the threatening might of the vast Soviet empire and its satellites, began to respond creatively to crimes committed during various types of wars and military conflicts globally.

Chapter 10

IHL: Soviet-Afghan War, Saddam Hussein, Ad Hoc Tribunals, and Guantánamo

The 1974–1977 Diplomatic Conference's success in getting an extremely diverse group of nations to approve the two *Protocols Additional* was remarkable. But their completion was just that—adherence and enforcement would prove to be much more difficult. Within a few years after the Diplomatic Conference ended, major wars broke out in Afghanistan and the Middle East that would seriously test the efficacy of these accords. This all took place in the midst of what was probably the greatest political upheaval in the second half of the twentieth century—the collapse of the Soviet satellite system in Eastern Europe and the Soviet Union itself. Though this was, for the most part, peaceful, it did breed wars of conflict, particularly in the Former Yugoslavia and parts of Russia, that would see considerable violations of IHL. But if there was a silver lining in any of this, it was that once the Cold War theoretically ended, so did those ideological barriers that had long prevented the international community from creating international judicial mechanisms to deal with grave breaches of the Geneva Conventions, acts of genocide, and war crimes. Between 1993 and 2002, the international community created three major tribunals—two ad hoc and one permanent—to address some of the major crimes committed in various conflicts in Europe, Africa, and Asia since the adoption of *Protocols Additional*.

The Soviet-Afghan War

Almost a century earlier, Rudyard Kipling wrote "The Young British Soldier" (1895), a poem that captured the difficulties and horrors the British faced during their two nineteenth-century wars in Afghanistan.

> When you're wounded and left on Afghanistan's plains,
> And the women come out to cut up what remains,

Jest roll to your rifle and blow out your brains
An' go to your Gawd like a soldier.
Go, go, go like a soldier,
Go, go, go like a soldier, Go, go, go like a soldier,
So-oldier-of-the Queen![1]

According to Lester Grau, while the various tribes in Afghanistan have traditionally

> never fought "to the knife" where one side attempts to annihilate the other completely...it is apparent that [when] one side is winning, the other side kicks out a rear guard and melts into the mountains. The rear guard as a distinct body takes the bulk of the casualties.

The Afghanis, he adds, "are capable of annihilation combat...when foreigners invade Afghanistan, as the British and the Soviets learned in the 19th and 20th centuries."[2]

The Soviet-Afghan War began just a few years after the completion of the *Protocols Additional*. What some inaccurately regard as Moscow's "Vietnam" became a horrific bloodbath that resulted in the deaths of as many as 75,000 Soviet troops, 18,000 pro-Soviet Afghan troops, and 75,000–90,000 Mujahedin. Between 1.25 to 2 million Afghans (out of a prewar population of about 15 million) also died during the war, while at least 750,000 were wounded during the conflict. And by the time it ended in 1989, another 5 million Afghanis had fled the country.[3]

According to the Afghanistan Justice Project, both sides

> committed crimes against humanity and serious war crimes [which]...included large-scale massacres, disappearances and summary executions of at least tens of thousands of Afghans, indiscriminate bombing and rocketing that killed hundreds of civilians, torture, mass rape and other atrocities. In the twenty-seven years since the war began, there has been no serious effort, international or domestic, to account for these crimes.[4]

M. Hassan Kakar charges that it was the Soviets who committed the worst crimes as part of what he calls their "program of genocide." This included the destruction of the agricultural system, "the dropping of booby traps from the air, the planting of mines, and the use of chemical substances."[5]

Yet this was not the type of war that the Kremlin intended to conduct when it invaded Afghanistan at the end of 1979 to counter what it feared was a "'possible political shift to the West'" by Hafizullah Amin, who had recently overthrown Nur-Mohammed Taraki, the head of the new pro-Soviet Democratic Republic of Afghanistan (DRA). Taraki's efforts to initiate Soviet-style antireligious and other reforms led to widespread violence and civil war. Backed by a growing Soviet military presence, Taraki transformed the country into "a giant prison."[6] Amin, who had studied in the United States, seemed, at least to the Kremlin, to "shy away from Moscow."[7] Consequently, Leonid Brezhnev and his aging circle of advisers decided to intervene, adopting the "Czechoslovak model: 'an invasion,' occupation of the capital's airport, an assault landing of the tank-borne infantry, and then the invasion of the army."[8] The Soviet goal was to topple the government, put its new man—Babrak Karmal—in power, "stabilize the situation," and strengthen the DRA's armed forces. Moscow hoped to withdraw most of its troops, which never numbered more than 115,000–125,000 soldiers and airmen, within three years.[9]

But once they entered Afghanistan, the Russians became bogged down in a counterinsurgency war against diverse, scattered guerrilla forces throughout the rugged countryside.

> The principal forms of combat were the raid, block and sweep, ambush, and those actions connected with convoy escort and convoy security.[10]

These were tactics, the Russians admitted, that were quite similar to those used during Britain's three wars in Afghanistan in the nineteenth and early twentieth centuries.[11] Oliver Roy adds that such tactics involved

> attrition and reprisals; the sealing of the Mujaheddin supply routes and the direct application of pressure on Pakistan through bombings and terrorist actions; and the penetration of the resistance movement.[12]

This "total war" approach brought widespread death and destruction in the four principal regions where the Soviet forces operated. But they quickly discovered that they were not prepared to fight "a long counterinsurgency effort in Afghanistan" since their armed forces were trained principally "to fight large-scale, high tempo offensive operations exploiting nuclear strikes on the northern European plain and China." What complicated all of this was that "the Soviets never really understood their enemy or the neighboring country in which they were fighting."[13]

Though Soviets tactics changed with the vicissitudes of the war, their most destructive one centered on destroying

> Mujahideen support in the rural countryside. They bombed granaries and rural villages, destroyed crops and irrigation systems, mined pasture and fields, destroyed herds and launched sweeps through rural areas—conscripting young men and destroying the infrastructure. The Soviet leadership, believing Mao Tse-tung's dictum that the guerrilla lives in the population like a fish in water, decided to kill the fish by draining off the water.

By 1985, most villagers had fled from the combat areas, which forced the rebels to establish their own supply bases in the countryside. Soviet tactics from then until the end of the war centered around the destruction of these supply facilities.[14] According to studies done by the United Nations, the Afghanistan Justice Project, and Hassan Kakar, in addition to destroying potential supplies for the Mujahidin, the attacks were also meant to convey "to a village and its neighbors as collectivities the message that supporting the resistance had a cost."[15]

The Soviets brought the full force of their massive military arsenal to bear in Afghanistan and added some new weapons to the mix such as toy bombs. A 1985 UN report noted that these bombs dispersed "hundreds of fragments similar to small blades," which resulted in "serious leg injuries and hand wounds which frequently result in amputation."[16] Equally insidious was the use of chemical weapons. Kakar reports that the Soviets used chemical agents during the early phase of the war. A Norwegian filmmaker reported on one chemical attack outside of the village of Charpur in the summer of 1980.

> In the morning we were woken up by helicopters [which were flying around]. Hurriedly we left the village, but left one man behind us; he was wounded and we could not carry him out. The helicopters dropped a couple of what we thought at that moment were bombs. The only thing we saw was a kind of explosion and a yellow cloud. The second wave of helicopters came in and bombed with chemical rockets. So, everything in the village was bombed. The [villager?] told me that the first wave was a gas tank...We came [back to] the village a couple of hours later. We found the man we [had] left behind dead. His face was swollen. We took him out and brought him to another place and came back the next morning and then the face was completely swollen, physically like what would have been dead for three or four weeks. It was really strange, and everybody in the group who was in the village was having blisters on his head, his face, [while] the face was swollen...Mycotoxins...are apparently being used in Afghanistan. That is a new kind of agent, rather hideous and extremely lethal. Riot control agents are apparently also being used, and there are some agents that have been reported and which had symptoms that are not fully understood which cause sudden onset of death without any prior symptoms.[17]

A year later, the United States, which spent hundreds of millions of dollars arming Mujahedin, accused the Soviets of transferring trichothecene mycotoxins to Afghanistan, Laos, and Afghanistan in violation of the 1925 Geneva Protocol that outlawed the "use of asphyxiating, poisonous or other gases," and the 1972 *Convention on the Prohibition of the Development, Production and Stockpiling of Bacteriological (Biological) and Toxin Weapons and Their Destruction.*[18] While it is difficult "to verify the use of chemical substances" in the early years of the war, the 1985 UN report cited a number of instances where Soviet and Afghan forces used gas in four provinces.[19] Two years earlier, Ricardo Fraile, a French expert on chemical warfare, testified before a series of hearings in Oslo, Norway, that while he could not say with certainty that the Soviets were using chemical weapons in Afghanistan, there was "an ever-growing bulk of evidence" that they were.[20] Several French studies in 1986 verified these charges, and noted that the Soviets also poisoned wells, causing the deaths of people and cattle.[21]

The Soviet's Afghan Allies, particularly the *Khadamat-e Aetla'at-e Dawlati* (KhAD), the Soviet-dominated Afghan secret police, were also complicit in committing "grave breaches" and war crimes, particularly against captives.[22] Particularly heinous were KhAD torture methods. According to one former KhAD officer, some of its favorite torture methods included

> electric shocks applied to the genitals of men and the breasts of women; tearing out fingernails, combined with electric shock; removing all toilet facilities from the prisoners' cells, so that after a certain time they were obliged to perform such functions in full view of their cell mates; the introduction of wooden objects into the anus, a practice used in particular with aged or respected prisoners; pulling out the beards of prisoners, particularly if they are old or religious figures; strangulation of prisoners to force open their mouths, which are then urinated into; the use of police dogs against

prisoners; hanging by the feet for an indefinite period; the rape of women, with their hands and feet tied, and the introduction of a variety of objects into the vagina.[23]

The United Nations also reported in 1985 that KhAD, which was under the supervision of Soviet KGB officers, often took part in the interrogations, which included psychological tortures,

> including mock executions, the rape of a member of the prisoner's family in his presence, and the pretense that the prisoners was to be freed.[24]

The Mujahedin also committed "grave breaches" and war crimes, though they are not as well documented. The Afghan Justice Project's *Casting Shadows* focused exclusively on Soviet war crimes, while Kakar's study on the first three years of the Soviet-Afghan War had little to say about the crimes of the Mujahedin. And the 1985 UN report simply notes that the rebels killed

> a number of civilians...in the explosion of a munitions depot on 27 August 1986 at Qargha in Kabul Province. In addition, a bomb explosion at the Jalalabad airport on 11 August 1986, killed approximately 16 persons and wounded several others. Leaders of the [anti-Soviet] opposition movements took credit for both of these incidents.[25]

Other sources, however, are a bit more revealing. *Crimes of War* mentions, for example, that

> a number of mujahidin groups also committed war crimes during this period. Many of those based in Pakistan who had the support of the Pakistani military and intelligence agencies operated with impunity and had considerable control over the Afghan refugee population. One of the most powerful of these was Hizb-I Islami, headed by Gulbuddin Hekmatyar. These mujahidin carried out assassinations and maintained secret detention facilities in Pakistan; persons detained there included Afghan refugees who opposed the mujahidin leaders, or who worked for foreign NGOs, especially those employing women.[26]

The Afghan Centre for Investigative Journalism (ACIJ) also has interviewed a number of Afghanis who were tortured and abused by the Mujahedin. One young woman, Rahela, who lived in Faryab Province, told the ACIJ that the Mujahedin attacked her family and kidnapped two of her sisters because the family was suspected of being communist sympathizers.[27] School teachers and government workers were viewed with considerable suspicion, and were on occasion kidnapped and tried by rebel "special courts," who often sentenced them to death.[28] Schools were targeted because Mujahedin saw them as centers for teaching Soviet and communist propaganda.[29]

One of the problems that various human rights groups faced in Afghanistan was limited access to areas under rebel and Soviet control, which made it difficult to document such crimes. In addition, they also found it hard to determine what was meant by "'resistance' as a whole," since "resistance" groups ranged from "barely organized desperate peasants" to more sophisticated, well-organized groups. Some of earliest crimes documented by these groups were the mistreatment of Soviet POWs.

According to Helsinki Watch, Afghan guerillas, adhering to "their traditional concept of revenge (*badal*) executed any captured Soviet soldiers." In 1981, Afghan resistance groups in Pakistan agreed to allow the International Committee of the Red Cross access to Soviet POWs, while the Soviets and guerillas in Afghanistan refused the ICRC such access.[30] The result was that, according to a 1985 Helsinski Watch report:

> Some resistance groups keep prisoners in abusive conditions, torture them, and execute them without distinguishing prisoners of war from other types of prisoners, such as captured spies.[31]

Human Rights Watch (HRW) reported a few years later that one rebel group, Hezb-i-Islami, used "terror squads" that captured suspected leftists, and brought then back to detention centers near Peshawar, Pakistan, where they tortured and killed them.[32]

> Hekmatyar [the head of Hezb-i-Islami] is regarded as ruthless, uncompromising and devious...The Hezb...is known to operate its own jails, where kidnapped mujahed opponents have been tortured and killed. While the other parties operate detention centres, they are normally reserved for Afghan communists or Soviet prisoners and not guerrilla antagonists.[33]

Most Afghan groups, though, treated Afghan captives better than Soviet prisoners, and saw the former "as potential allies rather than enemies." In fact, there were even stories about the rebels giving Afghan captives "pocket money to pay for expenses" to return home after their release.[34] This was not the case with captured Afghani government officers, particularly communist party members, who were imprisoned or executed. The same was true for members of KhAD, who were usually tortured and, in some cases, executed after a trial by an Islamic court.[35]

Unfortunately, efforts to bring Soviet or Afghan war criminals to justice for such crimes has been difficult. Though the Soviet Union and Afghanistan ratified the 1949 Geneva Conventions in the 1950s, the Russians did not ratify *Additional Protocol I* until 1989. Afghanistan did the same a decade later. Soviet Russia also ratified the 1925 Geneva Protocol on the use of chemical agents a few years after it went into force, but stated that it would only be applicable to other states who had also ratified it. On the other hand, the Soviet Union and Afghanistan both ratified the 1972 biological toxins convention several years before the Russian invasion in 1979. However, with the exception of the brief accord with the ICRC about Soviet POWs in 1984, both countries barely gave lip service to their provisions. On the other hand, there are indications that the Russians did prosecute some of their own troops who committed the "most infamous Soviet crimes against Afghans, though many more were ignored."[36]

In contrast, there were international efforts to bring Soviet and Afghan war criminals to justice. In 2004, Dutch authorities arrested two former high-ranking Afghan KhAD officers—Habibullah Jalalzoy and Heshamuddin Hesam—who were living in exile in the Netherlands, and charged them with war crimes and crimes against humanity during the Soviet-Afghan war. A few years earlier, a special Dutch immigration unit began an investigation of both men to see if Article 1F of the 1951/1967 *Convention and Protocol Relating to the Status of Refugees* was applicable.[37] It was not if there were

> serious reasons for considering that he has committed a crime against peace, a war crime, or a crime against humanity, as defined in the international instruments drawn up to make provision in respect to such crimes.[38]

Once the 1F unit completed its investigations, it turned both cases over to the Office of the Prosecutor for further investigation, which in turn gave them to the Dutch National Police's National Investigation Team for War Crimes. The cases were then brought before the Hague District Court, which tried both men from September 19 to October 14, 2005.[39]

They were prosecuted under the Dutch International Criminal Offences Act, which gave the court and the prosecution "universal criminal jurisdiction over war crimes committed in non-international armed conflicts."[40] About 20 witnesses testified about the torture they suffered at the hands of both men, who were convicted of numerous crimes and sentenced to 9 (Jalalzoy) and 12 (Hesam) years in prison. A Dutch Court of Appeal upheld the convictions but dismissed several of the charges. It also upheld the right of Dutch courts to try individuals accused of war crimes committed during non-international armed conflicts under common article 3 of the 1949 Geneva Conventions. The Dutch Supreme Court confirmed these decisions in 2008.[41] On the other hand, the Hague District Court acquitted another KhAD agent, Abdullah F., of similar crimes in 2005, ruling that

> the question of whether the defendant had "effective control" [over his subordinates' acts of violence and torture against the victims] cannot be answered affirmatively with a sufficient degree of certainty.[42]

This has not ended the question of bringing alleged Afghan war criminals to justice, particularly in Afghanistan. In the spring of 2012, Afghan protestors, who burned images of President Hamid Karzai, accused the country's leaders and the United States of "ignoring past abuses... [and] of appointing alleged war criminals to top government posts rather than trying them for war crimes."[43]

Iraq and Saddam Hussein

Eight and a half months after the Soviets invaded Afghanistan, Saddam Hussein, Iraq's new, autocratic president, invaded Iran, beginning what would be one of the deadliest wars in modern Middle Eastern history. Backed by Saudi Arabia and Kuwait, the invasion had many goals, but the principal one was to thwart the possibility of an Iranian-led religious revolution from sweeping into Iraq, particularly in the Kurdish-Shia areas of the country. Though estimates vary widely, as many as half a million Iranians and Iraqis were killed or wounded in the fighting.[44] The most serious violations of international law centered around Iraqi use of chemical agents during this devastating conflict. Initially, Iraq used these weapons to counter

Iranian tactics that involved sending large waves of Iranian troops into battle against Iraqi forces. But what began as a defensive tactic developed, over time, into an Iraqi strategy using jets and helicopters to drop shells filled with various forms of mustard gas and nerve agents such as tabun on Iranian forces.[45]

A 1984 UN investigation verified Iraq's use of chemical weapons, while a later CIA study documented specific instances of Iraqi use of these agents between 1983 and 1988. The CIA report stated that "Iraqi forces killed or injured more than 20,000 people delivering chemical agents," while the Iranian government claimed in a 1995 report that "over 60,000 veterans of the war with Iraq" were receiving medical treatment for injuries caused by such chemical agents.[46] Another source claims that during the course of the war, the Iraqis "bombarded some 2,000 villages in Iran" with a specially concocted gas compound that included "hydrogen cyanide, mustard gas, Sarin, and Tabun."[47]

While all of these attacks were ghastly, what got the most attention internationalally were the Iraqi assaults against Kurdish villages in northern Iraq in 1987 and 1988. The Kurds that lived in this sensitive region along the Iran-Iraq border had mixed loyalties, and by 1987, the pro-Iranian Kurdish Democratic Party had control of most of the northern border of Iraq. Early that year, Saddam Hussein appointed his cousin, Ali Hassan al-Majid ("Chemical Ali"), governor of northern Iraq, with power to do whatever was necessary to secure the region. He initiated the "spoils" (al-Anfal) campaign that "reached a level of brutality and killing so high and wreaked such devastation on settled life, even for a regime widely known for its brutality, that it finally resulted in international outrage and charges of genocide."[48]

Particularly heinous was the March 18, 1988, attack on the Kurdish village of Halabja, taken only a few days earlier by Iranian and Patriotic Union of Kurdistan forces. On the evening of March 16, the Iraqis began a massive bombardment of the village of 70,000 using a "hydrogen cyanide compound." Fortunately, most of the villagers had fled before the assault began. Estimates are that the Iraqis killed 3,500–8,000 Kurds in the attack, including civilians, and injured another 7,000.[49] Though it is difficult to know how many Kurds died in Saddam Hussein's "scorched earth campaign," figures range from 50,000 to 100,000. It is also estimated that the Iraqis destroyed 4,000 Kurdish villages and displaced or resettled 1.5 million Kurds between 1982 and 1988, most of this during the al-Anfal campaign.[50]

Until 1988, the international reaction to the war crimes in the Iran-Iraq war was, at best, tepid. The 1984 UN investigation of Iraq's use of chemical weapons did result in UN Security Council Resolution (SCR) 582 two years later that deplored

> the escalation of the conflict, especially territorial incursions, the bombing of purely civilian centres, attacks on neutral shipping or civilian aircraft, the violation of international humanitarian law and other laws of armed conflict and, in particular, the use of chemical weapons contrary to obligations under the 1925 Geneva Protocol; [It] calls upon Iran and Iraq to observe an immediate cease-fire, a cessation of all hostilities on land, at sea and in the air and withdrawal of all forces to the internationally recognized boundaries without delay.[51]

To its credit, the UN had been trying to do what it could to end the conflict since 1984. SCR 582 was followed in 1987 by SCR 598, which again called for an immediate cease-fire, and restated the above sections of SCR 582. Though Hussein's government accepted the terms of SCR 598, Iran refused to do so because it thought that the international community had not done enough to condemn Iraq for its war crimes, instead believing that Iran was the "aggressor" in the conflict.[52]

All of this changed after the Halabja attack. The UN adopted SCR 612, and later, SCR 620, which expressed dismay at the use of chemical weapons in violation of the 1925 Geneva accords on chemical warfare.[53] In the end, what finally convinced Iran to accept SCR 598 and begin peace talks was the intense, Washington-sponsored "diplomatic, military, and economic campaign" against Iran in the aftermath of the controversial Irangate scandal, in which the United States sold arms to Iran to help support Contra guerillas in a civil war in Nicaragua. A cease-fire was declared on August 20, 1988, followed by still unsuccessful peace talks.[54]

This would all change after Hussein, burdened by an $80 billion war debt, invaded Kuwait in the summer of 1990. Saudi Arabia, fearful that it would be Hussein's next target, asked for US assistance, and Washington warned Hussein to withdraw his forces immediately from Kuwait.[55] The United States was backed by several United Nations' Security Council Resolutions such as SCR 678 (November 29, 1990), which also demanded Iraq's withdrawal, and authorized "member states co-operating with Kuwait to use all necessary means" to back up the resolution.[56] When Hussein refused to heed the United Nations' warning, a US-led coalition began a six-week aerial assault against Iraq in early 1991 that devastated the country's military, economic, political, and communications infrastructure. On February 24, Allied ground forces moved into Kuwait, and quickly drove the Iraqis back across the border. Three days later, Hussein agreed to a cease-fire, which the United Nations rejected until he accepted all of the terms of SCRs 686 and 687. The former stipulated that Iraq accept all previous SCRs, and

> rescind immediately its actions purporting to annex Kuwait, accept in principle its liability under international law for any loss, damage or injury in regard to Kuwait and third states and their nationals, as a result of the invasion and illegal occupation by Iraq.[57]

It also stipulated that Iraq release all Kuwait and "third-State nationals," including POWs and the bodies of the deceased said nationals, to the ICRC. In addition, Iraq was to help in the location of all Iraqi

> mines, booby traps, and other explosives as well as any chemical and biological weapons and material in Kuwait.[58]

SCR 687 went further and warned Iraq, particularly in light of Hussein's earlier threats to develop nuclear weapons and use chemical weapons and ballistic missiles, to reaffirm its obligations under the 1925 Geneva Protocol, and accept the destruction of

> all chemical and biological weapons and all stocks of agents and all related subsystems and components and all research, development, support and manufacturing facilities related thereto; all ballistic missiles with a greater range than one hundred and fifty kilometres, and related major parts and repair and production facilities...[and] reaffirm unconditionally its obligations under the Treaty on the Non-Proliferation of Nuclear Weapons of 1 July 1968...[It also stipulated that] Iraq shall unconditionally agree not to acquire or develop nuclear weapons or nuclear weapons-usable material or subsystems or components or any research, development, support or manufacturing facilities related to the above.[59]

SCR 687 also required Hussein to agree to full cooperation with the International Atomic Energy Commission to identify, locate, destroy, remove, and neutralize such weapons.[60]

Hussein agreed to these terms but did everything possible later to thwart them, which resulted in a new US-led invasion and occupation of Iraq in the spring of 2003. While there is some disagreement about the various reasons that led the Bush administration to invade Iraq, the key ones centered around the accusation that his regime was linked to the 9/11 al-Qaida attacks on the United States, and that he was developing weapons of mass destruction in violation of SCR 687. Though we now know that the latter was not the case, Hussein hinted that he had such weapons, somehow thinking it would be a deterrent to further international action against Iraq. The reverse was true, and by the fall of 2002, a US-led coalition was making preparations to invade Iraq and remove Saddam Hussein from power, with or without UN support. The invasion began on March 17, 2003, with most fighting over within three weeks. The search for Hussein, however, took months, and he was finally captured, "like a rat in a hole," near his hometown of Tikriti by members of the United States' Fourth Infantry Division.[61]

Several days before his capture, the American-dominated Allies' Coalition Provisional Authority of Iraq (ACPAI) issued the Statute of the Iraq Special Tribunal (SIST), which was later voided and replaced by the Iraqi High Criminal Court Law on the eve of the trial of Hussein and seven other defendants.[62] This did little to change the fact that the tribunal was an "American creation" though not run as an "American court." [63] The SIST was a marriage of major international statutes such as the 1948 Genocide Convention and the 1949 Geneva Conventions with older Iraqi law. The result was a document whose "breadth and vagueness . . . makes them [its clauses] susceptible to politicized interpretation and application, and therefore could be regarded as political offenses."[64] Investigative judges, for example, were to handle all pretrial investigations,[65] and prepare a dossier to help determine if there was sufficient evidence to go to trial. The investigative judge controlled this process, including the right of the defense to be present during the collection of evidence. The defense also had the right to submit comments for the investigative dossier. If the case went to trial, then everything in the dossier was considered valid, including the testimony of witnesses. Once an investigative judge had completed his investigation, he could issue an indictment. The case could then be sent to the Iraqi Higher Criminal Court (IHCC), a five-judge panel that fully controlled the proceedings, including the selection of witnesses. A Cassation Panel or Court handled all appeals and could preserve or alter a lower court's decision, including a retrial.[66]

Saddam Hussein's first trial began on October 19, 2005, and included seven other defendants:

Saddam Hussein. President of Iraq, 1979–2003. *Death.*
Barzan al-Tikriti. Saddam Hussein's half-brother and former head of Iraqi intelligence. *Death plus two ten-year terms of imprisonment.*
Awad Hamd al-Bandar. Former president of the Revolutionary Court. *Death.*
Taha Yasin Ramadan. Former vice president and head of popular army. *Life plus three prisons terms of 7–10 years.*

Abd Allah al-Ruwaid. Former Baath party official in Al-Dujail. *15 years.*

Mizher al-Ruwaid. Son of Abd and Baath party official in Al-Dujail. *15 and 7 years.*

Ali Dayih Ali. Former Baath party official in Al-Dujail. *15 years.*

Muhammed Azzawi Ali. Former Baath party official in Al-Dujail. *Charges dismissed.*[67]

They were each charged with various roles in the trial, imprisonment, torture, and murder of 148 Shiites from Dujail in retaliation for an assassination attempt on Hussein's life in 1982. The 13-month, televised trial was plagued by a number of problems that seriously undermined the "centrality of the rule of law in the Iraqi context."[68] Security was almost nonexistent during the trial, and five persons who worked for the court were killed before it began. Several defense lawyers were also murdered, which prompted some of their peers to quit. Those who remained on the defense team often knew little about applicable criminal and international law, while the court's Defense Office functioned essentially as a "'legal aid' office for the indigent accused."[69]

Even worse, four of the five original judges stepped down, replaced by new judges who were unfamiliar with the case and lacked the experience to conduct high-level criminal proceedings. They also, at times, lacked the demeanor and the skills to maintain order in the courtroom—a problem compounded by Saddam Hussein's efforts to do whatever possible to disrupt the trial. He had carefully followed the trial of Slobodan Milošević, and saw the former Serbian leader's behavior before the International Criminal Tribunal for the Former Yugoslavia (ICTY) as a "blueprint" for his own antics in Baghdad. In the end, the judges allowed the courtroom to become a "soap box" for the political opinions of the defendants. Their defense team added to this unstable environment by staging boycotts and "walk-outs" that often left their clients "to fend for themselves."[70]

The prosecution was equally inept and did not think it necessary fully to prove the guilt of each defendant. Chief prosecutor Ja'afar al-Moussawi, for example, was convinced that each defendant was part of a joint criminal enterprise in planning the Dujail murders, but presented little evidence in court to prove it. He also chose not to call expert witnesses to document the important interrelationships between the various organs of state and their command structure vis-à-vis the crimes. Instead, the principal focus during the trial was the crimes themselves instead of "who orchestrated them."[71]

In the end, though, these problems did not prevent the court from finding Hussein and six of the other defendants guilty of the Dujail crimes. The tribunal sentenced Hussein, Barzan al-Tikriti, and al-Bandar to death, Ramadan to life, and the Rawaids and Ali to lesser terms. It dismissed charges against Muhammed Ali. The court rejected Hussein's argument that as Iraq's leader, he had the right during wartime to take actions against a town that was populated by terrorists and others who tried to assassinate him. The court argued that his actions in Dujail were "'not necessary to stop an immediate and imminent danger,'" and "were disproportionate to the threat."[72] After the verdict was read, Hussein cried out,

God curse the enemies of the occupation...Death to the enemies of the nation![73]

Hussein appealed the verdict to the Cassation Court, which rejected it in late 2007.[74]

Internationally, the trial was viewed as a legal fiasco. Human Rights Watch (HRW), which had observers at the trial, concluded that the

> court's conduct . . . reflects a basic lack of understanding of fundamental fair trial principles, and how to uphold them in the conduct of a relatively complex trial. The result is a trial that did not meet key fair trial standards. Under the circumstances, the soundness of the verdict is questionable.[75]

The International Center for Transitional Justice, which also had observers at the trial, added that such problems would

> fundamentally undermine the contribution of the trial of Saddam Hussein and his associates to the transition in Iraq. Instead of arriving at a conclusive historical record, the proceedings are in danger of being questioned on their factual determination and fairness for years to come.[76]

Fortunately, the second trial of Saddam Hussein and his six codefendants from August 21, 2006, to December 5, 2006 and January 8, 2007 to June 24, 2007, went much better. Hussein and "Chemical Ali" were charged with genocide, while the rest were charged with crimes committed during the *al-Anfal* campaign.[77]

Saddam Hussein. President of Iraq, 1979–2003. *Death.*

Ali Hassan al-Majid. Cousin of Saddam Hussein and architect of the *al-Anfal* campaign. *Death.*

Sultan Hashem Ahmed al-Ta'i. Former commander of I Corps, army chief of staff, and defense minister. *Death.*

Hussein Rashid al-Tikriti. Former Army deputy chief for operations. *Death.*

Sabir Abd al-Aziz al-Douri. Former general director of Military Intelligence Service. *Life.*

Farhan Mutlaq al-Jabouri. Former military director of Military Intelligence Service of northern and eastern regions. *Life.*

Taher Tawfiq al-Ani. Former governor of Mosul and secretary of Northern Affairs Committee under al-Majid. *Acquitted.*[78]

The second *Hussein et al.* trial took place in two phases. The first centered around the testimony of 76 witnesses as well as a number of expert witnesses from the United States, who presented forensic evidence about what was found in the various mass grave sites in the *al-Anfal* region.[79] Soon after this phase began, the presiding judge, Abdallah al-Amiri, was replaced by Muhammed Uraybi al-Khalifa, after Minqith al-Fatoon, the chief prosecutor, accused al-Amiri of pro-Hussein sentiments.[80]

The defense's principal argument throughout the trial was that the tribunal did not have the authority to try any of the defendants and that the Kurds that died during the *al-Anfal* campaign were simply "unfortunate" victims of "legitimate efforts to force Iranian troops from the area."[81] Hussein, ever moody, staged periodic outbursts throughout the proceedings, at one point yelling that the judges were "agents of Iran and Zionism." Judge al-Khalifa had little patience with such behavior, and had the former dictator removed from the court on a number of occasions.[82] This phase of the trial ended when Hussein began his appeal of the Dujail verdict, which was reached on November 5. It was rejected on December 26, and four days later, he was hanged at an Iraqi army base on the outskirts of Baghdad in a circus-like atmosphere. As he was led to the scaffold, Hussein had an angry exchange with one of his guards.

> "You have destroyed us. You have killed us. You have made us live in destitution [the guard screamed]."
>
> "I have saved you from destitution and misery and destroyed your enemies, the Persians and Americans," Saddam responded.
>
> "God damn you," the guard said.
>
> "God damn you," responded Saddam.[83]

When the *Al-Anfal* trial resumed in January, the court dropped all charges against Hussein, much to the chagrin of many who felt that the case against him should be continued. His execution also cast a pall over the proceedings, which continued for another six months. The prosecution had completed its case before the trial recessed in November, so the second phase focused principally on the defendants' statements and defense arguments. Each of them was allowed one day in court to address the judges. During his session, Ali Hassan al-Majid argued that the *al-Anfal* operations were necessary to save Iraq from "internal and external enemies," while Hussein Rashid stated that he was just following orders. Sultan Hashem Ahmed al-Ta'i made the same argument, while Sabir al-Douri said that he did not give any orders relating to *al-Anfal* military activities. When presented with documents that contradicted this, he said they were forged or that he did not have the time to read them before signing them. Farhan Mutlaq al-Jabouri said he knew nothing about the gas and military attacks, and that military intelligence had no role in any of this. Tahir Tawtia al-'Aani testified that he had been away from his office as governor throughout the campaign and knew no more about it than "any ordinary Iraqi."[84] Though the defense did call nine witnesses, only five showed up, and none of them had anything to say substantively about the charges against the remaining defendants.[85]

The final phase of the trial took place between April 2 and May 10, when the prosecution made its final arguments, followed by those of the defendants. The trial reconvened on June 24, when the court issued its verdict. Ali Hassan al-Majid was convicted and condemned to death on 13 different counts including various "forms of genocide," crimes against humanity, war crimes, and confiscation of property. Sultan Hashem Ahmed al-Ta'i and Hussein Rashid received multiple death and life sentences, while Farhan Mutlaq al-Jabouri and Sabir al-Douri received multiple life and lesser sentences for their similar crimes. The court dismissed the charges against Taher Tawfiq al-Ani for "lack of evidence."[86] Each of those convicted unsuccessfully appealed their sentences, though, to date, the Iraqi government has only executed al-Majid.[87]

The ICTY, the ICJ, and War in the Former Yugoslavia

The legal proceedings against Saddam Hussein ended after his execution in Baghdad at the end of 2006. Ten and a half months earlier, former Serbian dictator

Slobodan Milošević, also on trial for war crimes, died in his sleep at the comfortable UN Detention Unit in the Hague. An autopsy revealed that Milošević had been manipulating drugs prescribed for a severe heart condition in the hope that the court would allow him to be treated in Moscow for severe high blood pressure. His trial before the International Criminal Tribunal for the Former Yugoslavia (ICTY) was terminated a few days later without a verdict.[88]

Hussein was a pathological, brutal dictator who used raw force time and again to build his savage regime. Milošević's crimes were born in the aftermath of the collapse of communism in the Former Yugoslavia and centered more around his role in trying to take advantage of Yugoslavia's decay to build a Greater Serbian state. He and his subordinates combined Serbian nationalistic themes with superior military forces to unleash a reign of militaristic terror in parts of the Former Yugoslavia that horrified the Western world. The worst of the fighting took place in multiethnic Bosnia and Herzegovina (BiH), which, at the time, had a population that was 43.7 percent Muslim (Bosniaks), 31.4 percent Serb, and 17.3 percent Croat.[89]

Between 1991 and 1995, fighting between Serbs, Croats, and Bosnia's large Muslim population almost destroyed Bosnia. Estimates are that 100,000–110,000 soldiers and civilians were killed in the conflict, 65 percent of them Bosnian Muslims. The war also forced 1.3 million refugees to flee BiH.[90] Most of the Muslims who were killed were victims of Serb forces operating in the region. Though Croat and Bosnian forces committed some of the atrocities, particularly during the early stages of the war, the CIA reported in 1995 that "Serb forces committed the worst and most numerous offenses." The controversial but influential CIA report also charged that,

> A range of reporting...indicates that ethnic Serb forces have carried out at least 90 percent of the destruction, displacement, and loss of life associated with ethnic cleansing. Croats and Muslims in Bosnia have also committed atrocities and forced other ethnic groups to flee—the Croat destruction of Mostar is one example—but the ethnic cleansing actions of the Bosnian Serbs are unrivaled in scale, intensity, and ferocity. We have no evidence that Croat and Muslims have planned or carried out calculated, large-scale ethnic cleansing.[91]

According to one CIA official with intimate knowledge of this highly classified report, while there was no conclusive evidence to support the accusation that Bosnian Serb and Serbian leaders played a direct role in the planning and execution of these "ethnic cleansing" crimes, it was possible that Pale (Bosnian Serb capital) and perhaps Belgrade "exercised a carefully veiled role in the purposeful destruction and dispersal of [the] non-Serb population."[92]

While the idea of "ethnic cleansing" gained currency during the Bosnian war, the practice of "cleansing" an area or region of all possible or potential opposition in a military context can be traced back to antiquity.[93] It was widely practiced in the twentieth century, particularly in Europe. The Carnegie Endowment for International Peace's study of the Balkan Wars of 1912–1913 stated, for example, that the "burning of villages and the exodus of the affected population is a normal and traditional incident of all Balkan Wars and insurrections."[94] The Armenian genocide began as an act of "ethnic cleansing" several years later when the Turks tried to rid eastern Anatolia of Armenians. And during World War II, the Germans "ethnically cleansed" parts of Poland and the Soviet Union to pave the way for the settlement of ethnic Germans in these newly acquired areas. After it ended, the Allies allowed nations in central and eastern Europe to drive out their ethnic German populations as an act of revenge for German atrocities committed during World War II.

The "ethnic cleansing" policies of the Serbs in the Bosnian war were strikingly comprehensive and multifaceted. They involved the complete purging of an ethnic community using a variety of administrative, propagandistic, and inhumane military measures to gain complete control over an area.[95] Such policies included rape—the most horribly intimate of war crimes. Estimates are that between 12,000 to 50,000 women were raped during the war, most of them Bosnian Muslims. What was particularly evil about these crimes was the creation of special "rape camps" where Bosniak women were repeatedly raped and sexually assaulted by Serbian soldiers, and then forced to return pregnant to their families in shame. Part of the reason for this practice was to impregnate Muslim women, thus defiling their cultural, ethnic, and religious heritage.[96]

While the question of rape and "rape camps" is controversial, the ICTY has successfully documented and prosecuted such crimes. In 2001, it found Dragoljub Kunarac, Radomir Kovać, and Zoran Vuković guilty of war crimes and crimes against humanity for their rape, torture, and enslavement of Bosniak women in Foča. Its judgment stated that the defendants set up special "rape camps" in the village where

> Muslim women and girls, mothers and daughters together, [were] robbed of the last vestiges of human dignity...where women and girls [were] treated like chattel, pieces of property at the arbitrary disposal of the Serb occupation forces, and more specifically, at the beck and call of the accused.

While the court ruled that it could find no evidence that such "systematic rape was employed as a 'weapon of war,'" meaning that rape was "understood to mean a kind of concerted approach or an order given to the Bosnian Serb forces to rape Muslim women as part of their combat activities," Serb forces did use rape "as an instrument of terror."[97]

The shocking nature of such crimes was what led the UN Security Council to create the ICTY in 1993. The same year, the Republic of Bosnia and Herzegovina filed a complaint against the Federal Republic of Yugoslavia (FRY) before the International Court of Justice (ICJ) in the Hague, claiming that Serbia and Montenegro violated articles 1–4 of the Genocide Convention.[98] Thirteen years later, the ICJ released its controversial decision, ruling that while the mass killings, principally by Serbian forces, were possibly "war crimes and crimes against humanity," they were not "acts of genocide prohibited by the Convention."[99] On the other hand, the ICJ ruled that the mass murders in Srebrenica in mid-July 1995, when Bosnian Serb forces butchered 8,000 Bosnian Muslim men and boys, were "acts of genocide" as defined by article 2 of the Genocide Convention.[100] It also criticized the Serbian government for its failure to prevent and punish this crime at Srebrenica.[101]

Antonio Cassese, the first president of the ICTY, called the decision "a judicial massacre" that was meant "to give something to everybody and leave everything as it was."[102] Two Serbian legal scholars, Vojin Dimitrejević and Marko Milanović, saw the case as "a true judicial drama" that "from its beginning to its end [was] at the mercy of political considerations outside the courtroom."[103] On the other hand, Anja Seibert-Fohr argues that the court relied too heavily in its decision on "criminal terms" and "did not adequately address the concept of state responsibility." This led it to rely on very high standards of proof "beyond reasonable doubt." Regardless, she concludes that its decision "was a very important landmark in the recognition of state responsibility under the Genocide Convention" that created a very "high threshold for special intent."[104]

The question of intent was one of the most intriguing aspects of the ICJ decision. It cited article 2 of the Genocide Convention, which listed various acts of genocide, noting that the commission of such crimes "comprises 'acts' and 'an intent.'"[105] It added that there were certain "mental" elements in such acts that went beyond mere discriminatory behavior. This included the "intent" to "destroy, in whole or in part, the group to which the victims of the genocide belong." But, to be genocide, it added, such actions "must be significant enough for its destruction to have an impact on the group as a whole," meaning the intent "must be to destroy at least a substantial part of the particular group."[106]

The ICTY has been far more forceful in its decisions on genocide. It has indicted 21 individuals for their role in the Srebrenica genocide, where Bosnian Serb forces mass murdered 7,000–8,000 Bosniak males in mid-July 1995. Between 1996 and 2001, the tribunal convicted Dražen Erdemović, Radislav Krstić, and Dragan Obrenović for their roles in the Srebrenica genocide. Erdemović pleaded guilty to the charges of "murder as a crime against humanity," and was sentenced to five years in prison. He claimed that if he had not participated in the murders of 70 Bosniaks, he would have been killed. Gen. Krstić, the chief of staff and deputy commander of the Bosnian Serb army's Drina corps, was found guilty of his involvement in two criminal plans—"to ethnically cleanse the Srebrenica enclave of all Muslim civilians and later to kill the military aged men of Srebrenica." He was convicted of murder, persecution, and genocide, and sentenced to 46 years in prison, a term later reduced to 35 years on appeal. Obrenović, deputy commander of a Drina Corps brigade during the massacre, was initially charged with genocide, murder, extermination, persecution, and inhumane acts. He later agreed to plead guilty in return for a reduction in charges to persecutions as "a crime against humanity," and was sentenced to 17 years imprisonment.[107] According to the ICTY, these and other trials have "established beyond a reasonable doubt that . . . the killing of 7,000 to 8,000 Bosnian Muslim prisoners was genocide."[108] Milošević was also charged with genocide and complicity in the Srebrenica massacre, though he died before he could be convicted. However, four years later, seven Serbian policemen and military leaders were found guilty of genocide and other crimes at Srebrenica, and sentenced to prison terms ranging from five years to life, with the prospect of further prosecution.[109]

But it was the Milošević trial, and now that of his co-conspirators, Radovan Karadžić and Ratko Mladić, that will hopefully reveal the depth of the Serbian leadership's involvement not only in the Srebrenica massacres, but also in the larger body of war crimes committed in the Yugoslav wars of the 1990s. Initially, Milošević was able to parlay his role as head of the rump Yugoslav state into that of a peacemaker. At the Dayton peace talks in 1995, which brought an end to the Bosnian war, he was seen as "the puppet master, pulling strings, directing the course of events" throughout Serbian-held territory.[110] Consequently, for the next few years he was able to distance himself from the proceedings in the Hague in large part because the tribunal had produced scant evidence linking him to the crimes in Bosnia and Croatia. However, he ultimately fell prey to his own ambitions, misrule, new atrocities in Kosovo, and the decision of two ICTY chief prosecutors, Louise Arbour and Carla del Ponte, to indict him for a multiplicity of crimes that ultimately led to his trial.[111]

What made Milošević's trial unique was that he was the "first former head of state tried for war crimes and violation of international humanitarian law, which is of itself an important precedent."[112] The pathway to Milošević's trial was paved years earlier when the politically ambitious Milošević sought to use the gradual collapse of the Yugoslav state in the mid- to late 1980s to tap into a resurgent wave of Serbian nationalism to create a new base of political power. In 1987, he told a group of disgruntled Kosovar Serbs who had complained of mistreatment at the hands of Kosovar Albanians:

> First I want to tell you, comrades, that you should stay here. This is your country, these are your houses, your fields and gardens, your memories. You are not going to abandon your lands because life is hard, because you are oppressed by injustice and humiliation. It has never been a characteristic of the Serbian and Montenegrin people to retreat in the face of obstacles, to demobilize when they should fight, to become demoralized when things are difficult. You should stay here, both for your ancestors and your descendants. Otherwise you would shame your ancestors and disappoint your descendants. But I do not suggest you stay here suffering and enduring a situation with which you are not satisfied. On the contrary! It should be changed, together with all progressive people here, in Serbia and Yugoslavia. *Yugoslavia does not exist without Kosovo! Yugoslavia would disintegrate without Kosovo! Yugoslavia and Serbia are not going to give up Kosovo!*[113]

Kosovo, a Serbian province with a predominantly Albanian Muslim population, was considered by many Serbs as their spiritual homeland. In 1986, a memorandum by the Serbian Academy of Sciences claimed that the Kosovar mistreatment of Serbs was "tantamount to the physical, political, legal, and cultural genocide of the Serbian people in Kosovo and Methohija." It ended by proclaiming that

> under the influence of the ruling ideology, the cultural heritage of the Serbian people is being alienated, usurped, invalidated, neglected, or wasted; their language is being suppressed and the Cyrillic alphabet is vanishing...No other Yugoslav nation has been so rudely denied its cultural and spiritual integrity as the Serbian people. No literary and artistic heritage has been so routed, pillaged, and plundered as the Serbian one.[114]

Milošević's game plan was to revive age-old dreams of a "Greater Serbia" that would bring together scattered Serbian populations throughout Yugoslavia into a Serbian "super" state. According to the 1991 census, 42 percent of Yugoslavia's Serbs lived outside of Serbia, about 1.3 million of them in Bosnia-Herzegovina (BiH).[115] Milošević began to put his game plan into action in the midst of the disintegration of Yugoslavia. In 1991, Slovenia and Croatia seceded from the Yugoslav federation, which led to a modest civil war between Serbia and Croatia. Meanwhile,

BiH adopted a "Memorandum on Sovereignty," followed by a successful, Serbian-boycotted Bosnian referendum on independence in early 1992. The new Bosnian Serb Republic (*Republika Srpska*; RS) responded to the referendum by attacking Sarajevo, the BiH capital.[116]

Civil war quickly spread throughout the Former Yugoslavia. All sides adopted "ethnic cleansing" campaigns, though the worst were initiated by the Serbs. By the summer of 1993, the Serbs were in control of over 70 percent of Bosnia and a portion of Croatia. The Bosnian Muslims and Croats responded the following spring with the creation of a Bosnian Federation (*Federacije Bosne I Hercegovine*).[117] The UN Security Council, acting under the authority of Chapter VII of the UN charter, which gave it the right to take "measures...to maintain or restore international peace and security,"[118] responded with SCR 827, which created an "international tribunal" for the "former Yugoslavia" to prosecute persons "for serious violations of international humanitarian law" as a way to "restore and maintain peace" in the Former Yugoslavia.[119]

In late 1994 and early 1995, it indicted Dragan Nikolić, the head of the Sušica concentration camp in Bosnia, and Duško Tadić, a Bosnian Serb politician, charging them with "grave breaches" of the 1949 Geneva Conventions and other crimes. Both were sentenced, after appeals, to 20 years imprisonment.[120] But its most important trials involved three key figures in the principal crimes of the Former Yugoslavia—Milošević, Karadžić, and Mladić. Though the latter were indicted in 1995, they were not arrested and extradited to the Hague until 2008 and 2011 respectively.[121] The ICTY also indicted Milošević in 1999 for various crimes in Kosovo, and two years later, amended the indictment to include crimes committed earlier in Bosnia and Croatia from 1991 to 1995. All three Serbian leaders, as well as several other co-indictees, were charged with criminal liability for involvement in a "joint criminal enterprise" that resulted in the commitment of various war crimes, crimes against humanity, and genocide from 1991 to 1995.[122]

Article 7 of the ICTY Statute, which deals with "individual criminal responsibility," states that

1. A person who planned, instigated, ordered, committed, or otherwise aided and abetted in the planning, preparation or execution of a crime [grave breaches; violations of laws or customs of war; genocide; crimes against humanity]...shall be individually responsible for the crime.
2. The official position of any accused person, whether as head of State or government or as a responsible Government official, shall not relieve such person of criminal responsibility nor mitigate punishment.
3. The fact that any of the acts referred to in articles 2 to 5 of the present Statute were committed by a subordinate does not relieve his superior of criminal responsibility if he knew or had to know that the subordinate was about to commit such acts or had done so and the superior failed to take the necessary and reasonable measures to prevent such acts or to punish the perpetrators thereof.
4. The fact that an accused person acted pursuant to an order of a Government or of a superior shall not relieve him of criminal responsibility, but may be considered in mitigation of punishment if the international tribunal determines that justice so requires.[123]

The challenge for the ICTY, and later, the International Criminal Tribunal for Rwanda (ICTR), was how to use the more narrow post–World War II military definitions of command responsibility and define them more broadly to apply equally to "all (military and civilian) superiors, thus 'superior responsibility.'"[124] Unfortunately, it has been difficult for both tribunals to prosecute individuals for "superior responsibility," which, unlike command responsibility, is applicable to the military and civilians.[125] One of the most controversial aspects of command responsibility is the question of *mens rea* or the applicable state of mind of a defendant. This has to be proven beyond a reasonable doubt and "cannot be presumed." Both the ICTY and the ICTR have rejected the idea of "a 'duty to know' on the part of a commander," and, while prosecutors do not have to prove specific knowledge of such crimes, they do have to prove that the superior had "'alarming information' in his possession...to prove that he 'had reason to know.'"[126]

This was the principal question that the justices faced in the 1997–1998 *Mucić et al. "Čelebići Camp"* (IT-96–21) trial. Col. Zejnil Delalić, the commander of the Bosnian Muslim 1st Tactical Group, was responsible, among other things, for the operation of a prison camp at Čelebići near Konjić, where Serb POWs were beaten and tortured. The tribunal stated in its judgment that "the essential elements of command responsibility for failure to act" were as follows.

(1) the existence of a superior–subordinate relationship;
(2) the superior knew or had reason to know that the criminal act was about to be or had been committed; and
(3) the superior failed to take necessary and reasonable measures to prevent the criminal act or punish the perpetrator thereof.[127]

Using these standards, the court found Delalić innocent, a decision later upheld on appeal. However, as Allison Danner and Jeremy Martinez have pointed out, if the Delalić case had been prosecuted five or six years later, it is possible that he and one of his codefendants, Hazim Delić, might have successfully been prosecuted for a category two joint criminal enterprise crime dealing with "'systems of ill-treatment,' primarily in concentration camps."[128]

Up until the Delalić case, one of the principal obstacles to the application of command responsibility was the nature of the superior–subordinate relationship. For the most part, post–World War II courts abandoned the traditional "*de jure* position of the accused," instead trying to determine the "effective control of the superior over his or her subordinates." It was the "effective control" issue laid out in the Delalić case that transformed the ICTY's perspective on command responsibility.[129] According to the Delalić judgment:

A position of command is indeed a necessary precondition of the imposition of command responsibility. However, this statement must be qualified by the recognition that the existence of such a position cannot be determined by reference to formal status alone. Instead, the factor that determines liability for this type of criminal responsibility is the actual possession or non-possession of powers of control over the actions of subordinates.[130]

This was one of the key challenges for the prosecution in the Milošević case. He was charged with individual and command responsibility for grave breaches of the Geneva Conventions of 1949, violations of the laws and customs of war, genocide, and crimes against humanity. Milošević was also indicted for participation in joint criminal enterprises in Kosovo, Croatia, and Bosnia, which included involvement in "a campaign of terror and violence" in Kosovo, and the "forcible removal" of non-Serbian populations in Croatia and Bosnia.[131] In the latter case, he was charged with genocide for working

> in concert with or through other individuals in the joint criminal enterprise. Each participant or coperpetrator within the joint criminal enterprise...significantly contributed to achieving the objective of the enterprise.[132]

The indictment added that as president of Serbia and leader of the Socialist Party of Serbia (*Socialistička partija Srbije*; SPS), Milošević "exercised effective control or substantial influences" over other members of the joint criminal enterprise.[133] This, in league with his effective command of the Yugoslav National Army (*Jugoslovenska Narodna Armija*; JNA), the Yugoslav Forces (*Vojska Jugoslavije*; VJ), the Ministry of Internal Affairs (*Ministarvsto Unutrašnijh Poslova*; MUP), and Serbia's paramilitary forces, meant that he played the key role in the "forcible removal" of non-Serbs from Bosnia. The indictment also alleged that Milošević, who controlled the state media, used it "to spread exaggerated or false messages of ethnically based attacks...intended to create an atmosphere of fear and hatred among Serbs living in Serbia" and elsewhere, "which contributed to the forcible removal of the majority of non-Serbs, principally Bosnian Muslims and Bosnian Croats, from large areas of Bosnia and Herzegovina."[134] The evidence presented in his trial well documented the close relationship between his military, MUP, and the various Serb paramilitary forces operating in Bosnia and elsewhere.[135]

Unfortunately, Milošević's death and the ICTY decision to end his trial a few days later "left a significant hole in the fabric of the development and solidification of international justice." On the other hand, his trial underscored the fact that heads of state could no longer "commit such atrocities" with "impunity."[136] Fortunately, the ICTY has successfully brought Karadžić and Mladić, Milošević's cohorts in crime, to trial. Hopefully, their trials will bring to light more about Milošević's role in the crimes committed in BiH. Karadžić was a founding member of the Serbian Democratic Party and the chairman of the Bosnian Serb Republic's National Security Council. In 1992, he became president of the Bosnian Serb state and the supreme commander of its armed forces. Mladić, his co-conspirator, was the main staff commander of the Bosnian Serb Army (*Vojska Republike Srpske;* VRS), and oversaw all operations of this force throughout most of the war in Bosnia.[137] Both men were charged with being co-conspirators in joint criminal enterprises that resulted in some of the most heinous crimes in the Yugoslav wars. They were indicted in 1995 on multiple counts of genocide and crimes against humanity for their "acts and omissions, and in concert with others," in the commission of "crimes against humanity by persecution of Bosnian Muslim and Bosnian Croat civilians on national, political, and religious grounds." The indictment said that they were

> criminally responsible for the unlawful confinement, murder, rape, sexual assault, torture, beating, robbery and inhumane treatment of civilians; the targeting of political leaders, intellectuals and professionals; the unlawful deportation and transfer of civilians; the unlawful shelling of civilians; the unlawful appropriation and plunder of real and personal property; the destruction of home and businesses; and the destruction of places of worship.[138]

They were also indicted for their role in the massacre at Srebrenica. The Srebrenica indictment pointed to the "superior authority" of both men, noting that they were "individually responsible" for the crimes committed there under article 7 of the ICTY Statute. They were specifically charged with 2 counts of genocide and 17 counts of crimes against humanity.[139] Karadžić's trial began in the spring of 2010 and is expected to be concluded in 2015. Mladić's trial began in the spring of 2012, and is expected to be over by the end of 2015 or mid-2016.

By the fall of 2013, the ICTY had indicted 161 war criminals and has 25 cases under appeal or on trial. It has concluded proceedings for 136 of the accused (18 acquitted; 69 sentenced; 13 referred to national jurisdiction; 36 indictments withdrawn or deceased). While some have questioned the value and cost of these proceedings, it is important to remember that they have played an important role in creating a new body of precedents and documentary evidence in international criminal law that provides details about some of the most heinous crimes in Europe since World War II.

Rwanda and the ICTR

A world away in Arusha, Tanzania, the ICTY's sister tribunal, the International Criminal Tribunal for Rwanda (ICTR), is also moving forward with its own investigations and trials of those allegedly involved in the Rwandan genocide in 1994. There are probably few crimes in modern history more tragic than the Rwandan genocide, which, like many of those during the Yugoslav wars, took place as the world looked on. In a little more than three months in the spring and summer of 1994, tens of thousands of Hutu *genocidaires*, many of them drawn from government forces, murdered 500,000–800,000 Tutsi tribesmen and 50,000 Hutus.[140] Beyond this were mass rapes of as many as 250,000–500,000 women. In fact, according to René Degni-Ségui, the United Nations' Special Rapporteur for Rwanda, women could "be regarded as the main victims of the massacres, since they were raped and massacred and subjected to other brutalities."[141]

In 1996, the UN Security Council passed SCR 955, which created the ICTR, to prosecute

> persons responsible for genocide and other serious violations of international humanitarian law committed in the territory of Rwanda and Rwandan citizens responsible

for genocide and other such violations committed in the territory of the neighbouring States, between 1 January 1994 and 31 December 1994.[142]

Though it drew heavily from the statute and precedents of the ICTY, the ICTR focused principally on acts of genocide and violations of common article 3, and not "grave breaches." But, like the ICTY, the ICTR also cited jurisdiction for crimes against humanity and laid out guidelines for questions of personal jurisdiction, individual criminal responsibility, and various other areas of jurisdiction.[143]

Over the past 17 years, the ICTR has completed 47 cases, has 15 on appeal, and has acquitted 12 detainees. Several detainees have passed away before judgment, while 10 cases have been transferred to national jurisdiction. It has also released two detainees for various reasons. Seven of those found guilty and imprisoned are now free, while nine indicted criminals are still at large. In addition, national and local courts (*gacaca*) have tried almost 10,000 Rwandans suspected of involvement in the 1994 genocide. Though impressive, the quality of justice in the *gacaca* trials is quite low. Complicating all of this is Rwanda's Disarmament, Demobilization and Reintegration (DDR) program, which has tried to reintegrate tens of thousands of combatants back into Rwandan society. This, and the fact that over 800,000 Rwandans have been implicated in the *gacaca* proceedings, has further raised questions about this admirable exercise in transitional justice.[144]

Many hoped that the ICTR would not face the same difficulties as the ICTY, which, in its early years, seemed trapped in the crosshairs of the ongoing political, ethnic, and military conflicts in the Former Yugoslav states. The Rwandan Patriotic Front (RPF), a guerrilla force made up principally of Tutsi refugees, ended the genocide when it took control of the country in July 1994. It has remained in control of the government since that time, and has proven to be an erstwhile friend of the ICTR. It has been able, through varying gestures of compliance and noncompliance, to exert "direct influence over the court's prosecutorial agenda by blocking the investigation of Tutsi war crimes committed against Hutu civilians in 1994." According to Victor Peskin, this has made "the ICTR a de facto 'victor's court' where Tutsi RPF suspects enjoy virtual immunity from prosecution."[145]

Tribal violence between the Hutus, who made up 85 percent of the population, the Tutsis (14 percent), and the Twa was an early part of post–World War II Rwandan history. Prior to 1939, the "ethnic" outlines of distinction between the Tutsi and Hutu were constructed more around a person's occupation as "a person rich in cattle"—Tutsi, or a Hutu, "a subordinate or follower of a more powerful person." Consequently, by the time that European colonists entered Rwanda in the late nineteenth century, these socioeconomic distinctions took on class connotations, with the Tutsi being seen as the power holding "pastoralists," and the Hutu their subjects. German and Belgian colonial rulers adopted these divisions, with the small Twa pygmy population seen as the third, outside class in Rwanda.[146]

Germany was the first colonial power to dominate Rwanda, followed by the Belgians during World War I. The latter treated Rwanda simply as a larger part of their Congo colony, and, like the Germans, regarded the Tutsi as the colony's Christian-educated "'racial aristocracy.'"[147] After World War II, the Hutus began to push for an end to racial discrimination and the dominance of the Tutsi in all areas of Rwandan life. This led to a Hutu revolution that gave the Hutus full control of the government.[148] After the revolution, some of the 130,000 Tutsis who had earlier fled to Burundi began to try to retake control of Rwanda. They used special guerrilla squads, the "cockroaches" (*inyenzi*), to raid border regions. The Hutu responded with widespread violence against Tutsi throughout Rwanda, killing as many as 10,000, and forcing many more into exile. In neighboring Burundi, which was controlled by a Tutsi minority, a Hutu rebellion in 1972 led to a "'selective genocide'" that resulted in the death of as many as 200,000 Hutu. Another 200,000 Hutu escaped into Rwanda.[149]

After he took power in 1960, Rwanda's Hutu president, Grégoire Kayibanda, described Rwanda as

> two nations in a single state... two nations between whom there is no intercourse and no sympathy, who are ignorant of each other's habits, thoughts and feelings as if they were dwellers of different zones, or inhabitants of different planets.[150]

He responded to the growing Tutsi threat with a harsh campaign that resulted in a mass migration of Tutsis out of the country. He was overthrown in 1973 by Gen. Juvénal Habyarimana, whose one-party dictatorship—the National Revolutionary Movement for Development (*Mouvement Révolutionnaire National pour le Développement*; MRND)—lasted until his death in 1994. Though Rwanda prospered during the early years of his reign, the economy collapsed in the late 1980s. In the midst of this crisis, hundreds of thousands of Tutsis in Uganda, Burundi, Zaire, and Tanzania began to clamor for a return to their homeland. They created the RPF to promote this idea as well as political reform in Rwanda. Habyarimana also faced growing opposition from moderate Hutus, whom he initially terrorized but later tried to assuage with constitutional changes that allowed the creation of opposition parties. At the same time, he began to strengthen his armed forces with the help of the French military. In 1992, he allowed the creation of a coalition government, though this did little to quiet his Hutu opponents, who established contact with Paul Kagame's RPF.[151]

Habyarimana loyalists responded by creating a network of activists throughout Rwanda driven by one ideal—"rid Rwanda of Hutu *ibyitso* (Tutsi 'accomplices')." A Hutu army memorandum went further, claiming the *ibyitso* were

> the Tutsi inside or outside the country, extremist and nostalgic for power, who have NEVER recognised and will NEVER recognize the realities of the 1959 social revolution and who wish to reconquer power by all means necessary including arms.[152]

What emerged was a "zero network" that, at least according to the Belgian ambassador to Rwanda, was intent on mass murdering all of the Tutsi. Part of the rationale of Hutu propaganda was "to stir up the fear that the Tutsi, in order to regain power, were prepared to slaughter Hutu en masse."[153] What followed was a government-sponsored series of mass killings euphemistically called "'clearing the brush'"[154] or, when it came to Tutsi women and children, "'pulling out the roots of the bad weeds.'"[155]

Ultimately, the French put pressure on Habyarimana to enter into negotiations with the RPF, which resulted in the Arusha Accords (August 4, 1993). They established

> the rule of law, the transitional institutions to govern until elections could be held, the repatriation of refugees, the resettlement of dis-placed persons, and the integration of the two opposing armies.[156]

Hutu extremists refused to accept the accords, while in neighboring Burundi, the murder of the newly elected, moderate Hutu president, Melchior Ndadaye, by radical Tutsi army officers, inspired a new wave of violence that resulted in the death of 150,000 Burundian Hutus and Tutsis, and the flight of 300,000 Hutus to Rwanda.[157] Hutus throughout the country were now convinced that the Tutsis were determined to take over Rwanda. Consequently, according to the ICTR indictment of Théoneste Bagorosa, the *directeur de cabinet* of the Rwandan Ministry of Defense, he and others began

> to work out a plan with the intent to exterminate the civilian Tutsi population and eliminate members of the opposition, so that they could remain in power. The components of this plan consisted of, among other things, recourse to hatred and ethnic violence, the training of and distribution of weapons [i.e., over 500,000 machetes] to militiamen as well as the preparation of lists of people to be eliminated. In executing the plan [Bagorosa and his codefendants] organized, ordered and participated in the massacres perpetrated against the Tutsi population and of moderate Hutu.[158]

In the midst of all of this, the UN Security Council created a peacekeeping force, the United Nations Assistance Mission for Rwanda (UNAMIR),

> to monitor the [Arusha] cease fire agreement, including establishment of an expanded demilitarized zone (DMZ) and demobilization procedures; monitor the security situation during the final period of the transitional Government's mandate leading up to elections; and assist with mine-clearance. The Mission would also investigate alleged non-compliance with any provisions of the peace agreement and provide security for the repatriation of Rwandese refugees and displaced persons. In addition, it would assist in the coordination of humanitarian assistance activities in conjunction with relief operations.[159]

The extremely small contingent of 2,548 UNAMIR multinational peacekeepers under Canadian Lt. Gen. Roméo Dallaire operated under strict UN principles of impartiality and use of force that limited its use of measures "of last resort." Similar restrictions would later partially cripple UNPROFOR "Dutchbat" peacekeepers at Srebrenica in BiH in1995.[160]

The situation in Rwanda eventually spun out of control after a missile attack killed President Habyarimana and everyone else onboard when his jet tried to land at Kigali airport on April 6, 1994. His killers were probably members of his inner circle, who then initiated the genocide that followed his murder.[161] The first victims of Bagorosa's carefully planned genocidal campaign were drawn from lists of prominent Hutus. Some were attacked by gangs in their homes or at roadblocks where they were killed on the spot. In addition,

> Burgomasters [*bourgmestres*, or mayors] and the prefectural staff provided logistical and financial support for the killing campaign. In addition to supplying communal vehicles, they requisitioned private vehicles to transport assailants and they provided the fuel both to run the vehicles and to burn Tutsi houses. They delivered the trucks and the bulldozers that made mass burials easier. Administrators and politicians paid for the "work" of assailants and, later, for the efforts of those who buried the bodies.[162]

The media, particularly the *Radio Télévision Libre des Milles Collines* (RTLM), played an important role in identifying potential victims and providing guidelines for carrying out the mass murders.[163] According to Dallaire, the radio in Rwanda "was akin to the voice of God, and if the radio called for violence, many Rwandans would respond, believing they were being sanctioned to commit these actions."[164] In its indictment of Ferdinand Nahimana, the head of RTLM, the ICTR charged him, along with three other co-conspirators, of working

> out a plan with the intent to exterminate the civilian population and eliminate the moderate Hutu. The components of the plan consisted of, among other things, the broadcasting of messages of ethnic hatred and incitement to violence, the training and distribution of weapons to militiamen, as well as the preparation of lists of people to be eliminated and the broadcasting of their identities. In executing the plan, they organized and ordered the massacres perpetrated against the Tutsi population and moderate Hutu, and at the same time incited, aided and participated in them.[165]

Though some scholars such as Scott Straus have questioned the importance of media in the genocide, particularly radio,[166] the ICTR considered it "a fundamental part of the [extermination/genocide] plan put in place" by Nahimana and his codefendants.[167]

Another tragic dimension of the planned genocide was rape. According to HRW, it was also the crime that had the least legal redress, particularly in Rwanda's regular court and *gacaca* systems.[168] Hutu propaganda depicted Tutsi women as

> devious and completely devoted to the interests of their fathers and brothers . . . [who] scorned Hutu men whom they found unworthy of their attention . . . Many assailants insulted [Tutsi] women for their supposed arrogance while they were raping them. If the assailants decided to spare the lives of the women, they regarded them as prizes they had won for themselves to be distributed to subordinates who had performed well in killing Tutsi. Some kept these women for weeks or months in sexual servitude.

Sometimes

> assailants mutilated women in the course of a rape or before killing them. They cut off breasts, punctured the vagina with spears, arrows, or pointed sticks, or cut off or disfigured body parts that looked particularly "Tutsi," such as long fingers or thin noses.[169]

In what some have called "'perhaps the most groundbreaking decision advancing gender jurisprudence worldwide,'"[170] the ICTR found Jean-Paul Akayesu, an educated mayor (*bourgmestre*) of the Taba commune, guilty in 1998 of two counts of genocide, and seven counts of crimes against humanity, including rape. His indictment stated that some of the crimes committed in Taba included

> acts of sexual violence [such as] forcible sexual penetration of the vagina, anus or oral cavity by a penis and/or the vagina or anus by some other objects and sexual abuse, such as forced nudity.[171]

These charges were backed by gruesome testimony during this trial, which lasted from January 9, 1997, until October 2, 1998. Witness J, a Tutsi woman, stated that

> her six year old daughter had been raped by three *interahamwe* [specially trained Hutu youth militia] when they came to kill her father...she had [also] heard that young girls were raped at the bureau command.

Shaharyar Khan, the Pakistani diplomat who was sent to Rwanda by the United Nations to try to halt the genocide, described *interahamwe* practices in his memoir, *The Shallow Graves of Rwanda*.

> The Interahamwe made a habit of killing young Tutsi children, in front of their parents, by first cutting off one arm, then the other. They would then gash the neck with a machete to bleed the child slowly to death but, while they were still alive, they would cut off the private parts and throw them at the faces of the terrified parents, who would then be murdered with slightly greater dispatch.[172]

Witness H added that Akayesu and other officials were often present when Tutsi women were raped just outside the mayor's offices.[173] Witness JJ, who fled her home after the genocide began, sought, like many other Tutsis, refuge at Taba's communal offices, but was driven away by the *interahamwe*. Desperate, they returned to the communal offices and begged Akayesu to kill them, since "they were so tired of it all."[174] He said that he did not have any bullets for this, and told them to leave. When they refused, the *interahamwe* took them into the forest and repeatedly beat and raped them. Witness JJ said

> that she was stripped of her clothing and raped in front of other people...the rapist, a young man armed with an axe and a long knife, penetrated her vagina with his penis... on this occasion she was raped twice.[175]

She testified that "'each time you encountered attackers they would rape you.'" Yet she and other Tutsi refugees thought that if they remained in the village center, the authorities would protect them. She finally realized that this would never happen after she heard Akayesu encourage the *interahamwe* to continue their mass rapes. As she was being taken inside the commune's cultural center to be raped, she heard Akayesu say loudly to the militiamen, "'Never ask me again what a Tutsi woman tastes like,' and 'Tomorrow they will be killed.'" Though she never saw Akayesu rape anyone, she testified that she thought that he had the authority to stop the mass rapes but did nothing.[176]

Witness KK testified that she heard Akayesu order the *interahamwe* to undress a young gymnast, Chatal, and forced her to "do gymnastics naked" in front of a large crowd. Afterwards, he told the militia to take her away and "'first of all make sure that you sleep with this girl.'"[177] Witness NN told the court that after her Hutu neighbors destroyed their home and killed her brother and father, they told her they would spare her daughters so "they could be raped." She begged them to kill the two girls instead. Her neighbor replied that "the 'principle was to make them suffer.'" They were then raped "in an 'atrocious' manner" and mocked afterward. The rapes by various men continued for several days and, after hiding for a week and a half, NN and her daughters sought refuge in the Taba village center because they had heard that Akayesu had ordered the killings to stop. Soon after arriving at the village, NN saw Akayesu watching the rape of another woman, and doing nothing to stop it.[178]

Another witness, PP, testified that Akayesu not only oversaw mass rapes, but also directed some of the murders. On one occasion, she told the court, she heard Akayesu tell one of the *interahamwe* to take three Tutsi women to Kinihira, a nearby "basin." Before they left, he told the militiamen,

> Take them to Kinihira. Don't you know where the killings take place, where the others have been killed?[179]

Once at Kinihira, the militiamen made the three women undress and "'run around and perform exercises' so that they could display the thighs of Tutsi women."[180] The *interahamwe* raped each woman before a crowd of about 200 people. One of the rapists, Pierre, told Alexia,

> "Let's see what the vagina of a Tutsi woman feels like." According to Witness PP, Alexia gave...Pierre her Bible before he raped her and told him, "Take this Bible because it's our memory, because you do not know what you are doing." Then one person held her neck, others took her by the shoulders and others held her thighs apart as numerous Interahamwe continued to rape her—Bongo after Pierre, and Hararurena after Bongo. According to the testimony, Alexia was pregnant. When she became weak she was turned over and lying on her stomach, she went into premature delivery during the rapes.

Once the militiamen were finished with Alexia,

> they then went on to rape Nishimwe, a young girl, and recalled lots of blood coming from her private parts after several men raped her. Louise was then raped by several Interahamwe while others held her down, and after the rapes, according to the testimony, all three women were placed on their stomachs and hit with sticks and killed.[181]

A number of male and female witnesses, some of them "in detention," testified that such rapes never took place and that Akayesu knew nothing about them. He said the same thing, and argued that he "was completely surprised by the allegations." In fact, Akayesu claimed, anyone who said women were raped in the commune "was lying." He admitted that he listened to Radio Rwanda and was aware that mass rapes were taking place elsewhere in the country. But, "he swore, in the name of God," the charges against him were trumped up and "that women were never raped within the premises of the bureau communal or on land belonging to the bureau communal or the commune." Moreover, he testified, such charges were fabricated by the "women's movement and women in Rwanda, who he described as 'worked up to agree that they have been raped.'"[182]

In reaching its momentous judgment, the court attempted to define rape, stating

> 597. that rape is a form of aggression and that the central elements of the crime of rape cannot be captured in a mechanical description of objects and body parts. The Convention against Torture and Other Cruel, Inhuman and Degrading Treatment or Punishment does not catalogue specific acts in its definition of torture, focusing rather on the conceptual framework of state sanctioned violence. Like torture, rape is used for such purposes as intimidation, degradation, humiliation, discrimination, punishment, control or destruction of a person. Like torture, rape is a violation of personal dignity, and rape in fact constitutes torture when inflicted by or at the instigation of or with the consent or acquiescence of a public official or other person acting in an official capacity.

> 598. The Chamber defines rape as a physical invasion of a sexual nature, committed on a person under circumstances which are coercive. Sexual violence which includes rape is considered to be any act of a sexual nature which is committed on a person under circumstances which are coercive. This act must be committed:

>> (a) as part of a widespread or systematic attack;
>> (b) on a civilian population;
>> (c) on certain catalogued discriminatory grounds, namely: national, ethnic, political, racial, or religious grounds.[183]

The ICTR repeated this definition later in its judgment, and stated that court testimony proved that Akayesu, or those in his presence or "at his instigation or with his consent or acquiescence," committed rapes, crimes that constituted "torture."[184]

From the tribunal's perspective, Akayesu

> had reason to know and in fact knew that acts of sexual violence were occurring on or near the premises of the bureau communal and that he took no measures to prevent these acts or punish the perpetrators of them.[185]

Consequently, it found that Akayesu, "by his own words, specifically ordered, instigated, aided and abetted" many of the rapes and "other inhumane acts which took place on or near the bureau communal premises of Taba." The tribunal found him guilty of these crimes[186] and also ruled that the crimes were genocidal because, in most cases, they "were accompanied with the intent to kill those [Tutsi] women." The tribunal was also satisfied beyond a reasonable doubt that Akayesu's involvement in such crimes was driven by the desire "to destroy the Tutsi group," which constituted the "crime of genocide," though not "complicity" to commit genocide. This made him "individually responsible for genocide."[187] He was sentenced to life imprisonment, a decision that was upheld on appeal. He is now imprisoned in Mali.[188]

Though the Akayesu trial's definition of rape was held up in several other ICTR cases—*Musema* (ICTR-96–13-T) and Niyitegeka (ICTR-96–14-T)[189]—*Musema* "demanded a high burden of proof for the crime of rape."[190] Subsequent ICTR and ICTY rulings have gone back and forth on the definition of rape. The ICTY *Prosecutor v. Dragoljub et al.* (IT-96–23-T & IT-96–23/1-T) stated that the

> *actus reus* [guilty act] of the crime of rape in international law is constituted by: the sexual penetration, however slight: (a) of the vagina or anus of the victim by the penis of the perpetrator or any other object used by the perpetrator; or (b) of the mouth of the victim by the penis of the perpetrator; where such sexual penetration occurs without the consent of the victim. Consent for this purpose must be consent given voluntarily, as a result of the victim's free will, assessed in the context of surrounding circumstances. The *mens rea* [state of mind] is the intention to effect this sexual penetration, and the knowledge that it occurs without the consent of the victim.[191]

Several ICTR trial chambers—*Prosecutor v. Kamuhanda* (ICTR-95–54A-T) and *Prosecutor v. Semanza* (ICTR-97–20-T)[192]—adopted this definition while *Prosecutor v. Muhimana* (ICTR-95–1B-T) ruled that

> the *Akayesu* definition and the *Kunarac* elements are not incompatible or substantially different in their application. Whereas *Akayesu* referred broadly to a "physical invasion of a sexual nature," *Kunarac* went on to articulate the parameters of what would constitute a physical invasion of a sexual nature amounting to rape.
>
> On the basis of the foregoing analysis, the Chamber endorses the conceptual definition of rape established in *Akayesu*, which encompasses the elements set out in *Kunarac*.[193]

Given the high level of proof established for prosecuting rape as a crime against humanity, the ICTR and the ICTY have adopted the idea of prosecuting the crimes of rape and sexual violence as joint criminal enterprises (JCE). While the standard of proof for such crimes remains high, the use of JCE allows prosecutors to win cases "without proving a specific nexus between the accused and the crimes happening on the ground if those crimes were clearly foreseeable by-products of a JCE involving genocidal intent or widespread and systematic attacks."[194] Though JCE is not mentioned in either the ICTR or ICYT statutes, the ICTR drew heavily from ICTY precedents in its application of JCE. *Nchamihigo* (ICTR-01–63-T) noted, for example, that JCE is "not a crime but a mode of liability," while *Mpambara* (ICTR-01–65-T) states that JCE is a "means of committing a crimes," and "not a crime in itself."[195]

The Appeals Chamber for *Gacumbitsi* (ICTR-2001–64-A), drawing upon ICTY precedents, identified two categories of JCE applicable to charges of murder, genocide, extermination, and rape. "The first (or basic) category encompasses cases in which 'all perpetrators, acting pursuant to a common purpose, possess the same criminal intention' to commit the crime charged." The chamber did not mention the second category, which deals principally with concentration camp scenarios. Category three, it went on, "concerns cases in which the crime charged, 'while outside the common purpose, is nevertheless a natural and foreseeable consequence of executing that common purpose."[196] Rebecca L. Haffajee notes that the burden of proof for category one remains quite high, since the prosecution had to prove that a common plan to create a crime existed at the time of its commission. In addition, she argues, there also has to be proof that the defendant played some role in some aspect of that plan, and assisted in committing the crime, even if they did not actually commit the act of rape or sexual violence. To prove category three, Haffajee adds, the prosecution has to show that the crime was "objectively a natural and foreseeable consequence of the execution of the JCE," and that the defendant, even after being aware subjectively that such a crime was possible, took part in the JCE.[197]

JCE, she concludes, must not be confused with complicity, conspiracy, or command responsibility. Complicity assumes assisting in the commission of a crime, while provable JCE cases treats all participants as principals in the commitment of such crimes. And even though conspiracy is similar to JCE's category one, the former carries a "lower burden of proof because it does not require evidence that the agreement to commit a crime actually results in the commission by any participant." JCE, she adds, is a "theory of liability," while conspiracy is a "freestanding crime." And though she admits that there is an "overlap" between JCE and command responsibility, what differentiates the two is that under JCE, there does not have to be a "superior-subordinate" relationship. Moreover, the agreement between the principals does not actually have to focus on the actual crime committed, though the crime does have to "be a natural and foreseeable by-product of that agreement."[198]

The Cambodian Genocide and the Extraordinary Chambers in the Courts of Cambodia (ECCC)

While the ICTY and the ICTR have had varying degrees of success bringing alleged war criminals to justice, this would not be the case for the Extraordinary Chambers in the Courts of Cambodia (ECCC), a hybrid tribunal created in 2003 to try the principal figures responsible for the horrible crimes committed by the Khmer Rouge in Cambodia from 1975 to 1979. These crimes took place after the Khmer Rouge took power in Cambodia in 1975, and began to purge the country of elements it deemed threatening or alien to its attempts completely to communize what they called Kampuchea. Though the Khmer Rouge only ruled Cambodia for four years, their mass murder program resulted in the deaths of as many as 1.7 million Cambodians. The search for justice for these crimes began soon after the Vietnamese invaded and occupied Cambodia in 1979, and drove Pol Pot's regime from power. Later that year, the Vietnamese-dominated government passed Decree Law No. 1, which set up a People's Revolutionary Tribunal at Phnom Penh

> to try the acts of genocide committed by the Pol Pot–Ieng Sary clique, planned massacres of groups of innocent people; expulsion of inhabitants of cities and villages in order to concentrate them and force them to do hard labor in conditions leading to their physical and mental destruction; wiping out religion; destroying political, cultural and social structures and social relations.[199]

This led to the trial of Pol Pot, Kampuchea's leader or "Brother No. 1," and Ieng Sary, his deputy foreign minister, *in absentia*. Though both men were convicted of various charges of "genocidal intent" and sentenced to death, the trial was seen by outside observers as nothing more than an attempt by the Vietnamese communists to discredit the Khmer Rouge. On the other hand, it established a precedent for future domestic trials in Cambodia of Khmer Rouge leaders who oversaw the mass murder of 21 percent of Kampuchea's population between 1975 and 1979.[200]

These initial Vietnamese efforts were complicated by the fact that the United States and China, fearful of Vietnamese efforts to dominate Southeast Asia, supported Khmer Rouge attempts to "destabilize" Cambodia and neutralize Vietnamese power in the region.[201] The result was a lengthy civil war that finally ended in 1991 with a peace accord that allowed the Khmer Rouge to remain a viable force in Cambodia. Their power waned dramatically in the face of two successful democratic elections in 1993 and 1998, and the death of Pol Pot. [202]

The United States, which had been pouring money into Cambodia in the hope that it would become a "'peaceful, stable, progressive country,'" took a leading role in supporting Cambodian efforts to seek justice for those responsible for what the United Nations considered genocide.[203] In 1994, President Bill Clinton signed the Cambodian Genocide Justice Act (1994) that stated:

> Consistent with international law, it is the policy of the United States to support efforts to bring to justice members of the Khmer Rouge for their crimes against humanity committed in Cambodia between April 17, 1975 and January 7, 1979.[204]

The US Department of State's East Asia and Pacific Affairs Desk created an Office of Cambodian Genocide Investigation that began to look into such crimes, and shared this evidence with the Cambodian government and any other national or international tribunal that sought to prosecute those responsible for genocide or crimes against humanity in Cambodia from 1975 to 1979.[205]

The Cambodian government of Hun Sen, a former Khmer Rouge officer who has ruled Cambodia since 1985, also asked the United Nations for similar help. Three years later, the United Nations created a legal advisory body, the Group of Experts on Cambodia, which suggested three options for bringing Khmer Rouge leaders to justice—an ad hoc UN-created tribunal, a "Cambodian tribunal under United Nations administration," or "an international tribunal established by a multinational treaty and trials in third States."[206] Phnom Penh responded by asking the United Nations to help in "drafting legislation that would provide for a special national court to try Khmer Rouge leaders and that would provide for foreign judges and prosecutors to participate in its proceedings."[207] In 2001, the Cambodian legislature, impatient with the slow pace of discussions with the United Nations on this question, passed the *Law on the Extraordinary Chambers* (LEC). The new law immediately created problems for the United Nations since it

> could spell doom for the minimal threshold of international standards of due process and the necessary protection of international personnel required by the United Nations.[208]

This led UN secretary general Kofi Annan to cancel talks with the Cambodian government over the question of creating a joint tribunal.[209] The principal reason was concern that the LEC would not guarantee that such a tribunal would follow "international standards of justice," including due process. This concern was compounded by the fact, at least from the United Nations' perspective, that Cambodian judges were "too corrupt and politicized" to conduct fair trials.[210]

There were those in the United Nations who disagreed with Annan's decision, and convinced Hun Sen to revise the LEC law to meet more rigid international legal standards. Talks resumed between the United Nations and the Cambodian government, which led to a 2003–2004 law—*Law on the Establishment of Extraordinary Chambers in the Courts of Cambodia (ECCC) for the Prosecution of Crimes Committed during the Period of Democratic Kampuchea,* that embraced the core legal concepts of the ICTY and the ICTR statutes.[211] Its focus was to try

> senior leaders of Democratic Kampuchea and those who were most responsible for the crimes and serious violations of Cambodian penal law, international humanitarian law and custom, and international conventions recognized by Cambodia, that were committed during the period from 17 April 1975 to 6 January 1979.[212]

The ECCC based its authority to conduct such trials on the 1956 Cambodian Penal Code, the Genocide Convention, and the Geneva Conventions. Article 29 of the ECCC law stipulated that any "suspect who planned, instigated, ordered, aided and abetted, or committed the crimes listed in articles 3–8" shall "be individually responsible for the crimes." A suspect's rank would not relieve him or her of criminal responsibility for these crimes. The same was true for the questions of command and superior responsibility.[213] The law created a Trial Chamber of five judges, which included three Cambodians (one of whom would serve as president), and a seven-member Supreme Court Chamber with four Cambodian judges, which served "both as an appellate chamber and [chamber of] final instance."[214] It stipulated that judges had to "have high moral character, a spirit of impartiality and integrity, and experience, particularly in criminal law or international law, including international humanitarian law and human rights law."[215] The tribunal would have two co-prosecutors—one Cambodian, and one non-Cambodian—while investigations would be handled by two investigating judges—one Cambodian and one non-Cambodian.[216] The trials would theoretically afford defendants the same legal protections and rights as other international tribunals, while the costs of running the tribunal would be shared by the Cambodian government and the United Nations Trust Fund (UNTF), which would solicit voluntary contributions from various UN members for this purpose.[217]

It took two years before the court became operable, and another three before it began its first trial. In 2007, Leang Chea and Robert Petit, the tribunal's co-prosecutors, filed an Introductory Submission to the court that focused on their investigations of the crimes committed by the Khmer Rouge. It stated that

> These crimes were committed as part of a common criminal plan constituting a systematic and unlawful denial of basic rights of the Cambodian population and the targeted persecution of specific groups. The purported motive of this common criminal plan was to effect a radical change of Cambodian society and ideological lines. Those responsible for these crimes and policies included senior leaders of the Democratic Kampuchea regime. The coprosecutors have identified and submitted for investigation 25 distinct factual situations of murder, torture, forcible transfer, unlawful detention, forced labor and religious, political and ethnic persecution as evidence of the crimes committed in the execution of this common plan. The factual allegation constitutes crimes against humanity, genocide, grave breaches of the Geneva

Conventions, homicide, torture, and religious persecution. The preliminary investigation has resulted in the identification of five suspects who committed, aided, abetted and/or bore superior responsibility for those crimes. The coprosecutors are satisfied that these suspects were senior leaders of Democratic Kampuchea and/or those most responsible for the crimes committed within the jurisdiction of the ECCC.[218]

Those indicted for these crimes were:

Case 001:
Kaing Guek Eav (alias, Duch). Chairman of the Khmer Rouge Security Center S-Phnom Penh. Found guilty of crimes against humanity and grave breaches of the Geneva Convention. *Sentenced to 35 years imprisonment (later 30). Changed, on final appeal, to life imprisonment with credit for time served.*[219]

Case 002:
Ieng Sary. Former Deputy Prime Minister for Foreign Affairs. Pol Pot's brother-in-law. Remained active in Khmer politics in exile after 1979. Convicted by 1979 tribunal of genocide. Charged with superior responsibility for crimes against humanity, genocide, and grave breaches. *Proceedings ended after death on March 14, 2013.*
Ieng Thirith. Wife of Ieng Sary. Minister of Social Affairs. Charged with having planned, instigated, and aided and abetted in crimes against humanity, genocide, and grave breaches of the Geneva Conventions. *Found medically unfit (dementia) to stand trial, released, and under "judicial supervision."*
Khieu Samphân (alias Hem Nân). Head of State. Confidante of Pol Pot. Charged with involvement in joint criminal enterprise and superior responsibility for having planned, instigated, ordered or aided and abetted crimes against humanity, genocide, and grave breaches of the Geneva Conventions. *Trial ongoing as of October 2013.*
Nuon Chea. Member of Standing Committee of the CPK (Communist Party, Kampuchea) and Chairman of People's Assembly. Responsible for party and state security. Charged with being involved in a joint criminal enterprise and superior responsibility for having planned, instigated, ordered, or aided and abetted in crimes against humanity, genocide, and grave breaches of the Geneva Conventions. *Found fit to stand trial after medical assessment in spring 2013.*[220]

Their trials have used the European "inquisitorial model of criminal procedure," drawn principally from France, which once ruled Cambodia. This model includes investigations by co-investigatory judges, the participation of the defendants in this process, the right of victims to play a role in the proceedings as "'civil parties,'" broader appellate rights, "court-driven" discovery, "literal rules of evidence," and the "creation of a *dossier* (a Case File)."[221] But the ECCC has taken these rights further, and, according to Gabriela González Rivas, who headed the tribunal's victims' unit, has given victims the right "to participate as parties." This gave them legal standing similar to those of the defendants, meaning that they can play a role in the investigation, have counsel, call witnesses, and question a defendant during a trial.

> Participation in these types of proceedings is a tool of empowerment...People can tell their story, feel that what happened to them is a consideration, a recognition that what happened to them shouldn't have happened.[222]

Another innovation in this trial was the introduction of the charge of joint criminal enterprise against Kaing Guek Eav (Comrade "Duch"), a low ranking official. According to Gregory Stanton, the founder of Genocide Watch, the reason for trying a lower ranking official first was quite simple. He's

> going to spill the beans on everybody else...He's converted to Christianity, and I'm convinced his conversion was genuine. He's said he wanted to confess to all the things he's done, and since then he's really talked.[223]

Initially, the tribunal refused to consider this charge against Kaing. However, it reversed its decision after a prosecutorial appeal, and a number of friends of the court (*amicus curiae*) briefs. One, written by Antonio Cassese, the first president of the ICTY, and three other well-known jurists, stated that from

> 1975–1979 there existed customary rules in international criminal law providing for three distinct modes of JCE liability. These rules were applicable to Cambodia. JCE may be applied by the Extraordinary Chambers in keeping with the principle *nullum crimen sine lege* [no crime or punishment without a law] and should be applied where appropriate to accurately reflect the full gravity of crimes and ensure consistency in uses of modes of liability in international criminal law.[224]

In its new judgment, the Cambodian court cited Nuremberg, ICTY, and other precedents to underscore what it argued was a JCE charge anchored in "customary international law." It added that article 29 of the ECCC Law, while not specifically mentioning JCE, mirrored ICTY and ICTR statutes on this question.[225]

Kaing's trial, which began with initial hearings on February 17, 2009, ended with closing statements on November 27, 2009. He was charged with crimes against humanity and grave breaches of the Geneva Conventions as well as "the national crimes of premeditated murder and torture. In the alternative, he is responsible by virtue of superior responsibility."[226] Evidence presented during his trial documented over 12,000 instances of such crimes. This is the reason that Richard Bernstein called him "one of the worst mass murderers of recent history."[227] Though Kaing had already admitted his guilt in pretrial statements, he apologized openly for his crimes in court on March 31, 2009.

> My name is Kaing Guek Eav. When I joined the revolution I used the name of Duch. I entered the revolution to liberate my own people, including my parents, my relatives, myself. That's why I was compelled to accept the task. At that time, in that regime, I saw no other alternative to solve the matter except to respect the discipline of the party. Sometimes we have to do a job we do not like. I would like to emphasize that I am responsible for the crimes committed at S-21, especially the torture and execution of the people there. I would like to express my regret and my heartfelt sorrow and loss for all the crimes committed by the CPK from 1975–1979.[228]

He did not personally kill any of those who were murdered at S-21, but led, planned, and supervised those that did. Those sent to S-21 were members of the Khmer Rouge who were suspected of being traitors, with each "destined for execution."[229]

Kaing became what Bernstein calls "a concierge of the machine of murder" who oversaw the torture and forced confessions of S-21's 14,000 prisoners. They were tortured until Duch was convinced that their confessions "were complete." Though most of what was in these confessions was false, they were meant to please the party leadership, who were motivated by a violent revolutionary zeal that blended "a mosaic of idealism and butchery, exaltation and horror, compassion and brutality."[230] Testimony throughout the trial documented Kaing's gruesome torture methods.

> The vast majority of persons interrogated at S21 were repeatedly and intentionally subjected to severe interrogation methods, which often resulted in serious physical injuries and severe mental harm...There is evidence of at least one coercive sexual penetration committed at S21, when an interrogator inserted a stick into a female prisoners' genitals...Beatings resulted in bleeding and multiple injuries such as broken limbs, loss of hearing, loss of teeth, scars and sometimes death...electrocution...caused the detainees to lose consciousness—and in certain cases to become impotent, delirious or to die. Placing a plastic bag over the detainees' head induced a sensation of suffocation and made them believe that they were dying. Death ensued in at least one instance. The Accused acknowledged that detainees were subjected to water boarding, which entailed pouring water into their nose to induce a sensation of suffocation and drowning.[231]

Kaing also admitted that there were times when the detainees were force-fed excrement. In the end, he testified, the goal of these methods was simple.[232]

> To force them to confess. Therefore, it was both the force physically, the physical pain, and with the scolding, with the verbal abuse, it contributed to the psychological suffering upon the confessors so that they would give in to confession.[233]

Given Kaing's admission of guilt, it was not difficult for the tribunal to find him guilty of the numerous charges against him. His defense team, though, argued that he was simply following "superior orders" while "under duress." It also noted that he had cooperated openly with the tribunal, had expressed remorse for his crimes, and could possibly be rehabilitated.[234] While the court rejected the claim of superior orders and duress as mitigating factors, it did think that Kaing's cooperation was an issue to consider in reaching its judgment. Consequently, though it convicted him of all charges, the court decided that there were enough mitigating circumstances to limit his sentence to "a finite term of imprisonment" instead of life. Consequently, it sentenced him to 35 years imprisonment but reduced it by five years because of his illegal detention by the Cambodian Military Court from 1999 to 2007.[235] He appealed this decision to the Supreme Court Chamber, which added an "additional conviction for the crimes against humanity of extermination (encompassing murder), enslavement, imprisonment, torture, and other inhumane acts."[236] It then sentenced him to life imprisonment.

The trial for Case 002 began several months earlier, though the proceedings against Ieng Sary ended after his death on March 14, 2013. The same was true for Ieng Thirith, who was declared mentally unfit to stand trial. The court considered a similar judgment for Nuon Chea after a detailed mental and physical investigation in the spring of 2013. It concluded:

> Notwithstanding the advanced age and frailty of the accused and the accused's precarious physical health, the testimony of the medical experts clearly indicate that the accused remains capable of participating in his own defence.[237]

Each of the defendants was charged with crimes against humanity, grave breaches of the Geneva Conventions, and genocide. The French co-investigating judge, Marcel Lemonde, stated that it was "'a more complex case even than the Nuremberg Trials.'" He added that he and his co-judge, Bunleng You, had put together a case file of over 350,000 pages that would lead to "a high judicial debate."[238] According to observers, if the trial was unsuccessful, it "would always remind people of the larger failures of the court and suggest that he [Duch] was a scapegoat."[239]

Case 002 proved more difficult to conduct, not only because of the death of Ieng Sary and his wife's dementia, but also because, unlike Case 001, which focused on crimes in S-21, crimes in Case 002 were committed throughout Cambodia. Leang Chea underscored the breadth of these crimes when she opened for the prosecution on November 21, 2011.

> The evidence we will put before you will show that starting on the 17th of April 1975 the Communist Party of Kampuchea turned Cambodia into a massive slave camp, reducing an entire nation to prisoners living under a system of brutality that defies belief to the present day. The forced evacuation of Cambodian cities, the enslavement of millions of people in forced labour camps; the smashing of hundreds of thousands of lives in notorious security centres and the killing fields; the extermination of minorities; the countless deaths from disease, exhaustion, abuse and starvation—these crimes ordered and orchestrated by the Accused, were among the worst horrors inflicted on any nation in modern history. Every Cambodian who was alive during this period was affected by the criminal system of oppression which these accused put in place. The death toll is staggering. The demographic experts appointed by the investigating Judges have estimated that between 1.7 and 2.2 million people died as a result of CPK rule. Approximately one in four Cambodians did not survive this regime.[240]

She followed up with a litany of specific horrors drawn from witness testimony and other evidence that documented these crimes. They were committed as part of the "common criminal plan to which the accused agree[d] and significantly contributed." The nature of these crimes, she went on, were also grave breaches of the Geneva Conventions. But this was not, she added, a trial of revenge. Instead, it was about "the ascertainment of the truth and the determination of guilt."[241]

> To the despots and perpetrators of atrocities around the world we will send this message; Justice never forgets...
> In the words of Buddha: "overcome the angry with non-anger. Overcome the wicked by goodness. Overcome the miser by generosity. Overcome the liar by truth."[242]

The following day, Nuon Chea took the stand, and blamed the alleged crimes on threats from Vietnamese agents. After thanking the court for the opportunity to explain his policies, he declared himself to be a Cambodian patriot who wanted "to pay my respects to our ancestors who sacrificed their flesh, blood, bone and life to defend our motherland."[243] He argued that he had been falsely accused and that "only certain facts are to be adjudicated by this Court."

> I must say only the body of the crocodile is to be discussed, not its head or the tails, which are the important parts of its daily activities.[244]

He claimed that the crimes detailed by Leang Chea and her new co-prosecutor, Andrew Cayley, in their opening remarks, were "not true."[245] But instead of addressing them, he told the court that he was motivated by a determination to fight against Vietnamese efforts "to destroy the revolution of the Kampuchean people and the development in Cambodia and its democracy."[246] His only goal, he added, had been

> to serve the interests of the nation and the people. May I be heard that oppression, injustice had compelled me to devote myself to fight for my country.
> I had to leave my family behind to liberate my motherland from colonialism and aggression and oppression by the forces, by the thieves who wished to steal our land and wipe Cambodia off the face of the world...we want to build in Cambodia a society that is clean, independent without any killing of people or genocide.[247]

He did allude to the crimes mentioned by Chea and Cayley, but argued that

> If we had shown mercy to these people, our nation would have been lost. We didn't kill many...We only killed the bad people, not the good.[248]

As expected, Ieng Sary refused to respond to the prosecutors' opening remarks, but did read a very brief opening statement on November 23. Wheelchair bound, he told the judges that he was exhausted and did not want to take part in the trial. However, "out of respect for this institution, I will continue to participate as I have always done so since I was charged, arrested, and brought to the ECCC detention facilities."[249]

Like Chea, Khieu Samphân dismissed the charges against him, arguing that they were based on nothing more than the "'guess-work'" of unnamed witnesses.[250] He reminded the court of the suffering that his country faced not only under the Khmer Rouge's predecessors, but also during the last years of the Vietnam War, when the

> United States carpeted the small Kampuchean territory with bombs, [which] outnumbered those numbers of bombs the alliance used during the Second World War everywhere, including the two big bombs dropped on Hiroshima and Nagasaki.[251]

Though it is difficult accurately to estimate the bombing tonnage and number of victims from these raids, Taylor Owen and Ben Kiernan estimate that the United States dropped 2.75 million tons of bombs on Cambodia from 1965 to 1973, compared to 2 million tons during World War II. Though some estimates place the number of Cambodians killed during these raids between 50,000 and 150,000, they think the "number of casualties is surely higher."[252]

Khieu added that he was not on the Standing Committee of the CPK, and that he was not part of a joint criminal enterprise. He knew nothing about the murders and had no role in the other crimes that he was charged with. And though he admitted that he "occupied an official senior position in Democratic Kampuchea," he was not "part of the decision-making process" and was not aware of "all that was happening in our country."[253]

The tragedy of the cases against Khieu and the other defendants is that they will probably be the last to be tried before the ECCC, since efforts to bring other alleged Cambodian war criminals to justice have been unsuccessful. In 2009, Robert Petit decided that there was ample evidence to open new cases against five suspects—Sou Met, former air force commander, and Meas Muth, former navy commander (Case 003)—and three Khmer Rouge regional officials—Aom An, Yim Tith, and Im Chen (Case 004). Leang Chea, his Cambodian counterpart, disagreed, saying that more indictments would be "destabilizing." Moreover, she thought that further trials would cost too much and "violate the spirit of the tribunal." Hun Sen agreed, and stated that he thought trying four or five people was sufficient. Peter Maguire, the author of *Facing Death in Cambodia*, said that he suspected that Hun's plan was just to try Kaing, and hoped that the other defendants, who were in their late seventies or early eighties, would die before their trials began.[254]

Petit overrode these objections, and submitted these cases to the pretrial chamber. Its three Cambodian judges opposed accepting the cases, a decision overridden by the two international judges, who referred it to the investigating judges, Siegfried Blunk of Germany and Bunleng You. They announced in the spring of 2011 that they had finished their investigation of Case 003, which was interpreted to mean it was closed. Many members of the United Nations' investigative staff resigned in protest, while Human Rights Watch demanded Blunk's resignation. Blunk did just that, though a new controversy soon developed over his replacement—Swiss jurist Laurent Kaspar-Ansermet. Cambodia's Supreme Council of Magistracy initially refused to accept his nomination by the United Nations, which the international organization called "'a matter of serious concern,'" and a violation of the 2003 agreement on trying Khmer Rouge war criminals.[255] Though the Cambodians relented, Kaspar-Ansermet soon resigned after he reopened Case 003, citing "an increasingly hostile work environment." Now that two of the four original defendants in Case 002 have died or have been declared medically unfit to stand trial, it is doubtful that any new cases will be brought before the ECCC. At best, when its deliberations end, the ECCC will have convicted three Khmer Rouge officials for the vast crimes committed in Cambodia from 1975 to 1979.[256]

Guantánamo

Though the crimes adjudicated by the ECCC are quite different from those before the US military commission tribunals at the Guantánamo naval base in Cuba, they have both been clouded by significant controversy. One of the more troublesome aspects of the 9/11 tragedy and the subsequent wars in Afghanistan and Iraq, at least legally speaking, have been questions about the torture of prisoners at the Joint Task Force Guantánamo prison in Cuba and elsewhere, and the decision to try some of the prisoners under the 1996 *War Crimes Act*. This law, which was passed with widespread support by both houses of Congress, gives the US government the right to prosecute anyone who commits a "war crime" against a member of the US Armed Forces or a US national. The law defines a "war crime" as any violation of the Geneva Convention of August 12, 1949, which deals with the "Protection of Civilian Persons in Time of War" and its *Protocol Additional* of June 8, 1977.[257]

Though the United States has been involved in a decades-long campaign against international terrorists, the al-Qaida attacks on September 11, 2001, traumatized a nation and a new president unprepared for suicide assaults against two cities—New York and Washington—that symbolized the great wealth and power of the United States. This was the first time since Pearl Harbor that foreign nationals wreaked such havoc on American soil. President George W. Bush quickly announced that the United States was now involved in an ongoing war on terror and on September 18 sent Congress *The Authorization for Use of Military Force* bill that gave him the authority

> to use all necessary and appropriate force against those nations, organizations, or persons he determines planned, authorized, committed, or aided the terrorist attacks that occurred on September 11, 2001, or harbored such organizations or persons, in order to prevent any future acts of international terrorism against the United States by such nations, organizations or persons.[258]

Passed by both houses of Congress, it provided the Bush White House with the vast authority it needed to wage a global war against a vast array of international enemies. Five weeks later, Congress expanded the president's authority by passing the controversial *USA Patriot Act*, which gave the executive branch vast authority to use the country's intelligence community

> to gather intelligence information and then to apprehend and bring to some sort of justice suspected terrorists and their supporters in the United States as well as abroad.[259]

A year later, at the White House's instigation, Congress passed the *Authorization for the Use of Military Force against Iraq Resolution of 2002* (October 16, 2002), which gave the president the power to wage war against Iraq because, it argued, that country was involved in the 9/11 attacks and had weapons of mass destruction. More specifically, it gave the president, in consultation with Congress, the right to

(1) defend the national security of the United States against the continuing threat posed by Iraq; and
(2) enforce all relevant United Nations Security Council resolutions regarding Iraq.[260]

According to the BBC, this legislation meant that President Bush "was fully authorized to use force 'as he sees fit.'"[261]

In the midst of all of this, the White House decided to intern newly captured detainees at Guantánamo Bay, Cuba (GBC). Though it considered other bases, it finally settled on this remote 45-square-mile outpost in Cuba because, according to a memorandum from two Department of Justice lawyers, Patrick Philbin and John Yoo, in late December 2001, it was legally beyond the reach of any federal court that might consider a *habeas corpus* petition from the detainees.[262] The Bush administration also developed a series of policies about the treatment of al-Qaida and Taliban detainees, who began to be sent to Guantánamo from Afghanistan in early 2002.[263] On February 7, 2002, President Bush decided that "none of the detainees held at Guantánamo would have any legal rights under the Geneva Conventions," while later that summer, the White House approved the use of water boarding and other "'enhanced interrogation techniques'" on "certain detainees held by the CIA."[264]

These were backed by a series of memos from the Department of Justice that supported these decisions for those suspected of belonging to al-Qaida and the Taliban. One, to White House Counsel Alberto R. Gonzales on August 1, 2002, stated that torture was an act that caused pain both "difficult to endure" as well as "mental harm." However, the memo went on, the 1984 *Convention against Torture and Other Cruel, Inhuman and Degrading Treatment or Punishment* (CAT), which the United States ratified in 1994, was not applicable to the interrogation and torture of al-Qaida members and "its Allies" because it "would represent an unconstitutional infringement of the President's authority to conduct war." Moreover, "under the current circumstances, necessity or self-defense may justify interrogation methods that might violate Section 2340A [18 U.S. Code]."[265] It then went on to analyze in detail the legal standing of a "defendant of torture" vis-à-vis sections 2340 and 2340A, which a 2004 Department of Justice memo explained was enacted by Congress "to carry out the United States' obligations under the CAT."[266] The 2004 memo explained that as long as an individual defendant showed "good faith" intentions that his torture methods would not cause prolonged physical or mental harm, then this "would negate" any charge that his intentions were a violation of sections 2340–2340A.[267] In the end, it concluded that the Justice Department's interpretation of Section 2340A was only applicable to "the most egregious conduct," or the "most heinous acts."[268] The memo concluded that

> necessity and self-defense could justify interrogation methods needed to elicit information to prevent a direct and imminent threat to the United States and its citizens.[269]

Actually, sections 2340 and 2340A carefully reflect article 1 of the CAT, which states that torture means any act by which severe pain or suffering, whether physical or mental, is intentionally inflicted on a person for such purposes as obtaining from him or a third person information or a confession, punishing him for an act he or a third person has committed or is suspected of having committed, or intimidating or coercing him or a third person, or for any reason based on discrimination of any kind, when such pain or suffering is inflicted by or at the instigation of or with the consent or acquiescence of a public official or other person acting in an official capacity. It does not include pain or suffering arising only from, inherent in, or incidental to lawful sanctions. [270]

Section 2340 says that torture is an

> act committed by a person acting under the color of law specifically intended to inflict severe physical or mental pain or suffering (other than pain or suffering incidental to lawful sanctions) upon another person within his custody or physical control.[271]

It goes on to define the various dimensions of such torture as that which causes "'severe mental pain or suffering'" threatened "imminent death," or threats against another person with such abuse, including the "administration or application of mind altering procedures calculated to disrupt profoundly the senses or personality." It concludes by noting that such strictures were applicable to all states within the United States plus the District of Columbia as well as "the commonwealths, territories, and possessions of the United States."[272] Section 2340A deals with those outside of the United States who commit such crimes, and states that they could be subject to a fine, not more than 20 years imprisonment or, in the case of the death of a detainee, life imprisonment or death. Such punishments were applicable not only to a US national, but anyone who "is present in the U.S. regardless of their nationality." Moreover, anyone involved in a conspiracy to commit such crimes could suffer the same penalties.[273]

While the August 2002 memo was respectful of the CAT and 18 U.S.C. 2340 and 2340A, its intention was to justify methods of interrogation that would normally be considered illegal under these statutes. Consequently, this analysis, in league with other Justice Department reports, helped convince Secretary of Defense Donald Rumsfeld to issue a secret memo on December 2, 2002, that gave military interrogators permission to use 15 techniques already in use by the CIA in its evolving network of "black site" interrogation centers around the world. Rumsfeld's memo divided these techniques into three categories.

Category I
incentive; yelling at detainee; deception; multiple interrogator techniques; interrogator identity.

Category II
stress positions for a maximum of four hours (e.g. standing) [in a note attached to this memo, Rumsfeld suggested 8–10 hours]; use of falsified documents or reports; isolation for up to 30 days (requires notice); interrogation outside of the standard interrogation booth; deprivation of light and auditory stimuli; hooding during transport & interrogation; use of 20 hour interrogations; removal of all comfort items; switching detainee from hot meal to MRE; removal of clothing; forced grooming (e.g. shaving); inducing stress by use of detainee's fears (e.g., dogs)

Category III
use of mild, non-injurious physical contact.[274]

According to Rumsfeld, he approved these new methods after interrogators at GBC asked for enhanced methods because they claimed they were getting nowhere using protocols laid out in the US Army's 1992 *Intelligence Interrogation* manual (FM 34–52).[275] The manual stated that interrogations had to done in a "lawful manner," and that any person interrogated, even if he was a suspected terrorist, was to be granted "P[O]W protection until their precise status had been determined by competent authority." Moreover, the manual prohibited "acts of violence or intimidation, including physical or mental torture, threats, insults, or exposure to inhumane treatment as a means or aid to interrogations."[276]

A draft of Rumsfeld's memo was sent to all branches of the military in October, and each raised concerns about these "enhanced methods." They argued that they might "'constitute criminal conduct'" that could possibly "'expose our service members to possible prosecution.'" The Army's JAG office added that "many of the techniques violated the provisions against torture and inhumane treatment of the International Criminal Court," and would "'not read well in either *The New York Times* or *The Cairo Times*.'" The head of the Department of Defense's Criminal Investigation Task Force warned that the use of such techniques "may subject service members to punitive articles of the Uniform Code of Military Justice." Such concerns led Capt. (now Rear Admiral) Jane Dalton, the counsel to the Joint Chiefs of Staff, to initiate a legal review of the Rumsfeld draft, which Williams Haynes, Rumsfeld's general counsel, told her to stop.[277]

The reference to the International Criminal Court or more specifically the 1998 Rome Statute that brought it into force in 2002 is particularly important. The Clinton administration signed the Rome Statute on December 31, 2000, though the Bush administration revoked this accession in the spring of 2002. Several months later, Senator Jesse Helms introduced the *American Service Members Protection Act*, which President Bush signed into law on August 2, 2002. Its stated purpose was to protect US citizens from prosecution by the ICC, and forbade all cooperation with it. It also placed restrictions on US participation in certain UN peacekeeping operations, and pledged that the United States would use all means possible to free any member of the Armed Forces or "certain other persons" detained for possible ICC prosecution.[278] Particularly troubling to the Bush White House was article 7. 1 (e) of the Rome Statute, which states that torture is a crime against humanity, which it defines as

> the intentional infliction of severe pain or suffering, whether physical or mental, upon a person in the custody or under the control of the accused; except that torture shall not include pain or suffering arising only from, inherent in or incidental to, lawful sanctions.[279]

Such actions by the US government, of course, deliberately placed the United States outside of the jurisdiction of the first permanent international criminal court in history, which had been created to "try and punish...the most serious violations of human rights in cases when national justice systems fail at the task." Though US opposition to the court would soften as more and more interrogation crimes surfaced, it has, to date, refused to become a party to the ICC.

Over time, GBC interrogators developed methods that went far beyond those listed in Rumsfeld's memo, and began using them on the alleged twentieth 9/11 hijacker, Mohammed al-Qahtani. They abused him so badly that the United States dropped charges against him in 2009 because his treatment met "the legal definition of torture."[280] Such illegal methods soon drew the attention of FBI agents, who were sent to Cuba to observe CIA techniques. One wrote in late 2002, "'You won't believe it [the abuses]!'" a reference to "the 'coercive tactics' being employed indiscriminately on the detainees." Other FBI agents not only questioned these brutal methods but also doubted their "'effectiveness.'"[281] Al-Qahtani, for example,

> was forced to wear a woman's bra and had a thong placed on his head during the course of the interrogation...[he was] told that his mother and sister were whores...[he was told] he was a homosexual, had homosexual tendencies, and that other detainees had

found out about these tendencies...On 20 December 02, an interrogator tied a leash to the subject...led him around the room, and forced him to perform a series of dog tricks.[282]

But GBC was not the only facility where such abuses were taking place. The ICRC released a report in early 2004 detailing similar mistreatment by military intelligence officers at the US military prison at Abu Ghraib outside of Baghdad. These included

beatings with hard objects...pressing the face into the ground with boots...being paraded naked outside cells in front of other persons deprived of their liberty, and guards, sometimes hooded or with women's underwear over the head...acts of humiliation such as being made to stand naked against the wall of the cell with arms raised or with women's underwear over the head for prolonged periods—while being laughed at by guards, including female guards, sometimes photographed in this position.[283]

Interestingly, the head of the military interrogation unit at Abu Ghraib, Capt. Carolyn Wood, had served in a similar position at Bagram air force base in Afghanistan, where "wholesale abuse of detainees...was rampant."[284] The abuses at Abu Ghraib were publicly exposed in a May 10, 2004, article in the *New Yorker* by Seymour Hersh, which was based on an earlier Department of Defense (DOD) investigation. The DOD report called what had taken place at Abu Ghraib in the fall of 2003 "acts of brutality and purposeless sadism." Photographs, which were later made public, revealed

abuses, unacceptable even in wartime, [that] were not part of authorized interrogations nor were they even directed at intelligence targets. They represent deviant behavior and a failure of military leadership and discipline.[285]

They included:

Breaking chemical lights and pouring the phosphoric liquid on detainees; pouring cold water on naked detainees; beating detainees with a broom handle and a chair; threatening male detainees with rape, allowing a military police guard to stitch the wound of a detainee who was injured after being slammed against the wall in his cell; sodomizing a detainee with a chemical light and perhaps a broom stick, and using military working dogs to frighten and intimidate detainees with threats of attack, and in one instance actually biting a detainee.[286]

International outrage forced President Bush to condemn such methods and issue a directive "that the United States not engage in torture." Later that year, the Justice Department withdrew the August 1, 2002, memorandum, and replaced it with a much less detailed one that said "torture is abhorrent both to American law and values and to international norms." It said that it was not necessary to revisit the question about the president's "power and the potential defenses to liability," and all that was necessary to address such abuses was to modify some of the earlier analysis and interpretation of 18 U.S.C. 2340–2340A.[287]

In 2006, Physicians for Human Rights did a detailed series of medical evaluations of 11 detainees who were captured in Afghanistan and later sent to Guantánamo, or were captured and imprisoned in Iraq. It concluded in its report that senior US officials approved "'take the gloves off'" torture methods that went "beyond the draconian methods approved at various times between 2002 and 2004." Retired Maj. Gen. Antonio Taguba, who conducted the army's investigation into the Abu Ghraib scandal, stated in the preface that

> there is no longer any doubt as to whether the current administration has committed war crimes. The only question that remains to be answered is whether those who ordered the use of torture will be held to account.[288]

For the most part, none were. The US Army dropped charges against the two officers in charge of the military police units at Bagram and Ghraib, while only one senior commander, Lt. Col. Steven Jordan, was court-martialed for eight charges for the crimes committed at the Iraqi military prison. He was only found guilty on one charge—"disobeying an order from General [George] Fay not to discuss his case with potential witnesses." Jordan's conviction was later overturned by the commanding general of the US Military District in Washington, while his immediate superior, Col. Thomas Pappas, was granted immunity from prosecution.[289]

Finally, on August 30, 2012, Attorney Gen. Eric Holder announced that the Justice Department would not prosecute any CIA operatives for the death of two prisoners in Afghanistan and Iraq because

> the admissible evidence would not be sufficient to obtain and sustain a conviction beyond a reasonable doubt.

This did not, Holder added, "resolve the broader questions regarding the propriety of the examined conduct." To date, only one former CIA agent, John C. Kiriakou, who has spoken openly about water boarding, is now awaiting trial, but not for torture. Instead, he is charged with disclosing the names of CIA agents who took part in the interrogations of al-Qaida detainees in Afghanistan.[290] A September 2, 2012, *New York Times* editorial criticized the Obama administration for its failure to look more closely into the abuses committed during the Bush administration.

> Not only have those responsible escaped criminal liability, but the administration has succeeded in denying victims of the harsh methods any day in court, using exaggerated claims of secrecy and executive power to get federal judges, who should know better, to toss out claims for civil relief. The broad denial of justice to victims disgraces both the administration and the courts.[291]

The revelations about prisoner abuse at Guantánamo and other US military prisons in 2004 had a transformative effect on their rights. Almost from the moment that the detainees began to arrive at GBC in 2002, their lawyers began filing cases in the US District Court of the District of Columbia to win basic due process and counsel rights for their clients, something they were initially denied by the Bush administration, who considered the detainees unlawful enemy aliens. The administration's basic argument in these cases was that

> regardless of whether there was an ongoing war, the courts did not have the jurisdiction or the authority even to hear the claims of the Guantánamo detainees *solely* because they were foreign citizens and Guantánamo was not in the sovereign territory of the United States.[292]

This ultimately led to the Supreme Court's *Rasul v. Bush* decision on June 24, 2004, which ruled that the detainees had the right to challenge "the legality of their detention at" GBC and the "'privilege of litigation' in U.S. courts."[293]

Three weeks later, conspiracy charges were filed against Salim Ahmed Hamdan in what was to be Guantánamo's first trial. The indictment read:

> Salem Ahmed Hamdan, in Afghanistan, Pakistan, Yemen and other countries, from on or about February 1996 to on or about November 24, 2001, willfully and knowingly joined an enterprise of persons who shared a common criminal purpose and conspired and agreed with Usama bin Laden, Saif al Adel, Dr. Ayman al Zawahiri (a/l/a "the Doctor"), Muhammed Atef, the al Qaida organization, known and unknown, to commit the following offenses triable by military commission: attacking civilians; attacking civilian objects; murder by an unprivileged belligerent; destruction of property by an unprivileged belligerent; and terrorism.

Hamdan was also accused of delivering weapons and ammunition to members of al-Qaida, and serving as bin Laden's driver.[294] In early September 2004, Hamdan's lawyers, Navy Lt. Cmdr. Charles Swift and Georgetown law professor Neal Katyal, filed a brief with the US District Court in Washington that argued that the Hamdan case established

> an unprecedented and dangerous expansion of Executive Branch authority cloaked in the exercise of the President's war powers...Far from the battlefield and remote from any zone of military occupation, the President has unilaterally created a military commission, justified by a so-called war on terrorism.[295]

Two months later, the District Court ruled that until it had been determined that Hamdan was "not entitled to POW status," he could only be tried by court-martial under the Uniform Code of Military Justice (UCMJ). It also ordered that he be released from solitary confinement and sent back into the general GBC population.[296]

This decision was quickly overturned by the United States Court of Appeals, District of Columbia Circuit, in the spring of 2005. It's brief decision stated that Congress had "authorized the military commission that will try Hamdan," and that such a military body was the "'competent tribunal'" to try him. It added that as a "stateless terrorist," he was not protected by the Geneva Conventions.[297] Hamdan's lawyers appealed this decision to the US Supreme Court, which reversed the Court of Appeals' ruling in a 5–3 decision on June 29, 2006. It argued that the "military commission at issue" is not specifically authorized by Congress and "lacks the power to proceed because its structure and procedures violate both the UCMJ and the four Geneva Conventions signed in 1949."[298]

Congress responded almost immediately by passing a *Military Commissions Act* that gave the president authority to create such tribunals. It defined lawful and unlawful enemy combatants, and stated that only the latter could be tried by such commissions. It also stipulated that the secretary of defense was to report any trials conducted by the commissions annually to Congress, and laid out the structure, procedure, and rules of such trials, including the exclusion of any statements "obtained by torture."[299] The procedures in such trials were to be based on those described for courts-martial in the UCMJ. The only exceptions were those regulations applicable to "speedy trials," "compulsory self-incrimination," and "pretrial investigation."[300] The decisions of the military commissions, which were to be made up of no less than five officers, required the "concurrence of two-thirds of the members present."[301]

The new law added that after judgment, a case would automatically be referred to a Court of Military Commission Review (CMCR). It also gave the United States Court of Appeals, District of Columbia Circuit, "exclusive jurisdiction to determine the validity of a final judgement" after it had been approved by the "convening authority [the Secretary of Defense or his designee]."[302] And while a military commission could impose the death penalty, it could not be carried out without the approval of the president, and then only after a full review of the decision before the court of appeals and the denial of a *writ of certiorari* by the Supreme Court.[303]

The new military commission law also listed 28 crimes that could be tried by the tribunals. Two dealt with "terrorism" and "providing material support for terrorism."[304] It also stated that "no individual in the custody or under the physical control of the United States government, regardless of nationality or physical location, shall be subject to cruel, inhuman, or degrading treatment or punishment."[305] On the other hand, detainees were denied the right to apply to federal courts for *habeas corpus* rights.[306] The Supreme Court declared this particular section of the law unconstitutional in *Boumediene v. Bush* in 2008, reminding Congress that in considering

> both the procedural and substantive standards used to impose detention to prevent acts of terrorism, the courts must accord proper deference to the political branches. However, security subsists, too, in fidelity to freedom's first principles, chief among them being freedom from arbitrary and unlawful restraint and the personal liberty that is secured by adherence to the separation of powers.[307]

President Barack Obama decided soon after he came into office in 2009 to review the procedures of the military commissions and the detainee program at GBC with an eye toward closing the prison there in January 2010. He ordered a halt to all proceedings except for some pretrial hearings and the trial of Ahmed Ghailani, which was moved to New York. Ghailani, who was charged with over 280 counts of murder and conspiracy for his role in the bombings of US embassies in Kenya and Tanzania in 1998, was acquitted of all but one charge—conspiring to destroy government property—by a federal jury in Manhattan on November 17, 2010, and later sentenced to life imprisonment.[308] The decision to transfer Ghailani's case to federal court jurisdiction was widely criticized, though the Obama administration stated after his trial that it was still committed to trying the GBC detainees in civilian courts, but not in New York.[309]

Congressional and public criticism of this decision ultimately led the White House to announce the following summer that it was thinking about restarting the military commission trials but with some changes, which led to a new *Military Commissions Act* (2009).[310] It renamed the CMCR the United States Court of Military Commission Review, and expanded its authority to allow it to consider the "factual sufficiency of the evidence," which brought its review authority in line with the appeals system of the UCMJ. It also gave the president the authority to appoint civilian judges to the military commissions with the approval of the Senate. The new law was also much more "protective of appellate judges" than the UCMJ.[311]

In early 2010, the Guantánamo Review Task Force (GRTF), made up of representatives from the Departments of Justice, Defense, State, and Homeland Security plus the Joints Chiefs of Staff and the office of the Director of National Intelligence, completed the first of several reviews of the "status of all individuals" in prison at GBC as well as the question of closing the prison facilities there. It noted that since 2002, 779 "individuals have been detained at Guantánamo in connection with the war against al-Qaida, the Taliban, and associated forces." Of this number, 530 had been released or transferred to 36 other countries, with only 242 still in US custody there. Of this number, 126 were approved for transfer, while 44 "were referred for prosecution either in federal court or a military commission." The cases against 36 of those in this latter group were active or under investigation. Six were scheduled to be prosecuted in federal court and 6 more by military commissions. Another 48 detainees were considered too dangerous for transfer and would "remain in detention under the government's authority under the Authorization for Use of Military Force passed by Congress in response to the attacks of September 11, 2001." These detainees could challenge their incarceration in federal court, and their cases would periodically be reviewed by the executive branch. Another 30 detainees from Yemen were to remain in "'conditional'" detention based on the current security environment in that country. While there were no plans to return them to Yemen, they could be transferred there or to another country "if the current moratorium on transfers to Yemen is lifted and other security conditions are met."[312]

The uncertain status of many of those approved for transfer as well as general prison conditions and other issues led to a hunger strike in early 2013 that ultimately saw 100 out of GBC's remaining 166 prisoners risk death to protest what they considered numerous wrongs, legal and otherwise, at the facility. The US decision to force-feed many of them with tubes forced through their noses into their stomachs has renewed criticism of the operations of GBC and the question of prisoner rights.[313]

The five most important and dangerous prisoners in GBC—Khalid Sheikh Mohammed; Ramzi bin al-Shibh; Walid Muhammed Salih Mubarak Bin Atash; Mustafa Ahmed al-Hawsawi; and Ali Abdul Aziz Ali— key figures in the 9/11 attacks, did not participate in these protests because they are held in a special high security part of the prison. The GRTF report stated that they would be tried in a New York federal court less than a mile away from ground zero.[314] This decision became part of the larger controversy over closing the GBC prison and moving the detainees to a new site in the United States. However, as the January 2010 closing date neared, it became clear that locating a site in the United States was becoming increasingly problematic. One of the biggest obstacles to this was local and congressional opposition to housing dangerous terrorists in any domestic US facility.[315] Of particular concern were those prisoners "who cannot be put on trial ['because of problems with evidence'] but are deemed too dangerous to transfer or let go."[316] By the summer of 2010, the Obama administration seemed to have given up the idea of closing the Guantánamo prison even though it had found a viable site in Thomson, Illinois. The White House blamed Congress for failing to support this initiative,[317] particularly after the latter passed new legislation that placed "new curbs on moving prisoners to the U.S. from Guantánamo for any trials."[318]

This forced the government to rethink its plan to try Khalid Sheik Mohammed and his four co-conspirators in the 9/11 attacks in federal court. In early 2011, the White House announced that it planned to resume military commission trials in Guantánamo. By the spring of 2012, the tribunals had convicted seven of the detainees of various war crimes, many getting sentences far more lenient than those that might have been imposed by civilian courts. According to Clive Stafford Smith, a lawyer for the British human rights group Reprieve, the reason was simple. Those convicted were so desperate to be freed that they agreed to plea bargains that "don't make up for the harsh treatment the men suffered in the past."[319]

Such leniency will probably not be the case for the five 9/11 conspirators who, as "unprivileged enemy belligerents," were charged with

> attacking civilians; attacking civilian objects; intentionally causing serious bodily injury; murder in violation of the law of war; destruction in violation of the law of war; hijacking or hazarding a vessel or aircraft; terrorism.

The 2011 military commission charge sheet for the five alleged terrorists listed the names of each of the 2,976 people who died during the 9/11 attacks on the World Trade Center, the Pentagon, and the "intentional crashing of United Airlines flight 93 in Shanksville, Pennsylvania."[320] The defendants are

Khalid Sheikh Mohammed (a.k.a. Mukhtar). Pakistan. Mastermind of the 9/11 attacks who proposed idea of attack to Osama bin Laden as early as 1996. Raised funds for the operation and trained them in Afghanistan and Pakistan. Captured by Pakistani intelligence services in 2003; transferred to US custody in 2007. Imprisoned at CIA "black site," 2003–2006.

Ramzi Bin al-Shibh. Yemen. Coordinator of the 9/11 plot who helped find flight schools for hijackers. Acted as an intermediary between Khalid Sheikh Mohammed and the hijackers in the U.S. Planned to be one of the original hijackers but failed to get U.S. visa. Captured in Pakistan in 2002 and transferred to US authority. Imprisoned at CIA "black site," 2002–2006.

Walid Muhammed Salih Mubarak Bin Atash (a.k.a. Khallad, Waleed bin Atash). Yemen. Senior al-Qaida operative who ran 9/11 training camp in Afghanistan. Allegedly bin Laden's bodyguard. Tied to U.S. embassy bombings and attack on *USS Cole*. Tested airline security on United Airlines flights between Bangkok and Hong Kong. Bin Laden selected him as one of the hijackers but detained in Yemen before 9/11. Captured in Pakistan in 2003 and transferred to U.S. Imprisoned at CIA "black site," 2003–2006.

Mustafa Ahmed Adam al-Hawsawi. Saudi Arabia. Al Qaida media committee member. Helped provide hijackers with funds, credit cards, and other resources. Captured in 2003 in Pakistan and transferred to U.S. authority. Imprisoned at CIA "black site," 2004–2006.

Ali Abdul Aziz Ali (a.k.a. Ammar al Baluchi). Pakistan. Nephew of KSM. Helped arrange travel for some of the hijackers to U.S. Provided them with $120,000 for flight training and other expenses in U.S. Captured in Pakistan in 2003 and transferred to U.S. authority. Imprisoned at CIA "black site," 2005–2006.[321]

They were each arraigned on May 5, 2012. Family members of the victims of the 9/11 attacks were invited to various military bases on the East Coast to see the arraignment beamed in from GBC on giant closed circuit TV screens. Though the actual trial had not begun by mid-August 2013, Brig. Gen. Mark S. Martins, the chief prosecutor for the military commissions at GBC, pledged that he intended to conduct a fair trial of the alleged conspirators. He admitted that earlier military commission trials had been flawed, but new reforms would assure the world that the system was "legitimate." Unfortunately, a shroud of secrecy enveloped many of the early proceedings, and the tribunal asserted it had the right to close sessions or stop the audio feed, which, according to one of the defense attorneys, Navy Cmdr. Walter Ruiz, seriously affected the defense's case. Consequently, he asked the court to hear his motion to dismiss all charges.[322]

When the arraignment sessions began, a few of the defendant's lawyers argued that the "process was rigged to lead to the execution of their clients," which led to a day-long process that was "sometimes chaotic."

> Throughout the arraignment, Khalid Sheikh Mohammed and the other four defendants refused to talk to, or even listen to the judge. Several delayed the hearings by praying, and one shouted to the judge that the guards at the prison might kill them. Another [Atash] was brought to the court in restraints and later took off his shirt, before insisting that the full charges be read aloud, which lasted into the night.[323]

Their protests seemed to be coordinated and were meant, according to one of the defense attorneys, James G. Connell III, as a means of "'peaceful resistance to an unjust system."[324] One of the key issues that will be brought up by the defense in the trial is the alleged torture and mistreatment of each of their clients since their capture. The ICRC interviewed each of the defendants in the fall of 2006 after their transfer from the CIA's High Value Detainee Program "black sites" to GBC. Khalid Sheikh Mohammed told the ICRC that he was repeatedly water boarded or "suffocated by water" and shackled into a standing posture for a month.

> I would be strapped to a special bed, which can be rotated into a vertical position. A cloth would be placed over my face. Water was then poured onto the cloth by one of the guards so that I could not breathe. This obviously could only be done for one or two minutes at a time. The cloth was then removed and the bed was put into a vertical position. The whole process was then repeated during about 1 hour.[325]

Ramzi Bin al-Shibh and Bin Atash reported similar treatment. The latter, along with Khalid Sheikh Mohammed, also spoke of being slammed into walls by their interrogators while wearing a thick "neck roll." They also discussed being beaten and kicked during interrogations or forced to go naked for extended periods of time.

Sleep deprivation and exposure to cold temperatures and cold water was also a common interrogation method. They were also shackled, handcuffed, and deprived of food for long periods of time.[326] Since the tribunal had already ruled that it would not allow the prosecution to present any evidence obtained through torture, the only reason for bringing it up is mitigation. But according to many of the victims' family members who viewed the first day of the proceedings, such treatment paled in comparison with the horrible deaths of their family members.[327] In the end, given the nature of the crimes committed on 9/11 and the ongoing war against international terrorism, the current trial of Khalid Sheikh Mohammed and his four coconspirators will do little to bring us closure or full insight into this dreadful crime. But, as William Shawcross, the son of Britain's top prosecutor at Nuremberg, Sir Hartley Shawcross, notes, perhaps it

> will be an important stage in the long and painful process of addressing our generation's most spectacular edition of barbarism.[328]

Conclusion

International attempts to seek justice for numerous war crimes committed since the 1970s have had mixed success. Again, politics would play a central role in this search for judicial reckoning, as evidenced by the limited success of the trials in Cambodia and Guantánamo. One could argue, though, that since these trials have not fully played out, their outcomes could result in some surprises. Efforts by the ad hoc tribunals in the Hague and Arusha have been far more successful, and meted out considerable justice to some of the worst perpetrators of the genocidal crimes in the Former Yugoslavia and Rwanda. What is remarkable about these tribunals is their deep commitment to due process rights for defendants, something often not afforded defendants in Nuremberg and Tokyo, and the unnamed thousands of defendants in the various post–World War II trials throughout Europe and Asia.

Their success can be attributed not only to the mature body of international humanitarian law and its associated precedents, but also the model provided by the Rome Statute and the International Criminal Court (ICC). This, coupled with the commitment of many of the Rome Statute signatory states and the United Nations to ensure that these trials be conducted in the most fair manner, has established a model that will set the standards for future international criminal trials that deal with violations of international humanitarian law.

Epilogue: The ICC

Despite the mixed success of various ad hoc tribunals to bring to justice war criminals globally, it is the ICC in the Hague that offers the greatest promise for investigating, trying, convicting, and, through such actions, deterring war crimes and genocide internationally. The idea of creating an international court to try war crimes and crimes against humanity came in the aftermath of World War I. Article 227 of the Treaty of Versailles called for the creation of a special court to try Kaiser Wilhelm II, though this idea never bore fruit. There was also talk in the 1930s of the creation of a special tribunal to deal with international crimes though nothing ever came of such suggestions.[1]

All of this changed in the aftermath of World War II and the IMT trials in Nuremberg and Tokyo. Article VI of the 1948 Genocide Convention stated that

> persons charged with genocide or any of the other acts enumerated in Article 3 [genocide; conspiracy to commit genocide; direct and public incitement to commit genocide; attempt to commit genocide; complicity in genocide] shall be tried by a competent tribunal of the State in the territory of which the act was committed, or by such international penal tribunal as may have jurisdiction with respect to those Contracting Parties which shall have accepted its jurisdiction.[2]

Simultaneously, the UN General Assembly asked its International Law Commission (ILC) to look into the prospect of creating an international tribunal to try persons accused of acts of genocide, and to see if this could be done through the creation of a criminal chamber for the International Court of Justice (World Court), a United Nations court that deals with disputes between nations. After a number of stops and starts, the ILC began seriously to work on the idea of creating an ICC in 1990. Eight years later, the UN General Assembly held a conference in Rome to discuss and hopefully approve what became known as the Rome Statute (July 17, 1988) of the ICC. Though 139 countries signed it, the Rome Statute needed 60 nations to ratify it before the ICC could become operational. The sixtieth ratification took place on April 11, 2002, and on July 1, 2002, the ICC came into being. Unfortunately, a number of countries that signed the Rome accord, such as the United States, the Russian Federation, Iraq, and Israel, have failed to ratify it. To date, 105 countries have become signatories of the ICC law and there are now hints that the United States is rethinking its relationship with the court.[3]

The ICC, which is located in the Hague in the Netherlands, can consider crimes committed only after the Rome Statute came into force in 2002. There are also various limits placed on its geographic jurisdiction. Cases can be referred to the court by a "State Power" or the UN Security Council. In addition, the ICC's prosecutor "may initiate charges acting *proprio motu*, that is, on his own initiative." Prosecution is limited to state parties, or countries that either ratified the Rome Statute or accepted the jurisdiction of the ICC.[4] Such cases must deal with one of four crimes—genocide, crimes against humanity, war crimes, and aggression.[5]

To date, four state parties—Uganda, the Democratic Republic of the Congo (DRC), the Central African Republic (CAF), and Mali have referred potential war crimes cases to the ICC. Pre-Trial Chamber II is currently hearing *The Prosecutor v. Joseph Kony, Vincent Otti, Okot Odhiambo and Dominic Ongwen.* Unfortunately, despite a $5 million reward for Kony, Odhiambo, and Ongwen, none of the four defendants, leaders of the Lord's Resistance Army (LRA), are in custody. They are accused of numerous war crimes including child abduction, sex slavery, and mutilation. The remnants of this 20-year-old guerilla group now roam a border region between South Sudan, the DRC, and CAF.[6]

The ICC's various trial chambers are currently hearing five cases involving war crimes in the DRC, and have reached decisions on two of them. The ICC has dropped charges in a third case—*The Prosecutor v. Callixte Mbarushimana*, but is moving forward with the case against Bosco Ntaganda, who turned himself in to the court in the spring of 2013. Ntaganda, a Congolese warlord nicknamed "The Terminator" because of "his reputation for extreme brutality,"[7] was charged in 2006 with three counts of war crimes under article 25 (3) of the Rome Statute involving the conscription of children under age 15 for combat, and 7 counts of "criminal responsibility as an indirect co-perpetrator" of war crimes and crimes against humanity including murder, rape, sexual slavery, attacks against civilians, and persecution.[8] Questions about what made him surrender go to the heart of one of the controversies about the impact of ICC charges on alleged war criminals not in ICC custody. It seems as though it was based partly on a split in his rebel group, M23, and the fact that the $5 million reward might have been enough to spur former members of his group to turn him in. There are also indications that the Rwandan government, which had long backed Ntaganda, now considered him a liability because of his criminal past. Regardless, he turned himself in at the American embassy in Rwanda, seemingly convinced that "this route may have offered [him] the least disadvantages."[9] Another alleged war criminal, Abu Garda, also turned himself in in 2009 in response to charges brought against him and four others in five ICC cases involving the situation in Darfur. Two other defendants, Abdallah Banda Abakaer Nourain and Saleh Mohammded Jerbo Jamus, turned themselves in to the court the following year. Their trial is scheduled to begin in 2014.[10]

But it is the case against Hassan Ahmad al-Bashir, president of Sudan, that has most tested the ability of the ICC to bring to justice national leaders involved in various war crimes and acts of genocide. Bashir, the first national leader to be indicted by the ICC, led a coup in 1989 that ousted Prime Minister Sadiq al-Mahdi, and named himself as his successor. Bashir began immediately to introduce Sharia law to parts of the country and initiated purges of the military, opposition parties, the media, and anything he deemed a threat to his government. Over time, a regional civil war spread nationwide, and rebels in Darfur took up arms against his government. Bashir responded by sending the devils on horseback (*Janjaweed*) into

Darfur. They ravaged the area and caused 400,000 deaths, displacing over 2.5 million people, almost half of Darfur's population.[11]

The ICC began to investigate Bashir's role in all of this in 2005, and in 2008 issued a warrant for his arrest. It charged him with five counts of crimes against humanity, two of war crimes, and three counts of genocide. In the first two sets of charges, he was charged with "individual criminal responsibility . . . as an indirect perpetrator for forcible transfer, torture, rape, and directing attacks against civilians." The genocide counts involved acts of bodily and mental harm as well as "inflicting on each target group conditions of life calculated to bring about the group's physical destruction."[12] To date, Bashir, who denies these charges, not only remains free but is still the president of Sudan. He has been able to garner support from various Arab and African leaders and numerous regional organizations in the Middle East and Africa.[13]

There are also cases pending before the ICC against alleged war criminals in the Côte d'Ivoire, Libya, and Kenya that have led to charges of bias on the part of the international tribunal, given that all of the active cases before it involve Africans. In early September 2013, the Kenyan parliament voted to consider withdrawing from the ICC to protest the indictments of Kenya's president, Uhuru Kenyatta, and his deputy, William Ruto.[14] Six weeks later, the African Union asked the ICC to postpone the trials of both men, arguing that "no sitting head of state should be prosecuted by an international tribune."[15] Such statements reflect growing African disillusionment with the ICC, particularly on the question of "sovereign immunity," and reflect what some see as "a vestige of imperialism."[16] Others such as Bishop Desmond Tutu, Kofi Annan, and Daniel Bekele of Human Rights Watch, disagree, warning that such moves would be "disincentives" to seek justice in future for acts of genocide and other war crimes in Africa and elsewhere.[17]

Charles Taylor, the former president of Liberia, was indicted and prosecuted by the Special Court for Sierra Leone for war crimes in Sierra Leone during his years in office. According to the charges, he supported and abetted rebel groups in Sierra Leone through weapons sales in a "blood for diamonds" trade that netted him millions of dollars. During his trial, which took place in the Hague because of security concerns in Sierra Leone, the prosecution put him "at the centre of a systematic campaign waged against civilians in Sierra Leone after 30 November 1996."[18] He was convicted in the spring of 2012 of "aiding and abetting, as well as planning, some of the most heinous and brutal crimes recorded in human history" and sentenced to 50 years in prison. His case is under appeal.[19] His conviction, the first of a former head of state since the end of World War II, underscores not only the vitality of international humanitarian law and the courts created to adjudicate the crimes specifically laid out in the various conventions and other bodies of law, but also the importance of such tribunals in the larger world of international law. They represent a major step forward in the ongoing maturation and enforcement of international humanitarian law.

Sit finis libri, non finis quaerendi

Notes

I   CRIMES OF WAR: ANTIQUITY TO THE MIDDLE AGES

1. *The Works of Mencius,* in James Legge, ed. and trans., *The Four Books: The Great Learning, Confucian Analects, the Doctrine of the Mean, the Works of Mencius* (Hong Kong: Hop Kuen Book, 1971), pp. 282–283; see also W. A. P. Martin, "Traces of International Law in Ancient China," *International Review,* Vol. 14 (January 1883), p. 69, who, paraphrasing Mencius, said that "the only foundation of national prosperity is justice and charity"; Hauiyu Wang also discusses this subject in "The Way of Heart: Mencius' Understanding of Justice," *Philosophy East & West,* Vol. 59, No. 3 (July 3, 2009), pp. 317–363.
2. Wilhelm G. Grewe, *The Epochs of International Law,* trans. and rev. Michael Byers (Berlin: Walter de Gruyter, 2000), p. 7.
3. Lassa Oppenheimer, *International Law: A Treatise,* ed. Arnold D. McNair, Vol. 1 (New York: Longmans, Green, 1905), pp. 4–5.
4. Eric Yong-Joong Lee, "Early Development of Modern International Law in East Asia—With Special Reference to China, Japan and Korea," *Journal of the History of International Law,* Vol. 4 (2002), p. 42.
5. Robert Cryer, *Prosecuting International Crimes: Selectivity and the International Criminal Law Regime* (Cambridge: Cambridge University Press, 2005), pp. 25–31.
6. R. P. Anand, "Universality of International Law: An Asian Perspective," *Essays in International Law,* No. 23 (2007), pp. 23, 38.
7. Michael Howard, "Constraints on Warfare," in Michael Howard, George J. Andreopoulos, and Mark R. Shulman, eds., *The Laws of War: Constraints on Warfare in the Western World* (New Haven: Yale University Press, 1994), p. 1.
8. Ibid., p. 186.
9. Ibid., p. 188.
10. William J. Hamblin, *Warfare in the Ancient Near East to 1600 BC: Holy Warriors at the Dawn of History* (London: Routledge, 2006), p. 46; *The Epic of Gilgamesh: The Babylonian Epic Poem and Other Texts in Akkadian and Sumerian,* trans. and intro. Andrew George (London: Penguin, 2000), xxxi.
11. Hamblin, *Warfare in the Ancient Near East,* p. 126.
12. *The Epic of Gilgamesh,* pp. 44–47.
13. Amnon Altman, "Tracing the Earliest Recorded Concepts of International Law: The Early Dynastic Period in Southern Mesopotamia," *Journal of the History of International Law,* Vol. 6 (2004), pp. 162–163.

14. Amnon Altman, "Tracing the Earliest Recorded Concepts of International Law (2): The Old Akkadian and Ur III Periods in Mesopotamia," *Journal of the History of International Law*, Vol. 7 (2005), pp. 125–126.

15. Hamblin, *Warfare in the Ancient Near East*, p. 112.

16. Amnon Altman, "The Role of the 'Historical Prologue' in the Hittite Vassal Treaties: An Early Experiment in Security Compliance," *Journal of the History of International Law*, Vol. 6 (2004), p. 49.

17. *Letters to the King of Mari: A New Translation, with Historical Introduction, Notes, and Commentary*, ed. and trans. Wolfgang Hempel (Winona Lake: Eisenbrauns, 2003), pp. 283, 298, 349, 355, 366, 368, 396, 479, 566, 606.

18. Ibid., p. 366.

19. Ibid., p. 177; for more on the controversy surrounding Hammurabi's treatment of Zimri-Lin and Mari, see Jack M. Sasson, "The King and I: A Mari King in Changing Perceptions," *Journal of the American Oriental Society*, Vol. 118, No. 4 (October–December 1998), pp. 460–462.

20. *The Code of Hammurabi*, ed. Richard Hooker, trans. L. W. King, pp. 1–39. http://www.xmarks.com/site/www.wsu.edu/~dee/MESO/CODE.HTM. For more on the ethical standards of Hammurabi's law code, see Morris Jastrow, Jr., *Aspects of Religious Belief and Practice in Babylonia and Assyria* (New York: Benjamin Blom, 1971), pp. 391–408.

21. Miriam Lichtheim, *Ancient Egyptian Literature: A Book of Readings* (Berkeley: University of California Press, 1973), p. 20.

22. Hamblin, *Warfare in the Ancient Near East*, p. 366.

23. Ibid., p. 327.

24. Ibid., p. 364.

25. Ibid.

26. Ibid.

27. Ibid, p. 365.

28. G. Maspéro, *Life in Ancient Egypt and Assyria* (New York: D. Appleton-Century, 1940), pp. 188–189.

29. Anthony J. Spalinger, *War in Ancient Egypt: The New Kingdom* (Oxford: Blackwell, 2005), pp. 164–165, 236–237.

30. A. Malamat, "Origins and the Formative Period," in H. H. Ben-Sasson, ed., *A History of the Jewish People* (Cambridge, MA: Harvard University Press, 1994), pp. 31–46.

31. Rabbi Joseph Telushkin, *Biblical Literacy: The Most Important People, Events, and Ideas in the Hebrew Bible* (New York: William Morrow, 1997), p. 165.

32. *Tanakh: The Holy Scriptures: The New JPS Translation according to the Traditional Hebrew Text* (Philadelphia: Jewish Publication Society, 1985), pp. 343–344.

33. H. Tadmor, "The Period of the First Temple, the Babylonian Exile and the Restoration," in Ben-Sasson, ed., *A History of the Jewish People*, pp. 107–109, 120–123, 132–133; Werner Keller, *The Bible as History*, trans. B. H. Rasmussen, 2nd rev. ed. (New York: William Morrow, 1981), p. 245.

34. Keller, *The Bible as History,* p. 245; A. T. Olmstead, *History of Assyria* (New York: Charles Scribner's Sons, 1923), p. 308.

35. Olmstead, *History of Assyria*, p. 308.

36. *Tanakh*, p. 600.

37. Ibid., p. 600.

38. Herodotus, *The History*, trans. David Grene (Chicago: University of Chicago Press, 1987), p. 193; Tadmor, "The Period of the First Temple," pp. 144–145; Keller, *The Bible as History*, pp. 260–261.

39. H. W. F. Saggs, *The Might that Was Assyria* (London: Sidgwick and Jackson, 1990), p. 248.

40. Ibid., pp. 261–262.

41. Georges Contenau, *Everyday Life in Babylon and Assyria* (New York: St. Martin's Press, 1954), p. 148.
42. Morton Cogan, *Imperialism and Religion: Assyria, Judah and Israel in the Eighth and Seventh Centuries B.C.E.* (Missoula: Society of Biblical Literature and Scholars Press, 1974), pp. 21–22; Simo Parpola, "National and Ethnic Identity in the Neo-Assyrian Empire and Assyrian Identity in Post-Empire Times," *Journal of Assyrian Academic Studies*, Vol. 18, No. 2 (2004), pp. 5–6, 8–10, 14.
43. Nigel Tallis, "Transport and Warfare," in John Curtis and Nigel Tallis, eds., *Forgotten Empire: The World of Ancient Persia* (Berkeley: University of California Press, 2005), p. 210.
44. Pierre Briant, *From Cyrus to Alexander: A History of the Persian Empire,* trans. Peter T. Daniels (Winona Lake: Eisenbrauns, 2002), p. 47.
45. Ibid., p. 47.
46. Tom Holland, *Persian Fire: The First World Empire and the Battle for the West* (New York: Doubleday, 2005), pp. 12, 14, 19.
47. Briant, *From Cyrus to Alexander*, p. 50.
48. Herodotus, *The History*, p. 278.
49. Thucydides, *The Peloponnesian War*, trans. Walter Blanco, ed. Walter Blanco and Jennifer Tolbert Roberts (New York: W. W. Norton, 1998), p. 122; Josiah Ober, "Classical Greek Times," in Michael Howard, George J. Andrepoulos, and Mark R. Shulman, eds., *The Laws of War: Constraints on Warfare in the Western World* (New Haven: Yale University Press, 1994), p. 13
50. Herodotus claimed that Xerxes's invasion force numbered 2,641,610 and, when you add the crews on Persian ships in the Aegean, 5,283,220 men. Herodotus, *The History,* pp. 534–536; a more contemporary estimate is that Xerxes's army ranged from 60,000 to 300,000 men. J. M. Cook, *The Persian Empire* (New York: Schocken Books, 1993), pp. 113–114; Briant, *From Cyrus to Alexander,* p. 527; Holland, *Persian Fire*, p. 394, n54.
51. Herodotus, *The History*, p. 469.
52. Ibid., pp. 553, 555; Nelson, *Persian Fire*, p. 294.
53. Herodotus, *The History*, pp. 553, 555, 650; Nelson, *Persian Fire*, p. 294.
54. Donald Kagan, *The Peloponnesian War* (New York: Penguin, 2003), pp. 114–117.
55. Frank Chalk and Kurt Jonassohn, *The History and Sociology of Genocide: Analyses and Case Studies* (New Haven: Yale University Press, 1990), pp. 65–73.
56. Kagan, *The Peloponnesian War*, p. 249.
57. Ibid., pp. 306–308.
58. Will Durant, *The Life of Greece* (New York: Simon and Schuster, 1939), p. 437.
59. James R. Ashley, *The Macedonian Empire; The Era of Warfare under Philip II and Alexander the Great, 359–323 B.C.* (Jefferson: McFarland, 1998), pp. 153–156; A. B. Bosworth, *Conquest and Empire: The Reign of Alexander the Great* (Cambridge: Cambridge University Press, 1988), pp. 5–19.
60. J. F. C. Fuller, *The Generalship of Alexander the Great* (London: Eyre & Spottiswoode, 1958), pp. 264–267.
61. Ashley, *The Macedonian Empire*, pp. 156, 177–180; James Romm, ed., *Alexander the Great: Selections from Arrian, Diodorus, Plutarch, and Quintus Curtius* (Indianapolis: Hackett Publishing Co., 2005), pp. 27–28.
62. Ashley, *The Macedonian Empire*, pp. 237–249; Bosworth, *Conquest and Empire*, pp. 66–67.
63. Bosworth, *Conquest and Empire*, pp. 92, 95–96.
64. Ashley, *The Macedonian Empire*, p. 306.
65. Ibid., pp. 307–309, 331.
66. Romila Thapar, *Early India: From the Origins to AD 1300* (Berkeley: University of California Press, 2003), pp. 175–178.

67. Roger Boesche, "Kautilya's *Arthaśāstra* on War and Diplomacy in Ancient India," *Journal of Military History*, Vol. 67 (January 2003), pp. 19, 30.
68. Ibid., p. 31.
69. Olga V. Butkevych, "History of Ancient International Law: Challenges and Prospects," *Journal of the History of International Law*, Vol. 5 (2003), p. 207.
70. Boesche, "Kautilya's *Arthaśāstra*," p. 34; Butkevych, "History of Ancient International Law," p. 207.
71. Romila Thapar, *Asoka and the Decline of the Mauryas*, 2nd ed. (Delhi: Oxford University Press, 1973), pp. 255–256.
72. Ibid., pp. 28–37, 166–169.
73. Romila, *Early India*, pp. 182–183.
74. Mark Edward Lewis, "Warring States Political History," in Michael Loewe and Edward L. Shaughnessy, *The Cambridge History of Ancient China: From the Origins of Civilization to 221 B.C.* (Cambridge: Cambridge University Press, 1999), pp. 587, 616.
75. Ibid., pp. 630–631; David Shepherd Nivison, "The Classical Philosophical Writings," in Loewe and Shaughnessy, *The Cambridge History of Ancient China*, pp. 752–783.
76. Lewis, "Warring States," p. 631.
77. Sun Tzu, *The Art of War: The New Translation*, trans. J. H. Huang (New York: Quill, 1993), pp. 23–24; Ralph D. Sawyer discusses the various theories about Sun Tzu and the history of *The Art of War* in his *The Seven Military Classics of Ancient China* (Boulder: Westview Press, 1993), pp. 149–153.
78. "Sun-tzu's Art of War," in *The Seven Military Classics of Ancient China*, trans. Ralph D. Sawyer (Boulder: Westview Press, 1993), p. 160; Sun Tzu, *The Art of War*, pp. 46–47.
79. Mark Edward Lewis, *The Early Chinese Empires: Qin and Han* (Cambridge, MA: Belknap Press of Harvard University Press, 2007), pp. 32, 50.
80. *Shang Jun Shu (The Book of the Lord Shang)*, Chapter 18 , p. 21; http://chinese.dsturgeon.net/text.pl?node'47226&if'en.
81. Robin D. S. Yates, "Law and the Military in Early China," in Nicola Di Cosmo, ed., *Military Culture in Imperial China* (Cambridge, MA: Harvard University Press, 2009), p. 32.
82. Derk Bodde, "The State and Empire of Ch'in," in Denis Twitchett and Michael Loewe, eds., *The Cambridge History of China*, Vol. 1: *The Ch'in and Han Empires, 221 B.C.– A.D. 220* (Cambridge: Cambridge University Press, 1986), pp. 99–100.
83. Lewis, *The Early Chinese Empires*, p. 101.
84. Sun Tzu, *The Art of War*, p. 48; Derk Bodde, *China's First Unifier: A Study of the Chi'in Dynasty as Seen in the Life of Li Ssŭ, 280?–208 B.C.* (Hong Kong: Hong Kong University Press, 1967), pp. 5–9; Arthur Cottrell, *The First Emperor of China* (New York: Holt, Rinehart, and Winston, 1981), pp. 141–145.
85. Li Yu-ning, ed., *The First Emperor of China* (White Plains: International Arts and Sciences Press, 1975), xiv.
86. Ssu-ma Ch'ien, "Basic Annals of Ch'in Shih-huang," in ibid., pp. 269–270.
87. Eric Yong-Joong Lee, "Early Development of Modern International Law in East Asia—With Special Reference to China, Japan, and Korea," *Journal of the History of International Law*, Vol. 4 (2002), p. 42.
88. Bodde, *China's First Unifier*, pp. 5–7, 82–84, 237.
89. Ibid., p. 237.
90. David A. Graff, *Medieval Chinese Warfare, 300–900* (London: Routledge, 2002), pp. 45–47.
91. Ibid., pp. 49–50.

92. Lewis, *The Early Chinese Empires,* pp. 115, 142–143. Michael Loewe, "The Former Han Dynasty," in Twitchett and Loewe, *The Cambridge History of China,* 1, p. 168; Yü Ying-Shih, "Han Foreign Relations," ibid., pp. 379, 460–462; Nishijima Sadao, "The Economic and Social History of Former Han," ibid., pp. 579–580; Paul Demiéville, "Philosophy and Religion from Han to Sui," ibid., p. 819

93. Antonio Santosuosso, *Soldiers, Citizens and the Symbols of War: From Classical Greece to Republican Rome, 500–167 B.C.* (Boulder: Westview Press, 1997), p. 152

94. Cicero, *On Duties,* ed. M. T. Griffin and E. M. Atkins (Cambridge: Cambridge University Press, 1991), pp. 14–15. Cicero stated that those "who were not cruel or savage in warfare should be spared," pp. 156–157.

95. Robert L. O'Connell, *The Ghosts of Cannae: Hannibal and the Darkest Hour of the Roman Republic* (New York: Random House, 2010), p. 116.

96. Ibid., p. 119; Gregory Daly, *Cannae: The Experience of Battle in the Second Punic War* (London: Routledge, 2002), p. 198.

97. O'Connell, *The Ghosts of Cannae,* p. 127.

98. Ibid., p. 160.

99. Theodor Mommsen states that there were 10,000 captives. *The History of Rome,* Vol. 2 (New York: Charles Scribner's Sons, 1895), p. 328; Brian Craven, *The Punic Wars* (New York: St. Martin's Press, 1980), p. 199.

100. Craven, *The Punic Wars,* pp. 260, 264; according to Charles E. Little, the origins of this phrase can be traced to a number of Roman writers who, over time, included it in the historic canon about the Punic Wars. Charles E. Little, "The Authenticity and Form of Cato's Saying 'Carthago delenda Est,'" *Classical Journal,* Vol. 29, No. 6 (March 1934), pp. 429–435; see also M. Dubuisson, "'*Delendo Est Carthago*': remise en question d'un stéréotype," in H. Devijver and E. Lipiński, eds., *Studia Phoenicia,* X: *Punic Wars* (Leuven: Vitgeverij Peeters, 1989), pp. 279–287.

101. Louis Rawlings, "Hannibal the Cannibal? Polybus on Barcid Atrocities," *Cardiff Historical Papers,* pp. 1–44; http://174.125.47.132/search?q-cache.neQxygYip9wJ:www.ct.ac.uk/hisar/resources/CHP9.

102. Craven, *The Punic Wars,* pp. 273–274.

103. Ibid., p. 285.

104. Santosuosso, *Soldiers, Citizens, and the Symbols of War,* p. 160.

105. Geoffrey Best, *Humanity in Warfare* (New York: Columbia University Press, 1980), p. 8.

106. Antonio Santosuosso, *Storm against the Heavens: Soldiers, Emperors, and Civilians in the Roman Empire* (Boulder: Westview Press, 2004), p. 63.

107. Cicero, *The Republic and The Laws,* trans. Niall Rudd (Oxford: Oxford University Press, 1998), p. 69.

108. Ibid., p. 65.

109. Michael Grant, *The Army of the Caesars* (New York: M. Evans, 1974), p. 67.

110. Julius Caesar, *Seven Commentaries on the Gallic War,* trans. Carolyn Hammond (New York: Oxford University Press, 1996), p. 151.

111. Ibid., pp. 193–194; Santosuosso, *Storm against the Heavens,* pp. 61–62.

112. Paul Johnson, *A History of the Jews* (New York: Harper & Row, 1987), pp. 105–110; M. Stern, "The Period of the Second Temple," in Ben-Sasson, ed., *A History of the Jewish People,* pp. 296–299.

113. Stern, "The Period of the Second Temple," pp. 299–300.

114. *The New Complete Works of Josephus,* trans. William Whiston (Grand Rapids: Kregel, 1999), pp. 763–764.

115. Ibid., pp. 905–906.

116. Ibid., pp. 930, 933; Shayne Cohen questions some parts of Josephus's story about the mass suicide of the Jews. "Masada: Literary Tradition, Archaeological Remains, and the Credibility of Josephus," *Journal of Jewish Studies*, Vol. 33 (Spring–Autumn, 1982), pp. 385–405.

117. Santosuosso, *Storm against the Heavens*, pp. 148, 152.

118. Will Durant, *Caesar and Christ: A History of Roman Civilization and of Christianity from Their Beginnings to A.D. 325* (New York: Simon and Schuster, 1944), p. 670.

119. John L. Esposito, *Islam: The Straight Path*, 3rd rev. ed. (New York: Oxford University Press, 2005), pp. 5–12, 40–48, 51–57.

120. Mahmoud A. Ayoub, "Qur'ān," in John L. Esposito, *The Oxford Encyclopedia of the Modern Islamic World*, Vol. 3 (Oxford: Oxford University Press, 1995), p. 385.

121. *The Qur'ān*, trans. Abdullah Yusuf Ali (Elmhurst, NY: Tahrike Tarsile Qur'ān, 2007), p. 216.

122. Ibid., pp. 20, 42, 112, 114, 120, 339, 343.

123. Ibid., pp. 17, 114, 116; Rudolph Peters, "Jihād," *The Oxford Encyclopedia of the Islamic World*, Vol. 2, pp. 369–373. Hugh Kennedy, *The Great Arab Conquests: How the Spread of Islam Changed the World We Lived In* (Cambridge: Da Capo Press, 2007), pp. 48–51.

124. Youssef H. Aboul-Enein and Sherifa Zuhur, *Islamic Rulings on Warfare* (Carlisle: Strategic Studies Institute, U.S. Army War College, 2004), p. 22.

125. John Kelsay, "Al-Shaybani and the Islamic Law of War," *Journal of Military Ethics*, Vol. 2, No. 1 (2003), p. 68.

126. Javaid Rehman, "The Concept of Jihād in Islamic International Law," *Journal of Conflict and Security Law*, Vol. 10, No. 3 (Winter 2005), p. 329.

127. Kennedy, *The Great Arab Conquests*, p. 41.

128. John Haldon, *Warfare, State and Society in the Byzantine World, 565–1204* (London: University College, 1999), pp. 21, 217–220.

129. Ibid., pp. 243–244.

130. Ibid., pp. 245–256.

131. John Julius Norwich, *A Short History of Byzantium* (New York: Alfred A. Knopf, 1997), pp. 228–230, 250–256.

132. Jane I. Smith, "Islam and Christendom: Historical, Cultural, and Religious Interaction from the Seventh to the Fifteenth Centuries," in John L. Esposito, ed., *The Oxford History of Islam* (Oxford: Oxford University Press, 1999), pp. 337–341; Will Durant, *The Age of Faith: A History of Medieval Civilization-Christian, Islamic, and Judaic-from Constantine to Dante: A.D. 325–1300* (New York: Simon and Schuster, 1950), pp. 585–613.

133. Sean McGlynn, *By Sword and Fire: Cruelty and Atrocity in Medieval Warfare* (London: Weidenfeld & Nicolson, 2008), p. 5.

134. Brian Todd Carey, Joshua B. Allfree, and John Cairns, *Warfare in the Medieval World* (Barnsley: Pen & Sword Books, 2006), p. 85.

135. Ibid., p. 85; McGlynn, *By Sword and Fire*, pp. 62–64.

136. McGlynn, *By Sword and Fire*, pp. 64–65; Maurice Keen, *Chivalry* (New Haven: Yale University Press, 1984), pp. 47–48.

137. Frederick H. Russell, *The Just War in the Middle Ages* (Cambridge: Cambridge University Press, 1975), pp. 35–36.

138. David Nicolle, *Crusader Warfare*, Vol. 1: *Byzantium, Europe and the Struggle for the Holy Land, 1050–1300* (London: Continuum, 2007), pp. 42, 49.

139. McGlynn, *By Sword and Fire*, pp. 152–161; Steven Runciman, *A History of the Crusades*, Vol. 1: *The First Crusade and the Foundation of the Kingdom of Jerusalem* (Cambridge: Cambridge University Press, 1951), pp. 286–287.

140. McGlynn, *By Sword and Fire*, pp. 156–157.

141. Antonio Santosuosso, *Barbarians, Marauders, and Infidels* (Boulder: Westview Press, 2004), p. 224; Runciman, *A History of the Crusades*, 1, pp. 234–235, says that the Crusaders butchered all of the "Turks" in Antioch.

142. Runciman, *A History of the Crusades*, 1, p. 75.

143. Ibid., pp. 64–65, 78.

144. Smith, "Islam and Christendom," p. 325.

145. Ibid., pp. 325–326.

146. Hannes Möhring, *Saladin: The Sultan and His Times, 1138–1193*, trans. David S. Bachrach (Baltimore: Johns Hopkins University Press, 2008), p. 13; Dr. A. R. Azzam, *Saladin* (Harlow: Pearson Longman, 2009), p. 186; Santosuosso, *Barbarian, Marauders, and Infidels*, p. 224; Esposito, *Islam*, p. 59.

147. Esposito, *Islam*, pp. 65–66; Malcolm Cameron Lyons and D. E. P. Jackson, *Saladin: The Politics of Holy War* (Cambridge: Cambridge University Press, 1982), pp. 354–361.

148. McGlynn, *By Sword and Fire*, p. 107.

149. Ibid., p. 106.

150. John T. Noonan, Jr., "Gratian Slept Here: The Changing Identity of the Father of the Systematic Study of Canon Law," *Traditio*, Vol. 35 (1979), pp. 145–146.

151. Cicero, *The Republic*, pp. 65, 69.

152. Russell, *The Just War in the Middle Ages*, pp. 16–39; James J. O'Donnell, *Augustine: A New Biography* (New York: HarperCollins, 2005), p. 259.

153. Russell, *The Just War*, p. 18.

154. Ibid., p. 19.

155. Ibid., pp. 60–61; see also Gratian, *The Treatise on Laws (Decretum DD 1–20)*, trans. Augustine Thompson and James Gordley (Washington, DC: Catholic University Press, 1993), p. 7.

156. Russell, *The Just War*, pp. 62–64.

157. James J. O'Donnell, *Augustine: A New Biography* (New York: HarperCollins, 2005), p. 259.

158. St. Thomas Aquinas, *Summa Theologica*, trans. Fathers of the English Dominican Province, Vol. 2 (New York: Benziger Brothers, 1947), pp. 1359–1362; for more on Aquinas's work, see Jean-Pierre Torrell, *Saint Thomas Aquinas*, Vol. 1: *The Person and His Work*, trans. Robert Royal (Washington, DC: Catholic University of American Press, 2005).

159. Gregory M. Reichberg, "Preventive War in Classical Just War Theory," *Journal of the History of International Law*, Vol. 9 (2007), p. 11.

160. *The Secret History of the Mongols: A Mongolian Epic Chronicle of the Thirteenth Century*, Vol. 1 (Leiden: Brill, 2004), p. 77.

161. Paul Ratchnevsky, *Genghis Khan: His Life and Legacy*, trans. and ed. Thomas Nivison Haining (Oxford: Blackwell, 1992), pp. 114–115.

162. A. A. Guber, *History of the Mongolian People's Republic* (Moscow: Nauka, 1973), pp. 106–109; Christopher Beckwith, *Empires of the Silk Road: A History of Central Eurasia from the Bronze Age to the Present* (Princeton: Princeton University Press, 2009), pp. 184–188.

163. Ratchnevsky, *Genghis Khan*, p. 130.

164. 'Ala-ad-Din 'Ata-Malik Juvaini, *The History of the World-Conqueror*, translated from the text of Mirza Muhammed Qazvini by John Andrew Boyle, Vol. 1 (Cambridge, MA: Harvard University Press, 1958), p. 152.

165. Michael Prawdin, *The Mongol Empire: Its Rise and Legacy*, trans. Eden and Cedar Paul (New York: Free Press, 1967), pp. 174–175.

166. *Matthew Paris's English History from the Year 1235 to 1273*, trans. The Rev. J. A. Giles, Vol. 2 (London: George Bell & Sons, 1893), pp. 28–29.

167. Edward D. Sokol, "Mongol Invasion of Russia," in Joseph L. Wieczynski, ed., *The Modern Encyclopedia of Russian and Soviet History*, Vol. 23 (Gulf Breeze: Academic International Press, 1981), p. 39; Nicholas V. Riasanovsky, *A History of Russia*, 5th ed. (New York: Oxford University Press, 1993), pp. 67–69.

168. Jeremiah Curtin, *The Mongols: A History* (Boston: Da Capo Press, 2003), p. 136.

169. Sokol, "Mongol Invasion of Russia," p. 40.

170. Riasanovsky, *A History of Russia*, p. 67.

171. *The Chronicle of Novgorod, 1016–1471*, trans. Robert Mitchell and Nevill Forbes (New York: AMS Press, 1970), p. 82.

172. George Vernadsky, *A History of Russia*, Vol. 3: *The Mongols and Russia* (New Haven: Yale University Press, 1953), p. 52; Sokol, "Mongol Invasion of Russia," pp. 41–42.

173. Charles J. Halperin, *Russia and the Golden Horde: The Mongol Impact on Medieval Russian History* (Bloomington: Indiana University Press, 1987), pp. 126–127; Vernadsky, *A History of Russia*, 3, pp. 333–390; David Nicolle, *Crusader Warfare*, Vol. 2: *Muslims, Mongols and the Struggle against the Crusades, 1050–1300 AD* (London: Continuum, 2007), p. 294.

174. Ruth Dunnel, "The Hsi Hsia," in Herbert Franke and Denis Twitchett, eds., *The Cambridge History of China*, Vol. 6: *Alien Regimes and Border States, 907–1368* (Cambridge: Cambridge University Press, 1994), pp. 213–214; David C. Wright, "The Northern Frontier," in Graff and Higham, *A Military History of China*, pp. 71–72.

175. Thomas Allen, "The Rise of the Mongolian Empire and Mongolian Rule in North China," in Frank and Twitchett, *The Cambridge History of China*, 6, pp. 386–388, 390–396, 403–411; Morris Rossabi, "The Reign of Khubilai Khan," ibid., pp. 417–436; Valerie Hansen, *The Open Empire: A History of China to 1600* (New York: W.W. Norton, 2000), p. 367.

2   WAR AND CRIMES IN CHINA AND POSTMEDIEVAL EUROPE

1. Edward L. Dreyer, *Early Ming China: A Political History, 1355–1435* (Stanford: Stanford University Press, 1982), pp. 18–64; Jonathan D. Spence, *The Search for Modern China* (New York: W. W. Norton, 1990), pp. 8–9.

2. Robin Higham and David A. Graff, "Introduction," in David A. Graff and Robin Higham, eds., *A Military History of China* (Boulder: Westview Press, 2002), p. 5.

3. Hok-lam Chan, "The Rise of Ming T'ai-tsu (1368–98): Facts and Fictions in Early Ming Official Historiography," *Journal of the American Oriental Society*, Vol. 95, No. 4 (1975), p. 699; Dreyer, *Early Ming China*, pp. 39–52. According to Dreyer, Zhu's forces, commanded by Ch'ang-ch'un, captured 3,000 prisoners and executed most of them.

4. David Morgan, *The Mongols*, 2nd ed. (Oxford: Blackwell, 2007), p. 178; Denis Twitchett and Tilemann Grimm, "The Cheng-t'ung, Ching-t'ai, and T'ien-shun Reigns, 1436–1464," in Frederick W. Mote and Denis Twitchett, eds., *The Cambridge History of China*. Vol. 7: *The Ming Dynasty, 1368–1644*, Part 1 (New York: Cambridge University Press, 1988), pp. 322–331; Dreyer, *Early Ming China*, pp. 71–76, 248.

5. Frederick W. Mote, "The Ch'eng-hua and Hung-chih Reigns, 1465–1505," in Mote and Twitchett, *The Cambridge History of Modern China*, 7, 1, pp. 375–376; Nicola di Cosmo, ed., *Military Culture in Imperial China* (Cambridge: Harvard University Press, 2011), p. 32; Michael Loewe, "The Western Han Army: Organization, Leadership, and Operation," ibid., p. 86.

6. Ray Huang, "The Lung-ch'ing and Wan-li Reigns, 15671620–," ibid., pp. 563–573; tension between China and Japan did nothing to lessen trade between both countries, which, even during the chaotic latter days of the Ming dynasty, was substantial. James W. Tong, *Disorder under Heaven: Collective Violence in the Ming Dynasty* (Stanford: Stanford University Press, 1991), p. 149.

7. James Bunyan Parsons, *The Peasant Rebellions of the Late Ming Dynasty* (Tuscon: University of Arizona Press, 1970), pp. 48–49.

8. Huang, "The Lung-ch'ing," pp. 563–573; Tong, *Disorder under Heaven*, p. 149.

9. Tong, *Disorder under Heaven*, p. 96.

10. Ibid., pp. 176–177.

11. Ibid., p. 177.

12. Ibid.

13. Ibid., p. 178.

14. Ibid., pp. 180–181.

15. Ibid., p. 181.

16. Immanuel C. Y. Hsü, *The Rise of Modern China*, 6th ed. (New York: Oxford University Press, 2000), pp. 21–23; Pei-kai Cheng, Michael Lestz, and Jonathan D. Spence, eds., *The Search for Modern China: A Documentary Collection* (New York: W. W. Norton, 1999), pp. 21–23.

17. Lynn A. Struve, "The Southern Ming, 1644–1662," in Mote and Twitchett, *The Cambridge History of China*, 7, 1 , pp. 656–657.

18. Lynn A. Struve, *Voices from the Ming-Qing Cataclysm* (New Haven: Yale University Press, 1993), pp. 29–30.

19. Ibid., p. 37.

20. Ibid.

21. Ibid., p. 40.

22. Ibid., p. 43.

23. Ibid.

24. Ibid., p. 45.

25. Ibid., p. 47.

26. Ibid., p. 48.

27. Joanna Waley-Cohen, *The Culture War in China: Empire and the Military under the Qing Dynasty* (London: I. B. Taurus, 2006), p. 1.

28. Joanna Waley-Cohen, "Commemorating War in Eighteenth Century China," *Modern Asian Studies*, Vol. 30, No. 4 (1996), pp. 871, 873.

29. Paul Lococo, Jr., "The Qing Empire," in Graff and Higham, *A Military History of China*, p. 127.

30. Jonathan Spence, "The K'ang-shi Reign," in Williard J. Peterson, ed., *The Cambridge History of China*, Vol. 9, Part 1 : *The Ch'ing Empire to 1800* (Cambridge: Cambridge University Press, 2002), p. 141.

31. Ibid., p. 143.

32. S. R. Gilbert, "Menzi's Art of War: The Kangxi Emperor Reforms the Qing Military Examinations," in di Cosmo, *Military Culture in Imperial China*, pp. 244–248.

33. *Mencius*, trans. D. C. Lan, rev. ed. (London: Penguin, 2004), pp. 5–7, 158.

34. Joanna Waley-Cohen, "Militarization of Culture in Eighteenth-Century China," in di Cosmo, *Military Culture in Imperial China*, p. 287.

35. Hsü, *Rise of Modern China*, p. 37.

36. Peter C. Perdue, *China Marches West: The Qing Conquest of Central Eurasia* (Cambridge, MA: Belknap Press of Harvard University Press, 2005), pp. 161–162, 166–171; Mark Mancall, *China at the Center: 300 Years of Foreign Policy* (New York: Free Press, 1984),

p. 77; Mark Mancall, *Russia and China: Their Diplomatic Relations to 1728* (Cambridge, MA: Harvard University Press, 1971), pp. 141–158.

37. Perdue, *China Marches West*, pp. 250–255, 571–574.

38. Ibid., pp. 257, 265–266, 268, 270–272.

39. Ibid., pp. 272–283.

40. Ibid., p. 283.

41. Ibid.

42. Ibid.

43. Pamela Kyle Crossley, "The Conquest Elite of the Ch'ing Empire," in Peterson, *The Cambridge History of China*, 9, 1, pp. 352–354.

44. Perdue, *China Marches West*, p. 284.

45. Ibid., p. 285.

46. Peter C. Perdue, "Military Mobilization in Seventeenth and Eighteenth-Century China, Russia, and Mongolia," *Modern Asian Studies*, Vol. 30, No. 4 (October 1996), p. 759.

47. Perdue, *China Marches West*, p. 285.

48. Christopher Beckwith, *Empires of the Silk Road: A History of Central Eurasia from the Bronze Age to the Present* (Princeton: Princeton University Press, 2009), p. 240.

49. E. W. Mote, *Imperial China, 900–1800* (Cambridge, MA: Harvard University Press, 1999), pp. 940–943; Spence, *Search for Modern China*, p. 94; Alexander Woodside, "The Ch'ien-Lung Reign," in Peterson, *The Cambridge History of China*, 9, 1, pp. 293–309.

50. John H. Langbein, *Torture and the Law of Proof: Europe and England in the Ancien Régime* (Chicago: University of Chicago Press, 2006), pp. 13–14; *Die Constitutio Criminalis Carolina*, pp. 2–3. http://www.latein-pagina.de/iexplorer/hexen1/carolina.htm.

51. Harold J. Berman, *Law and Revolution*, Vol. 2: *The Impact of the Protestant Reformations on the Western Legal Traditions* (Cambridge, MA: Belknap Press of Harvard University Press, 2003), pp. 137–141, 145–146.

52. Richard Marius, *Martin Luther: The Christian between God and Death* (Cambridge, MA: Belknap Press of Harvard University Press, 1999), p. 267; Luther's concept of the "priesthood of the individual believer" can be found in his *Von der Freiheit eines Christenmenschen* (The Freedom of a Christian). The paradox can be found early in Luther's essay when he states that "a Christian man is the most free lord of all, and subject to none, a Christian man is the most dutiful servant of all, and subject to every one"; http://wsu.edu/~dee/REFORM/FREEDOM.HTN.

53. Ibid., pp. 73–77, 148.

54. Diarmaid MacCulloch, *The Reformation* (New York: Viking, 2004), pp. 154–155.

55. Barbara B. Diefendorf, *Beneath the Cross: Catholics and Huguenots in Sixteenth-Century Paris* (New York: Oxford University Press, 1991), pp. 177, 327; James Westfall Thompson notes in his *The Wars of Religion in France, 1559–1576: The Huguenots, Catherine de Medici, and Philip II* (Chicago: University of Chicago Press, 1909), p. 450, that figures for the number of dead in Paris ranged from 1,000 to 10,000.

56. C. V. Wedgwood, *The Thirty Years War* (New York: Anchor Books, 1961), p. 491.

57. David A. Bell, *The First Total War: Napoleon's Europe and the Birth of Warfare as We Know It* (Boston: Houghton Mifflin, 2007), p. 37.

58. Stephen C. Neff, *War and the Law of Nations: A General History* (Cambridge: Cambridge University Press, 2005), p. 87.

59. Michael Roberts, *Gustavus Adolphus: A History of Sweden, 1611–1632*, Vol. 2: *Gustavus Adolphus: A History of Sweden, 1626–1632* (London: Longmans, Green, 1958), pp. 240–243; American military legal scholars offer different opinions about the importance of Gustav II's Articles of War. William Winthrop, the "'Blackstone' of Military Law," credits Gustav's Articles with forming the basis of modern military law and lists all 167 articles in the Appendix of his classic, *Military Law and Precedents*, 2nd ed. (Washington, DC: Government Printing Office, 1920), pp. 907–917. Lt. Col. William

R. Hagan, who wrote the introduction to the above reprint of Winthrop's study, will have none of this. He concludes that "Gustavus Adolphus was an important, but not a revolutionary, figure in the development of military law." "Overlooked Textbooks Jettison Some Durable Military Law Legends," *Military Law Review*, No. 163 (1986), p. 200; what adds to this controversy are the different versions of Gustav's laws of war. Winthrop listed 167 articles in his study, while Kenneth Ögren states that the Articles of War had 150 articles. He says that seven dealt with humanitarian issues, but then specifically cites six in his article. The difference seems to center around a revised set of the articles issued by Gustav just before his death in 1632. The new articles had clauses that tried to strengthen discipline in his army. "Humanitarian Law in the Articles of War Decreed in 1621 by King Gustavus II Adolphus of Sweden," *International Review of the Red Cross*, No. 313 (1996), pp. 1–3, http://www.icrc.org/Web/Eng/siteeng0.nsf/html/57JN8D.

60. Geoff Mortimer, *Eyewitness Accounts of the Thirty Years War 1618–48* (New York: Palgrave Macmillan, 2002), p. 3. For an example of the power of the press, particularly as it relates to propaganda, see Martin Roberts's discussion of the spread of Protestant efforts to spread the anti-imperial document, *Appellatio ad Caesarem* (Appeal to Caesar), to influence public opinion in the German states. Roberts, *Gustavus Adolphus II*, 2, p. 423.

61. Neff, *War and the Law of Nations*, p. 32.

62. Ibid., p. 85.

63. Hugo Grotius, *The Rights of War and Peace*, Book 2, ed., Richard Tuck, from the edition of Jean Barbeyrac (Indianapolis: Liberty Fund, 2005), p. 1021.

64. Theodore Meron, *War Crimes Law Comes of Age: Essays* (Oxford: Clarendon Press, 1998), p. 124.

65. Roberts, *Gustavus Adolphus*, pp. 423, 639.

66. Grotius, *The Rights of War and Peace*, 2, pp. 395–419.

67. Neff, *War and the Law of Nations*, p. 97.

68. Simon Chesterman, *Just War or Just Peace: Humanitarian Intervention and International Law* (Oxford: Oxford University Press, 2001), p. 13.

69. Peter Gay, *The Enlightenment: An Interpretation: The Rise of Modern Paganism* (New York: W. W. Norton, 1995), pp. 9, 256.

70. Ibid., p. 321.

71. John Locke, *An Essay Concerning Human Understanding*. Abridged and edited with an Introduction and Notes, Kenneth P. Winkler (Indianapolis: Hackett, 1996), pp. 11–12, 30–32, 39.

72. John Locke, *Two Treatises of Government and a Letter Concerning Toleration*, ed. Ian Shapiro (New Haven: Yale University Press, 2003), pp.101, 166, 172.

73. Ibid., pp. 224, 249.

74. Jean Jacques Rousseau, *The Social Contract and Later Political Writings*, ed. and trans. Victor Gourevitch (Cambridge: Cambridge University Press, 1997), pp. 44–46.

75. Ibid., pp. 44–47.

76. Ibid., pp. 166–167.

77. Paul Bushkovitch, *Peter the Great; The Struggle for Power, 1671–1725* (Cambridge: Cambridge University Press, 2001), pp. 183–187, 223–226, 231–241, 244–245, 250–254, 270, 280–292, 426; Lindsey Hughes, *Russia in the Age of Peter the Great* (New Haven: Yale University Press, 1998), pp. 17–18, 26–57; Frans G. Bengtsson, *The Sword Does Not Jest: The Heroic Life of King Charles XII of Sweden*, trans. Naomi Walford (New York: St. Martin's Press, 1960), pp. 74–95, 245–260, 269–286, 302–388.

78. David Bell, *The First Total War: Napoleon's Europe and the Birth of Warfare as We Know It* (Boston: Houghton Mifflin, 2007), pp. 25, 37.

79. Ibid., pp. 30–37.

80. Ibid., p. 48.

81. Ibid., p. 37.

82. Ibid., p. 41.

83. Ibid., pp. 42–44.

84. Robert B. Asprey, *Frederick the Great: The Magnificent Enigma* (New York: History Book Club, 1999), pp. 440, 451.

85. Geoffrey Parker, *The Military Revolution: Military Innovation and the Rise of the West, 1500–1800* (Cambridge: Cambridge University Press, 1996), p. 147.

86. Asprey, *Frederick the Great*, pp. 458, 474–475, 481, 482.

87. Ibid., p. 369.

88. Ibid., pp. 369–370.

89. Parker, *The Military Revolution*, p. 151.

90. Ibid., p.151; Bengtsson, *The Sword Does Not Jest*, p. 269, notes that Karl XII had another 30,000 troops stationed across the southeastern Baltic coast; Hughes, *Russia in the Age of Peter the Great*, p. 39; A. A. Malinovskii states that Karl XII had a force of about 30,000 men. "Poltava, Battle of (1709)," in Joseph L. Wieczynski, ed., *The Modern Encyclopedia of Russian and Soviet History*, Vol. 29 (Gulf Breeze: Academic International Press, 1982), p. 24; Alan Schom, *Napoleon Bonaparte: A Life* (New York: HarperCollins, 1997), p. 595; Livi Bacci Massimo, *The Population of Europe: A History*, trans. Cynthia De Nardi Ipsen and Carl Ipsen (Oxford: Blackwell, 2000), p. 8.

91. Quincy Wright, "Review of *Jus Gentium Methodo Scientifica Pertractatum*," *American Journal of International Law*, Vol. 29 (1935), pp. 552–554.

92. Peter Senn, "What Is the Place of Christian Wolff in the History of the Social Sciences?" *European Journal of Law and Economics*, Vol.4, No. 2 (1997), p. 179.

93. Christian Wolff, *Jus Gentium Methodo Scientifica Pertractatum*, 2, trans. Joseph H. Drake (Oxford: Clarendon Press, 1934), pp. 314–315.

94. Ibid., p. 292.

95. Ibid., p. 382.

96. Ibid., p. 411.

97. Ibid.

98. Ibid., p. 414.

99. Ibid., pp. 414–415.

100. Ibid., p. 424.

101. Ibid., p. 427.

102. Ibid., p. 429.

103. Ibid., p. 438.

104. Ibid., pp. 439–440.

105. Ibid., p. 449. It is interesting to compare Wolff's succinct yet legally clear discussion of this issue with Grotius's more turgid, antiquity-based discussion. See Grotius, *The Rights of War and Peace*, Book 3, pp. 1300–1302.

106. Wolff, *Jus Gentium*, pp. 450–451.

107. Ibid., p. 452.

108. Emer de Vattel, *The Law of Nations*, ed. Béla Kapossy and Richard Whatmore (Indianapolis: Liberty Fund, 2008), p. 562. The full title of Vattel's work was *Le droit des gens: Ou Principes de la loi naturelle, appliqués à la conduite & aux affaires des nations & des souverains* (The Law of Nations, or Principles of the Law of Nature, Applied to the Conduct and Affairs of Nations and Sovereigns).

109. Nicholas Greenwood Onuf, "*Civitas Maxima*: Wolff, Vattel, and the Fate of Republicanism," *American Journal of International Law*, Vol. 88 (1994), p. 280; Vattel, *The Law of Nations*, p. 12.

110. Wolff, *Jus Gentium*, pp. 487–489, 491.

111. Ibid., pp. 513–514.
112. Onuf, "*Civitas Maxima*," p. 282.
113. Senn, "What Is the Place of Christian Wolff," p. 179.
114. Vattel, *The Law of Nations*, pp. 10–13
115. Onuf, "*Civitas Maxima*," pp. 296–297.
116. Ibid., p. 283.
117. Abraham C. Weinfeld, "What Did the Framers of the Federal Constitution Mean by 'Agreements or Compacts'?" *University of Chicago Law Review*, Vol. 3, No. 3 (April 1936), p. 461.
118. Brian Richardson, *The Non-Vattelian Origins of America's Engagement with Public International Law* (NYU School of Law Legal History Colloquium, December 6, 2011), pp. 1–2.
119. *Sosa v. Alvarez-Machain et al.*, *Certiorari* to the United States Court of Appeals for the Ninth Circuit, No. 03–339, Argued March 30, 2004, Decided June 29, 2004, p. 8; http://caselaw.lp.findlaw.com/cgi-bin/getcase.pl?court'us&vol'000&invol'03–339.
120. Richardson, *The Non-Vattelian Origins*, pp. 4–5.
121. James Kent, *Commentaries on American Law*, 15th ed., Jon Roland, 1997–2002, p. 18; http://www.constitution.org/jk/jk_000.htm.
122. Neff, *War and the Law of Nations*, p. 112.
123. Vattel, *The Law of Nations*, p. 482.
124. Ibid., pp. 567, 570.
125. Bell, *The First Total War*, pp. 6–7.
126. Michael Howard, "The Influence of Clausewitz," in Carl von Clausewitz, *On War*, trans. and ed. Michael Howard and Peter Paret (New York: Alfred A. Knopf, 1993), p. 38.
127. Ibid., p. 701.
128. Ibid., p. 704.
129. Simon Schama, *Citizens: A Chronicle of the French Revolution* (New York: Alfred A. Knopf, 1989), pp. 589–591, 605–609, 612.
130. Gunther Rothenberg, "The Age of Napoleon," in Michael Howard, George J. Andreopoulos, and Mark R. Shulman, eds., *The Laws of War: Constraints on Warfare in the Western World* (New Haven: Yale University Press, 1994), pp. 87–88.
131. Schama, *Citizens*, pp. 619, 63–636, 706, 755–759; Georges Lefebvre, *The French Revolution from Its Origins to 1793,* trans. Elizabeth Moss Evanson (London: Routledge & Kegan Paul, 1962), pp. 241–243, 271–272.
132. Bell, *The First Total War*, pp. 162–171.
133. Schama, *Citizens*, p. 788.
134. Donald Greer, *The Incidence of the Terror during the French Revolution: A Statistical Interpretation* (Cambridge, MA: Harvard University Press, 1936), pp. 60, 64.
135. Schama, *Citizens*, p. 791.
136. Ibid., p. 792.
137. Bell, *The First Total War*, p. 156.
138. Ibid., p. 184.
139. Ibid., pp. 184–185.
140. Ibid., pp. 186–189.
141. Ibid., pp. 189–190.
142. Ibid., p. 7; Adam Zamoyski, *1812: Napoleon's Fatal March* (New York: Harper Perennial, 2005), p. 536; David G. Chandler, *The Campaigns of Napoleon: The Mind and Method of History's Greatest Soldier* (New York: Scribner, 1996), xxix.
143. Schom, *Napoleon Bonaparte*, pp. 234, 299; Chandler, *The Campaigns of Napoleon*, pp. 265–267; Bell, *First Total War*, p. 251.
144. Schom, *Napoleon Bonaparte*, pp. 396–397, 399, 413; Chandler, *The Campaigns of Napoleon*, pp. 384–385, 431–432; Rothenberg, "The Age of Napoleon," pp. 89–91.

145. Rothenberg, "The Age of Napoleon," pp. 89–91.

146. There are different estimates not only about French losses, but also about the number of French troops that invaded Russia. David G. Chandler states in his *The Campaigns of Napoleon*, pp. 852–853, that 655,000 French troops "crossed the Vistula in the summer of 1812," and only 93,000 returned to Poland. Losses included 370,000 battlefield deaths and 200,000 French POWs. Over half would perish while prisoners of the Russians; Alan Schom states in his *Napoleon Bonaparte*, pp. 643–644, that only 43,000 French troops made it back into Poland, while Adam Zamoyski states in his *1812*, pp. 233–234, that 120,000 French troops stumbled back into Poland at the end of 1812; Rothenberg, "The Age of Napoleon," pp. 89–90, 97.

147. Bell, *The First Total War*, pp. 260–261.

148. Zamoyski, *1812*, p. 443.

149. Ibid., p. 443.

150. Ibid, p. 445.

151. Ibid., p. 451.

152. Ibid., pp. 484–485.

153. Chandler, *Campaigns of Napoleon*, pp. 852–853; Schom, *Napoleon Bonaparte*, pp. 634–644; Zamoyski, *1812*, pp. 233–234; Rothenberg, *Age of Napoleon*, pp. 89–90, 97.

154. Bell, *Total War*, p. 261; Zamoyski, *1812*, pp. 233–234.

155. Louis Antoine Fauvelet de Bourrienne, *Memoirs of Napoleon Bonaparte*, ed. R. W. Phipps, Vol. 8 (New York: Charles Scribner's Sons, 1891), p. 315; Schom, *Napoleon Bonaparte*, pp. 644–669, 680; Chandler, *The Campaigns of Napoleon*, pp. 916, 924, 932–933, 936, said Napoleon had 260,000 men under his command, but had only 177,000 on the battlefield. The Allies faced him with 300,000 men ready for battle; Harold Nicolson, *The Congress of Vienna: A Study in Allied Unity, 1812–1822* (Gloucester: Peter Smith, 1973), pp. 39, 58, 83–101, 179–181, 193–195, 198–199, 235–239, 258.

156. Nicolson, *The Congress of Vienna*, p. 225.

157. *Declaration of the Powers against Napoleon*, March 13, 1815, pp. 1–2; http://www.napoleon-series.org/research/government/diplomatic/c_declaration.html.

158. Chandler, *The Campaigns of Napoleon*, pp. 1090–1091; Nicolson, *The Congress of Vienna*, pp. 100–101, 238–239; Schom, *Napoleon Bonaparte*, pp. 765–766.

159. Gary Jonathan Bass, *Stay the Hand of Vengeance: The Politics of War Crimes Tribunals* (Princeton: Princeton University Press, 2000), p. 55.

160. Ibid., pp. 49–50.

161. Ibid., p. 50.

162. Ibid., p. 50.

163. *The Treaty of Versailles* (June 28, 1919), Part 8 , Penalties, Article 227, 1, http://history.acusd.edu/gen/versaillestreaty/ver231.html.

3   COLONIALISM: THE AMERICAS, ASIA, AND AFRICA

1. S. C. Gwyne, *Empire of the Summer Moon: Quanah Parker and the Rise and Fall of the Comanches, the Most Powerful Indian Tribe in American History* (New York: Scribner, 2010), pp. 36–41.

2. Kelly F. Himmel, *The Conquest of the Karankawas and the Tonkawas, 1821–1859* (College Station: Texas A & M Press, 1999), p. 84.

3. Ibid., pp. 84–85.

4. Ibid., pp. 85–86; Dee Brown, *Bury My Heart at Wounded Knee: An Indian History of the American West* (New York: Henry Holt, 1970), pp. 269–270.

5. Brown, *Bury My Heart at Wounded Knee*, pp. 86–87.

6. Ibid., pp. 89–91.

7. Russell Thornton, *American Indian Holocaust and Survival: A Population History since 1492* (Norman: University of Oklahoma Press, 1987), p. 43.

8. Ibid., pp. 149–150; Brown, *Bury My Heart at Wounded Knee*, pp. 434–438.

9. Thornton, *American Indian Holocaust and Survival*, pp. 150–155; Brown, *Bury My Heart at Wounded Knee*, pp. 439–445.

10. *The Indian Removal Act of 1830*, May 26, 1830, p. 1, http//www.civics-online.org/library/formatted/texts/indian_act.html.

11. Alexis de Tocqueville, "Letters from America," trans. Frederick Brown, *Hudson Review*, Vol. 62, No. 3 (Autumn 2009), pp. 390–391.

12. Ibid., p. 391.

13. Ibid., pp. 390–393.

14. Thornton, *American Indian Holocaust and Survival*, p. 114.

15. De Tocqueville, "Letters from America," p. 391.

16. Ibid., pp. 390–392.

17. Marco Polo, *The Travels of Marco Polo* (New York: Orion Press, 1958). See, for example, his description of the rewards offered to Kublai Khan's chief generals and the khan's vast treasure, pp. 118, 125.

18. John A. Crow, *The Epic of Latin America,* 4th ed. (Berkeley: University of California Press, 1992), p. 67.

19. Charles C. Mann, *1491: New Revelations of the Americas before Columbus* (New York: Vintage Books, 2006), pp. 131–133.

20. William H. Prescott, *The Conquest of Mexico* (New York: Doubleday, Doran, 1934), pp. 167–168.

21. Bernal Díaz del Castillo, *The Discovery and Conquest of Mexico, 1517–1521*, trans. A. P. Maudslay (New York: Farrar, Straus, and Cudahy, 1956), pp. 178–179.

22. Ibid., pp. 190–191.

23. Ibid., p. 213.

24. Ross Hassig, *Aztec Warfare: Imperial Expansion and Political Control* (Norman: University of Oklahoma Press, 1988), p. 121.

25. Ibid., pp. 249–250.

26. Ibid., p. 121.

27. Del Castillo, *The Discovery and Conquest of Mexico,* pp. 219–220.

28. Ibid., p. 221.

29. Ibid., pp. 225–231, 380; Crow, *The Epic of Latin America,* pp. 82–85; Prescott, *The Conquest of Mexico*, pp. 401, 412, 524–525; Del Castillo, *The Discovery and Conquest of Mexico*, pp. 415–429.

30. Del Castillo, *The Discovery and Conquest of Mexico,* p. 431.

31. Ibid., p. 436.

32. Ibid., p. 525.

33. Ibid., p. 449.

34. Hugh Thomas, *Conquest: Montezuma, Cortés and the Fall of Mexico* (New York: Simon & Schuster, 1993), p. 525.

35. Ibid., pp. 528–529.

36. Davíd Carrasco, *City of Sacrifice: The Aztec Empire and the Role of Violence in Civilization* (Boston: Beacon Press, 1999), p. 221.

37. Thomas, *Conquest*, pp. 318–320, 545–546, 586–587, 594.

38. Richard F. Townsend, *The Aztecs* (London: Thames and Hudson, 1992), p. 42.

39. William H. Prescott, *History of the Conquest of Mexico and History of the Conquest of Peru* (New York: Cooper Square Press, 2000), pp. 940–942.

40. Ibid., pp. 945–946.

41. Ibid., pp. 947–948; Crow, *The Epic of Latin America*, pp. 99–100.

42. Prescott, *History of the Conquest of Mexico and Peru*, pp. 969–974.

43. Ibid., pp. 974–976 n33; Crow, *The Epic of Latin America*, p. 101.

44. Robin Blackburn, *The Making of New World Slavery: From the Baroque to the Modern, 1492–1800* (London: Verso, 1998), p. 134.

45. Bartolomé de las Casas, *A Short Account of the Destruction of the Indies*, ed. and trans. Nigel Griffin (London: Penguin Books, 1992), xx.

46. Ibid., p. 29.

47. Thornton, *American Indian Holocaust and Survival*, p. 22; Blackburn, *The Making of New World Slavery*, p. 132.

48. Blackburn, *The Making of New World Slavery*, p. 132.

49. Ward Churchill, *Indians Are Us? Culture and Genocide in Native North America* (Monroe, ME: Common Courage Press, 1994), p. 38; Thornton, *American Indian Holocaust and Survival*, p. 43; David E. Stannard, *American Holocaust: The Conquest of the New World* (New York: Oxford University Press, 1992), p. 146.

50. Thornton, *American Indian Holocaust and Survival*, pp. 43–44.

51. Ibid., pp. 47, 49.

52. D. E. Mungello, *The Great Encounter of China and the West, 1500–1800*, 2nd ed. (Lanham: Rowan & Littlefield, 2005), p. 15.

53. Mark Mancall, *China at the Center: 300 Years of Foreign Policy* (New York: Free Press, 1984), p. 15.

54. Mungello, *The Great Encounter*, pp. 3–4.

55. Mancall, *China at the Center*, pp. 21–22, 26.

56. Mungello, *The Great Encounter*, p. 3.

57. Mancall, *China at the Center*, p. 15.

58. Mungello, *The Great Encounter*, p. 6.

59. Ibid., pp. 72–73, 7.

60. Ibid., p. 81; Manfred Barthel, *The Jesuits: History and Legend of the Society of Jesus*, trans. Mark Howson (New York: William Morrow, 1984), pp. 41, 47–48; J. Peter Nixon, "Ignatius for the Perplexed," *Commonweal*, June 4, 2010, p. 25.

61. Barthel, *The Jesuits*, pp. 178, 182, 189; Andrew C. Ross, *A Vision Betrayed: The Jesuits in Japan and China, 1542–1742* (Maryknoll: Orbis Books, 1994), pp. 14–31.

62. Ross, *A Vision Betrayed*, p. 120.

63. Ibid., p. 130.

64. Mancall, *China in the Center*, pp. 82–83.

65. Ross, *A Vision Betrayed*, p. 145.

66. Barthel, *The Jesuits*, p. 192.

67. Ross, *A Vision Betrayed*, p. 153; one of these books was the *Xiguo Jifa*, which showed Chinese scholars how to build a "memory palace" to enhance their memory skills, something important when studying for the complex state Confucian exams. See Jonathan D. Spence, *The Memory Palace of Mataeo Ricci* (New York: Viking, 1984), for more details about Ricci's work in this field.

68. George H. Dunne, *Generation of Giants: The Story of the Jesuits in China in the Last Decades of the Ming Dynasty* (Notre Dame: University of Notre Dame Press, 1962), p. 245; Mungello, *The Great Encounter*, pp. 24–26.

69. J. S. Cummins, *A Question of Rites: Friar Domingo Navarrete and the Jesuits in China* (Hauts: Scolar Press, 1993), p. 233.

70. Mancall, *China at the Center*, pp. 84–87; Mungello, *The Great Encounter*, pp. 26–30; Barthel, *The Jesuits*, pp. 194–198; Cummins, *A Question of Rites*, pp. 238–239; Ross, *A Vision Betrayed*, pp. 190–198.

71. Ross, *A Vision Betrayed*, pp. 204, 206.

72. Immanuel C. Y. Hsü, *The Rise of Modern China*, 6th ed. (New York: Oxford University Press, 2000), p. 106.

73. Ibid., pp. 139–141.
74. Hsü, *Rise of Modern China*, pp. 154–155; J. L. Cranmer-Byng, "Lord Macartney's Embassy to Peking in 1793," *Journal of Oriental Studies*, Vol. 4, Nos. 1–2 (1957), pp. 117–120.
75. Hsü, *Rise of Modern China*, pp. 155–160; James L. Hevia, *Cherishing Men from Afar: Qing Guest Ritual and the Macartney Embassy of 1793* (Durham: Duke University Press, 1995), pp. 97–102.
76. "The First Imperial Edict, September 1793," in Pei-kai Chang, Michael Lestz, and Jonathan D. Spence, eds., *The Search for Modern China: A Documentary Collection* (New York: W. W. Norton, 1999), pp. 104–106; Cranmer-Byng, "Lord Macartney's Embassy to Peking in 1793," pp. 136–137.
77. "The Second Edict, September 1793," in Chang, Lestz, and Spence, eds., *The Search for Modern China*, pp. 106–109; Hevia, *Cherishing Men from Afar*, pp. 193–195.
78. Jack Beeching, *The Chinese Opium Wars* (San Diego: Harcourt Brace Jovanovich, 1975), p. 19.
79. Hsü, *Rise of Modern China*, pp. 171, 173.
80. Ibid., pp. 168–174, 176–178; Chang, Lestz, and Spence, *Search for Modern China*, pp. 110–122; Beeching, *The Chinese Opium Wars*, pp. 66–67.
81. "Commissioner Lin; Letter to Queen Victoria, 1839," in William H. McNeil and Mitsuko Iriye, eds., *Modern Asia and Africa: Readings in World History*, Vol. 9 (New York: Oxford University Press, 1971), pp. 111–118; Beeching, *The Chinese Opium Wars*, pp. 74–93.
82. Beeching, *The Chinese Opium Wars*, p. 98.
83. Edgar Holt, *The Opium Wars in China* (London: Putnam, 1964), pp. 98–100.
84. Beeching, *The Chinese Opium Wars*, pp. 131–152.
85. Hsü, *Rise of Modern China*, pp. 188–190.
86. Ibid., pp. 190–191.
87. Ping-ti Ho, *Studies on the Population of China, 1368–1953* (Cambridge, MA: Harvard University Press, 1959), pp. 64, 278, 282.
88. Maochun Yu, "The Taiping Rebellion: A Military Assessment of Revolution and Counterrevolution," in David A. Graff and Robin Higham, eds., *A Military History of China* (Lexington: University of Kentucky Press, 2012), p. 135; Jonathan Spence, *God's Chinese Son: The Taiping Heavenly Kingdom of Hong Xiuquan* (New York: W. W. Norton, 1996), pp. 23–24, 59–60.
89. Hsü, *Rise of Modern China*, pp. 127–128; John King Fairbank and Merle Goldman, *China: A New History*, 2nd ed. (Cambridge, MA: Belknap Press of Harvard University Press, 2006), p. 207.
90. Franz Michael, *Taiping Rebellion: History and Documents*, Vol. 1 (Seattle: University of Washington Press, 1966), pp. 112–113; Spence, *God's Chinese Son*, pp. 126–128, 171–180.
91. John K. Fairbank, "The Creation of the Treaty System," in John K. Fairbank, ed., *The Cambridge History of China*, Vol. 10: *Late Ch'ing, 1800–1911*, Part1 (London: Cambridge University Press, 1978), p. 237.
92. J. Y. Wong, *Deadly Dreams: Opium, Imperialism, and the Arrow War, 1856–1860* (Cambridge: Cambridge University Press, 1998), pp. 43–66, 69–83, 87–90.
93. Ibid., p. 97.
94. Ibid., pp. 91–97; Beeching, *The Chinese Opium Wars*, p. 221.
95. Holt, *The Opium Wars in China*, p. 197.
96. Beeching, *The Chinese Opium Wars*, p. 224.
97. Wong, *Deadly Dreams*, pp. 43–44, 459–461; Hsü, *Rise of Modern China*, p. 206.
98. S. Y. Teng, *The Taiping Rebellion and the Western Powers* (London: Oxford University Press, 1971), pp. 244–250, 261–263; Hsü, *Rise of Modern China*, pp. 210–211.

99. Hsü, *Rise of Modern China*, pp. 213–216.

100. Michael, *Taiping Rebellion*, 1, p. 174.

101. Fairbank and Goldman, *China*, pp. 213–214; Beeching, *The Chinese Opium Wars*, pp. 199–200, 286–287, 305–306; John King Fairbank, *The Great Chinese Revolution, 1800–1985* (New York: Harper & Row, 1986), p. 81. For Taiping regulations on the conduct of its armies, see Spence, *God's Chinese Son*, pp. 147–148, 165–168.

102. Hsü, *Rise of Modern China*, pp. 355, 361–379.

103. Ibid., pp. 373–380, 387–406; Jonathan D. Spence, *The Search for Modern China* (New York: W. W. Norton, 1990), pp. 230–235.

104. Joseph W. Esherick, *The Origins of the Boxer Rebellion* (Berkeley: University of California Press, 1987), pp. 123–124; Joseph E. Schrecker, *Imperialism and Chinese Nationalism: Germany in Shantung* (Cambridge, MA: Harvard University Press, 1971), pp. 91, 130–139; *The Yi Ho Tuan Movement of 1900* (Peking: Foreign Languages Press, 1976), pp. 1–14; Giles MacDonough, *The Last Kaiser: The Life of Wilhelm II* (New York: St. Martin's Press, 2000), pp. 234–235.

105. Nat Brandt, *Massacre in Shansi* (Syracuse: Syracuse University Press, 1994), p. 233.

106. Ibid., pp. 231–232.

107. Ibid., pp. 223–233; Victor Purcell, *The Boxer Uprising: A Background Study* (Cambridge: Cambridge University Press, 1963), pp. 240–262. The contingent of foreign troops was made up of 8,000 Japanese, 4,800 Russian, 3,000 British, 2,100 American, 800 French, 58 Austrian, and 53 Italian soldiers.

108. Brandt, *Massacre in Shansi*, p. 277; Hsü, *Rise of Modern China*, pp. 400–401.

109. Purcell, *The Boxer Uprising*, p. 261.

110. William L. Langer, *The Diplomacy of Imperialism, 1890–1902*, Vol. 2 (New York: 1935), p. 704; Purcell, *The Boxer Uprising*, pp. 261–262.

111. Douglas M. Peers, *India under Colonial Rule: 1700–1885* (Harlow: Pearson Longman, 2006), pp. 21–22, 36.

112. Bruce B. Lawrence, "The Eastward Journey of Muslim Kingship," in John L. Esposito, ed., *The Oxford History of Islam* (Oxford: Oxford University Press, 1999), pp. 396–397.

113. Sir Mortimer Wheeler and A. L. Basham, "Ancient and Hindu India," in Vincent A. Smith and Percival Spear, eds., *The Oxford History of India*, 4th ed. (New Delhi: Oxford University Press, 1958), p. 207.

114. Romila Thapar, *A History of India*, Vol. 1 (Harmondsworth: Penguin Books, 1966), pp. 233–234.

115. Lawrence, "The Eastward Journey of Muslim Kingship," p. 397; Wheeler and Basham, "Ancient and Hindu India," pp. 208–209.

116. Lawrence, "The Eastward Journey of Muslim Kingship," pp. 398–399; Thapar, *A History of India*, pp. 234–235.

117. J. B. Hanison, "The Muslim Period," in Smith and Spear, *Oxford History of India*, pp. 232–233.

118. Ibid., pp. 234–235; Hajime Nakamura, *Gotama Buddha: A Biography Based on the Most Reliable Texts*, trans. Gaynor Sekimori, Vol. 1 (Tokyo: Kosei, 2000), p. 127.

119. Ibid., pp. 235–236.

120. Stanley Wolpert, *A New History of India* (New York: Oxford University Press, 1977), p. 109; Lawrence, "The Eastward Journey of Muslim Kingship," p. 399.

121. J. B. Harrison, "India in the Muslim Period," in Smith and Spear, *Oxford History of India*, p. 237.

122. Michael Prawdin, *The Mongol Empire: Its Rise and Legacy*, trans. Eden and Cedar Paul (New York: Free Press, 1967), pp. 194–199; Harrison, "India in the Muslim Period," p. 239; Edward Dennis Sokol, "Tamerlane (1336–1405)," in Joseph L. Wieczynski, ed., *The Modern Encyclopedia of Russian and Soviet History*, Vol. 38 (Gulf Breeze: Academic International Press, 1984), p. 166.

123. Justin Marozzi, *Tamerlane: Sword of Islam, Conqueror of the World* (Cambridge: Da Capo, 2006), p. 264.

124. Ibid., p. 271.

125. Ibid., p. 271.

126. Wolpert, *A New History of India*, p. 119; Beatrice Forbes Manz, *The Rise and Rule of Tamerlane* (New York: Cambridge University Press, 1989), p. 72; Marozzi, *Tamerlane*, pp. 270–272.

127. Marozzi, *Tamerlane*, p. 274.

128. Wolpert, *A New History of India*, p. 121.

129. Ibid., pp. 124–125.

130. Ashirbadi Lal Srivastava, *The Mughal Empire (1526–1803)*, 5th rev. ed. (Agra: Shiva Lal Agarwal, 1966), p. 141.

131. Wolpert, *A New History of India*, p. 155.

132. Srivastava, *The Mughal Empire*, pp. 301–303; John F. Richards, *The Mughal Empire* (Cambridge: Cambridge University Press, 1996), pp. 129–130; R. P. Tripathi, *Rise and Fall of the Mughal Empire* (Allahabad: Central Book Depot, 1976), pp. 442–445.

133. Srivastava, *The Mughal Empire*, pp. 328–332.

134. Richards, *The Mughal Empire*, pp. 158–161; Wolpert, *A New History of India*, p. 157.

135. Richards, *The Mughal Empire*, pp. 171–172, 217–218.

136. Ibid., p. 222.

137. Ibid., pp. 222–223.

138. Wolpert, *A New History of India*, p. 167.

139. Richards, *The Mughal Empire*, p. 290.

140. Percival Spear, *A History of India*, Vol. 2 (London: Penguin, 1990), pp. 62–65.

141. Denis Judd, *The Lion and the Tiger: The Rise and the Fall of the British Raj, 1600–1947* (Oxford: Oxford University Press, 2004), p. 9.

142. Douglas M. Peers, *India under Colonial Rule: 1700-1885* (Harrow: Pearson Longman, 2006), pp. 22–23; Judd, *The Lion and the Tiger*, pp. 17–18.

143. Wolpert, *A New History of India*, p. 179; Peers, *India under Colonial Rule*, p. 28.

144. Lawrence James, *Raj: The Making and Unmaking of British India* (New York: St. Martin's Griffin, 1997), p. 39.

145. Wolpert, *A New History of India*, pp. 185–186.

146. James, *Raj*, p. 49.

147. Ibid., p. 49.

148. Ibid., p. 64.

149. Ibid., p. 65.

150. Ibid., p. 81.

151. Ibid., p. 93.

152. Ibid., p. 97.

153. Ibid., p. 97.

154. Ibid., p. 121; Peers, *India under Colonial Rule*, p. 39, says the British had 300,000 troops in India by this time.

155. Peers, *India under Colonial Rule*, pp. 51–52.

156. James, *Raj*, p. 135.

157. Ibid., p. 136.

158. Peers, *India under Colonial Rule*, p. 64.

159. Ibid., pp. 65–66.

160. Ibid., p. 64.

161. Ibid., pp. 65–66.

162. James, *Raj*, pp. 234–240.

163. Andrew Ward, *Our Bones Are Scattered: The Cawnpore Massacre and the Indian Mutiny of 1857* (New York: Henry Holt, 1996), pp. 428–429.

164. Ibid., 437.
165. Ibid., 442.
166. James, *Raj*, p. 256.
167. Ibid., p. 286.
168. Ibid., p. 256.
169. Ibid., p. 259.
170. Ibid., pp. 260–261.
171. Ward, *Our Bones Are Scattered*, pp. 500–501.
172. Peers, *India under Colonial Rule*, p. 71.
173. James, *Raj*, p. 293; Peers, *Indian under Colonial Rule*, pp. 74–75.
174. Spear, A *History of India*, pp. 149–150; James, *Raj*, p. 326.
175. Judd, *The Lion and the Tiger*, p. 86.
176. Ibid., p. 87.
177. James, *Raj*, p. 297.
178. John Reader, *Africa: A Biography of the Continent* (New York: Vantage Books, 1999), xi.
179. Dr. Marimba Ani, "To Be Afrikan," *BRC-News*, September 9, 1999, p. 1; http://www.hartford-hwp.com/archives/30/084.html. Dr. Ani first used this term, which is drawn from the *Kiswahili*, in her classic work *Let the Circle Be Unbroken: The Implications of African Spirituality in the Diaspora* (Trenton: Red Sea Press, 1994).
180. Nathan Nunn, "The Long-Term Effects of Africa's Slave Trades," *Quarterly Journal of Economics*, Vol. 123, No. 1 (February 2008), pp. 140–142.
181. Philip D. Curtin, *The Atlantic Slave Trade: A Census* (Madison: University of Wisconsin Press, 1969), p. 268.
182. Nunn, "The Long-Term Effects of Africa's Slave Trades," p. 152.
183. Paul E. Lovejoy, "The Volume of the Atlantic Slave Trade: A Synthesis," *The Journal of African History*, Vol. 23, No. 4 (1982), pp. 478, 483; Curtin's estimates are much lower, *The Atlantic Slave Trade*, p. 211.
184. Milton Meltzer, *Slavery: A World History*, Vol. 2 (New York: Da Capo, 1993), p. 17; C. C. Wrigley, "Historicism in Africa: Slavery and State Formation," *African Affairs*, Vol. 70, No. 279 (April 1971), p. 114; J. D. Fage, "Slavery and the Slave Trade in the Context of West African History," *Journal of African History*, Vol. 10, No. 3 (1969), p. 402; John Thornton, *Africa and Africans in the Making of the Atlantic World, 1400–1800*, 2nd ed. (Cambridge: Cambridge University Press, 1998), p. 99; David Henige, "Measuring the Immeasurable: The Atlantic Slave Trade, West African Population and the Pyrrhonian Critic," *Journal of African History: Special Issue in Honour of J. D. Fage*, Vol. 27, No. 2 (1986), pp. 300–301; John K. Thornton, "The Art of War in Angola, 1575–1680," in Douglas M. Peers, ed., *War and Empire: Contact and Conflict between European and Non-European Military and Maritime Forces and Cultures* (Aldershot: Ashgate, 1997), pp. 81–90, 117, 121; Paul E. Lovejoy, *Transformations in Slavery: A History of Slavery in Africa* (Cambridge: Cambridge University Press, 1983), p. 70.
185. Reader, *Africa*, p. 361.
186. Lovejoy, *Transformations in Slavery*, p. 478; Eric Williams, *From Columbus to Castro: The History of the Caribbean, 1492–1969* (London: André Deutsch, 1970), pp. 280, 382.
187. *Declaration of Independence*, July 4, 1776. The Avalon Project. Yale Law School. http://avalon.law.yale.edu/18th_century/declare.asp; *Declaration of Rights and Duties of Man and Citizen*, Constitution of the Year III (1795), p. 1, http://chnm.gmu.edu/revolution/d/298.
188. Williams, *From Columbus to Castro*, pp. 280–281; Lovejoy, *Transformations in Slavery*, p. 140; Meltzer, *Slavery*, 2, p. 245.
189. Williams, *From Columbus to Castro*, pp. 280–281, 292–302; "The Effort of Portugal to Abolish Slavery," *New York Times*, May 24, 1869, p. 4. Lovejoy, *Transformations in Slavery*, p. 140; Meltzer, *Slavery*, 2, p. 245.

190. Thomas Pakenham, *The Scramble for Africa: White Man's Conquest of the Dark Continent from 1876 to 1912* (New York: Harper Collins, 2003), p. 1.

191. Adam Hochschild, *King Leopold's Ghost: A Story of Greed, Terror, and Heroism in Colonial Africa* (Boston: Houghton Mifflin, 1999), pp. 29–31, 57–58.

192. Pakenham, *The Scramble for Africa*, pp. 38–39.

193. Hochschild, *King Leopold's Ghost*, pp. 65–67.

194. Ibid., pp. 68–69.

195. Fritz Stern, *Gold and Iron: Bismarck, Bleichröder, and the Building of the German Empire* (New York: Vintage Books, 1979), pp. 402–409; Hochschild, *King Leopold's Ghost*, pp. 75–87; Pakenham, *The Scramble for Africa*, pp. 254–255.

196. Hochschild, *King Leopold's Ghost*, pp. 225, 233, 282.

197. Joseph Conrad, *Heart of Darkness* (New York: Dell, 1960), p. 89.

198. Séamas Ó Síocháin and Michael O'Sullivan, eds., *The Eyes of Another Race: Roger Casement's Congo Report and 1903 Diary* (Dublin: University College Dublin Press, 2003), pp. 1, 28–32. This volume contains not only Casement's full official report but also his 1903 diary detailing his research travels in the Congo; Hochschild, *King Leopold's Ghost*, pp. 250–259.

199. Stern, *Gold and Iron*, pp. 410–411.

200. Ibid., p. 411.

201. Pakenham, *The Scramble for Africa*, pp. 608–609.

202. Ibid., pp. 609–610.

203. Ibid., p. 615.

204. Ibid., p. 611.

205. Ibid., p. 615.

206. Isabel V. Hull, *Absolute Destruction: Military Culture and the Practices of War in Imperial Germany* (Ithaca: Cornell University Press, 2005), pp. 332–333.

207. Elizabeth Elbourne, *Blood Ground Colonialism, Missions, and the Contest for Christianity in the Cape Colony and Britain, 1799–1853* (Montreal: McGill-Queens University Press, 2002), p. 78; Adrian Greaves, *Crossing the Buffalo; The Zulu War of 1879* (London: Weidenfeld & Nicolson, 2005), pp. 23–30.

208. Noël Mostert, *Frontiers: The Epic of South Africa's Creation and the Tragedy of the Xhosa People* (New York: Alfred A Knopf, 1992), p. 678.

209. A. G. Visser, "Amakeia," p. 1; http://www.poemhunter.com/poem/amakeia; Mostert, *Frontiers*, p. 670.

210. Mostert, *Frontiers*, pp. 688–708, 751.

211. Ibid., p. 759.

212. Ibid., pp. 759–760.

213. Denis Judd and Keith Surridge, *The Boer War* (New York: Palgrave Macmillan, 2003), pp. 20–21.

214. John Laband, *The Transvaal Rebellion: The First Boer War, 1880–1881* (Harlow: Pearson Longman, 2005), pp. 12–14.

215. Judd and Surridge, *The Boer War*, p. 25.

216. Ibid., p. 25.

217. Ibid., pp. 25–26.

218. Ibid., pp. 28–29.

219. Christopher M. Paulin, *White Men's Dreams, Black Men's Blood: African Labor and British Expansionism in Southern Africa, 1877–1895* (Trenton: Africa World Press, 2001), pp. 68–70; Richard Cope, *Ploughshare of War: The Origins of the Anglo-Zulu War of 1879* (Pietermaritzburg: University of Natal Press, 1999), pp. 3, 235.

220. Ibid., p. 237.

221. Ibid., pp. 223, 235–236, 237–238.

222. Ibid., pp. 243–244.

223. Greaves, *Crossing the Buffalo*, pp. 118–134.

224. John Laband, *Kingdom in Crisis: The Zulu Response to the British Invasion of 1879* (Manchester: Manchester University Press, 1992), p. 87.

225. Ibid., p. 88.

226. Ibid., pp. 107–108.

227. Cope, *Ploughshare of War*, p. 250.

228. Laband, *Kingdom in Crisis*, pp. 207–229.

229. Ibid., p. 230.

230. Greaves, *Crossing the Buffalo*, pp. 330–332.

231. Cope, *Ploughshare of War*, pp. 254–255.

232. John Laband, *The Transvaal Rebellion: The First Boer War, 1880–1881* (Harlow: Pearson Longman, 2005), pp. 21, 198–210; Thomas Pakenham, *The Boer War* (New York: Random House, 1979), pp. 33–34. Judd and Surridge, *The Boer War*, pp. 33, 46.

233. Judd and Surridge, *The Boer War*, p. 49.

234. Pakenham, *The Scramble for Africa*, pp. 567–568, 571–575.

235. Pakenham, *The Boer War*, p. 522.

236. Judd and Surridge, *The Boer War*, pp. 193–194; Pakenham, *The Boer War*, p. 522.

237. Pakenham, *The Boer War*, p. 523.

238. Ibid., p. 529.

239. Pakenham, *The Scramble for Africa*, pp. 577–578.

240. Barbara Harlow and Mia Carter, eds., *Archives of Empire*, Vol. 2: *The Scramble for Africa* (Durham: Duke University Press, 2003), pp. 668, 670.

241. Pakenham, *The Boer War*, pp. 533–534; Pakenham, *The Scramble for Africa*, p. 578.

242. Pakenham, *The Boer War*, pp. 539–540.

243. David Rubenstein, *A Different World for Women: The Life of Millicent Garrett Fawcett* (Columbus: Ohio State University Press, 1991), pp. 121–127; Pakenham, *The Boer War*, pp. 546–549.

244. Judd and Surridge, *The Boer War*, pp. 298–299; Pakenham, *The Boer War*, p. 571.

245. Peter Gay, *The Cultivation of Hatred*, Vol. 3: *The Bourgeois Experience—Victoria to Freud* (New York: W. W. Norton, 1993), pp. 85–86.

246. Robert Blake, *A History of Rhodesia* (New York: Alfred A. Knopf, 1978), p. 104.

247. Gay, *The Cultivation of Hatred*, 3, p. 87; L. H. Gann, *A History of Southern Rhodesia: Early Days to 1934* (London: Chatto & Windus, 1965), pp. 115–120; Blake, *A History of Rhodesia*, pp. 102–114.

248. Hull, *Absolute Destruction*, p. 332.

4   BIRTH OF THE MODERN LAWS OF WAR—LIEBER TO VERSAILLES

1. *Arthur Conan Doyle: A Life in Letters*, ed. Jon Lellenberg, Daniel Stashower, and Charles Foley (New York: Penguin, 2007), pp. 433–436.

2. Arthur Conan Doyle, *The Great Boer War* (1902). The Gutenberg Ebook Project (Ebook #3069), pp. 259–260; http://www.gutenberg.org/files/3069/3069-h/3069-h.htm.

3. Ibid., pp. 45–46; 74.

4. Ibid., p. 48; *Laws and Customs of War on Land* (Hague II), July 29, 1899, The Avalon Project at Yale Law School, pp. 9–10; http://www.yale.edu/lawweb/avalon/lawofwar/hague02.htm..

5. Doyle, *The Great Boer War*, pp. 51–52, 58, 68; *Laws and Customs of War on Land* (Hague II), p. 9.

6. Doyle, *The Great Boer War*, pp. 70, 75; *Laws and Customs of War on Land* (Hague II),p. 4.

7. Elihu Root, *Addresses on International Subjects* (Cambridge, MA: Harvard University Press, 1916), p. 103.

8. Martii Koskenniemi, *The Gentle Civilizer of Nations: The Rise and Fall of International Law, 1870–1960* (Cambridge: Cambridge University Press, 2002), pp. 39–40.

9. Frank Freidel, *Francis Lieber: Nineteenth Century Liberal* (Gloucester: Peter Smith, 1968), pp. 13–17, 30–34, 43–46, 50–52, 115–143, 282–286, 292–293, 368–369.

10. Ibid., pp. 282, 309, 314, 318. 320.

11. Ibid., p. 320.

12. Ibid., p. 323.

13. Ibid., pp. 323–324.

14. James Turner Johnson, "Lieber and the Theory of War," in Charles R. Mack and Henry H. Lesesne, eds., *Francis Lieber and the Culture of the Mind* (Columbia: University of South Carolina Press, 2005), p. 64.

15. Ibid., p. 63.

16. Freidel, *Francis Lieber*, pp. 328–329; Halleck's massive two-volume history of international law, *International Law*, Vol. 1, and *International Law; or Rule Regulating the Intercourse of States in Peace and War*, Vol. 2 (Memphis: General Books, 2010), is an impressive history of international law going back to antiquity. First published in 1861, it was updated in 1878 to include major international events and developments since the date of its first publication.

17. Francis Lieber, "Guerilla Parties Considered with Reference to the Laws and Usages of War," in Richard Shelly Hartigan, *Lieber's Code and the Law of War* (Chicago: Precedent, 1983), pp. 35–36, 41–43.

18. Freidel, *Francis Lieber*, p. 331.

19. Ibid., pp. 331–335.

20. Root, *Addresses on International Subjects*, p. 92.

21. Theodor Meron, *War Crimes Law Comes of Age: Essays* (Oxford: Clarendon Press, 2006), pp. 132–133, 135.

22. *The 1863 Laws of War Being the Articles of War (1806), General Orders 100, General Orders 49, and Extracts of Revised Army Regulations of 1861* (Mechanicsburg: Stackpole Books, 2005), pp. 36–37, 39–40, 43.

23. Ibid., pp. 45–48, 51–66.

24. Michael Burlingame, *Abraham Lincoln: A Life*, Vol. 2 (Baltimore: Johns Hopkins University Press, 2008), p. 541.

25. *The Life and Letters of Francis Lieber*, ed. Thomas Sergeant Perry (Boston: James R. Osgood, 1882), pp. 333–334.

26. Betsy Baker Röben, "The Method Behind Bluntschli's 'Modern' International Law," *Journal of the History of International Law*, Vol. 4 (2002), pp. 249, 251.

27. Koskenniemi, *The Gentle Civilizer of Nations*, pp. 39–42.

28. *The Life and Letters of Francis Lieber*, pp. 366, 379–380, 384–385, 388–389, 390–391, 398, 401, 409, 411–413; *Convention for the Amelioration of the Condition of the Wounded in Armies in the Field*, Geneva, August 22, 1864, p. 1; http://www.icrc.org/ihl.nsf/webprint/120-FULL?OpenDocument; Koskenniemi, *The Gentle Civilizer of Nations*, p. 39.

29. Geoffrey Wawro, *The Franco-Prussian War: The German Conquest of France in 1870–1871* (Cambridge: Cambridge University Press, 2003), p. 237.

30. Otto Friedrich, *Blood and Iron: From Bismarck to Hitler; The Von Moltke Family's Impact on German History* (New York: HarperPerennial, 1995), p. 188.

31. Ibid., pp. 188–189.
32. Thomas Rohkämer, "Daily Life at the Front," in Stig Förster and Jörg Nagler, eds., *On the Road to Total War: The American Civil War and the German Wars of Unification, 1861–1871* (Washington and Cambridge: German Historical Institute and Cambridge University Press, 1997), p. 507.
33. Manfred Messerschmidt, "The Prussian Army from Reform to War," ibid., p. 277.
34. Ibid., p. 279.
35. John Horne and Alan Kramer, *German Atrocities, 1914: A History of Denial* (New Haven: Yale University Press, 2001), pp. 94, 151–152.
36. Ibid., pp. 41–42; *Statutes,* Institut de droit international, September 10, 1873, Article 1.
37. V. V. Pustogarov, *Our Martens: F. F. Martens, International Lawyer and Architect of Peace,* ed. and trans. W. E. Butler (The Hague: Kluwer Law International, 2000), pp. 108–109.
38. Karma Nabulsi, *Traditions of War: Occupation, Resistance, and the Law* (Oxford: Oxford University Press, 1999), pp. 3–4.
39. Ibid., pp. 6–8.
40. *The 1863 Laws of War,* pp. 33–52; *Project of an International Declaration Concerning the Laws and Customs of War,* Brussels, August 27, 1874, pp. 1–4; http://www.icrc.org/ihl. nsf/WebPrint/135-FULL?OpenDocument.
41. Dietrich Schindler, "J. C. Bluntschli's Contribution to the Law of War," in M. G. Kohen and Marcelo Kohen, eds., *Promoting Justice, Human Rights and Conflict Resolution through International Law* (Leiden: Brill, 2007), p. 454.
42. Ibid., p. 454; *The Laws of War on Land. Oxford.* September 9, 1880, p. 1. http://www. icrc.org/ihl/nsf/FULL/140?OpenDocument.
43. *The Laws of War on Land,* p. 1.
44. Ibid., p. 1.
45. Ibid., p. 1.
46. Nabulsi, *Traditions of War,* p. 9.
47. Ibid., pp. 9, 94.
48. Thomas Erskine Holland, *Letters to "The Times'" upon War and Neutrality, 1881–1920* (Middlesex: Echo Library, 2006), p. 28.
49. Ibid., p. 33.
50. Sidney Bradshaw Fay, *The Origins of the World War,* 2nd ed. (New York: Macmillan, 1949), pp. 32–49.
51. Arthur Eyffinger, *The Peace Palace: Residence for Justice—Domicile of Learning* (The Hague: Carnegie Foundation, 1988), p. 10; "World Expenditures for Armaments," *Literary Digest,* February 23, 1935, p. 42.
52. Theodore H. Von Laue, *Sergei Witte and the Industrialization of Russia* (New York: Columbia University Press, 1963), pp. 45–46, 155–156; Grant Dawson, "Preventing 'A Great Moral Evil': Jean de Bloch's *The Future of War* as Anti-revolutionary Pacifism," *Journal of Contemporary History,* Vol. 37, No. 1 (2002), pp. 56; T. H. E. Travers, "Technology, Tactics, and Morale: Jean de Bloch, the Boer War, and British Military Theory, 1900–1914," *Journal of Modern History,* Vol. 51, No. 2 (June 1979), pp. 265–267.
53. Giles Macdonogh, *The Last Kaiser: The Life of Wilhelm II* (New York: St. Martin's Press, 2000), p. 237; Barbara W. Tuchman, *The Proud Tower: A Portrait of the World before the War 1819–1914* (New York: Ballantine Books, 1996), p. 278.
54. Eyffinger, *The Peace Palace,* p. 9.
55. Pustogarov, *Our Martens,* p. 162.
56. Stephen Barcroft, "The Hague Peace Conference of 1899," *Irish Studies in International Affairs,* Vol. 3, No. 1 (1989), p. 59.

57. Eyffinger, *The Peace Palace*, p. 12.

58. Ibid., p. 17; Pustogarov, *Our Martens*, pp. 162–167.

59. Eyffinger, *The Peace Palace*, pp. 17–18.

60. Ibid., pp. 24–25; Barcroft, "The Hague Peace Conference of 1899," pp. 63–65.

61. Pustogarov, *Our Martens*, p. 168.

62. Eyffinger, *The Peace Palace*, p. 29.

63. Ibid., p. 29.

64. Robert K. Massie, *Dreadnought: Britain, Germany, and the Coming of the Great War* (New York: Random House, 1991), p. 430.

65. *The Proceedings of the Hague Peace Conferences: The Conference of 1899* (New York: Oxford University Press, 1920), p. 90.

66. Ibid., pp. 394–407.

67. Ibid., pp. 564–578.

68. Ibid., pp. 45–54.

69. Ibid., p. 54.

70. *Laws and Customs of War on Land* (Hague II), pp. 2–3.

71. Meron, *War Crimes Law Comes of Age*, p. 10.

72. Barcroft, "The Hague Peace Conference of 1899," p. 65.

73. *Laws and Customs of War on Land* (Hague II), pp. 688–694, 712–713, 735, 755.

74. Ibid., pp. 91–93.

75. Ibid., pp. 228–234.

76. Ibid., pp. 220–221.

77. Eyffinger, *The Peace Palace*, p. 35.

78. Ibid., p. 35; *International Commission of Inquiry Reports: Great Britain-Russia, North Sea Incident Inquiry. "The Dogger Bank Case,"* November 25, 1904–February 26, 1905, p. 1; James Brown Scott, *The Hague Court Reports: Comprising Awards, Accompanied by Syllabi, the Agreements of Arbitration, and Other Documents in Each Case Submitted to the Permanent Court of Arbitrations* (Buffalo: William S. Hein, 2004), pp. 403–411; P. Hamilton, *International Arbitration & Dispute Resolution* (Dordrecht: Kulwer Law International, 1999), pp. 298–301.

79. Pustogarov, *Our Martens*, p. 281.

80. J. N. Westwood, *Russia against Japan, 1904–05: A New Look at the Russo-Japanese War* (Albany: State University of New York Press, 1986), pp. 154–155.

81. F. De Martens, "The Portsmouth Peace Conference," *North American Review*, Vol. 181, No. 588 (November 1905), p. 642.

82. Westwood, *Russia against Japan*, pp. 157–159; Eugene P. Trani, *The Treaty of Portsmouth: An Adventure in American Diplomacy* (Lexington: University of Kentucky Press, 1969), p. 142; The Nobel Peace Prize 1906, Theodore Roosevelt, "Acceptance Speech," Herbert H. D. Peirce, December 10, 1906, pp. 1–2. http://nobelprize.org/nobel_prizes/peace/laureates/1906/roosevelt-acceptance.html.

83. "Official Correspondence Relating to the Second Conference," James Brown Scott, ed., *Texts of the Peace Conferences at The Hague, 1899 and 1907* (Boston: Ginn, 1908), pp. 93–106; Eyffinger, *The Peace Palace*, pp. 77–78.

84. *Convention for the Amelioration of the Condition of the Wounded and Sick in Armies in the Field*, Geneva, July 6, 1906, pp. 1–6; http://www.icrc.org/ihl.nsf/WebPrint/180-FULL?OpenDocument; Scott, *Texts of the Peace Conferences*, p. 267.

85. Roger Chickering, *Imperial Germany and a World without War: The Peace Movement and German Society, 1892–1914* (Princeton: Princeton University Press, 1975), pp. 229–230.

86. Scott, *Texts of the Peace Conferences at The Hague*, p. 137; Eyffinger, *The Peace Palace*, p. 86.

87. Eyffinger, *The Peace Palace*, p. 87.

88. William I. Hull, *The Two Hague Conferences and Their Contributions to International Law* (Boston: Ginn & Company for the International School of Peace, 1908), p. 480.

89. Scott, *Texts of the Peace Conferences*, p. 198.

90. Hull, *The Two Hague Conferences*, pp. 479–487; Eyffinger, *The Peace Palace*, p. 88.

91. Hull, *The Two Hague Conferences*, pp. 69–70; Scott, *Texts of the Peace Conferences*, p. 104.

92. Hull, *The Two Hague Conferences*, p. 71.

93. Scott, *Texts of the Peace Conferences*, p. 2.

94. Hull, *The Two Hague Conferences*, pp. 71–75.

95. Scott, *Texts of the Peace Conferences*, p. 138.

96. Ibid., pp. 203–331.

97. Eyffinger, *The Peace Palace*, p. 91.

98. Hull, *The Two Hague Conferences*, pp. 464, 496–503.

99. Alan Kramer, *Dynamic of Destruction: Culture and Mass Killing in the First World War* (Oxford: Oxford University Press, 2007), p. 5.

100. Aleksandr Solzhenitsyn, *August 1914: The Red Wheel, Knot I*, trans. H. T. Willets (New York: Noonday Press, 1989), p. 46.

101. G. J. Meyer, *The Story of the Great War, 1914 to 1918* (New York: Bantam Dell, 2007), p. 705; Ian F. W. Beckett, *The Great War*, 2nd ed. (Harlow: Pearson Longman, 2007), pp. 643–644.

102. Beckett, *The Great War*, p. 438.

103. John Keegan, *The First World War* (New York: Alfred A. Knopf, 1999), p. 423; Colin Nicolson, *The First World War, Europe 1914–1918* (Harlow: Longman, 2001), p. 248; Jean-Yves Le Naour, *The Living Unknown Soldier: A Story of Grief and the Great War* (New York: Henry Holt, 2005).

104. W. Bruce Lincoln, *Passage through Armageddon: The Russians in War & Revolution, 1914–1918* (New York: Simon and Schuster, 1986), p. 480; Beckett, *The Great War*, p. 521; Keegan, *The First World War*, p. 423; Nicolson, *The First World War*, p. 248; Col. Gen. G. F. Krivosheev, ed., *Soviet Casualties and Combat Losses in the Twentieth Century* (London: Greenhill Books, 1997), pp. 7–8; Mark Ferro, *Nicholas II: Last of the Tsars*, trans. Brian Pearce (Oxford: Oxford University Press, 1995), pp. 235–236.

105. Beckett, *The Great War*, p. 40; Keegan, *The First World War*, p. 423; Nicolson, *The First World War*, p. 248; Erik Jan Zürcher, "Between Death and Desertion: The Experience of the Ottoman Soldier in World War I," *Turcica*, Vol. 28 (1996), p. 256.

106. Ernst Simmel, "War Neuroses and 'Psychic Trauma,'" in Anton Kaes, Martin Jay, and Edward Dimenberg, eds., *The Weimar Republic Sourcebook* (Berkeley: University of California Press, 1995), p. 7.

107. Alan Palmer, *Twilight of the Habsburgs: The Life and Times of Emperor Francis Joseph* (New York: Grove Press, 1994), pp. 346–347.

108. Erik J. Zürcher, *Turkey: A Modern History*, new rev. ed. (London: I. B. Taurus, 2001), pp. 138–172; Lord Kinross, *The Ottoman Centuries: The Rise and Fall of the Turkish Empire* (New York: Morrow Quill, 1977), pp. 608–609; Stanford Shaw, *History of the Ottoman Empire*, Vol. 2: *Reform, Revolution, and Republic. The Rise of Modern Turkey, 1808–1975* (Cambridge: Cambridge University Press, 1977), pp. 340–372.

109. John Horne and Alan Kramer, *German Atrocities, 1914: A History of Denial* (New Haven: Yale University Press, 2001), p. 74.

110. James F. Willis, *Prologue to Nuremberg: The Politics and Diplomacy of Punishing War Criminals of the First World War* (Westport: Greenwood Press, 1982), pp. 29–35, 40–41.

111. Gerd Hankel, *Die Leipziger Prozesse: Deutsche Kriegsverbrechen und ihre strafrechtliche Verfolgung nach dem Ersten Weltkrieg* (Hamburg: Hamburger Edition, 2003), p. 15; Alan

Kramer, "The First Wave of International War Crimes Trials: Istanbul and Leipzig," *European Review*, Vol. 14, No. 4 (2006), p. 447.

112. Macdonogh, *The Last Kaiser*, pp. 410–412, 459.

113. Willis, *Prologue to Nuremberg*, p. 58.

114. Gary Jonathan Bass, *Stay the Hand of Vengeance: The Politics of War Crimes Tribunals* (Princeton: Princeton University Press, 2002), p. 71.

115. Ibid., pp. 70–71.

116. Willis, *Prologue to Nuremberg*, p. 58.

117. Ibid.

118. Bass, *Stay the Hand of Vengeance*, pp. 73–74, 99–100.

119. "Commission on the Responsibility of the Authors of the War and on Enforcement of Penalties," Report Presented to the Preliminary Peace Conference. March 29, 1919, *American Journal of International Law*, Vol. 14, No. 1 (January–April 1920), p. 95.

120. Ibid., p. 98.

121. Ibid., p. 107.

122. Ibid., p. 115.

123. Ibid., p. 117.

124. Ibid., pp. 119–120, 122–123.

125. Ibid., pp. 146–147.

126. Ibid., pp. 129, 151–152.

127. Paul Mantoux, *The Deliberations of the Council of Four (March 24–June 28, 1919): Notes of the Official Interpreter*, trans. Arthur S. Link, Vol. 1 (Princeton: Princeton University Press, 1992), pp. 118–122, 187–195.

128. Ibid., p. 189.

129. Ibid., p. 262.

130. Ibid., p. 406.

131. Ibid., pp. 407, 410.

132. Ibid., pp. 414–415.

133. Ibid., pp. 446–449.

134. Ibid., p. 517; *The Treaty of Versailles (June 28, 1919)*, Part 7 , Penalties, Articles 227–230; http://history.acused.edu/gen/text/versaillestreaty/ver227.html; ibid., Part 8 , Reparation Section, General Provisions, Article 231, p. 1.

135. Mantoux, *The Deliberations of the Council of Four*, p. 517; Jürgen Matthäus, "The Lessons of Leipzig," in Patricia Heberer and Jürgen Matthäus, eds., *Atrocities on Trial: Historical Perspectives on the Politics of Prosecuting War Crimes* (Lincoln: University of Nebraska Press, 2008), p. 8.

136. Mantoux, *The Deliberations of the Council of Four*, pp. 462–463.

137. Ibid., pp. 559–560.

138. Jan Willem Schulte Nordholt, trans. Herbert H. Rowen, *Woodrow Wilson: A Life for World Peace* (Berkeley: University of California Press, 1991), p. 358.

139. Willis, *Prologue to Nuremberg*, pp. 98–108.

140. Ibid., p. 111.

141. Macdonogh, *The Last Kaiser*, p. 425.

142. Willis, *Prologue to Nuremberg*, p. 112; Macdonogh, *The Last Kaiser*, pp. 427–459.

143. Horne and Kramer, *German Atrocities*, pp. 338–339.

144. John W. Wheeler-Bennett, *Hindenburg: The Wooden Titan* (London: Macmillan, 1967), p. 238; Willis, *Prologue to Nuremberg*, pp. 115–116.

145. Ian Kershaw, *Hitler: 1889–1936 Hubris* (New York: W. W. Norton, 1998), p. 115; David Clay Large, *Where Ghosts Walked: Munich's Road to the Third Reich* (New York: W. W. Norton, 1997), p. 122.

146. Horne and Kramer, *German Atrocities*, pp. 340–341.

147. Ibid., pp. 341–342.

148. Claud Mullins, *The Leipzig Trials: An Account of the War Criminals' Trials and a Study of German Mentality* (London: H. F. & G. Witherby, 1921), pp. 67, 87, 97, 104–107; Hankel, *Die Leipziger Prozesse*, pp. 333–339, 420–422.

149. Tony Bridgland, *Outrage at Sea: Naval Atrocities in the First World War* (Barnsley: Leo Cooper, 2002), pp. 181–182.

150. Mullins, *The Leipzig Trials*, pp. 132–133; Hankel, *Die Leipziger Prozesse*, pp. 465–470.

151. Mullins, *The Leipzig Trials*, pp. 135–149; Horne and Kramer, *German Atrocities*, p. 348; Hankel, *Die Leipziger Prozesse*, pp. 108–113, 117–123.

152. Mullins, *The Leipzig Trials*, pp. 151–168; Hankel, *Die Leipziger Prozesse*, pp. 100, 123–142; Horne and Kramer, *German Atrocities*, pp. 352–353.

153. Alan Kramer, "The First Wave of International War Crimes Trials: Istanbul and Leipzig," *European Review*, Vol. 14, No. 4 (October 2006), pp. 448–449.

154. Hankel, *Die Leipziger Prozesse*, pp. 228–259.

155. Kramer, "The First Wave," pp. 507–517; Horne and Kramer, *German Atrocities, 1914*, p. 351; Matthäus, "The Lessons of Leipzig," pp. 19–20.

156. Kershaw, *Hitler, 1889–1936: Hubris*, p. 379; Franz von Papen, *Memoirs*, trans. Brian Conwell (New York: E. Dalton, 1953), p. 257.

157. Kershaw, *Hitler, 1889–1936: Hubris*, pp. 194–210.

158. Erich Raeder, *My Life*, trans. Henry W. Drexel (Annapolis: United States Naval Institute, 1960), p. 109; Keith W. Bird, *Erich Raeder: Admiral of the Third Reich* (Annapolis: Naval Institute Press, 2006), p. 41.

159. Willis, *Prologue to Nuremberg*, p. 114; Office of United States Chief of Counsel for Prosecution of Axis Criminality, *Nazi Conspiracy and Aggression: Opinion and Judgement* (Washington, DC: US Government Printing Office, 1947), pp. 142–144.

160. The number of victims remains controversial to this day. A London newspaper, the *Westminster Gazette,* reported in the fall of 1915 that 800,000 Armenians had already been massacred, while the official British study on the genocide, *The Treatment of Armenians in the Ottoman Empire 1915–16*, estimated 600,000 deaths. In 1919, the Turkish government, which had begun its own investigation of the crimes, suggested that the number of victims was 800,000. Turkish historian Taner Akçam accepts this figure though Peter Balakian and Vahakn Dadrian estimate that more than a million Armenians died during World War I.

161. Center for Strategic Research, *The Armenian "Genocide": Facts & Figures* (Ankara: Center for Strategic Research, 2007), pp. 3–4.

162. Ronald Grigor Suny, *Looking toward Ararat: Armenia in Modern History* (Bloomington: Indian University Press, 1993), pp. 8–11, 17; Simon Payaslian, *The History of Armenia* (New York: Palgrave Macmillan, 2007), pp. 34–35; Vahan M. Kurkjian, *A History of Armenia* (New York: Armenia General Benevolent Union, 1958), pp. 118–121.

163. Suny, *Looking toward Ararat*, pp. 17, 22, 24; Payaslian, *The Modern History of Armenia*, pp. 103, 110–112; Shaw, *History of the Ottoman Empire and Modern Turkey*, 2, p. 200.

164. Ferro, *Nicholas II*, p. 75.

165. Payaslian, *The History of Armenia*, p. 113.

166. Erich Eyck, *Bismarck and the German Empire* (New York: W. W. Norton, 1968), pp. 243–252; *The Preliminary Treaty of Peace, Signed at Stefano* (March 17, 1878), pp. 4, 8. http:// pages.uoregon.edu/kimball/1878mr17.SanStef.trt.htm; Shaw, *History of the Ottoman Empire and Modern Turkey*, 2, pp. 200–201; Gerard Chaliand, "Introduction," in Gerard Chaliand, ed., *A People without a Country: The Kurds and Kurdistan*, trans. Michael Pallis (New York: Olive Branch Press, 1993), p. 8; Kendal, "The Kurds under the Ottoman Empire," ibid., pp. 14–24; Walter Kolarz, *Russia and Her Colonies* (Hamden: Archon Books, 1967), pp. 182–183; Robert H. Hewsen, "Circassians," in Joseph L. Wieczynski, ed., *The Modern Encyclopedia of Russian and Soviet History*, Vol. 7 (Gulf Breeze: Academic International Press, 1978), pp. 131–133.

167. Payaslian, *The History of Armenia*, pp. 116–117; "The Treaty of Berlin," 1878. *Modern History Source Book*, p. 2. http://www.fordham.edu/halsall/mod/1878berlin.html; Shaw, *History of the Ottoman Empire and Modern Turkey*, Vol. 2, pp. 190–191.

168. Shaw, *History of the Ottoman Empire and Modern Turkey*, 2, pp. 156–158, 257, 259–260.

169. Ibid., pp. 202–203; Suny, *Looking toward Ararat*, pp. 98–100; Guenter Lewy, unfortunately viewed by some as a Turkish apologist because he does not consider the massacres in 1915–1916 a genocide, also agrees about the general ineffectiveness of the Armenian revolutionary movement and its lack of appeal to Armenians in Anatolia. *The Armenian Massacres in Ottoman Turkey: A Disputed Genocide* (Salt Lake City: The University of Utah Press, 2005), pp. 11–15.

170. Peter Balakian, *The Burning Tigris: The Armenian Genocide and America's Response* (New York: HarperCollins, 2003), p. 55.

171. Ibid., p. 56.

172. Ibid., p. 56.

173. Ibid., p. 61.

174. Lewy, *The Armenian Massacres in Ottoman Turkey*, pp. 20–26; Payaslian states in *The History of Armenia*, p. 120, that the death toll was 100,000–300,000, while other sources suggest a death toll of 80,000–300,000. Taner Akçam, *A Shameful Act: The Armenian Genocide and the Question of Turkish Responsibility*, trans. Paul Bessemer (New York: Metropolitan Books, 2006), pp. 40–43; Vakhan N. Dadrian, *The History of the Armenian Genocide: Ethnic Conflict from the Balkans to Anatolia to the Caucasus* (New York: Berghan Books, 1995), pp. 113–157; Donald Bloxham, *The Great Game of Genocide: Imperialism, Nationalism, and the Destruction of the Ottoman Armenians* (Oxford: Oxford University Press, 2005), pp. 51–53.

175. "Another Armenian Holocaust," *New York Times*, September 10, 1895, p. 1.

176. Akçam, *A Shameful Act*, p. 43.

177. Payaslian, *The History of Armenia*, p. 123.

178. Shaw, *History of the Ottoman Empire and Modern Turkey*, 2, p. 255.

179. Ibid., 2, pp. 255, 266–267; Erik K. Zürcher, *Turkey: A Modern History*, 3rd ed. (London: I.B. Tauris, 2004), pp. 90–94.

180. Akçam, *A Shameful Act*, pp. 69–70; Dadrian, *The History of the Armenian Genocide*, pp. 181–182; "C. H. M. Doughty-Wylie to Sir G. Lowther," Report, Inclosure 1 in No. 83, Adana, April 21, 1909, pp. 1–8, in Wolfgang and Sigrid Gust, ed., *A Documentary of the Armenian Genocide in World War I*, www.armenocide.net.; "Sir G. Lowther to Sir Edward Grey," Constantinople, May 4, 1909, No. 324, ibid., p. 6; "Vice Consul C.H.M. Doughty-Wylie to Sir. G. Lowther," Report, Inclosure 5 in No. 96, Adana, May 4, 1909, ibid., p. 2; "The Vice Consul C.H.M. Doughty-Wylie to Sir G. Lowther," Report, Inclosure 3 in No. 103, Adana, May 7, 1909, ibid., p. 2; "Sir G. Lowther to Sir Edward Grey," Report No. 138 (No. 442), Therapia, June 15, 1909, and Inclosure 2 in No. 138, *Memorandum by the Rev. S.H. Kennedy Respecting the Siege and Relief of Durtyol*, ibid., pp. 1–8; "Sir G. Lowther to Sir Edward Grey," Report No. 48 (No. 639), Constantinople, August 8, 1909, ibid., pp. 1–7.

181. Zürcher, *Turkey*, pp. 100–105.

182. Akçam, *A Shameful Act*, pp. 85–87.

183. Ibid., pp. 87–89.

184. Zürcher, *Turkey*, pp. 116–119; Shaw, *History of the Ottoman Empire and Modern Turkey*, 2, pp. 201, 310, 312, 315; Akçam, *A Shameful Act*, pp. 113–116; Roger Ford, *Eden to Armageddon: World War I in the Middle East* (New York: Pegasus Books, 2010), pp. 121–137.

185. Zürcher, *Turkey*, p. 121.

186. Martin Gilbert, *Churchill: A Life* (New York: Henry Holt, 1991), pp. 299–312; Richard Toye, *Churchill's Empire: The World that Made Him and the World He Made* (New York:

Henry Holt, 2010), pp. 131–134; Jeffrey Grey, *A Military History of Australia*, 3rd ed. (Cambridge: Cambridge University Press, 2008), pp. 92–102.

187. Akçam, *A Shameful Act*, pp. 125–129.

188. Ibid., p. 159; Vahakn N. Dadrian, *The History of the Armenian Genocide: Ethnic Conflict from the Balkans to Anatolia to the Caucasus*, 6th ed. (New York: Bergaham Books, 1995), p. 221; Balakian, *The Burning Tigris*, pp. 182–183.

189. Henry Morgenthau, *Ambassador Morgenthau's Story: A Personal Account of the Armenian Genocide* (New York: Cosimo Classics, 2008), pp. 210–211.

190. Ibid., p. 213.

191. Ibid., pp. 213–214.

192. Grigoris Balakian, *Armenian Golgotha*, trans. Peter Balakian with Aris Sevag (New York: Alfred A. Knopf, 2009), pp. 84–85.

193. Ibid., p. 88.

194. "From the Consul in Adana (Buege) to the Embassy in Constantinople," May 18, 1915, Gust, *A Documentation of the Armenian Genocide in World War I*, p. 1; "From Johannes Lepsius to the Foreign Office," June 22, 1915, ibid., p. 2.

195. "Notes by the Consul General in the German Embassy in Constantinople," June 30, 1915, ibid., p. 1.

196. "From the Administrator in Aleppo (Hoffmann) to the Embassy in Constantinople," October 18, 1915, ibid., p. 1.

197. "From the Consul General (Bergfeld) to the Reichskanzler (Bethmann Hollweg)," July 9, 1915, ibid., p. 2.

198. "Petition Submitted by an Armenian to the Embassy in Constantinople," August 19, 1915, ibid., p. 2.

199. "From the Consul in Aleppo (Roessler) to the Reichskanzler (Bethamnn Hollweg)," January 3, 1916, ibid., p. 1.

200. Morgenthau, *Ambassador Morgenthau's Story*, p. 210.

201. Ibid., pp. 217–220.

202. Ibid., pp. 220–221.

203. Viscount Bryce, *The Treatment of Armenians in the Ottoman Empire, 1915–16: Documents Presented to Viscount Grey of Fallodon, Secretary of State for Foreign Affairs* (London: His Majesty's Stationery Office, 1916), pp. 6–7.

204. Ibid., p. 9.

205. "From the Consul in Aleppo (Roessler) to the Reichskanzler (Bethmann Hollweg)," September 20, 1916, K. No. 93/No. 2669, Gust, *A Documentation of the Armenian Genocide*, p. 6; "From the Consul in Damascus (Loytved Hardegg) to the Embassy in Constantinople," Damascus, May 30, 1916, ibid., p. 1.

206. "From the Consul in Aleppo (Roessler) to the Reichskanzler (Bethmann Hollweg)," February 9, 1916, No. 366/K. No. 18, ibid., pp. 3–4.

207. "From the Consul in Aleppo (Roessler) to the Reichskanzler (Bethmann Hollweg)," Aleppo, September 20, 1916, K. No. 93/No. 2669, ibid., p. 7.

208. "From the Ambassador on Extraordinary Mission in Constantinople (Wolff-Metternich) to the Reichskanzler (Bethmann Hollweg)," July 22, 1916, No. 409, ibid., p. 1.

209. "From the Consul in Aleppo (Roessler) to the Reichskanzler (Bethmann Hollweg)," July 29, 1916, K. No. 79/No. 2135, ibid., p. 1.

210. Ibid., pp. 1–3.

211. Ibid., p. 3.

212. "From the Chargé d'affaires in Aleppo (Hoffmann) to the Embassy in Constantinople," September 5, 1916, No. 578 (B.N. 2535), ibid., 2 pp.

213. "From the Consul in Aleppo (Roessler) to the Reichskanzler (Bethmann Hollweg)," November 5, 1916, K. No. 104/No. 3045, ibid., p. 3.

214. "From the Consul in Aleppo (Roessler) to the Reichskanzler (Bethmann Hollweg)," May 14, 1917, K. No. 56/No. 923, ibid., p. 1.

215. "From the Consul in Aleppo (Roessler) to the Reichskanzler (Bethmann Hollweg)," April 27, 1916, K. No. 47/No. 1189, ibid., p. 2; "From the Ambassador in Extraordinary Mission in Constantinople (Wolff-Metterniuch) to the Reichskanzler (Bethmann Hollweg)," July 10, 1916, No. 368, ibid., p. 1.

216. Shaw, *History of the Ottoman Empire and Modern Turkey*, 2, pp. 318–319.

217. Bass, *Stay the Hand of Vengeance*, pp. 116–117.

218. Akçam, *A Shameful Act*, p. 214.

219. Bass, *Stay the Hand of Vengeance*, p. 117.

220. Balakian, *The Burning Tigris*, p. 278; Simon Payaslian, *United States Policy toward the Armenian Question and the Armenian Genocide* (New York: Palgrave Macmillan, 2005), pp. 89–95.

221. Bryce, *The Treatment of Armenians in the Ottoman Empire, 1915–16*, pp. 1–684, *passim*.

222. "From the Ambassador in Constantinople (Wangenheim) to the Reichskanzler (Bethmann Hollweg)," May 27, 1915, No. 324, Gust, *A Documentation of the Armenian Genocide*, p. 1.

223. "From the Ambassador in Extraordinary Mission in Constantinople (Wolff-Metternich) to the Reichskanzler (Bethmann Hollweg)," December 7, 1915, No. 711, ibid., pp. 1–2; Ellery Cory Stowell, *The Diplomacy of the War of 1914* (New York: Houghton Mifflin, 1915), p. 551.

224. "From the Ambassador in Extraordinary Mission in Constantinople," December 7, 1915, No. 7, Gust, *A Documentation of the Armenian Genocide*, pp. 2–3.

225. Wolfgang and Sigrid Gust, "Introduction." *The Armenian Genocide 1915/16: Documents from the Political Archives of the German Foreign Office*, pp. 74–76. http://www.armeno-cide.de/armenocide/armgende.nsf/WebStart-En?OpenFrameset.

226. Bloxham, *The Great Game of Genocide*, p. 187; Balakian, *The Burning Tigris*, p. 296; Payaslian, *United States Policy toward the Armenian Question*, pp. 95–103, 116–128; John Milton Cooper, Jr., argues that Wilson was extremely sensitive to the plight of the Armenians, but was limited by practical considerations in terms of what he could do to help the Armenians during wartime. "A Friend in Power? Woodrow Wilson and Armenia," in Jay Winter, *American and the Armenian Genocide of 1915* (Cambridge: Cambridge University Press, 2003), pp. 103–112.

227. Shaw, *History of the Ottoman Empire and Modern Turkey*, 2, pp. 320–321.

228. James Brown Scott, ed., *Official Statements of War Aims and Peace Proposals: December 1916 to November 1918* (Washington, DC: Carnegie Endowment for International Peace, 1921), pp. 12–15, 37.

229. Arnold J. Toynbee, *The Murderous Tyranny of the Turks* (New York: George H. Doran, 1917), title page.

230. "Woodrow Wilson Speech before a Joint Session of Congress," January 8, 1918. The *Fourteen Points* are included in the speech, pp. 1–5; http://wwi.lib.byu.edu/index.php/President_Wilson=s_Fourteen_Points.

231. "Commission on the Responsibility of the Authors of the War and on Enforcement of Penalties," *The American Journal of International Law*, Vol. 14, Nos. 1/2 (January-April 1920), pp. 104–107, 112–115.

232. Akçam, *A Shameful Act*, pp. 217–221; Dadrian, *The History of the Armenian Genocide*, pp. 306–308; Bass, *Stay the Hand of Vengeance*, pp. 117–123.

233. Bass, *Stay the Hand of Vengeance*, pp. 124–125, 293.

234. Ibid., pp. 125–126.

235. Ibid., pp. 126–127.

236. Ibid., p. 129.
237. Vajhan N. Dadrian, "Genocide as a Problem of National and International Law: The World War I Armenian Case and Its Contemporary Legal Ramifications," *Yale Journal of International Law*, Vol. 14, No. 2 (Summer 1989), p. 285.
238. Ibid., p. 128, 135; Shaw, *History of the Ottoman Empire and Modern Turkey*, 2, p. 358.
239. *The Treaty of Peace between the Allied and Associated Powers and Turkey signed at Sèvres*, August10, 1920, Part IV, Article 144, and Part VII, Articles 226–230; http://history. acusd.edu/gen/versaillestreaty.html,.
240. Ibid., pp. 130–143; Dadrian, *History of the Armenian Genocide*, pp. 310–311.
241. Republic of Turkey, Ministry of Foreign Affairs, 8. Declaration of Amnesty [Treaty of Lausanne, July 24, 1923], p. 2; http://www.mfa.gov.tr/common/print.htm.
242. Akçam, *A Shameful Act*, p. 365.
243. Telford Taylor, *The Anatomy of the Nuremberg Trials: A Personal Memoir* (Boston: Little, Brown, 1992), p. 18.

5   PEACE, LAW, AND THE CRIMES OF WORLD WAR II

1. H. G. Wells, *The War that Will End War* (London: Frank & Cecil Palmer, 1914), p. 11; Adrian Gregory, *The Last Great War: British Society and the First World War* (Cambridge: Cambridge University Press, 2008), p. 5.
2. Kathleen Hall Jamieson, *Eloquence in an Electronic Age: The Transformation of Political Speechmaking* (New York: Oxford University Press, 1988), p. 99.
3. John Milton Cooper, Jr., *Woodrow Wilson: A Biography* (New York: Alfred A. Knopf, 2009), pp. 251, 263.
4. Jan Willen Schulte Nordholt, *Woodrow Wilson: A Life for World Peace* (Berkeley: University of California Press, 1991), p. 144.
5. Cooper, *Woodrow Wilson*, pp. 175–176.
6. Ibid., p. 342.
7. G. J. Meyer, *A World Undone: The Story of the Great War, 1914 to 1918* (New York: Delta, 2007), pp. 481–483.
8. "Address of President Woodrow Wilson to the United States Senate," January 22, 1917, p. 2. http://www.firstworldwar.com/source/peacewithoutvictory.htp.
9. Cooper, *Woodrow Wilson*, p. 362.
10. "Address of President Woodrow Wilson," pp. 2–3.
11. Cooper, *Woodrow Wilson*, pp. 449–452.
12. Margaret MacMillan, *Paris 1919: Six Months that Changed the World* (New York: Random House, 2002), pp. 14–15.
13. Ibid., pp. 15–16.
14. Woodrow Wilson, "State of the Union Address," December 2, 1918, pp. 3, 6–7. http://www.infoplease.com/t/hist/state-of-the-union/130.html; Cooper, *Woodrow Wilson*, pp. 454–459, 474–475, 494, 502.
15. F. P. Walters, *A History of the League of Nations*, Vol. 1 (London: Oxford University Press, 1952), pp. 4–14.
16. *The Covenant of the League of Nations* (including Amendments adopted to December 1924). The Avalon Project, Yale University, p. 1; http://avalon.law.yale.edu/20th_century/leagcov.asp.
17. Ibid., pp. 1–2.
18. Ibid.
19. Ibid., pp. 2–3.
20. Ibid., pp. 3–4.

21. Ibid., p. 4.

22. Cooper, *Woodrow Wilson*, p. 474.

23. Andrew Webster, "From Versailles to Geneva: The Many Forms of Interwar Disarmament," *Journal of Strategic Studies*, Vol. 29, No. 2 (April 2006), pp. 226–227.

24. *The Treaty of Versailles*, June 28, 1919. The Avalon Project, Yale University, p. 1; http://avalon.law.yale.edu/imt/partv.asp.

25. Peter Jackson, "France and the Problems of Security and International Disarmament after the First World War," *Journal of Strategic Studies*, Vol. 29, No. 2 (April 2006), p. 247.

26. Ibid., p. 262; David M. Crowe, *The Holocaust: Roots, History, and Aftermath* (Boulder: Westview Press, 2008), p. 96.

27. Andrew Barros, "Disarmament as a Weapon: Anglo-French Relations and the Problems of Enforcing German Disarmament, 1919–28," *Journal of Strategic Studies*, Vol. 29, No. 2 (April 2006), pp. 306–307.

28. Ibid., p. 304.

29. Erik Goldstein, *The First World War Peace Settlements, 1919–1925* (London: Longman, 2002), pp. 76–78.

30. "Treaty between the United States of America, the British Empire, France, Italy, and Japan, Signed at Washington, February 6, 1922," *Papers Relating to the Foreign Relations of the US, 1922*, Vol. 1 (Washington, DC: US Government Printing Office, 1922), pp. 247–266; Michael Graham Fry, "The Specific Dominions and the Washington Naval Conference, 1921–22," in Erik Goldstein and John Maurer, eds., *The Washington Conference, 1921–22: Naval Rivalry, East Asian Stability and the Road to Pearl Harbor* (London: Frank Cass, 1994), pp. 89–90; Goldstein, *The First World War Peace Settlements*, p. 78.

31. "International Treaty for the Limitation and Reduction of Naval Armament," October 27, 1930, London, pp. 1–21; http://www.microworks.net/pacific/road_to_war/london_treaty.htm.

32. Gordon M. Berger, "Politics and Mobilization in Japan, 1931–1945," in Peter Duus, ed., *The Cambridge History of Japan*, Vol. 6 (Cambridge: Cambridge University Press, 2008), pp. 105–106.

33. *Protocol for the Pacific Settlement of International Disputes*, October 2, 1924, pp. 1–6. http://refworld.org/docid/40421A204.html; Goldstein, *The First World War Peace Settlements*, pp. 86–90.

34. Walters, *History of the League of Nations*, 2, pp. 384–387; *General Act for the Pacific Settlement of International Disputes*, Adopted by the Assembly [of the League of Nations], September 26, 1928. *Transactions of the Grotius Society*, Vol. 16, "Problems of Peace and War, Papers Read before the Society in the Year 1930," pp. 143–153; for an assessment of this accord, see Miroslas Gonsiorowski, "Political Arbitration under the General Act for the Pacific Settlement of International Disputes," *American Journal of International Law*, Vol. 27, No. 3 (July 1933), pp. 469–490.

35. *Protocol for the Prohibition of the Use of Asphyxiating, Poisonous or Other Gases, and of Bacteriological Methods of Warfare*, Geneva, June 17, 1925, p. 1; http://www.icrc.org/ihl.nsf/FULL/280?OpenDocument.

36. Webster, "From Versailles to Geneva," p. 237.

37. Walters, *History of the League of Nations*, 2, pp. 500–501.

38. Ibid., pp. 502–510.

39. Ibid., p. 511.

40. Thomas Davies, "France and the World Disarmament Conference of 1932–1934," *Diplomacy and Statecraft*, Vol. 15, No. 4 (2004), pp. 767–768; Walters, *History of the League of Nations*, 2, pp. 514–515.

41. Max Domarus, ed., *Hitler: Speeches and Proclamations, 1932–1945: The Chronicle of a Dictatorship*, Vol. 1: *The Years 1932 to 1934* (Wauconda, IL: Bolchazy-Carducci, 1990), p. 234.

42. Ian Kershaw, *Hitler: 1889–1936 Hubris* (New York: W. W. Norton, 1998), pp. 490–491.

43. Walters, *History of the League of Nations*, 2, pp. 542–543; Davies, "France and the World Disarmament Conference," pp. 768–769.

44. Gerhard L. Weinberg, *The Foreign Policy of Hitler's Germany: Diplomatic Revolution in Europe, 1933–36* (Chicago: University of Chicago Press, 1970), p. 46.

45. Kershaw, *Hitler:1889–1936 Hubris,* pp. 441–446.

46. Weinberg, *The Foreign Policy of Hitler's Germany, 1933–36*, p. 44.

47. Kershaw, *Hitler: 1899–1936 Hubris*, p. 491.

48. Walters, *History of the League of Nations*, 2, pp. 544–546; Kershaw, *Hitler: 1899–1936 Hubris*, p. 491.

49. "Message of President Roosevelt to the Congress, May 16, 1933," US Department of State, *Peace and War: United States Foreign Policy, 1931–1941*, Vol. 8 (Washington, DC: US Government Printing Office, 1943), pp. 178, 179 n13, 180–182, 348.

50. Domarus, *Hitler: Speeches and Proclamations*, 1, pp. 326–327.

51. Ibid., pp. 330–331.

52. Ibid., pp. 331–333.

53. Ralf Georg Reuth, *Goebbels*, trans. Krishna Winston (New York: Harcourt Brace, 1993), p. 188.

54. Wolfram Wette, "Ideology, Propaganda, and Internal Politics in Reconditioning the War Policy of the Third Reich," in Wilhelm Diest, Manfred Messerschmidt, Hans-Erich Volkmann, and Wolfram Wette, eds., *Germany and the Second World War*, Vol. 1: *The Build-up of German Aggression*, trans. P. S. Fall, Dean S. McMurry, and Ewald Osers (Oxford: Oxford University Press, 2000), p. 98.

55. Walters, *History of the League of Nations*, 2, p. 549.

56. Ibid., pp. 548–550; Weinberg, *The Foreign Policy of Nazi Germany, 1933–36*, 163–166; Kershaw, *Hitler, 188–1936 Hubris*, pp. 493–494.

57. Domarus, *Hitler: Speeches and Proclamations*, 1, pp. 364–365.

58. Telford Taylor, *The Anatomy of the Nuremberg Trials: A Personal Memoir* (Boston: Little, Brown, 1992), p. 22.

59. Office of United States Chief of Counsel for Prosecution of Axis Criminality, *Nazi Conspiracy and Aggression*, Vol. 1 (Washington, DC: US Government Printing Office, 1946), p. 5.

60. *Documents on the Tokyo International Military Tribunal: Charter, Indictment and Judgements*, Neil Boister and Robert Cryer, eds. (Oxford: Oxford University Press, 2008), pp. 5–6, 8, 16–33.

61. Ibid., xxxiii.

62. Marius B. Jansen, *The Making of Modern Japan* (Cambridge, MA: Belknap Press of Harvard University Press, 2000), pp. 289, 335, 367–368.

63. Ibid., pp. 398–399.

64. Robert B. Edgerton, *Warriors of the Rising Sun* (New York: W. W. Norton, 1997), p. 323.

65. Ibid., p. 324.

66. Ibid., pp. 389–397.

67. Ibid., pp. 399–400.

68. Mark R. Peattie, "The Japanese Colonial Empire, 1895–1945," in Peter Duus, ed., *The Cambridge History of Japan*, Vol. 6, pp. 224–228.

69. Ikuhiko Hata, "Continental Expansion, 1905–1941," ibid., 280–281.

70. Jansen, *The Making of Modern Japan*, pp. 515–516; Thomas H. Buckely, "The Icarus Factor: The American Pursuit of Myth in Naval Arms Control, 1921–36," in Goldstein and Maurer, *The Washington Conference, 1921–22*, pp. 132–133.

71. Hata, "Continental Expansion," pp. 284–285.

72. Ibid., pp. 285–287.

73. Ibid., pp. 288–289; Jansen, *The Making of Modern Japan*, pp. 562–563, 577–579.

74. *Documents on the Tokyo International Military Tribunal*, pp. 34–35.

75. Hata, "Continental Expansion," pp. 291–295; Jansen, *The Making of Modern Japan*, pp. 577–584.

76. Hata, "Continental Expansion," p. 297; Immanuel C. Y. Hsü, *The Rise of Modern China*, 6th ed. (New York: Oxford University Press, 2000), p. 550.

77. Walters, *A History of the League of Nations*, 2, p. 465.

78. Ibid., p. 470; *The Covenant of the League of Nations*, p. 3.

79. Walters, *A History of the League of Nations*, 2, pp. 470–471.

80. Ibid., p. 472.

81. Ibid., pp. 472–474.

82. Ibid., p. 474; Jonathan Fenby, *Chiang Kai-shek: China's Generalissimo and the Nation He Lost* (New York: Carroll & Graf, 2003), pp. 203–204; Jay Taylor, *The Generalissimo: Chiang Kai-shek and the Struggle for Modern China* (Cambridge, MA: Belknap Press of Harvard University Press, 2009), pp. 93–94.

83. Hata, "Continental Expansion," p. 296; Walters, *A History of the League of Nations*, 2, pp. 475, 477.

84. Walters, *A History of the League of Nations*, 2, pp. 480–481.

85. Taylor, *The Generalissimo*, p. 98; Fenby, *Chiang Kai-shek*, pp. 208–209.

86. Fenby, *Chiang Kai-shek*, p. 209

87. Donald A. Jordan, *China's Trial by Fire: The Shanghai War of 1932* (Ann Arbor: University of Michigan Press, 2001), pp. 47–49.

88. Fenby, *Chiang Kai-shek*, p. 214.

89. Walters, *A History of the League of Nations,* 2, pp. 487–488.

90. Ibid., p. 494.

91. Ibid.

92. Ibid.

93. Ibid., pp. 488–494.

94. Hata, "Continental Expansionism," p. 298.

95. Jansen, *The Making of Modern Japan*, p. 596.

96. James B. Crowley, *Japan's Quest for Autonomy: National Security and Foreign Policy, 1930–1938* (Princeton: Princeton University Press, 1966), p. 195.

97. Hata, "Continental Expansionism," pp. 300, 302.

98. Richard Pankhurst, "Italian Fascist War Crimes in Ethiopia: A History of Their Discussion, from the League of Nations to the United Nations (1936–1949)," *Northeast African Studies*, Vol. 6, Nos. 1–2 (1999) (New Series), p. 83.

99. Gordon M. Berger, "Politics and Mobilization in Japan, 1931–1945," in Duus, *The Cambridge History of Japan*, Vol. 6, p. 118.

100. Ibid., pp. 119–120.

101. Ibid., p. 124.

102. Taylor, *The Generalissimo*, p. 143.

103. Ibid., pp. 145–150.

104. *Documents on the Tokyo International Military Tribunal*, p. 537; Iris Chang, *Rape of Nanjing: The Forgotten Holocaust of World War II* (New York: Basic Books, 1997), p. 4; Peter Li, "The Nanjing Holocaust: Memory, Trauma, and Reconciliation," in Peter Li,

ed., *Japanese War Crimes: The Search for Justice* (New Brunswick: Transaction, 2003), p. 231. The Japanese claim that their forces committed only 38,000–42,000 "illegal murders" in Nanjing.

105. *The Tokyo Major War Crimes Trial: The Records of the International Military Tribunal for the Far East with an Authoritative Commentary and Comprehensive Guide*, R. John Pritchard, ed., Vol. 7 (Lewiston, NY: Edward Mellen Press, 1981), pp. 2526, 2531–2532.

106. Ibid., pp. 2535–2537.

107. Ibid., p. 2538.

108. Ibid., p. 2568.

109. Ibid., p. 2572.

110. Ibid., p. 2573.

111. *Tokyo Major War Crimes Trial*, 103, 49605–49606; Joshua A. Fogel, "Introduction: The Nanjing Massacre in History," in Joshua A. Fogel, ed., *The Nanjing Massacre in History and Historiography* (Berkeley: University of California Press, 2000), p. 6; Chang, *Rape of Nanjing*, p. 89.

112. *Tokyo Major War Crimes Trial*, 103, pp. 49607–49608; R. J. Rummel, *China's Bloody Century: Genocide and Mass Murder since 1900* (New Brunswick: Transaction, 1991), pp. 133, 149, 156.

113. Walters, *A History of the League of Nations*, 2, pp. 731–737; Fenby, *Chiang Kai-shek*, pp. 302, 309.

114. Alvin D. Coox, "The Pacific War," in Duus, *The Cambridge History of Japan*, Vol. 6, pp. 319–322.

115. Yuma Totani, *The Tokyo War Crimes Trial: The Pursuit of Justice in the Wake of World War II* (Cambridge: Harvard University Press, 2008), p. 152.

116. Saburō Ienaga, *The Pacific War: A Critical Perspective on Japan's Role in World War II* (New York: Pantheon Books, 1978), p. 184.

117. Totani, *The Tokyo War Crimes Trial*, pp. 152–153.

118. International Citizens' Forum on War Crimes and Redress, "Seeking Reconciliation and Peace for the 21st Century," Tokyo, December 10–12, 1999, pp. 1–7; http://www.vcn.bc.ca/alpha/icf.htm; Yue-him Tam, "Report on the International Citizens' Forum on War Crimes & Redress—Seeking Peace & Reconciliation for the 21st Century," pp. 3–4. http://www.vcn.bc.ca/alpha/ICFfinal.htm.

119. Rumi Sakamoto, "The Women's International War Crimes Tribunal on Japan's Military Sexual Slavery: A Legal and Feminist Approach to the 'Comfort Women's Issue,'" *New Zealand Journal of Asian Studies*, Vol. 3, No. 1 (June 2001), p. 49.

120. Yayori Matsdui, "Women's International War Crimes Tribunal on Japan's Military Sexual Slavery: Memory, Identity, and Society," in Li, *Japanese War Crimes*, pp. 262–263.

121. Ibid., p. 263.

122. Hata, "Continental Expansion," in Duus, *The Cambridge History of Modern Japan*, Vol. 6, pp. 309–310; Coox, "The Pacific War," ibid., pp. 324–328.

123. Coox, "The Pacific War," ibid., pp. 328–349; Jansen, *The Making of Modern Japan*, pp. 625–629, 632–642.

124. *Tokyo Major War Crimes Trial*, 103, p. 49594; These are the same figures used by Yuki Tanaka in *Hidden Horrors: Japanese War Crimes in World War II* (Boulder: Westview Press, 1998), p. 4.

125. *Tokyo Major War Crimes Trial*, 103, pp. 49593–49594.

126. Ibid., pp. 49621–49624; Peter Li, "Japan's Biochemical Warfare and Experimentation in China," in Li, *Japanese War Crimes*, pp. 294–295.

127. Michael Norman and Elizabeth M. Norman, *Tears in the Darkness: The Story of the Bataan Death and Its Aftermath* (New York: Farrar, Straus and Giroux, 2009), pp. 174–176.

128. Ibid., p. 176.

129. Ibid.

130. John W. Dower, *War without Mercy: Race & Power in the Pacific* (New York: Pantheon Books, 1986), p. 234; Tanaka, *Hidden Horrors*, pp. 28–29.

131. Dower, *War without Mercy*, pp. 184–185.

132. Ibid., pp. 234–235, 237.

133. Ibid., p. 260.

134. Ibid., p. 274.

135. Australian Government, Department of Veterans' Affairs, "Burma-Thailand Railway," p. 1; http://www.dva.gov.au/commems_oawg/OAWG/war_memorials/overseas_memorials/thai.

136. *Tokyo Major War Crimes Trial*, 103, pp. 49656–49657.

137. Ibid., p. 49663.

138. The United Nations War Crimes Commission, *Law Reports of Trials of War Criminals*, Vol. 4 (London: Untied Nations War Crimes Commission and His Majesty's Stationery Office, 1948), pp. 4–5.

139. Ibid., pp. 5–6.

140. Tien-wei Wu, "A Preliminary Review of Studies of Japanese Biological Warfare Unit 731 in the United States," *Free Republic*, September 23, 2001, pp. 4–5.

141. Nicholas D. Kristof, "Unmasking Horror—A Special Report: Japan Confronting Gruesome War Atrocity," *New York Times*, March 17, 1995, p. 1, http://query.nytimes.com/gst/fullpage.html?res=990CE2D71630F934A25750C0A9639582.

142. Sheldon H. Harris, "Japanese Biomedical Experimentation during the World-War-II Era," in Edmund D. Pelegrino, Anthony E. Hartle, and Edmund G. Howe, eds., *Military Medical Ethics*, Vol. 2 (Falls Church, VA, and Washington, DC: Office of the Surgeon General, United States Army and Borden Institute, Walter Reed Army Medical Center, 2003), p. 486.

143. Ibid., pp. 485–486.

144. Wu, "A Preliminary Review of Japanese Biological Warfare Unit 731," p. 2; Peter Li, "Japan's Biochemical Warfare and Experimentation in China," in Li, *Japanese War Crimes*, p. 292.

145. Harris, "Japanese Biomedical Experimentation during the World War–II Era," pp. 477, 484.

146. Sheldon H. Harris, *Factories of Death: Japanese Biological Warfare, 1932–1945, and the American Cover-Up* (London: Routledge, 1994), pp. 69–70.

147. Harris, "Japanese Biomedical Experimentation," p. 489.

148. Ibid.

149. Ibid.

150. Ibid.

151. Ibid.

152. Ibid., pp. 208–209.

153. Ibid.

154. Ibid., p. 218.

155. Ibid., pp. 218–219.

156. Ibid., pp. 221–222.

157. Joachim C. Fest, *Hitler*, trans. Richard and Clara Winston (New York: Harcourt Brace Jovanovich, 1974), p. 119; Kershaw, *Hitler 1889–1936*, pp. 133, 156; Klaus Fischer, *Nazi Germany* (New York: Continuum, 1995), p. 130.

158. Kershaw, *Hitler 1889–1936*, p. 133.

159. Adolf Hitler, *Hitler's Letters and Notes*, comp. Werner Maser, trans. Arnold Pomerans (New York: Bantam, 1976), p. 211.

160. Adolf Hitler, *Mein Kampf*, trans. Ralph Manheim (Boston: Houghton Mifflin, 1943), p. 382.

161. Kershaw, *Hitler, 1889–1936*, p. 245.

162. Richard J. Evans, *The Coming of the Third Reich* (New York: Penguin, 2004), pp. 234–237; Michael Burleigh, *The Third Reich: A New History* (New York: Hill and Wang, 2000), pp. 122–128; Jackson J. Spielvogel, *Hitler and Nazi Germany: A History*, 3rd ed. (Upper Saddle River: Prentice Hall, 1988), p. 53.

163. Kershaw, *Hitler 1889–1936*, pp. 327, 339, 366, 371; Thomas Childers, *The Nazi Voter: The Social Foundations of Fascism in Germany, 1919–1933* (Chapel Hill: University of North Carolina Press, 1983), p. 194; Burleigh, *The Third Reich*, pp. 139–143; Evans, *The Coming of the Third Reich*, pp. 255–262, 277–283, 292–295.

164. John W. Wheeler-Bennett, *Hindenburg: The Wooden Titan* (London: Macmillan, 1967), pp. 359–360; Burleigh, *The Third Reich*, pp. 144–145.

165. Wheeler-Bennett, *Hindenburg*, pp. 428–436; Evans, *The Coming of the Third Reich*, pp. 301–308, Franz von Papen, *Memoirs*, trans. Brian Conwell (New York: E. Dalton, 1953), p. 257.

166. Ralf Georg Reuth, *Goebbels*, trans. Kirshna Winston (New York: Harcourt Brace & World, 1993), p. 191; Karl A. Schleunes, *The Twisted Road to Auschwitz: Nazi Policy toward German Jews, 1933–1939* (Urbana: University of Illinois Press, 1990), p. 114.

167. Kershaw, *Hitler 1889–1936*, p. 567; Karl A. Schleunes, ed., *Legislating the Holocaust: The Berhard Loesener Memoirs and Supporting Documents*, trans. Carol Scherer (Boulder: Westview Press, 2001), pp. 154–155; Robert Proctor, *Racial Hygiene: Medicine under the Nazis* (Cambridge, MA: Harvard University Press, 1988), p. 132; Michael Burleigh and Wolfgang Wippermann, *The Racial State: Germany 1933–1945* (Cambridge: Cambridge University Press, 1991), p. 41.

168. Hitler, *Mein Kampf*, p. 255.

169. Crowe, *The Holocaust*, pp. 132–133.

170. Wim Willens, *In Search of the True Gypsy: From Enlightenment to the Final Solution*, trans. Don Bloch (London: Frank Cass, 1997), pp. 196–292; Guenther Lewy, *The Nazi Persecution of the Gypsies* (New York: Oxford University Press, 2000), pp. 6–9; Angus Fraser, *The Gypsies* (Oxford: Blackwell, 1992), p. 253; Gilad Margalit, *Germany and Its Gypsies: A Post-Auschwitz Ordeal* (Madison: University of Wisconsin Press, 2002), p. 32.

171. Michael Zimmermann, *Rassenutopie und Genzoid: Die nationalsozialistische "Lösung der Zigeunerfrage"* (Hamburg: Hans Christian Verlag, 1996), p. 149; Margalit, *Germany and Its Gypsies*, p. 36.

172. Lewy, *Nazi Persecution of the Gypsies*, pp. 47–48, 51–52; Margalit, *Germany and Its Gypsies*, p. 35; Frank Sparing, "The Gypsy Camps," in Karola Fings, Herbert Heuss, and Frank Sparing, eds., *From "Race Science" to the Camps: The Gypsies during the Second World War* (Hatfield, UK: University of Hertfordshire Press, 1997), pp. 54, 56.

173. Schleunes, *Twisted Road to Auschwitz*, p. 145; David Cesarani, *Becoming Eichmann: Rethinking the Life, Crimes, and Trial of a "Desk Murderer"* (Cambridge, MA: Da Capo Press, 2006), pp. 57, 67; Ian Kershaw, *Hitler: 1936–1945 Nemesis* (New York: W. W. Norton, 2000), pp. 129–130; Crowe, *The Holocaust*, pp. 124–125.

174. Anthony Read and David Fisher, *Kristallnacht: The Unleashing of the Holocaust* (New York: Peter Bedrick Books, 1989), pp. 133, 141, 153, 162; David Bankier, *The Germans and the Final Solution: Public Opinion under the Nazis* (Oxford: Blackwell, 1996), pp. 85–88.

175. Jeremy Noakes and Geoffrey Pridham, eds., *Foreign Policy, War and Racial Extermination*, Vol. 2: *Nazism, 1919–1945: A History of Documents and Eyewitness Accounts* (New York: Schocken Books, 1988), p. 1049.

176. David M. Crowe, *The Baltic States and the Great Powers: Foreign Relations, 1938–1940* (Boulder: Westview Press, 1993), pp. 68–81; David M. Crowe, *Oskar Schindler: The Untold Account of His Life, Wartime Activities, and the True Story Behind "The List"*

(Boulder: Westview Press, 2004), pp. 66–69; Heinz Höhne, *Canaris*, trans. J. Maxwell Brownjohn (New York: Doubleday, 1979), pp. 351–353; Telford Taylor, *Sword and Swastika: Generals and Nazis in the Third Reich* (New York: Barnes and Noble, 1952), p. 315; Gerhard L. Weinberg, *Foreign Policy of Hitler's Germany, 1937–1939: Starting World War II* (Chicago: University of Chicago Press, 1980), pp. 646–652; Pat Taggart, "Poland," in Editors of *Command Magazine, Hitler's Army: The Evolution and Structure of German Forces* (Conshohcken, PA: Da Capo Press, 2003), p. 220.

177. Henry Friedlander, *The Origins of Nazi Genocide: From Euthanasia to the Final Solution* (Chapel Hill: University of North Carolina Press, 1995), pp. 22, 39, 50; Michael Burleigh, *Death and Deliverance: "Euthanasia" in Germany, 1900–1945* (Cambridge: Cambridge University Press, 1994), pp. 94–95.

178. Burleigh, *Death and Deliverance*, p. 112; *Trial of War Criminals before the Nuremberg Military Tribunals under Control Council Law No. 10, "The Medical Case,"* Vol. 1 (Washington, DC: US Government Printing Office), pp. 846–850; Friedlander, *Origins of Nazi Genocide*, pp. 81–82; Noakes and Pridham, *Foreign Policy, War and Racial Extermination*, Vol. 2, p. 1038.

179. Kershaw, *Hitler, 1936–1945*, pp. 234–235, 244; Louis L. Snyder, ed., *Hitler's Third Reich: A Documentary History* (Chicago: Nelson-Hall, 1981), p. 329; Hans Umbreit, "Stages in the Territorial 'New Order' in Europe," in Berhard R. Kroener, Rolf-Dieter Müller, and Hans Umbreit, eds., and John Brownjohn et al., trans., *Germany and the Second World War*, Vol. 5: *Organization and Mobilization of the German Sphere of Power*, Part 1 , *Wartime Administration, Economy, and Manpower Resources, 1939–1941* (Oxford: Clarendon Press, 2000), p. 41.

180. Richard C. Lukas, *Forgotten Holocaust: The Poles under German Occupation, 1939–1944* (New York: Hippocrene Books, 1990), p. 3.

181. Crowe, *The Holocaust*, p. 162.

182. Ibid., pp. 162–163.

183. Ibid., pp. 159, 167–182.

184. Hitler, *Mein Kampf*, p. 382.

185. Richard J. Evans, *The Third Reich at War* (New York: Penguin Press, 2009), pp. 160–161.

186. Norman Rich, *Hitler's War Aims: Ideology, the Nazi State, and the Course of Expansion* (New York: W. W. Norton, 1973), p. 212.

187. Noakes and Pridham, *Foreign Policy, War, and Racial Extermination*, 2, p. 1090; Yitzhak Arad, Yisrael Gutman, and Abraham Margaliot, eds., *Documents on the Holocaust*, trans. Lea Ber Don (Lincoln and Jerusalem: University of Nebraska Press and Yad Vashem, 1999), p. 376.

188. Crowe, *The Holocaust*, p. 197.

189. Christopher R. Browning, *The Origins of the Final Solution: The Evolution of Nazi Jewish Policy, September 1939–March 1942* (Lincoln and Jerusalem: University of Nebraska Press and Yad Vashem, 2004), p. 244.

190. Yitzhak Arad, Shmuel Krakowski, and Shmuel Spector, eds., *The Einsatzgruppen Reports* (New York: Holocaust Library, 1989), pp. 14–15.

191. Richard Rhodes, *Masters of Death: The SS-Einsatzgruppen and the Invention of the Holocaust* (New York: Alfred A. Knopf, 2002), p. 64.

192. Jan T. Gross, *Neighbors: The Destruction of the Jewish Community in Jedwabne, Poland* (Princeton: Princeton University Press, 2001), pp. 96–101.

193. Browning, *Origins of the Final Solution*, p. 309.

194. Rudolf Höss, *Death Dealer: The Memoirs of the SS Kommandant at Auschwitz*, ed. Steven Paskuly (New York: Da Capo Press, 1996), pp. 27–28.

195. Noakes and Pridham, *Foreign Policy, War and Racial Extermination*, 2, p. 1104.

196. Crowe, *The Holocaust*, p. 228.

197. Ibid., pp. 232–234.

198. Browning, *Origins of the Final Solution*, pp. 404, 408–409; Noakes and Pridham, *Foreign Policy, War, and Racial Extermination*, 2, p. 1104; *Die Tagebücher von Joseph Goebbels*, Part 2 : *Diktate 1941–1945*, Vol. 2, *Oktober–Dezember 1941*, ed. Elke Frölich (Munich: K. G. Saur, 1996), pp. 408–409; State of Israel, Ministry of Justice, *The Trial of Adolf Eichmann: Record of Proceedings in the District Court of Jerusalem*, Vol. 4 (Jerusalem: Israel State Archives and Yad Vashem, 1994), pp. 1799, 1826; *Minutes of the Wannsee Conference*, January 20, 1942, pp. 1–14; http://prorev.com/wannsee.htm

199. Crowe, *The Holocaust*, p. 239.

200. Franciszek Piper, *Auschwitz: How Many Perished, Jews, Poles, Gypsies...* (Kraków: Poligrafia, 1991), p. 52.

201. Otto Friedrich, *The Kingdom of Auschwitz, 1940–1945* (New York: Harper Perennial, 1994), p. 32.

202. Robert Jay Lifton and Amy Hackett, "Nazi Doctors," in Yisrael Gutman and Michael Berenbaum, eds., *Anatomy of the Auschwitz Death Camp* (Bloomington: Indiana University Press, 1994), p. 306.

203. Crowe, *The Holocaust*, pp. 258–261.

204. Dr. Miklos Nyiszli, *Auschwitz: A Doctor's Eyewitness Account*, trans. Tibere Kremer and Richard Seaver (Greenwich: Fawcett, 1960), pp. 50–51.

205. Barbara Distel and Ruth Jakusch, eds., *Concentration Camp Dachau, 1933–1945* (Munich: Comité International de Dachau, 1978), p. 46; Paul Berben, *Dachau, 1933–1945: The Official History* (London: Comité International de Dachau, 1975), p. 2; Office of US Chief of Counsel, Subsequent Proceedings Division, APO 124–A, *Staff Evidence Analysis, Criminal Organizations*, Document No. 085, February 9, 1942, pp. 2–3, Mazal Library; http://www.mazal.org/N/series/NO-0085000–.htm; *Trials of War Criminals before the Nuernberg Military* Tribunals,1, pp. 460–461.

206. Jozo Tomasevich, *War and Revolution in Yugoslavia, 1941–1945* (Stanford: Stanford University Press, 2001), pp. 380, 383–384, 593, 738: Lisa M. Adeli, "From Jasenova to Yugoslavism: Ethnic Persecution in Croatia during World War II" (PhD dissertation, University of Arizona, 2004), pp. 40–41; Božo Švarc, "The Testimony of a Survivor of Jadovno and Jasenovac," in Barry M. Lituchy, ed., *Jasenovac and the Holocaust in Yugoslavia: Analysis and Survivor Testimonies* (New York: Jasenovac Research Institute, 2006), p. 141; Sadik Darron, "Recollections of Jasenovac," ibid., pp. 178, 180.

207. "Defining the Legal Position of the Jews in Slovakia," September 11, 1941, http://www.jewishvirtuallibrary.org/source/Holocaust/definingjewbud.html; Jörg Hoensch, "The Slovak Republic, 1939–1945," in Victor S. Mamatey and Radomir Luža, eds., *A History of the Czechoslovak Republic, 1918–1948* (Princeton: Princeton University Press, 1973), p. 291; Livia Rothkirchen, "The Slovak Regime: A Reassessment of the Halt to the Deportations." *East Central Europe*, Vol. 1, Nos. 1–2 (1983), pp. 3–13; Milena Hübschmannová, "Roma in the So-Called Slovak State (1939–45)," in Donald Kenrick, ed., *The Final Chapter*, Vol. 3: *The Gypsies during the Second World War* (Hatfield: University of Hertfordshire Press, 2006), pp. 25, 37.

208. "Executive Summery," *Final Report of the International Commission on the Holocaust in Romania* (November 11, 2004, Bucharest, Romania), p. 1, http://www.yad.vahsem.org.il/about_yad/what_new/data_whats_new/report/html.

209. Ibid., p. 1; Chapter 8, "Roma," ibid., pp. 3, 13–14, 17, 18; Radu Ioanid, *The Holocaust in Romania: The Destruction of Jews and Gypsies under the Antonescu Regime, 1940–1944* (Chicago: Ivan R. Dee, 2000), pp. 19, 53, 227; Donald Kenrick and Grattan

Puxon, *The Destiny of Europe's Gypsies* (New York: Basic Books, 1972), p. 129; David M. Crowe, *A History of the Gypsies of Eastern Europe and Russia* (Boulder: Westview Press, 2007), p. 134.

210. Crowe, *The Holocaust*, p. 449.

211. Randolph L. Braham, *The Politics of Genocide: The Holocaust in Hungary*, Vol. 1 (New York: Columbia University Press, 1994), pp. 54, 127, 158, 179; Cesarani, *Becoming Eichmann*, pp. 160, 162; John Bierman, *Righteous Gentile: The Story of Raoul Wallenberg, Missing Hero of the Holocaust* (New York: Viking, 1981), p. 91; Crowe, *History of the Gypsies*, p. 90; Katalin Katz, "The Roma of Hungary during the Second World War," in Kenrick, *The Final Chapter*, pp. 70–71, 83.

212. Nicola Labanca, "Colonial Rule, Colonial Repression and War Crimes in the Italian Colonies," *Journal of Modern Italian Studies*, Vol. 3, No. 4 (2004), p. 304.

213. The United Nations War Crimes Commission, *History of the United Nations War Crimes Commission and the Development of the Laws of War* (Buffalo: William S. Hein, 2006), p. 189.

214. Ibid., pp. 189–190.

215. Cristiano Andrea Ristuccia, *1935 Sanctions against Italy: Would Coal and Crude Oil Have Made a Difference* (Oxford: Linacre College, 2006), p. 3.

216. Lidia Santarelli, "Muted Violence: Italian War Crimes in Occupied Greece," *Journal of Modern Italian Studies*, Vol. 9, No. 3 (2004), pp. 285–288, 293.

217. Ibid., p. 290.

218. Ibid., pp. 291–292.

219. H. James Burgwyn, "General Roatta's War against the Partisans in Yugoslavia: 1942," *Journal of Modern Italian Studies*, Vol. 9, No. 3 (2004), pp. 316–317.

220. Ibid., p. 318.

221. Ibid., p. 318.

222. Ibid., p. 322.

223. Santarelli, "Muted Violence," p. 282.

224. Susan Zuccotti, *The Italians and the Holocaust: Persecution, Rescue, and Survival* (Lincoln: University of Nebraska Press, 1988), pp. 25, 109; R. J. B. Bosworth, *Mussolini's Italy: Life and the Fascist Dictatorship, 1915–1945* (New York: Penguin, 2006), pp. 243, 421; Emil Ludwig, *Talks with Mussolini*, trans. Eden and Cedar Paul (Boston: Little, Brown, 1933), pp. 69–71; Aaron Gillette, "The Origins of the 'Manifesto of Racial Scientists,'" *Journal of Modern Italian Studies*, Vol. 6, No. 3 (2001), pp. 305, 314–315, 318–319; Crowe, *The Holocaust*, pp. 311–314.

225. Michael R. Marrus and Robert O. Paxton, *Vichy France and the Jews* (Stanford: Stanford University Press, 1995), pp. 36, 39, 88; Richard Cobb, *French and Germans, Germans and French: A Personal Interpretation of France under Two Occupations, 1914–1918/1940–1944* (Cambridge: Brandeis University Press, 1983), p. 60; Crowe, *The Holocaust*, pp. 288–291.

226. The Institute of National Remembrance, Decision to Commence Investigation into Katyn Massacre, December 1, 2004, p. 1; http://www.ipn.gov.pl/portal/en/2/77/Decision_to_commence_investigation_into-Katyn...; Luke Harding, "Russia Posts Katyn Massacre Documents Online," *Guardian*, Guardianuk, April 28, 2010, pp. 1–2; http://www.guardian.co.uk/world/2010/apr/28/katyn-massacre-russia-documetns-web/print; Allen Paul, *Katyn: The Untold Story of Stalin's Polish Massacre* (New York: Charles Scribner's Sons, 1991), p. 114; Andrzej Paczkowski and Karel Bartošek, "The Other Europe: Victim of Communism," in Stéphane Courtois, Nicolas Werth, Jean-Louis Panné, Andrzej Paczkowski, Karel Bartošek, and Jean-Louis Margolin, eds., *The Black Book of Communism: Crimes, Terror, Repression* (Cambridge, MA: Harvard University Press, 1999), pp. 367–372.

227. Crowe, *The Baltic States*, pp. 150–175.

228. Francine Hirsch, "The Soviets at Nuremberg: International Law, Propaganda, and the Making of the Postwar Order," *American Historical Review*, Vol. 113, No. 3 (June 2008), pp. 704–705, 711.

229. Crowe, *The Baltic States*, p. 178.

230. Nicolas Werth, "A State against Its People: Violence, Repression, and Terror in the Soviet Union," in Courtois et al., *The Black Book of Communism*, p. 213.

6   THE NUREMBERG IMT TRIAL

1. Diana Lary, *The Chinese People at War: Human Suffering and Social Transformation, 1937–1945* (Cambridge: Cambridge University Press, 2010), p. 197.

2. Ibid., pp. 197–199.

3. Ibid., pp. 202–208.

4. Ibid., p. 1; R. J. Rummell, *China's Bloody Century: Genocide and Mass Murder since 1900* (New Brunswick: Transaction, 2007), pp. 112, 120, 133; Col. Gen. G. F. Krivosheev, *Soviet Casualties and Combat Losses in the Twentieth Century* (London: Greenhill Books, 1997), pp. 83, 86–87.

5. Gerhard Weinberg, *A World at Arms: A Global History of World War II* (Cambridge: Cambridge University Press, 1994), p. 894; John Ellis, *World War II: A Statistical Survey* (New York: Facts on File, 1993), pp. 253–255; David M. Crowe, *The Holocaust: Roots, History, and Aftermath* (Boulder: Westview Press, 2008), pp. 162, 447.

6. George Ginsburgs, "Laws of War and War Crimes on the Russian Front during World War II: The Soviet View," *Soviet Studies*, Vol. 11, No. 3 (January 1960), p. 254.

7. Ibid., p. 255.

8. Alexander Victor Prusin, "'Fascists Criminals to the Gallows!': The Holocaust and Soviet War Crimes Trials, December 1945–February 1946," *Holocaust and Genocide Studies*, Vol. 17, No. 1 (Spring 2003), p. 2.

9. Ibid., pp. 2–3.

10. The United Nations War Crimes Commission, *History of the United Nations War Crimes Commission and the Development of the Laws of War* (London: United Nations War Crimes Commission, 1948), p. 88.

11. Ibid., p. 3.

12. Edmund Jan Osmanczyk and Anthony Mango, eds., *Encyclopedia of the United Nations and International Agreements*, Vol. 4 (London: Routledge, 2004), p. 2663; The United Nations War Crimes Commission, *History of the United Nations War Crimes Commission*, p. 90.

13. Marina Sorokino, "People and Procedures: Toward a History of the Investigation of Nazi Crimes in the USSR," *Kritika: Explorations in Russian and Eurasian History*, Vol. 6, No. 4 (Fall 2005), pp. 801–806; Prusin, "Fascist Criminals to the Gallows!" p. 3.

14. The United Nations War Crimes Commission, *History of the United Nations War Crimes Commission*, pp. 91–94.

15. Ibid., pp. 95–98.

16. Ibid., pp. 98–104; Telford Taylor, *The Anatomy of the Nuremberg Trials: A Personal Memoir* (Boston: Little, Brown, 1992), pp. 26–27; The United Nations War Crimes Commission, *History of the United Nations War Crimes Commission*, pp. 109–127.

17. "Moscow Declaration on Atrocities," by President Roosevelt, Mr. Winston Churchill, and Marshal Stalin, issued on November 1, 1943, p. 1; http://www.ena.lu/moscow_declaration_atrocities_november_1943-2-13571.

18. Taylor, *The Anatomy of the Nuremberg Trials*, p. 28.

19. Winston R. Churchill, *Closing the Ring* (Boston: Houghton Mifflin, 1951), pp. 373–374.
20. John L. Chase, "The Development of the Morgenthau Plan through the Quebec Conference," *Journal of Politics*, Vol. 16, No. 2 (May 1954), p. 336.
21. Ibid., pp. 336–337.
22. Ibid., p. 337.
23. Jenkins, *Churchill*, p. 754.
24. Gilbert, *Churchill*, p. 793.
25. Taylor, *The Anatomy of the Nuremberg Trials*, pp. 30–31.
26. *Suggested Post-Surrender Program for Germany* [Morgenthau Plan], September 1, 1944, Appendix B, pp. 2–3; http://docs.fdrlibrary.marist.edu/psf/box31/a297a07.html.
27. Ibid., p. 2.
28. Ibid., pp. 2–3.
29. Taylor, *The Anatomy of the Nuremberg Trials*, p. 31.
30. Ibid., p. 31.
31. Marina Sorokina, "People and Procedures: Toward a History of the Investigation of Nazi Crimes in the USSR," *Kritika: Exploration in Russian and Eurasian History*, Vol. 6, No. 4 (Fall 2005), pp. 824–825.
32. Ibid., pp. 816–817; Prusin, "Fascist Criminals to the Gallows!" p. 3.
33. Sorokina, "People and Procedures," p. 826; Francine Hirsch, "The Soviets at Nuremberg: International Law, Propaganda, and the Making of the Postwar Order," *American Historical Review*, Vol. 113, No. 3 (June 2008), p. 711.
34. Prusin, "Fascist Criminals to the Gallows," pp. 3–4; George Ginsburgs, *Moscow's Road to Nuremberg: The Soviet Background to the Trial* (The Hague: Kluwer Law International, 1996), p. 45.
35. Prusin, "Fascist Criminals to the Gallows!" pp. 3–4.
36. Ginsburgs, *Moscow's Road to Nuremberg*, p. 46.
37. Ibid., pp. 47–48.
38. Hirsch, "The Soviets at Nuremberg," p. 713.
39. "Ube˙." "Voennaya Literatura"; http://militera.lib.ru/prose/russia/erenburg_lgz/091.html; S. M. Plokhy, *Yalta: The Price of Peace* (New York: Viking, 2010), p. 205.
40. Plokhy, *Yalta*, p. 205; Harriman makes no mention of this conversation in his memoirs. W. Averell Harriman and Elie Abel, *Special Envoy to Churchill and Stalin, 1941–1946* (New York: Random House, 1975). In fact, the only mention of Ehrenburg came during a conversation with Stalin at the end of 1945 during a discussion of Soviet occupation policies in Romania and Bulgaria, when the Soviet leader told Harriman if he had problems with such policies, he would call on Ehrenburg to publish his views on the matter, p. 524.
41. Plokhy, *Yalta*, p. 252.
42. Ibid., p. 252; Gilbert, *Churchill*, p. 821.
43. Robert Beitzell, ed., *Tehran, Yalta, Potsdam: The Soviet Protocols* (Hattiesburg: Academic International, 1970), pp. 128, 138.
44. Plokhy, *Yalta*, p. 253.
45. Taylor *The Anatomy of the Nuremberg Trials*, p. 32.
46. Ibid., pp. 32–33.
47. Ibid., p. 34.
48. Ibid., p. 35.
49. Ibid.
50. Ibid., p. 36.
51. Ibid.
52. Ibid.

53. Ibid.
54. Ibid., pp. 36–37.
55. Hirsch, "The Soviets at Nuremberg," pp. 707–708.
56. Smith, *American Road to Nuremberg*, p. 96.
57. Ibid., pp. 49–52; The United Nations War Crimes Commission, *History of the United Nations War Crimes Commission*, pp. 180–185.
58. Smith, *American Road to Nuremberg*, pp. 51–52.
59. Ibid., pp. 99–101.
60. Ibid., pp. 108–113.
61. Arieh J. Kochavi, *Prelude to Nuremberg: Allied War Crimes Policy and the Question of Punishment* (Chapel Hill: University of North Carolina Press, 1998), p. 161.
62. Ibid., pp. 161–164.
63. Taylor, *The Anatomy of the Nuremberg Trials*, p. 39.
64. *Report to the President by Mr. Jackson, October 7, 1946.* The Avalon Project, Yale Law School; http://avalon.law.yale.edu/imt/jack63.asp.
65. *Charter of the International Military Tribunal*, Office of United States Chief of Counsel for Prosecution of Axis Criminality, *Nazi Conspiracy and Aggression*, Vol. 1 (Washington, DC: US Government Printing Office, 1946), p. 6.
66. Ibid., pp. 1–12.
67. "The Rule of Law among Nations," *Temple Law Quarterly*, Vol. 19 (1945), pp. 140–141 (italics added).
68. "American Draft of Definitive Proposal, Presented to Foreign Ministers at San Francisco," April 1945, The Avalon Project, Yale Law School, pp. 1–3; http://avalon.yale.edu/imt/jack04.asp; "Memorandum of Proposals for the Prosecution and Punishment of Certain War Criminals and Other Offenders," April 30, 1945, pp. 1–5; http://avalon.law.yale.edu/imt/jacko5.asp.
69. "Justice Jackson's Report to President Truman on the Legal Basis for Trial of War Criminals," *Temple Law Review*, Vol. 19 (1945), pp. 147–149.
70. Taylor, *The Anatomy of the Nuremberg Trials*, p. 47.
71. International Conference on Military Trials: London 1945. "Report to the President by Mr. Justice Jackson, June 6, 1945," p. 1. The Avalon Project, Yale Law School; http://avalon.law.yale.edu/imt/jack08.asp.
72. Ibid., p. 1.
73. Ginsburgs, *Moscow's Road to Nuremberg*, p. 107.
74. International Conference on Military Trials, "Minutes of Conference Session of June 26, 1945," p. 1; http://avalon.law.yale.edu/jack13.asp; *Memorandum to President Roosevelt from the Secretaries of State and War and the Attorney General*, January 22, 1945. The Avalon Project, Yale Law School, p. 2; http://avalon.law.yale.edu/imt/jack01.asp; Whitney R. Harris, *Tyranny on Trial: The Trial of the Major German War Criminals at the End of World War II at Nuremberg, Germany, 1945–1946* (Dallas: Southern Methodist University Press, 1999), pp. 11–22; Taylor, *The Anatomy of the Nuremberg Trials*, pp. 59–67.
75. "Minutes of Conference Session of June 26, 1945," p. 3.
76. Ibid., p. 4.
77. International Conference on Military Trials, "Minutes of Conference Session of July 2, 1945," pp. 2–6; http://avalon.law.yale.edu/imt/jack20.asp.
78. International Conference on Military Tribunals, "Minutes of Conference Session of July 3, 1945," pp. 1–6; http://avalon.law.yale.edu/imt/jack21.asp; International Conference on Military Trials, "Minutes of Conference Session of July 17, 1945," pp. 7–8; http://avalon.law.yale.edu/imt/jack32.asp.

79. "Minutes of Conference Session of July 17, 1945," pp. 7–8; International Conference on Military Trials, "Minutes of Conference Session of July 19, 1945," p. 6; http://avalon.law.yale.edu/imt/jack37.asp; International Conference on Military Trials, "Minutes of Conference Session of July 23, 1945," pp. 5–7; http://avalon.law.yale.edu/imt/jack44.asp; Taylor, *The Anatomy of the Nuremberg Trials*, p. 62.

80. Taylor, *The Anatomy of the Nuremberg Trials*, p. 65; International Conference on Military Trials, "Definition of 'Aggression' Suggested by American Delegation as Basis of Discussion," July 19, 1945, p. 1; http://avalon.law.yale.edu/imt/jackson36.asp.

81. International Conference on Military Trials, "Redraft of Definition of 'Crimes,' Submitted by Soviet Delegation," July 23, 1945, p. 1; http://avalon.law.yale.edu/jack43.asp.

82. International Conference on Military Trials, "Minutes of Conference Session of July 25, 1945," p. 3; http://avalon.law.yale.edu/imt/jack51.asp.

83. Taylor, *The Anatomy of the Nuremberg Trials*, p. 68.

84. Ibid., p. 64.

85. *Agreements of the Berlin (Potsdam) Conference, July 17–August 2, 1945: Protocol of the Proceedings, August 1, 1945*, p. 6; http://www.pbs.org/wghb/amex/truman/psources/ps_potsdam.html.

86. International Conference on Military Trials, "Minutes of the Conference of July 23, 1945," pp. 5–7; International Conference on Military Trials, "Minutes of Conference Session of August 2, 1945," pp. 1–9; http://avalon.law.yale.edu/imt/jackson59.asp.

87. *London Agreement of August 8th, 1945*, International Military Tribunal, *Trial of the Major War Criminals before the International Military Tribunal, Nuremberg 14 November 1945–1 October 1946*, Vol. 1 (Nuremberg: International Military Tribunal, 1947), pp. 8–9.

88. *Charter of the International Military Tribunal*, ibid., pp. 10–11.

89. Ibid., p. 11.

90. Ibid., pp. 12–14.

91. Ibid., pp. 14–16.

92. Taylor, *The Anatomy of the Nuremberg Trials*, pp. 79–80, 85–90.

93. Crowe, *The Holocaust*, p. 399.

94. Taylor, *The Anatomy of the Nuremberg Trials*, pp. 97–99. *The Nuremberg Epilogue* (Moscow: Progress, 1971), pp. 16–17.

95. Ann Tusa and John Tusa, *The Nuremberg Trial* (New York: Skyhorse Publishing, 2010), p. 108.

96. Ibid., p. 108; Taylor, *The Anatomy of the Nuremberg Trials*, pp. 113–115; *Nazi Conspiracy and Aggression: Opinion and Judgement* (Washington, DC: US Government Printing Office, 1947), pp. 105–106.

97. *Nazi Conspiracy and Aggression*, p. 103.

98. Ibid., p. 103; John Cooper, *Raphael Lemkin and the Struggle for the Genocide Convention* (London: Palgrave Macmillan, 2008), pp. 62–65; *Nazi Conspiracy and Aggression*, 1, p. 31.

99. *Nazi Conspiracy and Aggression*, 1, pp. 13–82.

100. Tusa, *The Nuremberg Trial*, pp. 117–120; "Minutes of the Opening Session of the Tribunal," at Berlin, October 18, 1945, pp. 1–2; http://avalon.law.yale.edu/imt/int-min.asp; "Rules of Procedure," October 29, 1945, pp. 1–3; http://avalon.law.yale.edu/imtrules.asp.

101. *Nazi Conspiracy and Aggression*, 1, pp. 94–95.

102. I was given a private tour of the courtroom, which was closed at the time, in May 2010, by Chief Judge Gerda-Marie Reitzenstein; Ray D'Addario and Klaus Kastner, *Der*

Nürnberger Prozess: Der Verfahren gegen die Hauptkriegsverbucher 1945–1946 mit 200 Abbildungen (Nürnberg: Verlag A. Hoffman, 1994), pp. 15, 17.

103. A. Poltorak, *The Nuremberg Epilogue* (Moscow: Progress, 1971), pp. 16–17.

104. *Nazi Conspiracy and Aggression*, 1, pp. 114–116.

105. Ibid., pp. 120–170.

106. Ibid., pp. 160–173.

107. Ibid., p. 173.

108. Albert Speer, *Inside the Third Reich: Memoirs*, trans. Richard and Clara Winston (New York: Macmillan, 1970), p. 513.

109. Taylor, *The Anatomy of the Nuremberg Trials*, pp. 173–177, 203.

110. Bradley F. Smith, *Reaching Judgement at Nuremberg* (New York: Basic Books, 1977), pp. 82–86.

111. Taylor, *The Anatomy of the Nuremberg Trials*, pp. 187–188.

112. Ibid., p. 188.

113. Tusa, *The Nuremberg Trial*, pp. 164–166.

114. Erich Raeder, *Grand Admiral: The Personal Memoir of the Commander in Chief of the German Navy from 1935 until His Break with Hitler in 1943*, trans. Henry W. Drexel (New York: Da Capo, 2001), pp. 390–391; Speer, *Inside the Third Reich*, p. 513.

115. Taylor, *The Anatomy of the Nuremberg Trials*, pp. 191–193, 198–199; Tusa, *The Nuremberg Trial*, pp. 167–168, 177–179, 180–182.

116. Ibid., pp. 100, 101, 106.

117. Taylor, *The Anatomy of the Nuremberg Trials*, pp. 191–193; Tusa, *The Nuremberg Trial*, pp. 177–179.

118. Tusa, *The Nuremberg Trial*, pp. 182–183; Taylor, *The Anatomy of the Nuremberg Trials*, pp. 262, 322–323.

119. Tusa, *The Nuremberg Trial*, pp. 182–183.

120. Ibid., p. 183.

121. Stephanie Berlin, "Memorandum for the Office of the Prosecutor," Issue 3. *The Tu Quoque Defense* (Cleveland: Case Western Reserve University School of Law International War Crimes Project, 2002), p. 4.

122. Tusa, *The Nuremberg Trial*, pp. 356–357.

123. Ibid., p. 191.

124. Taylor, *The Anatomy of the Nuremberg Trials*, p. 299.

125. Ibid., p. 306.

126. Ibid.

127. International Military Tribunal, *Trial of the Major War Criminals before the International Military Tribunal: Nuremberg 14 November 1945–1 October 1946*, Vol. 7 (Nuremberg: International Military Tribunal, 1947), p. 168 [hereafter IMT, *TMWC*].

128. Ibid., pp. 171–172.

129. Ibid, p. 172.

130. Ibid., p. 173.

131. Ibid., p. 175.

132. Ibid., p. 193.

133. Tusa, *The Nuremberg Trial*, p. 196.

134. IMT, *TMWC*, 7, pp. 260–261.

135. Ibid., pp. 282–283, 288, 293–295, 298–304.

136. Ibid., pp. 562–602.

137. Taylor, *The Anatomy of the Nuremberg Trials*, p. 316.

138. IMT, *TMWC*, 8, pp. 293–299.

139. Ibid., pp. 309–317, 319–322.

140. Ibid., pp. 322, 324–331; Crowe, *The Holocaust*, pp. 241, 247.

141. IMT, *TMWC*, 8, pp. 333, 337–338.

142. Ibid., pp. 331–332.

143. Dmitri Volkogonov, *Stalin: Triumph and Tragedy*, trans. Harold Shukman (New York: Grove Weidenfeld, 1988), pp. 486–487; Robert Service, *Stalin: A Biography* (Cambridge: Belknap Press, 2004), pp. 253, 256,267–268, 287.

144. Taylor, *The Anatomy of the Nuremberg Trials*, pp. 319–321.

145. Tusa, *The Nuremberg Trial*, p. 269.

146. IMT, *TMWC*, 9, pp. 1–234; Taylor, *The Anatomy of the Nuremberg Trials*, pp. 238–239; Tusa, *The Nuremberg Trial*, pp. 270–271.

147. IMT, *TMWC*, 9, pp. 235, 401.

148. Ibid., pp. 361–363.

149. David Patrick Maxwell Fyfe Kilmuir, *Political Adventure: The Memoirs of the Earl of Kilmuir* (London: Weidenfeld and Nicolson, 1964), p. 112.

150. Ibid., pp. 112–113.

151. Biddle, *In Brief Authority*, pp. 409–410.

152. Ibid., pp. 410–411.

153. IMT, *TMWC*, 9, p. 417.

154. Ibid., pp. 417, 420, 431.

155. Ibid., p. 507.

156. Ibid., p. 673.

157. Ibid., p. 514.

158. Ibid., p. 519.

159. Ibid., p. 544.

160. Ibid., pp. 545–555.

161. Ibid., pp. 577–579.

162. Taylor, *The Anatomy of the Nuremberg Trials*, p. 344.

163. Ibid., p. 345.

164. Tusa, *The Nuremberg Trial*, p. 288.

165. IMT, *TMWC*, 9, pp. 621–627.

166. Ibid., pp. 628, 630–31.

167. Ibid., pp. 634, 635.

168. Ibid., pp. 642–643.

169. Ibid., pp. 644–646.

170. Ibid., pp. 611–612.

171. Ibid., pp. 617–619.

172. Tusa, *The Nuremberg Trial*, p. 294.

173. IMT, *TMWC*, 10, pp. 205–206.

174. IMT, *TMWC*, 11, p. 25.

175. Ibid., 11, p. 45.

176. Ibid., pp. 50–54.

177. IMT, *TMWC*, 4, p. 292.

178. Ibid., pp. 322–335, 353.

179. Ibid., p. 354.

180. Ibid., pp. 354–355.

181. IMT, *TMWC*, 11, pp. 399–402, 403, 406–409.

182. Ibid., p. 416.

183. Crowe, *The Holocaust*, pp. 227, 235, 237.

184. IMT, *TMWC*, 11, p. 444.

185. Tusa, *The Nuremberg Trial*, p. 321.

186. IMT, *TMWC*, 11, pp. 535–537, 552–557.

187. Ibid., 12, p. 7.

188. Ibid., p. 7.
189. Ibid., p. 8.
190. Ibid., p. 13.
191. Michael E. Antonio, "Arbitrariness and the Death Penalty: How the Defendant's Appearance during Trial Influences Capital Jurors' Punishment Decision," *Behavioral Sciences and the Law*, Vol. 24 (2006), p. 232.
192. S. Ettinger, "The Modern Period," in H. H. Ben-Sasson, ed., *A History of the Jewish People* (Cambridge, MA: Harvard University Press, 1994), p. 875.
193. Richard Overy, *Interrogations: The Nazi Elite in Allied Hands, 1945* (New York: Viking, 2001), pp. 35–37.
194. Ibid., p. 37.
195. *Nazi Conspiracy and Aggression*, 1, p. 66.
196. Taylor, *The Anatomy of the Nuremberg Trials*, p. 376.
197. Ibid., p. 380.
198. Ibid., pp. 178, 186.
199. Ibid., pp. 379–380, 385, 390, 410, 414–416.
200. Tusa, *The Nuremberg Trial*, pp. 335–336.
201. Overy, *Interrogations*, p. 186; G. M. Gilbert, *Nuremberg Diary* (New York: Da Capo, 1995), pp. 73–74; Tusa, *The Nuremberg Trial*, p. 333.
202. Ibid., p. 160.
203. Biddle, *In Brief Authority*, p. 447.
204. Rebecca West, *A Train of Powder* (New York: Viking, 1946), p. 5.
205. Tusa, *The Nuremberg Trial*, p. 334.
206. Ibid., p. 457.
207. Ibid.
208. Biddle, *In Brief Authority*, p. 443.
209. Gitta Sereny, *Albert Speer: His Battle with Truth* (New York: Vantage Books, 1996), p. 704; Dan van der Vat, *The Good Nazi: The Life and Lies of Albert Speer* (Boston: Houghton Mifflin, 1997), pp. 364–369.
210. Joachim Fest, *Speer; The Final Verdict*, trans. Ewald Osers and Alexandra Dring (New York: Harcourt, 1999), pp. 287, 289.
211. Taylor, *The Anatomy of the Nuremberg Trials*, pp. 449–451; Tusa, *The Nuremberg Trial*, p. 393.
212. IMT, *TMWC*, 14, p. 621; IMT, *TMWC*, 15, pp. 64, 127, 136, 137, 139.
213. Tusa, *The Nuremberg Trial*, p. 381.
214. Ibid, p. 433.
215. Ibid., pp. 437–438, 441–443.
216. Ibid., p. 457.
217. Ibid., pp. 441–443, 446, 479–481, 517.
218. Ibid., p. 481.
219. Ibid., p. 482.
220. IMT, *TMWC*, 16, p. 488.
221. Ibid., pp. 493–495.
222. Sereny, *Albert Speer*, p. 478.
223. IMT, *TMWC*, 16, pp. 556–561, 563.
224. Fest, *Speer*, pp. 288–289.
225. Bradley F. Smith, *Reaching Judgement at Nuremberg* (New York: Basic Books, 1977), pp. 222–223.
226. IMT, *TMWC*, 15, p. 64.
227. *Nazi Conspiracy and Aggression; Opinion and Judgement*, p. 148.
228. Crowe, *The Holocaust*, p.197.

229. IMT, *TMWC*, 4, pp. 439–442.
230. Ibid., p. 442.
231. Ibid., p. 443.
232. Ibid., pp. 443–444.
233. IMT, *TMWC*, 15, pp. 298, 316; Jonathan F. Vance, "Men in Manacles: The Shackling of Prisoners of War, 1942–1943," *Journal of Military History*, Vol. 59, No. 3 (July 1995), pp. 483–485.
234. Ibid., pp. 320–321.
235. Ibid., p. 323.
236. Ibid, pp. 341, 504–505; Antony Beevor, *The Fall of Berlin 1945* (New York: Viking, 2002), pp. 409–410; Ralf Blank, "Wartime Daily Life and the Air War on the Home Front," in Jörg Echternkamp, ed., *Germany and the Second World War*, Vol. 9/1: *German Wartime Society 1939–1945: Politicization, Disintegration, and the Struggle for Survival*, trans. Derry Cook-Radmore, Ewald Osers, Barry Swerin, and Barbara Wilson (Oxford: Clarendon Press, 2008), pp. 458–476.
237. IMT, *TMWC*, 15, pp. 341–342.
238. Ibid., pp. 468, 479.
239. Ibid., p. 479.
240. Ulrich Herbert, *Hitler's Foreign Workers: Enforced Foreign Labor in Germany under the Third Reich*, trans. William Templar (Cambridge: Cambridge University Press, 1997), p. 298.
241. IMT, *TMWC*, 15, p. 658, 659; IMT, *TMWC*, 16, p. 75.
242. IMT, *TMWC*, 16, p. 3.
243. Crowe, *The Holocaust*, p. 447.
244. *Nazi Conspiracy and Aggression: Opinion and Judgement*, pp. 152–153.
245. Ibid, p. 163.
246. Kershaw, *Hitler, 1936–1945: Nemesis*, pp. 572, 714–716.
247. IMT, *TMWC*, 17, p. 261.
248. Ibid., pp. 261–267, 271–371, 382–383, 447–453; Kershaw, *Hitler, 1936–1945*, p. 833.
249. IMT, *TMWC*, 19, pp. 427–429.
250. Ibid., p. 448.
251. Ibid., p. 433.
252. Ibid., p. 452.
253. Ibid., pp. 466–467.
254. Ibid., pp. 494, 497, 498, 515.
255. Ibid., pp. 494–515.
256. Ibid., pp. 494–528.
257. Ibid., p. 528.
258. Taylor, *The Anatomy of the Nuremberg Trials*, pp. 494, 497.
259. Ibid., p. 570.
260. IMT, *TMWC*, 20, p. 14.
261. Ibid., p. 14.
262. IMT, *TMWC*, 8, 355; "Constitution of the IMT," p. 2. The Avalon Project, Yale Law School; http:///avalon.law.yale.edu/imt/imtconst.asp.
263. IMT, *TMWC*, 8, p. 355.
264. Ibid., p. 364.
265. Charter of the IMT, p. 2.
266. IMT, *TMWC*, 8, p. 366.
267. Ibid., p. 374.
268. Ibid., pp. 371–374.

269. IMT, *TMWC before the IMT, Nuremberg, 14 November 1945–1 October 1946,* "Colonel Neave Report: Final Report on the Evidence of Witnesses for the Defense Organizations Alleged to Be Criminal, Heard before a Commission Appointed by the Tribunal Pursuant to Para. 4 of the Order of the 13th of March, 1946," Vol. 42 (Nuremberg: IMT, 1949), p. 1.

270. "Colonel Neave Report," p. 2.

271. Ibid., pp. 3–4.

272. *Nazi Conspiracy and Aggression,* pp. 68–73.

273. Taylor, *The Anatomy of the Nuremberg Trials,* p. 507.

274. Ibid., p. 494.

275. Ibid., p. 535.

276. IMT, *TMWC,* 4, p. 161.

277. Ibid., pp. 177, 180.

278. Ibid., p. 212.

279. Ibid., pp. 216–226.

280. Ibid., p. 229.

281. Tusa, *The Nuremberg Trial,* p. 433; IMT, *TMWC,* 21, pp. 583–585.

282. Ibid., p. 593.

283. Ibid.

284. Ibid., pp. 595–596.

285. Ibid., p. 597.

286. IMT, *TMWC,* 21, pp. 610–611.

287. Ibid., pp. 613, 615.

288. Ibid., p. 614.

289. Ibid., p. 616.

290. Taylor, *The Anatomy of the Nuremberg Trials,* p. 517; Crowe, *Holocaust,* pp. 409–410.

291. Tusa, *Nuremberg Trial,* p. 435; Taylor, *The Anatomy of the Nuremberg Trials,* p. 517.

292. Taylor, *The Anatomy of the Nuremberg Trials,* pp. 392, 411.

293. Ibid., pp. 440–441.

294. Hamburg Institute for Social Research, *The German Army and Genocide: Crimes against War Prisoners, Jews, and Other Civilians, 1939–1944* (New York: New Press, 1999), pp. 7, 14; Crowe, *The Holocaust,* 201–202.

295. IMT, *TMWC,* 4, pp. 478–479.

296. Ibid., p. 483.

297. Ibid., p. 484.

298. Taylor, *The Anatomy of the Nuremberg Trials,* p. 518; NCA, 1, pp. 72–73; IMT, *TMWC,* 20, pp. 584–585, 599–600.

299. IMT, *TMWC,* 22, pp. 44–45.

300. Ibid., pp. 46–51.

301. Klaus P. Fischer, *Nazi Germany: A New History* (New York: Continuum, 1995), p. 312; Martin Broszat, *The Hitler State* (New York: Longman, 1981), pp. 280–282.

302. IMT, *TMWC,* 22, pp. 96–97.

303. Ibid., p. 97.

304. Ibid., pp. 98–99.

305. *NCA: Opinion and Judgement,* p. 104.

306. IMT, *TMWC,* 22, pp. 1–169.

307. Ibid., p. 176.

308. Ibid., pp. 176–178.

309. IMT, *TMWC,* 22, p. 223.

310. Ibid., pp. 269–270.

311. Ibid., pp. 309–310, 363.

312. Ibid., p. 365.
313. Ibid., p. 368.
314. IMT, *TMWC*, 22, p. 384.
315. Ibid., p. 386.
316. Ibid., p. 406.
317. Ibid., p. 407.
318. Ibid., p. 410.
319. Taylor, *The Anatomy of the Nuremberg Trials*, p. 549; Biddle, *In Brief Authority*, p. 465.
320. *Nazi Conspiracy and Aggression*, pp. 4–5.
321. Taylor, *The Anatomy of the Nuremberg Trials*, p. 456.
322. Biddle, *In Brief Authority*, p. 473.
323. Taylor, *The Anatomy of the Nuremberg Trials,* p. 550.
324. Biddle, *In Brief Authority*, pp. 466, 468; Taylor, *The Anatomy of the Nuremberg Trials*, p. 550.
325. Biddle, *In Brief Authority*, p. 468; Taylor, *The Anatomy of the Nuremberg Trials*, p. 554; *MEMORANDUM*, "Minutes of the Conference in the Reich Chancellery," November 5, 1937, in Max Domarus, ed., *Hitler: Speeches and Proclamations, 1932–1945: The Chronicle of a Dictatorship*, Vol. 2: *The Years 1935 to 1938* (Wauconda, IL: Bolchazy-Carducci, 1992), pp. 963–972.
326. Taylor, *The Anatomy of the Nuremberg Trials*, p. 555.
327. Tusa, *The Nuremberg Trial*, p. 450; *Nazi Conspiracy and Aggression: Opinion and Judgement*, pp. 16–46.
328. Biddle, *In Brief Authority*, p. 471.
329. Ibid., p. 472.
330. *Nazi Conspiracy and Aggression: Opinion and Judgement*, p. 85.
331. Tusa, *The Nuremberg Trial*, p. 450.
332. Taylor, *The Anatomy of the Nuremberg Trials*, p. 559; Tusa, *The Nuremberg Trial*, p. 458.
333. Tusa, *The Nuremberg Trial*, pp. 458–459.
334. Ibid., pp. 457–458.
335. Taylor, *The Anatomy of the Nuremberg Trials*, p. 563; Tusa, *The Nuremberg Trial*, p. 460.
336. *Nazi Conspiracy and Aggression: Opinion and Judgement*, p. 140.
337. Ibid., p. 475.
338. Tusa, *The Nuremberg Trial*, p. 463.
339. Taylor, *The Anatomy of the Nuremberg Trials*, pp. 565–566.
340. *Nazi Conspiracy and Aggression*, pp. 166–182, 189–190.
341. Taylor, *The Anatomy of the Nuremberg Trials*, pp. 601–611, 616–618; Tusa, *The Nuremberg Trial*, pp. 477–487.

7 THE TOKYO IMT TRIAL

1. *The Tokyo Major War Crimes Trial: The Records of the International Military Tribunal for the Far East*, R. John Pritchard, ed. and comp., Vol. 2 (Lewiston, NY: Edward Mellen Press, 1998), xxv.
2. The United Nations War Crimes Commission, *History of the United Nations War Crimes Commission and the Development of the Laws of War* (Buffalo: William S. Hein, 2006), p. 91.
3. Neil Boister and Robert Cryer, *The Tokyo International Military Tribunal: A Reappraisal* [hereafter *The Tokyo IMT*] (Oxford: Oxford University Press, 2008), p. 18.
4. Benjamin B. Ferencz, "War Crimes Trials: The Holocaust and the Rule of Law," in *In Pursuit of Justice: Examining the Evidence of the Holocaust* (Washington, DC: United States Holocaust Memorial Museum, 1995), p. 16.

5. *Cairo Communiqué*, December 1, 1943, 1 p.
6. Mark Eykholt, "Aggression, Victimization, and Chinese Historiography of the Nanjing Massacre," in Joshua A. Fogel, ed., *The Nanjing Massacre in History and Historiography* (Berkeley: University of California Press, 2000), pp. 18–19.
7. *History of the United Nations War Crimes Commission*, pp. 129–130.
8. Jeffrey Grey, *A Military History of Australia*, 3rd ed. (Cambridge: Cambridge University Press, 2008), pp. 178, 192–195; Yuma Totani, *The Tokyo War Crimes Tribunal: The Pursuit of Justice in the Wake of World War II* (Cambridge, MA: Harvard University Press, 2008), p. 14; *History of the United Nations War Crimes Commission*, pp. 153–154; Boister and Cryer, *The Tokyo IMT*, p. 19; Gerhard L. Weinberg, *A World at Arms: A Global History of World War II* (Cambridge: Cambridge University Press, 1994), pp. 842–843.
9. Philip R. Piccigallo, *The Japanese on Trial: Allied War Crimes Operations in the East, 1945–1951* (Austin: University of Texas Press, 1979), p. 4.
10. *Documents on the Tokyo International Military Tribunal: Creation, Indictment and Judgements* [hereafter *Documents on the Tokyo IMT*], Neil Boister and Robert Cryer, eds. (Oxford: Oxford University Press, 2008), pp. 1–2.
11. Ibid., p. 1.
12. Edward Behr, *Hirohito; Beyond the Myth* (New York: Villard Books, 1989), pp. 295–300; Herbert P. Bix, *Hirohito and the Making of Modern Japan* (New York: HarperCollins, 2000), pp. 493–496, 499–519; Boister and Cryer, *The Tokyo IMT*, p. 21. Japan and the Soviet Union signed a neutrality pact in 1941. Stalin denounced it in the spring of 1945, and declared war on Japan on August 8, 1945.
13. Marius B. Jansen, *The Making of Modern Japan* (Cambridge, MA: Belknap Press of Harvard University Press, 2000), p. 666.
14. William Manchester, *American Caesar: Douglas MacArthur, 1880–1964* (Boston: Little Brown, 1978), pp. 453–454.
15. "Japan's Instrument of Surrender," in *Documents on the Tokyo IMT*, pp. 3–4.
16. Boister and Cryer, *The Tokyo IMT*, pp. 21–22; Totani, *The Tokyo War Crimes Trial*, p. 28.
17. State-War-Navy Coordinating Committee, *Political-Military Priorities in the Far East: United States Initial Post-Defeat Policy Relating to Japan, SWNCC 150/3, 22 August 1945*, p. 6. http://www.ndl.go.jp/constitution/e/shiryo/o1/020/020_0071.html.
18. Zachary D. Kaufman, "The Nuremberg Tribunal v. the Tokyo Tribunal: Designs, Staffs, and Operations," *John Marshal Law Review*, Vol. 43 (Spring 2010), pp. 754–755.
19. Boister and Cryer, *The Tokyo IMT*, pp. 22–23; Totani, *The Tokyo War Crimes Tribunal*, pp. 21–22.
20. Totani, *The Tokyo War Crimes Tribunal*, p. 23.
21. Ibid., pp. 23–24.
22. Ibid., p. 24.
23. D. Clayton James, *The Years of MacArthur*, Vol. 3: *Triumph and Disaster, 1945–1964* (Boston: Houghton Mifflin, 1985), p. 102.
24. Ibid., p. 94.
25. United Nations War Crimes Commission, *Law Reports of Trials of War Criminals* [hereafter UNWCC, *Law Reports*], Vol. 4 (London: The United Nations War Crimes Commission by His Majesty's Stationery Office, 1948), pp. 3–4.
26. Gary D. Solis, *The Law of Armed Conflict: International Humanitarian Law in War* (Cambridge: Cambridge University Press, 2010), p. 383.
27. Peter Maguire, *Law and War: International Law & American History*, rev. ed. (New York: Columbia University Press, 2010), p. 107.
28. UNWCC, *Law Reports*, 4, pp. 37–63.
29. Douglas MacArthur, *Reminiscences* (New York: McGraw-Hill, 1964), p. 146.

30. Hampton Sides, "The Trial of General Homma," *American Heritage Magazine*, Vol. 58, No. 1 (February/March 2007), pp. 2, 17–19; http://www.americanheritage.com/print/61812.
31. *Application of Masaharu HOMMA v. Lieutenant General Wilhelm D. Styer, Commanding General, United States Army Forces, Western Pacific. No. 93. Misc and no. 818*. 327 U.S. 759 (1946), pp. 1–9; http://supreme.justia.com/us/327/759/case.html.
32. MacArthur, *Reminiscences*, pp. 295–298.
33. Sides, "The Trial of General Homma," p. 19.
34. James, *The Years of MacArthur*, 3, p. 101.
35. Boister and Cryer, *The Tokyo IMT*, pp. 25–27; *Documents on the Tokyo IMT*, pp. 5–15.
36. James, *The Years of MacArthur*, p. 102.
37. Ibid., pp. 102–103; Totani, *The Tokyo War Crimes Trial*, pp. 28–32.
38. MacArthur, *Reminiscences*, p. 318.
39. "Exchange of Letters regarding the 1945 Surrender of Japan," August 10–11, 1945, p. 1; http://www.international.ucla.edu/eas/documents/surrender-exch.htm.
40. Totani, *The Tokyo War Crimes Trial*, pp. 44–50.
41. "Exchange of Letters," p. 2.
42. Noah Berlin, "Constitutional Conflict with the Japanese Imperial Role: Accession, Yasukuni Shrine, and Obligatory Reformation," *Journal of Constitutional Law*, Vol. 1, No. 2 (Fall 1998), p. 391.
43. MacArthur, *Reminiscences*, pp. 279–280.
44. Ibid., p. 288.
45. Berlin, "Constitutional Conflict," p. 395.
46. Ibid., p. 395; MacArthur, *Reminiscences*, p. 287.
47. John W. Dower, *Embracing Defeat: Japan in the Wake of World War II* (New York: W. W. Norton, 1999), pp. 295–296.
48. Max Hastings, *Retribution: The Battle for Japan, 1944–45* (New York: Alfred A. Knopf, 2008), p. 39.
49. MacArthur, *Reminiscences*, p. 288.
50. Bix, *Hirohito*, pp. 584–586.
51. Berlin, "Constitutional Conflict," p. 396.
52. Totani, *The Tokyo War Crimes Trial*, p. 53.
53. Dower, *Embracing Defeat*, p. 295.
54. Totani, *The Tokyo War Crimes Trial*, p. 55.
55. Ibid., pp. 54–58.
56. "Charter of the International Military Tribunal for the Far East (April 26, 1946)," *Documents on the Tokyo IMT*, pp. 7–15.
57. Ibid., p. 7.
58. Boister and Cryer, *The Tokyo IMT*, p. 283.
59. B. V. A. Röling and Antonio Cassese, *The Tokyo Trial and Beyond* (Cambridge: Polity Press, 1993), p. 30.
60. Boister and Cryer, *The Tokyo IMT*, pp. 82–83.
61. Totani, *The Tokyo War Crimes Trial*, pp. 31–34.
62. Behr, *Hirohito*, p. 345.
63. Totani, *The Tokyo War Crimes Trial*, p. 269 n29.
64. Ibid., p. 346.
65. Dower, *Embracing Defeat*, p. 326.
66. *Tokyo Major War Crimes Trial*, 13, p. 31331.
67. Ibid., 77, pp. 36779–36781.
68. *Documents on the Tokyo IMT*, pp. 638–639.
69. Ibid., p. 676.

70. Dower, *Embracing Defeat*, pp. 326–327, 329.

71. Boister and Cryer, *The Tokyo IMT*, p. 67.

72. *Documents on the Tokyo IMT*, p. 8.

73. Ibid., pp. 34–46.

74. Totani, *The Tokyo War Crimes Trial*, pp. 66–67.

75. Boister and Cryer, *The Tokyo IMT*, pp. 53–54.

76. Totani, *The Tokyo War Crimes Trial*, pp. 22, 67.

77. Ibid., pp. 68–69.

78. Ibid., pp. 63, 69–70.

79. Ibid., pp. 22–23, 70–77.

80. A. S. Comyns-Carr, "The Judgement of the International Military Tribunal for the Far East," *Transactions of the Grotius Society*, Vol. 34 (1948), p. 142.

81. Boister and Cryer, *The Tokyo IMT*, p. 157.

82. Totani, *The Tokyo War Crimes Trial*, pp. 105–107.

83. Ibid., pp. 107–108.

84. *Tokyo Major War Crimes Trial*, 28, p. 12861.

85. "Opening Statement of the Prosecution," *Trial of Japanese War Criminals: Documents* (Washington, DC: US Government Printing Office, 1946), p. 4.

86. *Documents on the Tokyo IMT*, pp. 16–56.

87. Ibid., pp. 56–69.

88. *Tokyo Major War Crimes Trial*, 2, pp. 308–315; Boister and Cryer, *The Tokyo IMT*, p. 72.

89. Dower, *Embracing Defeat*, p. 461.

90. Röling and Cassese, *The Tokyo Trial*, p. 20.

91. Fred L. Borch, "Sitting in Judgement: Myron C. Cramer's Experiences in the Trials of German Saboteurs and Japanese War Leaders," *Prologue*, Vol. 41, No. 2 (Summer 2009), p. 38.

92. Boister and Cryer, *The Tokyo IMT*, p. 75.

93. Ibid., pp. 79–80.

94. Ibid., pp. 81–82.

95. Ibid., pp. 90.

96. Ibid., pp. 72–73, 90–91.

97. Dower, *Embracing Defeat*, p. 458.

98. Röling and Cassese, *The Tokyo Trial and Beyond*, pp. 36–37; *Tokyo Major War Crimes Trial*, 2, xl.

99. *Tokyo Major War Crimes Trial*, 2, xl.

100. Ibid., xliii.

101. Boister and Cryer, *The Tokyo IMT*, p. 73.

102. Ibid., pp. 97–98.

103. *Documents on the Tokyo IMT*, pp. 63–69. These counts were those accepted by the judges in their final judgment.

104. Boister and Cryer, *The Tokyo IMT*, p. 104.

105. Kobori Keiichiro, *The Tokyo Trials: The Unheard Defense* (Rockport: New English History Press, 2003), p. 48.

106. Jansen, *The Making of Modern Japan*, p. 419; Bix, *Hirohito*, pp. 171–172, 174–176; Behr, *Hirohito*, p. 155.

107. Boister and Cryer, *The Tokyo IMT*, pp. 92, 113; Bix, *Hirohito*, p. 602.

108. Behr, *Hirohito*, pp. 226–231

109. Totani, *The Tokyo War Crimes Trial*, pp. 37–38; *Tokyo Major War Crimes Trial*, 64–65, pp. 30711–31211.

110. *Major Tokyo War Crimes Trial*, 34, pp. 16187, 16190.

111. Ibid., pp. 16188–16189.
112. Bix, *Hirohito*, pp. 430–431.
113. Ibid., pp. 431–433.
114. *Tokyo Major War Crimes Trial*, 34, pp. 16192–16194.
115. Ibid., 79, p. 37297.
116. Ibid., pp. 37927–37303.
117. Ibid., 81, p. 38692.
118. Ibid., pp. 38681–39701.
119. Ibid., 74, p. 35475; ibid., 81, pp. 38915–38916.
120. Ibid., 81, p. 38920.
121. Ibid., pp. 38932–38933.
122. Ibid., p. 38935.
123. Ibid.
124. Ibid., pp. 38936–38937.
125. Ibid., pp. 41047–41095.
126. Ibid., pp. 410082–41086.
127. Ibid., p. 46424.
128. Ibid., p. 46425.
129. Ibid.
130. Ibid., pp. 46426–46427, 46432–46436.
131. Ibid., pp. 46458–46459.
132. Ibid., pp. 46460–46461.
133. Ibid., p. 46461.
134. Ibid., p. 46462.
135. Ibid., p. 46463.
136. Edwin P. Hoyt, *Warlord: Tōjō against the World* (Lanham: Scarborough House, 1993), pp. 7–64 *passim*; Courtney Browne, *Tōjō: The Last Banzai* (New York: Holt, Rinehart and Winston, 1967), pp. 22–105 *passim*.
137. *Documents on the Tokyo IMT*, pp. 16–34, 62–63, 69.
138. *Tokyo Major War Crimes Trial*, 76, pp. 36412–36413.
139. "Hideki Tōjō's Prison Diary," *Hoseki* (August–September 1991), p. 4, http://www.translationcentraljp.com/article.html.
140. *Tokyo Major War Crimes Trial*, 76, pp. 36534–36535.
141. Hoyt, *Warlord*, pp. 229–230.
142. *Tokyo Major War Crimes Trial*, 76, p. 36508.
143. Boister and Cryer, *The Tokyo IMT*, p. 76.
144. *Tokyo Major War Crimes Trial*, 76, p. 36535.
145. Ibid., p. 36569.
146. Ibid., p. 36570.
147. Ibid., p. 36571.
148. Ibid., p. 36572.
149. Ibid., pp. 36573–36583.
150. Ibid., p. 36587.
151. Ibid., p. 36590.
152. Ibid., p. 36591.
153. Ibid., pp. 36647–36648.
154. Ibid., p. 36649.
155. Ibid., pp. 36649–36650.
156. Ibid., pp. 36653–36654.
157. *Documents on the Tokyo IMT*, p. 624.
158. *Tokyo Major War Crimes Trial*, 76, pp. 36421–36422.

159. Boister and Cryer, *The Tokyo IMT*, p. 179.
160. *Tokyo Major War Crimes Trial*, 9, p. 3892.
161. Ibid., p. 4610.
162. Boister and Cryer, *The Tokyo IMT*, pp.153–154.
163. *Tokyo Major War Crimes Trial*, 7, pp. 2621–2622.
164. Ibid., 11, pp. 4612–4613.
165. Ibid., pp. 4614–4615.
166. Ibid., p. 4629–4635.
167. Ibid., p. 4638.
168. Ibid., p. 4642.
169. Boister and Cryer, *The Tokyo IMT*, pp. 157–158.
170. *Tokyo Major War Crimes Trial*, 27, 12576.
171. Ibid., p.12577.
172. Boister and Cryer, *The Tokyo IMT*, p.158.
173. *Tokyo Major War Crimes Trial*, 27, pp. 12468–12469.
174. Ibid., 32, p. 15035.
175. Ibid., p. 15037.
176. Ibid., p. 15040.
177. Yuki Tanaka, *Hidden Horrors: Japanese War Crimes in World War II* (Boulder: Westview Press, 1998), p. 127.
178. Ibid., pp. 129–130.
179. Boister and Cryer, *The Tokyo IMT,* p. 162.
180. Ibid., p. 163.
181. C. M. Turnbull, *A History of Singapore, 1819–1975* (Kuala Lumpur: Oxford University Press, 1977), pp. 181, 186–187, 193–194, says that the number could have been as high as 25,000; Tanaka, *Hidden Horrors*, pp. 81–82.
182. Totani, *The Tokyo War Crimes Trial*, pp. 163–164; Hayashi Hirofumi, "British War Crimes Trials of Japanese," *Science and the Humanities*, No. 31 (July 2001), p. 4; http://www32.ocn.ne.jp/~eng08.htm
183. *Tokyo Major War Crimes Trial*, 29, pp. 13456–13547.
184. Ibid., pp. 13457–13458.
185. Tanaka, *Hidden Horrors,* p. 27.
186. Ibid., p. 27.
187. Ibid., pp. 29–30.
188. Ibid., pp. 45–60; *Tokyo Major War Crimes Trial*, 29, 3422–13424.
189. Totani, *The Tokyo War Crimes Trial*, p. 174.
190. Saburō Ienaga, *The Pacific War, 1931–1945: A Critical Perspective on Japan's Role in World War II* (New York: Pantheon, 1978), p. 176.
191. *History of the United Nations War Crimes Commission*, p. 518.
192. Totani, *The Tokyo War Crimes Trial*, p. 175; Dower, *Embracing Defeat*, pp. 551–553.
193. *Tokyo Major War Crimes Trial*, 29, 13526–13528, 13651–13652; Totani, *The Tokyo War Crimes Trial*, pp. 176–177.
194. Totani, *The Tokyo War Crimes Trial*, pp. 177–178.
195. Ibid., p.178.
196. Ibid., pp. 179–180.
197. The Women's International War Crimes Tribunal for the Trial of Japan's Military Sexual Slavery, Case No. PT-2000-1-T, January 31, 2002, *The Prosecutors and the Peoples of the Asia-Pacific Region v. Hirohito Emperor Showa et al.: Judgement*, p. 17.
198. Yayori Matsui, "Women's International War Crimes Tribunal on Japan's Military Sexual Slavery: Memory, Identity, and Society," in Li, *Japanese War Crimes*, p. 270.
199. *Tokyo Major War Crimes Tribunal*, 35, p. 16268.

200. Ibid., p. 16271.
201. Ibid., pp. 16272–16277; ibid., 36, p. 16997.
202. Totani, *The Tokyo War Crimes Trial*, p. 182.
203. C. Hosoya, N. Andō, Y. Ōnuma, and R. Minear, *The Tokyo War Crimes Trial: An International Symposium* (Tokyo: Kodansha International, 1986), p. 93.
204. *Tokyo Major War Crimes Tribunal*, 88, p. 42115.
205. Ibid., pp. 42201–42202.
206. Ibid., pp. 42203–42204.
207. Ibid., p. 42078.
208. Ibid., p. 42187–42188.
209. *Tokyo Major War Crimes Trial*, 37, p. 17017.
210. Ibid., pp. 17017–17018.
211. Ibid., p. 17019.
212. Ibid., p. 17021.
213. Ibid., p. 17024.
214. Ibid.
215. Ibid., pp. 17024–17025.
216. Ibid., p. 17026.
217. Ibid., p. 17028.
218. Ibid., pp. 17034–17035.
219. Ibid., p. 17036.
220. Ibid.
221. Ibid., pp. 17036–17037.
222. Ibid., pp. 17040–17041.
223. Ibid., p. 17057.
224. Ibid., p. 17058.
225. Ibid., pp. 17058–17059.
226. Ibid., p. 17060.
227. Ibid., pp. 17060–17061.
228. Ibid., p.17086.
229. Ibid., pp. 17086–17087.
230. *Tokyo Major War Crimes Trial*, 88, pp. 42113–42114.
231. Ibid., p. 42114.
232. Ibid., pp. 42114–42115.
233. Ibid., p. 42119.
234. Ibid., p. 42113.
235. Ibid., 2, pp. 402–403.
236. Ibid., 83, p. 39954.
237. Ibid., 35, p. 16419.
238. Ibid., 59, p. 28278.
239. *Nazi Conspiracy and Aggression: Opinion and Judgement*, pp. 85–86.
240. Ibid., p. 107.
241. *Tokyo Major War Crimes Trial*, 88, pp. 42135–42136.
242. Ibid., 2, pp. 396, 402.
243. Ibid., 88, p. 42136.
244. Ibid., p. 42137.
245. Ibid., pp. 42140–42141.
246. *Marino v. United States*, 91F. ed 691–699, 113 A.L.R. 975 (9 Cir. 1937; Cr. Code "37, 18 U.S.C.A." 88, p. 726; Department of Justice of the United States of America, *Pre-Trial Brief on the Law of Conspiracy,* in *Tokyo Major War Crimes Trial*, 123A, pp. 74–78; Sir Robert Samuel Wright, *The Law of Conspiracies and Agreements* (Ithaca: Cornell

University Press, 2009), pp. 5–18; Peter Gillies, *The Law of Criminal Conspiracy* (Annandale: Federation Press, 1990), pp. 79–83.

247. *Tokyo Major War Crimes Trial*, 37, p. 17060.
248. Ibid., pp. 17060–17061.
249. Ibid., pp. 17086–17087.
250. Ibid., pp. 17061, 17076.
251. Ibid., 88, pp. 42120–42128.
252. Ibid., pp. 42200–42201.
253. Ibid., p. 42202.
254. Ibid., 89, pp. 42494–42513.
255. Boister and Cryer, *The Tokyo IMT*, p. 184.
256. *Tokyo Major War Crimes Trial*, 2, p. 201.
257. Ibid., 88, p. 42257.
258. Ibid., p. 42258.
259. Ibid., pp. 42258–42259.
260. Ibid., 90, p. 43046.
261. Ibid., pp. 43046–43057.
262. Ibid., p. 43053.
263. Ibid., p. 43054.
264. Ibid., p. 43056.
265. Ibid., p. 43058.
266. Ibid., pp. 43058–43059.
267. Ibid., pp. 43060–43111.
268. Ibid., pp. 43051, 43111–43112.
269. Ibid., pp. 43111–43112; *Hearings before the Committee on Foreign Relations, United States Senate, Seventieth Congress, Second Session on the General Pact for the Renunciation of War Signed at Paris August 27, 1928*. December 7 and 11, 1928, Part 1, p. 9; http://avalon. law.yale.edu/20th_century/kbhear.asp.
270. *Tokyo Major War Crimes Trial*, 90, pp. 43111–43136.
271. Ibid., p. 43136.
272. Ibid., p. 43158.
273. Ibid., p. 43160.
274. Ibid., p. 384.
275. Boister and Cryer, *The Tokyo IMT*, p. 279.
276. Ōnuma Yasuaki, "The Tokyo Trial: Between Law and Reason," in Hosoya et al., *The Tokyo War Crimes Trial*, p. 47; Madoka Futamura, *War Crimes Tribunals and Transitional Justice: The Tokyo Trial and the Nuremberg Legacy* (London: Routledge, 2008), p. 72.
277. *Tokyo Major War Crimes Trial*, 2, p. 189.
278. Ibid., 101, p. 48499.
279. Ibid., 109, *Pal Opinion*, p. 1225.
280. Ibid., 105, *Pal Opinion*, p. 37.
281. Ibid., 106, *Pal Opinion*, p. 527.
282. Ibid., 105, *Janarilla Opinion*, p. 33.
283. Ibid., 101, p. 48512(a).
284. *Documents on the Tokyo IMT*, lxiii.
285. Röling and Cassese, *The Tokyo Trial and Beyond*, pp. 28–29; *Documents on the Tokyo IMT*, lxiv.
286. *Documents on the Tokyo IMT*, lxv–lxvii.
287. *Tokyo Major War Crimes Trial*, 101, p. 48439.
288. Ibid., p. 48440; Boister and Cryer, *Documents on the Tokyo IMT*, p. 8.
289. *Tokyo Major War Crimes Trial*, 101, pp. 48430–48431.

290. Kayoko Takeda, *Interpreting the Tokyo War Crimes Tribunal: A Sociopolitical Analysis* (Ottawa: University of Ottawa Press, 2010), pp. 50–51.

291. United Nations Audiovisual Library of International Law, pp. 1–3; www.org/law/avl; Boister and Cryer, *The Tokyo IMT*, p. 136; *Documents on the Tokyo IMT*, p. lxxii.

292. *Tokyo Major War Crimes Trial*, 103, pp. 49575–49576.

293. Boister and Cryer, *The Tokyo IMT*, p. 128.

294. *Tokyo Major War Crimes Trial*, 101, pp. 48438–48439.

295. Ibid., 103, p. 49772.

296. *Documents on the Tokyo IMT*, pp. 18, 24–27, 32–33.

297. Ibid., xliv–xlv.

298. Ibid., pp. 632–639.

299. Ibid., pp. 676–677.

300. Ibid., p. 677.

301. Ibid., p. 677.

302. Ibid., pp. 775–807.

303. Ibid., p. 775.

304. Ashis Nandy, "The Other Within: The Strange Case of Radhabinod Pal's Judgement on Culpability," *New Literary History*, Vol. 23, No. 1 (Winter 1992), p. 60.

305. Ibid., p. 48.

306. Ibid., pp. 53–54.

307. *Documents on the Tokyo IMT*, pp. 854, 859, 880.

308. Ibid., p. 819.

309. Ibid. p. 827.

310. Ibid., pp. 837, 829.

311. Ibid., p. 834.

312. Ibid, pp. 914–915.

313. Ibid., pp. 903–904.

314. Ibid., p. 867.

315. Ibid., p. 923.

316. Ibid., pp. 1302–1303.

317. Ibid., p. 1304.

318. Ibid., pp. 1306, 1308.

319. Ibid., p. 1312.

320. Ibid., p. 1312.

321. Ibid., p. 1326.

322. Ibid., p. 1328.

323. Ibid., p. 1329.

324. Ibid., pp. 1329–1230

325. Ibid., pp. 1331–1332.

326. Ibid., pp. 1332–1333.

327. Ibid., p. 1343.

328. Ibid., p. 1354.

329. Ibid., p. 1371.

330. Ibid., pp. 1373, 1378–1379.

331. Ibid., p. 1391.

332. Ibid., p. 1394.

333. Ibid., p. 1395.

334. Ibid., pp. 1398, 1402–1403.

335. Ibid., p. 1420.

336. Ibid., p. 1422.

337. Ibid., p. 1426.

8   POST–WORLD WAR II NATIONAL TRIALS
IN EUROPE AND ASIA

1. United Nations War Crimes Commission, *History of the United Nations War Crimes Commission and the Development of the Laws of War* (Buffalo: William S. Hein, 2006), p. 518.

2. David M. Crowe, *The Holocaust: The Roots, History, and Aftermath* (Boulder: Westview Press, 2008), pp. 413–414.

3. Ibid., p. 409.

4. "Control Council Directive No. 38: The Arrest and Punishment of War Criminals, Nazis and Militarists and the Internment, Control and Surveillance of Potentially Dangerous Germans," in Office of Military Government for Germany (US), *Denazification: Report of the Military Governor (1 April 1947–30 April 1948),* No. 34, pp. 14–26.

5. Konrad H. Jarausch, *After Hitler: Recivilizing Germans, 1945–1995* (Oxford: Oxford University Press, 2006), p. 54.

6. Dick de Mildt, *In the Name of the People: Perpetrators of Genocide in the Reflection of the Post-War Prosecution in West Germany* (The Hague: Martinus Nijhoff, 1996), pp. 18–19.

7. Frank M. Buscher, *The U.S. War Crimes Trial Program in Germany, 1946–1955* (New York: Greenwood, 1989), p. 2.

8. United Nations War Crimes Commission, *Law Reports of Trials of War Criminals,* Vol. 1 [hereafter *UNWCC, Law Reports*] (Buffalo: William S. Hein, 1997), p. 52.

9. Ibid., pp. 112–113.

10. Ibid., pp. 113–114.

11. Office of the Judge Advocate General of the Army, *A Manual for Courts-Martial U.S. Army, 1928: Corrected to April 20, 1943* (Washington, DC: US Government Printing Office, 1943), pp. 7–9.

12. UNWCC, *Law Reports,* 1, p. 120.

13. Office of the Judge Advocate General, *A Manual,* p. 40; United Nations War Crimes Commission, *Law Reports,* 1, p. 116.

14. UNWCC, *Law Reports,* 1, pp. 116–117.

15. Ibid., p. 117.

16. Ibid., pp. 117–118.

17. Ibid., p. 118.

18. Ibid., p. 119.

19. Ibid., pp. 119–120.

20. Ibid., pp. 120–121.

21. *United States v. Peter Kohn, Matthias Gierens and Matthias,* Case No. 12–2422, June 5, 1945, Ahrweiler, Germany, pp. 1–4. ICWC (Forschungs- und Dokumentationszewntrum für Kriegsverbrucherprozesse), Source 000–012–2422.

22. Ibid., p. 4.

23. Ibid., p. 5.

24. Ibid., pp. 5–6.

25. Ibid., pp. 7–8.

26. Ibid., pp. 8–10.

27. *United States v. Peter Back,* Case No. 12–2422–1, 16 June 1945, Ahrweiler, Germany, pp. 1–8. ICWC, Source 000–012–2422–001,

28. Review of Record of Trial by Military Commission in the Cases of *United States v. Lieutenant Gunther Thiele and United States v. Grenadier Georg Steinert, both Members of the German Army, Tried by Common Trial.* June 22, 1945, Case No. 12–494, Source No. 000–012–0494, ICWC, pp. 4–5; *United States v. Johann Schwaren. Review and*

Recommendations, Case No. 12–494–1, November 3, 1947, Source No. 000–012–0494–001, ICWC, pp. 1–2.

29. Review of *United States v. Theile and Steinert*, p. 6.

30. Ibid., p. 7.

31. Ibid., pp. 10–11.

32. Ibid., p. 13.

33. Ibid., p. 13.

34. *Trials of War Criminals before the Nuernberg Military Tribunals under Control Council Law No. 10*, Vol. 1 (Washington, DC: US Government Printing Office, 1949), xx–xxvii.

35. Ibid., 4, p. 286.

36. Ibid., p. 356.

37. Crowe, *The Holocaust*, pp. 403–404.

38. Ibid., p. 404.

39. Office of US Chief of Counsel, Subsequent Proceedings Division, APO 124-A. *Staff Evidence Analysis, Criminal Organizations*. Document No. -085, February 9, 1942, pp. 2–3. The Mazal Library; http://www.mazal.org/N)-series/NO-0085–000.htm.

40. *Trials of War Criminals before the Nuernberg Military Tribunals under Control Council Law No. 10*, 4, pp. 460–461.

41. Crowe, *The Holocaust*, p. 406.

42. *Declaration of Geneva* (1948 and 1968). The World Medical Association; http://www.wma.net/e/policy/c8.htm.

43. Crowe, *The Holocaust*, p. 406.

44. Ibid., pp. 406–407.

45. Institute of Criminal Law, University of Amsterdam, "Introduction," *The Dachau Trials: Trials by U.S. Army Courts in Europe, 1945–1948*, p. 1; http://www1.jur.uva.nl/junsv/JUNSVEng/DTRR/Dachau%20trials%20intro.htm.

46. Ibid., p. 1.

47. Deputy Theater Judge Advocates Office, War Crimes Branch, United States Forces, European Theater, *United States v. Martin Gottfried Weiss et al.*, March 1946), pp. 1–2. ICWC, Source 000–050–0002.

48. Ibid., pp. 2, 29–55.

49. Ibid., pp. 9, 11–16.

50. UNWCC, *Law Reports*, 11, pp. 9–10.

51. Ibid., pp. 3, 84–85.

52. Paul Berben, *Dachau, 1933–45: The Official History* (London: Comitéde Dachau, 1975), pp. 201, 228; Barbara Distel and Ruth Jakusch, eds., *Concentration Camp Dachau, 1933–1945* (Munich: Comité de Dachau, 1978), p. 212.

53. Willi Mernyi and Florian Wenniger, *Die Befreiung des KZ Mauthausen: Berichte und Dokumente* (Vienna: Verlag des Österreichschen Gewerkschaftsbundes GmbH, 2006), pp. 22; Tomaz Jardim, *The Mauthausen Trial: American Military Justice in Germany* (Cambridge, MA: Harvard University Press, 2012), p. 60; Benyamin Eckstein, "Mauthausen," in Israel Gutman, ed., *Encyclopedia of the Holocaust*, Vol. 3 (New York: Macmillan, 1990), p. 952.

54. *United States v. Hans Altfuldisch et al.*, Case No. 000.50.5. Deputy Judge Advocate's Office, 7708 War Crime Group, Headquarters European Command, Review and Recommendations of the Deputy Judge Advocate for War Crimes, March 1946, p. 4. ICWC, Source 000–050–0005.

55. Ibid., p. 7.

56. Ibid., pp. 7–8.

57. Jardim, *The Mauthausen Trial*, pp. 54–55.

58. *United States v. Hans Altfuldisch et al.*, p. 48.
59. Jardim, *The Mauthausen Trial,* p. 146.
60. *United States v. Hans Altfuldisch et al.,* pp. 24, 48–49, 70–72, 78–79; Jardim, *The Mauthausen Trial*, pp. 197, 199.
61. Royal Warrant, June 18, 1945, p. 1; UNWCC, *Law Reports*, 1, p. 105.
62. Ibid., p. 107.
63. United Nations War Crimes Commission, *History of the United Nations War Crimes Commission*, p. 518.
64. UNWCC, *Law Reports*, 2, p. 1.
65. Ibid., pp. 4, 101.
66. Crowe, *The Holocaust*, p. 407.
67. UNWCC, *Law Reports*, 2, p. 14.
68. Ibid., pp. 407–408.
69. UNWCC, *Law Reports*, 2, pp. 62–63.
70. Ibid., p. 2.
71. Ibid., p. 35.
72. UNWCC, *Law Reports*, 2, pp. 1–2.
73. Ibid., pp. 2–3.
74. Ibid., p. 3.
75. Ibid., pp. 121–125.
76. Wilhelm Lindsey. "Zyklon B, Auschwitz und der Prozeß gegen Dr. Bruno Tesch," *Vierteljahreshelfe für freie Geschichtsforschung*, http:vho.org/vffg/2001/2/lindsey/69–188. html.
77. UNWCC, *Law Reports*, 1, pp. 95, 97.
78. Ibid., p. 101.
79. Ibid., pp. 102–103.
80. UNWCC, *Law Reports*, 11, pp. 18–29.
81. Ibid., 8, pp. 9–14.
82. Henry Rousso, "Did the Purge Achieve Its Goals?" in Richard J. Golsan, ed., *Memory, the Holocaust, and French Justice: The Bousquet and Touvier Affairs* (Hanover: University Press of New England, 1996), p. 101.
83. Crowe, *The Holocaust*, p. 415.
84. Rousso, "Did the Purge Achieve Its Goals?" p. 118.
85. Crowe, *The Holocaust*, p. 415.
86. Ibid., p. 415.
87. Richard J. Golsan, "Introduction," in Golsan, *Memory, the Holocaust, and French Justice*, p. 24.
88. UNWCC, *Law Reports*, 3, p. 93.
89. Ibid., pp. 93–99.
90. Ibid., 3, pp. 23–24.
91. Ibid., p. 25.
92. Ibid., pp. 30–35.
93. Ibid., pp. 24–49.
94. Ibid., p. 72.
95. "Control Council Directive No. 38," p. 17.
96. Jeffrey Herf, *Divided Memory: The Nazi Past in the Two Germanies* (Cambridge: Harvard University Press, 1997), pp. 72–73.
97. Christiane Wilke, "Recognizing Victimhood," Law and Humanities Junior Scholar Interdisciplinary Workshop, June 6–7, 2006, p. 6; http://www.law.columbia.edu/null/wilke+-+Long?exclusive=filemgr.downloadfile_id=97928showthumb=o.

98. Mark Elliot, "Andrei Vlasov: Red Army General in Hitler's Service," *Military Affairs*, Vol. 42, No. 2 (1982), p. 84; Nikolai Tolstoy, *Victims of Yalta* (London: Corgi Books, 1979), pp. 397, 468, 515. Tolstoy's figures are slightly higher than those provided by Col. Gen. G. F. Krivosheev in his *Soviet Casualties and Combat Losses in the Twentieth*, trans. Christine Barnard (London: Greenhill Books, 1997), pp. 85, 91–92.

99. Alexander Victor Prusin, "Fascist Criminals to the Gallows! The Holocaust and Soviet War Crimes Trials, December 1944–February 1945," *Holocaust and Genocide Studies*, Vol. 17, No. 1 (Spring 2003), pp. 3–4.

100. George Ginsburgs, "Law of War and War Crimes on the Russian Front during World War Two: The Soviet View," *Soviet Studies*, Vol. 11, No. 3 (January 1960), p. 263.

101. Ibid., p. 264.

102. The Moscow Conference, October 1943: *Joint Four-Nation Declaration*. The Avalon Project at Yale Law School, p. 4; http://www.yale.eduy/lawweb/avalon/wwil/moscow.htm.

103. Ginsburgs, "Law of War and Crimes on the Russian Front during World War Two," p. 269.

104. *Moscow Trial of 16 Polish Diversionists: June 18–21, 1945* (London: M. W. Books, 1945), pp. 2, 67–69.

105. Crowe, *The Holocaust*, p. 427.

106. Wilfried Strik-Strikfeldt, *Against Stalin and Hitler: Memoirs of the Russian Liberation Movement, 1941–1945*, trans. David Footman (New York: John Day, 1973), p. 69.

107. Crowe, *The Holocaust*, p. 428.

108. Ibid., pp. 159, 162.

109. Ulrich Herbert, *Hitler's Foreign Workers: Enforced Foreign Labor in Germany under the Third Reich*, trans. William Templer (Cambridge: Cambridge University Press, 1997), p. 462.

110. Alexander Prusin, "Poland's Nuremberg: The Seven Court Cases of the Supreme National Tribunal, 1946–1948," *Holocaust and Genocide Studies*, Vol. 24, No. 1 (Spring 2010), p. 1.

111. Crowe, *The Holocaust*, p. 423.

112. UNWCC, *Law Reports*, 7, p. 82.

113. Ibid., pp. 82–83; Prusin, "Fascist Criminals"; ibid., p. 3.

114. UNWCC, *Law Reports*, 7, p. 83.

115. United Nations War Crimes Commission, *Law Reports of Trials of War Criminals: Four Genocide Trials* (New York: Harold Fertig, 1992), pp. 70–72.

116. Ibid., pp. 102–106.

117. Ibid., pp. 112–116.

118. UNWCC, *Law Reports*, 7, pp. 1–3; the full story of Göth's arrest and interrogation by the SS is told in David M. Crowe's *Oskar Schindler: The Untold Account of His Life, Wartime Activities, and the True Story behind the List* (Boulder: Westview, 2004), pp. 349–360.

119. Mietek Pemper, *The Road to Rescue: The Untold Story of Schindler's List*, trans. David Dollenmayer (New York: Other Press, 2008), p. 41.

120. Nachman Blumental et al., eds., *Proces Ludobójcy Amona Leopolda Goetha przed Najwyższy Trybunał Narodowy* (Warszawa: Centralna Żcydowska Komisja Historyczna przy Centralnym Komitecie Żydów w Polsce, 1947), p. 70.

121. Aleksander Bieberstein, *Zagłada Żydów w Krakowie* (Kraków: Wydawnictwo Literackie, 1985), p. 141.

122. UNWCC, *Law Reports*, 7, pp. 5–8.

123. Ibid., p. 9.

124. Ibid., p. 10.
125. Ibid., pp. 4, 10.
126. Ibid., p. 17.
127. Ibid., pp. 11, 17.
128. Ibid., p. 17.
129. Ibid., pp. 17–18.
130. Rudolph Höss, *Death Dealer: The Memoirs of the SS Kommandant at Auschwitz*, ed. Steven Paskuly, trans. Andrew Pollinger (New York: Da Capo, 1996), p. 189.
131. United Nations War Crimes Commission, *History of the United Nations War Crimes Commission*, p. 518; ICWC, *Dokumente: Datenbank (Auszug)*, "Yokohama Trials."
132. UNWCC, *Law Reports*, 1, pp. 71–73.
133. Ibid., p. 76.
134. Ibid., pp. 73–74.
135. Ibid., p. 74.
136. Ibid.
137. Ibid.
138. Ibid., pp. 76–80.
139. Review of the Staff Judge Advocate, *United States of America v. Isao Fukuhara*, Yokohama, Japan, May 4, 1946, Case. No. 6, p. 2. ICWC. *Dokumente: Datenbank (Auszug)*. "Yokohama Trials."
140. Ibid., p. 2.
141. Ibid., p. 5.
142. Ibid., pp. 2, 6.
143. Ibid., p. 7.
144. Ibid.
145. Ibid.
146. Ibid., pp. 9–10.
147. Yun Xia, "*Traitors to the Chinese Race (Hanjian)": Political and Cultural Campaigns against Collaborators during the Sino-Japanese War of 1937–1945* (Seattle: Department of History, University of Washington, 2010), p. 1.
148. Ibid., p. 292.
149. Dongyoun Hwang, "Wartime Collaboration in Question: An Examination of the Postwar Trials of the Chinese Collaborators," *Inter-Asia Cultural Studies*, Vol. 6, No. 1 (2005), p. 75.
150. Charles D. Musgrove, "Cheering the Traitor: The Post-War Trial of Chen Bijun, April 1946," *Twentieth Century China*, Vol. 30, No. 2 (April 2005), p. 7.
151. Xia, *Traitors to the Chinese Race*, p. 293.
152. M. Kajimoto, *The Nanjing Atrocities: The Postwar Judgement: II. Nanking War Crimes Tribunal*, p. 1; http://www.nankingatrocities.net/Tribunals/nanjing_02.htm; Xia, "*Traitors to the Chinese Race*," p. 292.
153. Xia, *Traitors to the Chinese Race*, p. 41; Xiaoyuan Liu, *A Partnership for Disorder: China, the United States, and Their Policies for the Postwar Disposition of the Japanese Empire, 1941–1945* (Cambridge: Cambridge University Press, 2002), p. 25.
154. Xia, *Traitors to the Chinese Race*, pp. 41–43.
155. Ibid., pp. 43–44.
156. Ibid., p. 46.
157. Ibid., Appendix A, pp. 305–306.
158. Ibid., xi–xii.
159. Musgrove, "Cheering the Traitor," p. 20.
160. Xia, *Traitors to the Chinese Race*, pp. 93–94.
161. Musgrove, "Cheering the Traitor," pp. 8–9.

162. Hwang, "Wartime Collaboration," p. 76.
163. Ibid., p. 76.
164. Ibid.
165. Ibid., p. 79.
166. Xia, *Traitors to the Chinese Race,* p. 90.
167. Ibid., pp. 79–80; Zanasi, "Globalizing *Hanjian,*" pp. 731–733.
168. Zanasi, "Globalizing *Hanjian,*" p. 738.
169. J. G. Shields, *The Extreme Right in France: From Pétain to Le Pen* (London: Routledge, 2007), p. 23.
170. Zanasi, "Globalizing *Hanjian,*" p. 738.
171. Jules Roy, *The Trial of Marshal Pétain,* trans. Robert Baldick (New York: Harper & Row, 1968), Chapter2 , p. 18.
172. Charles Williams, *Pétain: How the Hero of France Became a Convicted Traitor and Changed the Course of History* (New York: Palgrave Macmillan, 2005), p. 249.
173. Hwang, "Wartime Collaboration," p. 80.
174. Ibid., p. 80.
175. Ibid., pp. 80–81.
176. Taylor, *The Generalissimo*, pp. 339–345.
177. Hwang, "Wartime Collaboration," p. 81.
178. Musgrove, "Cheering the Traitor," p. 6.
179. Hwang, "Wartime Collaboration," p. 77.
180. Musgrove, "Cheering the Traitor," p. 9.
181. Ibid., pp. 9–10.
182. Marie-Claire Bergère, *Sun Yat-sen,* trans. Janet Lloyd (Stanford: Stanford University Press, 1998), pp. 405, 433; Jonathan Fenby, *Chiang Kai-shek: China's Generalissimo and the Nation He Lost* (New York: Carroll & Graf, 2004), pp. 90–94.
183. John Hunter Boyle, *China and Japan at War, 1937–1945: The Politics of Collaboration* (Stanford: Stanford University Press, 1972), pp. 19–20; Fenby, *Chiang Kai-shek*, pp. 274–275.
184. Pei-kai Cheng and Michael Lestz with Jonathan D. Spence, eds., *The Search for Modern China: A Documentary Collection* (New York: W. W. Norton, 1999), p. 330.
185. Taylor, *The Generalissimo*, pp. 153–154.
186. Fenby, *Chiang Kai-shek*, p. 343; Musgrove, "Cheering the Traitor," p. 13; Frederick Wakeman, Jr., *Spymaster: Dai Li and the Chinese Secret Service* (Berkeley: University of California Press, 2003), p. 337.
187. Musgrove, "Cheering the Traitor," p. 12.
188. Ibid., pp. 12–13.
189. Ibid., p. 16.
190. Ibid., pp. 14–15; Diana Lary, *The Chinese People at War: Human Suffering and Social Transformation, 1937–1945* (Cambridge: Cambridge University Press, 2010), pp. 117–121.
191. Keith Schoppa, *In a Sea of Bitterness: Refugees during the Sino-Japanese War* (Cambridge, MA: Harvard University Press, 2011), p. 309.
192. Musgrove, "Cheering the Dictator," p. 16.
193. Ibid., p. 16.
194. Ibid., p. 17.
195. Ibid., pp. 17–18.
196. Ibid., p. 18.
197. Ibid., pp. 9, 18.
198. Taylor, *The Generalissimo*, p. 357.
199. Musgrove, "Cheering the Dictator," p. 19.

200. Ibid., p. 19.
201. Boyle, *China and Japan at War*, p. 362.
202. Xia, *Traitors to the Chinese Race*, pp. 203–209; Musgrove, "Cheering the Dictator," p. 20.
203. Musgrove, "Cheering the Dictator," p. 21.
204. Ibid., p. 22.
205. Boyle, *China and Japan at War*, p. 362.
206. Bergère, *Sun Yat-sen*, p. 432.
207. Musgrove, "Cheering the Dictator," pp. 24–25.
208. Xia, *Traitors to the Chinese Race*, p. 293.
209. Piccigallo, *The Japanese on Trial*, p. 162; UNWCC, *Law Reports*, 5, pp. 8–9.
210. UNWCC, *Law Reports*, 5, pp. 1–5.
211. Ibid., pp. 22–23.
212. Ibid., pp. 4–24.
213. Ibid., p. 60.
214. Ibid.
215. Ibid., pp. 61–62.
216. Ibid., pp. 62–63.
217. Ibid., pp. 63–64.
218. Ibid, p. 66.
219. Ibid., p. 67; Wayne G. Johnson, "The Execution of Major Houck," *118th Tactical Reconnaissance Squadron*, p. 1; http://www.118trs.com/david-houck/execution-of-major-houck.
220. UNWCC, *Law Reports*, 5, p. 70.
221. Richard Fuller, *Japanese Generals, 1926–1945* (Atglen, PA: Schiffer Military History, 2011), p. 211; John Mark Carroll, *A Concise History of Hong Kong* (Lanham: Rowman and Littlefield, 2007), p. 131.
222. Piccigallo, *The Japanese on Trial*, p. 162.
223. Xia, *Traitors to the Chinese Race*, p. 45.
224. UNWCC, *Law Reports*, 14, pp. 3, 152; Klaus Mühlhahn, *Criminal Justice in China* (Cambridge, MA: Harvard University Press, 2009), pp. 63–64.
225. UNWCC, *Law Reports*, 14, p. 152.
226. Ibid., p. 1.
227. Taylor, *The Generalissimo*, pp. 113–114; UNWCC, *Law Reports*, 14, p. 1.
228. UNWCC, *Law Reports*, 14, pp. 1–2.
229. Ibid., p. 2; *International Protocol, 1901*. Signed at Peking, September 7, 1901, p. 5.
230. UNWWC, *Law Reports*, 14, p. 2; *International Protocol, 1901*, pp. 19–21.
231. UNWCC, *Law Reports*, 14, p. 4.
232. Ibid., p. 2, 7; Fuller, *Japanese Generals* p. 177; Piccigallo, *The Japanese on Trial*, p. 165.
233. Chang, *The Rape of Nanking*, p. 50.
234. Masahiro Yamamoto, *Nanking: Anatomy of an Atrocity* (Westport: Praeger, 2000), p. 106.
235. Daqing Yang, "The Challenges of the Nanjing Massacre: Reflections on Historical Inquiry," in Joshua A. Fogel, ed., *The Nanjing Massacre in History and Historiography* (Berkeley: University of California Press, 2000), pp. 149–150.
236. David Bergamini, *Japan's Imperial Conspiracy* (New York: Pocket Books, 1972), p. 16.
237. Chang, *The Rape of Nanjing*, p. 37.
238. Bix, *Hirohito*, p. 333.
239. Yamamoto, *Nanking*, p. 194; M. Kajimoto, "The Postwar Judgement: Nanking War Crimes Tribunal," *Nanjing Atrocities*, p. 1; http://www.nankingatrocities.net/Tribunals/nanjing_02.htm.
240. Yamamoto, *Nanking*, p. 194.

241. Chang, *The Rape of Nanking*, p. 171; Yamamoto, *Nanking*, p. 195.
242. Yamamoto, *Nanking*, p. 195.
243. Chang, *The Rape of Nanking*, p. 172.
244. M. Kajimoto, "The Postwar Judgement," p. 2.
245. Piccigallo, *The Japanese on Trial*, p. 166.
246. Bix, *Hirohito*, pp. 365–366.
247. Ibid., p. 362.
248. Taylor, *The Generalissimo*, p. 315; Ronald H. Spector, *In the Ruins of Empire: The Japanese Surrender and the Battle for Postwar Asia* (New York: Random House, 2008), pp. 38–40.
249. John Hunter Boyle, *China and Japan at War, 1937–1945: The Politics of Collaboration* (Stanford: Stanford University Press, 1972), p. 327.
250. Spector, *In the Ruins of Empire*, p. 41.
251. Ibid., p. 41.
252. Donald G. Gillin and Charles Etter, "Staying On: Japanese Soldiers and Civilians in China, 1945–1949," *Journal of Asian Studies*, Vol. 42, No. 3 (May 1983), pp. 501, 502.
253. Piccigallo, *The Japanese on Trial*, p. 166.
254. Ibid., p. 166.
255. Ibid.
256. Ibid., pp. 166–167.
257. Ibid., p. 167.
258. Ibid.
259. Taylor, *The Generalissimo*, pp. 394–396.
260. Piccigallo, *The Japanese on Trial*, p. 167.
261. Taylor, *The Generalissimo*, p. 424.
262. Ibid., p. 452; Bix, *Hirohito*, p. 595.
263. Piccigallo, *The Japanese on Trial*, p. 255 n53.
264. John L. Ginn, *Sugamo Prison, Tokyo: An Account of the Trial and Sentencing of Japanese War Criminals in 1948, by a U.S. Participant* (Jefferson: MacFarland, 1992), pp. 10–12.
265. Piccigallo, *The Japanese on Trial*, p. 167.
266. Communist Party of China, "On the Ordering the Reactionary Kuomintang Government to Re-Arrest Yasuji Okamura, Former Commander-in-Chief of the Japanese Forces of Aggression in China, and to Arrest the Kuomintang Civil War Criminals: Statement by the Spokesman for the Communist Party of China," January 28, 1949, *Selected Works of Mao Tse-tung*, Vol. 4 (Peking: Foreign Languages Press, 1969), p. 327.
267. Communist Party of China, "Peace Terms Must Include the Punishment of Japanese War Criminals and Kuomintang War Criminals—Statement by the Spokesman for the Communist Party of China," February 5, 1949, 4, ibid., pp. 333–335.
268. Boyle, *China and Japan at War*, p. 331; Richard Fuller, *Shōkan: Hirohito's Samurais* (London: Arms and Armour, 1992), pp. 179–180.
269. Xia, *Traitors to the Chinese Race*, pp. 297–298.
270. Ibid., p. 298.
271. John King Fairbank and Merle Goldman, *China: A New History*, 2nd ed. (Cambridge, MA: Belknap Press of Harvard University Press, 2006), pp. 323–325.
272. Xia, *Traitors to the Chinese Race*, pp. 299–300; Mühlhahn, *Criminal Justice*, p. 167.
273. Mühlhahn, *Criminal Justice*, pp. 176, 274.
274. Xia, *Traitors to the Chinese Race*, pp. 300–301.
275. Gillin and Etter, "Japanese Soldier and Civilians," pp. 511–512.
276. Adam Cathcart and Patricia Nash, "War Criminals and the Road to Sino-Japanese Normalization: Zhou Enlai and the Shenyang Trials, 1954–1956," *Twentieth Century China*, Vol. 34, No. 2 (April 2008), pp. 92–93.

277. Justin Jacobs, "Preparing the People for Mass Clemency: The 1956 Japanese War Crimes Trials in Shenyang and Taiyuan," *China Quarterly*, Vol. 205 (March 2011), p. 156.
278. Ibid., pp. 153–154, 157.
279. Ibid., pp. 160–161.
280. Ibid., p. 162.
281. Cathcart and Nash, "War Criminals," pp. 95–97.
282. Ibid., p. 97.
283. Ibid., 98–99.
284. Ibid., p. 99.
285. Jacobs, "Preparing the People for Mass Clemency," pp. 163–164, 166.
286. Cathcart and Nash, "War Criminals," pp. 100–101.
287. Ibid., 101–102; Natsuko Fukue, "Imperial Army Vet Haunted by Horrors in China,"*Japan Times*, May 9, 2009, p. 1; http://www.japantimes.co.jp/print/nn20090409w1.html.
288. Cathcart and Nash, "War Criminals," p. 103; China Fushun War Criminals Management Center, *Place of New Life of Japanese War Criminals* (Beijing: China Intercontinental Press, 2005), p. 26.
289. Cathcart and Nash, "War Criminals," pp. 103–105.
290. Jacobs, "Preparing the People for Mass Clemency," p. 168.
291. Ibid., p. 170.
292. Ibid., p. 169.
293. Ibid., pp. 170–171.
294. Natsuko, "Imperial Army War Vet," pp. 1, 3.

9 The Genocide and Geneva Conventions: Eichmann, Lemkin, Tibet, Guatemala, and the Korean War

1. CGH, "Holocaust Death Camp Guard Demjanjuk Found Guilty," *Spiegel Online*, May 12, 2011, p. 1; http://spiegel.de/international/germany/five-years-for-helping-the-ss-holocaust-death-.
2. David M. Crowe, *The Holocaust: Roots, History, and Aftermath* (Boulder: Westview Press, 2008), pp. 434–435.
3. Gisela Griedrichsen, "The Deeper Meaning of the Demjanjuk Verdict," trans. Paul Cohen, *Spiegel Online*, p. 2; http://www.spiegel.de/international/germany/it-was-clear-what-happened-the-deeper-meaning.
4. State of Israel, Ministry of Justice, *The Trial of Adolf Eichmann: Record of Proceedings in the District Court of Jerusalem*, Vol. 1 (Jerusalem: Ministry of Justice, 1992), pp. 3–9; *Nazis and Nazi Collaborators (Punishment) Law*, 5710–1950, August 1, 1950, Israel Ministry of Foreign Affairs, pp. 1–6; http://www.mfa.gov.il/MFA/MFAArchive/1950_1959/N azis+and+Nazi+Collaborators+punishment.
5. State of Israel, *The Trial of Adolf Eichmann*, ibid., 5, pp. 2082–2093.
6. Ibid., pp. 2243–2244.
7. Ibid., pp. 2341–2343, 2345–2347, 2353, 2357–58.
8. Ibid., p. 2369.
9. David Cesarani, *Becoming Eichmann: Rethinking the Life, Crimes, and Trial of a "Desk Murderer"* (Cambridge: Da Capo, 2006), pp. 319–323.
10. State of Israel, *The Trial of Adolf Eichmann*, 5:2089.
11. United Nations, General Assembly, "Resolutions Adopted by the General Assembly during Its First Session," Resolutions 95 (I), "Affirmation of the Principles of International Law Recognized by the Charter of the Nürnberg Tribunal," December 11, 1946, and Resolution 96 (I), "The Crime of Genocide," December 11, 1946, pp. 188–189; http://www.un.org/documents/ga/res/1/ares.1.htm.

12. State of Israel, *The Trial of Adolf Eichmann*, 1, 551–552; see similar arguments in ibid., 5, 2244, 2331.
13. Ibid., 5, 2050.
14. Ibid., 5, 2092.
15. Ibid., 5, 2186; see also pp. 2348–2349.
16. Hanna Yablonka, *The State of Israel v. Adolf Eichmann*, trans. David Herman (New York: Schocken Books, 2004), p. 31.
17. State of Israel, *Nazi and Nazi Collaborators Law*, 1950, pp. 1–6.
18. John Cooper, *Raphael Lemkin and the Struggle for the Genocide Convention* (New York: Palgrave Macmillan, 2008), pp. 32, 40.
19. Raphael Lemkin, *Axis Rule in Occupied Europe: Laws of Occupation, Analysis of Government, Proposals for Redress*, 2nd ed. (Clark, NJ: Lawbook Exchange, 2008), pp. 79–82.
20. Ibid., pp. 79–80.
21. Ibid., p. 80.
22. Eyal Benvenisti, *The International Law of Occupation* (New York: Oxford University Press, 2012), p. 24.
23. Lemkin, *Axis Rule*, p. 81.
24. Ibid., pp. 82–90.
25. Ibid., p. 90.
26. Ibid., pp. 93–94; Cooper, *Raphael Lemkin*, pp. 18–19.
27. Cooper, *Raphael Lemkin*, pp. 56–63.
28. Raphael Lemkin, *Totally Unofficial: The Autobiography of Raphael*, ed. by Donna-Lee Frieze (New Haven: Yale University Press, 2013), pp. 118–120; there are modest references to Lemkin's work with Jackson's team in London and Nuremberg. Lemkin seems to have spent most of his brief time in Nuremberg working with Telford Taylor.
29. Telford Taylor, *The Anatomy of the Nuremberg Trials* (Boston: Little, Brown, 1992), p. 103.
30. Office of United States Chief of Counsel for Prosecution of Axis Criminality, *Nazi Conspiracy and Aggression*, Vol. 1 (Washington, DC: US Government Printing Office, 1946), pp. 31–32.
31. Cooper, *Raphael Lemkin*, p. 67; Peter Padfield, *Hess: The Führer's Disciple* (London: Cassell, 2001), p. 91. Padfield discusses Haushofer's relationship with Hess in some depth throughout this study.
32. Cooper, *Raphael Lemkin*, p. 68.
33. Ibid., pp. 67–69.
34. Samantha Power, *"A Problem from Hell": America and the Age of Genocide* (New York: Harper Perennial, 2002), pp. 49–50.
35. Lemkin, *Totally Unofficial*, pp. 118–120; Cooper, *Raphael Lemkin*, p. 77.
36. Cooper, *Raphael Lemkin*, pp. 78–81.
37. William A. Schabas, *Genocide in International Law: The Crime of Crimes*, 2nd ed. (Cambridge: Cambridge University Press, 2009), pp. 52–60.
38. Ibid., pp. 59–60.
39. Ibid., p. 61.
40. Ibid., p. 62.
41. Ibid., pp. 62–63.
42. Ibid., pp. 69–70.
43. Lemkin, *Totally Unofficial*, pp. 118–179; Cooper, *Raphael Lemkin*, pp. 119, 122.
44. Lemkin, *Totally Unofficial*, p. 172; Cooper, *Raphael Lemkin*, p. 159.
45. Schabas, *Genocide in International Law*, pp. 77–89.
46. United Nations, General Assembly, Resolution 260 (III), *Convention for the Prevention and Punishment of the Crime of Genocide*, December 9, 1948, pp. 174–178; http://www.un.org/documents/ga/res/3/ares3.htm.
47. Ibid., pp. 174–175.

48. Ibid., p. 175.

49. Jia Wei Wang and Nyima Gyaincain, *The Historical Status of China's Tibet* (Beijing: China Intercontinental Press, 2008), pp. 21, 30, 45.

50. Dalai Lama, *The Autobiography of the Dalai Lama* (New York: HarperCollins,1990), p. 11; Glenn H. Mullin, *The Fourteen Dalai Lamas: A Sacred Legacy of Reincarnation* (Santa Fe: Clear Light, 2011), pp. 143–147; John Powers, *Introduction to Tibetan Buddhism*, rev. ed. (Ithaca: Snow Lion, 2007), pp. 164–165; Tom A. Grunfeld, *The Making of Modern Tibet,* rev. ed. (Armonk: M. E. Sharpe, 1996), pp. 40–42; Matthew T. Kapstein, *The Tibetans* (Malden: Blackwell, 2006), pp. 131–133; Hugh Richardson, "The Dalai Lamas," in Alex McKay, ed., *The History of Tibet*, Vol. 2: *The Medieval Period to c. 850–1895, the Development of Buddhist Paramouncy* (London: Routledge, 2003), pp. 557–558; Luciano Petech, "The Dalai Lamas and Regents of Tibet: A Chronological Study," in ibid., 2, p. 569; Wei Jing, *100 Questions about Tibet* (Beijing: Beijing Review Press, 1989), p. 9.

51. Matthew T. Kapstein, *The Tibetans* (Malden: Blackwell, 2006), p. 3.

52. Melvin C. Goldstein, "The Revival of Monastic Life in Drepung Monastery," in Melvyn C. Goldstein and Matthew T. Kapstein, eds., *Buddhism in Contemporary Tibet: Religious Revival and Cultural Identity* (Berkeley: University of California Press, 1998), pp. 1–2, 15–16; Central Tibetan Administration and the Tibetan Centre for Human Rights and Democracy, *China's Attempts to Wipe Out the Language and Culture of Tibet: Tibetan Response to China's White Paper of 25 September 2008* (Dharamsala: Central Tibetan Administration and Tibetan Centre for Human Rights, 2008), p. 41.

53. Melvin C. Goldstein, *A History of Modern Tibet*, Vol. 1 (Berkeley: University of California Press, 1989), pp. 206–211, 244.

54. Dalai Lama, *Freedom in Exile*, pp. 98–99, 110, 114–119, 122; Geoffrey Samuel, *Civilized Shamans: Buddhism in Tibetan Societies* (Washington: Smithsonian Institution Press, 1993), pp. 380–381; Warren W. Smith, *Tibet's Last Stand? The Tibetan Uprising of 2008 and China's Response* (Lanham: Rowman & Littlefield, 2010), pp. 64–65; Grunfeld, *The Making of Modern Tibet*, pp. 131–132; Tsetsen Shakya, *The Dragon in the Land of the Snows: A History of Modern Tibet since 1947* (New York: Penguin, 1999), pp. 140–141.

55. Shakya, *The Dragon in the Land of the Snows*, pp. 155–156, 161, 163–184, 186–200, 204–207; Dalai Lama, *My Land and My People: The Original Autobiography of His Holiness the Dalai Lama* (New York: Grand Central, 1997), pp. 130–144, 156–157, 170–178; Tubten Khétsun, *Memories of Life in Lhasa under Chinese Rule*, trans. Matthew Akester (New York: Columbia University Press, 2008), pp. 24–29; Dalai Lama, *Freedom in Exile,* pp. 98–99, 110, 114–119, 122, 130–144; Grunfeld, *The Making of Modern Tibet*, p. 139.

56. Shakya, *The Dragon in the Land of the Snows*, p. 223.

57. International Commission of Jurists, *Tibet and the Chinese People's Republic: A Report to the International Commission of Jurists by Its Legal Inquiry Committee on Tibet* (Geneva: International Commission of Jurists, 1960), p. 226.

58. Ibid., p. 232.

59. Ibid., pp. 242, 248.

60. Ibid., p. 277.

61. Ibid., pp. 242, 255, 259, 267, 269–272.

62. Ibid., p. 3.

63. Ibid., p. 13.

64. Ibid., pp. 13-14.

65. Norman M. Naimark, *Stalin's Genocides* (Princeton: Princeton University Press, 2010), pp. 130–137; Robert Conquest, *The Harvest of Sorrow: Soviet Collectivization and the*

Terror-Famine (New York: Oxford University Press, 1986), pp. 299–301; Col. Gen. G. F. Krivosheev, ed., *Soviet Casualties and Combat Losses in the Twentieth Century* (London: Greenhill Books, 1997), pp. 83–90; Timothy Snyder, "Stalin & Hitler: Mass Murder by Starvation," *New York Review of Books*, June 21, 2012, p. 51.

66. R. J. Rummell, *China's Bloody Century: Genocide and Mass Murder since 1900* (New Brunswick: Transaction, 2007), p. 314; R. J. Rummell, "Getting My Reestimate of Mao's Democide Out," Democratic Peace Blog, November 30, 2005, pp. 1–2; http://democraticpeace.wordpress.com/2008/11/24/getting-my-estimate-of-maos-democide-out/; Rummell came out with new statistics partly in response to Jung Chang and Jon Halliday's controversial book, *Mao: The Unknown Story* (New York: Alfred A. Knopf, 2005), p. 3, who estimated Chinese deaths during this period at over 70 million; Jean-Lous Margolin, "China: A Long March into Night," in Stéphanier Courtois, Nicholas Werth, Jean-Louis Panné, Andrej Packowski, Karel Bartošek, and Jean-Louis Margolin, eds., *The Black Book of Communism: Crimes, Terror, Repression,* trans. Jonathan Murphy and Mark Kramer (Cambridge, MA: Harvard University Press, 1999), pp. 463–464; Judith Banister, *China's Changing Population* (Stanford: Stanford University Press, 1987), pp. 85, 87, 118. Basil Ashton, Kenneth Hill, Alan Piazza, and Robin Zeits, "Famine in China, 1958–61," in Dudley L. Poston, Jr., and David Yaukey, eds. *The Population of Modern China* (New York: Plenum Press, 1992), p. 252.

67. Government of Tibet-in-Exile, *Tibet: Proving Truth from Facts* (Dharamsala: Government of Tibet-in-Exile, 1996), p. 24; Rummell, *China's Bloody Century*, pp. 272–273; Patrick French, *Tibet, Tibet: A Personal History of a Lost Land* (New York: Vintage, 2003), pp. 279–283, 304–305.

68. French, *Tibet, Tibet,* pp. 304–305, 322, 352; Barry Sautman, "'Demographic Annihilation' and Tibet," in Barry Sautman and June Teufel Dreyer, eds., *Contemporary Tibet; Politics, Development, and Society in a Disputed Region* (Armonk: M.E. Sharpe, 2006), p. 246; Yan Hao, "Tibetan Population in China: Myths and Facts Re-examined," *Asian Ethnicity,* Vol. I, No. 1 (2000), pp. 15, 19–22, 33, 35.

69. Robert Barnett, "What Were the Conditions Regarding Human Rights in Tibet before Democratic Reform?" in Anne-Marie Blondeau and Katia Buffetrille, eds., *Authenticating Tibet: Answers to China's 100 Questions* (Berkeley: University of California Press, 2008), pp. 87–92.

70. Dalai Lama, *Five Point Peace Plan*, Address to the US Congressional Human Rights Caucus, September 21, 1987, The Office of His Holiness the Dalai Lama, pp. 1–7; http://www.dalai.lama.com/messages/tibet/five-point-peace-plan.

71. Dalai Lama, *Freedom in Exile*, pp. 260–261; Melvyn C. Goldstein, *The Snow Lion and the Dragon: China, Tibet, and the Dalai Lama* (Berkeley: University of California Press, 1997), pp. 91–93.

72. Congressional-Executive Commission on China, *Annual Report: 2009* (Washington, DC: US Government Printing Office, 2009), 2009, pp. 3–4; Kapstein, *The Tibetans*, p. 149.

73. Xiangrui Liu and Daqiong, "Gala Marks Emancipation of Serfs," *China Daily*, March 29, 2012, p. 6; Zhong Liu and Chu Lizhong, *China's Tibet* (Beijing: China Intercontinental Press, 2000), pp. 1–11; Chang-hao Hsi and Kao Yuan-met, *Tibet Leaps Forward* (Peking: Foreign Languages Press, 1977), pp. 21–26.

74. Jing, *100 Questions about Tibet*, p. 49.

75. Ibid., Section 10 , p. 1.

76. Information Office of the State Council of the People's Republic of China, *Fifty Years of Democratic Reform in Tibet* (Beijing: Information Office of the State Council of the People's Republic of China, 2009), Conclusion (b), p. 1.

77. Government of Tibet-in-Exile, *Tibet*, Human Rights Section, pp. 1–3; Religion and National Identity Section, pp. 2, 7; French, *Tibet, Tibet*, pp. 279–283.

78. Jing, *100 Questions about Tibet*, pp. 58–59.

79. Congressional-Executive Commission on China, *Annual Report 2004* (Washington, DC: US Government Printing Office, 2004), p. 41; Congressional-Executive Commission on China, *Annual Report 2003* (Washington, DC: US Government Printing Office, 2003), p. 81; Congressional-Executive Committee on China, *Annual Report 2005* (Washington, DC: US Government Printing Office, 2005), pp. 108–109.

80. Voice of America, "China Intensifies Resettlement of Tibetan Nomads," *VOANews.com*, August 28, 2009, pp. 1–2; http://www.printthis.clickability.com/pt/cpt?action=cpt&title=China+Intensifies+Resettlement; Congressional-Executive Committee on China, *Annual Report 2008* (Washington, DC: US Government Printing Office, 2008), p. 192.

81. Andrew M. Fischer, "Subsistence and Rural Livelihood Strategies in Tibet under Rapid Economic and Social Transition," *Journal of the International Association of Tibetan Studies*, No. 4 (December 2008), pp. 32–33, 40–41.

82. Smith, *Tibet's Last Stand?*, pp. 40–75.

83. Information Office of the State Council of the People's Republic of China, *White Paper: Protection and Development of Tibetan Culture* (Beijing: Information Office of the State Council of the People's Republic of China, 2008), p. 1.

84. Central Tibetan Administration, *China's Attempts to Wipe out the Language and Culture of Tibet*, pp. 68–69.

85. Andrew Jacobs, "Chinese Officials Direct a Day of Mourning for a Quake's Victims," *New York Times*, April 22, 2010, p. A12.

86. "China Mum on Dalai Lama's Request to Visit Quake-Hit Areas," *DNA*, April 20, 2010, p. 1; http://www.dnaindia.com/dnaprint910.php?newsid=1373593; "From Whence Cometh My Help," *Economist*, May 1, 2010, p. 42.

87. Congressional-Executive Committee on China, *Annual Report 2010* (Washington, DC: US Government Printing Office, 2010), pp. 215–216, 218, 220–224.

88. Jason Burke, "One Tibetan Woman's Tragic Path to Self-Immolation," *Nomad Rights*, March 27, 2012, pp. 1–4; http://nomadrights.org/2012/04/one-tibetan-womans-tragic-path-to-self-immolation/. "Petition Questions Legality of Chinese-Language Policy for Tibetans," *Tibetan Review*, January 14, 2011, p. 1; http://www.tibetanreview.net/news.php?id=8119

89. Barbara Demick, "Self-Immolations in Tibet Show No Sign of Slowing," *Los Angeles Times*, March 10, 2012, p. 1; Sruthi Gottipat and Rick Gladstone, "Tibetan Exile Sets Self Afire in Protest Act," *New York Times*, March 27, 2012, p. A4; Jim Yardley, "Before Talks in Capital, India Tightens Security in Tibetan Districts," *New York Times*, March 29, 2012, p. A12.

90. Andrew Jacobs, "China: Tibetan Dies in Protest Fire," *New York Times*, June 16, 2012, p. A9.

91. Andrew Jacobs, "Self-Immolations in Tibet as China Tightens Grip," *New York Times*, March 23, 2012, p. A6.

92. Ibid.

93. "Behind the Immolations," *China Daily*, December 10, 2012, p. 11.

94. "Two More Deaths Take Self-Immolations Count to 94," *Tibetan Review*, December 10, 2012, p. 1; http://www.tibetanreview.net/news.php?id=11556&.

95. ICRC, *Convention on the Prevention and Punishment of the Crime of Genocide*, p. 1; International Criminal Court, *Rome Statute of the International Criminal Court* (The Hague: International Criminal Court, 2002), pp. 22–23.

96. Schabas, *Genocide in International Law*, pp. 256–257, 264–267.

97. Matthew Lippman, "Genocide," in M. Cherif Bassiouni, ed., *International Criminal Law*, Volume 1: *Sources, Subjects, and Contents*, 3rd ed. (Leiden: Martinus Nijhoff, 2008), p. 418.

98. William A. Schabas, *An Introduction to the International Criminal Court*, 3rd ed. (Cambridge: Cambridge University Press, 2007), pp. 101–105.

99. *Declaration of the Rights of Person Belonging to National or Ethnic, Religious and Linguistic Minorities*. Adopted by the General Assembly Resolution 47/135 of December 18, 1992, pp 1–2; *United Nations Declaration of the Rights of Indigenous Peoples, Official Records of the General Assembly, Sixty-Second Session*, September 13, 2007, p. 5.

100. John A. Crow, *The Epic of Latin America*, 3rd ed. (Berkeley: University of California Press, 1992), p. 17.

101. Charles C. Mann, *1491: New Revelations of the Americas before Columbus* (New York: Vintage Books, 2006), pp. 276–277, 309–314; UNHCR, *Refworld*, "World Directory of Minorities and Indigenous Peoples—Guatemala: Overview, July 2008, p. 1; http://ww.unhcr.org/refworld/country,COUNTRYPROF,GTM,4954ce19c,0.html.

102. Bartolomé de las Casas, *A Short Account of the Destruction of the Indies*, ed. and trans. Nigel Griffin (London: Penguin, 2004), pp. 55–56, 122.

103. Ibid., pp. 55–56; Maureen E. Shea, *Culture and Customs of Guatemala* (Westport: Greenwood Press, 2001), p. 4; Karine Vanthuyne, "Becoming Maya? The Politics and Pragmatics of 'Being Indigenous' in Postgenocide Guatemala," *PoLAR: Political and Legal Anthropology Review*, Vol. 32, No. 2 (2009), p. 196.

104. Shea, *Culture and Customs of Guatemala*, p. 5.

105. Greg Gandin, *The Blood of Guatemala: A History of Race and Nation* (Durham: Duke University Press, 2000), pp. 238–239.

106. Shea, *Culture and Customs of Guatemala*, p. 6.

107. Gandin, *The Blood of Guatemala*, p. 135; Shea, *Culture and Customs of Guatemala*, p. 8.

108. Gandin, *The Blood of Guatemala*, p. 142.

109. Julie A. Charlip, "Central America in Upheaval," in Thomas H. Holloway, ed., *A Companion to Latin American History* (Chichester: Wiley-Blackwell, 2011), pp. 417–418; Grandin, *The Blood of Guatemala*, p. 119.

110. Grandin, *The Blood of Guatemala*, pp. 177, 179.

111. Shea, *Culture and Customs of Guatemala*, p. 8.

112. Richard H. Immerman, *The CIA in Guatemala: The Foreign Policy of Intervention* (Austin: University of Texas Press, 1982), p. 75.

113. Ibid., p. 71.

114. Ibid., *The CIA in Guatemala*, pp. 80–81, 200, 241.

115. Ibid., pp. 81–82, 101, 133, 173–175; Gandin, *The Blood of Guatemala*, p. 202.

116. *Guatemala: Memory of Silence, Report of the Commission for Historical Clarification: Conclusions and Recommendations*, p. 18; http://shr.aaas.org/guatemala/ceh/report/english/toc.html.; see also *Memory of Silence: The Guatemalan Truth Commission Report*, ed. Daniel Rothenberg (New York: Palgrave Macmillan, 2012), pp. 142–144, 185–187; *Guatemala. Never Again! Recovery of Historical Memory Project. The Official Report of the Human Rights Office, Archdiocese of Guatemala* (Maryknoll, NY: Orbis Books, 1999), pp. 4, 18, 20, 24.

117. *Guatemala: Memory of Silence*, pp. 14, 26, 29, 86, p. 180.

118. Ibid., pp. 29, 31.

119. *Guatemala. Never Again!*, pp. 116–117.

120. Victoria Sanford, *Buried Secrets: Truth and Human Rights in Guatemala* (New York: Palgrave Macmillan, 2003), pp. 160–161.

121. Etelle Higonnet, *Quiet Genocide: Guatemala, 1981–1983* (Piscataway: Transaction, 2009), p. 47.

122. Sanford, *Buried Secrets*, pp. 114–115.

123. Virginia Garrard-Burnett, *Terror in the Land of the Holy Spirit: Guatemala under General Efraín Ríos Montt, 1982–1983* (Oxford: Oxford University Press, 2010), pp. 34, 39.

124. Ibid., pp. 86–87.
125. Ibid., 86–87; *Guatemala. Never Again!*, pp. 218–22.
126. Garrard-Burnett, *Terror in the Land of the Holy Spirit*, p. 91.
127. Ibid, pp. 88–93.
128. Ibid, pp. 93–94.
129. Ibid., p. 94.
130. Ibid., pp. 95–96.
131. *Guatemala: Memory of Silence,* p. 14.
132. Ibid., p. 3.
133. Ibid., p. 9.
134. Ibid., p. 205; International Committee of the Red Cross, "Guatemala: Practice Relating to Rule 158, Section B. Prohibition on Amnesty for War Crimes," p. 1; http://www.icrc.org/customary-ihl/eng/docs/v2_cou_gt_rule159.
135. *Guatemala: Memory of Silence*, pp. 63–64.
136. Ibid., p. 64.
137. Ibid., pp. 67–75.
138. Ibid., p. 76.
139. Ibid., p. 77.
140. Ibid.
141. Ibid.
142. Ibid.
143. Ibid., p. 78; *Convention for the Prevention and Punishment of the Crime of Genocide*, pp. 1–2.
144. Kate Doyle, "The Pursuit of Justice in Guatemala," National Security Archive Electronic Briefing Book, No. 373, March 23, 2012, p. 2.; http://www.gwu.edu/~nsaarchiv/NSAEBB/NSAEBB373/index.htm.
145. *Guatemala: Memory of Silence*, p. 42.
146. Ibid., pp. 216–217.
147. Ibid., pp. 218–219.
148. Ibid., pp. 218–220.
149. Peace Pledge Union, "Guatemala: After the Genocide," p. 1; http://www.ppu.org.uk/genocide/g_guatemala2.html.
150. Larry Rohter, "Old Footage Haunts General and a Director," *New York Times*, September 9, 2011, p. AR10; "Genocide-Linked General Otto Pérez Molina Poised to Become Guatemala's Next President," *Democracy Now*, September 15, 2011, pp. 1–4; http://www.democracynow.org/2011/15/genocide_linked_general_otto_prez_molina; Damien Cave, "Desperate Guatemalans Embrace an 'Iron Fist,'" *New York Times*, September 9, 2011, p. A1; Annie Bird, "'Genocidal' General Wins Presidential Elections in Guatemala," CETRI, November 9, 2011, pp. 1–3; http://www.cetri.be/spip.php?page=imprimer&id_article=2364; Lauren Casarik, "Guatemala: Reconciliation or Retrenchment? Upholding Human Rights in Guatemala Should be the US' First Priority to Avoid Its Past Mistakes," *Al Jazeera*, January 13, 2012, pp. 1–3; http://www.aljazeera.com/indepth/opinion/2012/01/2012110113757722207.html; Kate Doyle, "Notes from the Evidence Project: Guatemala Government to Dismantle Its 'Archives of Peace,'" NS Archives, June 1, 2012, pp. 1–2; http://nsarchive.wordpress.com/2012/06/01/guatemalan-government-closes-peaqce-ardchives/; Guatemalan Human Rights Commission/USA, "GHRC Denounces Closure of Peace Archives Directorate in Guatemala//GHRC denuncia clausura de la Dirección de los Archivos de la Paz," June 4, 2012, pp. 1–3; http://ghrcusa.wordpress.com/tag/ooto-perez-molina/; Laura Carlsen, "Genocide on Trial in Guatemala," *Nation*, February 29, 2012, pp. 1–2; http://www.thenation.com/print/article/a66526/genocide-trial-guatemala.

151. Doyle, "The Pursuit of Justice in Guatemala," p. 3.

152. David Baluarte and Erin Chlopak, "The Case of Myrna Mack Chang: Overcoming Institutional Impunity in Guatemala," *Human Rights Brief*, Vol. 10, No. 3 (2003), p. 11.

153. Ibid., p. 12.

154. Ibid., pp. 11–13; Committee on Human Rights, "Case Information: Myrna Elizabeth Mack Chang," p. 1; http://www7.nationalacademies.org/humanrights/Cases/CHR_043981.htm.

155. Doyle, "The Pursuit of Justice in Guatemala," p. 3.

156. Mike McDonald, "Guatemala's Military Man, Nicaragua's Revolutionary," *Americas Quarterly*, pp. 1–3; http://americasquarterly.org/Mcdonald; Doyle, "The Pursuit of Justice in Guatemala," p. 3; Programa de las Naciones Unidas para el Desarrollo, "Reconciliation and Transitional Justice in Guatemala," October 11, 2011, p. 3; http://www.pnud.org.gt/frmNewsDetailsRaspx?idnoticia=58.

157. *Guatemala: Memory of Silence*, pp. 103–104.

158. Center for Justice and Accountability, "The Dos Erres Massacre," p. 1. http://cja.org/article.php?list=type&type=459&printsafe=1.

159. Doyle, "The Pursuit of Justice in Guatemala," pp. 3–4.

160. Garrard-Burnett, *Terror in the Land of the Holy Spirit*, p. 90.

161. Lauren Wolfe, "Reckoning with a Genocide in Guatemala," *Atlantic*, February 2012, pp. 1–2; http://www.theatlantic.com/international/print/2012/02/reckoning-with-a-genocide-in-guatemala; Elisabeth Malkin, "Accused of Atrocities, Guatemala's Ex-Dictator Chooses Silence," *New York Times*, January 26, 2012, p. A11; EFE, "Guatemalan Ex-Strongman Charged with Crimes against Humanity," *Latin American Herald Tribune*, July 5, 2012, p. 1; http://www.laht.com/article.asp?ArticleId=465956&CategoryId=23558.

162. Laura Carlsen, "Genocide on Trial in Guatemala," *Nation*, February 29, 2012, p. 2; http://thenation.com/print/article/166526/genocide-trial-guatemala.

163. Mike McDonald, "Former Guatemala Dictator to Face Massacre Charges," Reuters, May 21, 2012, p. 1; http://www.reuters.com/assests/print?aid=USBRE84L02V20120522.

164. "2nd Genocide Charge against Rios Montt," *Central American Politics*, May 22, 2012, p. 1; http://centralamercian politics.blogspot.com/2012/05/2nd-genocide-charge-against-rios-montt.

165. Naomi Roht-Arriaza and Alumdena Bernabeu, "The Guatemalan Genocide Case in Spain," Center for Latin American Studies, UC Berkeley, Fall 2008, p. 1.

166. María del Carmen Márquez Carrasco and Joaquín Alcaide Fernández, "In re Pinochet. Spanish National Court, Criminal Division (Plenary Session), Case 19/97. November 4, 1998, Case 1/98, November 5, 1998," *American Journal of International Law*, Vol. 93, No. 3 (July 1999), p. 692. After a 16-month legal battle, Foreign Minister Jack Straw decided to send Pinochet back to Chile for health reasons (Pinochet had initially come to London to seek medical care). Though the Chilean Congress granted him immunity from prosecution, the Court of Appeal of Santiago stripped him of this, and in late 2000 a Santiago court indicted him for kidnapping. He was never brought to trial for health reasons and in 2002 all charges were dropped against him. When it was discovered that the claims of ill health was a ruse, he was reindicted in late 2004 and placed under house arrest. Over the next few years, his status was argued in a number of court cases, and in 2006 he was again placed under house arrest and indicted for new crimes. He died on December 10, 2006, while still under house arrest.

167. Naomi Roht-Arriaza and Almudena Bernabeu, "The Guatemala Genocide Case," *Berkeley Review of Latin American Studies* (Fall 2008), pp. 1–2.

168. Ibid., p. 2.

169. Ibid., p. 2.

170. The Center for Justice & Accountability, "What We Do," p. 1, http://www.cja.org.section.php?id=86.

171. Roht-Arriaza and Bernabeu, "The Guatemala Genocide Case," p. 3.

172. Central Court of Instruction, Number Five, National Court, Madrid, *Proceedings: Summary, Terrorism and Genocide. "Operational Condor,"* December 10, 1998, pp. 1–5; Center for Justice & Accountability, *Cabello v. Fernandez-Larios,* 402F.3d 1148 (llth Cir. 2005), pp. 1–3. http://www.cja.org/article.php?list=type&type=32; for more on the Pinochet case, see Madeleine Davis, ed., *The Pinochet Case: Origins, Progress, and Implications* (London: Institute of Latin American Studies, 2003); Ariel Dorfman, *Exorcising: The Incredible Unending Trial of General Augusto Pinochet* (New York: Seven Stories Press, 2002); Peter Kornbluh, *The Pinochet File: A Declassified Dossier on Atrocity and Accountability* (New York: New Press, 2003); Naomi Roht-Arriaza, *The Pinochet Effect: Transnational Justice in the Age of Human Rights* (Philadelphia: University of Pennsylvania Press, 2005); Steven J. Stern, *Reckoning with Pinochet; The Memory Question in Democratic Chile, 1989–2006* (Durham: Duke University Press, 2010).

173. Roht-Arriaza and Bernabeu, "The Guatemalan Genocide Case," p. 2.

174. The National Security Archives, The George Washington University, "Summaries of Genocide Proceedings before the Spanish Federal Court, Round One," February 4–8, 2008, p. 4. http://www.gwu.edu/~nsarchiv/guatemala/genocide/round1.htm.

175. Ibid., pp. 4–5.

176. Ibid., p. 8.

177. Ibid.

178. The National Security Archive, The George Washington University, "Summaries of Genocide Proceedings before the Spanish National Court, Round Two," May 26–30, 2008, p. 7. http://www.gwu.edu/~nsarchiv/guatemala/genocide/index.htm.

179. Ibid., p. 9.

180. Ibid., pp. 23–24.

181. Kate Doyle, "Guatemala: Justice for Rios Montt's Victims?" *Latin America Bureau*, April 2, 2012, pp. 3–4. http://www/lab.org.uk/index.php?option=com_content&view=article&id=1325:guatemala-.

182. Elisabeth Malkin, "Ex-Dictator Is Ordered to Trial in Guatemalan War Crimes Case," *New York Times,* January 28, 2013, pp. 1–2; http://www.nytimes.com/2013/01/29/world/americas/ex-dictator-is-ordered-to-trial-in-guatemala.

183. Anita Isaacs, "On the Brink of Justice in Guatemala," *New York Times,* March 27, 2013, pp. 1–2; http://www.nytimes.com/2013/03/28/opinion/on-the-brink-of-justice-in-guatemala.html; Elisabeth Malkin, "In Testimony, Guatemalans Give Account of Suffering," *New York Times,* April 14, 2013, pp. 1–3; http://www.nytimes.com/2013/04/15/world/americas/in-rios-montt-trial-guatemalans-give-a.

184. Mike McDonald, "Guatemala Trial of Rios Montt Has Likely Collapsed," Reuters, March 21, 2013, p. 1. www.reuters.com/article/2013/5/22/us-guatemala-riosmontt_idUSBRE9401N20130522.

185. Dietrich Schindler, "Significance of the Geneva Conventions for the Contemporary World," *International Review of the Red Cross*, No. 836 (December 31, 1999), pp. 2, 7 n4. http://www.icrc.org/eng/resources/documents/misc/57jq6t.htm; Françoise Bouchet-Saulnier, *The Practical Guide to Humanitarian Law,* Second English Language Edition, ed. and trans. Laura Brav and Clémentine Olivier (Lanham: Rowman & Littlefield, 2007), p. 121.

186. Gary D. Solis, *The Law of Armed Conflict: International Humanitarian Law in War* (Cambridge: Cambridge University Press, 2010), p. 83.

187. International Committee of the Red Cross, *What Is International Humanitarian Law?* (Geneva: International Committee of the Red Cross 2004), p. 1.

188. Solis, *The Law of Armed Conflict*, p. 23.

189. Ibid., p. 27.

190. Steven R. Ratner and Jason R. Abrams, *Accountability for Human Rights Atrocities in International Law: Beyond the Nuremberg Legacy*, 2nd ed. (Oxford: Oxford University Press, 2001), p. 10.

191. Solis, *The Law of Armed Conflict*, p. 25.

192. Theodor Meron, "The Humanization of Humanitarian Law," *American Journal of International Law*, Vol. 94, No. 2 (April 2000), p. 240; Solis, *The Law of Armed Conflict*, p. 25.

193. M. Cherif Bassiouni, "Introduction to International Humanitarian Law," in M. Cherif Bassiouni, ed., *International Criminal Law*, Vol. 1, 3rd ed. (Leiden: Martinus Nijhoff, 2008), p. 290.

194. Ibid., pp. 269–270; Adam Roberts and Richard Guelff, eds., *Documents on the Laws of War*, 3rd ed. (Oxford: Oxford University Press, 2000), p. 69.

195. Bassiouni, "Introduction to International Humanitarian Law," pp. 280–281, 284–285, 287.

196. Ibid., pp. 284–285.

197. David P. Forsythe, "Legal Management of International War: The 1977 Protocol on Non-International Armed Conflicts," *American Journal of International Law*, Vol. 72, No. 2 (April 1978), p. 273; Allison Marston Danner, "When Courts Make Law: How the International Criminals Recast the Laws of War," *Vanderbilt Law Review*, Vol. 59, No. 1 (January 2006), p. 12; Solis, *The Law of Armed Conflict*, p. 98.

198. Philippe Abplanalp, "The International Conferences of the Red Cross as a Factor for the Development of International Humanitarian Law and the Cohesion of the International Red Cross and Red Crescent Movement," *International Review of the Red Cross*, No. 308 (October 10, 1995), pp. 7–9; http://www.icrc.org/eng/resources/documents/misc/57jmr9.htm.

199. "Draft Convention for the Protection of Civilian Populations against New Engines of War," Amsterdam, August 29–September 2, 1938, pp. 1–5; http://www.icrc.org/ihl.nsf/FULL/345?OpenDocument.

200. "Charter of the United Nations," June 26, 1945, p. 1; http://www.un.org/en/documents/charter/preamble.shtml.

201. Schindler, "Significance of the Geneva Conventions," p. 2.

202. The Universal Declaration of Human Rights, December 10, 1945, Preamble, p. 1; http://www.un.org/en/documents/udhr/.

203. Abplanalp, "The International Conferences of the Red Cross," p. 8.

204. International Committee of the Red Cross, *The Geneva Conventions of August 12, 1949* (Geneva: International Committee of the Red Cross, 2009), p. 3; Geoffrey Best, *War & Law since 1945* (Oxford: Oxford University Press, 1994), pp. 80–81.

205. International Committee of the Red Cross, *Report on the Work of the Conference of Government Experts for the Study of the Conventions for the Protection of War Victims (Geneva, April 14–1946)* (Geneva: International Committee of the Red Cross, 1947), pp. 1–2.

206. Ibid., p. 8.

207. Ibid.

208. Ibid.

209. Ibid., pp. 8–11, 67–68, 269, 299; Best, *War & Law*, pp. 89–90.

210. Abplanalp, "The International Conferences of the Red Cross," p. 9; *Seventeenth International Red Cross Conference: Report* (Geneva: International Committee of the Red Cross, 1949), pp. 8–17.

211. *Seventeenth International Red Cross Conference*, pp. 92–93.

212. *Final Record of the Diplomatic Conference of Geneva of 1949*, Vol. 1 (Berne: Federal Political Department, 1963), pp. 158–172.

213. International Committee of the Red Cross, *The Geneva Conventions of August 12, 1949* (Geneva: International Committee of the Red Cross, 2009), pp. 23–221 *passim*. The conventions are also available on the ICRC's website.

214. Jean S. Pictet, ed., *The Geneva Conventions of 12 August 1949*, Vol. 3: *Geneva Convention Relative to the Treatment of the Prisoners of War* (Geneva: International Committee of the Red Cross, 1960), pp. 29–30.

215. Ibid, p. 30.

216. Ibid., p. 31.

217. Ibid.

218. Ibid.

219. *Final Record*, 2, B, p. 9.

220. Ibid., pp. 10–11.

221. Ibid, p. 12.

222. Ibid., pp. 13–14.

223. Ibid., p. 41.

224. Ibid.

225. Ibid., p. 44.

226. Ibid, pp. 46, 77–78.

227. International Committee of the Red Cross, *Remarks and Proposals Submitted by the International Committee of the Red Cross: Documents for the Consideration of Governments Invited by the Swiss Federal Council to Attend the Diplomatic Conference at Geneva (April 21, 1949)* (Geneva: International Committee of the Red Cross, 1949), p. 8.

228. Pictet, *The Geneva Conventions*, 3, p. 33.

229. Ibid., pp. 33–34.

230. *Final Record*, 2, B, pp. 331–339.

231. ICRC, *The Geneva Conventions of August 12, 1949*, pp. 24, 52, 75–76, 154.

232. Ibid., p. 23.

233. Jean S. Pictet, ed., *Commentary*, 1: *Geneva Convention for the Amelioration of the Condition of the Wounded and Sick in Armed Forces in the Field* (Geneva: International Committee of the Red Cross, 1952), p. 357.

234. Ibid., p. 358

235. Ibid.

236. Best, *War & Law*, p. 164.

237. Ibid., pp. 162–163.

238. International Committee of the Red Cross, *Remarks and Proposals Submitted by the International Committee of the Red Cross* (Geneva: International Committee of the Red Cross, 1949), p. 18.

239. Ibid., p. 20

240. Ibid., p. 21.

241. Best, *War & Law*, p. 165.

242. ICRC, *Remarks*, p. 43.

243. Ibid., p. 21.

244. Ibid., p. 19.

245. Ibid., p. 21.

246. Ibid., p. 22.

247. ICRC, *The Geneva Conventions of August 12, 1949*, pp. 43, 69.

248. Ibid., p. 131.

249. Ibid., p. 211.

250. Best, *War & Law*, p. 166.

251. David Halberstam, *The Coldest Winter: America and the Korean War* (New York: Hyperion, 2007), p. 1; D. Clayton James, *The Years of MacArthur*, Vol. 3: *Triumph and Disaster, 1945–1964* (Boston: Houghton Mifflin, 1985), pp. 418–419.

252. James, *The Years of MacArthur*, 3, pp. 389–400.

253. Halberstam, *The Coldest Winter*, pp. 1, 4.

254. United Nations Security Council, 83 (1950). Resolution of June 27, 1950 [S/1511]. *Security Council Resolutions—1950* (New York: United Nations, 1950), p. 5; Resolution of July 7, 1950 [S/1588], ibid., pp. 4–5. UNSC Resolution of July 31, 1950 [S/1657], ibid., p. 6.

255. Halberstam, *The Coldest Winter*, 9, 311, 345; Kuo-kang Shao, *Zhou Enlai and the Foundations of Chinese Foreign Policy* (New York: St. Martin's Press, 1996), pp. 180–182.

256. Robert Service, *Stalin: A Biography* (Cambridge, MA: Harvard University Press, 2004), pp. 552–557; Simon Sebag Montefiore, *Stalin: The Court of the Red Tsar* (New York: Alfred A. Knopf, 2004), pp. 607–609; Jung Chang, *Mao: The Unknown Story* (New York: Alfred A. Knopf, 2005), pp. 365–367.

257. Shao, *Zhou Enlai*, p. 182.

258. Halberstam, *The Coldest Winter*, p. 628

259. Ibid., p. 630.

260. Don Kirk, "Truth But No Reconciliation," *International Justice Tribune*, No. 121, February 2, 2011, p. 1; Choe Sang-Hun, "South Korean Commission Details Civilian Massacres Early in 1950s War," *New York Times*, November 27, 2009, pp. A5, A8.

261. Charles J. Hanley and Hyung-Jin Kim, "South Korea Shuts Down Korean-War Human Rights Probe, Largely Absolves U.S.," Associated Press, July 11, 2010, pp. 1–2; http://blog.cleveland.com/world_impact/print.html?entry=/2010/07south_korea-shuts-do; Choe Sang-Hun, "Korean War's Lost Chapter: South Korea Says U.S. Killed Hundreds of Civilians," *New York Times*, August 3, 2008, pp. 6, 10; Geoffrey Cain, "Is Time Running Out to Dig Up South Korea's Mass Graves?" *Time*, November 27, 2009, pp. 1–3. http://www.time.com/time/printout/0,8816,1943075,00.html.

262. Choe Sang-Hun, "An Abductee's Daughter Speaks Out about an Unhealed Korean Wound," *New York Times*, December 4, 2011, p. 16.

263. Darius Rajali, *Torture and Democracy* (Princeton: Princeton University Press, 2007), p. 84.

264. *Korean War Atrocities: Report of the Committee on Government Operations Made through Its Permanent Subcommittee on Investigations by Its Subcommittee on Korean War Atrocities Pursuant to S. Res. 40* (Washington, DC: United States Government Printing Office, 1954) p. 15.

265. Rajali, *Torture and Democracy*, p. 85.

266. Ibid., p. 85.

267. *Korean War Atrocities*, pp. 4–9.

268. Ibid., pp. 3–4.

269. Ibid., pp. 4, 6.

270. Ibid., pp. 4–5; Philip D. Chinnery, *Korean Atrocity! Forgotten War Crimes, 1950–1953* (Annapolis: US Naval Institute Press, 2001), pp. 56–73.

271. *Korean War Atrocities*, p. 15.

272. ICRC, *The Geneva Conventions of August 12, 1949*, p. 79.

273. David P. Forsythe and Barbara Ann J. Rieffer-Flanagan, *The International Committee of the Red Cross: A Neutral Humanitarian Actor* (London: Routledge, 2007), p. 19; Best, *War & Law*, p. 352; Elizabeth Schafer, "Red Cross, International," in Stanley Sander, ed., *The Korean War: An Encyclopedia* (London: Routledge, 1995), pp. 291–292.

274. ICRC, *The Geneva Conventions of August 12, 1949*, p. 123.

275. Jan P. Charmatz and Harold M. Wit, "Repatriation of Prisoners of War and the 1949 Geneva Convention," *Yale Law Journal*, Vol. 62, No. 3 (February 1953), pp. 391–392, 394–395; S. M. Plokhy, *Yalta: The Price of Peace* (New York; Penguin Books, 2010), pp. 293–305; many of the 2 million Soviet POWs, now considered collaborators, disappeared into Stalin's Gulag. Nikolai Tolstoy, *Victims of Yalta* (London: Corgi Books, 1978), pp. 46, 49, 468, 498–499.

276. Sookyung Lee, "Hardly Known, Not Yet Forgotten, South Korean POWs Tell Their Story," trans. Greg Scarlatoiu, Radio Free Asia, January 25, 2007, p. 1; http://www.rfa.org/english/news/social/korea_pow-20070125.html. William Paul Skelton, *American Ex-Prisoners of War* (Washington, DC: Department of Veterans Affairs, 2002), pp. 30, 34.

277. Schindler, "Significance of the Geneva Conventions," p. 2.

278. Yves Sandoz, Christophe Swinarski, and Bruno Zimmermann, eds., *Commentary on the Additional Protocols of 8 June 1977 to the Geneva Conventions of 12 August 1949* (Geneva: Martimus Nijhoff Publishers, 1987), xxv–xvii; Draft *Rules for the Limitation of the Dangers Incurred by the Civilian Population in Time of War* (Geneva: International Committee of the Red Cross, 1956), pp. 1–4. http:www.icrc.org/ihl.nsf/WebPrint/420-FULL?OpenDocument.

279. Sandoz et al., *Commentary*, xvii; International Committee of the Red Cross, *Final Record Covering the Draft Rules for the Limitation of the Dangers Incurred by the Civilian Population in Time of War* (Geneva: International Committee of the Red Cross, 1958), pp. 1–184 *passim*.

280. "Resolutions Adopted by the XXth Convention of the International Committee of the Red Cross," *International Review of the Red Cross*, No. 56 (November 1965), p. 575.

281. *Final Act of the International Conference on Human Rights, Teheran, 22 April to 13 May 1968* (New York: United Nations, 1968), p. 18.

282. Ibid.

283. Roland Burke, "From Individual Right to National Development: The First UN International Conference on Human Rights, Tehran, 1968," *Journal of World History*, Vol. 19, No. 3 (September 2008), p. 277.

284. "Respect for Human Rights in Armed Conflicts: Resolution 2444 (XXIII) of the United Nations General Assembly," December 19, 1968, p. 1; http://www.icrc.org/ihl.nsf/FULL/440?OpenDocument.

285. Schindler, "Significance of the Geneva Conventions," p. 3.

286. Sandoz et al., *Commentary*, xviii.

287. International Committee of the Red Cross, *Rules Applicable in Guerrilla Warfare* (Geneva: International Committee of the Red Cross, 1971), p. 50.

288. Ibid., p. 51.

289. Noelle Higgins, "The Application of International Law to Wars of National Liberation," *Journal of Humanitarian Assistance* (April 2004), p. 34.

290. Sandoz et al., *Commentary*, xviii.

291. Ibid., xviii.

292. Ibid., xix.

293. Solis, *The Law of Armed Conflict*, p. 120; *Official Records of the Diplomatic Conference on the Reaffirmation and Development of International Humanitarian Law Applicable in Armed Conflicts: Geneva (1974–1977)*, Vol. 2 (Berne: Federal Political Department, 1978), pp. 351–404.

294. Sandoz et al., *Commentary*, xix.

295. Ibid., ix.

296. ICRC, *Protocols Additional to the Geneva Conventions of 12 August 1949* (Geneva: International Committee of the Red Cross, 1977), p. 4.
297. Higgins, "The Application of International Law," p. 37.
298. Solis, *The Law of Armed Conflict*, p. 123.
299. Higgins, "The Application of International Law," p. 39.
300. Solis, *The Law of Armed Conflict*, p. 125.
301. ICRC, *The Geneva Conventions of August 12, 1949*, p. 47; Solis, *The Law of Armed Conflict*.
302. ICRC, *The Geneva Conventions of August 12, 1949*, p. 31.
303. Philip Sutter, "The Continuing Role for Belligerent Reprisals," *Journal of Conflict and Security Law*, Vol. 13, No. 1 (Spring 2008), p. 111; Solis, *The Law of Armed Conflict*, p. 126.
304. David A. Bagley, "Ratification of Protocol I to the Geneva Conventions of 1949 by the Untied States: Discussion and Suggestions for the American Lawyer-Citizen," *Loyola of Los Angeles International and Comparative Law Review*, Vol. 11, No. 3 (1989), pp. 450–451.
305. Abraham D, Sofaer, "The Rationale for the United States Decision Not to Ratify Protocol I to the Geneva Conventions on the Protection of War Victims," *American Journal of International Law*, Vol. 82, No. 4 (October 1988), p. 785.
306. Hans-Peter Gasser, "An Appeal for Ratification by the United States," *American Journal of International Law*, Vol. 81, No. 4 (October 1987), p. 914.
307. Ibid., p. 915.
308. Ibid.
309. Ibid., p. 917.
310. Ibid., pp. 920–921.
311. Ibid., pp. 921–922.
312. Maj. Gen. George S. Prugh, "Application of Geneva Conventions to Prisoners of War," *Law at War: Vietnam Studies, 1964–1973* (Washington, DC: Department of the Army, 1975), pp. 1–2; http://lawofwar.org/vietnam_pow_policy.htm.
313. Solis, *The Law of Armed Conflict*, p. 134.
314. Ibid., p. 135.
315. ICRC, *Protocols Additional to the Geneva Conventions of 12 August 1949*, pp. 36–37.
316. Ibid., pp. 40–41.
317. Ibid., pp. 62–63.
318. Ibid., pp. 11–12.
319. Alison Marston Danner, "When Courts Make Law: How the International Criminal Tribunals Recast the Laws of War," *Vanderbilt Law review*, Vol. 59, No. 1 (January 2006)," p. 16.
320. Ibid.
321. Solis, *The Law of Armed Conflict*, p. 129.
322. Jelena Pejic, "The Protective Scope of Common Article 3: More Than Meets the Eye," *International Review of the Red Cross*, Vol. 93, No. 881 (March 2011), p. 198.
323. ICRC, *Protocols Additional to the Geneva Conventions of 12 August 1949*, pp. 92, 94; Solis, *The Law of Armed Conflict*, pp. 130–131.
324. ICRC, *Protocols Additional to the Geneva Conventions of 12 August 1949*, p. 97; Solis, *The Law of Armed Conflict*, p. 131.
325. ICRC, *Protocols Additional to the Geneva Conventions of 12 August 1949*, p. 90.
326. Roberts and Guelff, *Documents on the Laws of War*, p. 482.
327. Theodor Meron, *The Humanization of International Law* (Leiden: Martinus Nijhhoff, 2006), pp. 30–31.

10   IHL: Soviet-Afghan War, Saddam Hussein, Ad Hoc Tribunals, and Guantánamo

1. *Collected Verse of Rudyard Kipling* (Toronto: Copp Clark, 1910), pp. 283–284.
2. Lester W. Grau, "The Soviet-Afghan War: A Superpower Mired in the Mountains," *Journal of Slavic Military Studies*, Vol. 17, No. 1 (2004), p. 130.
3. Gregory Feifer, *The Great Gamble: The Soviet War in Afghanistan* (New York: HarperCollins, 2009), p. 4; Sylvain Boulouque, "Communism in Afghanistan," in Stéphane Courtois Nicolas Werth, Jean-Louis Panné, Andrzej Paczkowski, Karol Bartošek, and Jean-Louis Margolin, *The Black Book of Communism*, trans. Jonathan Murphy and Mark Kramer (Cambridge, MA: Harvard University Press, 1999), pp. 717, 725.
4. The Afghanistan Justice Project, *Casting Shadows: War Crimes and Crimes against Humanity, 1978–2001* (Kabul: Afghanistan Justice Project, 2005), p. 4.
5. M. Kassan Kakar, *Afghanistan: The Soviet Invasion and the Afghan Response, 1979–1982* (Berkeley: University of California Press, 1995), pp. 213, 215–216.
6. Boulouque, "Communism in Afghanistan," pp. 712–713.
7. Ibid., p. 714.
8. Mikhail Heller and Aleksandr Nekrich, *Utopia in Power; The History of the Soviet Union from 1917 to the Present*, trans. Phyllis B. Carlos (New York: Summit Books, 1986), p. 692.
9. Lester W. Grau and Michael A. Gress, eds. and trans., *The Soviet-Afghan War: How a Super Power Fought and Lost: The Russian General Staff* (Lawrence: University Press of Kansas, 2002), xxii–xxiii.
10. Ibid., pp. 305–306.
11. Ibid., 311.
12. Oliver Roy, *The Lessons of the Soviet/Afghan War*, Adelphi Papers 259 (London: Brassey's, 1991), p. 20.
13. Grau and Gress, *The Soviet-Afghan War*, p. 310.
14. Ali Ahmad Jalali and Lester W. Grau, *The Other Side of the Mountain: Mujahideen Tactics in the Soviet-Afghan War* (Quantico: United States Marine Corps Studies and Analysis Division, 1999), xix–xx.
15. Julian Geran Pilon, "The Report that the U.N. Wants to Suppress: Soviet Atrocities in Afghanistan," Heritage Foundation, No. 556 (January 12, 1987), pp. 8–9; Afghan Justice Project, *Casting Shadows*, p. 41; Kakar, *Afghanistan*, pp. 129–135.
16. Pilon, "The Report," pp. 9, 12.
17. Kakar, *Afghanistan*, pp. 247–248.
18. Josef Goldblat, "The Biological Weapons Convention—An Overview," *International Review of the Red Cross*, No. 318 (June 30, 1997), pp. 7–8.
19. Kakar, *Afghanistan*, p. 247; Pilon, "The Report," pp. 9–10.
20. Kakar, *Afghanistan*, p. 249.
21. Boulouque, "Communism in Afghanistan," pp. 718–719.
22. Pilon, "The Report," p. 7.
23. Boulouque, "Communism in Afghanistan," p. 721.
24. Ibid., p. 721.
25. Pilon, "The Report," p. 11.
26. Patricia Grossman, "Afghanistan," in *Crimes of War 2.0: What the Public Should Know* (New York: W. W. Norton, 2007), pp. 30–36.
27. "Two Sisters Lost, Thirty Years Gone," Interview of Rahela by Afghan Centre for Investigative Journalism; http://www.iwpr.org.af/two-sisters-lost-years-gone.
28. "Under Mujahideen, Teachers as Targets," Interview of Sher Ahmad by Afghan Centre for Investigative Journalism; http://www.iwpr.org.af/under-mujahideen-teachers-as-targets.

29. Helsinki Watch, *"Tears, Blood and Cries": Human Rights in Afghanistan since the Invasion, 1979–1984* (New York: Helsinki Watch, 1984), pp. 209–210.

30. Ibid., pp. 195–199.

31. Helsinki Watch and Asia Watch, *To Die in Afghanistan (A Supplement to "Tears, Blood and Crimes": Human Rights in Afghanistan since the Invasion 1979 to 1984)* (New York: Helsinki Watch and Asia Watch, 1985), p. 93.

32. Olivier Roy, *The Lessons of the Soviet/Afghan War* (London: Brassey's, 1991), pp. 57–59.

33. Helsinki Watch, *By All Parties to the Conflict: Violations of the Laws of War in Afghanistan* (New York: Helsinki Watch, 1988), pp. 37–39.

34. Helsinki Watch, *Tears, Blood and Cries,* p. 199.

35. Ibid., pp. 199–207.

36. Grau and Gress, *The Soviet-Afghan War,* p. 314.

37. "Habibullah Jalalzoy," *Trial,* n.d., p. 1; http://www.trial-ch.org/en/resources/trial-watch/trial-watch/profiles/profile/392/action/show; "Heshamuddin Hesam," *Trial,* n.d., p. 1; http://www.trial-ch.org/en/resources/trial-watch/trial-watch/profiles/profile/391/action/show; Jürgen Schurr and Carla Ferstman, *Strategies for the Effective Investigation and Prosecution of Serious International Crimes: The Practice of Specialised War Crimes Units* (Paris: International Federation for Human Rights, 2010), p. 13.

38. United Nations, *Convention and Protocol Relating to the Status of Refugees,* 1951 and 1967, p. 16.

39. Schurr and Ferstman, "Strategies for the Effective Investigation and Prosecution of Serious International Crimes," p. 14.

40. Cedric Ryngaert, "Another Afghan Case in the Hague District Court: Universal Jurisdiction over Violations of Common Article 3," *The Hague Justice Portal,* September 13, 2007, p. 1.

41. Ibid., p. 1; *Appeal Judgement in the Case of Habibullah Jalalzoy,* January 29, 2007, Ruling, Docket No. 22–006132–05, Court of Appeal in The Hague, *The Hague Justice Portal,* pp. 4–5; http://www.icrc.org/customary-ihl/eng/docs/v2_cou_nl_rule158; "Dutch Supreme Court Rejects Appeals of Afghan Intelligence Officers," *The Hague Justice Portal,* July 8, 2008, p. 1.

42. Ryngaert, "Another Afghan Case," p. 7.

43. "Protestors and Afghan War-Crimes Trials," United Press International, April 30, 2012, p. 1; http://www.upi.com/TOP_News/World-News/2012/04/30/Protestors-want-Afghan-war-cri.

44. Dilip Hiro, *The Longest War: The Iran-Iraq Military Conflict* (New York: Routledge, 1992), pp. 27–37, 250, estimates that total war dead is, conservatively, 262,000 Iranians and 105,000 Iraqis. Official Iranian estimates claim that 194,931 Iranians died during the war, while the Iraqi government claimed afterward that 800,000 were killed during the conflict; Charles Tripp says over 250,000 Iraqis died during the war. *A History of Iraq* (Cambridge: Cambridge: Cambridge University Press), p. 239; Phebe Marr, *The Modern History of Iraq* (Boulder: Westview Press, 2004), p. 207. Marr says that Iraq suffered 380,000 casualties, 125,00 dead, and 255,000 wounded.

45. Javed Ali, "Chemical Weapons and the Iran-Iraq War: A Case Study of Noncompliance," *The Nonproliferation Review,* Vol. 8, No. 1 (Spring 2001) pp. 43–49.

46. Central Intelligence Agency, *Iraqi's Weapons of Mass Destruction Programs* (Washington, DC: Central Intelligence Agency, 2002), pp. 8–9; "News Chronology," *Chemical Weapons Convention Bulletin,* No. 28 (June 1995), p. 20.

47. Kenneth R. Timmermann, *The Death Lobby: How the West Armed Iraq* (Boston: Houghton Mifflin, 1991), p. 146.

48. Marr, *The Modern History of Iraq,* p. 200; this was not the first instance of such brutality. In 1982, Shiite Muslim rebels tried to assassinate Saddam Hussein while he was

riding through the village of Dujail. In retaliation, Hussein ordered the execution of 148 Dujaili residents, including many children.

49. Timmerman, *The Death Lobby*, pp. 293–294; Ali, "Chemical Weapons and the Iran-Iraq War," p. 52.

50. Marr, *The Modern History of Iraq*, p. 202; in 2005, the district court in the Hague declared the *al-Anfal* campaign an act of genocide as defined by the 1948 Genocide Convention during the trial of Franz van Anraat, who was accused of selling Iraq chemicals that were used against the Kurds. The charge against Anraat was later changed to war crimes.

51. UN Security Council, *Resolution 582*, February 24, 1986, p. 1.

52. UN Security Council, *Resolution 598*, July 20, 1987, pp. 1–2; Ali, "Chemical Weapons and the Iran-Iraq War," pp. 52–53.

53. UN Security Council, *Resolution 598*, pp. 1–2; UN Security Council, *Resolution 612*, May 9, 1988, p. 1; UN Security Council, *Resolution 620*, August 26, 1988, pp. 1–2.

54. Hiro, *The Longest War*, 240, 248, 270.

55. Tripp, *A History of Iraq*, pp. 239–244.

56. UN Security Council, *Resolution 660*, August 2, 1990, pp. 1–2; UN Security Council, *Resolution 678*, November 29, 1990, pp. 1–2.

57. UN Security Council, *Resolution 686*, March 2, 1991, pp. 1–3.

58. Ibid., p. 2.

59. UN Security Council, *Resolution 687*, April 3, 1991, pp. 1–3.

60. Ibid., p. 3.

61. Tripp, *A History of Iraq*, pp. 239–246, 267–275.

62. Nehal Bhuta, *Judging Dujail: The First Trial before the Iraqi High Tribunal* (New York: Human Rights Watch, 2006), p. 8; Asser Institute, "The Iraqi High Tribunal," p. 1; http://www.asser.nl/default.aspx?site_id=9&level1=13336&level2=13375&level 3=13419.

63. Miranda Sissons, "And Now from the Green Zone…Reflections on the Iraq Tribunal's Dujail Trial," *Ethics & International Affairs*, Vol. 20, No. 4 (2006), pp. 3, 5.

64. Bhuta, *Judging Dujail*, p. 8; "Iraqi High Criminal Court Law," *Al-Waqa'I Al-Iraqiya*, No. 4006, October 18, 2005, pp. 1–23 *passim*.

65. "Iraqi High Criminal Court Law," p. 6.

66. Ibid., pp. 9–23; Bhuta, *Judging Dujail*, pp. 9–10.

67. Marieke Wierda and Miranda Sissons, *Briefing Paper: Dujail: Trial and Error?* (New York: International Center for Transitional Justice, 2006), p. 1.

68. Ibid., p. 8.

69. Bhuta, *Judging Dujail*, pp. 20–22, 24, 30–31.

70. Wierda and Sissons, *Briefing Paper*, pp. 8–9; Michael A. Newton and Michael P. Scharf, *Enemy of the State: The Trial and Execution of Saddam Hussein* (New York: St. Martin's Press, 2008), pp. 109–110.

71. Wierda and Sissons, *Briefing Paper*, p. 10.

72. Michael P. Scharf, "The Iraqi High Tribunal: A Viable Experiment in International Justice," *Journal of International Criminal Justice*, Vol. 5, No. 2 (May 2007), p. 261.

73. Newton and Scharf, *Enemy of the State*, pp. 171–172.

74. Michael A. Kelly, *Ghosts of Halabja: Saddam Hussein and the Kurdish Genocide* (Westport: Praeger Security International, 2008), p. 90.

75. Ibid., p. 88.

76. Wierda and Sissons, Briefing Paper, p. 15.

77. Bill van Esveld, "The Complainant Phase of the Anfal Trial," International Center for International Justice, Update Number One, January 1, 2009, p. 5.

78. Kelly, *Ghosts of Halabja*, p. 81; "Chemical Ali's Sentenced to Hang," *BBC News*, June 24, 2007, pp. 1–2; http://newsvote.bbc.co.uk/mpapps/pagetools/print/news.bbc.co.uk/2/hi/ middle_east/62339.

79. Esveld, "The Complainant Phase," pp. 5–6; Kelly, *Ghosts of Halabja*, pp. 82–89.

80. Esveld, "The Complainant Phase," 6; Kelly, *Ghosts of Halabja*, p. 84.

81. Kelly, *Ghosts of Halabja*, pp. 81, 83.

82. Ibid., pp. 84–85.

83. Ibid., p. 90.

84. Clark Gard, "The Defense Phase and Closing Stages of the Anfal Trial: Update Number Three," International Center for Transitional Justice, January 1, 2009, pp. 6–9.

85. Ibid., p. 11.

86. Ibid., pp. 18–21.

87. The Iraqi High Tribunal, The Appellate Chamber, Baghdad, Iraq, September 4, 2007, pp. 1–28 *passim*; "Iraqi Lawmakers against Execution of Top Officials in Saddam Regime," Xinhua, July 16, 2011, p. 1; http://news/xinhuanet.com/english2010/world/2011-07-/16/c_13989694.htm.

88. Judith Armatta, *Twilight of Impunity: The War Crimes Trial of Slobodan Milosevic* (Durham: Duke University Press, 2020), pp. 426–428.

89. Steven L. Burg and Paul S. Shoup, *The War in Bosnia-Herzegovina: Ethnic Conflict and International Intervention* (Armonk: M. E. Sharpe, 1999), p. 27.

90. Sarajevo's Research and Documentation Center (*Istraživačko Dokumentacioni Centar*) estimated in its *Human Losses in Bosnia and Herzegovina 91–95* (2007) that 39,684 civilians and 57,523 soldiers were killed during the conflict. Of this number, 66 percent were Bosnian Muslims. Slides 1–32. Ewa Tabean and Jakub Bijak, "War Related Deaths in the 1992 Armed Conflicts in Bosnia and Herzegovina: A Critique of Previous Estimates and Recent Deaths," *European Journal of Population*, Vol. 21 (2005), pp. 206, 210.

91. Central Intelligence Agency, *Serb Ethnic Cleansing* (Eur. 94–1008C/S, December 1994), p. 3; http://www.foia.cia.gov/browse_docs_full.asp.

92. Central Intelligence Agency Balkan Task Force, *Atrocities in Bosnia: A Regional Overview*, December 22, 1995, pp. 2–9; http://www.foia.cia.gov/browse_docs_fullasp; Roger Cohen, "CIA Report on Bosnia Blames Serbs for 90% of the War Crimes," *New York Times*, March 9, 1995, pp. 1–2. http://www.nytimes.com/1995/03/09world/cia-report-on-bosnia-blames-serbs-for-90-; Steven L. Burg and Paul S. Shoup, *The War in Bosnia-Herzegovina: Ethnic Conflict and International Intervention* (Armonk: M. E. Sharpe, 2000), pp. 324–328.

93. Drazen Petrovic, "Ethnic Cleansing—An Attempt at Methodology," *European Journal of International Law*, Vol. 5 (1994), p. 343; Andrew Bell-Fialkoff, "A Brief History of Ethnic Cleansing," *Foreign Affairs*, Vol. 72, No. 110 (1992–1993), pp. 111–112.

94. Carnegie Endowment for International Peace, *The Other Balkan Wars* (Washington, DC: Carnegie Endowment for International Peace, 1993), pp. 73, 269.

95. Petrovic, "Ethnic Cleansing," pp. 345–348.

96. Alexandra Stiglmayer, "The Rapes in Bosnia-Herzegovina," in Alexandra Stiglmayer, ed., *Mass Rape: The War against Women in Bosnia-Herzegovina*, trans. Marion Faber (Lincoln: University of Nebraska Press, 1994), pp. 82–169; Burg and Shoup, *War in Bosnia-Herzegovina*, p. 170; Mary Valentich, "Rape Revisited: Sexual Violence against Women in the Former Yugoslavia," *Canadian Journal of Human Sexuality*, Vol. 3, No. 1 (Spring 1994), pp. 53–57.

97. ICTY, *Judgement of Trial Chamber II in the Kunarac, Kovać and Vuković Case*, February 22, 2001 (JL/P.I.S./566-e), pp. 1–2; *Prosecutor v. Dragoljub Kunarac, Radomir Kovac and Zoran Vukovic: Judgement*, February 22, 2001 (IT-96–23-T & IT 96–23/1-T), pp. 209–257.

98. *Application of the Convention on the Prevention and Punishment of Genocide (Bosnia and Herzegovina v. Yugoslavia [Serbia and Montenegro])*, March 20, 1993 (General List No. 91), pp. 8–9, 51–64.

99. International Court of Justice, *Case Concerning the Convention on the Prevention and Punishment of the Crimes of Genocide (Bosnia and Herzegovina v. Serbia and Montenegro)*, *Judgement*, February 26, 2007, General List No. 91, The Hague, pp. 55, 98 [hereafter *Bosnia v. Serbia*, Case 91].

100. Ibid., pp. 106, 108.

101. Ibid., pp. 158, 161, 165–166.

102. Antonio Cassese, "A Judicial Massacre," February 27, 2007, *guardian.co.uk*, p. 1; http:// www.guardian.co.uk/commentsfree/2007/feb27/thejudicialmassacreofsrebr/print. Cassese expanded on these comments in his "On the Use of Criminal Law Notions in Determining State Responsibility for Genocide," *Journal of International Criminal Justice*, Vol. 5 (2007), pp. 875–887.

103. Vojin Dimitrijević and Marko Milanović, "The Strange Story of the Bosnian Genocide Case," *Leiden Journal of International Law*, Vol. 21 (2008), p. 66.

104. Anja Seibert-Fohr, "The ICJ Judgement in the Bosnian Genocide Case and Beyond: A Need to Reconceptualize?" *Working Papers* (February 20, 2009) (Heidelberg: Max Planck Society for the Advancement of the Sciences—Max Planck Institute for Comparative Public Law and International Law, 2009), pp. 8–9, 14–15; see also Andrea Gattini, "Evidentiary Issues in the ICJ's Genocide Judgement," *Journal of International Criminal Justice*, Vol. 5 (2007), pp. 889–904.

105. *Bosnia v. Serbia*, Case 91, p. 69.

106. Ibid., pp. 69–70, 73–74.

107. ICTY, "Pilica Farm" (IT-96–22): *Dražen Erdemivić*, pp. 1–5; ICTY, "Srebrenica-Drina Corps" (IT-98–33): *Radislav Krstić*, pp. 1–10; ICTY, "Srebrenica" (IT-02–60/2): *Dragan Obrenović*, pp. 1–6.

108. ICTY, *Outreach*, "Facts on Srebrenica," pp. 1–2; http://www.un.org.icty/index-b.html.

109. "Seven Convicted over 1995 Srebrenica Massacre," June 10, 2010, CNN, p. 1; http:// edition.cnn.com/2010/WORLD/europe/06/10/hague.srebrenica/veredict/?hpt=T1.

110. Judith Armatta, *Twilight of Impunity: The War Crimes Trial, Slobodan Milosevic* (Durham: Duke University Press, 2010), p. 206.

111. Carla del Ponte and Chuck Sudetic, *Madame Prosecutor: Confrontations with Humanity's Worst Criminals and the Culture of Impunity: A Memoir* (New York: Other Press, 2009), pp. 89–90.

112. Sara Darehshori, *Weighing the Evidence: Lessons from the Slobodan Milosevic Trial* (New York: Human Rights Watch, 2006), p. 5.

113. Tim Judah, *The Serbs: History, Myth & the Destruction of Yugoslavia* (New Haven: Yale University Press, 1997), p. 29.

114. Sabrina P. Ramet, *The Three Yugoslavias: State Building and Legitimation, 1918–2005* (Washington, DC, and Bloomington: Wilson Center Press and Indiana University Press, 2006), pp. 320–321.

115. Ibid., pp. 99–100, 145–146; Judah, *The Serbs*, pp. 314–317.

116. Ramet, *The Three Yugoslavias*, pp. 416–417, 427.

117. David M. Crowe, *A History of the Gypsies of Eastern Europe and Russia*, 2nd ed. (New York: Palgrave Macmillan, 2007), pp. 231–232.

118. *Charter of the United Nations*, Chapter 7 , p. 1; http://www.un.org/en/documents/charter/chapter7.shtml

119. UN Security Council, *Resolution 827*, May 25, 1993, S/RES/827 (1993), p. 1.

120. *ICTY v. Dragan Nikolić "Sušica Camp" (IT-94–2)*, Case Information Sheet, pp. 1–6; *ICTY v. Duško Tadić "Prejedor"* (IT-94–1), Case Information Sheet, pp. 1–6.

121. ICTY, *History*, pp. 1–2; http://www.icty.org/sid/95.

122. ICTY, *Slobodan Milošević: "Kosovo, Croatia and Bosnia"* (IT-02–54), Case Information Sheet, pp. 1–8.

123. United Nations, *Updated Statute of the International Criminal Tribunal for the Former Yugoslavia*, September 2009, p. 6.

124. Beatrice I. Bonafe, "Finding a Proper Role for Command Responsibility," *Journal of International Criminal Justice*, Vol. 5 (2007), pp. 604–605.

125. Ibid., pp. 601–605; ICTY *Judgment, Delalic et al.* (I.T-96–21) "Celebici" (November 16, 1998), Part III C, Applicable Law, pp. 5–23; http://www.ess.uwe.ac.uk/documents/part3c.htm.

126. Bonafe, "Finding a Proper Role for Command Responsibility," pp. 605–607.

127. ICTY *Judgment: Prosecutor v. Zenjil Delalic, Zdravko Muci (also known as "Pavo," Hazim Delic, and Esad Lando (also known as "Zinga")*, November 16, 1998 (Case No. IT-96–21-T), pp. 56–61, 136.

128. Allison Marston Danner and Jeremy S. Martinez, *Guilty Associations: Joint Criminal Enterprise, Command Responsibility and the Development of International Criminal Law* (Nashville and Stanford: Public Law & Legal Theory Working Paper Series. Working Paper No. 04–09 and Research Paper No. 87, March 2004), pp. 28, 54; ICTY *Prosecutor v. Duško Tadić: Sentencing Judgement*, July 14, 1997, pp. 1–41.

129. Bonafe, "Finding a Proper Role for Command Responsibility," pp. 608–609.

130. ICTY *Judgment, Delalic et al.*, Part III C: Applicable Law, Para. 370.

131. ICTY, *The Prosecutor of the Tribunal against Slobodan Milosevic et al.: Indictment* (Kosovo), May 22, 1999, p. 15; http://www.christuxrex.org/www2/china/indictment.html; ICTY, *The Prosecutor of the Tribunal against Slobodan Milošević: Indictment* (Case No. IT-01-xxx; Croatia), September 27, 2001, pp. 2–5; ICTY, *The Prosecutor of the Tribunal against Slobodan Milošević: Indictment* (Case No. IT-01–51-I; Bosnia), November 22, 2001, pp. 2–3.

132. Ibid., p. 3.

133. ICTY, *The Prosecutor of the Tribunal against Slobodan Milošević: Indictment*, November 22, 2001, pp. 1–7.

134. Ibid., pp. 2–8.

135. ICTY, *Prosecutor v. Milošević*, December 16, 2003, pp. 30494–30495, 30496.

136. Gideon Boas, *The Milošević Trial: Lessons for the Conduct of Complex International Criminal Proceedings* (Cambridge: Cambridge University Press, 2007), p. 1.

137. *ICTY v. Radovan Karadžić* (Case No. IT-95–5/18), Case Information Sheet, p. 1; http://www.icty.org/x/cases/karadzic/cis/en/cis_karadzic_pdf; *ICTY v. Ratko Mladić* (IT-09-92), Case Information Sheet, p. 1; http://www.icty.org/x/cases/mladic/cis/en/cis_mladic_en.pdf.

138. ICTY, *The Prosecutor of the Tribunal against Radovan Karadžić and Ratko Mladić: Indictment* (Case No. IT-95-5-1), July 1995, p. 3.

139. Ibid., November 14, 1995, pp. 5–9.

140. Paul D. Williams, *War & Conflict in Africa* (Cambridge: Polity Press, 2011), p. 125.

141. United Nations, Economic and Social Council, Commission on Human Rights, *Report on the Human Rights in Rwanda*, January 29, 1996, E/CN.4/1996/68 (New York: United Nations, 1996), pp. 5–6.

142. UN Security Council, *Resolution 955*, S/RES/955 (1994), November 8, 1994, pp. 1–15; UN Security Council, *Resolution 977*, S/RES/977 (1995), February 22, 1995, p.1.

143. *Updated Statute of the International Criminal Tribunal for the Former Yugoslavia*, September 2009, pp. 5–7; UN Security Council, *Resolution 955* (1994), pp. 3–6.

144. United Nations Office of the Special Adviser on Africa, *DDR and Transitional Justice*, 13–14, 30–31; for more on the controversies surrounding the ICTR, see Del Ponte, *Madame Prosecutor*; courts in Belgium and Switzerland have also convicted a handful of individuals for crimes committed in Rwanda.

145. Victor Peskin, *International Justice and the Balkans: Virtual Trials and the Struggle for State Cooperation* (Cambridge: Cambridge University Press, 2008), p. 152.

146. Alison des Forges, *Leave None to Tell the Story* (New York: Human Rights Watch, 1999), pp. 32–33; Alain Destexhe, *Rwanda and Genocide in the Twentieth Century*, trans. Alison Marschner (New York: New York University Press, 1995), pp. 38–39.

147. John Reader, *Africa: A Biography of the Continent* (New York: Vintage Books, 1998), pp. 616–621, 633–636.

148. Ibid., pp. 635–636.

149. Ibid., pp. 487–488.

150. Martin Meredith, *The Fate of Africa: A History of Fifty Years of Independence* (New York: Public Affairs, 2005), pp. 486–487.

151. Ibid., pp. 488–496; Gérard Prunier, *The Rwanda Crisis: History of a Genocide* (New York: Columbia University Press, 1995), pp. 90–91.

152. Meredith, *The Fate of Africa*, p. 496.

153. Ibid., pp. 497–498.

154. Human Rights Watch, *Beyond the Rhetoric: Continuing Human Rights Abuses in Rwanda*, Vol. 5, No. 7 (June 1, 1993), p. 4; http://www.unhcr.org/cgi-bin/texis/vtx/refworld/rwmain?page=printdoc&docid=3ae6.

155. Meredith, *The Fate of Africa*, p. 499.

156. Des Forges, *Leave None to Tell the Story*, p. 124.

157. Prunier, *The Rwanda Crisis*, p. 199; Meredith, *The Fate of Africa*, p. 500.

158. International Criminal Tribunal for Rwanda, *The Prosecutor against Théoneste Bagorosa: Amended Indictment* (Case No. ICTR-96–7-I) August 12, 1999, p. 18; Meredith, *The Fate of Africa*, p. 501.

159. United Nations, *Rwanda—UNAMIR: Background*, p. 4; http://www.un.org/en/peace-keeping/missions/past/unamirFT.htm..

160. United Nations, *United Nations Peacekeeping Operations: Principle and Guidelines* (New York: United Nations, 2008), pp. 33–36; Ramet, *The Three Yugoslavias*, pp. 459–460; Dzevad Sabljakovic, "Srebrenica Evidence Kept under Wraps," *Institute for War and Peace Reporting*, pp. 1–4. http://iwpr.net.

161. Prunier, *The Rwanda Crisis*, p. 223.

162. Des Forges, *Leave None to Tell the Story*, p. 512.

163. Ibid., p. 248.

164. Romeó Dallaire, *Shake Hands with the Devil: The Failure of Humanity in Rwanda* (New York: Da Capo, 2003), p. 272.

165. ICTR, *The Prosecutor against Ferdinand Nahimana: Amended Indictments* (Case no. ICTR-99-52), November 5, 1999, p. 15.

166. Scott Straus, *The Order of Genocide: Race, Power, and War in Rwanda* (Ithaca: Cornell University Press, 2006), p. 231; Scott Straus, "What Is the Relationship between Hate Radio and Violence? Rethinking Rwanda's 'Radio Machete,'" *Politics & Society*, Vol. 35, No. 4 (December 2007), pp. 610, 632.

167. ICTR, *Prosecutor against Nahimana*, p. 15.

168. Human Rights Watch, *Struggling to Survive: Barriers to Justice for Rape Victims in Rwanda* (New York: Human Rights Watch, 2004), p. 1.

169. Des Forges, *Leave None to Tell the Story*, p. 215.

170. Rebecca L. Haffajee, "Prosecuting Crimes of Rape and Sexual Violence at the ICTR: The Application of Joint Criminal Enterprise Theory," *Harvard Journal of Law & Gender*, Vol. 29, No. 1 (2006), p. 206.

171. ICTR, *Prosecutor against Jean-Paul Akayesu* (Case No.: ICTR-96–4-I), June 6, 1997, p. 2.

172. Dallaire, *Shake Hands with the Devil*, p. 462.

173. ICTR, *The Prosecutor versus Jean-Paul Akayesu: Judgement* (Case No. ICTR-96–4-T), September 2, 1998, p. 107.

174. Ibid., p. 108.

175. Ibid., p. 109.

176. Ibid.

177. Ibid., p. 111.
178. Ibid., pp. 112–113.
179. Ibid., pp. 113–114.
180. Ibid., p. 114.
181. Ibid.
182. Ibid., pp. 115–117.
183. Ibid., p. 149.
184. Ibid., p. 166.
185. Ibid., p. 168.
186. Ibid., pp. 169.
187. Ibid., p. 172.
188. ICTR, *The Prosecutor of the Tribunal against Jean-Paul Akayesu: Sentencing*, October 2, 1998, p. 10; ICTR, *The Prosecutor v. Jean-Paul Akayesu: Appeal Judgement*, June 1, 2001, pp. 1–7.
189. ICTR, *Summary of the Judgement in the Alfred Musema Case* (Case No. ICTR-96–13-T), January 27, 2000, p. 7; ICTR, *The Prosecutor v. Eliézer Niyitegeka: Judgement and Sentence* (Case No. ICTR-96–14-T), May 16, 2003, pp. 1–3; Human Rights Watch, *Genocide, War Crimes and Crimes against Humanity: A Digest of the Case Law of the International Criminal Tribunal for Rwanda* (New York: Human Rights Watch, 2010), p. 129.
190. Haffajee, "Prosecuting Crimes of Rape," p. 208.
191. ICTY, *Prosecutor v. Dragoljub Kunarac, Radomir Kovac and Zoran Vukovic* (Case Nos. IT-96–23-T and IT-96–23/1-T), February 22, 2001, pp. 155–156.
192. ICTR, *Prosecutor v. Jean de Dieu Kamuhanda* (Case No. ICTR-95–54A-T), January 22, 2004, pp. 120–121; ICTR, *Prosecutor v. Laurent Semanza* (Case No. ICTR-97–20-T), May 15, 2003, pp. 1–6; Human Rights Watch, *Genocide, War Crimes and Crimes against Humanity*, p. 129.
193. ICTR, *Prosecutor v. Mikaeli Muhimana* (Case No. ICTR-95–1B-T), April 28, 2005, p. 101; Haffajee, "Prosecuting Crimes of Rape," pp. 210–211.
194. Haffajee, "Prosecuting Crimes of Rape," p. 212.
195. ICTR, *Prosecutor v. Siméon Nchamhigo* (Case No. ICTR-01–63-T), November 12, 2008, p. 69; *Prosecutor v. Jean Mpambara* (Case No. ICTR-01–65-T), September 11, 2006, p. 5.
196. ICTR, *Sylvestre Gacumbitsi v. Prosecutor* (Case No. ICTR-2001–64-A), July 7, 2006, p. 58; Haffajee, "Prosecuting Crimes of Rape," pp. 213–214.
197. Haffajee, "Prosecuting Crimes of Rape," p. 214.
198. Ibid., pp. 215–216.
199. Wolfgang Form, "Justice 30 Years Later? The Cambodian Special Tribunal for the Punishment of Crimes against Humanity by the Khmer Rouge," in David M. Crowe, ed., *Crimes of State Past and Present: Government-Sponsored Atrocities and International Legal Responses* (Abingdon: Routledge, 2011), p. 141.
200. Howard J. De Nike, John Quigley, and Kenneth J. Robinson, eds., *Genocide in Cambodia: Documents from the Trial of Pol Pot and Ieng Sary* (Philadelphia: University of Pennsylvania Press, 2000), pp. 8, 17–18, 523–549.
201. Ibid., p. 140; Sophia Quinn-Judge, "Victory on the Battlefield; Isolation in Asia: Vietnam's Cambodian Decade, 1979–1989," in Odd Arne Westad and Sophie Quinn-Judge, eds., *The Third Indochina War: Conflict between China, Vietnam and Cambodia, 1972–79* (Abingdon: Routledge, 2006), p. 218.
202. Kenton Clymer, *Troubled Relations: The United States and Cambodia since 1870* (Dekalb: Northern Illinois University Press, 2007), pp. 182–2001; Quinn-Judge, "Victory on the Battlefield," pp. 226–227; Philip Short, *Pol Pot: Anatomy of a Nightmare* (New York: Henry Holt, 2004), p. 442.

203. Clymer, *Troubled Relations*, p. 206.

204. US Congress, *Cambodian Genocide Justice Act* (U.S.C. 2656, Part D, Sections 571–574), 1994, p. 1. http://cybercambodia.com/dachs/cgja.html; Howard Ball, *Prosecuting War Crimes and Genocide: The Twentieth-Century Experience* (Lawrence: University of Kansas Press, 1999), pp. 116–117.

205. *Cambodian Genocide Justice Act*, p. 1.

206. United Nations, *Report of the Group of Experts for Cambodia Established Pursuant to General Assembly Resolution 52/135*, March 15, 1999, p. 2.

207. United Nations, *Procedural History: Agreement between the UN and the Royal Government of Cambodia concerning the Prosecution under Cambodian Law of Crimes Committed during the Period of Democratic Kampuchea*, Phnom Penh, June 6, 2003, pp. 1–2; http://untreaty.un.org/cod/avl/ha/abunac/abunac.html.

208. David Scheffer, "The Extraordinary Chambers in the Courts of Cambodia," in M. Cherif Bassiouni, ed., *International Criminal Law*, Vol. 3: *International Enforcement*, 3rd ed. (Leiden: Martinus Nijhoff, 2008), p. 235.

209. Ibid., p. 236; Suzannah Linton, "Safeguarding the Independence and Impartiality of the Cambodian Extraordinary Chambers," *Journal of International Criminal Justice*, Vol. 4 (2006), pp. 329–330.

210. Form, "Justice 30 Years Later?" p. 145.

211. Scheffer, "The Extraordinary Chambers," pp. 236–238; Robert Petit and Anees Ahmed, "A Review of the Jurisprudence of the Khmer Rouge Tribunal," *Northwestern Journal of International Human Rights*, Vol. 8, No. 2 (Spring 2010), p. 166.

212. *Law on the Establishment of Extraordinary Chambers in the Courts of Cambodia for the Prosecution of Crimes Committed during the Period of Democratic Kampuchea*, October 27, 2004, p. 2.

213. Ibid., p. 8.

214. Ibid., p. 3.

215. Ibid..

216. Ibid., pp. 6, 8.

217. Ibid., pp. 4–7, 9–10, 12–13; Scheffer, "The Extraordinary Chambers," p. 238.

218. Extraordinary Chambers in the Courts of Cambodia, Office of the Co-Prosecutors, *Statement of the Co-Prosecutors*, Phnom Penh, July 18, 2007, pp. 1–5.

219. Ibid., "Case 001," May 2012, p. 1.

220. Ibid., pp. 1–2; ECCC, "Case 002," May 2012, p. 1; ECCC, "Biography: Kaing Guek Eav"; "Biography: Ieng Sary"; "Biography: Ieng Thirith"; "Biography: Khieu Samphan"; "Biography: Nuon Chea," 2011. http://www.eccc.gov.kh/en/indicted-person/; ECCC, *The Court Reporter*, April 2013, pp. 1, 4–5.

221. Petit and Ahmed, "A Review," p. 169.

222. Seth Mydans, "In Khmer Rouge Trial, Victims Will Not Stand Idly By," *New York Times*, June 17, 2008, p. A6.

223. Richard Bernstein, "At Last, Justice for a Monster," *The New York Review of Books*, April 9, 2009, p. 39.

224. *Amicus Curiae* Brief of Professor Antonio Cassese and Members of the *Journal of International Criminal Justice* on Joint Criminal Enterprise Doctrine (Case No. 001/18–07–2007-ECCC/OCIJ (PTC 02), October 27, 2008, p. 39.

225. ECCC, *Judgment* (Case No./Dossier No. 001/18–07–2007/ECCC/TC), July 26, 2010, p. 177.

226. Ibid., p. 3.

227. Bernstein, "At Last, Justice for a Monster," p. 38.

228. Thierry Cruvellier, "Cambodia: Reflections on the Duch Trial," *Crimes of War*, p. 1; http://www.crimesofwar.org/commentary/regions/cambodia-reflections-on-the-duch-trial/;

Seth Mydans, "Khmer Rouge Defendant Apologizes for Atrocities," *New York Times*, April 1, 2009, p. A8.

229. ECCC, Judgment, July 26, 2010, p. 65.
230. Philip Short, *Pol Pot: Anatomy of a Nightmare* (New York: Henry Holt, 2004), p. 281.
231. ECCC, Judgment, July 26, 2010, pp. 84–85.
232. Ibid., p. 86.
233. Ibid, p. 89.
234. Ibid., p. 208.
235. Ibid., p. 216.
236. ECCC, Supreme Court Chamber, *Appeal Judgement* (Case File/Dossier No. 001/18–07–2007-ECCC/SC), February 3, 2012, p. 320.
237. ECCC, *The Court Report*, April 2013, pp. 1, 4–5.
238. "Khmer Rouge Tribunal Indicts 4 Senior leaders," *USA Today*, September 17, 2010, p. 5A.
239. Seth Mydans, "Four Khmer Rouge Leaders Are Indicted," *New York Times*, September 17, 2010, p. A9.
240. ECCC, Trial Chamber, *Transcript of Trial Proceedings Public* (Case File No. 002/19–09–2007-ECCC/TC), November 21, 2011, p. 16.
241. Ibid., p. 105.
242. Ibid., pp. 106–108.
243. ECCC, *Transcript of Trial Proceedings Public* (Case File No. 002/19–09–2007-ECCC/TC), November 22, 2011, p. 77.
244. Ibid., p. 77.
245. Ibid., p. 111.
246. Ibid., p. 79.
247. Ibid., p. 111.
248. Seth Mydans, "Defendant Says Khmer Rouge's Aim Was to Protect Cambodia from Vietnam," *New York Times*, November 23, 2011, p. A8.
249. ECCC, *Transcript of Trial Proceedings Public* (Case File No. 002/19–09–2007-ECCC/TC), November 23, 2011, pp. 4–5.
250. Ibid., p. 9.
251. Ibid., p. 12.
252. Taylor Owen and Ben Kiernan, "Bombs over Cambodia," *Walrus* (October 2006), pp. 63, 67.
253. ECCC, *Transcript*, November 23, 2011, pp. 16–18.
254. Seth Mydans, "Efforts to Limit Khmer Rouge Trials Decried," *New York Times*, February 1, 2009, p. A8.
255. Reuters, "Cambodia: U.N. Assails Rejection of Khmer Rouge Tribunal Judge," *New York Times*, January 21, 2012, p. A6.
256. Beth Van Schaack, "Big News from the ECC," *Trial Observer*, October 22, 2011, p. 1; http://www.cambodiatribunal.org/blog/2011/10/big-nees-eccc; Human Rights Watch, *Cambodia: Judges Investigating Khmer Rouge Crimes Should Resign* (New York: Human Rights Watch, 2011), pp. 1–7; Christopher Dearing, "As ECCC Resumes, Cases 003 and 004 Remain Inconclusive," *Cambodia Daily*, July 18, 2012, pp. 1–4.
257. US Congress, *War Crimes Act of 1996*, 18 U.S.C.2441, pp. 1–3.
258. *Authorization for Use of Military Force*, September 18, 2001, 107 Congress, Public Law 107–40 [S.J. RES 23].
259. Howard Ball, *Bush, the Detainees, & the Constitution: The Battle over Presidential Power in the War on Terror* (Lawrence: University Press of Kansas, 2007), p. 13.
260. US Congress, *Authorization for Use of Military Force against Iraq Resolution of 2002*, October 16, 2002, Public Law 107–243, 107th Congress, pp. 2, 4.

261. Ball, *Bush, the Detainees, & the Constitution*, p. 12.

262. Patrick F. Philbin and John C. Yoo, US Department of Justice, Office of Legal Counsel, Memorandum for William J. Haynes, 2. "Possible Habeas Jurisdiction over Aliens Held in Guantanamo Bay, Cuba," December 28, 2001, pp. 1–9.

263. Donald Rumsfeld, *Known and Unknown: Memoir* (New York: Sentinel, 2011), p. 567.

264. Philippe Sands, "The Complicit General," *New York Review of Books*, September 24, 2009, p. 20.

265. US Department of Justice, Office of Legal Counsel, "Memorandum for Alberto R. Gonzales, Counsel to the President: Re: Standards of Conduct for Interrogation under 18 U.S.C. §2340–2340*A*," August 1, 2002, pp. 1–2.

266. Department of Justice, Memorandum Opinion for the Deputy Attorney General, "Legal Standards Applicable under 18 U.S.C. §2340–2340A," p. 2; http://www.justice.gov/olc/18usc23402340a2.htm.

267. Ibid., p. 8.

268. Ibid., p. 22.

269. Ibid., p. 39.

270. Office of the United States High Commissioner for Human Rights, *Convention against Torture and Other Cruel, Inhuman or Degrading Treatment or Punishment*, Adopted by the General Assembly, Resolution 39/46, December 10, 1984, Entry into Force, June 26, 1987, p. 1; http://www.2.ohchr.org/english/law/cat.htm.

271. 18 U.S.C. §2340, p. 1, *Find Law*, http://codes.lp.findlaw.com/uscode/18/I/113C/2340.

272. Ibid.

273. 18 U.S.C. §2340A, p. 1, *Find Law*, http://codes.IP.findlaw.com/uscode/18/I/113C/2340A.

274. "GTMO Interrogation Techniques," p. 1; ww.gsu.edu/~nsarchiv/NSAEBB; "Dec. 2, 2002—Memo from the Department of Defense Summarizing Approved Methods of Interrogation, with Annotation from Secretary of Defense Donald Rumsfeld," National Security Archive, *The Interrogation Documents: Debating U.S. Policy and Methods*, July 13, 2004, p. 1;http://www.gwu.edu/~nsarchiv/NSAEBB/NSAEBB127.

275. Rumsfeld, *Known and Unknown*, p. 576.

276. Headquarters, Department of the Army, *FM-34-52. Intelligence Interrogation* (Washington, DC: Department of the Army, 1992), pp. 1–6, I-8.

277. Sands, "The Complicit General," p. 22; Ball, *Bush, the Detainees*, pp. 66–68.

278. US Department of State, *American Service-Members' Protection Act*, August 2, 2002, pp. 1–8. http://www.state.gov/t/pm/rls/othr/misc/23425.htm.

279. William A. Schabas, *An Introduction to the International Criminal Court*, 3rd ed. (Cambridge: Cambridge University Press, 2007), ix, pp. 384–385.

280. Bob Woodward, "Detainee Tortured, Says U.S. Official," *Washington Post*, January 14, 2009, p. 1; http://www.washingtonpost.com/wp-dyn/content/article/2009/01/13/AR2009011303372_pf.

281. Ball, *Bush, the Detainees*, pp. 69–70.

282. Jameel Jaffer and Amrit Soingh, *Administration of Torture: A Documentary Record from Washington to Abu Ghraib and Beyond* (New York: Columbia University Press, 2007), p. 116.

283. International Committee of the Red Cross, *Report of the International Committee of the Red Cross (ICRC) on the Treatment by the Coalition Forces of Prisoners of War and Other Protected Persons by the Geneva Conventions in Iraq during Arrest, Internment and Interrogation* (Geneva: International Committee of the Red Cross, 2004), pp. 12–13.

284. William C. Peters, "Adjudication Deferred: Command Responsibility for War Crimes and US Military Justice from My Lai to Haditha and Beyond," in Crowe, *Crimes of State*, p. 180.

285. Independent Panel to Review DOD Detention Operations, *Final Report of the Independent Panel to Review DoD Detention Operations* (Washington, DC: Department of Defense, 2004), p. 5.

286. Seymour M. Hersh, "Torture at Abu Ghraid: American Soldiers Brutalized Iraqis. How Far Up Does the Responsibility Go?" *New Yorker*, May 10, 2004, p. 2; http://www.newyorker.com/archive/2004/05/10/040510fa_fact?printable=true.

287. Department of Justice, "Memorandum Opinion for the Deputy Attorney General," December 30, 2004, pp. 1–2.

288. Physicians for Human Rights, *Broken Laws, Broken Lives: Medical Evidence of Torture by US Personnel and Its Impact* (Cambridge: Physicians for Human Rights, 2008), viii, p. 1.

289. Peters, "Adjudication Deferred," pp. 180–183.

290. Scott Shane, "No Charges Filed on Harsh Tactics Used by the C.I.A.," *New York Times*, August 31, 2012, pp. A1–3; Evan Perez and Siobhan Gorman, "Justice Department Closes Probe of CIA Prison Deaths," *Wall Street Journal*, August 31, 2012, p. A8.

291. "No Penalty for Torture," *New York Times*, September 2, 2012, p. A22.

292. Mark P. Denbeaux and Jonathan Hafetz, eds., *The Guantánamo Lawyers: Inside a Prison, Outside the Law* (New York: New York University Press, 2009), pp. 30–31.

293. Supreme Court of the United States, *Sahfiq Rasul et al., Petitioners v. George W. Bush* (03–334) and *Fawzi Khalid Abdullah Fahad Al Odah et al. v. United States et al.* (03–343) *on Writs of Certiorari to the United States Court of Appeals for the District of Columbia*, June 28, 2004, pp. 15–16.

294. Jonathan Mahler, *The Challenge: Hamdan v. Rumsfeld and the Fight over Presidential Power* (New York: Farrar, Straus and Giroux, 20008), pp. 131–132.

295. Ibid., pp. 145–146.

296. United States District Court for the District of Columbia, *Salim Ahmed Hamdan v. Donald H. Rumsfeld* (No. CIV.A.04–1519 JR), November 8, 2004, pp. 1, 12; http://scholar.google.com.scholar_case?case=15985349136804769594&hl=en&as_sdt=2&.

297. United States Court of Appeals, *Salim Ahmed Hamdan v. Donald H. Rumsfeld et al.* (Case No. 04–5393). Appeal from the United States District Court for the District of Columbia (04cv01519), July 15, 2005, pp. 9, 13–19; Mahler, *The Challenge*, pp. 191–192.

298. Supreme Court of the United States, *Hamdan v. Rumsfeld et al.*, *Certiorari* to the United States Court of Appeals for the District of Columbia Circuit, June 29, 2006, pp. 1–2, 3–4, 25–30, 49–72.

299. US Congress, *Military Commission Act of 2006*, Public Law 109–366 (120 STAT. 2600), 109th Congress, October 17, 2006, p. 2608.

300. Ibid., p. 2602.

301. Ibid., p. 2616.

302. Ibid., pp. 2621–2622.

303. Ibid., p. 2623.

304. Ibid., pp. 2629–2630.

305. Ibid., pp. 2617, 2635.

306. Ibid., pp. 2635–2636.

307. Supreme Court of the United States, *Boumediene et al. v. Bush, President of the United States, et al.*, *Certiorari* to the United States Court of Appeals for the District of Columbia Circuit (No. 06–1195), June 12, 2008, pp. 8–41, 68–70.

308. Benjamin Weiser, "U.S. Jury Acquits Former Detainee of Most Charges," November 18, 2010, pp. A1, A26; Benjamin Weiser and Charlie Savage, "At Terror Trial, Big Questions Were Avoided," *New York Times*, November 19, 2010, pp. A1, A18.

309. Mimi Hall, Kevin Johnson, and David Jackson, "Detainee's Acquittal Sparks Debate over Civilian Trials," *USA Today*, November 19, 2010, p. 5A; Benjamin Weiser, "Life Sentence without Parole for Former Detainee," *New York Times*, January 26, 2011, pp. A18–A19.

310. Eper Finn, "Guantanamo Bay Detainee Brought to U.S. for Trial," *Washington Post*, June 10, 2009, p. 1. http://www.washington[post.com/wp-dyn/content/article/2009/06/09/AR2009060900401.

311. Office of Military Commissions, "U.S. Court of Military Commissions Review (USCMRC) History," p. 2. http://www.mc.mil/ABOUTUS/USCMCRHistory.aspx.

312. Guantanamo Review Task Force, *Final Report* (Washington, DC: Guantánamo Review Task Force, January 22, 2010), i–ii, pp. 1, 11.

313. "Enough to Make You Gag," *Economist*, May 4, 2013, pp. 12, 14; "The Oubliette," ibid., pp. 27–28.

314. Ibid., pp. 13, 21.

315. Peter Baker and David Johnston, "Guantánamo Deadline May Be Missed," *New York Times*, September 29, 2009, p. A27.

316. David Stout, "House Allows Guantánamo to Transfer Some to U.S.," *New York Times*, October 16, 2009, p. A17.

317. Evan Perez and Timothy W. Martin, "Illinois Prison Weighed for Transfers," *Wall Street Journal*, November 16, 2009, p. A4; Charles Savage, "Closing Guantánamo Fades as a Priority," *New York Times*, June 26, 2010, p. A13.

318. Evan Perez, "U.S. to Press Ahead on Guantanamo Trials," *Wall Street Journal*, January 21, 2011, p. A3.

319. Ben Fox, "Gitmo War Crimes Court Surprises Some Observers," *Star Tribune*, March 5, 2012, pp. 1–2; http://www.startribune.com/printarticle/?id=141395783.

320. Office of Military Commissions, Criminal Investigation Task Force (CITF), May 31, 2011, pp. 1–21.

321. Guantanamo Review Task Force, *Final Report*, p. 21; National Commission on Terrorist Attacks upon the United States, *The 9/11 Commission Report* (Washington, DC: US Government Printing Office, 2010), pp. 434–436; Peter Finn and Carrie Johnson, "Mastermind of Sept. 11 Faces N.Y. Murder Trial," *Boston Globe*, November 14, 2009, pp. A1, A4; International Committee of the Red Cross, *ICRC Report on the Treatment of Fourteen "High Value Detainees" in CIA Custody* (Washington, DC: International Committee of the Red Cross, 2007), pp. 5, 10–13, 14, 16–18, 22, 31–37.

322. The Associated Press, "9/11 Families Prepare for Start of Trials," *News & Record*, May 4, 2012, p. A13; Charlie Savage, "At Guantánamo, Trial for 9/11 Defendants, and for a Revamped Tribunal," *New York Times*, May 5, 2012, p. A12; Jess Bravin, "Sept. 11 Suspects Face Gitmo Hearing," *Wall Street Journal*, May 5–6, 2012, p. A3.

323. Charlie Savage, "9/11 Defendants Were Protesting 'Unjust System' at Hearing, Their Lawyers Say," *New York Times*, May 7, 2012, p. A12.

324. Ibid., p. A12.

325. International Committee of the Red Cross, *ICRC Report on the Treatment of Fourteen "High Value Detainees,"* p. 10.

326. Ibid., pp. 1–19.

327. The Associated Press, "9/11 Families Watch 1st Hearing," *News & Record*, May 6, 2012, p. A2; Peter Finn, "9/11 Detainees Worked to Disrupt Opening of Arraignment at Guantanamo Bay," *Washington Post*, May 5, 2012, pp. 1–4; http://www. washington-post.com/world/national-security/911-detainees-seek-to-disrupt-opening.

328. William Shawcross, *Justice and the Enemy: Nuremberg, 9/11, and the Trial of Khalid Sheikh Mohammed* (New York: Public Affairs, 2011), pp. 203–204.

Epilogue: The ICC

1. William S. Schabas, *An Introduction to the International Criminal Court*, 3rd ed. (Cambridge: Cambridge University Press, 2007), pp. 3–5.
2. *Convention on the Prevention and Punishment of the Crimes of Genocide*, December 9, 1948. United Nations General Assembly; http://www.hrweb.org/legal/genocide.html.
3. Schabas, *International Criminal Court*, pp. 5–23, 465–469. A complete copy of the Rome Statute can be found in pp. 381–464.
4. *Rome Statute*, Articles 1–16; Schabas, *International Criminal Court*, pp. 141–143.
5. *Rome Statute*, Article 5, Sections (a)–(c). Articles 6–8 define each of these crimes more specifically.
6. Reuters, "Reward Offered for Information on Kony," *New York Times*, April 3, 2013, p. A11.
7. Marlise Simons, "Congolese Rebel Commander Tells War Crimes Court He Was Just a 'Soldier,'" *New York Times*, March 27, 2013, p. A8.
8. International Criminal Court, *The Prosecutor v. Bosco Ntaganda* (ICC-01/04–02/06). Pretrial, pp. 1–2; http://www.icc-cpi.int/en_menus/icc/situations and cases/situations/situ.
9. Simons, "Congolese Rebel Commander," p. A8.
10. ICC, "Situations and Cases," pp. 1–2; http://www.icc-cpi.int/menus/ICC/Situations+and-cases/.
11. Mahmood Mamdani, *Saviors and Survivors: Darfur, Politics, and the War on Terror* (New York: Pantheon, 2009), pp. 193–205; Gérard Prunier, *Darfur: A 21st Century Genocide*, 3rd ed. (New York: Cornell University Press, 2008), pp. 54–81; Kofi Annan, *Interventions: A Life in War and Peace* (New York: Penguin, 2012), pp. 120–121.
12. ICC, *The Prosecutor v. Omar Hassan Ahmad al Bashir* (ICC-02/05–01/09), *Pretrial*, http://www.icc-cpi.int/en_menus/icc/situations and cases/situ.
13. Alexis Arieff, Rhoda Margesson, Marjorie Ann Browne, and Matthew C. Weed, *International Criminal Court Cases in Africa: Status and Policy Issues* (Washington, DC: Congressional Research Service, 2011), pp. 14, 16–17.
14. Catherine Soi, "Kenya Parliament Vote to withdraw from jurisdiction of International Criminal Court, as President and Deputy face charges," *Al Jazeera*, September 5, 2013, p. 2; http://www. aljazeera.com/news/africa/2013/09/2013/951510273559326.
15. Nicholas Kulish and Benno Muchler, "African Union Urges International Court to Delay President's Trial," *The New York Times*, October 13, 2013, p. 1.
16. Tom Odula, "African Union Says International Court Cannot Try Kenyan Leader," *The Washington Post*, October 13, 2013, p. A19.
17. Javier Blas, "African States Seek Immunity from Prosecution for Serving Leaders," *Financial Times*, October 14, 2013, p. 4.
18. "Taylor, Charles," The Hague Justice Portal, p. 1; http://www.haguejusticeportal.net/index.php?id=6414.
19. Marlise Simons and J. David Goodman, "Ex-Liberian Gets 50 Years for War Crimes," *New York Times*, May 30, 2012, p. 1; http://www.nytimes.com/2012/05/31/world/africa/charles-taylor-sentence.

Bibliography

The bibliography for this book can be found online at:

http://us.macmillan.com/warcrimesgenocideandjustice

Index

Printed and bound in the United States of America